Contents

Research
Report
25

Teaching and Learning Irish in Primary School

A Review of Research and Development

John Harris

Lelia Murtagh

Institiúid
Teangeolaíochta
Éireann

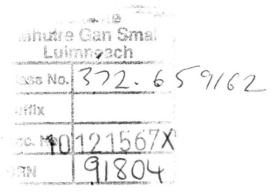
ISBN 0-946452-96-2

Institiúid Teangeolaíochta Éireann
31, Fitzwilliam Place
Dublin 2

Cover design by Mark Loughran, Identikit
Printed by Colour Books.

Acknowledgements

Many people helped us in the preparation of this report and in carrying out the research and development work on which it is based. We are particularly indebted to those who participated in the *Twenty-Classes Study*: teachers, pupils, parents and inspectors. The teachers permitted us unusually open access to all aspects of their work. Not only did they allow us into their classrooms to observe and record Irish lessons in progress but they also agreed to the pupils themselves and their parents being surveyed confidentially regarding their views on Irish in primary school. We are very grateful to the pupils for their generous response to the various demands which the study made on them and to their parents who responded to our questionnaire. We would also like to thank the primary school inspectors who collected all the data.

We are greatly indebted to the teachers, one hundred and ten in all, who participated in the *Communicative Materials Project* and the *Teaching through Irish Project*. The teachers tried out draft lessons in their own classrooms and also travelled regularly to meet ITÉ staff to discuss guidelines and teaching materials. We would also like to thank the teachers who worked full-time on these projects - ITÉ Project Officers Pádraig Ó Néill, Máire Uí Dhufaigh and Seán Mac Giollabhuí. We are also indebted to Dr. Eoghan Ó Súilleabháin, Departmental Inspector in the Department of Education and Science who made a significant contribution to the work. Thanks are also due to the Irish Curriculum Committees in the National Council for Curriculum and Assessment, and particularly the Chairpersons, Nollaig Feirtéir and Proinsias Ó Brodlaigh, on whose initiative the *Communicative Materials Project* was carried out.

We would like to thank the Department of Education and Science for funding the *Twenty Classes Study* and the *Communicative Materials Project*. Special thanks are due to Seán Ó Fiachra, Deputy Chief Inspector and Breandán Ó Coinghéallaigh, former Assistant Chief Inspector. We are also grateful to Dr. Robert Gardner, The University of Western Ontario, for permission to adapt the Attitude/Motivation Test Battery and for his advice on interpreting our own data.

Our colleagues in ITÉ contributed to the report in many ways. Our thanks go to Dónall Ó Baoill and Íosold Ní Dheirg who were consistently generous in their advice on matters relating to Irish. We are grateful to Donncha Ó Cróinín who read sections of the report in draft form and advised us on the compilation of the indices. We are also grateful to him and to Seán Ó Dubhda for technical support. We would like to thank Seán Ó Cathalláin, Mary Conway, Pól Ó Canainn and Annette Byrne who proof-read individual chapters. Thanks are due also to Pádraig Ó Riagáin and Tina Hickey for their advice on various occasions.

We are grateful to Deirdre Ní Bhaoill for laying out and producing the text for the lesson materials in the *Communicative Materials Project* and the *Teaching through Irish Project*, and for helping to prepare the final manuscript for the present report. Thanks are also due to Peig Ní Mhuirí, Máire Ní Éafa, Áine Ní Chonghaile and Orla Ní Chanainn for their help.

Finally, we are particularly indebted to Dr. Eoghan Mac Aogáin, Director of ITÉ, for commenting on an earlier version of the report and for his advice and generous support at all stages of the work.

1 Introduction

1.1 Background

The imminent publication of the new curriculum in Irish for primary schools brings to a close a period of great uncertainty about the teaching of the language. A central feature of that uncertainty has been the gradual decline over a long period in confidence in the *Nuachúrsaí*, the official Department of Education audio-visual courses for teaching the spoken language based on the *Buntús* research (Ireland: Department of Education, 1978). In 1978, for example, a national survey conducted by Institiúid Teangeolaíochta Éireann (ITÉ) showed that 58.8% of sixth-grade teachers were using the '*Nuachúrsaí* only' to teach Irish, while 33.6% were using the *Nuachúrsaí* in combination with the older ABC method . By 1985, the proportions were 29.4% for the '*Nuachúrsaí* alone' and 58.8% for the *Nuachúrsaí* in combination with the ABC (Harris and Murtagh, 1988b). Despite the indications here of teachers returning to an older method, it is nevertheless clear that the *Nuachúrsaí* were still very dominant at this stage. Only 2.5% of sixth-grade teachers in 1978 and 6.7% in 1985, for example, were using their 'own method' (Harris and Murtagh, 1988b). There is general agreement, if not precise data, that confidence in the *Nuachúrsaí* and their use has continued to decline in the interim (Irish National Teachers' Organisation, 1998b).

In 1990, the Review Body on the Primary Curriculum recommended a new syllabus for Irish. The following year a representative Curriculum Committee in the National Council for Curriculum and Assessment (NCCA) began work on the syllabus, completing their work in June 1998. In the meantime, new Irish course-books and workbooks have been produced by the major educational publishers, and there have been a number of other developments such as the appearance of *Modh an Aoibhnis* (Ó Conchúir and Ó Súilleabháin, 1991) and the guidelines and sample materials for a communicative approach to teaching Irish produced by ITÉ (Harris, Uí Dhufaigh, Ó Néill and Ó Súilleabháin, 1996a, Harris, Ó Néill, Uí Dhufaigh, and Ó Súilleabháin, 1996b). Nevertheless, there is little doubt that the approach of the majority of teachers is still very much dominated by the structural-linguistic syllabus which lay at the base of the audio-visual approach, and by the narrative emphasis in materials with which the *Nuachúrsaí* were associated. Two years ago a survey by the Irish National Teachers' Organisation (INTO, 1996a: 52) showed that, of eleven subject areas, Irish was the one causing most concern, with 'practically four out of every five teachers stating that change is urgently required'. By comparison, Mathematics was cited by only 30% of teachers, the area of concern associated with the next largest percentage. The most recent report on Irish from the INTO (1998a,b) makes it clear again that the major work of developing teaching materials for the new communicative curriculum has yet to begin in earnest.

The gradual abandonment of the audio-visual approach, and the anticipation of a change to a more communicative approach to teaching, has been mirrored by changes in the kind of research on Irish conducted by ITÉ. The earlier national surveys which we carried out in the late seventies and eighties - when the audio-visual approach and the *Nuachúrsaí* were dominant - focused on monitoring achievement and standards (Harris, 1984; Harris and Murtagh, 1988a,b). As the task of developing a new, more communicative curriculum assumed greater prominence, however, we have switched to smaller-scale studies which engage us more closely with the specific problems of teachers, pupils and parents (e.g. Harris and Murtagh, 1991,1992; Harris *et al*, 1996a,b; Harris and Mac Giollabhuí, 1998a,b,c). Carrying out new national surveys of achievement would not have made a useful contribution to our understanding at a time of apparently little real change in schools. The detailed, close-up picture of the teaching and learning of Irish which has emerged from this more recent ITÉ work, however, is fully consistent with the broad interpretative parameters established by the earlier national surveys.

Three of the later studies will be mentioned briefly at this point - they are described in more detail later. The *Twenty-Classes Study*, carried out in 1989, consisted of a broad-based study of the teaching and learning of Irish in twenty sixth-grade classes in ordinary schools nationally. It was funded by the Department of Education and was carried out in anticipation of the work of the NCCA Irish Curriculum Committee on the new curriculum. It was intended as a resource for that committee as it began its deliberations. Educational publishers and others who would be responsible later on for producing courses and teaching materials for the new curriculum were also expected to make use of it. The study used classroom observation and questionnaire-type instruments to collect information on the teaching and learning of Irish and to investigate the views and attitudes of pupils and parents, information which had never previously been collected. Among the problems identified in the *Twenty-Classes Study*, particularly among pupils and classes with low levels of achievement in Irish, were apathy/disinterest in relation to Irish, difficulty in understanding the teacher or lesson, low esteem and anxiety about speaking Irish, dissatisfaction with lessons and materials and lack of active support from parents. The study also examined the degree of emphasis on communication as opposed to traditional language practice in different classes and the frequency with which different types of pupils spoke in the Irish class.

The *Communicative Materials Project* (1993 to 1996) was carried out at the instigation of the NCCA Irish Curriculum Committee and was again funded by the Department of Education and Science. The work was carried out in ITÉ and was directed by John Harris, who had also served as an advisor to the NCCA Irish Curriculum Committee. The other members of the Working Group were two primary-school teachers who were seconded to the project and a primary-school inspector who participated on a part-time basis. This was a practically-oriented project, designed to find out exactly what a communicative approach to teaching Irish at primary level might entail, how it might be received by teachers and what problems might arise in implementing it. It involved teachers of all grades from a wide variety of schools coming together in workshops over a two-year period to discuss, tryout and revise draft communicative materials in Irish. Teachers from ordinary primary schools and those from Gaeltacht schools formed separate groups. The project also tried to find practical ways of responding to the various difficulties associated with Irish which had been identified in the *Twenty-Classes Study*. What the new communicative materials appeared to do for weaker pupils was to provide them with some of the positive experiences which had previously been confined to more able pupils: a chance to use Irish for real communication, the experience of making real progress in Irish and the opportunity to have that progress acknowledged. It will be clear from this that the *Twenty-Classes Study* and the *Communicative Materials Project* were the 'research' and 'development' phases respectively of the same basic enterprise.

The third project, the *Teaching through Irish Project*, was funded and executed by ITÉ over a two year period (1995-1997). It involved teachers and researchers working jointly on the development of materials for teaching Science and Art through Irish to pupils in ordinary schools who were learning Irish just as one subject. This was the first time that teachers' experience of Irish-medium teaching in ordinary schools had been formally investigated or that specific teaching guidelines had been developed (Harris and Mac Giollabhuí, 1998a,b,c). There were a number of reasons for carrying out the project and for its timing. First, teaching through Irish probably represents the most truly communicative use of Irish which is possible in a classroom context. Indeed, teaching content through the target language has long been seen as highly desirable in communicative foreign-language teaching but has been difficult to initiate and promote. Second, given that teaching through Irish has always been a component of the Irish programme in a significant minority of primary schools, it is desirable as the new communicative curriculum is implemented that teachers who are prepared, on a voluntary basis, to teach all or part of any subject through Irish should be supported. There has been an absence of materials up to now, however, which took systematic account of the linguistic requirements of pupils who do not have high levels of achievement in Irish and of the particular demands which this approach makes on teachers. ITÉ research has shown that even fairly limited amounts of Irish-medium teaching produce high levels of achievement in Irish (Harris, 1983; Harris and Murtagh, 1988b).

There can be little doubt about the potential scale of the change which the new curriculum will usher in, or about the sense of expectation with which it will be examined after such a long period of dissatisfaction. It is an opportune time, then, to look back at the audio-visual era and forward to the communicative era, and to determine the conditions for, and prospects of, success for the new curriculum. Our goal in the present report, therefore, is to review research relating to the teaching and learning of Irish in ordinary schools. We use the *Twenty-Classes Study* as the organising framework for the report because it is by far the broadest and most comprehensive examination we have conducted of the range of factors which are involved in teaching Irish in primary school. Within this framework, however, we also present information and data derived both from more recent work (the *Communicative Materials Project* and to a lesser extent the *Teaching through Irish Project*) and from the earlier ITÉ national surveys.

It must be emphasised that we are not presenting here the results of a new national survey based on quantitative data. We are reviewing a range of different studies conducted over the last 10 years, basing our main arguments on a combination of quantitative and qualitative information. The *Twenty-Classes Study* was carried out a considerable time ago, for example, and was the subject of two earlier reports to the Department of Education (Harris and Murtagh, 1991,1992). Accounts of the classroom observation work in that study have also appeared as individual chapters in different books (Harris and Murtagh, 1996, 1997) and some of the pupil-attitude data appear in Harris (1991). For the present report, however, we have conducted a more ambitious and comprehensive re-analysis of all the data in the *Twenty-Classes Study*. This allows us to identify new connections between a wide variety of factors, such as pupil attitude/motivation, parental attitudes and practices, materials used in the Irish lesson, types of language activities used in teaching, forms of classroom organisation, teacher mode of involvement and levels of pupil interest and participation in class. The reanalysis was prompted in part by new questions arising from our work with teachers in the *Communicative Materials Project* and the *Teaching through Irish Project.* The latter ongoing work with teachers also gave us ample opportunity to check the continuing validity and relevance of our conclusions. The result is that we are bringing together here a whole range of data about the teaching and learning of Irish in primary school which have not previously been published.

It should also be pointed out that, in many respects, the teaching of Irish has been in a state of suspension since the NCCA Irish Curriculum Committee began its work in 1991. Thus, while some of the surface details of teaching may have changed since the *Twenty-Classes Study* was carried out, the essentials almost certainly have not. Indeed, it is generally accepted that real change comes very slowly in the area of second- and foreign-language teaching anyway. Teaching and materials can sometimes acquire a communicative veneer, as it were, while the underlying approach remains quite traditional (Beretta, 1992). This is simply because the educational circumstances and classroom dynamics which cause existing approaches to be adopted are very powerful and are not easy to change. We show in Chapter 9, for example, the complexity and difficulty of trying to change basic classroom interaction patterns which might lead to an improvement in the class participation of pupils with lower levels of ability in Irish.

The present report serves a number of other purposes. First, while the *Communicative Materials Project* was the subject of two reports comprising guidelines for teachers and examples of communicative lessons (Harris *et al.*, 1996a,b), these reports were entirely in Irish. Thus, it may be useful to have an account of the project here for those not directly involved in Irish as well as for those outside Ireland with a particular academic or other interest in the language. Second, the report presents for the first time a full description of a number of new instruments for studying the teaching and learning of Irish in primary school. These instruments are likely to prove useful in the context of research on the implementation of the new curriculum. And third, we include in appendices here a variety of information which, combined with the quantitative data, produce a more complete picture of Irish in primary school: extensive transcripts of segments of the Irish lessons, a representative list of the spontaneous comments of pupils about learning Irish and a list of the observations of parents about their children learning Irish.

A major concern of the report will be to try to establish what is needed to make the introduction of the new curriculum a success. The *Twenty-Classes Study* and the *Communicative Materials Project* allow us to look forward into the prospective communicative language-teaching era in different ways. The *Twenty-Classes Study* anticipates some of the beneficial effects and difficulties which are likely to accompany the introduction of the new approach by comparing existing classes which are more or less communicative in orientation. These comparisons suggest that the portents for the new curriculum are good - pupil attitudes are better, their attention and interest are enhanced and achievement in Irish is higher in those classes which spend more time on communication. The *Communicative Materials Project* allows us to test out a communicative approach in an even more explicit, concrete way by identifying which specific tasks and materials help teachers to teach communicatively and which activities pupils like.

We will argue, however, that many of the problems associated with the teaching and learning of Irish in primary school will not be solved by the simple fact of introducing a communicative curriculum, although some of them may be considerably ameliorated by such an approach. Difficulties which have sometimes been attributed, perhaps too casually, to the unsuitability of the audio-visual method, such as poor pupil attitudes to learning Irish or difficulties in understanding the lesson, probably have multiple origins and will almost certainly require action above and beyond a switch to a communicative curriculum. Other problems such as pupils receiving insufficient acknowledgment from parents of their efforts to learn Irish may require different initiatives again.

It is also critical, however, to recognise and develop what is good about the Irish programme in primary school at present. Indeed, some of its most valuable features probably have very little to do with teaching method as conventionally understood but are features of what we have elsewhere called the second-language character (as opposed to the foreign-language character) of the programme - the tendency to teach Irish largely through Irish, to use Irish for real communication in class and school, to use Irish to teach parts of other subjects in some schools and the fact that nearly all parents have at least a little Irish (Harris, 1991). The kind of communicative materials which are developed for teaching Irish as a core subject, and for teaching parts of other subjects through Irish, as well as the quality of the support and in-service training provided for teachers, will determine in large measure whether these desirable features of the Irish programme are retained and developed in future.

No matter what aspect of the teaching and learning of Irish we examine in this report - the development of teaching materials, pupils' attitudes or parental involvement - the evidence constantly either gestures towards or reflects relationships with the world outside the school. Very often the evidence is of discontinuity or fracture between the school and life outside it - materials which are not considered modern or realistic by pupils, parents who are not actively supportive. Many of these difficulties have their origins, at least in part, in the second-language minority status of Irish.   But if discontinuity and fragmentation summarise the conditions at present, cohesion and partnership, we argue, should characterise the response.   At the moment the resources deployed in supporting Irish at primary level are not commensurate either with the challenges faced by the teacher or with the results implicitly expected. We propose, therefore, in the concluding section of this report (1) that the complex interaction between the work of ordinary primary schools and life outside, as far as Irish is concerned, should become the subject of a long-term exercise in educational and language planning. This would involve research, development and creative work designed to provide solutions to the challenges presented by the sociolinguistic situation in which these schools operate; and (2) that a broad-based partnership and inter-agency approach, with teachers at its centre, would be taken to this work. While part of the responsibility of such a body would be to provide resources for teaching and learning Irish, it would also be concerned with enlisting parental and community support and with mobilising and coordinating the efforts of those institutions and organisations which have the potential to enhance the work of the school. It is desirable that the focus should be specifically on schools, since initiatives and strategies at a national level designed to promote the language have not proved either strong enough or specific enough, given the sociolinguistic facts of Irish usage, to capitalise on and consolidate the achievements of ordinary schools.

It scarcely needs to be said that any initiative of this kind can only succeed if it takes full account of the perspective and needs of teachers and enlists their support. Teachers represent a huge resource for Irish, both in terms of their own ability in and personal commitment to the language and their professional role in teaching it. The Committee on Irish Language Attitudes Research survey (CLAR, 1975) and the INTO (1985a) survey showed that teachers were 'more supportive of Irish, more proficient in the language and more likely to use Irish than the general population' (Ó Riagáin, 1986: 13). In addition, substantial majorities of teachers were enthusiastic about teaching Irish and said their attitudes to teaching it were as favourable as when they began their careers or had become more favourable. But 81% of teachers felt the results obtained did not reflect the amount of time spent teaching Irish. Those who had become less favourable cited the syllabus, the position of Irish in Irish society, lack of pupil motivation and lack of parental support (INTO, 1985a: 14; INTO, 1998b: 11). It can be argued that, in the interim, as they have waited for the new curriculum and new materials, teachers have gone through a period of even greater uncertainty and discouragement (INTO, 1998b).

We believe that a well coordinated support system of the kind outlined above is the best way to respond to these problems. Whatever arrangements are adopted, the goal should be that over the next year or two teachers would see evidence (1) that there was a better balance between the effort they are putting into teaching Irish and the level of success achieved in the classroom, (2) that responsibility for promoting the language was more widely and more equally shared and (3) that teachers' efforts and achievements in relation to Irish were more generously recognised. In relation to the latter point, it is worth noting in passing that the vast majority of parents in the *Twenty-Classes Study*, responding in terms of their own children's performance, felt that the school was 'doing everything possible' as far as Irish was concerned.

The more ambitious programme of support that we are proposing for ordinary primary schools, however, would also provide a boost for Irish generally. We are perhaps more used to thinking of the *Naíonraí* (all-Irish preschools) or *Gaelscoileanna* (all-Irish primary schools) as linguistic magnets around which activities involving Irish, or Irish-speaking networks, might accumulate. But, as we argue in Chapter 5, ordinary primary schools also have this potential, although the language base from which they begin might be lower. We have only to reflect on the fact that on any given weekday between 9 a.m. and 11 a.m., ordinary primary schools around the country account for a considerable proportion of all the Irish being spoken outside *Gaeltacht* (Irish-speaking) areas. We must investigate more systematically, therefore, how to work outwards from that base in order to develop support for the language more generally. In other words, we must recognise clearly, in terms of the research and action agenda it implies, that ordinary primary schools comprise one of the great engines of Irish-language promotion.

1.2 Three research-and-development projects on Irish

We turn now to a description of the purpose and background of the three main studies which are the focus of the present report. The methodology of the first and most important of these, the *Twenty-Classes Study*, is described in more detail in Chapter 2. In the concluding section of this chapter we describe the organisation of the report.

1.2.1 The Twenty-Classes Study

The national surveys of achievement in spoken Irish conducted by ITÉ and the Curriculum Unit of the Department during the late 1970's and 1980's were useful in determining the extent to which the objectives of the curriculum in Irish were being attained in ordinary, all-Irish and Gaeltacht primary schools (Harris, 1982, 1983, 1984; Harris and Murtagh, 1987, 1988a, 1988b). They also provided objective information on changes in standards over time, and on the relationship between achievement in spoken Irish and a variety of factors such as pupil general academic ability, home use of Irish and the amount of Irish-medium teaching conducted in the school. This information was complemented by the substantial body of data on teachers' perceptions of the teaching of Irish in the 1984 INTO survey (INTO, 1985a). But much more research remained to be done. The role of parental attitudes, pupil attitudes and interests, and many other factors likely to determine success and failure in learning to speak Irish, had yet to be studied. Most importantly, we had little objective information on how Irish was taught - our information was limited to anecdote and individual case studies.

But new national surveys would not be an appropriate or effective way to obtain this information. National surveys, of their nature, require the sampling and testing of large numbers of pupils. Thus, they have to be confined to relatively narrow aspects of achievement in Irish: they cannot be used to collect detailed process-type information on teaching and learning. If national surveys were to attempt to collect such a range of data, the burden they would place on school time and resources would be unacceptable. In addition, the volume of data-analysis and interpretation involved would be prohibitive. The *Twenty-Classes Study* (originally titled *Scéim Phíolótach i dteagasc na Gaeilge*) was designed to overcome some of these problems by confining itself to a detailed examination of a small number of contrasting schools/classes. The field work was carried out by members of the Department's Primary School Inspectorate. The study had three main aims:

1. to describe the range of conditions under which spoken Irish is taught and learned by studying a small number of diverse classes,
2. to describe the teaching and learning of Irish in this small group of classes in more detail, and from a greater number of different perspectives than had ever been done hitherto,
3. to develop the instruments and observation procedures necessary to collect the new kinds of data implied by (2) above.

Our intention was that the data collected would be a resource for anyone concerned with the range of social, educational and linguistic conditions under which Irish is taught. Thus, it might be useful, for example, to those engaged in the development of courses and syllabuses in Irish, in the assembly of information packages for parents and so on. As it turned out, we subsequently made exactly this kind of use of the data ourselves when we undertook the *Communicative Materials Project* at the invitation of the Department of Education and Science and the NCCA. The development of new instruments, however, was also a central part of the work. In the present report, for example, we describe the development of a new instrument which provides a measure of different aspects of pupils' attitudes to Irish and their interest in learning Irish and foreign languages. We also demonstrate the feasibility - working through the school and with the teacher's agreement - of investigating parents' attitudes to Irish and the school, and parents' own practices in relation to such matters as praising their child's achievement in Irish and helping with Irish homework. In addition, we present data on the teachers' assessment of their pupils' ability in Irish, interest in Irish, and difficulty with Irish. Particularly significant are the two new classroom-observation instruments designed to record the activities and dynamics of the typical Irish language lesson at sixth-grade. This 'process' type information on the teaching of Irish is entirely new. Brief descriptions of all the instruments used are given in Chapter 2, with more detailed descriptions being presented in later chapters.

It is important to know, of course, if the data provided by these new instruments really do help to explain variations in achievement in spoken Irish in individual pupils or classes. Consequently, we also report here the results of a variety of correlation and regression analyses designed to answer this question. Information gathered by our instruments is also related to a number of background variables such as social class (a variable which had not previously been studied in relation to spoken Irish at primary level), pupil general academic ability, gender, the urban/rural location of the school and size of sixth-grade group.

In order to make the study more useful, we have 'calibrated', as it were, the Irish achievement of the 20 sixth-grade classes in terms of the achievement of classes nationally (Harris and Murtagh, 1988a). Thus, when we examine data on pupil attitudes, levels of interest or teaching activities in each of the 20 classes, we can interpret these data in terms of how good or bad the Irish achievement of each class is compared to classes nationally. Implicitly, our goal throughout is to predict the achievement in spoken Irish of the twenty classes, by showing how variables combine to determine the level of success achieved in each class. This means trying to show the manner in which favourable social, educational or attitudinal factors come together to produce a high level of achievement in spoken Irish in some classes, while corresponding unfavourable circumstances in others produce low levels of achievement. Our aim, however, is not to explain achievement in an isolated class-by-class way, but instead to show how achievement in a particular class fits into a broader pattern spanning groups of adjacent or similar classes. We will also be looking, from time to time, at classes which seem to go against the grain, classes which upset otherwise strong trends, and try to identify what exceptional factors may be at work. While our approach occasionally involves the presentation of rather large tables, we believe nevertheless that this serves some of the practical purposes outlined earlier rather better than summary tables.

It must be borne in mind too that we have collected no data relating to a number of factors which are relevant to Irish in primary school, particularly information relating to teachers and teaching. For example, issues such as teaching skill, teaching effectiveness or the quality of the teacher's Irish were not considered anywhere in this research. It would be quite wrong, therefore, to attempt to draw conclusions about any of these issues on the basis either of the quantitative data or of the lesson transcripts here.

1.2.2 *The Communicative Materials Project*

The *Communicative Materials Project* was carried out by ITÉ in close cooperation with the NCCA Irish Curriculum Committee (Harris *et al.*, 1996a,b). The goal was to produce guidelines and sample materials for a primary-school programme which would adopt a broadly communicative approach. We were conscious of the need for this exploratory work, knowing that a long period of experimentation and debate had also preceded the adoption of a communicative approach to modern languages and to Irish at post-primary (e.g. ITÉ, 1980). Notwithstanding the pioneering work of Sinéad Ní Neachtain (Norton, 1984a,b), there had been no really large-scale, systematic attempt prior to this to investigate the relevance of the new ideas about communicative teaching to Irish at primary level. The absence of such experimentation was a matter of concern to the NCCA Irish Curriculum Committee because, they reasoned, it would be difficult for commercial publishers to proceed promptly with the production of materials following the publication of the new curriculum, if practical work on guidelines and sample materials had not been carried out in advance.

Apart from introducing a new emphasis on communication in teaching and learning Irish, the *Communicative Materials Project* also attempted to find solutions to the range of problems identified in the *Twenty-Classes Study*. Among the problems in question - though not necessarily present in all classes or schools - were low levels of class attention and class interest, pupils' difficulty in understanding the lesson, pupils' reluctance to speak in class, pupils' lack of confidence in their own ability to succeed at Irish and lack of active support from parents.

The *Communicative Materials Project* itself was conducted at two main levels. Level 1 involved teachers and pupils in junior grades (junior infants to grade 2) classes. Level 2 concentrated on the senior grades (3-6). Altogether, there were over 60 teachers from *Galltacht* (English speaking areas) and *Gaeltacht* schools. Galltacht and Gaeltacht teachers met separately with the ITÉ Working Group. The account here focuses only on ordinary Galltacht schools. The final report on the project, however, argues that children who are native speakers of Irish, and who receive their whole education through Irish, have linguistic and communicative needs beyond those of pupils in ordinary schools. Consequently, it proposes that additional teaching materials be made available for Gaeltacht schools

In the initial meeting with teachers, the basic principles of the communicative approach to second-language teaching were outlined. The contrast between communication /meaning-negotiation and language practice was explained (see Chapter 6). The emphasis was to be on using Irish in the classroom in ways which simulated the 'naturalness' of first-language acquisition and which maximised opportunities for 'life-like' rehearsal of the language (Mitchell, 1994). Teachers were given a draft unit appropriate to their particular grade(s) and they discussed it in small groups along with one or more members of the ITÉ Working Group. A few weeks were then set aside for testing out the prepared unit in the classroom. During this time teachers completed a simple questionnaire on each lesson, recording progress and difficulties in using the materials.

Although communication and meaning negotiation was paramount, an emphasis on form was still maintained. This secondary goal was realised by first drawing pupils' attention to the relevant grammatical forms in the context of a communicative activity. This was then followed up by activities which involved more formal analysis and practice of the target structure. Language structures were not practised in a formal manner, however, until their communicative significance had already been illustrated. We made no attempt to replace the existing language-practice activities of teachers but simply asked them to integrate the new materials and ideas with their own approach as they saw fit. Neither did we dissuade teachers from using their existing reading schemes, though we did add some communicative reading tasks.

Lessons mainly consisted of communicative activities incorporating the four skills of listening, speaking, reading and writing. Where possible, authentic materials in the form of texts, street signs, notices, menus, application forms etc. were used. Authentic materials related to our cultural and literary heritage, such as songs, poems and place names, were also used. In the junior grades, the emphasis was on listening activities in which real messages in Irish had to be understood and responded to. Versions of stories at two levels of difficulty, some of them on audio tape, were made available to accommodate classes of varying ability in Irish.

A central goal was to promote a positive attitude to learning Irish and to make the learning process itself more enjoyable and interesting. Communicative games and tasks, in which the pupil must use simple Irish in a purposeful way in order to participate effectively, feature strongly in the materials. In some games, different pupils or groups of pupils have different pieces of simple information, and they have to communicate with each other in Irish in order combine the information necessary to succeed in the game. Social-interaction-based activities (e.g. role-play, sketches and drama) also play a major part, as does the acquisition of real new information or skills - e.g. learning Irish dances such as *Ballaí Luimnigh* through Irish. Everywhere in the materials, the pupils' own lives are to the fore and there is a sustained effort to ensure that the situations, characters and, as far as possible, speech and communication styles are consistent with pupils' interests and daily experience. This latter aspect of the work was the one that required the most thought. Substantial investment and research will continue to be needed in the years ahead if courses and materials in Irish which are realistic and which appeal to pupils are to be produced. The final report on the *Communicative Materials Project* makes the point that creative writers and other artists have a considerable contribution to make in this area.

Another problem was how to develop lessons and materials which would stimulate and engage those pupils with low levels of achievement in Irish, while providing some challenge for those with a better command of Irish. To ensure that this problem would be confronted head-on, teachers from a wide range of schools, including those in disadvantaged areas, were invited to participate in the project. Given the poor attitude/motivation results for pupils with low levels of ability in Irish (see Chapters 3 and 4 here) we set out to provide experiences which we hoped would allow all pupils to say 'I'm good at Irish' or 'I can speak Irish'. Experience to date suggests that this aspect of the project was an unqualified success - a frequent remark made by teachers who have used the materials is that even those children who were very weak at Irish were, for the first time, actually requesting that the Irish class begin. We also encouraged teachers to find ways of defining and explicitly marking pupils' progress as they gradually develop communicative proficiency in Irish. To this end, a communicative objective was set out at the beginning of each of the lessons supplied to the teachers. Finally, we tried to provide for more able pupils and classes in a systematic way. For example, a feature of all units was the inclusion of *Dúshláin Bhreise* so called because of the added challenge which these optional activities posed.

Teachers were exhorted not to correct pupils' errors during communicative activities but to do it later. Pupils were to be encouraged in every way to use whatever Irish they had at their disposal in order to understand or transmit messages. This meant learning to tolerate uncertainty and to take risks in situations where communicative difficulties were encountered. Pupils, in other words, were to be helped to develop 'strategic competence'. More generally, the teacher was urged to cultivate a tolerant, supportive, affirmative atmosphere in class which would promote a high level of pupil participation and personal expression.

Although spoken Irish was the major focus of the units, communicative reading and writing activities were also included. The traditional approach to reading - as a separate activity based mainly on narratives from graded readers - was replaced by reading activities which used a much greater range of texts, authentic texts where possible. These reading activities were integrated with the other three skill areas of listening, speaking and writing within a particular unit/exercise. In the early grades, special reading activities/games were designed to raise pupils' awareness of the sound/symbol relationships in Irish and to foster word recognition skills. Despite the new emphasis on integrated reading activities, however, it was stressed that the use of children's literature in Irish (from the school library) would still play a significant role in promoting literacy skills and in encouraging pupils to become independent readers. Activities which involved writing were generally not introduced in any systematic way until the senior grades. The emphasis was on functional writing e.g. writing birthday-party invitations, letters seeking information on Irish (Summer) Colleges or writing in a diary.

At the end of this initial period, teachers and researchers met in ITÉ to discuss teachers' reactions to the process of implementation and their assessment of the materials. We also solicited their opinions about more general issues, such as why they had not used communicative materials before now. Some of the issues were considered in small working groups, others in large-group discussions involving all teachers. Recommendations and comments arising from these discussions, augmented by questionnaire data, were used to redraft the sample units.

The Chairpersons and one or more members of the NCCA Irish Curriculum Committees attended all these meetings and participated in the work. The members of the ITÉ Working Group were also members of the NCCA Committee, and of various subcommittees, during all this time. Thus, a high level of information exchange between ITÉ and the NCCA was maintained as work on syllabus definition and the development of the communicative materials proceeded in tandem.

At the end of this and each subsequent meeting, teachers were given new lessons, accompanied by whatever pictorial or other materials, such as audio or video tapes, were required. Then, the cycle of trial, evaluation and redrafting started over again. Lessons and units were developed around some of the main themes set out in the draft new curriculum for Irish (e.g. Myself, Food, School, Pastimes and Special Occasions).

The final versions of the sample units were published in two reports (Harris *et al.*, 1996a,b). An audio tape containing material for various lessons accompanied each report. Substantial numbers of sample lessons were provided at each grade level e.g. a total of over 130 lessons are included for grades 3-6. An example of one of these lessons is set out in Appendix 1.1. The reports also included guidelines for implementing a communicative approach to teaching Irish as well as detailed specifications for the production and format of courses and teaching materials following the introduction of the new curriculum. They also deal with issues such as the importance of using children on audio and video tapes, and of employing native speakers of Irish - though not necessarily always from Gaeltacht areas - to record lesson material. It was never intended that these reports would constitute anything like a definitive statement on a communicative approach to Irish at primary level, but that they would serve as a contribution to ongoing debate and development.

The NCCA Irish Curriculum Committees were anxious that the reports should be available to teachers who were interested in examining the guidelines and in trying out the materials. It was felt that the broad-based consultative process which had been adopted up to then would be strengthened if a greater number of teachers could try out the materials and offer their opinions on them before the new course and syllabus took final shape. The distribution of the reports would also help to maintain the momentum for change by facilitating the early emergence of a number of teachers who were familiar with the practical classroom implications of the new approach and by preparing some of the groundwork for in-service courses which would be required later on. Recognising this, the Department of Education and Science provided funds to ITÉ to allow the free distribution of 500 copies of each of the two reports to those concerned with Irish in primary school and with the development of the new curriculum. In addition, 1400 copies of the report for junior classes and about 1300 copies of the report for senior classes have been purchased directly from ITÉ by individual teachers and schools.

1.2.3 *The Teaching through Irish Project*

This project was initiated just as the *Communicative Materials Project* was being completed. Perhaps it should be made clear straight away that we did not undertake it with the expectation that anything other than a small minority of teachers in ordinary schools would initially be interested in teaching entire school subjects through Irish. We felt, however, that it was important to begin this work and we believed that it could contribute to the development of Irish-language teaching in a number of significant ways as the new curriculum was introduced. Earlier research by ITÉ has shown that pupils in ordinary schools who are taught some aspects of the curriculum (apart from Irish) through Irish have substantially higher levels of achievement in spoken Irish than other pupils (Harris, 1983). More importantly, pupils of all levels of academic ability, as measured by an English-language verbal-reasoning test, have higher levels of achievement in Irish if they are in classes which are exposed to some Irish-medium teaching (Harris, 1993; Harris and Murtagh, 1988b). The Department of Education has had a policy for many years also of generally encouraging this approach. Despite this official policy, materials in Irish, specifically geared to the linguistic needs of pupils in ordinary schools, and to the requirements of teachers who are embarking on Irish-medium teaching for the first time, have never been made available.

The project involved ITÉ researchers working regularly with 50 third- and fourth-grade teachers over a two-year period to develop full courses in Science and Art through the medium of Irish. The teachers came from a wide variety of ordinary schools, including those in disadvantaged areas. The vast majority of them had no previous experience in teaching through Irish. Separate groups of teachers in Dublin and Tullamore met us in workshop sessions where we explained and discussed our proposals and distributed sample lessons. Having tried out the materials in their own classrooms, the teachers returned and discussed progress and completed questionnaires concerning the lessons. The lessons were then revised on the basis of this information. The teachers found the approach both enjoyable and rewarding and the courses are now on general sale.

None of the material consisted of translations or adaptations of existing courses in English. Instead, every aspect of each lesson was planned and developed with the particular needs of pupils and teachers in ordinary schools in mind. We choose Art because so many of the activities appropriate to the subject at this level involve language use which is located in a practical, concrete context. Science was chosen as the other subject in the knowledge that it would make greater demands on pupils in terms of vocabulary and perhaps use of language. On the positive side, we expected that pupils would have a high level of interest in this subject since they had not been taught Science before. In addition, since Science is only now being introduced as a subject for the first time in the new primary curriculum, the teacher would not have taught the subject through English before. Thus, in this respect at least, an entirely fresh start through the medium of Irish would be facilitated.

In the case of Science, we produced a teacher's handbook and a pupil's book, while in Art we produced just a teacher's handbook. Each handbook contained a general introduction to the whole question of teaching through Irish as well as guidelines for dealing with various difficulties which might arise. The material for each lesson was in three parts. The first consisted of background material including (i) a statement of the objective of the lesson, (ii) materials required, (iii) a list of the main vocabulary items involved (Irish and English), and (iv) a list of informal phrases or idioms that might be useful to the teacher during the lesson. The pupil book in Science included a pictorial vocabulary in Irish at the beginning of each lesson.

The second part of the material in the teacher's handbook consisted of an outline of the main steps in the lesson, usually illustrated, including a full script for the teacher. The aim was to anticipate some of the difficulties which would be presented by the limited linguistic ability of pupils, and to suggest possible ways around these difficulties. The availability of the prepared material had the effect of freeing teachers from some of the minute-by-minute decisions about the lesson to be taught, thus allowing them to attend more fully to classroom dynamics. In particular, they could devote more of their creative energy to responding to the individual needs of pupils who were learning through Irish for the first time. We expected and encouraged teachers to depart from the script. Nevertheless, there was general agreement that having the lesson planned in advance in this way was a major factor in the success of the project. The third part of the prepared material consisted of an optional development of the basic theme for more able classes. Examples of Science and Art lessons are set out in Appendix 1.2.

The guidelines made it clear that the materials provided could be used in any way that the teacher saw fit, but we suggested, after some general discussion, a number of principles that might be followed. We proposed, for example, that initially teachers would accept questions from pupils in English but answer them in simple Irish. In the longer term, teachers might rephrase in Irish the questions which had been posed in English by pupils. Discussions in English between pupils should also be permitted initially, but pupils should gradually be encouraged to use Irish. It was agreed that understanding and enjoyment of the subject were paramount considerations.

We believe that the provision of materials which are specifically designed for teaching pupils in ordinary schools through Irish is important in a number of ways. First, it is clear from the ITÉ surveys conducted in the 1970's and 1980's, as well as from the *Twenty-Classes Study* (see Chapter 2, section 2.4.4), that a limited programme of Irish-medium instruction is an essential ingredient in the success of those classes in ordinary schools which have really high levels of achievement in Irish - in some classes stretching all the way up to the mean level of performance attained in all-Irish schools. Even though the percentage of such schools nationally may be small, they make a significant contribution to the overall performance of ordinary schools in relation to Irish. Providing high-quality, specifically-designed Irish-medium materials also helps to maintain this traditional diversity in the ordinary primary schools' programme. The proven and deserved success of all-Irish schools should not have the unintended effect over time of creating an expectation that ordinary schools are homogeneously 'Irish-as-a-subject-only' in character.

There is perhaps a slightly greater danger of that happening as we adopt a communicative approach to teaching Irish. Communicative language teaching originated in foreign languages at post-primary, where the tradition of teaching parts or all of other subjects through the target language has never become really established. Thus, while we have much to learn from that valuable foreign-language teaching experience, we must also recognise that that tradition has tended to locate communication in the target language within the core lesson. It would be ironic, of course, if the element of the primary-school programme which involves the most truly communicative use of Irish were to fall into disuse as a 'more communicative' core programme came into being.

Admittedly, content-based teaching has grown in recent years as an adjunct to, and as a development of, communicative language teaching. Content-based teaching involves working out from the core subject, incorporating elements of other subjects into the teaching of the target language. This is a very desirable strategy and indeed we have adopted it to a significant extent in the *Communicative Materials Project*. But we believe that the bolder approach of attempting to teach a whole subject, such as Science or Art, through Irish has distinct advantages. The more radical approach obliges us to investigate the whole range of mechanisms by which sometimes complex information can be transmitted using relatively limited linguistic resources. It also identifies a broader range of topics suitable for integration with the core Irish lesson, topics which would almost certainly not come to light with a more piecemeal approach. In any case, one way of using the new materials would be for teachers to select certain *elements* of these Irish-medium lessons for inclusion in a conventional communicative approach - e.g. '*ag déanamh cárta na Nollag*' in the case of Art or '*ag úsáid uisce*' in the case of Science. Such elements could be readily integrated into the regular Irish lesson because the prepared materials have been specifically designed to accommodate the linguistic capabilities of pupils in ordinary schools. On the basis of that potential alone, a case can be made for repeating the *Teaching through Irish* experiment with other school subjects.

Finally, the suggestion has occasionally been made that there might be sufficient demand at some stage for a bilingual programme which was intermediate between 'ordinary' and 'all-Irish' programmes, if suitable structures were set in place (Harris, 1984; Mac Mathúna, 1985). Perhaps the best way of establishing the potential demand for such a programme would be to first conduct a pilot scheme backed up by a full range of specifically designed materials and in-service provision over a period of a few years. We return to this issue in Chapter 10. In any event, the communicative syllabus in Irish now being introduced, and the teaching materials which will follow from it, should inject a new vitality into the Irish lesson in ordinary schools. If, during this period of change, the tradition of using the language as a means of school and class communication, and to some extent as a medium of instruction, can be strengthened, the prospects are promising.

1.3 Organisation of the report

The *Twenty-Classes Study* provides the basic structure for the remainder of the report. The information and data from that study can be conveniently organised into chapters dealing with discrete topics such as pupils' views on the Irish lesson, parents' views and practices in relation to Irish and pupil participation in class. The data in each chapter come from different instruments or different parts of instruments. The account in each chapter is complete in itself although we often make cross references to findings elsewhere in the report. Discussion of the *Communicative Materials Project* or other ITÉ projects are incorporated within this structure. A key factor maintaining continuity between the chapters is that in presenting each new kind of data, we always list the 20 classes in the same order ranked from 1 (highest) to 20 (lowest) in terms of achievement in spoken Irish. Thus, individual classes can be identified throughout by their rank number, facilitating comparisons between different kinds of information for the same classes.

While we use statistical procedures such as correlation-regression and analysis of variance to show how data from the various instruments (observation schedules, attitude questionnaires and general ability tests) can help to explain high and low levels of achievement in Irish, we do not attempt to present a grand model of achievement in Irish. Our focus instead is on making the maximum use of the quantitative data and qualitative information to produce the most complete account possible of the teaching and learning of Irish. The development of a comprehensive statistical model to predict achievement, using all the different kinds of data here, is better deferred to another occasion. It should also be noted that when we quote statistical tests, the purpose is to distinguish between more and less important results in the study itself rather than to make claims about the existence of effects in the population.

We conclude here with a brief outline of the remaining chapters. In Chapter 2, we show how each of the classes in the *Twenty-Classes Study* fits into the national picture, by comparing data on *Pupil achievement in Irish*, *Social-class* and *Pupil general academic ability*. Data on a number of other variables are also presented. We show that, despite their small number, these twenty classes provide quite a good reflection of classes nationally.

The next two chapters examine pupils' affective reactions to Irish and to the process of learning it. In Chapter 3 we try to establish how positive or negative are the various components of pupils' Irish attitude/motivation and how each of these components are related to achievement in Irish. Chapter 4 provides an account of the Irish lesson in pupils' own words. Pupils were responding to questions about what they liked, disliked or would like to change. The report includes a sample of these comments, along with an analysis of the themes and how they varied from class to class.

In Chapter 5 we describe an investigation of parents' views and practices in relation to Irish and the teaching of Irish to their children. The sample of parents was limited to those in Dublin and surrounding areas.

In the next four chapters (6-9) we describe the development and application of two new classroom-observation instruments for analysing the teaching and learning of Irish. Chapter 6 begins with a review of current research on the classroom processes presumed to be responsible for successful second-language learning. It also gives an account of the development of the *Irish Lesson Analysis System - ILAS*. Chapter 7 and Chapter 8 describe the use of *ILAS* by primary school inspectors as they observed the teaching and learning of Irish. Because of the volume of data collected, Chapter 7 is confined to just three *ILAS* dimensions *Topic*, *Language activity* and *Materials*. Chapter 8 deals with the three remaining dimensions - *Pupil behaviour*, *Teacher mode of involvement* and *Classroom organisation*. The main focus is on the proportion of class time and the proportion of lesson segments which are devoted to the various language activities, topics etc. as the lesson proceeds. We also examined how class attention and interest vary according to changes in language activity and in other dimensions of the lesson. Chapter 9 provides an analysis of pupil participation and language use during the Irish lesson. This was based on classroom observation of individual pupils by primary school inspectors using the *Pupil Communicative Behaviour Record - PCBR*. There were three target pupils in each class - one at each of three different levels of ability in Irish (high/middle/low).

Finally, Chapter 10 is divided into two main sections. The first summarises the findings of the report, chapter by chapter. The second considers the implications for the kind of support structure which is now required for Irish in primary school.

2 The Twenty-Classes Study in a national context

2.1 Introduction

This chapter describes the methodology of the *Twenty-Classes Study* and presents a range of background information which is necessary to determine how much weight, if any, can be attached to our findings. While our goal was to represent the diversity of educational, social and linguistic circumstances under which Irish is taught, the selection of classes was fundamentally informal. It is important, then, that we present data which give some indication of how well the characteristics of the selected pupils and classes compare to the population nationally. Obviously, the closer the match, the more confidence we can have in the relevance of our findings. The degree of correspondence with the national profile is particularly important in the case of achievement in spoken Irish. But two other variables, academic ability and social class, are also important to the extent that previous research has shown that they are related to achievement in Irish.

We want to establish two kinds of representativeness: (a) that average *Pupil achievement in Irish, Pupil general academic ability* and *Social class* in the selected sixth-grade classes do not differ substantially from the national population and (b) that the selected classes as a group represent the full range of achievement in Irish nationally, while maintaining an overall balance between weak and strong classes. These two emphases in the analyses - on pupils and on classes - are maintained throughout each of the following chapters in which we present the data from the new instruments.

We also have a number of secondary aims. One of these is to establish the extent to which the smaller sub-group of classes involved in the Parents' Survey (see Chapter 5) differ from the larger group of twenty classes (what we call the *Total Sample*) as well as from classes nationally. Another task is to provide a more complete picture of the selected classes by presenting data relating to a number of socio-demographic and educational variables. Among these variables, all of which have been linked in previous research to achievement in Irish, are class size, gender composition of classes, urban-rural and regional location, Irish-medium instruction and course method used to teach Irish (Harris, 1983). Finally, we present data on teachers' perceptions of pupils' ability in Irish, interest in Irish and their experience of difficulty with different school subjects. These teacher-perception data provide the necessary background for other information to be presented in later chapters.

2.1.1 Overview of research on achievement in spoken Irish

We begin with a brief account of research on achievement in Irish at primary level. Three issues are examined: the extent to which curricular objectives in spoken Irish are attained; how standards have changed in the last few decades; and the social, educational and other factors which affect achievement.

School achievement in Irish

Taking the attainment of curricular objectives in spoken Irish first, national surveys conducted by ITÉ in the late 1970's and 1980's showed that an average of about one-third of pupils in ordinary schools attained mastery of each of the curricular objectives in spoken Irish at sixth, fourth and second grade. The tests were of the criterion-referenced kind and were based on the *Nuachúrsaí*, the official Department of Education conversation courses in Irish for primary schools (Ireland: Department of Education, 1978). Another one-third of pupils, on average, made at least minimal progress in relation to each of the objectives at each grade, but did not attain mastery. And one-third of pupils, on average, failed to make even minimal progress in relation to each of the objectives at each grade (Harris, 1982, 1983, 1984, 1988; Harris and Murtagh, 1988a,b). The fact that the various proportions remained reasonably stable as the objectives become more demanding at successive grades suggests that proficiency in spoken Irish grows steadily during the primary school years. The proportions failing to attain mastery or to make even minimal progress in relation to objectives at each grade, however, indicate the existence of a substantial gap between the level of performance in spoken Irish which the curriculum implicitly aims at and the actual level of performance which is attained by most pupils.

In the context of this performance gap, it is notable that early work by Kellaghan, Macnamara and Neuman (1969) indicated that pupils were more likely to be judged by teachers to have difficulty with mathematics and Irish generally than with English. Primary school pupils were also likely to rate themselves lower in Irish (spoken, reading and writing) than in mathematics or English relative to their classmates (Kellaghan, Madaus and Airasian, 1982). More recently, a study by the Department of Education (Ireland: Department of Education, 1994a), which explored the gender gap in Irish primary schools reported that the subjects teachers most frequently perceived pupils as requiring additional help with are mathematics and Irish.

Changes in standards of attainment in Irish

The second main issue concerns changes in standards of attainment. Research conducted in the 1970's and early 1980's indicated that standards of achievement in Irish were generally holding up well in the junior grades of primary school but were declining in the senior grades and at post primary. The findings were based on data relating to teachers' perceptions, scores on standardised reading-tests and public-examination grades (Ó Domhnalláin and Ó Gliasáin, 1976; INTO, 1976; Fontes and Kellaghan, 1977; Greaney,

1978; Ó Riagáin, 1982; Bord na Gaeilge, 1986). A comparison between ITÉ national surveys of achievement in spoken Irish at primary level conducted in 1978 and 1985, however, revealed a modest but statistically significant increase in the mean percentage of pupils attaining mastery of each of the sixth-grade objectives over the seven year period (Harris and Murtagh, 1988a).

General ability and social class
The third issue is the influence of various factors on pupil achievement in Irish and attitude to Irish. We begin with general academic ability and social class and then proceed to a number of other factors, including gender, regional/urban-rural location, size of sixth-grade group in class, home language and amount of Irish-medium instruction at school. The relationship between, on the one hand, general academic ability and social class and, on the other, second-language achievement, is complex. Many of the difficulties centre on the definition and measurement of general academic ability and social class. While a full analysis of these issues is beyond the scope of this report, it will be useful to draw attention to a few points before we examine the Irish studies which try to link these variables to achievement in Irish.

First, there is the difficulty that measures of general academic ability, such as tests of verbal reasoning in the mother tongue, tend to have a strong linguistic orientation anyway. In addition, verbal intelligence, reasoning and language aptitude, are considered to be the major components of overall intelligence, though these three components also have strong relationships with one another (Gardner and Lambert, 1972; Wesche, Edwards and Wells, 1982; Skehan, 1982, 1998; Sasaki, 1993). Moreover, there is considerable controversy regarding the notion of 'ability' as a fixed entity and, indeed, about the validity of the construct of ability/intelligence itself (Lynch, 1985; Boyle, 1987; Gardner, 1993). Finally, there is the complication that the two main variables under discussion, general academic ability as measured by a verbal reasoning test and social class, are themselves related (Kellaghan and Macnamara, 1972).

There is substantial evidence from Ireland and elsewhere (Genesse, 1976; Carroll, 1979) of a strong link between pupils' general academic ability and second-language achievement generally. A number of studies conducted in Irish primary schools show significant positive associations between general academic ability, as measured by a test of verbal reasoning in English, and achievement in both Irish reading (Martin and Kellaghan, 1977; Fontes, Kellaghan and O Brien, 1981) and spoken Irish (Harris and Murtagh, 1988b). Verbal reasoning has also been found to correlate strongly with success in Irish in public examinations at post-primary level (Greaney and Kellaghan, 1984).

Various national and international studies have also indicated that social-class background is positively linked to general educational outcomes, including second-language achievement and attitude (Burstall, 1975, 1979; Martin and Kellaghan, 1977; Hannan, Breen *et al.*, 1983; Skehan, 1990). In interpreting such findings, it should be borne in mind that social class tends to be primarily defined, as it is in the present study, in terms of parents' occupation. It has been argued, however, that the really critical factors in determining success in school life are 'cultural capital' indices such as parental values, attitudes, tastes, beliefs and linguistic practices (Bourdieu, 1974, 1977; Lynch, 1985). In the account of the Parents' Survey in Chapter 5 we describe the effects of such home factors on children's achievement in, and attitude to, Irish. National surveys of Irish ability and use of Irish among the adult population have also identified significant positive associations between social class and both ability to speak Irish and attitude to Irish (CLAR, 1975; Ó Riagáin, 1997).

One other general point here is that the influence of general ability and social class may vary according to the type of second-language proficiency being considered. Cummins (1984) makes a distinction between Cognitive Academic Language Proficiency (CALP) - consisting of linguistic knowledge and literacy skills required for academic work - and Basic Interpersonal Communicative Skills (BICS) - the skills required for oral fluency and sociolinguistic appropriateness. CALP is thought to be more dependent on cognitive ability or 'intelligence' than BICS is. Evidence to support the validity of the distinction comes mainly from studies of immersion programmes (Genesee, 1976, 1987). In general, the evidence is that the development of BICS is relatively independent of IQ. In later grades of primary school, however, as programmes become more academic in orientation, thereby calling more on CALP skills, IQ becomes a more powerful predictor of second-language achievement. Ellis (1994) suggests that the advantage of higher social class is more likely to be seen in formal language learning (CALP) than when a programme emphasizes communicative language skills (BICS).

Demographic, educational and other factors.
We turn now from general academic ability and social class to the other factors which have been linked to achievement generally and to Irish in particular. First, research on gender differences in second-language achievement indicates that girls, by and large, do better than boys as far as both verbal skills generally and second-language achievement are concerned (Maccoby and Jacklin, 1974; Burstall, 1975). In the case of Irish, tests of reading confirm the superior performance of girls over boys (Martin and Kellaghan, 1977). The ITÉ surveys of spoken Irish (Harris, 1984; Harris and Murtagh, 1988a) consistently show that more girls than boys attain mastery of grade-related objectives in spoken Irish. Published examination statistics for the three years 1992-1994 also show that girls regularly outperform boys in Irish in both the junior and Leaving Certificate examinations (Department of Education, 1993, 1994b, 1995a). More girls than boys opt for higher level papers, more girls receive honours and fewer girls fail.

The earlier mentioned study exploring gender differences (Department of Education, 1994a) showed that sixth-grade teachers in mixed schools perceived boys as needing assistance with Irish more frequently than girls: 76% of teachers said girls need additional assistance with Irish, but 94% said that boys need such assistance. Gender differences in attitudes to learning a second language have also been recorded in a number of studies

(Gardner and Lambert, 1972; Burstall, 1975; Pritchard, 1987). In general the results indicate that girls are more favourably disposed to learning a foreign language than boys. Although little research has been done on gender and attitudes specifically to learning Irish, a study of secondary school students in Cork City and County noted that girls were more positively oriented towards learning Irish than boys (Ó Fathaigh, 1991).

Regional/locational factors have also been found to influence achievement. In the 1978 sixth-grade survey of spoken Irish, Harris (1983) reported that classes in the Dublin region and in city locations generally had significantly lower levels of achievement in Irish than classes in other regions/locations - classes in Munster were best overall. In addition, smaller sixth-grade classes were associated with significantly higher levels of achievement in Irish.

Home use of Irish is also an important factor. A recent national survey on languages in Ireland reports that Irish is never spoken in over two-thirds of Irish homes (Ó Riagáin and Ó Gliasáin, 1994). While the opportunities for children outside the Gaeltacht to use Irish at home are fairly limited, therefore, various ITÉ surveys have confirmed the positive effects of even moderate home use of Irish on pupil achievement in the language (Harris, 1984; Harris and Murtagh, 1988a,b).

Finally, there is evidence that target-language use outside the language lesson proper can positively influence proficiency. Quite aside from the high levels of achievement found in all-Irish primary schools (Harris, 1984; Harris and Murtagh, 1988a), there is also evidence, as we mentioned in Chapter 1, that at least some Irish-medium instruction in ordinary schools leads to higher levels of achievement than is found in schools/classes where it is not used at all. In the 1978 ITÉ sixth-grade survey, Irish-medium instruction in ordinary schools emerged as a strong predictor of achievement in spoken Irish (Harris, 1983). Similar results were found in the 1985 sixth-grade replication study: the overall mean percentage attaining mastery of sixth-grade objectives was substantially different depending on the amount of Irish-medium instruction received: no Irish-medium instruction (30.4%, on average, mastered each objective); less than one-hour of Irish-medium instruction per week (36.1%, on average, mastered each objective); one hour or more such instruction (48.7%, on average, mastered each objective) (Harris and Murtagh, 1988b).

2.2 Methodology of the study

2.2.1 Sample

The intention was to select 20 sixth-grade classes from a wide variety of ordinary schools. Gaeltacht and all-Irish schools were not included. It was not intended that the schools selected would be in any sense exceptional, or that the sixth-grade classes would have exceptional teachers. We wanted a group of classes that would represent the full range of social, educational and linguistic conditions under which Irish is taught in primary schools at present. The following is the initial list of the possibilities we compiled:

a) Schools in disadvantaged areas
b) Schools in areas with a predominantly urban working class population
c) Schools following the *Nuachúrsaí* (audio-visual) method in a strict fashion
d) Schools using the ABC (traditional aural-oral) method
e) Schools in which a special emphasis is placed on the communicative dimension in teaching spoken Irish as a subject
f) Schools which use commercially produced workbooks as a regular part of the Irish lesson
g) Schools in which there is a substantial amount of Irish-medium teaching or Irish-medium communication
h) Schools where there is a particularly high level of involvement or interest by parents in the teaching of Irish or in the school generally.

Apart from these requirements, we also wanted a geographical spread of classes, covering all major regions of the country, and including both urban and rural locations. Most importantly, as the list above suggests, we wanted to adequately represent both high Irish-achievement and low Irish-achievement classes, and to balance these two types of classes against each other as far as possible. Ideally, the characteristics of the 20 classes selected, as a group, would not depart too radically from the picture nationally in terms of important variables such as achievement in spoken Irish, general academic ability and social-class composition.

Random selection of the small number of classes to be studied from a list of all sixth-grade classes in the country would almost certainly not have resulted in satisfactory coverage of the range of variables just mentioned. A stratified random sample would not have been feasible either, because the number of cells involved would be extremely large. We decided, therefore, to compile an initial list of 40 classes which would more than fulfill our requirements under the eight main headings above as well as in relation to the socio-demographic and other variables mentioned. The final 20 classes would be selected from this list. Lists of schools containing data on the kind of variables of interest to us here - level of parental support, Irish-medium teaching and so on - are simply not readily available. Thus, in developing the initial list of 40 classes we relied heavily on the knowledge and advice of Primary School Inspectors who were familiar with schools and classes around the country. The inspectors sent us detailed information on each of the 40 schools, including data on class size, gender composition, social background of pupils, pupil academic ability, parental involvement, Irish-language teaching methods and so on. While this information was extremely useful in compiling the basic list of classes and in making our final selection, it should be emphasized that it played no part at all in the study itself. All analyses and interpretation reported here are based on data collected directly from parents, pupils and teachers using objective research instruments.

In selecting the final 20 schools, therefore, we attended to the emerging profile of the sample as a whole over all of the variables of interest. We wanted the final sample to approximate a random national sample, with strata corresponding to the key variables. The results are presented in Table 2.1 and in later tables. Our approach did not mean that schools chosen on the basis of one category could not also sometimes represent other categories. For example, a sixth-grade class chosen because the school was located in an area with a predominantly urban working-class population (Category B in Table 2.1), might also happen to be using the *Nuachúrsaí* in a strict fashion (Category C). This particular class would not be counted again under Category C, however, because 'method' was not the main basis on which it was originally chosen.

Note that in a similar way categories relating to 'following the *Nuachúrsaí* (audio-visual) method in a strict fashion' or placing a 'special emphasis on the communicative dimension' were not mutually exclusive either. Our concern was that classes with the various defined characteristics would not be omitted. While our selection of classes did not aspire to be truly representative of the whole range of methods used to teach Irish, it was hoped that the number of factors taken into account in selection would produce a good cross-section of teaching approaches.

Because the study would make greater than usual demands on pupils, teachers and schools, we did not expect that all the schools/classes initially chosen would be able to accommodate us when we approached them. In the event, however, only one of the classes originally selected was unable to take part. This class was replaced by its nearest equivalent. In addition, some schools which we thought at first would be suitable under one or other of the headings in Table 2.1, turned out later not to be suitable due to other characteristics of the schools/classes which were of concern to us, such as the number of pupils, the location of the school, social-class composition or other factors. For example, while a school in a 'country' location might be basically suitable under a particular heading (e.g. Category D in the case of a teacher who used the ABC method), we might be unable to include it if we already had too many country schools under other category headings.

It will be clear from this that the final sample selected involved compromises, though we did manage to represent each of the eight main categories initially defined by at least two classes/schools. Probably the most significant shortcoming was that we did not succeed in balancing numbers of boys and girls. Of the twenty classes, nine came from mixed-sex schools, eight from girls schools and three from boys schools. Overall, 35% of the pupils were boys and 65% were girls. On the positive side, despite this imbalance, the achievement in spoken Irish of the pupils as a whole turned out to be reasonably close to the national average (See Tables 2.2 - 2.4 below).

The first two columns in Table 2.1 show that the *Total Sample* of 20 classes in the present study contains 534 pupils. Only seven of these classes (236 pupils), are included in the survey of parents which is the basis of Chapter 5. Details on the classes included in the Parent Survey are shown in Columns 3 and 4. We limited the Parent Survey in this way because we were unsure if the questionnaire used, and the system for distributing and collecting it, would be either effective or acceptable to teachers. Only classes in Dublin and nearby counties were involved so that the researchers could visit any of the schools at short notice if difficulties arose. In fact, there were no problems of any kind. Completed questionnaires were returned by 83.9% of parents (n = 198) and it is these parents and their children who provide the data presented later.

Table 2.1
Number of sixth-grade pupils and classes in 'Total' and 'Parent' samples by school type.

School Type N=	Total Sample*		Parent Sample	
	Classes	*Pupils*	*Classes*	*Pupils*
(A) Schools in disadvantaged areas	3	98	1	34
(B) Schools in areas with a predominantly urban working class population	3	106	1	39
(C) Schools following the *Nuachúrsaí* (audio-visual method) in a strict fashion	3	75	1	32
(D) Schools using the *ABC* method	2	22	-	-
(E) Schools in which a special emphasis is placed on the communicative dimension in teaching spoken Irish as a subject	3	55	1	30
(F) Schools which use commercially produced course books as a regular part of the Irish lesson	2	68	1	39
(G) Schools in which there is a substantial amount of Irish-medium teaching or Irish-medium communication	2	48	-	-
(H) Schools where there is a particularly high level of involvement or interest by parents in the teaching of Irish or in the school generally	2	62	2	62
Total	*20*	*534*	*7*	*236*

* 'Total Sample' consists of 20 classes (n (pupils) = 534). Seven of these classes were involved in the Parent Survey.

2.2.2 Instruments

Although ten instruments in all were originally used to collect data from parents, pupils and teachers in the present study (see Figure 1 below), not all of the instruments are equally important. Indeed two of them (marked with a single asterisk) contribute little or no data to the present report. Three of the instruments, the ability and achievement tests, were developed prior to the *Twenty-Classes Study* - these are marked with a double asterisk.

Figure 1 Instruments used in the Twenty-Classes Study listed in order of administration

1.	*Pupil Questionnaire*: A measure of pupil Irish attitude/motivation. Pupils recorded their reactions to 77 statements about Irish, learning Irish and interest in second/ foreign languages. These results are described in Chapter 3. Responses to three write-in items (78-80) are described in Chapter 4.
2.	*Teacher's Rankings of Pupils (Áireamh an Mhúinteora de réir cumais)*: The class teacher rated each individual pupil's (a) ability in Irish (b) interest in Irish and (c) difficulty with aspects of Irish, English and Mathematics. In addition, the teacher provided basic information on the parent's/ guardian's occupation/employment status (Instrument and results described below).
3.	*Irish Lesson Analysis System (ILAS)*: A direct classroom observation instrument concerned with teaching and learning activities in the Irish lesson. Observer No. 1 classified the main segments of classroom activity according to five dimensions (topic, language activity, pupil behaviour, teacher mode of involvement, classroom organisation). The instrument itself is described in detail in Chapter 6 and the results in Chapters 7 & 8.
4.	*Pupil Communicative Behaviour Record (PCBR)*: A classroom observation instrument designed to describe pupil behaviour during the Irish lesson. Observer No. 2 recorded the general behaviour and language use of three pre-selected pupils. The instrument and the results are described in Chapter 9.
5.	*Observers' Global Rating of Lesson*: At the end of each lesson Observers 1 & 2 jointly filled in a check list which related to that lesson which gave a global description of classroom activity and pupil/teacher behaviour.
6.	*Teacher Questionnaire (Céistiúchán don Oide)*: Information on the teacher's own views and practices in relation to teaching and learning Irish.
7.	**Béaltriail Ghaeilge ITÉ-VI (Sixth-grade test of spoken Irish)*: Criterion-referenced test of achievement in spoken Irish for sixth-grade pupils.
8.	**Béaltriail Ghaeilge ITÉ-II (Second-grade test of spoken Irish)*: Only the *Communication* subtest from the second-grade test was used.
9.	**Drumcondra Verbal Reasoning Test (DVRT)*: Pupils general academic ability was measured by this test in English.
10.	*Parents' Questionnaire*: Parents were asked for their views on Irish and the teaching of Irish in primary school (29 items). (Results in Chapter 5).

* Only a few items from these instruments are used in the present report. ** Existing instruments.

Numbers on the left hand side (column 1) of Figure 1 indicate the order in which the instruments were administered. This is followed by a brief description of the instrument, the person providing the information (pupils, teachers, inspectors or parents) and an indication of the chapter in which the results are described. The order of administration was determined by a number of factors. For example, the *Pupil Questionnaire* was administered first so that the somewhat exceptional focus on Irish during the classroom observation work, or the process of answering the test of spoken Irish, would not affect pupil responses to the attitudinal items. The Irish test (*Béaltriail Ghaeilge ITÉ*) and the *Drumcondra Verbal Reasoning Test* (*DVRT*) were delayed until after the classroom observation phase of the study in case the former would create a 'test' or 'examination' set in the pupils' minds. Such a set might lead them to interpret the observation as a further form of testing - something which would not be desirable as we wanted the lesson to be as unaffected by the observers' presence as possible. It should also be noted that the classroom observation instruments (the *ILAS* and the *PCBR*), although numbered sequentially in the above list were in fact administered concurrently by different observers (inspectors). In addition, each observer independently made a separate audio tape-recording of each of the two lessons. Instructions (in Irish) to the observers regarding the administration of the various instruments may be found in Appendix 2.1.

The overall strategy of the study, it will be recalled, was to interpret the data from a number of new instruments in the context of data derived from existing instruments which had been used in previous studies. The main focus of the report apart from the present chapter, therefore, is on the data derived from four newly-constructed instruments - *Pupil Questionnaire, ILAS, PCBR* and *Parents' Questionnaire* (no's 1, 3, 4 & 10). The advantage of introducing data from the three existing instruments (no's 7-9) measuring Irish achievement and general academic ability is that previous studies in which some of them feature (e.g. Harris and Murtagh, 1987, 1988b) provide comparative data at a national level which allow us to make at least a rough-and-ready assessment of how representative or otherwise pupils and classes in the present study are as a group.

Data from the *Teacher's Rankings of Pupils* presented in the present chapter also provide important contextual information necessary for the interpretation of data from the new instruments in later chapters: (a) teachers' perceptions of pupil difficulty with and interest in Irish and (b) basic data on the occupational status of parents to be used for the *Social class* scale.

Two other new instruments developed and administered in the course of this study were (5) the *Observers' Global Rating of the Lesson* and (6) the *Teacher Questionnaire*. These two instruments were intended merely to provide us with a 'fall-back' option in case one of the other instruments either failed entirely or yielded information which was ambiguous or deficient in some way. In the event, only three items from these instruments (two from the *Teacher Questionnaire* and one from the *Observers' Global Rating of the Lesson*) were used in interpreting results from the main instruments.

With the exception of actual pupil tests of Irish achievement (ITÉ tests) and general academic ability (*DVRT*), all other instruments on which this report is based may be seen in the various appendices.

We will now describe each of these instruments in more detail.

2.2.3 *The Pupil Questionnaire*

The *Pupil Questionnaire* (Appendix 3.2) consisted of 77 items measuring various dimensions of pupils' attitude to Irish and motivation to learn it. The items were used to develop 11 scales, nine of which related to Irish attitude/motivation, one related to the pupil's self-assessed ability in Irish and another to the extent to which Irish is used in the home. Many of the items, and the scales derived from them, are based to a greater or lesser extent on those used in the *Attitude/Motivation Test Battery (AMTB)* described by Gardner *et al.*, 1979. A five point Likert response format (Likert, 1932) was used for all items. Each item stem was read aloud by the inspector to avoid reading difficulties. More details on the questionnaire and its administration are given in Chapters 3.

In three items at the end of the *Pupil Questionnaire* pupils were also asked to write in their own words what they liked, disliked or would like to change in the Irish lesson. Chapter 4 describes the analysis and categorisation of these pupil assessments of the Irish lesson. Actual pupil responses to these open-ended items may be seen in Appendix 4.

2.2.4 *Teacher's Rankings of Pupils*

Each of the twenty class-teachers involved in the study was asked to complete a report sheet for the class (*Teacher's Rankings of Pupils / Áireamh an Mhúinteora ar na Daltaí de Réir Cumais*). Full instructions in Irish and English were given (see Appendix 2.2). The report sheet requested:

   (a) the teacher's perception of each pupil's ability in Irish (high, medium, low),
   (b) the teacher's perception of the pupil's interest in Irish (very high, high, medium, low, very low),
   (c) whether the teacher perceived the pupil as having difficulty in the following subject areas - Spoken Irish, Irish Reading, Irish Writing, Spoken English, English Reading, English Writing and Mathematics (difficulty, no difficulty),
   (d) a description of the parent's/guardian's occupation and employment status (employed /unemployed).

Regarding (a) above, it may be noted that a reason for asking the teachers to rate ability in Irish is that the application of one of the direct observation instruments (the *PCBR*) required that we would be able to identify in advance one pupil each of high, middle, and low ability in Irish. Each of these pupils would then be the focus of the Observer's attention at different times. The teacher's assessment of ability in Irish was required because at that stage the test of achievement in spoken Irish had not yet been administered.

The written instructions to the teacher regarding the information required at (d) above indicated that it was important as it was needed in order to rate pupils on a social class scale and that it would be treated as strictly confidential. The following two items of information were sought only on the *main earner*, whether that was the father, mother, or male or female guardian:

1. *Full Title of the parent's or guardian's occupation* (or former occupation if retired, redundant or unemployed), whichever parent was the main earner. For example, if the father was unemployed but the mother was employed, then she would be regarded as the main earner. The teacher was also asked to state whether the parent who was the main earner was, at that time, unemployed (i.e. receiving financial assistance from the state), and to indicate whether this was long-term (more than 2 years) or short-term (less than 2 years). If in doubt about how to classify a particular occupation, teachers were asked to simply give as much information as possible and to write any explanatory notes necessary in the margin.

2. *Type of Work Done*: It was pointed out that although the title itself might often be self-explanatory, more detail would sometimes be needed on the type of work done. For example, if the job title listed was 'Civil Servant', the type of work done might be that of a clerical assistant, tax inspector or staff officer etc. To give some idea of the kind of information required, the following examples were listed:
   Full Title: Civil Servant (Retired).
   Type of Work Done: Administrative Officer, Department of Finance.
   Full Title: Small farmer/part time barman.
   Type of Work Done: 40 acres mixed farming/works in hotel at night.
   Full Title: Factory worker (long-term unemployed).
   Type of Work Done: Machinist in clothing factory.
   Full Title: Farmer.
   Type of Work: 120/150 acres mixed farming.
   Full Title: Nurse.
   Type of Work Done: Private Nursing Home for the elderly.

In the case of the seven classes which participated in the Parents' Survey, we also had information directly from the parents themselves concerning occupation and employment (See Q.2 of the *Parents' Questionnaire* - Appendix 5.3). Priority was given to the information provided by the parents in these cases.

2.2.5 *Irish Lesson Analysis System (ILAS)*

The *Irish Lesson Analysis System (ILAS)* was designed to describe the structure and composition of the Irish lesson. This instrument was a modification and extension of the lesson analysis system developed by Mitchell, Parkinson and Johnstone (1981) at the University of Stirling which sets out detailed guidance for classifying the pedagogic units of the foreign-language lesson in terms of a number of critical dimensions, such as topic, language activity, teacher and pupil involvement, and classroom organisation. In Chapter 6 we describe how the Stirling system was adapted for use in a second-language (Irish) classroom, and the manner in which some categories of dimensions were altered, and other categories and dimensions added. Chapter 6 also describes the application of the *ILAS* in our classroom observation study. Transcripts showing how the system was applied may be found in Appendix 6.4.

2.2.6 *Pupil Communicative Behaviour Record (PCBR)*

Unlike the *ILAS* just described which categorised classroom teaching activities, the *Pupil Communicative Behaviour Record (PCBR)* focused on recording pupils' behaviour in the Irish classroom. We were particularly concerned with coding various communicative dimensions of individual pupil speech. In order to do this we adapted some of the major features of an observation instrument specifically designed to record the communicative aspects of language teaching *COLT* (*Communicative Orientation of Language Teaching*) - Part II (Allen, Fröhlich and Spada, 1984).

In applying the *PCBR*, selected pupils of different ability levels in Irish were observed for three minute intervals followed by a two minute period during which their behaviours were recorded under a number of headings. Individual (non-choral) speech was coded in terms of the language used (English/Irish), the length of the utterance, its function (question/answer), the nature of the contribution made by the pupil (predictable /unpredictable) and the interaction type involved (pupil-pupil/pupil-teacher). If the pupil remained silent the extent to which he/she was attentive or disruptive was noted. Finally, the occurrences of 'other' behaviours such as writing, reading or choral speech during the observation unit were also recorded.

Each of these descriptive categories is set out in full in Chapter 9. The difficulties in coding and in interpreting behaviours and the manner in which problems were eventually resolved is also described. In addition, Chapter 9 presents results on the application of the *PCBR* in the present study of 20 classes. Coding guidelines for the *PCBR*, and the *PCBR* coding sheet, may be found in Appendix 9.

2.2.7 *Observers' Global Rating of Lesson.*

The *Observers' Global Rating of Lesson (OGRL)* comprising 37 items was completed jointly by Observer 1 and Observer 2 at the end of each lesson. The *OGRL* provided a 'high-inference' (relatively subjective) global rating of certain classroom processes and teacher and pupil behaviour, the information being recorded after the completion of the Irish lesson. It was intended that data derived from it would only be used if the two, 'low-inference', 'on-line', classroom-observation instruments described above were to prove unworkable. The two more objective observation instruments functioned so well, however, that the *OGRL*, which covered more or less the same events and processes but in a less satisfactory way, was largely redundant. In Chapter 9, however, we do use information from one item (see Appendix 2.3) from the *OGRL*.

2.2.8 Teacher Questionnaire

The *Teacher Questionnaire* was designed to collect some background information on the teacher, his/her attitude to Irish and the teaching of Irish, general practice in relation to the Irish class, and reactions to the observation work. Data relating to only four items, however, are used in the report (see Appendices 2.4 & 2.5). In Chapter 4 we refer briefly to class-based information on (a) course-method employed in the teaching of Irish (item 17) and (b) to time spent teaching through Irish (item 32). In Chapter 6 we discuss the teachers' reactions to the observation work (items 69 & 70). In addition, we occasionally used information from the *Teacher Questionnaire* in an informal way. For example, in coding audio-taped lessons using the *ILAS* system (Chapter 6) reference to the completed *Teacher Questionnaire* for a particular class helped to confirm which textbook was being used. More detailed analyses of replies to the remaining questions would not have been useful given that we only had 20 classes. We were also conscious of the fact that teachers' views on Irish had already been extensively surveyed by the INTO (1985a).

2.2.9 Sixth-grade test of spoken Irish (Béaltriail Ghaeilge ITÉ-VI)

This criterion-referenced test of achievement in spoken Irish (Harris, Murtagh, Hickey, De Nais and Ó Domhnalláin, 1985) was designed to show whether pupils had attained mastery of particular behavioural objectives. These objectives were carefully tailored to the content of the *Nuachúrsaí* lesson for 5th and 6th grades. There were two parts to the test - a 'listening' section and a 'speaking' section. Objectives will be identified by brief names such as *General comprehension of speech, Pronunciation* and *Fluency of oral description*. A full list of objectives may be found in Table 2.2. All items used to test the 'listening' section were in multiple-choice form and were presented on a cassette tape to entire class-groups of pupils. The 'speaking' section was individually administered to each pupil in a face-to-face interview with an examiner (inspector). Examiners could give instructions in Irish or English, whichever language would best ensure that the pupil understood the task. The items themselves, however, were entirely in Irish.

It was decided to administer items relating to the second-grade *Communication* objective (Harris, Hickey, Ní Chonaill, and Murtagh, 1982) to a corresponding sample of sixth-grade pupils as was done in the 1985 survey (Harris and Murtagh, 1988a). The addition of this objective (see next section for a description) to the sixth-grade test necessitated the division of the speaking section into two parts, so as to reduce the demands which lengthy individual testing would make on pupils. Each pupil in the present study, therefore, was administered approximately half of the speaking items in a manner similar to that adopted at second grade (Harris, 1984). The group of speaking items (Part A or Part B) assigned to a particular pupil was decided randomly.

Two levels of performance in relation to each objective were distinguished: 'mastery' and 'minimal progress'. The proportion of items correct which counted as mastery was 75%. This level was decided before any testing began and was based in part on the judgments of a group of primary-school inspectors using a modified version of the Angoff method (Angoff, 1971; Livingston and Zieky, 1982). Minimal progress was defined as 40% correct responding. Most of the data to be presented here consist of the percentage of pupils who master each objective. Mastery and minimal progress as they apply here are discussed in detail in Harris (1984).

2.2.10 Second-grade 'Communication' objective (Béaltriail Ghaeilge ITÉ-II)

In the case of *Communication* (18 items), the emphasis was on assessing the pupil's ability to communicate in simple spoken Irish, well within the linguistic limits defined by the *Nuachúrsaí* at the second-grade level. For a fuller description see Harris and Murtagh (1988a). In order to ensure consistency of scoring at second and sixth grade, examiners were directed to adhere to the same scoring guidelines set out for the *Communication* objective at second grade and to evaluate the performance of sixth-grade pupils on exactly the same basis as they would evaluate second-grade pupils.

2.2.11 Drumcondra Verbal Reasoning Test (DVRT)

The *Drumcondra Verbal Reasoning Test* (Gorman, 1968) measures the ability to use and reason with verbal symbols in English. It contains sections on analogies, word opposites, identification of concepts as belonging to a particular category, and problems of inductive and deductive reasoning. The test was originally standardised on a national sample of Irish pupils aged approximately 10 to 13 years in 1967. Because of the gradual drift upwards in raw scores which has taken place in succeeding years, unpublished norms based on a new standardisation of the test in the late 1970's were used in the present study. Based on the later restandardisation the test had a mean standard score (SS) of 100 and a standard deviation (SD) of 15.

The *DVRT* was the last instrument to be administered. Instructions to inspectors (Appendix 2.1) suggested that a half day be set aside for its administration.

2.2.12 The Parents' Questionnaire

The 29-item *Parents' Questionnaire* (Appendix 5.3) was designed to gather information from parents on their social and linguistic background, their child and Irish, the school and Irish, and homework. The parent received the questionnaire from the school, in a sealed envelope, via his/her child. The questions were organised under four main headings:

Questions 1-7: *Background*: General background information on the parents, such as occupation, use of Irish in the home and parents' general attitude to Irish and Irish teaching.

Questions 8-12: *Your child and Irish*: Parents' feelings about their children learning Irish and the attitudes towards learning Irish they try to encourage in their children.

Questions 13-22: *The school and Irish*: Parents' knowledge of, and views on, the teaching of Irish in the school.

Questions 23-28   *Homework*: Parents' emphasis on, and involvement in, homework; in particular, Irish homework.

Further details on the administration of the *Parents' Questionnaire* are given in Chapter 5.

2.3 Pupils in the present study compared to pupils nationally

We now turn to the presentation of background data on the pupils and classes in the *Twenty-Classes Study*. In this section, we compare our pupils with pupils nationally. In the next section (2.4), we examine data on classes. The present section is organised in terms of: four topics: (a) *Pupil achievement in Irish,* (b) *Pupil general academic ability (DVRT)*, (c) *Social class*, and (d) *Pupil difficulty with Irish* and *Pupil interest in Irish* as rated/perceived by the class teacher.

2.3.1 Achievement in spoken Irish

The percentage of pupils in the 20 classes (*Total Sample*) who attain mastery of each of the sixth-grade objectives in spoken Irish are given in the first column of Table 2.2. Results for the second-grade *Communication* objective are also presented. It should be noted that the *Communication* objective has been excluded when calculating mean percentages attaining mastery (last row of Table 2.2). The mastery data are based only on those pupils who were present for all the Irish 'listening' items at least. Because the number of pupils in our sample is relatively small, we decided to include those pupils who sat the 'listening' test even if they were absent for the 'speaking' test. Thus, while the total number of pupils in the 20 classes is 534 (Table 2.1), only data for 483 is available for the 'listening' test, and somewhat fewer (n = 466) in the case of the 'speaking test' (Part A = 237; Part B = 229) (Table 2.2).

Objectives which do not involve a precise knowledge of grammar and morphology, namely *Sound discrimination, Pronunciation, Fluency of oral description, General comprehension of speech* and the second-grade *Communication* objective are the ones most frequently mastered. These five objectives also had the highest percentages of pupils attaining mastery in the 1985 national survey (Harris and Murtagh, 1988a). Likewise, the least frequently mastered objectives in both the present study and the 1985 national survey are the two relating to the use and recognition of the correct tense and person forms of verbs *(Understanding the morphology of verbs,* and *Control of the morphology of verbs)*, and those relating to the morphology of nouns *(Understanding the morphology of nouns* and *Control of the morphology of nouns)*. Less than 20% of pupils attain mastery of each of these four objectives. Just about half the pupils (50.7%) attain mastery of the second-grade *Communication* objective, a proportion which is very close to that found in the 1985 national survey (54.2%).

Table 2.2
Percentages of sixth-grade pupils in the present study ('Total Sample' of 20 classes) attaining mastery of objectives in spoken Irish, making minimal progress and failing to make minimal progress.

Objectives	attain mastery	make *only* minimal progress	fail to make minimal progress
Percentages of pupils who...			
Listening Test $N_{(a+b)} = 483$			
1. Sound discrimination	86.3	11.8	1.9
2. Listening vocabulary	29.4	49.3	21.3
3. General comprehension of speech	37.5	47.8	14.7
4. Understanding the morphology of verbs	18.6	44.1	37.3
5. " " " prepositions	32.5	58.2	9.3
6. " " " qualifiers	25.3	52.6	22.2
7. " " " nouns	15.1	59.2	25.7
Speaking Test			
A. $N_a = 237*$			
8. Pronunciation	65.4	26.2	8.4
9. Speaking vocabulary	24.1	21.9	54.0
10. Control of the morphology of verbs	16.0	14.3	69.6
11. " " " prepositions	29.5	38.4	32.1
12. " " " qualifiers	27.8	38.4	33.8
13. " " " nouns	19.8	45.1	35.0
B. $N_b = 229*$			
14. Control of the syntax of statements	20.1	28.4	51.5
15. " " " of questions	22.7	21.8	55.5
16. Fluency of oral description	52.4	20.5	27.1
Second-grade 'Communication' objective	*50.7*	*16.2*	*33.2*
Mean % of pupils attaining mastery of each of three levels of performance on 16 sixth-grade objectives	*32.7*	*36.1*	*31.2*

*Not all pupils who were present for the listening test received the speaking test. Thus $N_a + N_b$ do not add to the total $N_{(a+b)}$.

Column 2 shows the percentages of pupils who made minimal progress (40% of the items correct), without attaining mastery, in relation to each objective. Column 3 shows the percentages of pupils who fail to make even minimal progress (< 40% of items correct). The results in column 3 show that failure to make even minimal progress is less likely for 'listening' objectives than for 'speaking' objectives. The four objectives which have the largest percentages of pupils failing to make even minimal progress are, in decreasing order of magnitude: *Control of the morphology of verbs*, *Control of the syntax of questions*, *Speaking vocabulary* and *Control of the syntax of statements* - all speaking objectives. These four objectives were also lowest in terms of mean percentages of pupils making at least 'minimal progress' in the 1985 study.

Finally, summary data in the last row of Table 2.2 show that, on average, less than one third (32.7%) of the pupils in the present study attain mastery of each of the 16 sixth-grade objectives. Just over thirty-six percent (36.1%) make only minimal progress in relation to each objective, and 31.2% fail to make minimal progress. Thus, overall 68.8% of pupils make *at least* minimal progress in relation to each objective, a figure which is a little lower than the corresponding proportion (73%) in the 1985 national survey of achievement (Harris and Murtagh, 1988a,b) which we mentioned in the introduction.

Table 2.3 compares the achievement of the 168 boys and 315 girls in the present study. On average, girls master objectives more often than boys, with a difference of 4.4% between the mean percentage of boys (29.8%) and the mean percentage of girls (34.2%) attaining mastery of each of the 16 objectives. The general tendency for girls to do better is maintained in 12 out of the 16 cases. While we do not present the national data broken down according to gender, it is interesting to note that the achievement of boys in the present study is very close to the national average for boys, while girls are somewhat lower than the national average for girls. The mean percentage of boys attaining mastery was 29.5% nationally in 1985 while the mean percentage of girls attaining mastery nationally was 38.6% (Harris and Murtagh, 1988b).

Table 2.3
Mean percentages of boys and girls in the present study attaining mastery of objectives in spoken Irish

		Mean percentage of pupils attaining mastery		
Objectives in spoken Irish n (pupils) =		*Boys* (168)	*Girls* (315)	*Difference Girls-Boys*
Mean percentage of pupils attaining mastery of each of 16 sixth-grade objectives		29.8	34.2	4.4

In Table 2.4 we set out the mean percentages of pupils who attain mastery of each objective in spoken Irish in the three groupings of classes in the present study as well as in the 1985 national survey (Harris and Murtagh, 1988a). The three groupings (columns 2-4) consist of *Total Sample*, *Parent Sample* and the *Rest*. The *Parent Sample* (pupils from seven classes involved in the Parent Survey) plus the *Rest* (pupils from the remaining 13 classes) together make up the *Total Sample*. It can be seen that the mean percentage of pupils attaining mastery of each objective is slightly lower in the *Total Sample* in the present study (32.7%) than in the *National Sample* (34.5%). The difference is not significant ($z = .85$; NS) (see Ferguson (1976) for test of significance between two proportions). This is a key result in terms of the representativeness of the classes in the study.

Table 2.4

Mean percentages of sixth-grade pupils in the 1985 National Survey* attaining mastery of objectives in spoken Irish compared with corresponding percentages in the Present Study ('Total Sample', 'Parent Sample' and 'Rest.)

			Present Study		
Objectives in spoken Irish n (pupils) =		*1985 National Sample ** (2,211)	*Total Sample* (483)	*'Parent Sample'* (182)	*The 'Rest'* (301)
Mean percentage of pupils attaining mastery of each of 16 sixth-grade objectives **		34.5	32.7	23.9	38.2

*Harris and Murtagh (1988a); ** see text for details of tests of significance between proportions.

It can also be seen that there is a substantially lower level of achievement among pupils associated with the *Parent Sample* compared to the *Total Sample*. Only 23.9% of pupils in the *Parent Sample* attain mastery of each of 16 objectives compared to a third (32.7%) in the *Total Sample*, a difference of 8.8%. A direct comparison between two groups such as these is problematical, however, since the *Total Sample* includes the *Parent Sample*. Instead, we carried out a test of the significance of the difference between the *Parent Sample* and the *Rest* as far as mean percentages attaining mastery of spoken Irish is concerned. The *Rest* (i.e. *Total Sample* minus *Parent Sample*) are those pupils whose parents either were not involved in the Parents' survey or, if they were, did not return completed questionnaires. The results show that pupils in the *Parent Sample* have a significantly lower level of achievement in Irish than both pupils in the *Rest* of the classes in the study ($z = 3.31$; $p<.01$) and pupils in the *National Sample* ($z = 3.33$; $p<.01$).

Clearly, then, there is little difference in practical terms between pupils in the *Total Sample* and the *National Sample* in terms of achievement in spoken Irish, and this is confirmed by the statistical test. Pupils in the *Parent Sample*, however, do have a substantially lower level of achievement in spoken Irish than either the *National Sample* or other pupils in the present study (i.e. the *Rest*).

2.3.2 Pupil general academic ability (DVRT)

Table 2.5 provides information on *Pupil general academic ability* as measured by the *DVRT* from the 1985 national survey (Harris and Murtagh, 1988a) alongside corresponding information for the *Total Sample* and the *Parent Sample* in the present study. The data in each case consist of the percentages of pupils who fall into each of five *DVRT* standard-score (SS) ranges. It will be noted that the percentages in each of the five score ranges for the *Total Sample* and the *Parent Sample* are similar to the corresponding percentages in the *National Sample*. The top ability range (*DVRT* > 120) is associated with a somewhat greater proportion of pupils in the *National Sample* (21.2%) than in either the *Total Sample* (16.3%) or the *Parent Sample* (15.1%) in the present study. This difference is compensated for by the somewhat greater proportions of pupils in the middle-ability ranges in the *Total Sample* and the *Parent Sample*.

Table 2.5
Percentage distribution of pupils in 'Total Sample' and 'Parent Sample' by *Pupil general academic ability* (*DVRT* Standard Score)

DVRT Standard Score (SS) n (pupils) =	1985* *National Sample* (2,134)	Present Study	
		'Total Sample' (465)	'Parent Sample' (172)
< = 90	9.8	10.5	9.9
> 90, < = 100	15.6	14.4	16.3
> 100, < = 110	21.2	28.6	26.2
> 110, < = 120	32.3	30.1	32.6
> 120	21.2	16.3	15.1
Mean *DVRT* SS **	108.6	107.1	107.0
Standard Deviation	(13.6)	(15.1)	(16.4)

* Harris and Murtagh, 1988a; ** see text for details of tests of significance (differences between means).

Mean *DVRT* standard scores (last row of Table 2.5) show that pupils in both the *Total Sample* and the *Parent Sample* have, on average, a marginally lower level of general academic ability (mean *DVRT* SS's are 107.1 and 107.0 respectively) than pupils in the 1985 *National Sample* (mean *DVRT* SS = 108.6). The difference between the *National*

Sample and the *Total Sample* is significant (t = 1.97; p < .05), but that between the *National Sample* and the *Parent Sample* is not (t = 1.25; NS).

Once again, we cannot usefully compare the *Parent Sample* with the *Total Sample* because the former is included in the latter. Thus, we compare instead the mean *DVRT* scores for the *Parent Sample* and the *Rest* (i.e. the *Total Sample* minus the *Parent Sample*). Not surprisingly, given the data in Table 2.5, the *Parent Sample* and the *Rest* do not differ significantly in terms of mean *DVRT* standard scores (t = 0.13; NS).

One of the main reasons for our interest in the *DVRT* scores is the expected connection to *Pupil achievement in spoken Irish*. The *DVRT* score ranges used in Table 2.5 are again used in Table 2.6 to show how *Pupil achievement in spoken Irish* varies according to *Pupil general academic ability*. Note that while 465 pupils took the *DVRT* test, somewhat fewer (n = 432) were present for both the *DVRT* and the test of spoken Irish (Table 2.6). This discrepancy is unlikely to affect the outcome since the additional pupils for whom we have information on *DVRT* but not on achievement in Irish are distributed proportionately over the five pupil-general-ability (*DVRT*) groups. The data in Table 2.6 indicates a strong tendency for the percentages of pupils attaining mastery to increase according to their level of general academic ability. This trend is also evident at the level of individual objectives though we do not show this detailed data in Table 2.6. This association between *Pupil general academic ability* and *Pupil achievement in spoken Irish* is consistent with data obtained in the 1985 national survey of sixth grade classes (Harris and Murtagh, 1988a).

Table 2.6
Mean percentages of sixth-grade pupils attaining mastery of objectives in spoken Irish according to *Pupil general academic ability* (*DVRT* SS)

	Pupil general academic ability (DVRT SS)				
	<=90	*91-100*	*101-110*	*111-120*	*>120*
Objectives in spoken Irish n (pupils) = 432	(49)	(65)	(123)	(127)	(68)
Mean percentage of pupils attaining mastery of each of 16 sixth-grade objectives	11.9	19.7	30.0	41.1	56.4

In brief, then, *Pupil general academic ability* is slightly though significantly lower in the *Total Sample* in the present study than nationally. Pupils in the *Parent Sample* do not differ either from the *National Sample* or the *Rest* of the pupils in the present study in terms of general academic ability. There is a strong association between level of *Pupil general academic ability* and *Pupil achievement in spoken Irish*.

2.3.3 Social class (Census data)

Information on parent's occupation and employment status was obtained from the teacher (see Appendix 2.2) and was also available from the *Parents' Questionnaire* in the case of the seven classes in the *Parent Sample*. Information was categorised according to the Central Statistics Office (CSO) social-class scale. This scale -

> "grouped the 213 occupations listed into *six* broad groups in such a way as to bring together as far as possible, people of similar social class. In general, each occupation group was assigned as a whole to one or other social class group. However, farmers (other than those specialising in horses, pigs or poultry) are assigned to a social class category on the basis of the acreage farmed." (CSO, 1986).

A code of 7 was used where the social class was unknown. Thus, the highest social class group had a rating of 1 and the lowest a rating of 7. CSO guidelines also stipulated that persons at work should be assigned to the social class category appropriate to their *present* occupation and employment status. Unemployed persons and retired persons should be classified according to the social class category corresponding to their former occupation. Other persons should be classified according to the social class category of the person on whom they were deemed to be dependent.

Brief descriptions of these seven *Social class* categories (scale 1-7) may be found in Table 2.7. Table 2.7 also compares the *Social class* distribution of the general population in the 1986 Census (CSO, 1993) with the *Social class* distribution of three groups of pupils in the present study: *Total Sample*, *Parent Sample* and the *Rest*. Looking at the percentages in the first two columns, it can be seen that there is a reasonably high degree of correspondence between the distribution pattern in the *Total Sample* and the Census. The greatest divergences involve *Social-class* groups 3 and 7, where differences of over 6% occur.

Columns 3 and 4 show the *Social class* distribution of the pupils associated with the *Parent Sample* (n=198) and with the *Rest* (n=334). The most notable differences here are that the *Parent Sample* has higher percentages of pupils in *Social class* group 1 and a lower percentage of pupils in group 7 than in the *Total Sample*, the *Rest* or the general population. Thus, the *Parent Sample* on this evidence appears to have a somewhat higher *Social class* rating overall than the others. We also compared mean *Social class* ratings for (a) the Census ($\overline{x}$ = 3.9) and the *Total Sample* ($\overline{x}$ = 4.2) (b) the *Parent Sample* ($\overline{x}$ = 3.8) and the *Rest* ($\overline{x}$ = 4.5) and (c) the Census ($\overline{x}$ = 3.9) and the *Parent Sample* ($\overline{x}$ = 3.8). The results indicate that, on average:

a) pupils in our *Total Sample* tend to come from significantly *lower* social class categories (numerically higher ratings) than pupils in the general population (t = 3.75, p < .01);

b) pupils from the *Parent Sample* come from significantly *higher* social class categories than the *Rest* of pupils (t = 4.28, p < .01);

c) pupils from the *Parent Sample* do not differ significantly from those in the general population in terms of social class (t = 1.42; NS).

Table 2.7
Social class distribution of pupils in the present study compared with the census* of population 1986.

			Present Study		
			'Total Sample'	*'Parent Sample'*	*The 'Rest'*
Social Class Group	n =	*Census** (3,540,643)	(532)	(198)	(334)
1. Higher Professional, Higher Managerial, Proprietors and Farmers farming 200 or more acres ....(HP)		9.9	9.4	14.1	6.6
2. Lower Professional, Lower Managerial, Proprietors and Farmers farming 100-199 acres ....(LP)		14.1	13.0	12.1	13.5
3. Other Non Manual and Farmers farming 50-59 acres ....(NM)		17.5	10.7	11.6	10.2
4. Skilled Manual and Farmers farming 30-49 acres ....(SM)		22.8	24.2	30.3	20.7
5. Semi-Skilled Manual and Farmers farming less than 30 acres ....(SS)		15.4	17.3	15.7	18.3
6. Unskilled Manual ....(UM)		10.2	8.6	10.1	7.8
7. Social Class Unknown ....(U)		10.1	16.7	6.1	23.1
Mean social class rating **		*3.9*	*4.2*	*3.8*	*4.5*
Standard Deviation		*3.6*	*1.9*	*1.7*	*1.9*

*Census of Population 1986: Classification of Occupations." (Ireland: Central Statistics Office, 1993).
** see text for details of tests of significance.

Table 2.8 shows the relationship between *Pupil achievement in spoken Irish* and *Social class*, a relationship which has not previously been examined in any study at primary level. Data consists of the mean percentages of pupils in the *Total Sample* attaining mastery of each of sixteen sixth-grade objectives in spoken Irish for each of the seven *Social-class* groups. There is a strong and relatively consistent trend for pupils rated higher in terms of *Social class* to have a higher level of achievement in spoken Irish. Only *Social class* group 7 slightly upsets the trend, with 21.7% on average attaining mastery as opposed to 20% in *Social class* group 6. A possible explanation for this will be offered below in the context of our discussion.

Comparing the data in Tables 2.6 and 2.8 it is notable that the range of achievement over the five categories of pupil general academic ability (mean percentages attaining mastery ranging from 11.9% to 56.4%) is greater than the range over the seven social class groups (20% to 50.7%). Correlation data presented in later chapters (see Chapters 3 & 5) confirm that there is a stronger relationship overall between *Pupil general academic ability* and *Pupil achievement in Irish* than between *Social class* and *Pupil achievement in Irish.*

Table 2.8
Mean percentages of pupils in the 'Total sample' (20 classes) attaining mastery of objectives in spoken Irish by social class of pupil

		Social class group						
		highest -- lowest						
		1	2	3	4	5	6	7
		HP*	LP	NM	SM	SSM	UM	U
Objectives in spoken Irish	n (pupils) =	(43)	(64)	(55)	(119)	(85)	(41)	(75)
Mean percentage of pupils attaining mastery of each of 16 sixth-grade objectives		50.7	47.7	38.5	30.0	28.3	20.0	21.7

* See previous table (Table 2.7) for *Social class* group titles.

2.3.4 Teacher's ratings of pupil interest in and difficulty with Irish

We turn now to teachers' ratings of pupils' difficulty with various aspects of Irish, English and mathematics and overall interest in Irish. We also examine the relationship between some of these judgments of teachers and the performance of pupils on the ITÉ sixth-grade test of spoken Irish. Before describing the results relating to difficulty and interest it should be noted that teachers also rated pupil ability in Irish. The ratings of ability, however, are of no general interest beyond their necessity for the selection of pupils in the *PCBR* because we had specified in the instructions to the teacher that pupils should be divided in terms of ability in Irish "into three groups of approximately equal size" (see Appendix 2.2).

Looking at the data for the *Total Sample* in Table 2.9 we see that of the seven subject areas listed, the two which teachers perceive most often as presenting difficulty for pupils, are *Spoken Irish* and *Irish Writing*. Half of all pupils in the present study are perceived as having difficulty with *Spoken Irish*, with a similar figure applying to *Irish Writing* (50.2%). The third aspect of Irish listed, *Irish Reading*, virtually ties with *Mathematics* for third place in a ranking of perceived difficulty (37% versus 37.8%). More are perceived by their class teacher as having difficulty with *English Writing* (33.8%) than with either *English Reading* (22.6%) or *Spoken English* (16.7%).

Turning now to a comparison between the *Parent Sample* (column 2) and the *Total Sample,* it can be seen that with one exception there are no really substantial differences in terms of how frequently teachers rate pupils as having difficulties in each of the subject areas. The exception is *English Writing* where the proportion of pupils in the *Total Sample* who have difficulty exceeds the proportion in the *Parent Sample* by 6.5%.

Table 2.9
Proportion of pupils who are perceived by their own teachers to have difficulty with particular school subjects and to exhibit various levels of interest in Irish.

		Percentage of pupils	
Teachers' perceptions of..	n =	*Total Sample* (532)	*Parent Sample* (198)
Pupils who have difficulty with			
Spoken Irish		50.0	47.5
Irish Reading		37.0	40.4
Irish Writing		50.2	48.0
Spoken English		16.7	16.2
English Reading		22.6	19.2
English Writing		33.8	27.3
Mathematics		37.8	39.9
Pupils' interest in Irish			
'Very high' / 'high' interest		34.2	32.3
'Fair' interest		30.5	30.3
'Very low' / 'low' interest		35.3	37.4

Summarising the data relating to perceived pupil interest in Irish in Table 2.9, we can say that 34.2% of pupils in the *Total Sample* are seen as having a high level of interest in

Irish (combining 'very high' and 'high' interest), 30.5% as having a 'fair' level of interest, while 35.3% are rated as having a low level of interest (combining 'low' and 'very low' interest). The results for teachers' ratings of pupil interest in Irish in the *Parent Sample* in column two are very similar to those for the *Total Sample* in column 1 - the maximum difference is 2.1% when adjacent categories are combined in the manner just indicated.

Finally, we computed Pearson correlations between a teacher's perceptions of pupil difficulty and interest in Irish, on the one hand and an objective measure of pupil achievement in Irish, on the other. A composite measure of *Pupil difficulty in Irish*, based on assessments of difficulties with speaking, reading and writing in Irish was used. The correlation values (data not shown in table) indicate that greater degrees of *Pupil difficulty in Irish* as perceived by the teacher are strongly associated with lower *Pupil achievement in Irish* ($r = -.57$). Higher levels of perceived *Pupil interest in Irish* are also strongly associated with higher *Pupil achievement in Irish* ($r = .56$). Greater perceived difficulty with Irish, or less interest in it, are also significantly associated with lower *Pupil general academic ability* ($r = -.48$ and $-.38$ respectively). Note, however, that the correlations with achievement in Irish are somewhat stronger than with academic ability, particularly in the case of *Pupil interest in Irish*.

In calculating these correlations, we have used scores on just the listening section of the ITÉ sixth-grade Irish test as a measure of *Pupil achievement in Irish* - as we do on many other occasions elsewhere in the study where correlations are involved. There are two reasons for using listening items only: (a) all pupils took the listening test, whereas each pupil only took Part A or Part B of the speaking test and (b) there is a very high degree of correspondence anyway between performance on listening and speaking items. In the present study, for example, the correlation between listening items and 'speaking A' items is .82 and between listening items and 'speaking B' items is .76. In the 1985 national survey, corresponding Pearson 'r' coefficients were .8 in both cases (Harris and Murtagh, 1988b). Feyten (1991) also reports that listening ability is a very good predictor of overall second-language proficiency.

2.4 The *Twenty-Classes Study* compared to classes nationally

Up to this point, we have been concerned with a description of the pupils in the study. We turn now to a description of the classes. While we will again focus on the variables already introduced such as achievement in Irish, we also present a range of additional data which apply only to classes/schools: class size, urban/rural and regional location and gender composition. We also include data on parental unemployment.

2.4.1 *Class achievement in Irish*

The classes in column 1 of Table 2.10 are ranked (1-20) according to the mean percentage of pupils attaining mastery of each of the objectives of the sixth-grade Irish test. These ranks serve as class I.D.'s and as a general presentational framework for class related data in the remainder of the report. Because achievement in spoken Irish is so central to our concerns, it will be useful in subsequent chapters to relate whatever new data is being presented - on attitudes, classroom processes or pupil behaviour - to this ranking of the 20 classes in terms of achievement in Irish.

Table 2.10
Twenty sixth-grade Irish classes: Achievement in spoken Irish of each class in the *Twenty-Classes Study* compared to classes nationally.

Class achievement in spoken Irish		
Twenty-Classes Study		*National Sample*
Rank (1= highest achievement)	*Mean % of pupils mastering each of 16 sixth-grade objectives*	*Percentage of pupils mastering 'General comprehension of speech'**	*Percentage of classes nationally whose achievement in spoken Irish is better than this class * (using the 'Class Mastery' Index)*
1	81.3	88	4%
2	76.9	83	16%
3	71.3	70	12%
4	67.2	88	13%
5	65.8	83	11%
6	63.8	90	6%
7	48.6	58	41%
D 8	41.4	31	61%
9	37.7	68	51%
10	37.4	49	52%
11	36.0	50	59%
12	31.3	52	71%
13	16.7	21	81%
14	15.6	18	90%
15	14.4	11	90%
D 16	13.1	19	93%
17	12.3	4	92%
18	10.41	0	98%
19	10.36	7	93%
D 20	6.6	0	98%

* See text for details and Harris & Murtagh, 1988a,b; 'D' = Officially classified as disadvantaged.
Rows with darker shading indicate classes in *Parent Sample*.

The first thing to be noted (Table 2.10, column 2) is simply the great diversity in Irish achievement among the classes - an average of 6.6% of pupils in Class 20 attain mastery of sixth-grade objectives compared to a mean percentage of 81.3% in Class 1. The 20 classes break down into three clearly distinct groups in terms of the mean percentages of pupils attaining mastery. It can be seen that between 63.8% and 81.3% of pupils in the 'top' six classes (high-Irish-achievement group), for example, attain mastery of each of the objectives in spoken Irish. But only 6.6% to 16.7% attain mastery in the eight low-Irish-achievement classes. It will be noted that there is a substantial gap between achievement in the high-Irish-achievement group and the next middle-Irish-achievement group. The latter contains six classes in which, on average, between 31.3% and 48.6% of pupils attain mastery of objectives. There is no overlap in the mean percentages of pupils attaining mastery in these three groups. In assessing the significance of these figures, it may be useful also to recall (Table 2.4) that in the ITÉ 1985 national survey the mean percentage of pupils who attained mastery of these same objectives was 34.5% (Harris and Murtagh, 1988a). Thus, the 'middle' group of classes in Table 2.10 is closest overall to the national average.

It may also be noted that three classes are prefaced by the letter 'D', denoting that they are in schools which are officially classified as disadvantaged. Two of these disadvantaged-school classes (ranks 16 and 20) are in the low-Irish-achievement group and the third (rank 8) is in the middle-Irish-achievement group. The mean percentage of pupils attaining mastery (41.4%) in the latter class is considerably greater than corresponding percentages in the two other disadvantaged classes - 13.1% in the case of Class 16 and 6.6% in the case of Class 20. Below we show (Table 2.11) that there are differences between Class 8 and the other two classes in disadvantaged-area schools in relation to a number of other important variables - *Pupil general academic ability, Social class of the majority of pupils* and *Percentage of parents who are long-term unemployed.*

Detailed information on each individual objective is not presented simply because of the volume of data which would be involved. To give a more immediate indication of the nature of pupil achievement in Irish in the twenty classes, we present (column 3) data relating to mastery of one particular objective, *General comprehension of speech.* A total of 25 items were used to test *General comprehension of speech.* Three different approaches to testing were used: (i) items requiring the pupil to identify which of four different drawings exactly matched the situation described in a simple spoken sentence, (ii) items requiring the pupil to listen to a statement and then to answer a spoken multiple-choice question concerning the speaker's identity, location, or feelings, the identity of the person addressed etc., (iii) items requiring the pupil to listen to a brief (60 + words) spoken description of an incident and then to answer a series of spoken multiple-choice questions involving the recovery of information or the making of simple inferences. As in the case of all other objectives tested, the linguistic and other content of items was carefully tailored to the content of the *Nuachúrsaí* lessons at fifth/sixth grade (Department of Education, 1978).

It can be seen that the percentages of pupils attaining mastery of this one objective across the 20 classes do not exhibit the smooth decline in *overall* achievement in spoken

Irish which is represented by the ranks in column 1. Nevertheless, it can be seen that there is no overlap between the high-, middle- and low-Irish-achievement groups of classes in the percentages attaining mastery of *General comprehension of speech*. So, for example, all the classes in the middle-Irish-achievement group have lower percentages of pupils attaining mastery of this objective than all classes in the high-Irish-achievement group. There is substantial variation in the percentages of pupils mastering the *Comprehension* objective, however, in the low-Irish-achievement group of classes (0%-21%). It will be noted that in each of two classes (Class 18 and Class 20) no pupil at all attains mastery of *Comprehension.*

Column 4 in Table 2.10 shows the percentage of classes in the 1985 *National Sample* whose achievement is *better* than each of the 20 classes in the present study using a 'class mastery' index (Harris and Murtagh, 1988b). Since the particular type of achievement data we have just been using (mean percentages attaining mastery) is not available for comparative purposes on a class-by-class basis for the 1985 ITÉ National survey, we had to compute the 'class mastery index', used in the 1985 survey, for the classes in the present study. The index consists of a weighted score assigned to each pupil on the basis of whether he/she has (a) attained *mastery* (b) made *minimal progress* or (c) failed to make *minimal progress* in relation to each of the 16 objectives (see section 2.2.9 for definitions of 'mastery' and 'minimal progress'). The mean of the individual weighted pupil scores is the value of the 'mastery index' for that class. The first thing to be noted is that the three main groupings of classes ('high' - ranks 1-6; 'middle' - ranks 7-12; and 'low' - ranks 13-20) remain the same whether we use the 'mean percentage attaining mastery' or the 'class mastery index'. There is no overlap in the percentages in column 4 for the three groups of classes - just as there were no overlaps in column 2. This lack of overlap in class achievement in Irish in the three groups prompted us to use this broad three-way grouping in illustrating the overall across-class trends in many other kinds of data in the remainder of this report.

Looking at the values of the class mastery index in column 4, it can be seen that the first six of the twenty classes in the present study (high-Irish achievement classes) represent roughly the top 16% of the population of classes nationally in terms of achievement in Irish: the classes ranked 7 - 12 (middle-Irish-achievement classes) represent the middle 30% or so of classes (41% - 71%) and the eight low-Irish-achievement classes (ranks 13 - 20) represent the lowest 20% or so. At the two extremes, 4% of classes nationally are better than the highest achieving class here (rank 1) in terms of achievement in spoken Irish, while 2% of classes nationally have lower levels of achievement than the lowest-achieving class here (rank 20).

None of the classes involved in the Parent Survey fall within the high-Irish-achievement group of classes. This confirms data from Table 2.4 showing overall mastery to be lower in the *Parent Sample* than in the *Rest*.

2.4.2 Class characteristics: Social class and general academic ability

Data on *Social class* and *Pupil general academic ability (DVRT)* are presented for each of the 20 classes in Table 2.11. Given the strong association noted earlier between each of these variables and *Pupil achievement in Irish*, we would also expect to observe differences in *Pupil general academic ability* and *Social class* across 20 classes ranked in terms of achievement in Irish. Taking *Social class* (columns 2-4), first, three different indicators are shown:

a) the *Social class* group (1-7) to which the majority of pupils' belong (column 2);
b) the mean of the pupils' *Social class* ratings (column 3);
c) the percentage of parents who are long-term unemployed (column 4). High levels of unemployment are associated with lower levels of education (Hannan and Shortall, 1991).

Table 2.11
Twenty sixth-grade Irish classes: *Social class* **and** *Pupil general academic ability*

Class achievement in spoken Irish Rank	Social Class*			Pupil general academic ability		
	Social class of majority of pupils	Mean rating (1=high, 7=low)	% parents long-term unemployed	Mean DVRT SS	SD	% pupils with DVRT SS <= 90
1	Semi/unskilled	4.5	0%	106.4	9.3	0%
2	Non-manual+	2.6	5%	113.2	22.6	8%
3	Skilled+	3.8	0%	105.0	12.0	22%
4	Non-manual+	3.9	0%	96.5	24.5	25%
5	Skilled+	3.8	8%	113.8	10.3	0%
6	Non-manual+	3.3	0%	108.9	13.4	11%
7	Skilled+	3.7	8%	112.4	8.7	0%
D 8	Semi/unskilled	5.1	24%	110.4	8.9	4%
9	Skilled+	4.2	0%	109.5	24.2	8%
10	Non-manual+	3.1	0%	109.6	10.4	9%
11	Skilled+	4.3	6%	105.6	8.5	6%
12	Non-manual+	2.6	0%	115.3	8.5	0%
13	Semi/unskilled	4.5	9%	101.7	10.0	7%
14	Unskilled	4.9	29%	105.5	10.7	9%
15	Skilled+	4.2	0%	101.8	10.5	13%
D16	Unskilled	5.5	35%	100.2	13.9	29%
17	Unskilled	5.7	17%	107.4	14.6	18%
18	Skilled+	4.3	28%	100.9	12.6	19%
19	Skilled+	3.8	0%	106.8	23.9	11%
D 20	Unskilled	5.9	50%	102.0	15.3	24%

* See text & Table 2.7 for a description of *Social class* scale. 'D' = Officially classified as disadvantaged.

There is a tendency for higher *Social-class* categories (i.e. numerically low ratings in column 3) to be associated with higher levels of achievement in Irish (i.e. numerically low ranks in column 1). This trend is also reflected in the dominant *Social-class* category (column 2) associated with high- and middle-Irish-achievement classes compared to the low-Irish-achievement classes. Note that (a) the only four classes in which the dominant category is 'unskilled' are also low-Irish-achievement classes and (b) none of the low-Irish-achievement classes have a majority of pupils associated with 'non-manual or higher' *Social class* categories. The tendency for higher *Social class* to be associated with higher achievement in Irish, however, is not entirely consistent. Thus, Class 1 (the best overall in terms of Irish) has roughly the same mean *Social class* rating (column 3) as half of the classes in the low-Irish-achievement group.

The third occupational/social class indicator (column 4) shows that in the case of five classes (ranks 8, 14, 16, 18 & 20), between a quarter and a half of the pupils have parents who are long-term unemployed. Of these, three classes are the ones already designated as being in disadvantaged areas (classes 8, 16, 20). It is worth noting, however, that in Class 8 the percentage of parents who are long-term unemployed (24%) is lower than it is in the other two disadvantaged area classes (35% and 50%). It will also be noted that the class ranked last (20) in terms of achievement is associated with the highest proportion of long-term unemployment (50% of parents).

Columns 5-7 contain information on two class-based indices of *Pupil general academic ability*: (a) mean *DVRT* standard scores of the sixth-grade pupils in each class and (b) the proportion of sixth-grade pupils in each class with *DVRT* standard scores of 90 or less i.e. those who score more than a standard deviation below the national *DVRT* mean (108.6) for sixth-grade pupils based on the 1985 ITÉ survey - see Table 2.5 and Harris and Murtagh (1988a). Looking at column 5, it can be seen that all of the eight classes in the low-Irish-achievement group have mean *DVRT* scores which are lower than the national mean of 108.6. By comparison, eight of the twelve classes in the combined high- and middle-Irish achievement groups have mean *DVRT* scores which are higher than the national mean.

A broadly similar pattern can be seen in the proportion of pupils with very low general academic ability (column 7). In three quarters of the low-Irish achievement classes, the percentages of pupils with a *DVRT* score <=90 reach double figures. In the high- and middle-Irish-achievement classes such low levels of *Pupil general academic ability* tend to be less common, although classes 3 and 4 do have 22% and 25% of pupils respectively with *DVRT*<=90.

Finally, it is worth drawing attention to differences in *DVRT* scores between Class 8 and the other two 'disadvantaged' classes (ranks 16 & 20). The former has a higher mean *DVRT* score (110.4) and fewer pupils with *DVRT* SS <=90 (4%) than either of the other two classes (mean *DVRT* scores = 100.2 & 102; Percentage of pupils with *DVRT* SS <=90: 29% and 24% respectively)

2.4.3 Class characteristics: Pupil interest in Irish and difficulty with Irish

Table 2.12 presents class level data on teachers' assessments of their pupils' interest in Irish and difficulties in various subject areas (see Appendix 2.2). In column 2, the proportions of pupils in each class who were perceived by their teachers to have either 'low' or 'very low' interest in Irish are given. The trend (combining the two categories) is for a greater percentage of pupils in low-Irish-achievement classes than in high-Irish-achievement classes to be rated as having 'low' interest in Irish. Only one class in the high-Irish-achievement group has more than 30% of the pupils showing a 'low' level of interest in Irish, while all classes in the low-Irish-achievement group have more than that proportion with 'low' interest in Irish.

Table 2.12
Twenty sixth-grade Irish classes: Low interest in Irish and difficulties in various subjects
(N pupils = 532)

Class achievement in spoken Irish Rank	low* interest in Irish	Percentage of pupils whom teacher perceives as having - difficulty in various subject areas				
		Spoken English	English reading	Maths	Irish reading	Spoken Irish
1	0	0	0	0	0	0
2	21	0	8	26	13	33
3	20	10	0	30	0	30
4	0	13	13	25	13	13
5	33	100	0	33	8	100
6	20	40	20	40	20	30
7	41	0	13	31	36	49
D 8	32	0	35	56	41	82
9	40	30	27	40	47	43
10	10	3	5	44	28	36
11	6	24	24	59	35	53
12	52	19	19	36	29	48
13	46	27	27	24	42	67
14	32	21	36	32	46	21
15	56	3	19	44	50	53
D 16	47	29	29	41	44	44
17	38	24	31	48	41	48
18	33	8	28	31	44	74
19	37	33	30	50	50	40
D 20	67	17	43	37	60	70

* Combination of 'low' and 'very low' categories from the teacher's ratings of *Pupil interest in Irish*.
'D' = Officially classified as disadvantaged.

Teachers' judgments of pupils' difficulties in English, Irish and Mathematics aggregated to the class level, are given in columns 3-7. Pupils are more likely to be perceived as having difficulty with *Mathematics, Irish Reading* and *Spoken Irish* than with *Spoken English* and *English Reading*. Notice, for example, the number of single-figure percentages in the columns relating to *Spoken English* and *English Reading*.

In general, teachers of low-Irish-achievement classes (ranks 13 - 20) rate more of their pupils as having problems with *English Reading* than do teachers of high-Irish-achievement classes. Half of the low-Irish-achievement classes have 30% or more of pupils rated as having difficulty with *English Reading*, while only one of the middle-Irish-achievement classes and none of the high-Irish-achievement classes have such large proportions. The highest proportion rated as having difficulty with *English Reading* (43%) occurs in the class with the lowest Irish achievement (rank 20).

Looking at perceived difficulty in Irish, note that teachers in 14 of the 20 classes judge more pupils as having difficulty with *Spoken Irish* than with *Irish Reading*. Generally, higher proportions of pupils in the low-Irish-achievement group of classes than in the high-Irish-achievement group have difficulty with *Spoken Irish*. Differences between the low- and middle-Irish-achievement groups, in relation to pupil difficulty with *Spoken Irish*, are less pronounced. But even in the high-Irish-achievement group the proportions remain substantial. In four of these (ranks 2, 3, 5, 6) teachers rated 30% or more of pupils as having difficulty with *Spoken Irish*. Incidentally, Class 1 is the only one of the 20 classes in which no pupil is judged to have difficulty with *Spoken Irish*. Our own test results, of course, reinforce this judgment. Recall that only 4% of classes nationally do better in spoken Irish than Class 1. The teacher of Class 1 reported no pupil difficulty in any other subject area either.

Finally in this regard it may be noted that in certain classes with higher than average levels of achievement in spoken Irish as measured by our objective tests, teachers nevertheless report large majorities as having difficulty with Irish. For example, in classes 5 & 8, teachers judge 100% and 82% of pupils respectively to have difficulty with *Spoken Irish* while our Irish test shows the mean percentage attaining mastery of objectives in spoken Irish for the same classes as 65.8% and 41.4% respectively - well above the national mean of 34.5%.

2.4.4 Class characteristics: Socio-demographic and teaching variables

Table 2.13 presents class-based information relating to four socio-demographic and school organizational factors: (i) the number of pupils in sixth grade, (ii) gender composition of sixth grade, (iii) regional location of school, (iv) urban/rural location of school.

In the case of the high-Irish-achievement classes (ranks 1-6) the presence of a constellation of features associated with small schools can be observed: gender composition is always 'mixed'; five of the six classes are in country locations and have small numbers of sixth-grade pupils. Larger sixth-grade groups, single sex classes and city/town locations are more common in the middle- and low-Irish-achievement groups of classes. Note that none of the Dublin schools, but both of the Connaught schools, are in the high-Irish-achievement group of classes.

Table 2.13
Twenty sixth-grade Irish classes:
Mastery of objectives in spoken Irish, size of sixth grade, gender composition and location

Class achievement in spoken Irish Rank	Number of pupils in sixth grade	Gender composition of sixth-grade class	Location: Region	Location: Urban/rural
1	8	Mixed	Connaught	Country
2	39	Mixed	Munster	City
3	10	Mixed	Munster	Country
4	8	Mixed	Leinster	Country
5	12	Mixed	Munster	Country
6	10	Mixed	Connaught	Country
7	39	Girls	Dublin	City
D 8	34	Girls	Munster	City
9	30	Mixed	Leinster	Country
10	39	Girls	Dublin	City
11	17	Girls	Munster	Town
12	31	Boys	Dublin	City
13	33	Girls	Ulster	Town
14	28	Girls	Leinster	Town
15	32	Girls	Leinster	Town
D 16	34	Mixed	Dublin	City
17	29	Boys	Munster	City
18	39	Girls	Dublin	City
19	30	Mixed	Leinster	Country
D 20	30	Boys	Munster	City

'D' = Officially classified as disadvantaged.

Class 2 in the high-Irish-achievement group represents an exception to the pattern in the other five classes in the group in that it has more pupils (39 pupils in sixth-grade) and is in a city location. Presumably socio-educational factors or in-class teaching factors must be involved. Two obvious candidates are *Social class* (jointly with class 12, it has the highest *Social class*) and above average *Pupil general academic ability* (mean *DVRT* SS = 113.2).

Finally, we refer briefly to teacher-report data (Appendix 2.4) relating to two class teaching characteristics: (i) the course-method used to teach Irish and (ii) the extent to which Irish medium-instruction is used. Table 2.14 shows that the *Nuachúrsaí* are used either alone (9 classes) or in combination with the traditional ABC method (4 classes) in thirteen of the 20 classes. Only one teacher uses the ABC method alone as the main course-method. The remaining six teachers reported using their 'own method'. None of the three main Irish-achievement groups of classes are strongly associated with any particular course method.

Table 2.14
Course-method used to teach Irish and extent of Irish-medium instruction in each of the 20 classes (Teacher's Report)

Class achievement in spoken Irish Rank	Course-method used*	Time each week spent teaching other subjects through Irish*
1	Nuachúrsaí	3-4 hours
2	Nuachúrsaí and ABC	2-3 hours
3	ABC	less than 1 hour
4	Own method	2-3 hours
5	Own method	less than 1 hour
6	Nuachúrsaí	less than 1 hour
7	Nuachúrsaí	no time
D 8	Own method	less than 1 hour
9	Nuachúrsaí	less than 1 hour
10	Nuachúrsaí	less than 1 hour
11	Own method	1-2 hours
12	Nuachúrsaí & ABC	less than 1 hour
13	Nuachúrsaí	less than 1 hour
14	Nuachúrsaí	less than 1 hour
15	Nuachúrsaí	no time
D.16	Nuachúrsaí	no time
17	Nuachúrsaí & ABC	no time
18	Nuachúrsaí & ABC	no time
19	Own method	no time
D 20	Own method	no time

*Teachers' report (Appendix 2.4: Q 32). 'D' = Officially classified as disadvantaged

Data in column 3 show that seven classes (35%) spend 'no time' teaching subjects other than Irish through Irish, nine classes (45%) spend less than one hour and four classes (20%) spend more than one hour teaching through Irish. It can also be seen that class achievement in Irish tends to increase with increasing amounts of Irish-medium instruction. Three of the six high-Irish-achievement classes spend at least two hours per week being taught other subjects through Irish, while five of the six middle-Irish-achievement classes spend at least some time being taught through Irish. By comparison six of the eight low-achievement classes spend 'no time' at all being taught through Irish.

2.5 Discussion

The results show that the crucial characteristics of our sample accord rather better with those of the national population than might reasonably have been expected with such a small group of classes and pupils. Admittedly, some of the differences are statistically significant but their magnitude suggests that, for present purposes, the degree of comparability with the national context is acceptable. This is not to deny that in certain other contexts, differences of the same magnitude might be of considerable practical significance - for example, if we had been measuring changes in achievement over time at a national level, or evaluating achievement gain scores associated with the implementation of a particular educational treatment.

Another positive outcome is that we can identify probable explanations for the two most substantial differences between our samples and the national picture, explanations which do not undermine confidence in the representativeness of the samples in other respects. The two differences in question consist of (a) *Social class* in the *Total Sample* being lower overall than that in the Census and (b) *Pupil achievement in Irish* in the *Parent Sample* being lower than in the national population. The first of these differences, relating to *Social class*, we attribute to the fact that the quality of information about occupational status was in certain respects unsatisfactory. The second difference, the lower achievement in Irish of pupils in the *Parent Sample,* can be accounted for by the predominance of Dublin schools in that sample. We will now examine these and other aspects of the results in more detail.

2.5.1 *Total Sample compared to the National Sample*

Two main kinds of representativeness are desired: (a) that average *Pupil achievement in Irish, Pupil general academic ability* and *Social class* in the selected sixth-grade classes would be similar to the national population, (b) that the classes would represent the full range of achievement in Irish and at the same time balance weak and strong classes. The results show that in terms of achievement in Irish, pupils in the *Total Sample* are representative of the population of sixth-grade pupils nationally. The mean percentage attaining mastery of sixth-grade objectives in Irish is not statistically different from the mean percentage nationally. There are close similarities too in the 'performance profiles' of pupils in the present study and nationally.

The class-level analysis indicates, in addition, that both in terms of the range of achievement in Irish across the classes, and the balance between classes with high, middle and low levels of achievement in Irish, the *Total sample* mirrors the national picture quite well. A 'class mastery' index showed that the 20 classes selected represent the top and bottom 15%-20% or so of classes nationally as well as the middle 30%. Equally important, there is no overlap in the mean levels of achievement in Irish of the individual classes in three groups. This clear division into three groups of classes provides us with a convenient presentational framework for the rest of the report. On the negative side, it must be acknowledged that very high-achieving and very low-achieving classes are overrepresented, though clearly these classes must be in general balance since mean Irish achievement does not differ significantly from the national picture.

Two other points are worth making about the class-based data. The first concerns the fact that the mean percentage of pupils attaining mastery of each objective in spoken Irish in the very highest achieving class is as high as 81.3%. An immediate question which arises is whether this is as high as the average in all-Irish schools? While we do not have data at a national level on achievement in spoken Irish at sixth-grade in all-Irish schools, we do have data at *second grade*. The mean percentage of second-grade all-Irish school pupils nationally who attain mastery of second-grade objectives is 83.8% (Harris and Murtagh, 1988a). Using this figure as a rough and ready indicator, it is not unreasonable to suggest that the level of achievement in spoken Irish in Class 1 in the present study may not be too far off the level attained in many all-Irish schools.

It is also of interest to note that 4% of sixth-grade classes in ordinary schools nationally, in our estimation, do as well or better than, Class 1. Admittedly, this can only be considered a crude estimate, given that the 'class mastery index' used for national comparisons does not produce exactly the same ranking of the 20 classes as the 'mean percentage attaining mastery' does. Nevertheless, the comparisons are sufficient to make the point that some ordinary schools produce very high levels of achievement in spoken Irish. Even if the proportion of such schools nationally is small, their absolute number ensures that they must make a considerable contribution to the general language revival effort.

The second point about the class-based data is that mastery of *General comprehension of speech* is attained so infrequently in low-Irish-achievement classes - it falls below 20% in all but one of these classes and is zero in two classes. This is important in that it explains why pupils in low-Irish-achievement classes so often express the desire that the Irish lesson would be 'easier to understand' (See Chapter 4, section 4.4.3). It is important to bear in mind, nevertheless, that failure to achieve mastery of an objective does not mean that the pupil has no proficiency at all. It simply means that a pupil could not comprehend Irish at a level sufficient to be judged to have attained mastery at a particular grade - in the present case, mastery of *General comprehension of speech* at the *sixth-grade* level.

Turning now to the other key variables, the results show that while *Pupil general academic ability* in the *Total Sample* is significantly lower than nationally, the difference in practical terms is quite small - the mean *DVRT* standard scores only differ by 1.5. In the case of *Social class*, pupils in the *Total Sample* come from significantly lower *Social class* backgrounds (numerically higher ratings) than the general population. While in most of the seven *Social class* categories there is a reasonably high degree of correspondence between the distribution pattern in the *Total Sample* and the Census, in social-class groups 3 and 7 differences of over 6% occur. We return to a more detailed examination of this result below.

2.5.2 *Parent Sample compared to the National Sample and the 'Rest'*

The results show that *Pupil achievement in Irish* in the *Parent Sample* is substantially lower than it is nationally. The mean percentage attaining mastery of each objective in spoken Irish is only 23.9% compared to 34.5% nationally, a difference which is also, of course, statistically significant. Predictably, *Pupil achievement in Irish* in the *Parent Sample* is also significantly lower than it is in the *Rest* of the classes (i.e. those not involved in the Parent survey). As a consequence, all the classes in the *Parent Sample* are in either the middle- or low-Irish-achievement groups. This outcome is entirely to be expected, however, since all the schools selected are either in Dublin or in the surrounding counties in East Leinster. Earlier research (Harris, 1983) has shown that Dublin classes have lower levels of achievement in spoken Irish than classes from other regions.

In the other two key respects of interest here, however, the *Parent Sample* does not differ from the situation nationally. Both *Pupil general academic ability (DVRT)* and *Social class* in the *Parent Sample* do not differ significantly from the *National Sample*. *Pupil general academic ability* in the *Parent Sample* also does not significantly differ from the *Rest* of the classes.

The results also show that pupils in the *Rest* of the classes come from significantly lower *Social class* backgrounds than either pupils nationally (Census) or pupils in the *Parent Sample*. Since pupils in the *Parent Sample*, as we noted a moment ago, do not differ from those nationally in terms of *Social class,* it must be the *Rest* of the classes which are depressing the profile of the *Total Sample* - to such an extent that *Social class* in the latter is significantly lower than it is nationally. We believe that this effect is largely an artifact of the quality of information about *Social class* which is available for the *Rest*.

The critical issue here is that a high proportion of pupils in the *Rest* (23.1%) are assigned to category 7, 'social class unknown', compared to only 6.1% in the *Parent Sample*. This difference originates in the fact that in the case of the *Parent Sample* we had precise information on occupations directly from the parents themselves, whereas in the *Rest* of the classes we had only indirect information from teachers. Where parents have been unemployed for a long time, it is clear that teachers did not have accurate information on previous occupation. This is confirmed by the fact that although the overall percentage who are long-term unemployed was actually higher in the *Parent Sample* than it was in the *Rest*, a disproportionate number of long-term unemployed parents were categorised as 'social class unknown' in the *Rest* sample (55%) compared to the *Parent Sample* (25%). The implication here is that some pupils in the *Rest* who were assigned a *Social class* rating of 7 would almost certainly have been assigned to a higher *Social class* category (i.e. a numerically lower rating) if more precise information on previous occupation had been available. The higher proportion of 'social class unknown' ratings in the *Rest* would have the effect of artificially depressing the overall *Social class* in the *Total Sample*. Other evidence for the interpretation here is the fact that a greater proportion of parents fall into the 'social class unknown' category in the *Total Sample*

(16.7%) than in the *Census* (10.1%). In all probability, then, the real *Social class* standing of pupils in the *Total Sample* is not very different from those nationally.

2.5.3 *Irish achievement, general academic ability and social class*

The results indicate clearly that lower *Pupil general academic ability* and lower *Social class* predominate among pupils and classes with low levels of achievement in Irish. The formal statistical analysis of these relationships using regression and correlation techniques is deferred until Chapters 3 and 5. Our goal here is simply to illustrate the nature and strength of these relationships more directly in order to indicate the range of conditions under which Irish is taught. The mean percentages of pupils attaining mastery of sixth-grade objectives in Irish shows a steady and substantial increase according to increasing levels of *Pupil general academic ability*. This confirms the strong relationship between these same variables found in previous studies (Harris and Murtagh, 1988b). At the class level also, very low levels of *Pupil general academic ability* (*DVRT* <=90) are much more common in low-Irish-achievement classes than in high- and middle-Irish-achievement classes.

Social class is also positively linked with *Pupil achievement in Irish*. More than twice the proportion of pupils in the highest *Social class* group (50.7%) than in the lowest *Social class* group (21.7%) attain mastery of each objective on the Irish test. Nevertheless, there are instances of individual classes which go against the pattern. For example, pupils in Class 1, which has the highest level of achievement in Irish of all, tend to fall into relatively lower *Social class* categories, 'semi-skilled' or 'unskilled'.

A slight break in the trend in Irish achievement across social-class groups occurs in the case of *Social class* group 7 where marginally more pupils attain mastery than in *Social class* group 6. This adds weight to our earlier suggestion that due to the quality of information on occupational status available for the *Rest* of the classes, some pupils who would normally have been assigned to higher (i.e. numerically lower) *Social class* groups were instead assigned to *Social class* group 7. The inclusion of these pupils enlarged the proportion in *Social class* group 7 as well as raising the Irish achievement of this group.

The remaining data to be discussed do not involve formal comparisons at a national level and are primarily intended to provide a richer picture of the diversity of the classes in the study. It should be noted, however, that the issue of comparability with the national picture is pursued further in Chapter 5 where we consider the goodness-of-fit between some new data on adult ability in Irish and use of Irish at home in the Parent Sample and equivalent sociolinguistic data at a national level from other studies.

2.5.4 *Pupil interest in and difficulty with Irish*

The teachers' ratings allow us to place performance in Irish in the context of performance in other subjects such as Mathematics or English reading without conducting a large amount of direct testing. The results show that teachers tend to judge large proportions of pupils as having difficulty with Irish. This is particularly so in the case of spoken Irish where half of all pupils are seen as having difficulty. Irish reading comes next with 37% being reported as having difficulty.

At the class level, teachers in half the low-Irish-achievement classes judge that between 53% and 74% of pupils have difficulty with spoken Irish. But even in the high-Irish-achievement group of classes, which are considerably better than the national average, substantial proportions of pupils are often perceived as having difficulty with this subject. In four of these classes (ranks 2, 3, 5, 6) teachers rated 30% or more of pupils as having difficulty. Class 1 is the only one of the 20 classes in which no pupil is judged to have difficulty with *Spoken Irish*. Our own test of spoken Irish, of course, reinforces this judgment - only 4% of classes nationally do better than Class 1.

One way of construing data on perceived pupil difficulty with school subjects is that they indicate the extent to which there is a gap between the level of performance expected by the teacher and the actual performance of pupils. Viewed in this way, the expectations-performance gap is particularly large in the case of spoken Irish and indeed mathematics. The ITÉ national surveys of achievement in spoken Irish mentioned earlier, which show that only a third of pupils, on average, attain mastery of each objective, have been interpreted as evidence that the expectations/performance gap may be too high in the case of Irish (Harris, 1984). The argument was that the expectations embodied in the *Nuachúrsaí* were simply too ambitious for most pupils. Note also that a substantial majority of teachers (71%) believe that the 'expectations of the syllabus in Irish cannot be achieved within the amount of time available' (INTO, 1985a: 9).

If high expectations are to have a positive influence on outcome, they must be accompanied by frequent opportunities for pupils to experience success in learning and also to receive feedback on their progress which is both affirmative and of a high quality. Otherwise, pupils' esteem in relation to their ability to develop speaking proficiency may suffer. As we shall see in subsequent chapters, substantial numbers of pupils, particularly in low-Irish-achievement classes, have a poor image of their ability in Irish and tend to experience anxiety about the Irish class.

High percentages of teachers report pupils as having difficulty in other subject areas as well as Irish - 37.8% in Mathematics, 33.8% in English writing and 22.6% in English reading. Data to be presented later show that parents are less likely than teachers to report that their child has difficulties with subjects in general (Chapter 5, Table 5.13).

Data at the class level indicate that socio-educational factors, including unemployment, can be associated with low levels of achievement in Irish as well as in English and other school subjects. For example, low-Irish-achievement classes are associated with lower social-class ratings and with higher levels of long-term parental unemployment than classes in the other two achievement groups. Furthermore, half of the low-Irish-achievement classes have 30% or more of pupils rated as having difficulty with *English Reading*, while only one of the middle-Irish-achievement classes and none of the high-Irish-achievement classes have such large proportions. The highest proportion rated as having difficulty with *English Reading* (43%) is the class with the lowest Irish achievement (rank 20).

Over a third of pupils overall (35.5%) are considered by their teachers to have 'low' interest in Irish. Once again, however, this proportion varies considerably across classes. Only one class in the high-Irish-achievement group has more than 30% of the pupils exhibiting a 'low' level of interest in Irish, while all classes in the low-Irish-achievement group have more than that proportion of pupils with 'low' interest in Irish. Data discussed more fully in Chapters 3 and 7 show that, in general terms at least, teachers' assessments of the level of interest in Irish in different classes tend to be consistent with those based on both pupils themselves and inspectors who observed the Irish lesson. For example, the two classes with the greatest proportion of pupils showing low interest in Irish as assessed by teachers (Classes 15 and 20 in Table 2.12) are also the ones with the least positive overall Irish attitude/motivation based on pupils' own reports (Chapter 3: Table 3.10).

Finally, the results show that there are high correlations between teacher's judgments of difficulty in Irish and interest in Irish, on the one hand, and actual *Pupil achievement in Irish* as measured by the ITÉ test of spoken Irish, on the other (r=-.57 & .56 respectively). This is consistent with evidence in the educational literature generally that teachers' perceptions correlate very well with objective measures (Egan and Archer, 1985).

2.5.5 Socio-demographic and teaching variables

In this concluding section, we consider data relating to a number of socio-demographic and teaching characteristics of the *Twenty-Classes* compared to sixth-grade classes nationally. In general, the data confirm that we have succeeded in including classes in our study which represent the whole range of values and categories of some of the major socio-demographic and educational variables relevant to the teaching and learning of Irish. In saying this we do not suggest, of course, that we have achieved the kind of balance and representativeness which would be produced by stratified random sampling.

We also show that the relationship between these characteristics and class achievement in Irish is at least broadly consistent with previous ITÉ research conducted at a national level (Harris, 1983; Harris and Murtagh, 1988b). In relation to location, for example, note that while none of the Dublin classes are in the high-Irish-achievement group of classes, both Connaught classes are. The link between class achievement in Irish and size of sixth-grade group is also consistent with national data i.e. higher achievement is associated with smaller sixth-grade groups (Harris, 1983). Combining the 'Nuachúrsaí alone' and 'Nuachúrsaí plus ABC' categories we find that 65% of teachers say they use the Nuachúrsaí as an important part of their main method of teaching Irish. This percentage compares to 88.2% in the 1985 ITÉ survey of sixth-grade teachers (Harris and Murtagh, 1988b). Correspondingly the proportion of teachers using their 'own' method in the *Twenty-Classes Study* (30%) is considerably up from the 6.7% in the 1985 survey. While it is not at all critical to our approach that the percentages for the various methods in the *Twenty-Classes Study* should reflect the situation nationally, it is interesting to note that these data are consistent with a continuation of the fall off in the proportion of teachers committed to the *Nuachúrsaí* which first became evident in the 1985 ITÉ survey (see Chapter 1).

More important, than this, however, is the likelihood that teachers' reports of 'main method' are not really an adequate basis on which to draw conclusions about classroom practice. One source of doubt arises from the fact that response to another *Teacher Questionnaire* item suggest that 'own method' can include some use of the *Nuachúrsaí*. In addition, classroom-observation data (Chapter 7) show that film strips and the projector are used in only 9.1% of lesson segments (12.1% of lesson time), the *Nuachúrsaí* handbook is used in only 10% of segments (12% of time), and that *Nuachúrsaí*-related topics are involved in only 10.9% of segments. One possible explanation for the apparent discrepancy between these direct-observation data and teachers' reports is that teachers may mean 'main' method in the sense that their basic approach is anchored in the *Nuachúrsaí* - without implying that they use *Nuachúrsaí* or audio-visual materials/aids very frequently. It must be borne in mind also that teachers are responding to a multiple-choice question here rather than describing their chosen method in their own words. Irrespective of the truth or otherwise of this, these data raise doubts about the usefulness of multiple-choice questions in obtaining high-quality information on course-method.

Finally, we turn to the issue of teaching through Irish. The *Twenty-Classes Study* data on the amount of Irish-medium instruction which is conducted accords moderately well with data collected at a national level. The main difference is that somewhat more Irish-medium instruction is conducted in the twenty classes than in classes nationally. The percentages for the main Irish-medium categories in the national sample are as follows: 45% of classes spend 'no time' on Irish-medium instruction, 38.2% spend less than one hour and 16.5% spend more than one hour. The corresponding data for the *Twenty-Classes Study* are 35% (no time), 45% (less than one hour) and 20% (more than one hour) (Harris and Murtagh, 1988b). All the high-Irish-achievement classes spend at least some time each week on Irish-medium instruction - in some cases a substantial amount - compared to only two of the eight low-Irish-achievement classes. We have already mentioned just how high achievement in Irish is in some ordinary schools. All this emphasises once again that Irish-medium teaching is critical to the generation of really high levels of achievement in Irish in ordinary schools. It also supports our conclusions from the *Teaching through Irish Project* that, as the new curriculum is introduced, it is important to provide teaching materials, in-service training and other support for those teachers who are prepared, on a voluntary basis, to conduct some Irish-medium instruction.

In the following chapters, our task will be to amplify the basic description of the teaching and learning of Irish in the *Twenty classes* which has been presented in the present chapter. This will involve an account of a wide range of factors, including pupil attitude/motivation, pupils' views of the Irish lesson and course materials, the views and practices of parents, the structure and content of the Irish lesson and pupil participation and language use in the classroom.

3   Pupils' attitude and motivation

3.1 Introduction

There are at least two general aspects to primary school pupils' attitude to Irish and their motivation to learn it which are of interest to those involved in primary education. First, there is the commonsense notion, supported by a fairly sizeable body of research, that pupils' attitude and motivation are important factors which determine success in second- and foreign-language learning (Gardner and MacIntyre, 1993). Second, the primary school programme, apart from the central specific aim of developing proficiency in Irish, also has a number of other goals related to the affective domain - namely, to develop a positive attitude to the Irish language itself and to the idea of speaking it; to foster a desire to continue studying the language; and, more generally, to develop an interest in learning other languages. It would be of some interest, therefore, to have available an instrument which would allow us to measure the strength of individual attitudes and motivation in relation both to Irish and the learning of Irish and, in turn, to establish how important such attitudes and motivation were in relation to the level of proficiency in spoken Irish which was achieved by pupils. In the absence of any existing instrument suitable for administration to primary school pupils, the *Pupil Questionnaire* used in the present study of pupils' attitudes to Irish was developed. Before describing the *Questionnaire* itself and the information which it yielded, it will be useful to briefly review research on attitude-motivation in relation to second-language learning generally and in relation to Irish in particular.

3.1.1 Affective variables in second-language learning

In the last few decades many studies have shown a link between affective factors such as pupil attitude and motivation, on the one hand, and achievement in the second language on the other. Gardner (1985a) has demonstrated that within the attitudinal domain, the major determinant of achievement is motivation (see also Lalonde and Gardner, 1985). It is believed that attitudinal variables associated with the target language group and a desire to integrate with that group are influential not so much because of the direct association of these variables with proficiency, but more because they serve as the basis for maintaining and supporting motivation in the lengthy task of acquiring competence in the second language. This view of motivation and the instrument used to measure it (*The Attitude/Motivation Test Battery*) forms the basis of the approach to assessing pupils' attitudes to Irish and learning Irish which is adopted in the present study.

The Attitude/Motivation Test Battery (AMTB)

The *Attitude/Motivation Test Battery* was initially conceptualized and designed to measure the major attitudinal and motivation factors which influence individuals in the course of learning another language. As far back as 1959, Gardner and Lambert showed a link between two independent factors, Language Aptitude and Social Motivation, and achievement in French among Canadian English-speaking high-school students (Gardner and Lambert, 1959). In the late seventies, Gardner and his colleagues set about formalising the composition and measurement of attitude and motivation in relation to second-language learning (Gardner, Clément, Smythe and Smythe, 1979). To this end they developed the *Attitude/Motivation Test Battery* (*AMTB*), a series of measures designed particularly for a Canadian context, with English-speaking children learning French in mind. The battery measured a number of affective components. Three attitude/motivational clusters - *Motivation, Integrativeness* and *Attitude toward the learning situation* - were defined in terms of a conceptual analysis of the variables and their relation to second-language learning.

The first cluster or component, *Motivation,* refers to an individual who (a) wants to achieve a particular goal, (b) devotes considerable effort to achieving this goal and (c) experiences satisfaction in the activities associated with achieving the goal. The corresponding measures associated with the concept of *Motivation* in the *AMTB* were (a) *Desire to learn the language* (b) *Motivational intensity to learn the language* (c) *Attitudes to learning the language.*

The second cluster, *Integrativeness* refers to those learner attributes which reflect a positive outlook toward the target language group, or out-groups in general, or a desire to meet with and possibly associate with members of those groups. In the *AMTB,* these attributes were represented by three measures (a) *Attitudes toward the target language group* (b) *Interest in foreign languages* and (c) *Integrative orientation*

The third cluster *Attitudes to the learning situation,* refers to the learners' affective reactions to the learning situation e.g. attitudes towards the teacher, the class, the textbooks, the language laboratory etc. In the *AMTB* these are measured by (a) *Evaluation of the language teacher* and (b) *Evaluation of the language course.*

Comparing the three logical groupings above, Gardner and Smythe (1981) and Lalonde and Gardner (1985) have found *Motivation* to be the best predictor of pupil behavioural outcomes related to second/foreign-language learning e.g. behavioural intention, self-ratings, teacher ratings, French grades and objective measures of achievement in French (L2). These findings are consistent with Gardner's (1979) socio-educational model of second-language acquisition which sees *Motivation* as having a direct influence on second-language achievement, whereas the two attitudinal measures *Integrativeness* and *Attitude toward the learning situation* have a direct influence on *Motivation* which in turn mediates their relationship with second-language achievement (Lalonde and Gardner, 1985).

Two other measures, *Instrumental orientation* and *Language anxiety* were also incorporated in Gardner's overall definition of Attitude/Motivation. In contrast to the *Integrative orientation* which reflects an overall interest in the target language speaking community, an *Instrumental orientation* is characterized by 'a desire to gain social recognition or economic advantages through knowledge of a foreign language' (Gardner and Lambert, 1972: 14).

Language anxiety refers to learners' anxiety reactions to situations in which they might make use of the target language. The negative effect of language anxiety on achievement in the target language has been well established (Gardner, Smythe, Clément and Gliksman, 1976; Gardner, 1985a, Horwitz, Horwitz, and Cope, 1986; Trylong, 1987; Gardner and MacIntyre, 1993).

The antithesis of the anxious student according to MacIntyre and Gardner (1991) is the self-confident one. Clément, Gardner and Smythe (1977, 1980) found that self-confidence, defined by a lack of language anxiety and by the presence of a positive self-rated proficiency in the second language, was positively related to second-language proficiency measures as well as to motivation. Recently MacIntyre, Noels and Clément (1997) noted significant intercorrelations between language anxiety, second-language self-ratings and actual second-language proficiency. The authors also reported that regression analysis, with actual proficiency level controlled, showed that anxious students tended to underestimate their competence (lower self-ratings) relative to the less anxious students who tended to overestimate their competence (higher self-ratings).

A *Parental encouragement* factor although not incorporated in the overall construct of Attitude/Motivation has, nonetheless, been linked to higher pupil achievement in the second language (Gardner and Smythe, 1981). This measure reflects the extent to which students feel their parents support them in their study of the target language.

Various studies have modified the original items from the *AMTB* or used comparable ones for use in different contexts such as the learning of English by French-speaking students in Canada (Clément, Gardner and Smythe, 1977), primary-school students learning English in Belize, Central America (Gordon, 1980) and American high-school students learning Spanish (Muchnick and Wolfe, 1982). Despite variation in context, these and other studies have shown positive relationships between affective factors, particularly motivation, and learner self-confidence and achievement in the second language (Gardner and MacIntyre, 1993).

A number of aspects of second-language acquisition, apart from achievement as such, are also thought to be influenced by language attitudes/motivation. For example, Gliksman, Gardner and Smythe (1982) have demonstrated that pupils who were more 'integratively motivated' tended to volunteer more answers in the second-language classroom, were more correct in their responses and were generally more interested during class than less integratively motivated students. Another factor which is thought to be affected by language attitudes/motivation is the extent to which learners persist with their study of a second language. Finally, a higher drop-out rate has been reported among students who were less motivated, or who held less favourable attitudes to the target language, than others (Bartley, 1970; Clément, Smythe and Gardner, 1978; Ramage, 1990).

3.1.2 Research on attitudes to learning Irish among school children

Although a substantial amount of attention has been given over the years to the public's attitudes towards Irish (CLAR, 1975; Ó Riagáin and Ó Gliasáin, 1994) considerably less research has been conducted on language attitudes among the school going population or on pupils' perceptions of the language learning process itself. What research has been done in this area has focused on pupils who have reached second level education. Three different surveys over a twenty year period give some broad indications of how students in early secondary school feel in relation to Irish and the teaching of Irish.

A small-scale survey of first-year secondary students (outside the Gaeltacht) was conducted in the early 1970's as part of the larger CLAR (1975) survey of public attitudes to the Irish language. The findings of this unpublished part of the survey showed a high level of commitment to Irish. The 83% answering a question regarding their feelings towards Irish is broken down as follows. Almost half (48%) of the students in the sample were in 'favour of Irish' or committed to supporting it, 18% had 'no particular feelings' while 17% were 'somewhat/strongly opposed' to it. The support for Irish in the educational system was less strong - only 15% of first years ranked Irish as the subject they found 'most enjoyable' while 19% listed Irish as the subject they'd most like to drop. Over half (55%) the pupils agreed with the statement 'I feel it is important to know Irish' and over two thirds agreed that they 'would like to be able to speak Irish well'.

At the start of the following decade a youth market survey (Bord na Gaeilge, 1982) on attitudes to the Irish language was conducted based on interviews with 1,000 young people. A separate analysis of 13-14 year olds (n=107), showed that while the proportion 'in favour' (49%) of Irish was broadly similar to the CLAR survey (first-year students) findings above, the proportion who had 'no particular feelings' (36%) was substantially higher than in the CLAR survey (18%). However, the proportion who were 'opposed' to Irish (12%) or said they 'didn't know' (3%) was lower than in the case of CLAR.

It is worth noting that almost three quarters (74%) of young teenagers in the Bord na Gaeilge study agreed that 'a knowledge of the Irish language is an advantage'. In relation to eleven or more school subjects, Irish and Mathematics emerged as the ones enjoyed least by students: 20% and 21% of students respectively. Since these students were just embarking on their secondary education, their expressed attitude to Irish is likely to reflect their experiences learning Irish during their primary-school years.

The third, and more up to date source of information on pupils' attitudes to Irish and learning Irish comes from a regional study of second and third year post-primary classes conducted in the mid-eighties (Ó Fathaigh, 1991). These students then are broadly similar in age to those in the Bord na Gaeilge study above. The sample consisted of 24 classes randomly selected from post-primary schools in the Cork area. Various scales based on Walberg's (1979) *Learning Environment Inventory* and Gardner *et al.*'s (1979) *Attitude/Motivation Test Battery* were used to assess dimensions of the pupils' attitude/motivation and behavioural intentions in learning Irish. While the results indicated an overall 'positive' attitude to the importance of Irish as an ethnic symbol and to the promotion of bilingualism, less positive attitudes were related to the learning process itself. For example, on a scale of 1-5, the students' mean item rating on an 'Attitude to Bilingualism' scale was 3.6 compared to only 2.5 on the scale 'Desire to Learn Irish'.

Ó Fathaigh (1991) also found that learners' background and affective variables were linked to achievement in Irish. Positive relationships with achievement were recorded for students' social-class background, frequency of use of spoken Irish, contact with Irish/Irish speakers, and their desire to learn Irish while a negative effect was found in the case of Irish-class anxiety. Gender differences in attitude/motivation were also reported by Ó Fathaigh with girls being significantly more positive than boys on eight of the nine attitude/motivation scales. Another aspect of the study assessed learners' perceptions of the actual process of learning Irish. The results showed that half of all pupils recorded 'low' levels of *satisfaction* with the Irish class while almost a third reported 'high' levels of *difficulty* with the Irish lesson and with coping with selected areas of Irish use.

3.1.3 The present study of Irish attitude/motivation

The purpose of the present chapter is to describe the development of a *Pupil Questionnaire* which will provide measures of different aspects of primary pupils' attitude/motivation in relation to Irish, and to learning Irish and foreign languages. We will the use this instrument to:

1. assess how good is attitude/motivation in relation to Irish among senior-grade primary school pupils by using an adapted form of the *AMTB*.
2. establish the extent of the variation in attitude/motivation to Irish from class to class and
3. investigate the relationships between pupil *Irish attitude/motivation*, social and cognitive background factors, on the one hand, and actual achievement in Irish, on the other. We also examine the relationship between social and cognitive factors and *Irish attitude/motivation*.

We begin with a description of the development and administration of the *Pupil Questionnaire*. Included are technical data on mean scores and reliability for the various scales as well as a description of how composite measures of pupil attitude and motivation were constructed from individual scales (Table 3.1-3.2).

Results are presented in three parts corresponding to the three main issues listed above. In Part 1 (Tables 3.3-3.9) we examine responses on selected attitude/motivation items, as well as mean item-scores for different scales, as a rough and ready way of determining how good is attitude/motivation in relation to Irish for the total sample of pupils. In Part 2 (Table 3.10) we examine variation in *Irish attitude/motivation* from class to class. This class-level analysis is limited to a small number of item-based and composite-measure-based indicators of pupils attitudes' to Irish and learning Irish, and to learning a second/foreign language. In Part 3 (Tables 3.11-3.13) we use correlation and regression analyses to assess the relationship between *Irish attitude/motivation* and a number of other social, linguistic and educational variables.

3.2 Development and administration of the *Pupil Questionnaire*

The 80 item *Pupil Questionnaire* was administered to all pupils in the Total Sample present on the day of administration (n=490). Full details of the instructions for administration may be found in Appendix 3.1. For economy of presentation, the items themselves along with the percentage of pupils choosing each response option are shown in Appendix 3.2. For presentation purposes also we have grouped items under appropriate scales. It should be noted, however, that items in the actual *Pupil Questionnaire* were not grouped according to scales or identified in any way but were presented in a scrambled order (see item numbers). All except the last three items on the questionnaire had a five-point Likert response format (Likert, 1972) ranging from 'strongly disagree' (1) to 'strongly agree' (5).

Sixty five of the items were used to develop nine attitude-motivation scales. These items, and the scales which were derived from them, are based to a greater or lesser extent on the *Attitude/Motivation Test Battery (AMTB)* described earlier (Gardner *et al.*, 1979). A description of the way in which the original *AMTB* was adapted for the present context of pupils learning Irish is outlined below.

The remaining 15 items on the *Pupil Questionnaire* break down into three other scales or thematic groupings which are not based on the *AMTB* at all. Nine of these items are used to form two new scales: an *Irish-ability self-concept* scale (6 items) and a non-attitudinal scale, *Use of Irish at home* (3 items). A *Miscellaneous* scale, comprising three items, sought background information on the pupils' ability (self-assessed) in *English Reading* and in *Mathematics*, and on their perceptions of how proud their parents are of the amount of Irish that they (the pupils) have learned at school.

The final three items on the questionnaire (items 78, 79 and 80) sought comments from the pupils on (a) what they liked in the Irish lesson, (b) what they disliked in the Irish lesson and, (c) how they would like to change the Irish lesson. These three 'write-in' items were open-ended and were designed to elicit the spontaneous reactions of pupils in relation to the Irish lesson *per se*. The analysis of the written responses to these three items (see Appendix 4) is dealt with in the next chapter.

We describe briefly below each of the main eleven Likert scales excluding the *Miscellaneous* and the 'write-in' items. It will be noted (Appendix 3.2) that some scales contain a mixture of positively and negatively worded items. In order to calculate a total score for each scale it was necessary to change the orientation of scores on negatively worded items. Thus, a score of 5 indicating 'strongly agree' on a negatively worded item was converted to a score of 1, a score of 4 on the same item would be converted to 2, etc. to make them equivalent to positively worded items. Items on the *Irish-lesson anxiety* scale, which are all negative in relation to the pupil's experience in learning of Irish (e.g. 'I get nervous and mixed up when I am speaking in my Irish class'), were not changed. Scores on these items were added together to give a scale score - the intention is to estimate the strength of this negative factor.

Irish Attitude/Motivation scales: AMTB based

Integrativeness scales

1. *Attitude to Irish speakers.* This scale consists of ten positively worded items about Irish speakers. A high score on this measure (maximum = 50) indicates a positive attitude towards Irish speakers.

2. *Integrative orientation to Irish.* The four items in this scale emphasise the importance of learning Irish in order to permit social interaction with Irish speakers. A high score on this scale (maximum = 20) indicates that a pupil favours integrative reasons for studying Irish.

3. *Interest in second/foreign languages.* This measure consists of ten positively worded items (maximum = 50) designed to assess pupils' general interest in studying other/foreign languages. No specific language is mentioned in the items.

Motivation scales

4. *Desire to learn Irish.* Seven Likert type items (maximum score = 35) are included in this scale with a high score indicating a strong desire to learn Irish. Four items are positively worded and three are negatively worded.

5. *Motivational intensity to learn Irish.* This measure consists of five Likert type items (maximum score = 25) which are designed to measure the intensity of a pupil's motivation to learn Irish, in terms of effort made in class, attention given to homework and so on. Three items are positively worded and two are negatively worded. A high score on this scale indicates that a pupil reports a high degree of effort being spent in acquiring the language.

6. *Attitude to learning Irish.* This is a ten item scale, five of the items being positively worded, and five expressing negative sentiments. A high score (maximum = 50) indicates a positive attitude towards learning Irish.

Other attitude/motivation scales

7. *Instrumental orientation to Irish.* Pupils are presented with four items which stress the pragmatic or utilitarian value of learning Irish. A high score (maximum = 20) indicates that the pupil endorses instrumental reasons for learning Irish.

8. *Irish-lesson anxiety.* A five item scale with a high score (maximum = 25) reflecting the pupil's degree of discomfort and lack of self-confidence while participating in the Irish class. A high score indicates a high level of anxiety.

9. *Parental encouragement.* These ten positively worded items assess the extent to which pupils feel their parents support them in their study of Irish. A high score (maximum = 50) indicates a high level of perceived parental encouragement.

Non-AMTB based scales

10. *Irish-ability self-concept.* This new scale comprising six positively worded items (maximum score = 30) was designed to assess pupils' perceptions of their own ability

in Irish. A high score indicates a positive self-concept in relation to Irish ability.

11. *Use of Irish at home.* A three item (2 positive and 1 negative) scale measuring the extent to which Irish is used in the family home.

3.2.1 *Adapting the AMTB scales to the Irish situation*

The version of the *AMTB* upon which we modelled our own *Pupil Questionnaire* was designed particularly for a Canadian context, with English-speaking children learning French in mind (Gardner *et al.*, 1979, Gardner, 1985a). It was validated and standardized on samples of 1,000 anglophone Canadian students in grades 7 to 11. Items or scales which were not suitable for the different context of pupils learning Irish, or which were not suitable for primary school pupils because of their format, are not included in the present *Pupil Questionnaire*.

Apart from the obvious difference in the language being referred to, Irish rather than French, there are four other main differences between the attitude-motivation items and scales used in the *AMTB* and those used in our *Pupil Questionnaire*:

(1) We used the same *five*-point Likert type format throughout, whereas the *AMTB* uses either a *seven*-point Likert format or a conventional multiple-choice format. The changes were made because pilot testing had convinced us that at least some primary school pupils found the *AMTB* format difficult.

(2) Each item-stem (statement) was read aloud by the Inspector administering the *Pupil Questionnaire* as well as being printed in the pupil's booklet. The original *AMTB* items are normally read silently by the students themselves. Our modification was necessary in order to exclude the possibility, given the children's age, of any reading difficulties interfering with responses.

(3) We made substantial changes in the wording of individual items in order to adapt them to the different sociolinguistic situation in the case of Irish, to make them conform to the variety of English spoken here, and to take account of the age of the pupils involved.

(4) A series of eight semantic differential scales in the original *AMTB* were designed to assess the students' *Attitude to the learning situation* (not to be confused with the rather similarly named motivational scale *Attitude to learning French)* i.e. their general evaluative reaction to their French teacher and to the French course they were pursuing. These scales were not considered suitable for use in our study, bearing in mind the pupils' age, the range of other data being collected and the relatively small number of teachers involved. Consequently, Irish scales equivalent to these *AMTB* scales were not developed. The three 'write-in' items at the end of the questionnaire, however, give pupils the opportunity to express their reactions to the learning situation in a more informal way (see Chapter 4).

Two examples from the original *AMTB* serve to illustrate how we modified the attitude-motivation items for the *Pupil Questionnaire*:

Original *AMTB* items:

'English Canadians should make a greater effort to learn the French language.'

Strongly Disagree	Moderately Disagree	Slightly Disagree	Neutral	Slightly Agree	Moderately Agree	Strongly Agree

'If there were French-speaking families in my neighbourhood, I would:'

   (a) never speak French with them
   (b) speak French with them sometimes
   (c) speak French with them as much as possible

Pupil Questionnaire version:

'People in our country who only speak English should try harder to learn the Irish language'.

Strongly Disagree	Slightly Disagree	Neutral	Slightly Agree	Strongly Agree

'If there were Irish-speaking families living near me, I would like to speak Irish to them.'

Strongly Disagree	Slightly Disagree	Neutral	Slightly Agree	Strongly Agree

Seven Irish attitude-motivation scales on the *Pupil Questionnaire* listed earlier correspond directly to those used in the Canadian *AMTB* in terms of the number of items used, general response format and content. Two scales, however, *Motivational intensity to learn Irish* and *Desire to learn Irish*, are modified versions of the original scales. Gardner *et al.*, (1979) had used a conventional multiple-choice format for these two scales. We converted them to a Likert type format as shown in the examples above.

The significance of some aspects of the terminology used in items on the *Interest in second/foreign languages* scale should be mentioned. While items on this scale in the original Canadian *AMTB* referred variously to 'another language', 'another country' or 'a foreign language', no specific language was ever mentioned. The same was true in the case of our *Pupil Questionnaire*. Following the example of the corresponding items in the *AMTB*, half of the items on the *Interest in second/foreign languages* scale in the *Pupil Questionnaire* use either the terms 'foreign language' or 'another country' while the other half refer to a 'language other than English'. Thus, a balance is maintained between the idea of a 'another language' consisting of a 'foreign language' or a 'second language'.

3.2.2 Administering the Pupil Questionnaire

The changes made in adapting the original Canadian *AMTB* in developing the *Pupil Questionnaire* also involved substantial modifications in the administration of the *Pupil Questionnaire* compared to the original *AMTB*. Pupils were told (see Appendix 3.1) that they were being asked to answer the *Questionnaire* so that we could find out more about how children learn Irish and what they think and feel about it. It was emphasised that there were no right or wrong answers.

In the case of the practice items, the examiner first wrote both the statement and answer options on the blackboard, and then read each aloud one or more times, as necessary. The examiner proceeded through the answer options each time from left to right and pointed to each option as it was spoken. This was to ensure, as far as possible, that poor readers would be able to identify the answer options simply from the left to right order once the items proper began. For the remainder of the items only the statement was read aloud.

The word 'neutral' was explained by saying that it meant 'when you are in between, when you don't agree or disagree'. The method for recording answers, simply drawing a circle around the chosen answer, was also demonstrated. Finally, since some of the items referred to foreign languages, the inspector asked the class a few questions initially to establish that pupils understood what a foreign language was.

The instructions (see Appendix 3.1) specified that the examiner, when reading the items aloud to the pupils, should use a normal speaking rate and tone. No time limit was set for administration of the *Pupil Questionnaire* items, but the aim was to proceed to the next item briskly once the last pupil had marked his or her answer.

No other instrument was administered on the day on which pupils responded to this questionnaire. It will recalled from Chapter 2 that the *Pupil Questionnaire* was the first of the three pupil instruments to be administered to pupils. This was done so as to ensure that the other aspects of the study (testing and observation) would not unduly influence the pupils' responses to the *Questionnaire* items.

3.2.3 *Mean scores and reliability of the Pupil Questionnaire scales*

Table 3.1 gives mean scores and reliability estimates for each of the main 11 scales i.e. excluding the *Miscellaneous* scale and the 'write-in' items. The reliability estimates consist of Cronbach's alpha (Cronbach, 1951) which indicates the extent to which each scale is internally consistent i.e. each item within the scale is measuring the same trait/dimension. The Cronbach coefficient is calculated on the basis of the average correlation between items and the number of items in each scale (Carmines and Zeller, 1979). This type of reliability is particularly important in the context of the present work given the extent to which we have rewritten the items on the original test to make them suitable for the Irish situation.

Inspection of column five of Table 3.1 reveals that, in general, the reliability of most scales is substantial except for *Instrumental orientation to Irish* (as indeed is also the case in corresponding scales on the original *AMTB*). We also present data on the range of values of Cronbach's alpha, found in 32 studies which used the *AMTB*, quoted in Gardner (1985a). It can be seen that where the internal consistency estimates for our own scales fall outside Gardner's range, the differences are small - no more than .05 in any case. The values for Scale 4 and Scale 5 - *Desire to learn Irish* and *Motivational intensity to learn Irish* are particularly good bearing in mind the fundamental change in item format which was necessary and the reduction which was made in item numbers. The reliability values for the two entirely new *ITÉ* scales, *Irish-ability self-concept* and *Use of Irish at home*, are also satisfactory.

Table 3.1

Mean scores and reliability estimates for eleven Irish attitude/motivation scales based on *Pupil Questionnaire* items.

Scales	Item mean score (1-5)	Scale Score (Min, Max)	Mean	SD	Reliability (Cronbach Alpha)	AMTB* Norms: (Alpha Ranges)
n (pupils)=484-490						
Irish Attitude/Motivation scales						
Integrativeness scales						
(1) Attitude to Irish speakers	3.7	(10,50)	37.1	6.9	.79	.84-.88
(2) Integrative orientation to Irish	3.6	(4,20)	14.5	3.8	.73	.78-.85
(3) Interest in second/foreign languages	4.3	(10,50)	42.5	6.3	.81	.81-.89
Motivation scales						
(4) Desire to learn Irish**	3.0	(7,35)	21.2	7.0	.82	.77-.87
(5) Motivational intensity to learn Irish**	3.2	(5,25)	15.8	4.4	.67	.71-.85
(6) Attitude to learning Irish	3.3	(10,50)	32.7	11.0	.93	.91-.95
Other scales						
(7) Instrumental orientation to Irish	3.2	(4,20)	12.8	3.6	.59	.51-.56
(8) Irish-lesson anxiety	2.9	(5,25)	14.4	5.1	.77	.76-.81
(9) Parental encouragement (pupil report)	3.5	(10,50)	34.9	8.9	.88	.89-.91
Non-AMTB based scales						
(10) Irish-ability self-concept (pupil report)	3.1	(6,30)	18.6	5.4	.79	
(11) Use of Irish at home (pupil report)	§	(3,15)	7.1	3.5	.72	

* AMTB = Attitude/Motivation Test Battery (Gardner et al., 1979). **Based on reduced AMTB scales
§ Not comparable to the item means for the attitude/motivation scales.

Column one of Table 3.1 lists the mean item score for all items on the various eleven scales. It will be noted that all three mean scores for *Integrativeness scale* items (3.7, 3.6, 4.3) are higher than the three mean scores for *Motivation scale* items (3.0, 3.2, 3.3). While the items on the two different sets of scales are not comparable in any sense the consistency with which pupils respond more positively to *Integrativeness* items compared to *Motivation* items reinforces the conceptual distinction between these two components i.e. that they capture different aspects of overall attitude/motivation.

3.2.4 Three composite Irish Attitude/Motivation indices

In order to demonstrate the relationship between attitudinal/motivational variables and second-language achievement, Gardner *et al.* (1979) derived a number of composite measures from the various individual scales of the *AMTB*. Three of these, *Motivation index, Integrativeness index,* and *Attitudes to the learning situation index* correspond to the attitude/motivation clusters mentioned earlier, while *Attitude/Motivation Index* was used as an overall measure of attitude motivation (Gardner and Smythe, 1981).

For the purposes of predicting achievement in Irish and comparing differences in attitudes/motivation to Irish between groups of pupils, we created three composite measures, keeping as close as possible to corresponding ones used by Gardner *et al.* (1979). These composite scales will be used later in the chapter to relate the major dimensions of pupils' Irish attitude/motivation to achievement in Irish and other educational, social and linguistic variables.

Table 3.2 summarises how Irish composite indices were computed from the Irish attitude/motivation scales already described, and gives means and standard deviations for each index. The *Integrativeness index* on the Irish *Pupil Questionnaire* was computed by summing the pupil's scores on the three scales *Attitude to Irish speakers, Integrative orientation to Irish* and *Interest in second/foreign languages*. The *Motivation index* on the Irish *Pupil Questionnaire* was computed by summing scores on the following scales: *Desire to learn Irish, Motivational intensity to learn Irish* and *Attitude to learning Irish*.

An overall *Irish attitude/motivation index* designed to incorporate the major attitudinal/motivational characteristics associated with proficiency in Irish was formed by first summing the raw scores on Scales 1, 2, 3, 4, 5, 6, and 7 (*Integrativeness index, Motivation index,* and the *Instrumental orientation to Irish scale*) and, then, subtracting the raw score for Scale 8 *(Irish-lesson anxiety)*. It should be noted that the *Irish attitude/motivation index* does not include another composite index, *Attitudes to the learning situation,* used in the original *AMTB* version. This was not possible, because as we pointed out earlier, we did not develop Irish equivalents of the semantic differential items relating to the teacher and the course on which this composite index was based. The overall *Irish attitude/motivation index* just defined is also used in various correlation and regression analyses later in the report.

Finally, in this regard, note that scale 7, the *Parental encouragement* scale, is not included either in any of the original Canadian *AMTB* composite indices or in our own Irish composite indices.

Table 3.2
Three composite Irish Attitude/Motivation Indices

Composite indices	Min, Max Scores	Mean	SD
Integrativeness index = *Sum* of each pupil's score on scales: *(1) Attitude to Irish speakers* *(2) Integrative orientation to Irish* *(3) Interest in second/foreign languages*	*(24,120)*	94.2	13.6
Motivation index = *Sum* of each pupil's score on scales: *(4) Desire to learn Irish* *(5) Motivational intensity to learn Irish* *(6) Attitude to learning Irish*	*(22,110)*	69.7	20.1
Irish Attitude/Motivation index = *Sum* of each pupil's score on *Integrativeness index* (above) *Motivation index* (above) *(7) Instrumental orientation to Irish* scale *Minus* each pupil's score on *(8) Irish-lesson anxiety* scale	*(25,245)*	162.5	33.9

3.3 Results

3.3.1 Part 1: Pupils' Irish attitude/motivation

Our primary purpose is to illustrate as directly as possible the nature and strength of pupils' attitudes to Irish itself and to the process of learning it. To do this, we examine two kinds of data (a) responses to individual items (Appendix 3.2) and groups of items and (b) comparisons of mean scale scores and mean item scores for different scales. We also examine aspects of pupil self-concept in relation to Irish, their perception of parental encouragement and informal use of Irish at home. Obviously, given the number of items and scales, a very large number of other issues could also be examined. For the purposes of the present report, however, we confine ourselves to the following:

(a) How positive is Irish attitude/motivation generally among primary school pupils? Are pupils' responses to *Integrativeness* items more or less positive than their responses to *Motivational* items. More specifically are pupils' responses to items on the *Attitude to learning Irish* scale more or less positive than their responses on the *Interest in second/foreign languages* scale.

(b) Irish-ability self-concept and Irish-lesson anxiety: How positive are pupils' perceptions of their own standing within the class in Irish compared to their perception of their standing in other subject areas such as English and Mathematics. Items used come from three different scales - *Irish-ability self-concept, Miscellaneous* and *Irish-lesson anxiety*.

(c) Pupils' perceptions of their (i) parents' interest in their schoolwork (ii) parents' pride in their child's achievement in Irish (iii) parents' willingness to help with Irish. Items used come from the *Parental encouragement* scale and the *Miscellaneous* group of items.

(d) Pupils' reports of the extent to which Irish is used generally or by their mothers/fathers in their home. Items come from the *Use of Irish at home* scale.

Integrativeness versus motivation: Irish and foreign languages.

The comparison between *Interest in second/foreign languages* and *Attitude to learning Irish* represent a contrast between *Integrativeness* and *Motivation* - between a general interest in learning another language and the actual experience of doing so. We examine responses to a number of individual items and also compare mean item scores for the two scales. While the items in the two scales are not equivalent in any precise way, a quick reading of them (Appendix 3.2.) will confirm that there are broad similarities between them.

Table 3.3 shows the percentages of pupils who agree ('strongly' or 'slightly') with a number of positive statements concerning the learning of Irish and second/foreign languages. It can be seen that the proportion of pupils exhibiting positive attitudes range from between only 42% - 49.6% on the three selected items on the *Attitude to learning Irish* scale, but from 74.1% to 81.5% on three broadly similar items from the *Interest in second/foreign languages* scale.

The trend for pupils' interest in the notion of learning second/foreign languages to be more positive generally than their evaluation of their existing experience of learning Irish is also indicated (see Table 3.1) by the higher item mean score (4.3) for *Interest in second/foreign languages* compared to *Attitude to learning Irish* (3.3). The mean scale scores for *Interest in second/foreign languages* (42.5, SD=6.3) and *Attitude to learning Irish* (32.7, SD=11.0) make the same point. Each of these two scales contains 10 items in the same Likert type format and in each case high scores indicate a more positive stance. More generally the item mean scores on *Integrativeness* scales (3.7, 3.6, 4.3) are higher than item mean scores on *Motivation* scales (3.0, 3.2, 3.3).

Responses to groups of items within some of the *Integrativeness* scales can vary (see full list of items Appendix 3.2). One of the more interesting comparisons is between groups of items which signify global, passive versus specific active involvement. Within the *Attitude to Irish speakers scale*, for example, statements referring to general cultural/national reasons for learning Irish receive the most approval: 88% of pupils agree both that 'The Irish language is an important part of Ireland and the Irish people' and that 'If Ireland lost the Irish language and the Irish way of life, it would be a great loss' (items 12 & 23) . In contrast, 52% agree with the statement 'The more I get to know people who speak Irish, the more I want to learn it' and only 42% agree that they 'would like to know more people who speak Irish' (items 6 & 49).   Two items within the *Integrative orientation to Irish scale* (items 37 & 27) reflect the same passive/active contrast. Over three quarters (76%) of pupils agree that it is important to learn Irish because it will help them 'to read Irish books and to understand Irish songs, stories and television programmes' while 54% agree that 'it is important for me to learn Irish because it will make it easier for me to take part in things like *Slógadh, feiseanna* and Irish music'.

Table 3.3
Percentages of pupils agreeing ('strongly' or 'slightly') with positive statements concerning the learning of Irish and second/foreign languages.

Selected questionnaire items	*n (pupils) = 490*	*Percentage of pupils agreeing*
Motivation: Attitude to learning Irish *		
'I really enjoy learning Irish.'		47.6
'I love learning Irish.'		42.0
'I want to learn as much Irish as possible.'		49.6
Integrativeness: Interest in second/foreign languages **		
'Learning another language, besides English, can be very enjoyable.'		74.1
'I would really like to learn a lot of foreign languages.'		81.5
'I would like to learn a foreign language in school even if I didn't *have* to do it.'		79.8

*Based on replies to items 20, 25, 51 respectively in the *Pupil Questionnaire*.
** Based on replies to items 21, 31, 50 respectively in the *Pupil Questionnaire*

Irish-ability self concept and Irish-lesson anxiety
Table 3.4 shows the proportions of pupils who agree and who disagree that they are better than most pupils in their class at different school subjects or aspects of subjects. The data are based on responses to five different questions on the *Pupil Questionnaire*, three from the *Irish-ability self-concept* scale and two from the *Miscellaneou*s group of items. What is interesting about these items is the view they provide of pupil's self concept in relation to Irish compared to other school subjects.

It is fairly clear from Table 3.4 that *English Reading* is the subject in relation to which pupils tend to have the most positive self-concept. Thus, 57.5% 'agree' that they are better than most pupils in their class in *English Reading*. The lowest proportion of pupils 'agreeing' that they are better than most pupils in the class (30.7%) is associated with *Speaking Irish*. *Mathematics* comes next with 36.7% 'agreeing' they are better than most in the class. *Irish Reading* and *Irish Writing* are intermediate between *Mathematics* and *English Reading* in terms of self-assessments of this kind. Another way of looking at this same question is to compare the disparities between the proportions of pupils 'agreeing' and the proportions 'disagreeing' for the various item statements (see the last two rows of Table 3.4). For example, only 30.7% agree they are better at 'speaking Irish', while 47.5% disagree - a difference of 16.8% in a negative direction. The gap between 'agree' and 'disagree' for *English Reading* is more than twice that (37.7%) and in a positive direction.

Table 3.4
Percentages of pupils agreeing and disagreeing with statements concerning the pupils' standing in different subject areas*.

Response options (n=490)	*'I am better than most pupils in my class at ....'*				
	English reading	*Maths*	*Irish reading*	*Irish writing*	*speaking Irish*
Strongly disagree	5.9	22.7	10.8	13.5	22.0
Slightly disagree	13.9	20.4	21.8	18.2	25.5
Neutral	22.4	19.6	23.5	30.0	21.6
Slightly agree	37.3	22.2	32.0	28.2	22.7
Strongly agree	20.2	14.5	11.4	9.8	8.0
No response	--	--	--	--	0.2
Combined categories					
slightly/strongly *Disagree*	19.8	43.1	32.6	31.7	47.5
slightly/strongly *Agree*	57.5	36.7	43.4	38.0	30.7

* The items in the first two columns (items 69 & 57) are from the *Miscellaneous* items. Those in the next three columns (items 76, 75 & 66) are from the *Irish-ability self-concept* scale

Table 3.5 confirms the relatively poor self-concept of many children in relation to their speaking ability in Irish, this time based on responses to a negatively worded item from the *Irish-lesson anxiety* scale ('I always feel that the rest of the pupils in my class are better at speaking Irish than I am'). With the 'neutral' category here attracting a smaller proportion of pupils than in the case of the earlier mentioned 'speaking Irish' item, there is a difference of more than 20% between the proportion agreeing that the rest of the class are better than they are (54.3%) and the proportion disagreeing (33.6%).

Table 3.5
Percentage of pupils agreeing and disagreeing with the statement 'I always feel the rest of the pupils in my class are better at speaking Irish than I am.'

Response options	n =490	'... the rest of the pupils ... are better at speaking Irish than I am'
Strongly disagree		12.2
Slightly disagree		21.4
Neutral		11.4
Slightly agree		31.2
Strongly agree		23.1
No response		0.6

*Based on responses to item 32 (*Irish-lesson anxiety* scale) in the *Pupil Questionnaire.*

Table 3.6 contains data from another item on the *Irish-ability self-concept* scale which confirms that pupil self-concept in relation to *Speaking Irish* is somewhat worse than it is in relation to *Mathematics*. Most pupils (60.6%) disagree that they are better at 'speaking Irish' than they are at 'doing Maths' - only 27.8% agree they are better at 'speaking Irish'.

Table 3.6
Percentage of pupils agreeing and disagreeing with the statement 'I am better at speaking Irish than I am at doing Maths.'

Response options	n =490	'I am better at speaking Irish than I am at doing Maths'*
Strongly disagree		38.6
Slightly disagree		22.0
Neutral		11.2
Slightly agree		12.7
Strongly agree		15.1
No response		0.4

*Based on responses to item 77 (*Irish-ability self-concept* scale) in the *Pupil Questionnaire* -

In response to another question on the *Irish-ability self-concept* scale (see Table 3.7) the majority of pupils (71%) agree that they understand most of what the teacher says in Irish at school, but a sizeable minority (21%) do have comprehension difficulties. Responses to items from the *Irish-lesson anxiety scale* (Appendix 3.2) indicate a high level of pupil anxiety when speaking out loud during the lesson. For example, 51.1% agree that they feel unsure when 'speaking out loud in Irish during the lesson' while similar proportions agree (54.3%) that they 'get nervous or mixed up when speaking in Irish class' (item 22 & 28). Just over a quarter of pupils (26.1%) are 'embarrassed' to put up their hand and say something aloud during the Irish lesson (item 9).

Table 3.7
Percentage of pupils agreeing and disagreeing with the statement 'I understand most of what the teacher says in Irish at school.'*

Response options	n =490	'I understand most of what the teacher says in Irish at school'
Strongly disagree		9.0
Slightly disagree		12.0
Neutral		7.6
Slightly agree		40.4
Strongly agree		30.6
No response		0.4

*Based on responses to item 73 (*Irish-ability self-concept* scale) in the *Pupil Questionnaire.*

Parental support
Table 3.8 summarises responses to items relating to pupils' perceptions of their parents' attitudes to Irish - two from the *Parental encouragement* scale and one from the *Miscellaneous* scale (see Appendix 3.2). A majority of pupils (62.1%) agree ('slightly'/'strongly') that their parents help them with their Irish, or are proud of how much Irish they have learned in school (57.6%); somewhat fewer children (48.5%) agree that their parents are 'very interested' in anything to do with their Irish schoolwork. What may be of more significance, however, is the proportion of children who record actual disagreement (slight or strong) with these positive statements, not being content simply to represent their position as 'neutral' - 22.6% of pupils *disagree* that their parents 'try to help them with their Irish'; 16.6% *disagree* that their parents 'are proud of how much Irish they have learned in school'; and 35.3% of the pupils *disagree* that their parents are 'very interested' in anything to do with their Irish schoolwork. In addition to those actually disagreeing with these positive statements, between 14.7% and 25.5% adopted a 'neutral stance'. Other items on the *Parental encouragement* scale present broadly the same picture. Note that we also investigate parental encouragement in Chapter 5, based in that case on the responses of the parents themselves.

Table 3.8
Percentages of pupils agreeing and disagreeing with positive statements concerning their parents' attitudes to pupils' Irish schoolwork*.

Response options n=490	'My parents are proud of how much Irish I have learned at school'	'My parents are usually very interested in anything to do with my Irish schoolwork'	'My parents try to help me with my Irish'
Strongly disagree	8.6	12.9	11.6
Slightly disagree	8.0	22.4	11.0
Neutral	25.5	15.3	14.7
Slightly agree	32.7	31.2	34.5
Strongly agree	24.9	17.3	27.6
No response	0.4		0.6

* Based on replies to item 65 (*Miscellaneous* items) and items 38 & 1 respectively (*Parental encouragement* scale) in the *Pupil Questionnaire*.

Table 3.9
Percentages of pupils agreeing and disagreeing with positive statements concerning the amount of Irish used at home*.

Response Options n=490	'My mother sometimes speaks Irish at home '	'My father sometimes speaks Irish at home'	'No one at home ever speaks Irish'
Strongly disagree	58.8	50.2	21.4
Slightly disagree	11.2	14.3	29.4
Neutral	7.1	9.2	6.1
Slightly agree	15.9	15.3	12.4
Strongly agree	6.3	9.0	30.0
No response	0.6	2.0	0.6

* Based on replies to items 55, 64, 74 (*Use of Irish at home* scale) in the *Pupil Questionnaire*.

Use of Irish at home
Table 3.9 shows pupils' responses to all three items on the non-*AMTB* based *Use of Irish at home* scale. Just under a quarter of pupils report that one parent at least 'sometimes' speaks Irish at home. Specifically, 22.2% of pupils 'agree' that their mother sometimes speaks Irish at home while 24.3% 'agree' that their father sometimes speaks Irish at home. Responses to the another item (column 3, Table 3.9) indicate at least infrequent use of Irish

in half of all pupils' homes: just over a half of pupils (50.8%) 'disagree' with the statement 'no one at home ever speaks Irish'.

Instrumental orientation to Irish
Many studies have shown that achievement in second language is facilitated if individuals are motivated by the pragmatic rewards of learning the language (Lukmani, 1972; Dörnyei, 1990; Gardner and McIntyre, 1991). Pragmatic/utilitarian reasons for learning the language (e.g. getting a job, becoming more knowledgeable, earning respect) are the basis of the *Instrumental orientation to Irish* scale. It may be noted that the item mean score (3.2) on this scale is lower than item mean scores for any of the *Integrativeness orientation to Irish* scales (3.7, 3.6, 4.3). This suggests that sixth-grade children are less likely to be motivated by instrumental reasons for learning Irish than by integrative ones. Dörnyei, (1994), however, argues that the pragmatic rewards of learning a second language may appear quite remote to young learners. It must be borne in mind, however, that *Instrumental orientation to Irish* was the least reliable of all the scales in the present study (as was also the case in respect of the corresponding *AMTB* scale).

3.3.2 *Part 2: Between-class variation in attitude/motivation*

In this section we assess the extent to which pupils' attitude to learning Irish and to the idea of learning a second/foreign language varies between classes. As in other between-class comparisons in this study, classes are listed according to their achievement in spoken Irish (column 1, Table 3.10). Three indicators (columns 2-4) derived from the *Pupil Questionnaire*, are used to illustrate the range of pupil attitudes to Irish and learning Irish across classes. The first indicator *Class attitude to Irish* (column two) consists of class ranks based on the mean pupil score on the *Irish attitude/motivation index* for each class (see Table 3.2). A rank of 1 indicates the class with the most positive pupil attitudes to Irish, and 20 the least positive. The second indicator (column 3) is based on the pupil's response to one *Pupil Questionnaire* item measuring general affective reaction to learning Irish: 'I really enjoy learning Irish'. The third indicator gives class ranks on the *Irish-lesson anxiety* scale.

By and large, classes in the high- and middle-Irish achievement groups have *Class attitude to Irish* ranks which indicate a more positive Irish attitude compared to those in the low-Irish-achievement group (column two). All but one of the classes in the low-Irish-achievement group have double-figure ranks. Yet there are notable exceptions to the overall trend, particularly in the high- and middle-Irish-achievement groups. For example, Class 2, with a high level of achievement in Irish, nevertheless has a *Class attitude to Irish* rank of only 10. Consistent with this also, only 49% of pupils in Class 2 agree with the statement 'I really enjoy learning Irish' - the lowest percentage for the high-Irish-achievement group (column 3). This same class, it may be recalled, is the only *city* class in the high-Irish-achievement group (the others are in country schools) and has the largest complement of sixth-grade pupils (n = 39) (Table 2.13). Two other examples of classes with relatively high levels of achievement in spoken Irish combined with somewhat less positive attitude/motivation in relation to Irish are Classes 4 and 7 which have ranks of 11 and 15 respectively on the *Class attitude to Irish* index. 'Pearson r' data in Chapter 7 (Table 7.6) confirms the strong positive association between *Class attitude to Irish* and *Class achievement in Irish* (r=.74; p<.01).

Table 3.10
Pupils' attitudes to learning Irish and a second/foreign language in 20 sixth-grade classes.

Class achievement in spoken Irish Rank	Pupil's attitude to Irish and to learning Irish in school			Interest in second/ foreign languages	
	Class attitude to Irish Rank (1=most positive)	'I really enjoy learning Irish' Percent agreeing**	Class Irish lesson anxiety Rank (1= most anxiety)	Class interest in second/foreign languages Rank (1=most interest)	'I would like to learn a foreign language...*' Percent agreeing**
1	1	100%	19	3	88%
2	10	49%	13	1	92%
3	2	89%	18	8	67%
4	11	75%	20	20	63%
5	6	58%	14	12	83%
6	3	56%	12	2	89%
7	15	30%	5	9	84%
D 8	8	55%	9	10	81%
9	4	74%	7	4	81%
10	9	59%	15	5	95%
11	5	77%	10	6	76%
12	13	31%	16	18	48%
13	7	67%	6	13	83%
14	14	17%	1	7	87%
15	20	40%	11	16	83%
D 16	17	41%	8	15	78%
17	16	35%	17	17	70%
18	12	49%	3	11	90%
19	18	33%	4	14	74%
D 20	19	18%	2	19	61%

*The full statement reads: 'I would like to learn a foreign language in school even if I didn't *have* to do it.'
** Percent agreeing = Percentage of pupils who 'slightly agree'/ 'strongly agree' with the item statement.
'D' = Officially classified as disadvantaged.

Overall, half of all classes have only a minority of pupils (less than 50%) agreeing that they enjoy learning Irish. Seven of these with a minority enjoying Irish are low-Irish-achievement classes. Two have less than 20% enjoying Irish. The proportion of pupils in Class 1 who say they really enjoy learning Irish speaks for itself: 100%.

The data on *Class Irish-lesson anxiety* (column four) are fairly predictable, indicating in general that the higher class achievement in spoken Irish is, the less likely pupils in the class are to experience anxiety in the Irish lesson. 'Pearson r' data presented in Chapter 7 (see Table 7.6) confirms this negative trend: the correlation between *Class Irish-lesson anxiety* and *Class achievement in Irish* (r=-.64) is statistically significant (p <.01).

The last two columns on the right of Table 3.10 contain two types of information on class interest in second/foreign languages: (i) the class mean on the *Interest in second/foreign-languages* scale and (ii) the percentage of pupils in each class who agree with the statement from that same scale 'I would like to learn a foreign language in school even if I didn't *have to* do it' (item 50).

Perhaps the most striking result in these columns is the consistency with which the majority of pupils agree with the positive statement about learning a foreign language: over 60% in 19 out of the 20 classes agree that they 'would like to learn a foreign language' (the exception being Class 12 which has only 48% of pupils agreeing). By contrast, only 6 out of 20 classes have over 60% of pupils agreeing that they 'really enjoy learning Irish' (column 3). Despite this trend and the high levels of support for learning a second/foreign language generally, half the classes in the high-achievement group (Ranks 1, 3, and 4) actually have a greater percentage of pupils who agree that they enjoy learning Irish (column 3) than agree they would like to learn a foreign language. In the low-Irish-achievement group of eight classes, in contrast, only one has a majority (class 13) who 'really enjoy learning Irish' while all of them have a majority who 'would like to learn a foreign language'.

3.3.3   Part 3: Attitudinal, linguistic, educational and socio-demographic variables.

We are concerned with two issues in this section: (1) the extent to which our correlational analyses of the attitude/motivation of sixth-grade Irish primary school pupils replicates the findings of equivalent analyses by Gardner (1979, 1985a), and (2) identifying some of the individual, socio-demographic and home factors which are related to, or explain variance in, pupil attitude and achievement (using regression analyses).

The predictor variables consist of background factors such as *Gender, Location, Social class* and *Pupil general academic ability (DVRT)* as well as measures of *Use of Irish at home* and *Parental encouragement* based on Pupil Questionnaire scales. The criterion variables are *Pupil achievement in Irish* and the *Irish attitude/motivation index.*

The *Irish attitude/motivation* index, as well as the component attitude/motivation scales, will also be used as predictor variables in accounting for variance in *Pupil achievement in Irish*.

Before proceeding to the correlation and regression analyses proper, a number of points must be made about the coding of predictor and criterion variables.

1. *Pupil achievement in Irish:* We use total listening score on the ITÉ test as our measure here since each pupil took the listening section of the test but only part of the speaking section.

2. *Gender:* Since pupils were coded as either 1 = boy or 2 = girl, the variable *Gender* can be treated in the same way as other continuous variables with the higher score of 2 in this case indicating girls.

3. *School location:* The nominal categories of this variable have to be recoded as sets of dummy variables. Each dummy variable can be seen as setting up a contrast between one category of a nominal scale (e.g. *city*) and all other categories of that variable (e.g. *town* and *country* considered together). In the case of multiple regression analyses, the number of dummy variables is one less than the number of categories in that variable. Where a simple correlation matrix such as that in Table 3.11 is concerned, however, it is desirable to represent each nominal variable category by a dummy variable (*city* versus the *rest; town* versus the *rest; country* versus the *rest)* for completeness of presentation (see Harris, 1983).

4. *Social class* is different to other continuous variables in that a higher numerical rating on the *Social class* scale actually indicates *lower* social class. Thus, where a positive relationship exists between *Social class* and a variable such as *Pupil achievement in Irish,* the actual *r* value in Table 3.11 is negative.

5. *Irish-lesson anxiety,* as we mentioned earlier, is designed to measure a negative dimension of pupil attitude/motivation in relation to Irish. Thus, while most other attitude/motivation scales and variables, such as *Pupil achievement in Irish* will yield positive r values, we would expect the majority of r's involving *Irish-lesson anxiety* to be negative.

The numbers of cases upon which the various coefficients are based also require some comment. The general rule is that we use all available data for each variable. Thus, where information on a variable is missing for particular individuals, the correlation coefficients involving that variable will be based on a reduced number of cases. In the case of the regression analysis reported below, however, listwise deletion was used in order to deal with missing data i.e. only cases for which data on *all* variables in the regression model are available are included in the equation. Consequently, the regression analyses are based on slightly smaller numbers.

Correlation analysis
Table 3.11 shows the zero order correlations between the entire set of factors which will concern us in the present section: *Pupil achievement in Irish;* background variables such as *Gender, Location* and *Social class; Pupil general academic ability;* and the various *Irish attitude/motivation* scales and composite indices.

Pupil achievement in Irish:
Looking down the first column of Table 3.11 it can be seen that all of the variables listed, except for *Instrumental orientation to learning Irish*, are significantly correlated with *Pupil achievement in Irish*. *Instrumental orientation to learning Irish* was the scale with the lowest internal consistency value in the present study (Cronbach alpha = .59) - something which Gardner (1985a) had also found in the case of the original *AMTB* scale.

Leaving aside *Irish-ability self-concept*, which predictably is highly correlated with *Pupil achievement in Irish*, the variables which are most strongly and positively related to *Pupil achievement in Irish* are, in order of importance, *Pupil general academic ability* (r=.47), *Irish attitude/motivation index* (r=.40) and *Motivation index* (r=.38). Thus, pupils of higher general academic ability, or who have a more positive overall attitude to Irish, or who are highly motivated to learn Irish, tend to have higher levels of achievement in spoken Irish.

Two general points are of interest here. One concerns the relative independence of the attitude/motivation and general academic ability of pupils, the other concerns the fact that motivational factors seem to be more strongly associated with pupils' level of achievement in Irish than attitudinal (integrativeness) factors are. Regarding the first point it may be noted that compared to the relatively high correlations of both *Pupil general academic ability* and *Irish attitude/motivation index* with *Pupil achievement in Irish* (.47 and .40 respectively), the correlation between these two predictor variables themselves (*Pupil general academic ability* and the *Irish attitude/motivation index*), while significant, is only .22 (see column 3, last row of Table 3.11).

Thus, on the basis of these correlation data in Table 3.11, we could reasonably hypothesize that *Irish attitude/motivation* probably adds a significant independent component, distinct from *Pupil general academic ability* (DVRT), to the prediction of *Pupil achievement in Irish*. The hierarchical regression analysis reported later provides confirmation of this.

Turning to the second general point made above, it can be seen (column one) that *Pupil achievement in Irish* has somewhat higher correlations with the motivation scales - *Motivational intensity to learn Irish* (.34), *Desire to learn Irish* (.34) and *Attitude to learning Irish* (.35) - than with the attitudinal (integrative) measures - *Attitude to Irish speakers* (.29), *Integrative orientation to learning Irish* (.25) and *Interest in second/foreign languages* (.22). The composite scales show the same pattern with the correlation between *Motivation index* and *Pupil achievement in Irish* (r=.38) being slightly higher than that between *Integrativeness index* and *Pupil achievement in Irish* (r=.32).

Again consistent with this, *Irish-ability self-concept* (row 19, Table 3.11), which might be seen as an alternative Irish achievement criterion measure, has much higher correlations values with the three basic motivation scales than with the three attitudinal/integrativeness scales (r = .51, .52, and .55 as opposed to r = .37, .32 and .23). Likewise, the correlation of *Irish-ability self-concept* with the *Motivation index* is .59, whereas it is only .38 with the *Integrativeness index*.

Table 3.11

Zero order correlations* between a criterion variable (*Pupil achievement in Irish*) and a number of predictor variables related to pupil's background and Irish/attitude motivation. N pupils (min=432; max=532)

	1	2	3	4	5	6	7	8	9	10	11	12	13	14	15	16	17	18	19	20
1 Pupil achievement in Irish (listening)																				
Background variables																				
2 Gender	10																			
3 Pupil general academic ability (DVRT)	47	-03																		
4 City location	-10	-13	10																	
5 Town location	-17	33	-13	-55																
6 Country location	26	-14	01	-67	-26															
7 Social class	-34	-05	-26	00	08	-07														
Integrativeness scales																				
8 Attitude to Irish speakers	29	05	20	-03	-13	15	-03													
9 Integrative orientation to learning Irish	25	06	15	-11	-06	18	-04	70												
10 Interest in second/foreign languages	22	19	23	-01	-04	04	-12	36	32											
11 Integrativeness index	32	13	25	-05	-10	14	-09	87	78	74										
Motivation scales																				
12 Desire to learn Irish	34	14	11	-10	-05	16	-13	63	57	26	60									
13 Motivational intensity to learn Irish	34	24	07	-20	06	18	-06	44	43	28	47	61								
14 Attitude to learning Irish	35	14	14	-13	-07	21	-08	68	64	28	67	79	64							
15 Motivation index	38	18	13	-15	-05	21	-10	70	65	33	70	91	78	95						
Other Attitude/Motivation scales																				
16 Instrumental orientation to Irish	06	-06	-03	-05	-12	16	05	45	49	23	47	33	18	39	38					
17 Irish-lesson anxiety	-28	05	-26	00	05	-04	09	-08	-10	04	-05	-24	-32	-34	-33	08				
18 Parental encouragement	14	12	06	-07	03	06	-15	47	50	34	53	47	39	47	51	44	07			
Irish Ability and Use scales																				
19 Irish-ability self-concept	44	11	22	-02	-13	14	-18	37	32	23	38	51	52	55	59	19	-44	25		
20 Use of Irish at home	34	11	14	-15	-02	19	-20	35	28	19	34	46	43	37	45	15	-15	41	30	
Overall Irish attitude/motivation																				
21 Irish attitude/motivation index	40	14	22	-10	-10	20	-10	81	75	49	86	86	73	91	95	49	-38	54	60	44

*Entries in shaded/bold print are significant at the .05 level.

Predictably, *Irish-lesson anxiety* is negatively correlated with *Pupil achievement in Irish* (r=-.28). In other words, pupils who experience more anxiety during the Irish lesson tend to have lower levels of achievement in spoken Irish. An indication that anxiety might negatively affect motivation is provided by the negative correlation between *Irish-lesson anxiety* and the *Motivation index* (r=-.33). The correlation between *Irish-lesson anxiety* and the *Integrativeness index* is not significant.

Gender, Location, Social class and Pupil general academic ability:
We now turn to the correlations involving the four background variables *Gender, Location, Social class* and *Pupil general academic ability*. An examination of the coefficients in column 3 of Table 3.11 shows that *Pupil general academic ability* is significantly correlated with *Social class* and *Location* variables as well as with all the *Irish attitude/motivation* scales excepting *Motivational intensity to learn Irish* and *Instrumental orientation to learn Irish*. Thus, pupils of higher general academic ability tend to have more positive attitudes and motivation in relation to learning Irish. Nevertheless, correlations involving attitude/motivation scales and *Pupil general academic ability* (column 3) tend not to be as high as corresponding correlations involving the same scales and *Pupil achievement in Irish* (column 1). The only exception is the correlation of *Pupil general academic ability* with *Interest in second/foreign languages* (r=.23) which is virtually the same as the latter's correlation with *Pupil achievement in Irish* (.22).

An examination of the correlations in column 7 of Table 3.11 shows that *Social class* is significantly, though not strongly, associated with some of the *Irish attitude/motivation* scales. Where the correlation is significant it indicates that pupils from higher social-class categories have a more positive attitude and motivation in relation to learning Irish. It will be noted, however, that *Social class* is more strongly associated with *Pupil achievement in Irish* (r=-.34) than with overall *Irish attitude/motivation* (r=-.10). *Social class* was also significantly correlated (r=-.20) with *Use of Irish at home* - pupils from higher social class backgrounds report more Irish at home.

Correlations involving the *Location* 'dummy' variables show that pupils in *country* schools (row/column 6) have significantly higher levels of *Pupil achievement in Irish* (r=.26), as well as overall more positive *Irish attitude/motivation* (r=.20), than pupils in schools in other locations.

Where correlations involving *Gender* are statistically significant (row/column 2), they indicate more positive attitudes and motivation in relation to learning Irish among girls. The correlation between *Gender* and the *Irish attitude/motivation index* is significant (r=.14).

Finally, it will be noted that the Pearson 'r' values involving *Interest in second/foreign languages* and the other five *Integrativeness* and *Motivation* scales (range: .26-.36) are consistently lower than the intercorrelations within the latter group of five (specifically Irish) affective scales (range: .43-.79). This suggests that in the present study *Interest in second/foreign languages*, although internally consistent, is measuring a somewhat different affective dimension than the other five scales which directly relate to Irish.

Use of Irish at home and Parental encouragement:
Pupil-reported *Use of Irish at home* is positively, and significantly correlated with *Pupil achievement in Irish* (.34) and even more strongly with *Irish attitude/motivation* (.44). Note also that the relationship between *Use of Irish at home* and *Motivation* (.45) is stronger than that between *Use of Irish at home* and *Integrativeness* (.34).

It can be seen from row 18 (Table 3.11) that while the correlation between *Parental encouragement* and *Pupil achievement in Irish* (.14) is significant, it is not nearly so strong as the correlation between *Parental encouragement* and *Irish attitude/motivation* (.54). Unlike *Use of Irish at home*, however, there is little difference between *Integrativeness* and *Motivation* indices, as far as their correlations with *Parental encouragement* are concerned (.53 & .51 respectively).

It will be noted that correlations involving the main integrative/motivation scales and *Parental encouragement* are higher (r's range from .34 - .51) than those between the same affective scales and *Use of Irish at home* (r's range from .19 - .46). *Use of Irish at home* and *Parental encouragement* are themselves strongly and positively correlated (r=.41).

Hierarchical regression analyses
As we have just seen in the matrix of correlations in Table 3.11, most of the Irish attitude/motivation scales are highly correlated with each other, especially those scales which form the basis for the *Motivation* and the *Integrativeness* composite indices. This latter result is evidence of the construct validity of the scales. From the point of view of predicting achievement in spoken Irish, however, the large Pearson 'r' coefficients between the various attitude/motivation scales pose a problem of multicollinearity. The regression procedures which we now describe try to avoid this problem by examining the strength of the linear relations between variables using a statistic called 'tolerance' and then removing some of these variables with low 'tolerances' (i.e. those which are highly correlated with other (independent) predictor variables in the regression equation).

Two basic regression analyses were carried out. The two analyses are of the same general form, at least as far as the first six predictor variables mentioned earlier are concerned. The only difference between them is which of the two criterion measures is being predicted: (a) *Pupil achievement in Irish* or (b) *Irish attitude/motivation index*. The predictors were selected on the basis of the strength of their correlations with *Pupil achievement in Irish* and/or with the *Irish attitude/motivation index* (Table 3.11).

In regression analyses of this kind, predictor variables which are considered to be logically prior to others are entered into the equation first. The order of entry of variables in the present case is intended to reflect the broader context within which each predictor variable might be expected to affect *Pupil achievement in Irish* and/or *Irish attitude/motivation*. The more immutable variables, in our case *Gender, Location, Social class* and *Pupil general academic ability* are entered at the beginning.

Hierarchical inclusion permits an assessment of the successive effects of the different predictors on the criterion. In other words, the increase in R^2 (see column 4 in Table 3.12 and 3.13) as each predictor is entered is interpretable in terms of additional criterion variance accounted for after the effects of the previously entered variables have been removed. This is necessary since the pattern of intercorrelations between the predictor variables themselves (Table 3.11) show that the variance explained by each predictor is very unlikely to be unique.

After these initial six predictors were entered, the subsequent form of each of the two regression analyses depended on which criterion variable was involved. Where *Pupil achievement in Irish* was the criterion variable, the last predictor(s) entered consisted of one or more measures of Irish attitude/motivation (see Table 3.12). In the second regression analysis, in which *Irish attitude/motivation index* itself was the criterion, no other predictor was entered (see Table 3.13).

In the first regression, in which *Pupil achievement in Irish* is the criterion, we tried three different ways (see Tables 3.12) of entering predictors relating to *Irish attitude/motivation*:

(i)   as a single predictor - overall *Irish attitude/motivation*
(ii) as three predictors (*Irish-lesson anxiety, Integrativeness index, Motivation index)* entered in stepwise fashion (Cohen and Cohen, 1975)
(iii) in the form of the six main attitude/motivation components plus *Irish-lesson anxiety.*

The purpose of including the individual scales as predictors is to obtain a more precise indication of the components of overall *Irish attitude/motivation* which contribute most to the variance explained.

Explained variance in achievement and attitude/motivation.
It will be useful to examine the two main regression analyses together in order to point out similarities and differences in the amount of criterion variance explained by the predictors in each case. It can be seen that the first six predictor variables explain a smaller proportion of variance in *Pupil achievement in Irish* (Table 3.12) than in *Irish attitude/motivation* (Table 3.13). The proportion of total variance explained by the first six predictors is 36.4% in the case of the *Pupil achievement in Irish* criterion, while for the *Irish attitude/motivation* criterion it is 42.1%, a difference of 5.7%. This relatively small difference in total variance explained masks a much greater difference in the way the variance in the two criterion variables is explained by the individual predictors. In order to see this, it will be useful to look separately at the first four predictor variables.

In the case of the *Pupil achievement in Irish* criterion, the first four predictors entered, *Gender, Location, Social class* and *Pupil general academic ability* account for the bulk of the variance explained: 33.4% out of the total of 36.4% (column 2, Table 3.12). In the case of the *Irish attitude/motivation* criterion, these same four predictors account for only 14.3% out of the total of 42.1% (column 2, Table 3.13). More specifically, both *Social class* and *Pupil general academic ability* explain substantial proportions of the variance when *Pupil achievement in Irish* is the criterion (6.9% and 14.9% respectively), but considerably less when *Irish attitude/motivation* is the criterion (0% and 5% respectively). *Location* also adds more to the variance explained in the case of *Pupil achievement in Irish* (11.2%) than in the case of *Irish attitude/motivation* (7.6%).

Table 3.12

Multiple regression of *Pupil achievement in Irish* (listening) on pupil background and attitude/motivation variables: Summary table

Predictor variables (n=399)	Multiple R	R^2	Adjusted R^2	R^2 change	F change	df	Sig F
Gender	.062	.004	.001	.004	1.51	1,397	NS
Location : country vs city : town vs city	.340	.116	.109	.112	25.00	1,395	.001
Social class	.430	.185	.177	.069	33.50	1,394	.001
Pupil general academic ability (DVRT)	.578	.334	.326	.149	87.87	1,393	.001
Use of Irish at home (pupil report)	.602	.363	.353	.029	17.84	1,392	.001
Parental encouragement (pupil report)	.603	.364	.353	.001	0.59	1,391	NS
Irish attitude/motivation index	.636	.405	.392	.041	26.59	1,390	.001

Irish attitude/motivation scales

	Multiple R	R^2	Adjusted R^2	R^2 change	F change	df	Sig F
(Order of entry 2 = Stepwise)							
Irish-lesson anxiety (excluded)							
Integrativeness index (excluded)							
Motivation index	.636	.404	.392	.040	26.28	1,390	.000

	Multiple R	R^2	Adjusted R^2	R^2 change	F change	df	Sig F
(Order of entry 3 - individual scales)							
Attitude to learning Irish	.627	.393	.380	.029	18.61	1,390	.001
Attitude to Irish speakers	.628	.394	.380	.001	0.61	1,389	NS
Integrative orientation to Irish	.628	.394	.378	.000	0.05	1,388	NS
Irish-lesson anxiety	.632	.400	.383	.006	3.88	1,387	.05
Interest in foreign/second languages	.635	.403	.384	.003	.83	1,386	NS
Desire to learn Irish	.637	.405	.385	.002	1.55	1,385	NS
Motivational intensity to learn Irish	.645	.416	.395	.011	7.14	1,384	.01

Table 3.13
Multiple regression of *Irish attitude/motivation* on pupil background variables:
Summary table

Predictor variables (n=399)	Multiple R	R^2	Adjusted R^2	R^2 change	F change	df	Sig F
Gender	.117	.014	.011	.014	5.54	1,397	.05
: country vs city							
Location: town vs city	.300	.090	.083	.076	16.52	1,395	.001
Social class	.306	.094	.084	.004	1.59	1,394	NS
Pupil general academic ability	.379	.143	.133	.050	22.89	1,393	.001
Use of Irish at home	.522	.272	.261	.129	69.42	1,392	.001
Parental encouragement	.649	.421	.411	.149	100.73	1,391	.001

The other major difference between the two regression analyses is that *Use of Irish at home* and *Parental encouragement* explain considerably more variance when the criterion is *Irish attitude/motivation* (12.9% and 14.9% respectively) than they do when the criterion is *Pupil achievement in Irish* (2.9% and 0.1% respectively).

We turn now to the attitude/motivation predictors. The first thing to be noted is that the final proportion of variance explained by *Irish attitude/motivation* in predicting *Pupil achievement in Irish* (Table 3.12) varies very little (4.0% to 5.2%) depending on how the attitude/motivation predictors are cast: (i) as the overall *Irish attitude/motivation index* (order of entry 1), (ii) as composite indices plus individual scale (stepwise entry 2), or (iii) as individual scales (order of entry 3). This is not surprising of course, since linear combinations of subsets of the same superset of variables are involved. The second aspect of interest is that, irrespective of how Irish attitude/motivation is cast, in terms of predictors, the additional variance in *Pupil achievement in Irish* which it explains is fairly modest once the other six variables are entered. The reason, of course, is that despite the substantial correlation between, for example, *Irish attitude/motivation index* and *Pupil achievement in Irish* (r=.40), *Irish attitude/motivation* is also strongly correlated with many of the six earlier-entered predictors in the regression analysis, particularly *Parental encouragement* (r=.54) and *Use of Irish in the home* (r=.44) (see Table 3.11).

As noted above the overall variance explained by the three-predictor forms of Irish attitude/motivation (order of entry 2) in the stepwise model (R^2 = 4%) is largely the same as that in the previous model (R^2 = 4.1%). The order in which these three variables are listed in Table 3.12 reflects their relative contribution to the variance explained - the *Motivation index* being the critical contributor (*Beta*=.255; p<.01 - not shown in table).

Data relating to order of entry 3 (the individual scales as predictors) show that *Attitude to learning Irish* and *Motivational intensity to learn Irish* are the most important components of motivation. *Irish-lesson anxiety* also makes a small but significant contribution. Two of these, it will be noted, are *Motivation* variables. None of the *Integrativeness* variables make significant contributions.

To summarise the results of the regression analyses, then, the first six predictor variables explain somewhat more criterion variance in *Irish attitude/motivation* than in *Pupil achievement in Irish*. The most important predictors in order of variance explained are *Pupil general academic ability*, *Location* and *Social class* in the case of *Pupil achievement in Irish*, and *Parental encouragement* and *Use of Irish at home* in the case of *Irish attitude/motivation*.

The *Irish attitude/motivation index*, when entered last in the regression equation, adds a further 4.1% to the variance explained in *Pupil achievement in Irish*. *Attitude to learning Irish*, *Motivational intensity to learn* and *Irish-lesson anxiety* were the most important affective components as far as predicting achievement in Irish was concerned.

3.4 Discussion

The two main questions around which the discussion will centre can be stated simply: (i) how positive or negative are the different components of *Irish attitude/motivation*; and (ii) how strongly are each of these affective components related to achievement in Irish? Within this framework we also discuss how factors such as *Irish ability self-concept*, *Irish-lesson anxiety*, *Parental encouragement* and *Use of Irish at home* relate to both *Irish attitude/motivation* and *Pupil achievement in Irish*. Finally, we consider the role of socio-demographic and academic factors.

3.4.1 How positive is Irish attitude/motivation among primary school pupils?

One of the first questions which anybody concerned with the teaching of Irish will expect to be answered on the basis of results such as ours is how positive or otherwise are the different aspects of pupils' attitude/motivation. It would be very useful to know, for example, how successful our own primary schools are in developing positive attitudes to Irish, compared to primary schools in other countries which have second- or foreign-language programmes. Or, looking at different aspects of attitude-motivation among Irish primary-school pupils, are attitudes to the Irish language itself (or to Irish speakers) more positive than attitudes to actually learning Irish? Interesting as questions such as these are, however, any attempt to answer them on the basis of the kinds of evidence we have here, poses difficulties.

The main problem is that we do not have comparative data relating to the various components of attitude-motivation either for Irish pupils (because this is a new instrument) or pupils elsewhere (because the substantial adaptation of item content and format make comparisons with corresponding scale scores from Canadian studies impossible). Since formal assessments are not possible, we are limited to informal comparisons and conclusions.

The kinds of informal comparisons we have made here include -

1. Comparing the percentages of pupils selecting different response options on individual items;
2. Comparing responses to different groups of items;
3. Comparing mean scale scores or mean item scores on different scales.

In the latter case, for example, we used the answer options on the five-point Likert scale as a rough and ready way of interpreting the mean item score for each affective component as tending, in general, to be positive, negative or neutral. On a positively-worded item, a mean item score of '1' or '2' (roughly equivalent to 'strongly/slightly disagree') would suggest a generally negative attitude, '3' (neutral) neither positive nor negative, and '4' or '5' ('slightly/strongly agree') a positive attitude. This kind of evidence permits us, at best, to illustrate tendencies rather than to justify definitive conclusions. This is because the reliability estimates which we cited in section 3.2.2 above attach to scales, not to items. Furthermore, the strength of the underlying attitudinal variables which the item stem (statement) represents, will vary from statement to statement and from scale to scale. At the same time, in the absence of any other objective data in this area, it would be desirable to at least draw attention to any trends in scale means and individual item responses which would help to illuminate primary-school pupils' affective response to Irish. It is in this spirit that we take an informal approach to the data in this section of the discussion. We limit ourselves to clearly consistent phenomena and to differences in percentages responding which, on commonsense grounds, are substantial.

We conclude that of the two main affective clusters studied, *Integrativeness* and *Motivation*, pupils' integrative attitudes are the more positive. That is to say, pupils are generally well disposed towards the Irish language itself and towards the idea of integrating with the Irish language 'group' - they tend to be favourable towards Irish speakers, they wish to be more closely associated with the Irish language and, in a broader context, they are open to other languages and language groups. In contrast, the components of *Motivation*, what might be paraphrased as commitment to actually learning Irish, are less positive. *Motivation* items and scales - focused on such things as the strength of pupils' desire to actually learn Irish, on the intensity of effort which they are prepared to commit to learning Irish, or on the amount of satisfaction which they experience in learning it - all these tend to elicit less positive responses. More specifically, all three components of *Integrativeness* have higher item mean scores (ranging from 3.6 to 4.3) than all three components of *Motivation* (ranging from 3.0 to 3.3). This is a reassurance that, despite the informality of the comparisons we are making, the overall trend is consistent.

3.4.2 Integrativeness: Attitudes to Irish speakers and the Irish language

It will be a source of some satisfaction to those involved in teaching and promoting Irish that, for the great majority of pupils in sixth class, integrative attitudes are relatively positive. Positive integrative attitudes are extremely important in the context of the broad societal attempts to promote bilingualism. Equally importantly, however, is that these attitudes help to maintain motivation during the long task of acquiring a language (Gardner, 1985b). The strong intercorrelations between *Integrativeness* scales and

Motivational scales in the present study emphasise the importance of cultural/integrative factors in maintaining motivation in primary school pupils. It is worth noting in passing that in certain socio-cultural contexts, such strong connections between *Integrativeness* and *Motivation* can break down. In a study of Israeli-Jewish students studying either Arabic or French as a foreign language, for example, Kraemer (1990) found that although overall motivation was a good predictor of achievement in the target language, integrative attitudes were not.

Looking more closely at the *Integrativeness* scales in our own case, we see that some of them secure more favourable responses than others. *Integrativeness* items which concern global, passive support for Irish tend to elicit more positive responses than those which mention specific or active personal involvement. Within the *Attitude to Irish speakers* scale, for example, items referring to general cultural or national reasons for valuing Irish obtain the most positive responses, while those referring to actual engagement with 'people who speak Irish' are less positive. Thus, 88% of pupils agree that 'The Irish language is an important part of Ireland and the Irish people' or 'If Ireland lost the Irish language and the Irish way of life, it would be a great loss'. In contrast, the percentages who agree with statements such as 'The more I get to know people who speak Irish, the more I want to learn it' or 'I would like to know more people who speak Irish' are in the forties or low fifties.

It may be significant, however, that in response to an item (item 54) from one of the *Motivation* scales (*Desire to learn Irish*), a higher percentage than those we have just mentioned agreed that 'If there were Irish speaking families living near me, I would like to speak Irish to them' (67%). Perhaps it is just that the earlier-mentioned *Integrativeness* items referring to 'people who speak Irish' conjure up too remote an eventuality for many pupils, while references to 'Irish-speaking families' living nearby suggest a context of use that is more immediate and real.

The passive/active distinction mentioned above also appears to have some relevance to another *Integrativeness* scale, *Integrative orientation to Irish*. The most favourable responses here are elicited by an item which refers to relatively passive activities: 76% of children agreed that 'It is important to learn Irish because it will help me to read Irish books and to understand Irish songs, stories and television programmes'. An item which appears to suggest more specific, active involvement - taking part in activities such as '*Slogadh, feiseanna* and Irish music' - secured a positive response from only 54% of pupils.

In all probability, the development and improvement of pupils' *Attitude to Irish speakers* and *Integrative orientation to Irish* are governed in part by home/social factors. One indication of this is the significant correlations between the various *Integrativeness* scales, on the one hand, and *Parental encouragement* on the other (r's range from .34 to .53). Significant correlations between the *Integrativeness* scales and *Use of Irish at home* (r's range from .19 to .35) support the same point.

But certain kinds of in-class factors very likely play a role in maintaining and improving integrative attitudes as well. Arguably, in-class activities and experiences could have a particularly important role in developing positive attitudes in a case such as Irish where most pupils have little or no contact with the language outside school. In the *Communicative Materials Project*, we investigated various approaches to the development of positive integrative attitudes. The communicative approach adopted in the project, as an alternative to the existing structural/audio-visual approach, placed considerable emphasis on Irish culture and authentic materials in a way that was intended to be enjoyable for pupils and relevant to their own lives. Among the activities included were learning Irish dancing, exploring the Irish-language origins of local Irish placenames and role-plays/drama related to trips to the Gaeltacht or Irish Summer Colleges. Such activities might be expected to improve pupils' integrative attitudes to the language and culture at the same time as making the learning process itself more enjoyable. More generally, however, it is important that questions such as why children learn Irish, what use might they expect to make of it and why it is of more general value, would be raised, and answered in a positive way, in the classroom. It would also be desirable that future research would explore pupils' understanding of the purpose of learning Irish and would establish how that is modified by different kinds of in-class experiences or by exposure to particular kinds of lesson materials. We return to some of these issues in the context of pupils' views in the next chapter.

3.4.3 Motivation to learn Irish versus attitude to foreign languages

One contrast between *Integrativeness* and *Motivation* consists of the affective reaction of pupils to second/foreign languages versus Irish. The particular interest provided by this contrast is that it introduces a comparative dimension into our interpretation of the data - a dimension which is otherwise missing from this aspect of the study. The results show that pupils' disposition to the general idea of learning a second/foreign language is more positive than their attitude to learning Irish. Specifically, while only between 42% - 50% of pupils agreed with positive statements about their experience of learning *Irish* (e.g. 'I love learning Irish'), 74% - 82% agreed with broadly similar items which relate to their desire to learn a *second* or *foreign language* (e.g. 'I would really like to learn a lot of foreign languages even if I didn't *have* to do it'). A similar pattern is reflected in the mean scores for these two scales, which have the same number of items. *Interest in second/foreign languages* has a mean of 42.5 while *Attitude to learning Irish* has a mean of only 32.7.

We must guard, however, against a simplistic reading of these data. First, we cannot interpret differences in item- or scale-score means, or differences in the percentages agreeing with positively stated items, without taking some account of the fact that *Interest in second/foreign languages* is measuring a component of *Integrativeness* (i.e. it concerns affective factors which are relatively removed from the learning situation) while *Attitude to learning Irish* is *Motivational* in character (i.e. embedded to some degree in the current language-learning situation). Second, we must give due weight to the fact that the vast majority of Irish children have either no direct experience at school of learning foreign languages, as opposed to Irish, and that learning a foreign language, therefore, may not be associated in their minds with the routine effort or labour required to learn any language.

In other words, the less favourable response to items on the Irish scale may be at least partially explainable in terms of the negative effects of the real and immediate effort currently being expended by the pupil in learning Irish.

To compare pupils' attitudes to learning Irish versus foreign languages on a truly appropriate basis, we would have to be able to investigate a situation where a foreign-language programme had already been in place for a number of years. We could then administer, for example, an *Attitude to learning French* scale, equivalent to the Irish one, which would measure pupils' satisfaction with the actual experience of learning French. It will be interesting to compare responses on such foreign-language and Irish scales when the new Pilot Project on Modern Languages at Primary School is implemented (Department of Education and Science, 1997).

Notwithstanding these caveats, the data do show unequivocally that the vast majority of pupils are positive about the *general* idea of learning second/foreign languages, in a context where neither Irish nor any specific foreign language is mentioned. What is striking about the results is the consistently high proportion of pupils, across nearly all classes, who want to learn foreign languages. Over 60% of pupils in 19 of the 20 classes (over 80% in most of these) agree with the statement 'I would like to learn a foreign language even if I didn't *have* to'. This is in marked contrast to pupils' response to the item 'I really enjoy learning Irish' where only 6 of 20 classes have as many as 60% of pupils agreeing. The preference gap between Irish and foreign languages is particularly clear among pupils in low-Irish-achievement classes. Only one of the eight low-Irish achievement classes has a majority of the pupils agreeing they enjoy learning Irish, while all of these same classes have a majority expressing a desire to learn a foreign language.

Overall, there is a strong positive relationship between *Class achievement in Irish* and *Irish attitude/motivation* (r=.74). Responses to one item gives an indication of the range of attitude/motivation over the 20 classes. The class with the highest level of achievement in Irish has 100% of pupils agreeing (slightly or strongly) that they 'really enjoy learning Irish'. In contrast, two of the low-Irish achievement classes have less than 20% of pupils agreeing with this statement. Clearly, the experience of learning Irish is not a satisfying one for most of those in low-achievement classes. This state of affairs, apart from being an educational concern in relation to the pupils themselves, also poses real problems for teachers day to day. Many causative factors, both home/social and in-classroom, may be responsible.

Parental attitudes are likely to have made a contribution to these pupils' attitudes. Data relating to *Parental encouragement,* discussed below, suggest that children detect lack of enthusiasm in their parents in relation to Irish. Results to be presented later in Chapter 5 also indicate that parental support for children in the task of learning Irish can be lukewarm or absent. In contrast, on the basis of volunteered comments (Table 5.20), parents seem well disposed to the idea of their children learning a foreign language: the most frequent theme (19% of parents) is that 'more time should be given to other subjects (e.g. Modern Continental Languages, computers or English), and/or less time spent on Irish'.

Of course, in-classroom factors are also likely to be extremely important in determining pupil *Attitude to learning Irish*. In fact, Gardner and Smythe (1981) suggest that as pupils get older and better trained in the target language, the language-learning situation becomes relatively more important in determining attitudes, while integrativeness (general attitudes to the language and speakers) tends to become less important. In other words, maintaining the pupil's motivation to learn Irish as he or she reaches the later grades in primary school probably means taking relatively more account of the actual enjoyment and experience of success which the language-learning process itself provides. In later chapters, we explore this issue further showing how aspects of the learning situation are perceived by pupils. We also examine (Chapter 7) how characteristics of the teaching approach relate to pupil attitude/motivation, self-concept and anxiety about speaking Irish in class. Based in part on our experiences in the *Communicative Materials Project*, we also suggest some of the changes in lesson content, forms of pupil-teacher interaction and classroom organisation which may help to improve pupils' affective response to learning Irish.

Before we leave this issue, it is worth noting that in half of the high-Irish-achievement classes, more pupils prefer the reality of learning Irish to the prospect of learning a foreign language (Table 3.10). Presumably, this represents an instance of success breeding success - high levels of achievement in Irish leading to positive attitudes to learning. Indeed, this is consistent with the current view of motivation (Burstall, Jamieson, Cohen and Hargreaves, 1974; Strong, 1984; Gardner and McIntyre, 1993). Gardner (1985b) suggests that the relationship between achievement and attitude/motivation is one of reciprocal causation i.e. motivation influences language achievement, and language achievement and the experience of learning the language, in turn, influences attitude/ motivation.

3.4.4 *Parental encouragement and home use of Irish*

A substantial minority of pupils do not believe that they have the active support and encouragement of their parents in the task of learning Irish. Proportions of pupils ranging from 20%-35% reject eight of the ten positively worded statements on the *Parental encouragement* scale (Appendix 3.2) which suggest that they do receive help and encouragement. For example, 22.6% of children disagree that their parents 'try to help' them with Irish, while 35.3% disagree that their parents 'are usually very interested in anything to do with' the pupils' Irish schoolwork. Responses to a *Miscellaneous* item show that 16.6% of pupils disagree that their parents 'are proud of how much Irish' the pupils have learned at school. An additional minority, ranging from 14.7% to 25.5% for the items just quoted, are only prepared to represent themselves as 'neutral' on the question of whether or not their parents are supportive.

Comparative data on pupils' perceptions of parental support for other school subjects is difficult to find. In the *Second International Assessment of Educational Progress*, however, 94% of 13 year-old Irish pupils report that their parents want them 'to do well' in mathematics (Martin, Hickey and Murchan, 1992). As we will show in Chapter 5, parents themselves report that they give less support to Irish, particularly spoken Irish, than to other school subjects.

About half the pupils report at least some use of Irish at home. This again is broadly consistent with the reports of parents themselves (Chapter 5), even though the parents survey is based on a smaller number of classes. Thus, 50.8% of pupils *disagreed* with the statement that 'no one at home ever speaks Irish', while 56.5% of *parents* report that Irish is used 'seldom' or more frequently. The correlational and regression data, discussed below, indicate the importance of both *Parental encouragement* and *Use of Irish at home* to children's attitudes and achievement.

Parents and pupils are broadly in agreement about the child's reaction to learning Irish: 42.9% of parents think their child 'likes' learning Irish (see Chapter 5: section 5.3.5) while, 47.6% of children themselves agree that they 'really enjoy learning Irish'. In addition, 42% of children agree that they 'love learning Irish' (Table 3.3) and the same proportion agree that 'learning Irish is really great' (Appendix 3.2: item 35).

3.4.5 Irish-ability self-concept

Items from the *Irish-ability self-concept* scale allow us to say what kind of opinion pupils have of their own ability in Irish. Other items on the *Pupil Questionnaire* allow us to compare this with the pupil's self-concept in English Reading and Mathematics. In the case of each of these items, the pupil is required to compare his/her own ability with that of 'most' of the other pupils in the class. Since the class is always the reference group, differences from subject to subject in the proportions agreeing or disagreeing with the various positive statements can be seen as reflecting 'self-concept' in relation to the subjects in question. The larger the percentage who agree that they are better than 'most pupils' in the class, the better the self-concept of pupils in relation to the subject in question.

The results show that pupils tend to have a poor estimation of their ability to speak Irish compared to other school subjects. The proportion of pupils agreeing that they are 'better' is smallest in the case of Speaking Irish (30.7%), a little larger for Mathematics (36.7%) and is greatest for English Reading (57.5%). Of the three specific aspects of Irish rated, pupils tend to have the most positive opinion about their achievements in Irish reading (43.4%). Kellaghan and Fontes (1988) who provide data on the self-concept of sixth-grade primary school pupils also found that, of all the curricular areas studied, spoken Irish was the one associated with the lowest self-ratings by pupils.

A range of both home/social factors and school/class factors probably contribute to the situation we have just described - i.e. the poor self-concept in relation to Speaking Irish, the better self-concept in relation to Irish Reading and the very positive self-concept in relation to English Reading. Among the home/social factors which correlation data suggest are related to *Irish-ability self-concept* are *Parental encouragement* and *Use of Irish at home*. Certainly, it would seem to be critical to the development of positive self-esteem in relation to any subject that pupils would experience success and a feeling of competence and that they would receive adult recognition and praise for their achievements both at home and in school. In relation to school-class factors the development of realistic expectations and achievable goals must also be an important part of maintaining self-esteem in this area. These issues are taken up in more detail in relation to speaking and reading Irish in subsequent chapters. In Chapter 4, for example, we consider the possibility that pupils acquire a more positive sense of success in Irish Reading, compared to Speaking Irish, simply by virtue of their day-by-day progress through the reader.

Pupil responses to one other item on the *Irish-ability self-concept* scale must be mentioned: 21% of pupils *disagree* that they 'understand most of what the teacher says in Irish at school'. Given the general agreement in applied linguistics in recent years about the importance of comprehensible input in first and second-language learning, a percentage as large as this, of pupils who claim comprehension difficulties in Irish class, is a matter for some concern. As we will see in Chapter 4, difficulty in understanding the lesson or teacher is a frequently recurring complaint of pupils in low-Irish achievement classes.

3.4.6 *Irish-lesson anxiety*

The *Irish-lesson anxiety* scale measures the extent to which pupils experience anxiety or discomfort about speaking Irish in class. In brief, the results show that somewhere between a quarter and just over a half of all pupils, depending on the particular question, admit to anxiety, lack of confidence or embarrassment about speaking Irish. Specifically, 26.1% agree that they are 'embarrassed' to put up their hand and say something aloud during the Irish lesson while 54.3% agree that they 'get nervous or mixed up when speaking in Irish class'. While we have no directly comparable data from other primary school second-/foreign-language programmes, relatively high levels of unease, particularly when speaking, are reported among second-level (Liu, 1989) and third-level second-language students (Horwitz *et al.*, 1986).

Higher *Irish-lesson anxiety* in pupils is associated with significantly lower levels of achievement in Irish (r =-.28). The fact that this result relates to anxiety about *speaking* Irish is interesting in the light of data to be presented later (Chapter 9) about the frequency with which different types of pupils speak individually in the Irish class. The data show that pupils with lower levels of achievement in Irish are less likely than others to make individual spoken contributions in the Irish. We also show directly that classes with generally higher levels of *Irish-lesson anxiety* have pupils with a generally lower propensity to speak aloud in Irish during the Irish lessons (r=-.54). Clearly, changes in lessons which would render the prospect of speaking less intimidating for less able pupils are desirable. Among the strategies recommended by Tsui (1996) are: (i) improving questioning strategies by giving pupils time to think about the question and formulate their answers, (ii) accepting a variety of answers, (iii) increasing peer support though group work, (iv) focusing on content rather than on form in activities, and (v) generally establishing good relationships with students. We take up these issues in more detail in Chapter 9.

Not surprisingly, *Irish-ability self-concept* and *Irish-lesson anxiety* are strongly and negatively correlated (-.44) - in other words, pupils with a good self-concept in relation to their Irish ability tend to have less anxiety about speaking Irish in class. Other correlation data suggest that somewhat different sets of factors may influence anxiety and self-concept. For example, while *Irish-ability self-concept* is significantly correlated with (a) *Parental encouragement* (b) the *Integrativeness index* and (c) the *Motivation index*, only the last of these, the *Motivation index*, is significantly correlated with *Irish-lesson anxiety*. This serves to reinforce the commonsense expectation that while *Irish-lesson anxiety* is mainly determined by 'in-class' factors or factors more closely related to the learning process, *Irish-ability self-concept* is determined by both home/social and in-class factors. Thus, more broad-based initiatives, extending beyond the school proper, may be needed to deal with the problems of pupils who have a poor self-concept in relation to their ability in Irish. The form which these initiatives might take are outlined in Chapter 5.

3.4.7 Relationships between affective, linguistic and ability variables

The correlation data are of interest in a number of ways. At the most basic level, they indicate which affective, linguistic and social factors are most closely related to each other. This, in turn, can supply preliminary indications about the kind of initiatives most likely to improve attitudes or achievement in Irish. Looking at the results very generally first, it is clear that Irish attitude/motivation is strongly related to the level of proficiency in Irish achieved by pupils. The strength of this relationship among Irish primary-school pupils compares favourably with the corresponding correlations between the *AMTB* and French grades quoted by Gardner (1985a). Of the 10 values from different studies listed by Gardner, only two exceed the value of the Pearson 'r' reported here (.40).

While all six main components of *Irish attitude/motivation* are also significantly correlated with achievement in Irish, the three components of the *Motivation* cluster are somewhat more strongly related ($r = .34$ to $.35$) to achievement than are the three components of *Integrativeness* ($r = .22$ to $.29$). Similar findings are reported by Gardner and Smythe (1981) in relation to the original *AMTB* indices. *Attitude to learning Irish* (a *Motivational* scale) is the component most closely related to achievement in Irish, while *Interest in second/foreign languages* (an *Integrativeness* scale) is the least strongly correlated.

Turning to the intercorrelations between the six main *Irish attitude/motivation* scales themselves, it is notable that those involving *Interest in second/foreign languages* are substantially lower (range of $r = .26 - .36$) than the others (range of $r = .43 - .79$). This suggests that the *Interest in second/foreign-languages* scale is tapping an aspect of pupils' affective reaction which is distinct from the various components of their attitude/motivation in relation to Irish. This pattern was not observed in the corresponding set of intercorrelations for comparable *AMTB* scales in Canada (Gardner, Lalonde and Pierson, 1983). Presumably, the sociolinguistic issues and distinctions, which the 'Irish' versus 'foreign languages' comparison represents for children here, are different to the ones which the 'French' versus 'foreign languages' comparison represents for Canadian students.

Pupil general academic ability is also strongly related to *Pupil achievement in Irish* ($r = .47$), but it is less strongly (though still significantly) related to *Irish attitude motivation* ($r = .22$). Similar findings have been reported in studies using the Canadian version of the

AMTB. Gardner (1985a) found that while the *AMTB* based *Attitude/Motivation Index* correlated significantly with French grades (i.e. achievement in French) in nine out of ten cases, it correlated significantly with overall academic performance (all subjects) in only two out of ten cases. He argues that this outcome - and of course the same logic would apply to our own broadly corresponding finding here - is evidence of the discriminant validity of the attitude/motivation index. Discriminant validity is a form of construct validity (i.e. it gives an indication of the psychological reality of the underlying concept). It is established when a scale does *not* correlate with other measures with which it should not relate if the underlying theory is correct (Gardner, 1985a).

3.4.8 Regression analyses

The regression analyses represent an attempt to quantify the relative contribution of a small number of key factors, discussed in Chapter 2, to *Irish attitude/motivation* and *Pupil achievement in Irish*. The factors consist of individual *(Gender, Pupil general academic ability)*, socio-demographic *(Location, Social class)* and home characteristics *(Parental encouragement* and *Use of Irish at home)*.

Briefly, the results show that the bulk of the explained variance in *Irish attitude/motivation* (27.8%) is attributable to the two home factors, *Parental encouragement* and *Use of Irish at home* which are entered last in the regression model. *Parental encouragement*, entered just prior to *Use of Irish at home* explains the most variance. Only 14.3% of the variance in *Irish attitude/motivation* is explained by the four individual and socio-demographic factors

This contrasts with the prediction of *Pupil achievement in Irish* where it is the four individual and socio-demographic factors (mainly *Pupil general academic ability, Location* and *Social class*) which account for most (33.4%) of the variance. The two home factors, *Use of Irish at home* and *Parental encouragement*, only contribute an additional 3% to the explained variance in this case.

When overall *Irish attitude/motivation* is entered after all these, as a single block, it makes a significant though not very large additional contribution (4.1%) to the variance explained in *Pupil achievement in Irish*. Two aspects of motivation (*Motivational intensity to learn Irish* and *Attitude to learning Irish*), together with *Irish-lesson anxiety*, are the most important components of *Irish attitude/motivation* as far as predicting *Pupil achievement in Irish* is concerned. This is consistent with Lalonde and Gardner (1985) who found that for 39 samples *Motivation* was overall the best predictor of (i) objective measures of French proficiency, (ii) grades in French, and (iii) behavioural intention to continue French study.

It must be noted that, as in most cases in the social sciences, the interpretation of regression analyses involves quite strong assumptions. In particular, the priority which is assigned to different predictors in 'explaining' attitude/motivation and achievement in Irish - e.g. entering variables such as *Social class* or *Location* before *Parental encouragement* - can have considerable effects on the outcome. In addition, in using attitude/motivation to predict achievement in Irish, an assumption of unidirectionality in causation is being made, whereas the true relationship may be one of reciprocity (Gardner, 1985b; Gardner and MacIntyre, 1993). The relative importance of attitude/motivation, compared to other socio-educational factors, in determining achievement in Irish cannot be equated in any simple fashion, therefore, with the proportion of variance 'explained' here. Given the kind of correlations which were observed in this study between socio-educational variables and affective variables, it may well be that some of the influence exerted by background variables such as *Social class, Location* and *Pupil general academic ability* on achievement in Irish is actually realised through affective factors.

It is also important to acknowledge that these particular regression analyses do not in any sense amount to a complete model of the factors contributing to either attitude/ motivation or achievement in Irish. Our regression analyses here are confined to predictors which are mainly extra-classroom in character, albeit ones which have been identified as important in previous studies (Harris, 1983; Ó Riagáin and Ó Gliasáin, 1994). They do not include, for example, any of the classroom-based variables which, elsewhere in the present study, are shown to be significantly associated with one or other aspect of *Irish attitude/motivation*. For example, we report later (Chapters 7-8) that those classes in which a greater proportion of time is spent on communicative language activities, or in which a smaller proportion of time is spent on reading-aloud language-practice, have significantly better overall *Irish attitude/motivation* and significantly lower *Irish-lesson anxiety* than other classes. We also show that more favourable *Class attitude to Irish* and lower levels of *Class Irish-lesson anxiety* are both strongly associated with higher levels of class interest in the Irish lesson (as judged by the observer). Clearly, these findings constitute at least *prima facie* evidence for the commonsense expectation that classroom-based or teaching-related events or processes can determine, or be determined by *Irish attitude/motivation* generally and by *Irish-lesson anxiety* in particular. We will return to the relationship between the teaching and classroom variables and *Irish attitude/motivation* in later chapters.

3.4.9 *Conclusion*

This is the first time that primary-school pupils' attitudes to the Irish language and their motivation to learn it have been investigated. The study has been successful both in terms of instrument development and the analysis of the relationship between attitude/motivation and achievement in Irish. The various adaptations of the original Canadian approach - e.g. having an administrator read each item aloud for the pupils and simplifying response options and format - seem to have dealt with the main practical difficulties that might have been expected. The central task for pupils - to register their opinions and attitudes - appears to have been carried out with ease. Indeed, one of the things revealed by the exercise is the subtlety and care with which pupils of this age can record their opinions and perceptions of the Irish language and of the process of learning it. Reading down through the response data on different questions, the evidence that pupils have detected, and taken account of the significance of, minor differences in wording is striking.

The study provides an account of different aspects of pupils' affective response to Irish and to the learning of Irish, showing in particular that pupils respond more positively to *Integrativeness* items than to *Motivation* items. It also confirms that attitude/ motivation is strongly related to pupil achievement in Irish and it identifies some of the factors which determine pupils' attitude/motivation. Finally, it gives an account of *Irish-lesson anxiety, Irish-self concept* and *Parental encouragement* and their relationship to other affective and achievement variables.

While the remediation of the problems in attitude and motivation recorded here is clearly important on educational grounds alone, the fact that the work of primary schools is central to societal effort to promote the wider use of Irish adds urgency to the search for solutions. At the very least, it emphasises the importance of according an even higher priority than in the past to the development in pupils of a positive attitude to Irish and to the learning of Irish. All pupils, including those who at present have lower levels of ability in Irish, should enjoy the experience of learning Irish, experience success in learning it, acquire a positive image of their own ability to learn and to speak the language, and should be free of undue anxiety about speaking in class. Any evaluation of the new curriculum should include the investigation of the affective dimension of learning Irish. The *Pupil Questionnaire* may have a useful role to play in that work.

4 Pupils' views on the Irish lesson in their own words

4.1 Introduction

In this chapter, we analyse pupils' views, expressed in their own words, on their experience of learning Irish. This approach acknowledges the trend in recent research to broaden the definition of motivation in relation to language learning. The attitude/motivation constructs associated with the earlier Gardner work are now considered too narrow. Tremblay and Gardner (1995), for example, argue for the inclusion of learner variables such as the extent to which learners set clearly defined goals, value the language course and are self-confident. Crookes and Schmidt (1991) propose that learner variables such as choice, engagement and persistence are also important components of motivational behaviour. The use of a wider range of instruments - observation, ethnographic and introspective measures - for the identification of these variables is also advocated.

One example of this kind of investigation is Pattison's (1989) study of pupil motivation in learning a foreign language which was conducted in four European countries, Holland, France, Great Britain and Austria. The findings indicate an overall pupil preference for oral activities - especially getting the chance to speak in smaller groups. Pupils, however, disliked 'the stress of speaking alone in front of the class, reciting or repeating given texts, learning by heart and speaking of things already known or evident'. Reading was the second most popular activity. Negative responses - what pupils disliked most - were most often linked with grammar. The present study in which pupils record what they 'dislike', 'like' and 'would like to change' about the Irish lesson brings this new perspective to the study of motivation in learning Irish.

4.2 Method

All pupils in the present study were asked to respond to three write-in items at the end of the *Pupil Questionnaire*:

- 'What I don't like about the Irish lesson.'
- 'What I do like about the Irish lesson.'
- 'How I would like to change the Irish lesson.'

The inspectors who administered the *Pupil Questionnaire* encouraged the children to respond frankly, explaining that we were particularly interested in their opinions and suggestions with regard to learning Irish (see Appendix 3.1). Every effort was made to ensure that the pupils felt free to express their real opinions. They were assured that their responses would be confidential - that no one in the school would be allowed to see their comments. They were also told that although we were asking for their name on the cover of the *Pupil Questionnaire*, we required this only to help us keep together that document and other questionnaires which they would be asked to answer on subsequent days.

Pupil comments were limited only by the space (four lines) on the questionnaire booklet assigned to each written reply. These write-in items, it will be recalled, did not contribute to any of the attitude scales or to the overall Attitude/Motivation index. It may be noted in passing that these items are less constrained than those used by Pattison (1989) as we sought pupil reactions to *any* aspect of the learning experience - not just learning activities.

4.3 Coding procedures and sampling of responses

In this section we describe how we transcribed pupils' responses, assigned them to different thematic categories, and selected a sample of responses for inclusion in the present report (see Appendix 4).

4.3.1 Categorising responses

There were 490 questionnaire booklets from which each pupil's hand-written responses were first transferred (without editing) into one large typed document and checked for accuracy of transcription. As a prelude to coding proper we read a few times through all responses pertaining to each of the three items, gradually building up and revising a list of the different types of issues or response elements covered. While many pupils mention only one issue in relation to each item, others wrote responses comprising a number of elements. Each of these elements was given equal status and assigned to a particular coding category. This initial list of more than fifty categories per item accounted for at least 90% of all pupils' responses on each item. These categories were subsequently combined to yield a more manageable and still useful set of 10-15 coding categories for each of the three items. This number appeared to reflect the pupils' responses in reasonable detail while allowing us to draw at least some general conclusions.

Needless to say, the development of categories is fundamentally subjective, irrespective of the care with which the coding itself is implemented. In addition, because the comments were made by children they are not always fully articulated and are sometimes couched in terms which refer to very specific aspects of their own classroom.

4.3.2 Selecting sample responses

In order to illustrate the form and content of pupil responses we selected, for each of the main categories, a sample of 10% of responses which contain elements relating to that category. This was not a random selection but was intended to illustrate the range of response elements within each category. This collection of sample responses may be found in Appendix 4.

Spelling and punctuation changes were made to the originals where necessary but the form of the pupil's response was otherwise left unchanged. Care was taken to ensure that schools or teachers could not be identified from the pupils' comments. Names of teachers or schools are replaced by <name of teacher> <name of school>. Irish words are written in italics and accompanied by a translation/explanation in curved brackets ( ) .

It will be noted that comments within some categories vary more than others. For example, in relation to the item 'What I don't like in the Irish class', comments in *Category G - Spelling exercises,* vary little in the way they are expressed, e.g. simply 'I don't like Irish spelling'. In contrast, comments in *Category C - Grammar-related activities,* are articulated in many different ways ('I don't like the *Briathra* (verbs)'; 'I don't like e.g. *aige, leis* (prepositional pronouns)'; 'I don't like Irish grammar...'; etc.).

Most responses were clear-cut enough to allow them to be easily assigned to a category. For example, in relation to item 78 'What I do not like in the Irish lesson' some pupils simply wrote 'Irish spelling', 'Irish reading', 'using filmstrips' etc. Others gave slightly more elaborate responses mentioning aspects of the lesson that accounted for their likes or dislikes e.g. 'I don't like when the teacher asks me a question because if I get it wrong I get embarrassed'. Inevitably, some comments were also ambiguous or imprecise i.e. it was not initially clear what exactly pupils were referring to. Sometimes a knowledge of the particular classroom or teaching practices generally is assumed by the pupil. In such cases we were usually able to resolve the uncertainties by consulting other background information on the teaching methods used in that class (e.g. the *Teacher's Questionnaire,* or the classroom observation data for that class), as well as, gleaning clues from the apparently equivalent but more detailed comments of other classmates.

Consider the following response, for example, (see Appendix 4, item 78, Category A, no 3) 'I don't like the *comhrá* and changing the sentences into the *aimsirí* (verb tenses)'. Here it is not possible to say straight away whether the term *comhrá* ('conversation') is being used here to refer to the use of the *Nuachúrsaí* or to Irish conversation practice or activities in general. *Comhrá* is often used by Irish pupils and teachers to refer to the *Nuachúrsaí* course-method (the official audio-visual course for teaching spoken Irish - Department of Education, 1978). In the present example, *comhrá* was interpreted as referring to the *Nuachúrsaí* because (a) information from the *Teacher Questionnaire* indicated that the *Nuachúrsaí* were the main course-method used in teaching oral Irish and (b) more elaborate responses from other classmates made it clear that *comhrá* was the term used by them when talking about material from the *Nuachúrsaí.*

In many instances, the sample responses included under a particular thematic category in Appendix 4 will contain elements which are also coded under other category headings. For example, in relation to pupil 'dislikes', the response 'I don't like Irish spellings, projector, verbs' (see Appendix 4, item 78, Category G, no 1) was not only coded as *Category G - Spelling exercises* but also as *Category A - Nuachúrsaí-related activities/materials* and *Category C - Grammar-related activities.*

4.4 Results: Themes, complaints and preferences

The main achievement of this part of the study is represented by the pupils' own comments, categorised by theme, samples of which are presented in Appendix 4. Reading through these comments, a number of issues and impressions quickly emerge. The function of the simple quantitative analyses we conducted is merely to make these initial impressions more explicit. The analysis has two main components (1) identifying the relative importance of different themes in pupils 'dislikes', 'likes' and desired 'changes' in the Irish lesson generally (i.e. when all pupils and classes are considered together) and (2) determining to what extent the emphasis on particular themes varied from class to class.

4.4.1 Analysis

The results are divided into two parts. In Part 1, data is presented on the frequency with which various themes, problems and preferences feature in pupils' responses to the Irish lesson. Tables 4.1 - 4.3 set out the percentages of pupil responses associated with each of the thematic categories. The left hand side of each table lists the coding categories (A-K) to which the various response elements were assigned. The percentage distribution of pupils is shown on the right hand side of the table.

The results indicate a very high response rate - approximately 95% of pupils who were administered the *Pupil Questionnaire* responded to all three items. It should be noted that since each pupil's response could contain elements which were coded in relation to more than one category, the percentages on the right side of each table add to more than 100%.

Part 2 contains data on variations from class to class. The relevant data are presented in Tables 4.4 - 4.6. The main focus is on how pupils 'dislikes, 'likes' and desired 'changes' in relation to the Irish lesson vary according to class achievement in spoken Irish. The format of presentation of data is the same for each table. As in earlier chapters, classes are listed in order of their achievement in spoken Irish (ranked from 1-20) and are grouped into high-, middle- and low-achievement-in-Irish classes. Column 2 contains teacher-reported information on the main course-method used in teaching oral Irish. The remaining right hand columns give the two most commonly occurring thematic categories associated with pupils' 'dislikes'/ 'likes'/ desired 'changes', along with the percentage of pupils associated with each category in each class.

4.4.2 Part 1: Pupils' 'dislikes', 'likes' and desired 'changes'

What the pupil 'dislikes' in the Irish lesson:
The percentage in the last row of Table 4.1 indicates that practically all pupils (99.4%) made at least some kind of response to this item. As the footnote to Table 4.1 indicates, however, response elements made by almost six per cent of pupils did not fit into any of our coding categories. The most common pupil 'dislike' in relation to the Irish lesson involves *Nuachúrsaí-related activities/materials* (*Category A*). Almost 30% of pupils

report disliking some aspect of the *Nuachúrsaí* (including 11% who mention the use of film strips/projector in particular).

Table 4.1
'Dislikes': Percentage distribution of pupils' responses according to 12 thematic categories

'What I don't like in the Irish lesson': **Thematic categories.** *	*Percentage of pupils' responses (n=490)*
(A) *Nuachúrsaí*-related activities/materials	29.4
(B) Difficulty in understanding generally	16.9
(C) Grammar-related activities	16.3
(D) Boring, old fashioned, repetitious course & materials	15.1
(E) Reading activities and specific readers	14.5
(F) Written exercises including essays, answers etc.	13.9
(G) Spelling exercises	10.2
(H) Irish-lesson anxiety, low self-esteem etc.	9.2
(I) Generally negative about the Irish lesson (e.g. 'dislike everything about it' /'waste of time')	9.4
(J) Generally positive about the Irish lesson (e.g. 'like everything about it' / 'not enough Irish')	4.9
(K) Drama/poems/songs	4.1
No comment	0.6

*Two minor categories 'Dislike teaching through Irish' (1.2%), 'Dislike stories' (0.4%) are not included in the table. Response elements from a further 5.9% of pupil responses were so diverse that they were assigned to the category 'Other'. See Appendix 4 for samples of actual pupil responses.

The next most common response category (almost 17% of pupils) relates to difficulty in understanding various aspects of the Irish lesson, (*Category B*). Pupils frequently mention the fact that they do not understand what the teacher is saying (see Appendix 4, item 78, category B).

Just over 16% of pupils had response elements which were coded as *Category C: Grammar-related activities*. As the sample responses for this category show (see Appendix 4), the dissatisfaction centres to a large extent on the various forms of verb practice in the Irish lesson.

Fifteen per cent of pupils dislike the lesson or the lessons materials because they are *boring, old fashioned or repetitious (Category D)*. Almost half of these pupils specifically complain about the 'boredom' aspect of Irish lessons. While it is impossible to discover exactly what aspects of the course the pupils have in mind here, answers to the other two write-in items (79 & 80) and information on course-method and materials for particular classes (from the *Teacher Questionnaire*) suggest that some of the dissatisfaction relates to the use of the *Nuachúrsaí*. In reality, then, *Category D* may be considered, in part, as an extension of *Category A*. The remarks about boredom are not surprising given that responses to an item from the *Attitude to Learning Irish* scale (see Appendix 3.2: item 46) show that 41% of pupils agree with the statement 'I think that learning Irish is boring' (17.3% 'strongly agree' while 23.3% 'slightly agree').

The next three categories (*Categories E, F and G*) relate to pupils' dislike of specific skill-related activities in the Irish lesson. Just over 14% of pupils do not like *Reading activities and specific readers (Category E)*. A dislike of *Written exercises including essays, answers etc. (Category F)* is mentioned by a similar proportion (13.9%) of pupils. Approximately one-tenth of all pupils specifically dislike traditional *Spelling exercises (Category G)*.

Categories H, I and J concern the affective dimension of learning Irish. *Irish-lesson anxiety, low self-esteem etc. (Category H)* are concerns for 9.2% of the pupils and are reflected in response elements such as 'I don't like when the teacher asks me a question because if I get it wrong I get embarrassed' and 'Because I am no good at it....'.

Generally negative statements about the Irish lesson (*Category I*) such as 'I don't like anything in Irish' or 'I think it is a waste of time' are made by 9.4% of pupils. In contrast 4.9% of pupils write 'generally positive' comments *(Category J)* such as 'I like everything about the Irish lesson '.

Finally, four per cent of pupils report disliking aspects of the Irish lesson which involve *Drama/poems/songs - Category K*.

To summarise, the main themes which arise in pupils' responses to the item 'What I don't like in the Irish lesson' are:

- dislike of the use of *Nuachúrsaí*-related activities/materials
- dislike not being able to understand what is going on in the Irish lesson
- dislike of the boring, old fashioned and repetitious nature of the course and materials
- dislike grammar-related activities, particularly verb practice
- dislike activities focusing on developing certain skill areas such as reading, writing and spelling
- dislike the anxiety and low self-esteem which pupils associate with learning Irish

What the pupil likes in the Irish lesson
In presenting the data relating to the item 'What I like in the Irish lesson', we occasionally draw comparisons below between the proportion of pupils who say they *like* a particular aspect of the Irish lesson (the present item) and the proportion who, in response to the previous item express *dislike* of similar aspects. While the categories may not always be exactly equivalent the comparisons illustrate the persistence of some themes across 'likes'

and 'dislikes'. As in the case of the previous item, there was a very high response rate to this item: 98% of pupils wrote a remark of some kind.

Table 4.2 shows that the most frequent response, from over a quarter of pupils (28.2%), mentions either reading activities or using named readers as aspects of the Irish lesson which they like *(Category A - Reading activities and specific readers)*. Despite this, it will be recalled that in a previous item a substantial minority of pupils (14.5%) specifically mentioned reading as something they did *not* like in the Irish lesson. Thus, nearly twice as many pupils report that they like reading as dislike it. It is worth noting that while pupils frequently mention that they liked Irish reading or specific readers, they rarely elaborate on the reasons why this was so (see Appendix 4, item 79: *Category A* sample responses). This is a point which we will return to later in the context of a discussion on the central role of Irish reading and reading aloud in the Irish classroom.

The second most popular aspect of the lesson (25.7% of pupils) is the informal use of spoken Irish in the non-language-practice contexts of *Conversation, games, drama, songs, poems (Category B)*. It will be recalled from the previous table that only 4.1% of pupils mentioned drama/poems/songs as activities they *disliked*.

Written exercises *(Category C - Written exercises including essays, answers, etc.)* are specified by 16.7% of pupils as aspects of the Irish lesson they like. It will be recalled from the previous item, that broadly similar proportions of pupils (13.9%) mentioned that they *disliked* such exercises.

One feature of the Irish lesson which pupils specifically like, and which was not mentioned among pupil 'dislikes', relates to stories *(Category D - Stories generally, picture stories, creative writing)* - just over 14% of pupil responses.

Category E - Oral Irish practice generally, answering questions accounts for just under one-tenth (9.6%) of responses. It should be pointed out here that a distinction was made in coding between *Category B* type responses referring to the 'informal use of spoken Irish' and references to its more formal oral practice *(Category E)*.

Nuachúrsaí-related activities/materials (Category F) are among the 'likes' responses mentioned by a small proportion of pupils (8.4%). Comparison with data from the previous item shows that more than three times as many pupils dislike such activities/materials as like them.

Eight per cent of pupils resist the positive tone of the item and state quite unequivocally that they like nothing in the Irish lesson *(Category G)*. This roughly matches the 9.4% of pupils who in response to the previous 'dislike' item were *Generally negative* about the Irish lesson.

Being able to understand, explanations, translations etc. (Category H) is an aspect of the Irish lesson that 7.6% of pupils like. Many of the response elements refer specifically to teacher explanations or translations of Irish words (see Appendix 4, item 79, *Category H* sample responses). This reinforces the evidence from the previous item where 16.9% of pupils (Table 4.1- *Category B*) disliked the fact that they had difficulty in understanding generally.

Table 4.2
'Likes': Percentage distribution of pupils' responses according to 12 thematic categories.

'What I <u>do</u> like in the Irish lesson': *Thematic categories**	*Percentage of pupils' responses (n=490)*
(A) Reading activities and specific readers.	28.2
(B) Conversation, games, drama, songs, poems	25.7
(C) Written exercises including essays, answers etc.	16.7
(D) Stories generally, picture stories, creative writing	14.3
(E) Oral Irish practice generally, answering questions	9.6
(F) *Nuachúrsaí*-related activities/materials	8.4
(G) Like nothing about Irish	8.0
(H) Being able to understand, explanations, translations etc.	7.6
(I) Spelling exercises	7.3
(J) Grammar-related activities	6.3
(K) Learning about our own language, culture, identity etc.	5.7
No comment	2.0

*Three minor categories, not listed above, each accounted for 2% or less of all pupil responses: 'Using a particular course-book' (2%), 'Humour/funny stories' (1.6%), 'Pupil likes everything about Irish' (1.4%). Response elements from another 10.4% of pupil responses were so diverse that they were simply included under a category called 'Other'. See Appendix 4 for samples of actual pupil responses.

Pupils appear to be divided about 'liking' or 'disliking' grammar and spelling, although dislike predominates. Table 4.1 shows that 16.3% of pupils dislike grammar-related activities while 10.2% of pupils dislike spelling exercises. In Table 4.2 it can be seen that only 6.3% of pupils like *Grammar-related activities (Category J)* while only 7.3% of pupils like *Spelling exercises (Category I)*.

Finally, the last category of 'likes' comments in Table 4.2 does not refer to pupils reactions to the Irish lesson *per se* but to their attitudes to the Irish language itself and its importance as an ethnic symbol. Just under six per cent of pupil responses are assigned to *Category K - Learning about our own language, culture, identity etc* (see Appendix 4, item 79, *Category K)*.

To summarise,

- Each of the two categories *(i) Reading activities and specific readers*, and *(ii) Conversations, games, drama, songs, poems* (informal use of spoken Irish), account for elements found in over a quarter of all pupils' 'likes' responses.
- The next most frequent 'likes' responses are *Written exercises* (16.7%), *Stories* (14.3%) and *Oral Irish generally, answering questions* (9.6%).
- Three categories which have equivalents on the 'dislikes' item, *Nuachúrsaí-related activities/materials*, *Spelling exercises* and *Grammar-related activities*, account for less than a tenth of pupils 'likes' responses.
- The *Generally negative* comments from a minority of pupils in response to the 'dislikes' item reemerge in the 'likes' item in the form of statements where pupils (8%) report that they *Like nothing about Irish* .
- Comprehensibility in the Irish lesson (*Being able to understand, explanations, translations etc.*), a theme which previously appeared in relation to pupils' 'dislikes', appears again in the 'likes' responses, although to a lesser extent (7.6% pupils).
- Just under six per cent of pupils write that they like learning about *Our own language, culture, identity etc.*

How the pupil would like to change the Irish lesson
In the last 'write-in' item, pupils are asked to say how they would like to change the Irish lesson. From Table 4.3 we see that even though the response rate is still very high (95.7%), slightly fewer pupils answer than in the case of the previous two items. There is, however, greater diversity in the kinds of responses made to this item compared to the previous items. In order to have a manageable set of categories, we include in Table 4.3 only those categories which account for responses from 4% or more of the pupils. Details on the remaining six minor categories are given in the footnote. Over 12% of responses could not be coded under any of the major or minor category headings in Table 4.3.

It will be noted that broadly similar themes appear in Table 4.3 as in the case of the previous two items relating to 'likes' and 'dislikes'. This present item more than the previous ones, however, probably captures best what pupils perceive as most fundamentally in need of change in the Irish lesson.

There appear to be three broad concerns - (i) course/lesson content, (ii) understanding/ comprehensibility and (iii) degree of emphasis (more or less) on Irish generally.

Looking at the first of these concerns, course content/materials, we see (Table 4.3) that just over 16% of pupils think the course should be *More modern, fun, realistic, non-sexist* (*Category A*). This proportion corresponds closely to the 15.1% of pupils who 'dislike' the Irish lesson because they find it *Boring, old fashioned, repetitious etc.* (Table 4.1). Another frequent recommendation (made by 13.6% of pupils) is that there should be *More conversation, drama, games, poems, and songs* (*Category C*). It will be recalled that a quarter of all pupils had mentioned these activities in the previous items as 'likes'.

Table 4.3
'Changes': Percentage distribution of pupils' responses according to 12 thematic categories.

'How I would like to change the Irish lesson': **Thematic categories***	*Percentage of pupils' responses (n=490)*
(A) Make it more modern, fun, realistic, non-sexist	16.1
(B) Make it easier to understand - more explanations/translations.	14.1
(C) More conversation, drama, games, poems, songs	13.6
(D) Would not like any change	12.9
(E) Less emphasis on Irish, including Irish homework	9.4
(F) New materials: (film strips/books/stories/pictures/readers/videos/TV*)*	8.8
(G) Dispense with *Nuachúrsaí* filmstrips/projector	6.1
(H) Less or no use at all of the *Nuachúrsaí*	4.9
(I) More time devoted to teaching Irish and/or more teaching through Irish	4.9
(J) Stop teaching Irish altogether	4.5
(K) More Irish reading	4.5
No comment	4.3

*Six minor categories not listed in the table each accounted for less than 4% of all pupil responses: 'Less grammar' (3.7%), 'Fewer/easier spellings' (2.2%), 'Less reading/use of specific readers' (2%), 'More grammar' (1.4%); 'Less writing' (2.2%), 'More writing' (1.6%). Response elements from 12.4% of pupil responses on this item were so diverse that they were included under a category called 'Other'. See Appendix 4 for samples of actual pupil responses

Skipping down to *Category F* in Table 4.3, we see that 8.8% of pupils would like *New materials* of one kind or another. New books, stories, film strips, videos and TV programmes were among the suggestions (see Appendix 4, item 80, *Category F* sample responses). Just over six per cent of pupils wish to *Dispense with Nuachúrsaí film strips/projector* (*Category G*) while a further 4.9% would like to see either *Less use* or *no use at all of the Nuachúrsaí* (*Category H*).

The second broad concern relates to pupil comprehension of the lesson. *Category B* responses express the wish that the Irish lesson would be made *Easier to understand, with more explanations/translations* (14.1% of responses). It may be recalled that 16.9% of pupils did *not like* the Irish lesson because they had difficulty understanding, and that 7.6% of pupils mentioned *Being able to understand, explanations, translations etc.* as aspects of the Irish lesson which they liked.

The third broad concern - degree of emphasis on Irish is represented by the response categories *J, E, D, & I*. These categories might be seen as points on a scale reflecting the extent of change which pupils would like to see in the emphasis on Irish generally. The points on this scale are *Stop teaching Irish altogether (Category J), Less emphasis on Irish, including Irish homework (Category E), Would not like any change (Category D)* and *More time devoted to Irish (Category I)*. The two lowest points on the scale indicate negative pupil reactions to the teaching of Irish - 4.5% of pupils would not like any Irish at all taught or would like it replaced with another subject *(Category J)* while over 9% of pupils would like to spend less class time on Irish or have less Irish homework *(Category E)*. On this hypothetical scale a substantial minority of pupils (13%) *Would not like any change (Category D)*. Inspection of comments by the latter pupils to adjacent 'dislikes' and 'likes' items indicate that, in all probability some of their 'no change' responses actually signify an apathetic/negative reaction. Thus, the true proportion of pupils who would not like to see any change in the Irish lesson because they are *happy* with things as they are, is likely to be much lower than 13%. An unambiguous positive statement, however, comes from the 4.9% of pupils who would like *More time devoted to teaching Irish, and/or more teaching through Irish (Category I)*.

Finally, a result which does not fit into the three broad areas of pupil concern above indicates that 4.5% of pupils would like to change the Irish lesson by having *More Irish reading (Category K)*. Thus, it appears that while twice as many pupils like reading as dislike it (see Tables 4.1 & 4.2), only a small minority of pupils would actually like *more* reading.

In summary, there were three main desired changes:
- Change the course content and/or materials so that they would be more modern, more fun, more realistic, non-sexist (16.1%); include more conversation, drama, games, poems and songs (14.1%) or, more generally, bring in new materials (8.8%). Some would like to see either an end to the *Nuachúrsaí* (6.1%) or a reduction in their use generally (4.9%).
- The concern with comprehensibility in the Irish lesson identified earlier in the context of pupils 'dislikes' and 'likes' surfaces again here in the form of pupils' desire to make the lesson easier to understand etc. (14.1%).
- Varying levels of support for the teaching of Irish, ranging from extreme negative responses requesting that the teaching of Irish be stopped (4.5%) to much more positive statements indicating a desire to have more time devoted to Irish (4.9%). The intermediate categories consist of a desire for less emphasis on Irish (9.4%) and a lack of interest in any change (12.9%).

4.4.3 Part 2: Between-class variation in pupil perception of the Irish lesson

The themes which emerge in pupils' 'dislikes', 'likes' and desired 'changes' in the Irish lesson are not equally emphasised in all classes. Our examination of these between-class differences in pupils' views will be informal and will focus on broad differences between the three main groups of classes used previously - high Irish-achievement classes, middle Irish-achievement classes and low Irish-achievement classes. Class achievement in spoken Irish is included in our analysis of pupils' views because previous research (Harris, 1983) and data in earlier chapters indicated that achievement in Irish was significantly correlated with both linguistic, educational and attitudinal variables. Given the nature of the data, we will confine our analysis to simple frequency counts.

In column two of each table we present information on the main course method used to teach Irish based on data from an item on the *Teacher Questionnaire*, as a background for the pupils' comments (see Appendix 2.4: item 17). As we noted earlier in Chapter 2 (section 2.4.5), however, the 'main method' cited here should be seen as giving only a rough-and-ready indication of classroom practice. Classroom-observation data in Chapter 7 suggest that in terms of both topic and materials, the *Nuachúrsaí* and audio-visual materials are used in only about 10% of lesson segments.

Pupil 'dislikes': Class variation
The first thing to be noted in Table 4.4 is that there is a clear difference between the three main groups of classes (high-, middle-, and low-Irish-achievement) in terms of the aspects of the Irish lesson which pupils most 'dislike'. Dislike of *Nuachúrsaí-related activities/materials (Category A)* is often associated with pupils in the middle-Irish-achievement group of classes. All but one class (rank 8) in this group have this as the most frequent 'dislike' response option. The tendency is also evident, though less pronounced, in the low-Irish-achievement group of classes (the most common response in class ranks 14 & 16 and the second most common in class ranks 13 & 17).

In contrast, *Category A* does not feature at all among the most common response categories in the high-Irish-achievement group. Classes in the latter group are more likely to dislike *Grammar-related activities* (class ranks 2, 3 & 6) or *Spelling activities* (class ranks 1, 4 & 5).

Grammar *(Category C)* and spelling *(Category G)* do not appear as common dislikes in any of the low-Irish-achievement group of classes. Instead, *Difficulty in understanding generally (Category B)* is much more likely to be cited. Looking at Table 4.4 again, it can be seen that five of the low-Irish-achievement classes have *Category B* as the first or second most common 'dislike' response category compared to only one class in the middle-Irish-achievement group and two classes in the high-Irish-achievement group.

Finally, it is worthwhile noting the thematic categories associated with the lowest ranking class in terms of achievement in Irish (rank 20). Looking at the last row of Table 4.4 we see that this is the only class where *Irish-lesson anxiety, low self-esteem etc. (Category H)* is the most common 'dislike' category (29% of pupils). A further 18% of pupils in this class were *Generally negative about the Irish lesson (Category I)*. These findings are consistent with results from our attitude/motivation data in Chapter 3 (see Table 3.10) which showed that this class has the second highest ranking on the *Irish-lesson anxiety* index and was the second lowest in terms of overall *Class attitude to Irish (Irish attitude/motivation)*.

Table 4.4
Pupils' dislikes: Class variation

Class achievement in spoken Irish Rank	Course-method used*	Percentage of pupils choosing			
		Most common response category		Second most common response category	
1	*Nuachúrsaí*	G. Spelling exercises	38%	B. Difficulty in understanding generally	38%
2	*Nuachúrsaí* & ABC	C. Grammar-related activities	32%	E. Reading activities & specific readers	22%
3	ABC	C. Grammar-related activities	44%	F. Written exercises including essays, answers etc.	22%
4	Own method	G. Spelling exercises	25%	J. Generally positive about Irish lesson	25%
5	Own method	G. Spelling exercises	50%	F. Written exercises ... 42% K. Drama/poems/songs.. 42%	
6	*Nuachúrsaí*	C. Grammar-related activities	33%	B. Difficulty in understanding generally	33%
7	*Nuachúrsaí*	A. *Nuachúrsaí*-related activities/materials	81%	D. Boring/old fashioned/ repetitious ...	62%
8 D	Own method	C. Grammar-related activities	32%	E. Reading activities & specific readers ...	19%
9	*Nuachúrsaí*	A. *Nuachúrsaí*-related activities/materials	48%	Grammar, Reading, Anxiety Categories C, E & H (15% each)	
10	*Nuachúrsaí*	A. *Nuachúrsaí*-related activities/materials	56%	C. Grammar-related activities	26%
11	Own method	A. *Nuachúrsaí*-related activities/materials	35%	F. Written exercises including essays, answers etc.	18%
12	*Nuachúrsaí* & ABC	A. *Nuachúrsaí*-related activities/materials	35%	B. Difficulty in understanding generally ..	31%
13	*Nuachúrsaí*	B. Difficulty in understand -ing generally	30%	A. *Nuachúrsaí*-related activities/materials	23%
14	*Nuachúrsaí*	A. *Nuachúrsaí*-related activities/materials	30%	B. Difficulty in understanding generally	30%
15	*Nuachúrsaí*	B. Difficulty in understanding generally	30%	D. Boring, old fashioned, repetitious etc.	27%
16 D	*Nuachúrsaí*	A. *Nuachúrsaí*-related activities/materials	41%	E. Reading activities & specific readers	30%
17	*Nuachúrsaí* & ABC	F. Written exercises including essays, answers etc.	30%	A. *Nuachúrsaí*-related activities/materials	22%
18	*Nuachúrsaí* & ABC	B. Difficulty in understanding generally	33%	D. Boring/old fashioned repetitious...	28%
19	Own method	B. Difficulty in understanding generally	33%	F. Written exercises including essays, answers etc.	26%
20 D	Own method	H. Irish-lesson anxiety /low self-esteem etc.	29%	I. Generally negative	18%

*Teacher's report (Appendix 2.4). Classroom observation data indicate that, over all classes, use of the *Nuachúrsaí*/audio-visual materials is at a fairly low level - about 10% of lesson segments (see section 2.4.5 and section 7.3.3 & 7.3.4).
'D' = Officially classified as disadvantaged.

Table 4.5
Pupils' likes: Class variation

Class achievement in spoken Irish Rank	Course-method used*	Percentage of pupils choosing			
		Most common response category		Second most common response category	
1	Nuachúrsaí	A. Reading activities & specific readers	38%	B. Conversation, games, drama, songs, poems	38%
2	Nuachúrsaí & ABC	B. Conversation, games, drama, songs, poems	43%	A. Reading activities & specific readers	19%
3	ABC	C. Written exercises including essays, answers, etc.	44%	B. Conversation, games, drama, songs, poems	44%
4	Own method	A. Reading activities & specific readers	25%	*Other /minor response categories*	25%
5	Own method	A. Reading activities & specific readers	50%	J. Grammar-related ...	42%
				B. Conversation, games ..	.42%
6	Nuachúrsaí	A. Reading activities & specific readers	67%	E. Oral Irish practice, answering questions	33%
7	Nuachúrsaí	A. Reading activities & specific readers	49%	B. Conversation, drama, games, songs, poems	43%
8 D	Own method	A. Reading activities & specific readers	52%	C. Written exercises including essays, answers etc.	45%
9	Nuachúrsaí	A. Reading activities & specific readers	30%	C. Written exercises including essays, answers etc.	19%
10	Nuachúrsaí	A. Reading activities & specific readers	46%	B. Conversation, games, drama, songs, poems	33%
11	Own method	B. Conversation, games, drama, songs, poems	41%	E. Oral Irish practice answering questions	29%
12	Nuachúrsaí & ABC	K. Learning about our own language, culture ...	21%	A. Reading activities & specific readers	14%
13	Nuachúrsaí	A. Reading activities & specific readers	50%	B. Conversation, games, drama, songs, poems	30%
14	Nuachúrsaí	B. Conversation, games drama, songs, poems	48%	F. *Nuachúrsaí*-related activities/materials	17%
15	Nuachúrsaí	H. Being able to understand, explanations ...	43%	A. Reading activities & specific readers	20%
16 D	Nuachúrsaí	A. Reading activities & specific readers	30%	E. Oral Irish practice	15%
				B. Conversation, games...	15%
17	Nuachúrsaí & ABC	D. Stories generally, picture stories, creative writing	26%	A. Reading activities & specific readers	17%
18	Nuachúrsaí & ABC	D. Stories generally, picture stories, creative writing	54%	B. Conversation, games, drama, songs, poems	28%
19	Own method	G. Like nothing about Irish	37%	C. Written exercises, including essays, answers etc.	15%
20 D	Own method	G. Like nothing about Irish	54%	A. Reading activities & specific readers	18%

*Teacher's report (Appendix 2.4). See footnote Table 4.4.
'D' = Officially classified as disadvantaged.

Table 4.6
Pupils' desired changes: Class variation

Class achievement in spoken Irish Rank	Course-method used*	Percentage of pupils choosing			
		Most common response category		*Second most common response category*	
1	*Nuachúrsaí*	K. More Irish reading	25%	I. More time devoted to teaching Irish ..	25%
2	*Nuachúrsaí & ABC*	C. More conversation, drama, games, poems, songs	24%	A. More it more modern, fun, realistic, non-sexist	19%
3	ABC	I. More time devoted to teaching Irish	33%	D. Would not like any change	22%
4	Own method	I. More time devoted to teaching Irish	25%	K. More Irish reading	25%
5	Own method	D. Would not like any change ..	25%	C. More conversation, drama, games, poems, songs	25%
6	*Nuachúrsaí*	H. Less/no use at all of the *Nuachúrsaí*	33%	B. Make it easier .. 22% E. Less emphasis on Irish ... 22%	
7	*Nuachúrsaí*	A. Make it more modern, fun, realistic, non-sexist	92%	F. New materials	24%
8 D	Own method	D. Would not like any change	42%	B. Make it easier .. 13% E. Less emphasis on Irish ... 13%	
9	*Nuachúrsaí*	H. Less/no use at all of the *Nuachúrsaí*	19%	C. More conversation, drama, games, poems, songs	19%
10	*Nuachúrsaí*	A. Make it more modern, fun realistic, non-sexist	23%	G. Dispense with *Nuachúrsaí* film strips/projector	23%
11	Own method	F. New materials	42%	A. Make it more modern ... 18% D. Would not like any change 18%	
12	*Nuachúrsaí & ABC*	D. Would not like any change	24%	B. Make it easier to understand more explanations	21%
13	*Nuachúrsaí*	C. More conversation, drama games, poems, songs	20%	B. Make it easier.. 13% I. More time devoted to 13%	
14	*Nuachúrsaí*	D. Would not like any change	26%	B. Make it easier to understand more explanations	17%
15	*Nuachúrsaí*	A. Make it more modern, fun realistic, non sexist	27%	B. Make it easier to .... 20% E. Less emphasis on Irish.. 20%	
16 D	*Nuachúrsaí*	J. Stop teaching Irish altogether	22%	G. Dispense with *Nuachúrsaí* film strips/projector	19%
17	*Nuachúrsaí & ABC*	B. Make it easier to understand more explanations ..	30%	No comment	26%
18	*Nuachúrsaí & ABC*	C. More conversation, drama games, poems, songs	23%	A. Make it more modern, fun, realistic, non-sexist	18%
19	Own method	B. Make it easier to understand more explanations ...	30%	J. Stop teaching Irish altogether	19%
20 D	Own method	D. Would not like any change	21%	B. Make it easier to understand more explanations	18%

*Teacher's report (Appendix 2.4). See footnote Table 4.4.
'D' = Officially classified as disadvantaged.

Pupil 'likes': Class variation

It will be recalled that the most common 'likes' category was *Category A - Reading activities and specific readers*. In Table 4.5 we see that this is also the most common response category in half of the 20 classes and the second most favoured in five of the remaining ones. Comparing the three main Irish-achievement groups, it can be seen that *Reading activities and specific readers* is cited slightly less often as a common 'like' response in the low-Irish-achievement group. *Category B (Conversation, drama, games, etc)*, the first or second most common 'likes' responses in eleven of the 20 classes' is not associated with any particular achievement group. The remaining 'likes' themes feature among the most common response categories in no more than two of the 20 classes.

Negative reactions to Irish *(Category G - Like nothing about Irish)* which go against the tone of the original question ('What I do like ...') constitute the dominant response in the two lowest ranking classes: 37% of pupils in class 19 and 54% of pupils in class 20 feel that they cannot say anything positive about the Irish lesson. However, others within their classes mention either written exercises (15%) or reading (18%) as aspects of the Irish lesson which they like.

Pupil's desire for 'changes': Class variation

The diversity of responses to the 'desired changes' is reflected at the class level in the wide range of response categories which appear in the two right hand columns of Table 4.6. Despite this diversity, certain patterns can be detected.

First, low-Irish-achievement classes are more likely than either of the other two Irish-achievement groups of classes to express a desire that in future the Irish lesson would be *Easier to understand, with more explanations etc. (Category B)*. In six of the eight low-Irish-achievement classes, in particular, this is the first or second most frequent response made by pupils.

Two other thematic categories which feature a number of times are *Category A (Make it more modern, fun, etc.)* and *Category C (More conversation, drama, games etc.)*. There is no clear tendency for these categories, however, to be particularly associated with any of the three Irish-achievement defined groups of classes.

There are a number of indications of a generally negative view of the Irish lesson in the low-Irish-achievement classes (ranks 13-20), while there are indications of a generally positive view in the high-Irish-achievement classes (ranks 1-6). For example, two classes (ranks 16 & 19) in the low-Irish achievement group feature the theme *Stop teaching Irish altogether (Category J)* as either the most common, or the second most common, response category (22%, 19% pupils respectively). *Less emphasis on Irish* was a common response (20% of pupils) in another low-Irish-achievement class (class 15). Over a quarter (26%) of pupils in yet another low-achievement class (rank 17) did not make any comment at all. It may be recalled from Chapter 3 that this particular class (rank 17 in terms of achievement in Irish) was ranked 16 in terms of overall *Class attitude to Irish (Irish attitude/motivation)*. A reasonable interpretation of the reluctance of pupils in this class to answer this item is the existence of a generally negative attitude to Irish.

Finally, 21% of pupils in class rank 20, and 26% of pupils in class rank 14, say they *Would not like any change* in the Irish lesson. Data on *Irish attitude/motivation* and *Irish-lesson anxiety* for these two classes (Chapter 3) would suggest that their apparent support for the *status quo* in relation to the Irish lesson is most likely masking an underlying disillusionment and sense of failure in relation to learning Irish. For example, class 20 was ranked 19th in terms of *Class attitude to Irish (*based on the *Irish attitude/motivation index)* and class 14 was ranked highest (rank of 1) of all classes on the *Irish-lesson anxiety index*.

One exception to the general trend for negative responses to be associated with low-achievement classes is class rank 13 - here, 13% of pupils want *More time devoted to teaching Irish and/or more teaching through Irish (Category I).*

In contrast to the low-Irish-achievement classes, generally positive statements about learning Irish dominate in the high-Irish-achievement classes. In three of these classes (ranks 1, 3, and 4) the first or second most commonly desired 'change' is *More time devoted to teaching Irish and/or more teaching through Irish (Category I).* This is particularly significant given that, based on teachers' reports (see Table 2.14), two of these classes (ranks 1 & 4) already teach other aspects of the curriculum through Irish for 2-4 hours a week.

4.5 Discussion

It is clear from our results that soliciting pupils views directly is a fruitful approach to investigating both the learning process itself and the role of affective factors in facilitating it. The advantage of using open-ended questions is that pupils' comments are not limited to their general views on Irish or the learning of Irish but extend to personal reactions to classroom processes and to specific activities and materials. We have identified a number of related themes running through the responses to the questions concerning 'dislikes', 'likes' and desired 'changes'. We have also identified certain patterns of association between the occurrence of these themes and class achievement in Irish. The discussion which follows centres around five issues: the significance of pupils' comments; the main themes evident in pupils' expressed 'dislikes', 'likes' and desire for 'change'; the suitability of lesson content and materials; comprehension difficulties and apathy in low-Irish-achievement classes; and the popularity of Irish reading.

4.5.1 The significance of pupils' comments
Two related issues arise in considering the significance of pupils' responses:

(a) Are the Irish pupils' comments valid indicators of how they feel about the Irish lesson - in much the same way that we would expect adult statements of this kind to be?

(b) What factors, other than pupils' own experiences and inclinations, are likely to colour their perceptions? Are there any factors unique to them as primary school pupils?

The first question hinges not so much on whether pupils' assessments of the Irish lesson are true or otherwise in an absolute sense, but whether they can be taken at face value as faithfully representing the pupils' own views. Pattison (1989: 43) mentions that when interpreting pupils' comments we must be aware of the 'subjective, changeable and idealistic' nature of the ideas and opinions which pupils express. While pupils may have some limitations regarding their ability to communicate their opinions in formal terms, we can find no evidence of any really fundamental differences between adults and pupils of this age in the kind of factors which affect the content and stability of their opinions. Their responses, while often vigorously expressed, are fundamentally measured and thoughtful, sometimes incorporating both positive and negative points. In addition, reasons very often are given for the assessment - e.g. criticism of the *Nuachúrsaí* may mention that the material is not up-to-date or realistic, or reluctance to speak in Irish in the class may be explained in terms of embarrassment or fear of making a mistake.

Regarding the second related issue above, we must ask if there are any exceptional influences from parents or peers. Parents will certainly influence pupils' general attitude to Irish. They may also communicate some overall assessment of current approaches to teaching Irish in school based on their own experience. They are probably unlikely, however, to be able to communicate a detailed assessment of the Irish lesson directly to their children simply because so much of the focus in the teaching of Irish is on oral work which is confined to the classroom. Irrespective of the truth or otherwise of these observations, the coherence, immediacy and detail of pupils' comments generally, suggest that their content is primarily determined by the their own personal experience.

This is not to deny that certain issues may become more focused through peer interaction or through specific work in class. A high proportion of pupils in one class, for example, cited dislike of the sexist nature of the *Nuachúrsaí* (Table 4.6, class rank 7) suggesting some prior exchange of views on the topic. Issues may also become more focused in pupils' minds through reading the preceding multiple-choice attitudinal items on the *Pupil Questionnaire* itself. Phenomena such as these, however, are as likely to affect the assessments of adults as of children.

4.5.2 *Main themes in 'dislikes', 'likes' and desire for 'change'*

A number of broad themes surface in pupils' comments: the suitability of lesson materials and content, pupil's inability to understand the lesson or the teacher, Irish reading, grammar/spelling, written exercises, the degree of emphasis on Irish generally, and low self-esteem or general discouragement in relation to learning Irish. In many instances the same basic concern takes different forms, and is reinforced, in each of the three questions ('dislike', 'like' and desire for 'change'). Take, for example, ability to understand the lesson or the teacher. Results show that 17% of pupils 'dislike' the fact that they have difficulty in understanding generally. Consistent with this, a proportion of pupils (7.6%) respond by saying that what they 'like' in the present lesson is being able to understand what is being said and having explanations or translations. Continuing the theme in the third question, 14.1% of pupils would like to 'change' the lesson so that it is easier to understand and so that more explanations or translations are provided. In this regard also, it may be recalled from Chapter 3 (section 3.4.5) that 21% of pupils did *not* accept that they understood 'most of what the teacher says in Irish in school'.

Sometimes a measure of disagreement emerges when we compare responses to the three questions. For example, just over 16% of pupils dislike 'grammar-related activities' while 6.3% like them; and 13.9% of pupils dislike written exercises while 16.7% like them. It is worth noting that while grammar is the most frequently mentioned pupil 'dislike' (26% of learners) in Pattison's (1989) study of young FL learners, it only ranks third in the present Irish study.

Finally, the salience of the more common themes varies across classes. For example, all classes in the high-Irish-achievement group have either grammar or spelling as the most commonly mentioned 'dislike' but these same aspects do not feature as a common 'dislike' in any of the low-Irish-achievement classes. It is also notable that differences between classes tend to be more obvious in response to the 'dislike' question. It is not clear why this should be so. One possibility is that pupils may make their most important points in response to the first question, which happens to deal with 'dislikes'. If that were the case, their responses to the remaining two questions might often tend to involve elaboration or clarification. Alternatively, perhaps, it is simply that 'dislikes' more easily come into focus for pupils, or even that 'dislikes' are in some way easier to articulate.

4.5.3 *Suitability of lesson content and materials*

Pupils clearly identify sources of dissatisfaction and propose definite remedies in relation to lesson content and materials. They dislike both *Nuachúrsaí-related activities and materials* (at almost 30% the most common theme of all) and the fact that the present courses/lessons are *boring old fashioned and repetitious* (15.1%). The objection to the *Nuachúrsaí* is reinforced in responses to the question about 'change' where 6.1% want to *dispense with film strips/projector* and 4.9% want *less or no use of the Nuachúrsaí*. In contrast, what pupils like are *conversations, games, drama, songs and poems* (25.7%). They also want to change the present course so that it has *more conversations, games, drama, songs and poems* (13.6%) and so that it is *more modern, more fun, more realistic, and non-sexist* (16.1%). More generally, they want *new materials* (8.8%).

It is possible that some of the negative feelings associated with the *Nuachúrsaí* are not only represented by those thematic categories which involve actual mention of the *Nuachúrsaí* (e.g. *Nuachúrsaí-related activities and materials*). The juxtaposition of responses sometimes suggests that the social/lifestyle content of the *Nuachúrsaí* is at least one of the targets of pupil dissatisfaction when they refer to the lesson being *boring, old-fashioned and repetitious*. We must also consider that pupils may sometimes mention the *Nuachúrsaí* as a defining example of a general approach they do not like, one in which language practice and repetition are dominant. But frequent mention of dislike of the *Nuachúrsaí* does not necessarily mean that the *Nuachúrsaí* - or audio-visual equipment - are employed for a large part of the Irish lesson in these classes. In Chapter 7, for example, we note that, over all lessons observed, only 9.1% of segments (12.1% of lesson time) involved the use of film strips. Use of *Nuachúrsaí* topics and of the *Nuachúrsaí* handbook likewise were found in only about 10% of segments. One other point of relevance is that we cannot discount the possibility that if the *Nuachúrsaí* content were more satisfactory - if the language/communication and visual content were *more modern, more fun, more realistic, non-sexist* - that some of the other aspects of the method, such as the use of the projector and film strips, might not be seen as quite so objectionable. Unfortunately, the kind of data available to us here simply does not allow us to tease out these complexities.

Use of the *Nuachúrsaí* is not always associated with negative pupil reaction - 8.4% of pupils actually like them. Nor are the objections equally strong in all classes. In particular, neither 'dislike' of *Nuachúrsaí-related activities and materials,* nor dislike of existing lessons/materials on the basis that they are *boring, old-fashioned or repetitious,* are common themes in any of the high-Irish-achievement classes. This is so, even though the *Nuachúrsaí* are used in at least some of these classes. In other words, the *Nuachúrsaí* do not appear to pose a real problem for pupils who are doing well at Irish already. But the two negative themes just mentioned do surface in the negative responses of middle- and low-Irish-achievement classes. Dislike of *Nuachúrsaí-related activities and materials,* for example, is a common theme in all but one of the middle-Irish-achievement classes and in half the low-Irish-achievement classes.

How can we account for this difference in pupils' experience of the *Nuachúrsaí?* One possibility is that in high-Irish-achievement classes the use of the *Nuachúrsaí* is embedded in a different language-learning context; another is that the *Nuachúrsaí* themselves are used in a different way. It is plausible to think, for example, that the greater emphasis on content-based (Irish-medium) teaching in high-Irish-achievement classes would have the effect of making the 'labour' that goes into *Nuachúrsaí*-based language practice more meaningful for pupils - the vocabulary and structures learned are put to real communicative use in studying other school subjects through Irish.

A related possibility is that there are different emphases on the various *Nuachúrsaí* lesson-steps in high-Irish-achievement classes. One of the complaints commonly made about the implementation of the *Nuachúrsaí* generally (INTO, 1985a) is that activities prescribed in the final 'step' of each lesson, titled 'Free creative conversation', were often not implemented due to the amount of time required by the earlier repetition-based and grammar-related lesson-steps. There is some indirect evidence from the classroom observation data to be presented later in Chapter 7 that this may be true of the classes in the present study. The evidence in question shows that high-Irish-achievement classes spend significantly more lesson time than other classes on activities involving real and simulated communication in Irish (similar to some 'free creative conversation' activities) and relatively less time on language practice (similar to the earlier non-communicative or language-practice lesson-steps in the audio-visual method).

Having said that, however, we must acknowledge that there may be no simple, consistent relationship between pupils' affective reaction to various aspects of the Irish lesson and actual achievement in Irish. The fact that pupils find the *Nuachúrsaí,* or indeed any other aspect of the teaching of Irish disagreeable, does not necessarily mean that the impact of their use on the learning of Irish is in every respect negative. Obviously, we must take expressions of dislike very seriously in any area of learning. Nevertheless, the articulation of a particular dislike may merely indicate that resistance to the routine effort of learning the language has become focused on that aspect of the course. One example of this, perhaps, is the fact that all high-Irish-achievement classes cite either spelling or grammar as their most common dislike while none of the low-Irish-achievement classes do. Yet we could hardly claim that grammar or spelling were, therefore, inadvisable in high-Irish-achievement classes. Indeed the pupils' success may in part be determined by just these activities. To put it another way, if Irish lessons or courses of a completely different kind to the present ones were introduced, some other elements of these new courses might well become the focus of pupil complaints.

What distinguishes objections to the *Nuachúrsaí* and the desire for new materials, however, is the pervasiveness of the themes - their re-occurrence in different forms in response to all three questions. This, together with the strength of feeling evident in many of the pupils' comments, leaves little doubt that what a substantial proportion of pupils really want is the replacement of the *Nuachúrsaí*. Evidence that dislike of the *Nuachúrsaí* is particularly concentrated in the middle-Irish-achievement group increases the importance of the issue because this group represents the largest proportion of classes nationally.

The implicit alternative to the *Nuachúrsaí* proposed by pupils - lessons and materials which emphasise *conversations, games, drama, songs and poems* and which are *more modern, more fun, more realistic, and non-sexist* - is interesting in two respects. First, it represents an orientation which is similar in important respects to the communicative approach to language teaching. Second, these preferences emerge in classes at all levels of achievement in Irish in the present study.

It is not surprising, then, that teachers involved in the *Communicative Materials Project* reported a very positive reaction to the new communicative materials from pupils. This is not to make any claims for the merits of these particular materials but simply to suggest that the communicative orientation probably responds to at least some of the difficulties and complaints mentioned by pupils here. One of the more challenging problems which the *Communicative Materials Project* faced was to produce materials which were modern, realistic and 'fun' and which would reflect the reality of the pupils' own life and experience. This meant identifying contexts of use, situations and speech styles in Irish which are sufficiently plausible and interesting that they would engage pupils - despite the paradox that spoken Irish of any kind may have little reality for pupils in these very same situations in their ordinary lives. This has always been a difficulty for course developers but arguably the challenge to respond to it is presented particularly clearly in a communicative approach (Harris *et al.*, 1996a,b). We return to this issue at the end of the report (section 10.4) where we consider some of the more practical implications for providing communicative materials in Irish.

4.5.4 *Difficulty in understanding and apathy in low-Irish-achievement classes*

Two concerns are frequently expressed by pupils in low-Irish achievement classes: (a) apathy, discouragement and a general desire to disengage from the learning of Irish and (b) inability to understand the lesson or teacher. The concerns emerge in response to all three write-in questions, but particularly in response to those relating to 'dislikes' and desired 'changes'. These same issues appear occasionally in middle- and high-Irish-achievement classes but to a considerably lesser extent. The 'apathy/negativity' themes are not entirely surprising given the evidence in Chapter 3 of higher Irish-lesson anxiety and less positive attitudes to Irish in low-Irish-achievement classes. The direct comments of pupils, however, are more revealing and more convincing than scores based on multiple-choice attitude items could ever be. In addition, they succeed in highlighting 'difficulty in understanding' as at least one important source of the apathy and negativity.

Sometimes both concerns ('apathy/negativity' and 'difficulty understanding') appear in a cause-effect relationship in pupils responses - 'I don't like Irish at all because I don't understand it ....'. More generally, however, we are making the assumption that because the two themes appear so frequently in low-Irish-achievement classes, there is in all probability a real link between them. 'Difficulty in understanding' is cited as a common 'dislike' in more than half the low-Irish-achievement classes. In addition, the provision of lessons which would be 'easier to understand' features as a common desired 'change' in three quarters of the low-achievement classes.

Apathy and a desire to disengage from the learning of Irish, expressed in a number of forms, appears as a common theme in response to the 'change' question: 'stop teaching Irish altogether' (two classes), have 'less emphasis on Irish' (one class), 'would not like any change' (two classes) and 'no comment' (one class). We interpret the latter two themes ('would not like any change' and 'no comment') as 'negative' when they occur in low-Irish-achievement classes on the basis of information on Irish-lesson anxiety and general Irish attitude-motivation in these classes. Similar themes of apathy and negativity appear in response to the 'dislike' and 'like' questions: anxiety and low self-esteem in relation to Irish (one class), 'generally negative about the Irish lesson' (one class), and 'like nothing about Irish' (two classes).

It is important not to either understate or overstate the scale of the problems revealed by these results. In the highest-ranking class within the low-Irish-achievement group, a frequently expressed desire was actually to have 'more time devoted to Irish and/or more teaching through Irish'. This was so despite the fact that pupils in this class were also frequently unhappy about difficulties in understanding and wanted lessons to be 'easier to understand'. It must be borne in mind also that the main group of low-Irish-achievement classes, in which apathy/negativity were common, fall just within the lowest 10% of classes nationally in terms of achievement in Irish. This should probably be interpreted as a minimum estimate, however, because classes in the range of achievement immediately above this main group are not adequately represented in the present study.

But even if the true proportion of low-Irish-achievement classes in which these problems occurred amounted to no more than 10% nationally, they would still represent a significant educational problem. At the most basic level, access to 'comprehensible input' is essential to success in second-language learning (Krashen, 1985, 1991). But the concern extends beyond the language learning process itself. The anxiety and even panic which primary school pupils can experience when they are 'put on the spot' by being asked to speak in front of the class is described vividly by Holt (1994). Where there are, in addition, problems in understanding, it is easy to see how the anxiety associated with the whole public-performance aspect of the Irish lesson could develop into apathy and discouragement. As one pupil says here (Appendix 4, item 78, category H): 'I don't like it when the teacher asks me questions because if I get it wrong I get embarrassed'. Another complains: '..I am no good at it and most other people that are good at it laugh at me.'

Of course, difficulties in understanding are unlikely to be the only cause of the apathy and negativity in low-Irish achievement classes. Among the common themes in at least some of these classes are dissatisfaction about the *boring, old-fashioned or repetitious* nature of existing materials and the desire to change the course to make it *more modern, more fun, more realistic, and non-sexist* and to include *more conversations, games, drama, songs and poems.* No doubt these issues would have been cited more often were it not for the fact that they are superseded in terms of pupil concern by the more important theme of 'difficulty in understanding'. Arguably, low-Irish-achievement classes are particularly badly affected by activities and materials which are not inherently interesting. Pupils with higher levels of achievement in Irish have the compensation of being able to 'shine' in the kind of whole-class, teacher-focused, oral language-practice which is common in most schools (see Chapters 7 - 9).

Holt (1994: 10) warns that a child who is bored may gradually devote less attention, energy and intelligence to school tasks, a pattern which over time can become so much a habit that the child begins to 'think of himself as stupid'. Classroom observation data to be presented in Chapters 7 - 9, give an indication of the price to be paid for the difficulties in understanding and apathy which we have just described: an unwillingness on the part of less able pupils to make individual contributions in class, a greater propensity to remain silent and a lower level of attentiveness to the lesson.

The experimental materials developed for the *Communicative Materials Project* represent one attempt to respond to problems of difficulty in understanding and apathy/disinterest. One of our aims was to devise activities, games, and tasks which would be within the linguistic and communicative competence of all pupils but which would also demand their attention and interest. In the first place, we tried to ensure that the basic communicative activity in each lesson was simple enough so that all pupils could understand and participate. In addition, we 'recycled' communicative functions and linguistic material from one lesson to the next but, critically, always in the context of a novel communicative task or activity. The recycling was, in part, a response to the common complaint made about the *Nuachúrsaí* from the beginning that too much new linguistic material appeared in each lesson, with the result that many pupils never succeeded in attaining mastery of it. To cater for more able pupils and classes, we included a range of more challenging activities (*Dushláin Bhreise*), activities which could be developed from or built on the basic lesson (see Appendix 1.1)

A number of other recommendations were made in the context of the *Communicative Materials Project* with the aim of increasing the involvement of less able pupils. One of these was that pupils would be encouraged to take chances and to try different approaches in order to get their message across in class. If pupils can accept that making mistakes is an essential part of learning a language, the prospect of speaking in class may become less daunting. Other approaches such as increasing the response wait-time for pupils and increasing the amount of group work, are mentioned in Chapters 8 and 9.

As mentioned earlier the current view of motivation is that setting clearly defined goals for learners and promoting feelings of self-efficacy can lead to higher levels of motivation. Consistent with this, teachers in the *Communicative Materials Project* were encouraged to tell pupils at the beginning of a lesson what they were about to learn and to summarise later what they had succeeded in learning or what they were able to 'do' in Irish. Pupils need some yardstick by which they can measure or mark their own progress, particularly in the case of oral work, so that they have the experience of gradually attaining mastery.

While we cannot claim that any specific one of these initiatives was successful, there is no doubt that our general strategy was welcomed by teachers in the *Communicative Materials Project*. A widespread opinion was that those pupils who were weaker at Irish benefitted particularly from the new approach. Pupils who had barely participated in the lesson previously were found to be joining enthusiastically in the new activities and were proud to be able to actually communicate in Irish. Reading through the spontaneous comments of pupils in the present study also, it becomes even more clear why the kind of new initiatives we have been talking about would receive a welcome generally: 'If we did more fun work, like plays, chatting and games, we would be more eager to work....'. Another says: 'I like Irish when you know what you're talking about and you don't get embarrassed in front of your friends. It's great fun when you know it' (see Appendix 4: item 79, category H).

4.5.5 *The popularity of Irish reading*

Reading activities and specific readers constitutes the most commonly expressed 'like' overall (28.2% of pupils). Despite this, a substantial proportion (14.5%) actually dislike reading. And only 4.5% actually want lessons which involve more reading. There is no clear evidence of variation between high-, middle- and low-Irish achievement classes as far as preferences for or against Irish reading are concerned. It may be noted in passing that while reading also ranked highly (second) among the 'likes' responses of young foreign-language learners in Pattison's (1989) study, the percentage (16%) was lower than in the Irish study.

No particularly strong reasons for either disliking or liking Irish reading emerge from the pupils' comments. Some of explanations given for *disliking* reading are 'not liking the stories, not being good at reading and not being able to understand'. Among the reasons given for *liking* reading are 'understanding' the material, having 'everything explained', 'not making a mistake', 'answering the questions' and 'reading aloud' (see Appendix 4). In general terms, of course, it should not be at all surprising that pupils would like Irish reading, assuming that the material was at an appropriate level of difficulty and was geared to their interests. Perhaps the material in readers is simply better geared to pupils' interests than the (orally-based) *Nuachúrsaí* material is. It may be worth noting that Bennett (1997) suggests that more recent readers may represent an improvement on previous textbooks - colourfully illustrated, modern topics relevant to the needs and interests of children, well balanced in terms of elements of culture, heritage and humour, religious themes, and depiction of male and female roles.

It is quite possible also that pupils may simply like some aspects, or kinds of, Irish reading and dislike others. One common activity in low-Irish-achievement classes, as the classroom observation data to be presented later in Chapter 8 shows, is language-practice type reading aloud. This kind of reading activity - round-robin practice reading would be one example - is associated with significantly *lower* class interest than other kinds of activities. This does not necessarily mean that pupils dislike all aspects of reading aloud. They might enjoy the performance aspect of reading aloud themselves, the sense of competence it gives them, and yet lose interest and become distracted when the focus is on their classmates reading.

One other reason why Irish reading might be favoured by pupils should be mentioned - namely that it is easier for pupils and their parents to perceive their progress in the case of reading than in the case of some other aspects of Irish. While this factor may be tangential to the experience of reading as such, it is potentially important. At the end of a lesson or series of lessons, pupils know just how many pages or stories they have 'got through'. In contrast to oral work, the targets in reading may appear clearer, more attainable and more real to pupils. Once again, it may be simply because of their measurability in this sense, that Irish reading achievements receive more approbation from parents than achievements in oral Irish (see Chapter 5: section 5.3.3).

Pupils probably get relatively few opportunities to demonstrate their progress in oral Irish outside school. This in turn may go some way towards explaining why - as we reported in Chapter 3 (section 3.3.1) - pupils' Irish ability self-concept is better for Irish reading than for spoken Irish. Where the oral-Irish component of the lesson consists almost entirely of language-practice activities, weaker pupils may gradually develop the feeling that they are making no progress in this area. Their experience may be that the ultimate goal of learning the language - using it for real spoken communication in the way they use English - is something never attained but always deferred to some vague future date. This reinforces the point made earlier about the need for a yardstick by which even the weakest pupils would be able to judge their progress in each aspect of Irish. The goal should be that all pupils would experience success in all areas of Irish, and that they would be told in clear terms of that progress.

5 Parents' views and practices

5.1 Introduction

We now have a considerable amount of information on public attitudes to Irish from the original Committee on Irish Language Attitudes Research survey (CLAR, 1975), the partial replications of that survey by Ó Riagáin and Ó Gliasáin (1984, 1994) and the 1985 Irish National Teachers' Organisation surveys (INTO, 1985a,b). All of these surveys indicate a high level of public support for Irish in general, as well as for the teaching of Irish in primary school. The INTO-commissioned study of public attitudes (INTO, 1985b) found significant support (84% of respondents) for the 'inclusion of Irish in the primary school curriculum' and for the amount of time spent teaching Irish (52% say it is just right while 22% would like more time).

In the most recent national study on language attitudes in Ireland, Ó Riagáin and Ó Gliasáin (1994: 24) report an 'upward shift in favour of maintaining the teaching of Irish to most Irish school children'. This conclusion was based on the increase, over two decades, in the proportion of respondents who reported that they would be 'sorry' if children stopped doing Irish in school. The proportions agreeing with this option grew from approximately 67% in 1973 to 78% and 76% respectively in the 1983 and 1993 surveys. Despite general support for the teaching of Irish, the latter surveys indicate that over two thirds of those interviewed agreed with the statements that *'children seldom learn enough Irish to use it after school'*, and that *'if Irish were taught better in the schools, more people would speak it'* while over half agreed that children *'resent having to learn Irish in school'*.

No information is available on attitudes to Irish specifically among parents who have children in primary school, or the manner in which these adult attitudes relate either to the attitudes of the children themselves or to their success in acquiring proficiency in speaking the language at school. Surveys of teachers, however, provide valuable indirect information on perceived parents' attitudes to the teaching of Irish. The INTO (1985a) survey showed that teachers who were less favourably disposed to teaching Irish considered the major demotivating influences to be the lack of (i) pupil motivation (80%), (ii) parental support (75%) and (iii) community backup (67%).

As part of an ITÉ national survey of achievement in Irish also carried out in 1985, sixth-grade primary teachers views on the teaching of Irish were also sought (Harris and Murtagh, 1988b). This included questions on how teachers perceived parents' attitudes to Irish and involvement in their children's education. Opinion was divided on the extent to which parents were involved in their child's education, with 58% of sixth-grade teachers reporting that parents played a 'small'/'reasonably small' role and the remainder saying that parents in general played a 'large'/'reasonably large' role. In terms of attitude to

Irish, over half of teachers (58%) considered parents to be 'neutral'. while almost a third (30%) thought that parents were 'favourable'/'very favourable'. Another 12% thought parents were 'negative'. Responses to two other questions indicated that teachers believed parents to be satisfied with their children's ability in Irish (93% 'satisfied'/'very satisfied') and with the amount of time being spent on Irish (85% 'satisfied').

5.1.1 *Parental involvement in education*
Any examination of parental involvement in the child's learning of Irish must be put in the context of more general issues and research relating to parents and education. These issues include (i) the growth of involvement by parents in education in Ireland in recent years, (ii) research relating to the effects of home background and parental involvement on educational progress and child development, (iii) the effect of intervention programmes which focus on parents and the home in the case of disadvantaged populations, and (iv) questions such as the amount and the effect of parental involvement in homework. In this section, we examine each of these areas briefly as a background to the present study of parental views and practices in relation to Irish.

The growth of parental involvement
In the last few decades the role of Irish parents in their children's education has been gradually expanding. The first positive step towards inclusiveness came in 1975 with the decision to have parents represented on Boards of Management. Another important development was the establishment of the National Parents' Council (NPC) in 1985. Since then the Council has worked to raise the profile of parents in education, seeking a role which involves consultation and partnership in the process. Its members have been represented on the *Primary Curriculum Review Body* (Department of Education, 1990a) and on the *Primary Education Review Body* (Department of Education, 1990b).

The present decade has also seen greater efforts by the Department of Education and Science to promote and extend parental involvement. In 1991 a Department circular to primary schools (see INTO, 1997) requested that a Parents' Association would be formed in association with the school (where one was not already in existence) and that as part of the overall school plan there be a 'clearly defined policy for productive parental involvement'. The White Paper on Education - *Charting our Education Future* (Department of Education, 1995b) - also emphasizes the partnership dimensions of education, the central role played by parents in this partnership and their right to 'active participation in their children's education'. The government pledges to promote the active participation of parents 'at every level of the education process', and gives formal recognition to the NPC as the representative body for parents, and states that each school will be required to develop a 'formal home-school links policy'. This policy is to be formulated in cooperation with the Parents' Association and is to include 'initiatives aimed at raising awareness of the parents' role in facilitating the child's learning, with particular advice on homework'. Other objectives are the provision of 'information and training in relevant instructional skills and the provision of formal education and training programmes for parents'. The proposed Education (No 2) Bill (1997), in a section devoted to Parents' Associations, reaffirms the role of parents and the duty of the boards of management to promote contact between the school, the parents and the community.

The INTO (1996b) support and acknowledge the importance of parental involvement on boards of management and in the general life of the school. More recently the organisation (INTO, 1997) has developed the debate on this issue of involvement, referring particularly to the need for the time and space in each school for parent-teacher contact, in-service education in this general area for teachers, formal opportunities to explain the curriculum to parents, and a school policy on homework.

Research on parental involvement

Three major reports on schooling in Britain all emphasize the importance of parental involvement in children's education (Plowden, 1967; Bullock, 1975; Cockroft, 1982). In particular, the Plowden Study showed that more of the variation in children's school achievement could be accounted for by variation in parents' attitudes than by either variation in material circumstances of homes or by variation in schools. The positive influence of parents' attitudes, interest and aspirations on their children's educational achievements has also been shown in numerous other studies (Miller, 1971; Osborne and Milbank, 1987; Mortimore, Sammons, Stoll, Lewis, and Ecob, 1988; Applebee, Langer, and Mullis, 1989). The relative influence of parental characteristics, parental involvement, home circumstance, however, is not clear. Marjoribanks (1979) who assessed studies across three continents emphasised the complexity of the 'network of interrelated family environment variables that are associated with children's cognitive and affective outcomes'.

There are indications that early home learning and the involvement of parents in schoolwork in the early years is particularly important for subsequent achievement in school (Tizard and Hughes, 1984). In a project involving parents in curriculum matters in the reception classes of infant schools, Dye (1989) reported that experimental groups of pupils experiencing parental involvement made significant gains in many areas - language development, understanding of basic concepts, concentration, social maturity, and mathematical skills. By comparison, control groups made few gains. Another study in which parents became involved in a structured way in the mathematics curriculum showed benefits not only in terms of the children's mathematical skills, but also in terms of the attitudes of parents and children to the subject itself (Merttens and Vass, 1987).

This positive evidence has prompted numerous intervention type programmes aimed particularly at disadvantaged populations. An early example of this was the Haringey Project (Tizard, Schofield and Hewison, 1982) which focussed on improving reading through parental involvement. The results showed a marked improvement in attitude toward and achievement in reading - even in the case of children who were 'below average' to start. Other projects (Hannon and Jackson, 1987; Tizard, Mortimore, and Burchell, 1988) where parents promoted reading in the home, however, showed no greater increase in children's reading achievement compared to controls. It has been posited (Macbeth,

1989; Toomey, 1993) that the crucial element for success in parental involvement programmes is careful planning and monitoring and constant support and backup from the school for parents.

Here in Ireland, a government initiative, known as 'The Home-School-Community Liaison Scheme' which aimed to involve parents from disadvantaged areas in their children's education was launched in 1990. This scheme, initially targeted 55 primary schools classified as disadvantaged but has since been extended to include more schools. Local coordinators were appointed to liaise between parents and teachers to 'establish confidence, trust, mutual support and cooperation between parents and teachers, thereby enhancing perceptions and attitudes to the social, behavioural, and educational advantage of the children' (Department of Education, 1990c). The main activities of these coordinators consisted of initiating parents' courses and activities, home visits and meetings with parents, teachers and pupils. Initial evaluations indicate several favourable outcomes (Ryan, 1995). Among these are more positive parental attitudes to the school, improved parent-teacher relations and increased parental involvement in children's homework. Although only very limited information is available on the impact of the programme on pupils themselves, reports from coordinators point to pupil benefits such as improved behaviour, improved attendance, improved scholastic achievement, greater care in school work, and more positive attitudes towards school and teachers, to themselves and to their parents.

In 1995, a four year, Irish-government and EU funded primary school Parents' Programme was set in place. This programme has enabled the NPC-Primary to provide a range of support and training for parents. The programme aims to have in place by the end of 1999 the personnel, materials and organisational arrangements required for the training and development of parents. Among the programmes implemented so far are - The Parents' Association Effectiveness Programme, Local Training Initiatives for Partnership and The Parenting for Learning Programme. One indication of the success of the various initiatives is the high degree of uptake: by the end of 1997, 10,000 parents had participated and had undertaken 150,000 hours of training and development (NPC, 1998).

Homework and parental involvement
Studies in Britain and the United States have indicated that homework itself is academically beneficial. Paschal, Weinstein and Walberg (1984) who conducted a 'quantitative synthesis' of 15 empirical studies revealed strong positive effects of homework on learning - though homework which was graded or contained teachers' comments produced stronger effects. A large scale study of adolescents in the United States (Keith, Reimers, Fehrman, Potterbaum, and Aubey, 1986) showed that, after controlling for ability and family background, individual pupils who spent more time on homework achieved higher results than average. A more recent British study (Holmes and Croll, 1989) reported that time spent on homework had a strong positive association with academic performance even after the student's general ability and social class background were controlled. Even though social class background was only weakly related to time

spent on homework, the link between time on homework and academic performance was considerably stronger for pupils from working class backgrounds. Another interesting finding was that the variable most strongly related with time spent on homework was the frequency with which parents signed their child's homework diary. It has been pointed out (Cooper, 1989; Hallam and Cowan, 1998) that the positive effects of time spent on homework are more clearly established at secondary level than at primary level.

A number of studies (e.g. Maertens and Johnson, 1972; Chen and Stevenson, 1989) show that parental help with homework boosts children's achievements. Other studies, however, show no effect or even negative associations. A study of maternal involvement in first and third grade children's homework (Levin, Levy-Schiff, Appelbaum-Peled, Katz, Komar, and Meiran, 1997) found no effect of help on the child's academic performance. They also found that weaker children received more help from their parents. Furthermore, their results indicated that helping with homework could be counterproductive, leading sometimes to helplessness, dependency or frustration on the part of the child. Epstein (1983) found that the time parents spent helping their child with homework correlated negatively with the child's reading achievement. There is evidence too that the extent of parental help may vary with the age of the child (Macbeth and Turner, 1990; Stevenson, Chen, and Uttal, 1990). Parents' lack of subject-matter knowledge may become an issue as children get older, especially in disadvantaged populations.

Unfortunately, there is rather little information available on the amount of time Irish children typically spend on homework, the extent to which parents are involved, or the possible impact of either of these factors on children's academic achievements. A study of achievement in mathematics and science in Ireland (Martin, Hickey and Murchan, 1992) conducted as part of the International Assessment of Educational Progress shows that practically all nine year olds (98%) say they are assigned homework each evening. While no figures were given for the average amount of time spent on homework generally, the report states that 'typically, 9 year olds in the study spend less than one hour completing their homework for all subjects each evening'. Whether the latter refers to all pupils in all countries or to Irish pupils only is not clear. Martin *et al.* (1992) also report that the group of students who received help with their homework did not achieve higher levels in mathematics than those who did not receive help. They surmise that it is the weaker students who are more likely to obtain help. This conclusion is consistent with the earlier mentioned Levin *et al.* (1997) study.

At the moment there are no official departmental guidelines relating to how much homework Irish primary school children should be assigned. Individual schools, however, tend to have a policy in relation to homework incorporated into the school plan. The NPC-Primary consider homework important because it 'represents a direct link between the home and school and, as such, should offer a very good opportunity for the development of practical partnership between parent, child and teacher' (NPC, 1991). The Council, however, would like more clarity regarding homework policy. They argue that parents need to have a clear understanding of the part they are expected to play in the child's homework, the amount and type of homework and the time to be allotted to it. They argue that it is important that parents have 'structured participation ..... in a directed way in areas such as reading and mathematics'. They are concerned at what they see as parents' low input in mathematics and Irish due to parents' lack of competence in these subjects.

Broadly similar opinions relating to homework are expressed by teachers. The recent INTO report (INTO, 1997: 26) points out that the regular checking of homework by parents serves a number of desirable educational objectives including a means of 'involving parents in their children's work in school' and providing them with the 'opportunity to see the work the child is doing in school and form their own judgments on how the child is progressing.' While the organisation believes that the type of homework to be set, how it is marked, and how long it should take are largely professional matters for the teachers/school, it also proposes that all schools should formulate homework policy in consultation with parents' representatives. The INTO calls on the Department, in consultation with parent and teacher representatives, to draw up guidelines on parental involvement in homework which would make clear the responsibilities of parents.

5.1.2 *The present study: Parents' attitudes and practices in relation to Irish*

The purpose of this part of the present study was (a) to investigate the possibility of collecting information on parental attitudes and practices in relation to Irish by means of a questionnaire sent to parents via the school and the individual child, and (b) to establish the usefulness of such information in explaining achievement in spoken Irish and attitude to Irish among sixth-grade pupils. The questionnaire was concerned with such issues as general parental attitudes to Irish and to the teaching of Irish, parental praise and encouragement of the child, parents' views of their own child's progress in Irish, parents' knowledge of how Irish is taught in school, parents' willingness to help with and supervise their child's Irish homework on a regular basis, and related issues.

One question of more general interest is how exactly, and why, the positive public attitudes to Irish documented in various surveys fail to be translated into pupil success in acquiring proficiency in the language at school - at least a level of success which would gain parental approval and acceptance. Needless to say, a study on such a modest scale as the present one cannot hope to do anything more than provide a partial or preliminary answer. The fact that we are using individual items rather than scales to represent important parental attitude variables, imposes obvious limits on the kinds of conclusions we can reach.

5.2 Method

5.2.1 *Development and administration of the Parents' Questionnaire.*

The *Parents' Questionnaire* (Appendix 5.3) consists of 29 items, mostly in multiple choice form, covering the parents' general and linguistic background, their child and Irish, the school and Irish, and homework. While questionnaires in this area are usually administered by a trained interviewer who makes direct contact with the adult respondent in question, this would not have been either a desirable or feasible approach in the present case. Since many of the questions related to the school which the respondent's child was attending or to the child's performance in that school, a direct approach to the parent without going through the school would have been inappropriate. We were fortunate, therefore, that the relevant class teachers and principals in all the schools approached readily gave their support to the idea of the individual children distributing the questionnaires to their parents (in sealed envelopes) and collecting them again later. While this approach was very successful in the present case, the implications for future work of this kind may very much depend on the nature and scope of particular projects. For example, although our testing and classroom observation work placed great demands on pupils and teachers, the very scale and detail of the work had the effect of generating a considerable amount of interest and goodwill over the course of the few days we were in the schools.

Clearly, in a situation like this, the perceived and actual confidentiality of the completed questionnaires is a critical issue. It will be useful, therefore, to describe briefly the instructions given to inspectors regarding the distribution and collection of copies of the *Parents' Questionnaire* (see Appendix 5.1) and the instructions given to the parents themselves (Appendix 5.2).

The inspector was asked to give each pupil a sealed envelope with an ID number in the top right hand corner to be brought home to his/her parents. Each envelope contained (a) a copy of the *Parents' Questionnaire* which had the same ID on the cover as on the above mentioned envelope; (b) an explanatory letter for parents; (c) a pre-addressed envelope for returning the completed questionnaire. Since each returned *Parents' Questionnaire* would have only an ID number on the cover, a 'List of ID's' was also to be prepared. The inspector was asked to distribute the envelope personally to the relevant pupil and to write either the child's first name or the parents' name on the envelope just before handing it to the child (in case any of the children themselves inadvertently mixed up their envelopes later on). It was emphasised to the children that they were to give the actual envelope they received to their parents. As a final precaution, the teacher was asked to write the pupils' initials (only) on each envelope as it was returned.

Although each envelope normally contained an English version of the *Parents' Questionnaire*, copies of the Irish version were also made available. If parents required the Irish version they were asked to note this on the returning envelope and an Irish version would be sent out. One Irish version was sent out without being explicitly requested since it was known that this would be the preferred version. No parent requested an Irish version. Each teacher and principal was also given a copy of the *Parents' Questionnaire* and covering letter and allowed time to examine them before any copies were distributed. The work was to proceed only if the teacher and principal had no objection.

The explanatory letter which accompanied the blank copy of each *Parents' Questionnaire* (see Appendix 5.2) told the parent that his/her child's class was being involved in a study of the teaching and learning of Irish. It was explained that the study was being carried out in a number of schools by the Department of Education in association with ITÉ. Since an important part of this work was to determine parents' views on the teaching and learning of Irish, they were being asked to answer the questions on the enclosed questionnaire. It was emphasised that it was the parents' personal opinions which were being sought and that there were no right or wrong answers.

The completed questionnaire was to be placed in an accompanying envelope, sealed, and given to the child to return to the school. It was explained that the parents' opinions were being sought for general research purposes only, and that the views expressed would have no effect either on the child or the school. An assurance was given that no pupil or parent would be identified and that only ITÉ researchers would see their replies. Finally, it was noted that the child's own teacher knew that the parent's opinion was being sought.

Directions to the parents printed inside each copy of the Questionnaire specified that it should be completed by the parent/guardian who had the greater involvement in the child's school work e.g. the parent who usually bought schoolbooks, supervised homework, attended meetings in the school etc. Where both parents were equally involved, either parent might complete it. The Questionnaire was to be completed by the parents themselves without consulting the child. It was also pointed out that references to 'the school' in various questions meant the school the child was attending at present.

5.2.2 Sample and response rate

The *Parents' Questionnaires* were distributed to only seven of the original twenty classes since we were unsure if the *Questionnaire* itself, and the system for distributing and collecting it, would be either effective or acceptable to teachers. All classes were in Dublin and surrounding areas. None of these classes happened to come from the 'high-Irish-achievement' group of classes: three were 'middle-Irish-achievement' classes and four were 'low-Irish-achievement' classes.

Of the 236 pupils in these seven classes, 198 or 84% of the parents returned completed Questionnaires. More mothers (67.7%) than fathers (27.8%) completed the Questionnaire (see Appendix 5.3, Q2). The response rate in different classes ranged from 65% in one of the disadvantaged schools to 100% in one of the schools selected on the basis of the high level of parental support/involvement which had been informally reported. A higher percentage of parents in the 'middle-Irish-achievement' group of classes responded to the questionnaire (range of between 93-100%) than in the 'low-Irish-achievement' group (65%-80%). By the time we had received sufficient returns from the parents associated with these seven classes to indicate that our approach was satisfactory, it was too late in the school year to extend the survey to the remaining schools.

One other important question to be considered is whether, within the 'Parent Sample' of classes, pupils whose parents completed the *Parents' Questionnaire* (n=198) differ in some way from the minority of pupils (n=38) whose parents did not respond. Table 5.1 looks at this question in terms of pupil achievement in Irish, pupil's general academic ability and social class. It is clear from the data presented that pupils whose parents did respond have a significantly higher level of achievement in spoken Irish, and come from a higher social class background (numerically lower social class ratings), than those pupils whose parents did not respond.   There is no significant difference in relation to pupil general academic ability.

Table 5.1
A comparison of pupil's achievement in spoken Irish, pupil's general ability and social class in two groups of sixth-grade pupils: (a) Those whose parents *responded* to the *Parents' Questionnaire* and (b) Those pupils whose parents *did not respond.*

	(a) Pupils whose parents *responded* to the Questionnaire *(n=198)*	(b) Pupils whose parents *did not respond* to the Questionnaire *(n=38)*	t-test t value	p
Pupil's achievement in Irish	*(n = 182)*	*(n = 32)*		
Mean listening score	41.1	33.4		
Standard Deviation	12.4	10.8	3.63	.001
Pupil's general academic ability	*(n = 172)*	*(n = 28)*		
Mean DVRT Standard Score	107.0	102.3		
Standard Deviation	16.4	14.7	1.56	NS
Parents' social class	*(n = 198)*	*(n = 37)*		
Mean rating (1= highest; 7= lowest)	3.8	5.0		
Standard Deviation	1.7	1.8	-3.71	.001

5.3 Results

5.3.1 Analysis of the data

Results of the Parent Survey are described under seven main headings:

1. Parental characteristics.
2. Parents' support for the pupil learning Irish.

3. Parents' contact with school and knowledge about Irish teaching.
4. Parents' perceptions of child's difficulties with Irish.
5. Parents and Irish homework.
6. Parents' general comments.
7. Predicting pupil attitude/motivation and achievement from parental data.

Under each of the first five headings, we analyse the data from a number of different perspectives (a) the distribution of parents' responses to items relating to the theme in question, (b) variations between 'middle-Irish-achievement' and 'low-Irish-achievement' classes as far as parents' views and practices are concerned, and (c) a correlation analysis of the relationship between views and practices, on the one hand, and *Pupil achievement in Irish* and *Pupil Irish attitude/motivation,* on the other. We conclude the Results section with a description of regression analyses which try to assess the relative importance of selected 'pupil' and 'parent' variables in predicting *Pupil achievement in Irish* and *Pupil Irish attitude/motivation.*

The following is a more detailed description of the presentation format for results relating to 1-5 above:

(a) *Percentage distribution of parents' responses to each item*

This data describes the percentage distribution of parents responses on selected questionnaire items. Occasionally, in the text, reference is made to items not presented in tabular form but which may be found in the item-by-item data in Appendix 5.3.

(b) *Class (school) variation in parent's responses*

The same format for presentation of these results is used as in Chapter 3. Column 1 of each table shows how each of the seven classes was ranked in terms of class achievement in spoken Irish. Alongside this is shown the distribution of responses for the relevant *Parents' Questionnaire* items. Only those items in which substantial variation across classes occurs are shown in tabular form.

(c) *Relationships between 'pupil' and 'parent' variables (correlations)*

The correlation analysis examines the relationships between individual-pupil and parent characteristics. All correlations may be found in one large table (Table 5.5) in section 5.3.2 below. The majority of the 'parent variables' selected for inclusion in this table are significantly correlated with at least one of the two main 'pupil' variables of interest - *Pupil achievement in Irish* and *Pupil Irish attitude/motivation.* In relation to *Pupil achievement in Irish*, we confine ourselves, as in the analysis in earlier chapters, to total 'listening score' on the sixth-grade ITÉ test of spoken Irish. We also draw attention to some of the potentially interesting interrelationships between *Parents' Questionnaire* items themselves - how parent characteristics and practices are related to each other. Only those correlation values which confirm/disconfirm the major significant trends and relationships in the data are mentioned in the text.

Note that we have included a number of background variables - *Pupil gender, Social class, Pupil general academic ability* - even though these had been previously examined in Chapters 2 and 3. They are included here because we now need to establish their significance in relation to parents' attitudes and practices. At this stage, however, it will be useful to note that whether based on seven classes or twenty classes, the major relationships all remain the same (Table 5.5. and Table 3.11) e.g. the relationship between *Social class* and *Pupil general academic ability* or between *Pupil general academic ability* and *Pupil achievement in Irish*. The relationship between *Social class* and *Pupil achievement in Irish* is weaker in the seven classes analysis than in the twenty classes analysis but it is still significant. The relationship between *Social class* and *Pupil Irish attitude/motivation,* which is barely significant in the twenty-class analysis, is no longer significant in the seven-class analysis.

The majority of *Questionnaire* items had a multiple-choice format in which parents selected one of a number of response options e.g. in the case of *Parent's own attitude to Irish* (see Appendix 5.3, Q5) five options ranging from 'strongly in favour' to 'strongly against it' were offered. In coding such variables, the common-sense notion of what constituted 'more', or a 'more positive' value, of the variable being measured was assigned a higher numerical value. Thus, in the case of the example above, a value of 5 was assigned to the positively worded option 'strongly in favour' and a value of '1' was assigned to the negatively worded option 'strongly against it' and so on. It will be recalled, however, that this general rule did *not* apply to *Social class*. *Social class,* which was negatively coded, retains the same form as in earlier chapters (see Chapters 2 and 3): the lowest social class is assigned a numerical value of '7' and the highest a value of '1'.

Finally, the remaining two headings, 6 and 7 above, concern parents' general comments and the use of regression methods to explain variance in pupil attitude/motivation and achievement from parental data. These matters are dealt with at the end of the results section.

5.3.2 *Parental characteristics*

In this section we look at parents' social class background (Appendix 5.3, Q2), ability to speak Irish (Appendix 5.3, Q6) and the extent to which Irish is used at home (Appendix 5.3, Q 7). It will be recalled (see Chapter 2: Table 2.7,) that the mean social class rating for parents in the present study (3.8) is very close to the mean rating (3.9) found in census data for the general population. The difference was not statistically significant.

Table 5.2 presents data on the self-assessed speaking ability in Irish of parents in this study alongside data for the general public from two national surveys conducted by ITÉ in 1983 and 1993 (Ó Riagáin and Ó Gliasáin, 1994). The comparison is facilitated by the fact that items on the *Parents' Questionnaire* relating to ability and use make use of response options which are similar to those used in the original CLAR (1975) survey and the later ITÉ surveys. The data show that while the different group/samples are relatively similar in terms of speaking ability at 'higher' levels of ability ('Parts of conversations' or better), at 'lower' levels of ability the parents in our study are better than the general public.

Table 5.2

Percentage distribution of parents in the present study compared to the national population according to self-reported ability to speak Irish

Ability to speak Irish	Present study (parents) (n = 198)*	ITÉ National Survey 1983 ** (n = 791)	ITÉ National Survey 1993 ** (n = 976)
No Irish	9.1	16	18
(Only*) the odd word**	20.7	32	32
A few simple sentences	41.4	19	17
Parts of conversations	22.2	20	22
Most conversations	4.0	10	9
Native speaker ability	4.0	3	2
No response/No information	1.5	-	-

* Based on Q6 of the *Parents' Questionnaire.* ** (see Ó Riagáin and Ó Gliasáin, 1994: 5)

Table 5.3

Percentage distribution of parents in the present study compared to the national population according to their self-reported use of Irish at home

Use of Irish at home (parents' report)	Present study (parents) * (n = 198)	ITÉ National Survey 1983 (n = 791)	ITÉ National Survey 1993 (n = 976)
Very often** / often	3.0	5	3
Occasionally	19.2	10	10
Seldom	34.3	16	16
Never	41.9	69	71
No response	2.0	---	---

* Based on Q7 of the *Parents' Questionnaire.* **The term 'always' was used in the two ITÉ National Surveys (see Ó Riagáin and Ó Gliasáin, 1994: 13)

About 30% of parents in the present study assess their ability as 'parts of conversations' or better (combining the three highest ability levels), while the corresponding percentage for the general public in both national surveys is 33%. A greater proportion of the general public report themselves as having 'no Irish' or only 'the odd word' (48% in 1983 and 50% in 1993) than our subsample of parents (29.8%). The largest difference between the two national samples and our group is in the proportions reporting their ability to speak Irish as 'a few simple sentences' - a much greater proportion of parents in the present study (41.4%) than in the general public (19% in 1983 and 17% in 1993) report their ability as 'a few simple sentences'.

Parents in the present study also report higher levels of Irish use in the home than has been recorded for the public in general (Ó Riagáin and Ó Gliasáin, 1994). Looking at Table 5.3, it can be seen that over a half (56.5%) of parents say Irish is used 'seldom' or more often at home compared to less than one third (29%-31%) of the general public. Likewise, while 69% and 71% respectively of the general public in the 1983 and 1993 ITÉ national surveys report that Irish is 'never' used in the home, the corresponding proportion for the 'Parent Sample' is only 41.9%.

The class-by-class analysis indicates a tendency for these two parental variables (*Parent's ability in Irish* and *Use of Irish at home*) to vary according to class achievement in spoken Irish. Data in Table 5.4 shows higher levels of ability in Irish among parents whose children are in middle-Irish-achievement classes than among those whose children are in the low-Irish-achievement classes. Specifically, between 39% and 48% of parents of children in the middle-Irish-achievement classes report that their own ability to speak Irish is at the level of 'parts of conversations or better', whereas only 5%-17% of parents of children in the low-Irish-achievement classes believe their ability in Irish to be this high. We omit the high-Irish-achievement classes from Table 5.4 because we have no parent data for that group (see Chapter 2: Table 2.10).

The proportions of parents in each of the seven classes who report that Irish is spoken 'occasionally' or more frequently at home are listed in the rightmost column of Table 5.4. Despite some tendency for more frequent home use to be associated with middle-Irish-achievement classes compared to low-Irish achievement classes the pattern is not consistent. For example, in Class 12 only 16% of parents say that Irish is used at least 'occasionally' in the home, even though this is the class with the highest parental ability in Irish (48% at the level of 'parts of conversations' or better).

These across-class patterns of association between *Parent's ability in Irish, Use of Irish at home* (parent's report) and *Pupil achievement in Irish* are broadly consistent with the correlation analysis based on individual parents/pupils (Table 5.5, rows 6 & 7). *Parent's ability in Irish*, and *Use of Irish at home* to a lesser extent, have significant correlations with *Pupil achievement in Irish* ($r=.36$ and $r=.19$ respectively). Only *Use of Irish at home*, however, is significantly correlated with *Pupil Irish attitude/motivation* ($r=.15$). We are also interested in connections between the two parent variables themselves: *Parent's ability in Irish* and *Use of Irish at home*. The data indicate that, notwithstanding a slight tendency for parents with higher ability in Irish to use Irish more frequently at home, the relationship ($r=.09$) is not significant.

Table 5.4
'Parent's ability in Irish' and 'Use of Irish in the home' for seven middle and low Irish-achievement classes.*

	Percentage of parents who report....	
*Class achievement in spoken Irish Rank***	*.. own ability to speak Irish as 'parts of conversations' or better*	*..Irish spoken in home 'occasionally' or more frequently*
7	-	-
D 8	-	-
9	39%	32%
10	42%	37%
11	-	-
12	48%	16%
13	-	-
14	-	-
15	12%	24%
D 16	5%	9%
17	-	-
18	13%	13%
19	17%	17%
D 20	-	-

* Based on responses to Questions No's 6, 7 respectively in the *Parents' Questionnaire*.   ** See Table 2.10
'D' = Officially classified as disadvantaged.

It can also be seen (column four, Table 5.5) that *Social class* is related to *Parent's ability in Irish* (r=-.35), but not to frequency of *Use of Irish at home* (r=-.07). Specifically, parents from higher social class backgrounds tend to have higher ability in Irish in our sample. It will be recalled from Chapter 3, however, that in the larger Total Sample, *Use of Irish at home* (this time reported by the pupil) was correlated with *Social class* (r=-.20) - higher *Social class* being associated with more *Use of Irish at home*.

There is a positive significant correlation (r=-.26) between *Social class* and *Pupil achievement in Irish*, but not between *Social class* and *Pupil Irish attitude/motivation*. It may be recalled from Chapter 3 that correlations based on the Total Sample of twenty classes showed a similar pattern - the association between *Social class* and *Pupil achievement in Irish* (r=-.36) being much stronger than between *Social class* and *Pupil Irish attitude/motivation* (r=-.10) (although the latter correlation was still just significant).

Table 5.5

Zero order correlations between two criterion variables (*Pupil achievement in Irish* and *Pupil Irish attitude/motivation*) and a number of pupil- and parent-related predictor variables. N pupils (min=161; max=198)

	1	2	3	4*	5	6	7	8	9	10	11	12	13	14	15	16
1 Pupil achievement in Irish																
2 Pupil Irish attitude/motivation (index)	**32**															
3 Pupil general academic ability (DVRT)	**46**	**34**														
4 Social class (negatively coded)	**-26**	03	**-28**													
5 Parent's ability in Irish	**36**	11	**21**	**-35**												
6 Use of Irish at home (parent's report)	**19**	**15**	**17**	-07	09											
7 Parent's own attitude to Irish	14	**25**	**17**	-02	**20**	**30**										
8 Parent's attitude to child being taught Irish	11	**27**	**12**	-02	11	**45**	**75**									
9 Attitude to learning Irish which parent encourages in the child	**18**	**16**	09	-10	**20**	**26**	**49**	**50**								
10 Parent praises any aspect of the child's Irish achievements	**15**	**29**	12	-02	11	**16**	10	12	**18**							
11 Parent's contact with school	-04	-06	-02	10	-01	-02	05	11	-02	06						
12 Parent's knowledge of how Irish is taught in school	**22**	**17**	**14**	**-20**	**37**	**16**	**26**	**20**	**16**	**17**	**14**					
13 Amount of time child spends on all homework (parent's report)	-10	00	07	08	-04	-01	-13	**-19**	-12	06	08	-09				
14 Parent supervises or helps with homework generally	-10	00	-07	05	-05	-09	03	00	02	**24**	10	**16**	**23**			
15 Parent usually helps with Mathematics	02	-06	-12	-04	12	03	-01	-08	-04	07	-10	07	**15**	**22**		
16 Parent usually helps with English	**-23**	-11	**-15**	04	-12	-14	-11	**-15**	-01	-01	-08	-08	05	**19**	02	
17 Parent usually helps with Irish	07	01	03	**-21**	**29**	02	09	06	**19**	04	**-13**	**14**	07	**21**	**20**	**24**

*Negatively coded variable. Decimal points omitted. Values printed in bold with shading are significant at the .05 level

5.3.3 *Parents' support for the pupil learning Irish*

In this section we look at a series of questions which relate in one way or another to the degree of support parents provide for the child learning Irish: the parent's own attitude to Irish, the parent's attitude to his/her own child being taught Irish in school, the attitude towards learning Irish in school which the parent tries to encourage in the child and the frequency with which the parent praises the child's achievements in different subjects including Irish.

Table 5.6
Percentage distribution of parents according to: (a) Their own general attitude to Irish
(b) Their attitude to Irish being taught to their child

Attitude	Parent's <u>own</u> general attitude to Irish (n = 198)	Parent's attitude to child being taught Irish (n = 198)
Strongly in favour	16.7	29.3
Somewhat in favour	47.5	46.0
No particular feelings	22.7	13.6
Somewhat against it	9.1	7.1
Strongly against it	2.5	2.0
No response	1.5	2.0

(Based on Q5 and Q8 of *Parents' Questionnaire*)

Combining the first two categories of responses in Table 5.6 it can be seen that 64.2% of parents describe their *own attitude* to Irish as 'strongly/somewhat in favour', while 75.3% are 'strongly/somewhat in favour' of their *child being taught Irish* in school. Substantial minorities of parents, however, report having 'no particular feelings' about Irish generally (22.7%) or about their child being taught Irish (13.6%). Only 11.6% are personally against Irish, and only 9.1% are against their child being taught the language in school (including 2% who are 'strongly against it'). Although there was no directly comparable question in the 1993 national survey (Ó Riagáin and Ó Gliasáin, 1994), replies to a related question *How would you feel if most children stopped doing Irish at school* showed that only 7% of respondents said they would be 'a little/very glad about it'.

As parents' own attitudes to Irish and their children being taught Irish are fairly consistent across classes, we do not present data for these items according to classes.

At the level of individual pupils our correlation data (Table 5.5) show that *Parent's own attitude to Irish* (row 7) is significantly related to both *Pupil achievement in Irish* (r=.14) and *Pupil Irish attitude/motivation* (r=.25). A similar pattern is seen in the case of *Parent's attitude to child being taught Irish* (row 8). But while the latter has a strong correlation (r=.27) with *Pupil Irish attitude/motivation* (column 3) the correlation between *Parent's attitude to child being taught Irish* and *Pupil achievement in Irish* just fails to reach significance (r=.11). As might be expected, there is a particularly strong positive correlation between *Parent's own attitude to Irish* and *Parent's attitude to the child being taught Irish* (r=.75). It is worth noting that *Parent's own attitude to Irish* is also significantly correlated with *Parent's ability in Irish* (r=.20) and to an even greater extent with *Use of Irish at home* (r=.30).

As well as being favourably disposed to Irish and to their child being taught Irish, parents are by and large satisfied with the amount of time spent on Irish and the school's efforts in relation to their child's Irish (Appendix 5.3, Q16). Almost three-quarters (73.7%) think the amount of time spent on Irish is *just right* while 15.2% think *less* time should be spent on Irish. Only 8.6% think *more* time should be spent on Irish. Most parents (83.3%) also agree that the school 'is doing everything possible' to improve their child's progress in Irish generally (Appendix 5.3, Q 21). Of the minority of 14.1% of parents who feel the school could do more, 6% cite the need for more emphasis on oral Irish. Others (1-2%) mention the need for individual attention, the need to make Irish more fun or more interesting, the need for more emphasis on Irish culture, and the need for more audio/visual equipment and language labs.

These generally favourable parental attitudes to Irish and the teaching of Irish do not, however, appear to translate readily into either specific encouragement for the child in relation to learning Irish at school or frequent praise for school achievement in Irish. Taking the question of encouragement (Table 5.7) first, it can be seen, for example, that 69.2% of parents 'leave it up to' the child to develop his/her own attitude to Irish while only 29.3% let their child know that Irish is 'very important'. Nevertheless, very few parents (1%) explicitly discourage their child 'from taking Irish seriously' even though, as we saw earlier, approximately one-tenth of parents have negative attitudes to the language in general (11.6%) and/or are against it being taught to their children (9.1%). The lack of encouragement given by many parents may be related to the fact that 65.7% of them think that Irish is 'of little' or 'no importance' as far as their child's future job is concerned (Appendix 5.3, Q9). Once again, since low levels of encouragement by parents are fairly consistent across the seven classes studied, no class level data is presented for these items. The correlation data in Table 5.5 show that the *Attitude to learning Irish which parent encourages in the child* (row 9) is significantly associated with both *Pupil achievement in Irish* (r=.18) and with *Pupil Irish attitude/motivation* (r=.16).

The extent to which parents praise their child's achievement in Irish and other subject areas may be seen in Table 5.8. Between 20% and 30% of parents 'hardly ever' praise their child's school achievements in *Irish reading*, *Oral/spoken Irish* or *Irish writing*. In fact, success in *Oral/spoken Irish* is the area of school achievement least likely to attract praise. By comparison, in the case of *English reading*, *English writing* and *Mathematics* only extremely small minorities of parents (2.5% - 5.1%) report themselves as 'hardly ever' praising their child's achievements.

Table 5.7
Percentage distribution of parents according to the general attitude towards learning Irish they try to encourage in their child

Attitude to Irish parent encourages in child	Percentage of parents (n = 198)
I let my child know that Irish is very important	29.3
I leave it up to my child to develop his/her own attitude to Irish	69.2
I discourage my child from taking Irish seriously	1.0
No response	0.5

(Based on Q12 of the *Parents' Questionnaire*)

Table 5.8
Percentage distribution of parents according the frequency with which they praise their children's school achievements in different subjects

Subjects (n = 198)	often	occasionally	hardly ever	No response
English reading	64.6	29.3	5.1	1.0
Mathematics	68.7	26.8	3.0	1.5
English writing	61.1	32.8	2.5	3.5
Project work	59.1	28.8	6.6	5.6
Irish reading	41.4	32.8	20.2	5.6
Oral/spoken Irish	33.8	28.8	30.3	7.1
Irish writing	41.9	31.8	20.2	6.1

Parent praises child's achievements ...

(Based on Q11 of the *Parents' Questionnaire*)

A class by class analysis (data not in tabular form) reveals that the two highest ranking of the seven classes in terms of their achievement in spoken Irish (classes 9 and 10) also rank highest in terms of the extent to which parents praise their child's achievement in *Irish reading* and *Spoken Irish*. Even in these two classes, however, *English reading* and

Mathematics are still more likely to be praised than achievements in any aspect of Irish. Row ten in Table 5.5 shows correlations involving a composite variable *Parent praises any aspect of child's Irish achievement.* In computing this variable instances of parents praising any aspect of the child's achievement in *Irish reading, Spoken Irish or Irish writing* was coded as 1, and all others (no praise) as 0. The results indicate this composite variable *Parent praises any aspect of child's Irish achievement* to be positively and significantly linked with both *Pupil achievement in Irish* (r=.15) and *Pupil Irish attitude/motivation* (r=.29).

5.3.4 Parents' contact with school and knowledge about Irish teaching

The next series of questions (Q's 13, 14, 17, and 22 in Appendix 5.3) relate to various aspects of the school and Irish as perceived by the parent.

Table 5.9 shows that practically all parents (95%) report having some contact with the school their child is attending: 67.7% have 'occasional' contact while 27.3% have 'a lot' of contact. Despite the high level of contact parents do not feel particularly well-informed about the way Irish is taught.

Table 5.9
Percentage distribution of parents according to the amount of contact they have with the school their child is attending?

Contact with school	Percentage of parents (n = 198)
No contact at all	-
Practically no contact	5.1
Occasional contact	67.7
A lot of contact	27.3

Based on Q13 of the *Parents' Questionnaire*

Table 5.10 shows that 56.6% of parents feel they know only 'a little' about how Irish is taught to their child while just over a quarter (25.3%) say they 'know nothing about how Irish is taught'. Only 17.7% of parents say they know 'quite a lot' about how Irish is taught. Other data not shown in tabular form (see Appendix 5.3: Q14) reveal that very high proportions of parents are 'happy' with the level of contact they have with the school (85.4%) and do not feel that they personally could 'give the school any practical support as far as the teaching of Irish is concerned - apart from what they are already doing (93.4%).

Table 5.10

Percentage distribution of parents according to how much they know about the way their child is taught Irish in school

Parent's knowledge of how child is taught Irish in school	Percentage of parents (n = 198)
I know nothing about how Irish is taught	25.3
I know a little about how Irish is taught	56.6
I know quite a lot about how Irish is taught	17.7
No response	0.5

(Based on Q17 of the *Parents' Questionnaire*)

Table 5.11 presents class level data on parents' contact with the school and knowledge of how Irish is taught. It can be seen that with the exception of Class 16 the level of contact which parents have with schools does not vary greatly across the seven classes. It can also be seen (column 3) that in three of the four low-Irish-achievement classes, the proportion who 'know nothing' about how Irish is taught to their child ranges from 36% to 46%, whereas it is less than 20% in all the middle-Irish-achievement classes. The proportions for class rank 16 are worth drawing attention to. This class has the most parents who report having 'a lot' of contact with the school (55%) and the most parents who know 'nothing' about how Irish is taught (46%). An additional 50% of parents in this class know only a 'little' about how Irish is taught.

Correlations in Table 5.5 (row 11) do not reveal any link between *Parent's contact with school* on the one hand, and either *Pupil achievement in Irish* or *Pupil Irish attitude/motivation*, on the other. There are, however, significant positive correlations between *Parent's knowledge of how Irish is taught in school* and both *Pupil achievement in Irish* (r=.22) and *Pupil Irish attitude/motivation* (r=.17). It is also worth noting significant correlations between, on the one hand, *Parent's knowledge of how Irish is taught in school*, and, on the other, a range of other parental variables such as *Parent's ability in Irish* (r=.37), *Parent's own attitude to Irish* (r=.26), *Parent's attitude to child being taught Irish* (r=.20), *Social class* (r=-.20), *Parent praises any aspect of child's Irish achievements* (r=.17), *Use of Irish at home* (r=.16), and *Parent's contact with school* (r=.14).

Table 5.11
Parent Survey: 'Parents' contact with the school' and 'Parents' knowledge of how Irish is taught' for seven middle and low Irish-achievement classes *

Class achievement in spoken Irish Rank	Percentage of parents who report....	
	..having 'a lot' of contact with their child's school	*..knowing 'nothing' about how child is taught Irish in school*
7	-	-
D 8	-	-
9	21%	11%
10	26%	16%
11	-	-
12	19%	19%
13	-	-
14	-	-
15	24%	40%
D 16	55%	46%
17	-	-
18	23%	36%
19	30%	17%
D 20	-	-

'D' = Officially classified as disadvantaged.
* Based on responses to Q13 and Q17 respectively in the *Parents' Questionnaire*.

One other issue can be dealt with under this heading - teaching through Irish. Table 5.12 shows the proportions of parents who report that the school their child attends teaches some subject, apart from Irish, through the medium of Irish. About three quarters of parents (74.2%) report that there is *no* Irish-medium instruction of any kind in their children's school and a further 16.7% do not know. Only 7.6% of parents report that there is *some* teaching through Irish. In a second part of this item parents who reported no Irish-medium instruction in their child's school were asked if they would be willing to support the idea of the school teaching a subject through Irish. Just under a quarter (24.2%) of all parents agreed that they would support Irish-medium instruction while just over a half (51.5%) would not support such an initiative.

Table 5.12
Percentage distribution of parents according to whether or not the schools their children attend teach any subjects, apart from Irish, through Irish, or whether the parents would support Irish-medium education*

Irish-medium education	Percentage of parents (n = 198)
(a) Does the school teach any subjects through Irish?	
Yes	7.6
No	74.2
I don't know	16.7
No response	1.5
(b) Would parent support the idea of the school teaching a subject through Irish?	
Parent would support Irish-medium	24.2**
Parent would *not* support Irish-medium	51.5
Parents not responding/Question not applicable	24.2

* Based on Q19 of the *Parents' Questionnaire*
** This percentage may include a small number of parents from the 'Yes'/'I don't know' category of Q19.

5.3.5 Parents' and teachers' perceptions of difficulties

The proportions of parents who feel that their child has difficulty with various school subjects are set out in Table 5.13 Some parents, of course, report difficulties with more than one subject. For purposes of comparison, the proportions of *class teachers* who perceive these same children as having difficulties in the same subject areas are also set out in Table 5.13. It should be noted that the teachers' ratings here are based only on those pupils whose parents completed the *Parents' Questionnaire* - unlike the ratings discussed in Chapter 2 (Table 2.9) which were based on all pupils and involved judgements by all teachers.

Over a quarter of parents perceive that their child has difficulty with *Spoken Irish* (26.8%) while a similar proportion perceive their child as having difficulty with *Mathematics* (27.8%). Substantially fewer - only between 6%-7% of parents - perceive their children as having difficulties with either *English reading* 6.1%) or *English writing* (6.6%). *Irish reading* (15.7%) and *Irish writing* (16.7%) are intermediate in terms of parent perceived pupil difficulty.

Table 5.13
Correspondence between teachers' perceptions and parents' perceptions of pupil difficulty with different subjects

Reported pupil difficulty with...	(n = 198)	*Percentage distribution of pupils*	
		Parents' perceptions	*Teachers' ratings*
Spoken Irish		26.8	47.5
Irish reading		15.7	40.4
Irish writing		16.7	48.0
Mathematics		27.8	39.9
English reading		6.1	19.2
English writing		6.6	27.3

(Based on Q20 of the *Parents' Questionnaire* and on Teachers' Ratings of individual pupils)

For all subjects listed in Table 5.13 it is clear that teachers perceive considerably more pupil difficulty than parents. The median proportion of pupils having difficulty over the six skills is 40.2% according to teachers, but only 16.2% according to parents. In addition, unlike parents - who are most likely to perceive difficulty with mathematics - teachers are most likely to perceive difficulty with *Irish writing* (48%), followed by *Spoken Irish* (47.5%), *Irish reading* (40.4%) and *Mathematics* (39.9%). Overall, both parents and teachers, however, perceive the three aspects of Irish as being associated with much more difficulty for pupils than the two aspects of English.

Responses to another item (Appendix 5.3, Q10) indicate that over a fifth of parents (21.7%) think their child 'dislikes learning Irish' while nearly another third (32.3%) report that their child has 'no particular feelings about learning Irish'. Of those parents who elaborated on why their child disliked learning Irish, 6% report that the child finds it difficult to learn, 5.5.% believe the child 'thinks it unnecessary/irrelevant' and 2.5% believe their child 'finds it boring'. On the positive side 42.9% of parents believe their child likes learning Irish .

5.3.6 Parents and Irish homework

In Tables 5.14 - 5.20 we examine the question of children's homework and Irish. This issue is of particular interest in the case of Irish, since homework provides perhaps the only significant opportunity for many parents and children to interact in Irish on a regular basis. Prior to this, no research appears to have been done on the subject.

Table 5.14 shows that three quarters (75.2%) of parents report that their child spends more than 40 minutes on *all* homework each night. In Table 5.15 it can be seen that two thirds (66.6%) of parents supervise or help with children's homework 'always' or 'often', while somewhat more (71.3%) sign their children's homework regularly. Few parents report that they 'seldom' or 'never' supervise (7.6%) or sign (6.5%) homework.

Table 5.14
Percentage distribution of parents according to the amount of time they report that their children spend, on average, on *all* homework each night?

Amount of time child spends on all homework, on average, each night	Percentage of parents (n = 198)
Less than or 40 minutes	20.7
Between 41-60 minutes	40.4
Between 61-100 minutes	22.2
More than 100 minutes	12.6
No response	4.0

(Based on Q23 of the *Parents' Questionnaire*)

Table 5.15
Percentage distribution of parents according to the frequency with which they supervise and with which they sign their children's homework

Frequency ..	Percentage of parents who...	
	supervise homework (n = 198)	sign homework (n = 198)
Always	23.2	46.0
Often	43.4	25.3
Occasionally	25.8	21.7
Seldom	5.6	2.5
Never	2.0	4.0
No response	--	0.5

(Based on Q25 and Q24 of the *Parents' Questionnaire*)

Our correlation analysis shows that the two homework-related variables, *Amount of time child spends on all homework* and *Parent supervises or helps with homework generally,* are *not* significantly linked to either *Pupil achievement in Irish* or *Pupil Irish attitude/motivation.* It may be noted in passing, however, that *Parent supervises or helps with homework generally* is significantly associated with *Amount of time child spends on all homework* (r=.23), as well as with two other parental variables *Parent praises any aspect of the child's Irish achievements* (r=.24), and *Parent's knowledge of how Irish is taught in school* (r=.16) (see row 14, Table 5.5).

The proportions of parents who help with homework in different subject areas are shown in Table 5.16. It can be seen that of the three main subjects, the lowest proportion of parents (34.8%) help with *Irish,* 47.5% help with *English* while the highest proportion (70.2%) help with *Mathematics.* Again, it may be noted that the relatively high frequency of perceived pupil difficulty with *Mathematics* (Table 5.13) is implicitly acknowledged in the high level of parental involvement in homework in this subject. This is not true to the same extent in *Irish.* In fact, parents report helping with *History/Geography* slightly more often (37.9%) than they do with *Irish* (34.8%). *Arts and Crafts,* and *Environmental Studies* are the areas in which parents are least likely to help their children.

Table 5.16
Percentage distribution of parents according to the various subjects with which they *usually* help their children.

Parent usually helps child with...	Percentage of parents (n = 198)
Mathematics	70.2
English	47.5
Irish	34.8
History/Geography	37.9
Environmental studies	13.1
Arts & Crafts	15.2

(Based on Q26 of the *Parents' Questionnaire*)

In a class level analysis (data not in tabular form) we examined the extent to which parents reported usually helping their children with (a) *Irish* (b) *English* and (c) *Mathematics* homework in each of the seven classes. In six of these classes, more parents report helping with *Mathematics* than with *Irish* or *English* homework. The highest percentages of parents reporting that they usually help with *Irish* homework are found in Class 12 (55% of parents) and Class 10 (47%) respectively. It is worth recalling (Table 5.4) that these two classes also rank first and second in terms of parental ability in Irish.

Looking at the correlation analysis it can be seen that of the three subject-specific homework variables (Table 5.5, rows 15-17) none is significantly related to *Pupil Irish attitude/motivation*. Only one, *Parent usually helps with English,* is significantly correlated with *Pupil achievement in Irish* and the relationship is negative (r=-.23). In other words, pupils whose parents usually help them with their *English* homework have lower levels of achievement in Irish than pupils who do not receive such help. Other results in Table 5.5 suggest that the reason for this lower Irish achievement may be connected with the kind of pupils who receive help with their *English* homework. Note, for example, that *Parent usually helps with English* is inversely related to *Pupil general academic ability (DVRT)* (r = -.15). That is to say, pupils receiving help with their *English* homework - and recall that these are sixth-grade pupils - tend to have lower general academic ability than other pupils. Bearing in mind the high positive correlation between *Pupil general academic ability* and *Pupil achievement in Irish* (.46), it is plausible to think that it is the low level of general academic ability which is the common factor underlying both lower achievement in Irish and the need for parental help/supervision in the case of *English* homework.

It is worth noting that *Parent usually helps with Irish* has significant correlations with two other parental variables - *Social class* (r=-.21) and *Parent's ability in Irish* (r=.29) (row 17, Table 5.5). Thus, parents who help their child with Irish homework tend to have higher ability in Irish themselves and come from higher social class backgrounds.

Table 5.17

Percentage distribution of parents according to the various aspects of Irish homework with which they *usually* help their children.

Parent usually helps child with ..	*Percentage of parents (n = 198)*
Irish reading	27.8
Irish writing	15.7
Oral/spoken Irish	9.1
Irish grammar	18.2
Irish poetry	8.6
Irish spelling	37.4

(Based on Q27 of the *Parents' Questionnaire*)

Table 5.17 shows that of the six main areas of Irish, *Irish spelling* is one with which parents usually help their children (37.4%). Help with *Irish reading* is also relatively common (27.8%). This is followed by *Irish grammar* (18.2% of parents) and *Irish writing* (15.7% of parents). Notwithstanding the fact that 26.8% of parents see spoken

Irish as an area of difficulty for their children it is the aspect of Irish with which parents are least likely to help: less than one in ten of parents report that they usually help with *Oral/spoken Irish* or *Irish Poetry* .

Parental help with particular aspects of Irish - *Irish reading, Oral/spoken Irish* and *Grammar* - are significantly related to a number of pupil and parent variables. Zero-order correlations in Table 5.18 show that *Parent usually helps with Irish reading* is significantly and negatively correlated with *Pupil achievement in Irish* (r=-.17), *Pupil general academic ability* (r=-.18) and *Parent's contact with school* (r=-.18). In other words, parents who help with Irish reading homework have significantly higher levels of contact with the school, have children who are of lower general academic ability and who have lower levels of achievement in Irish.

Table 5.18
Zero-order correlations* between the aspect of Irish homework with which parent usually helps and a number of pupil and parent variables. N pupils (min=172; max=198)

Parent usually helps child with Irish	Pupil achievement in spoken Irish	Pupil Irish attitude/ motivation index	Pupil general academic ability (DVRT)	Social class**	Parent's ability in Irish	Attitude to learning Irish which parent encourages in child	Parent's contact with school	Parent's knowledge of how Irish is taught in school
Reading	**-17**	-06	**-18**	03	09	09	**-18**	05
Oral/Spoken	00	01	03	03	**13**	**21**	-07	09
Grammar	11 §	**13**	**13**	-03	**36**	**15**	-10	**18**

* Decimal points omitted. Values printed in bold with shading are significant at the .05 level. § p = .06;
** Negatively coded.

Parent usually helps with Irish grammar, in contrast, has a positive correlation with *Pupil achievement in Irish* which approaches significance (r=.11; p=.06) and is significantly associated with more positive *Pupil Irish attitude/motivation* (r=.13) and with higher *Pupil general academic ability* (r=.13). It is also positively linked with a higher standing in relation to *Parent's ability in Irish* (r=.36), *Parent's knowledge of how Irish is taught in school* (r=.18) and *Attitude to learning Irish which parent encourages in child* (r=.15).

The reasons parents give for not helping with Irish homework are outlined in Table 5.19. These percentages were calculated on the basis of all parents who responded to the questionnaire. The 40.9% of parents who did not give reasons (last row of Table 5.19) is composed of those (34.8%) who had already reported that they did help with Irish homework (Table 5.16) and those who did not respond to this item for other reasons.

Table 5.19
Percentage distribution of parents according to the main reasons why they do *not* help with their children's Irish homework.

Reason why parent does not help with *Irish* homework	Percentage of parents (n = 198)
Parent is not interested in school work generally	0.0
Parent does not have enough time usually	3.5
Parent does not agree with Irish being taught	1.5
Parent is not very good at Irish herself/himself	43.9
Volunteered Reasons	
(a) Parent says child does not need help	8.6
(b) Other reasons	1.5
No response/not applicable	40.9

(Based on Q28 of the *Parents' Questionnaire*)

The most common reason (43.9%) parents give for not helping with Irish homework is that they 'are not very good at Irish' themselves. Just under 9% (8.6%) of parents say that their child 'does not need help'. This latter reason was not offered as a response option on the main item itself but was simply volunteered by parents under the 'Other reasons' category. It is reasonable to think that if it had been presented as an option, it would have been selected more often. The option 'I don't have enough time usually' was selected by a small number of parents (3.5%) while even fewer (1.5%) reported not helping because they 'don't agree with Irish being taught'. No parent reported lack of 'interest in schoolwork generally' on their own part as a reason for not helping.

5.3.7 Parents' general comments

Table 5.20 summarises the general comments which were volunteered by parents in response to Question 29. Of the 198 parents who completed the *Parents' Questionnaire*, 89 (or 45%) offered comments (see Appendix 5.4). As in the case of pupils' comments described in (Chapter 4), each parent's written reply could involve more than one response element. It may be noted, however, that the majority contain only one response element, with the maximum number being three. Eleven coding categories were used to classify responses. These codes are defined in Table 5.20 under the five broad thematic headings:

(i) Irish in competition with other subjects, (ii) Support/lack of support for the teaching of Irish, (iii) Concern about methods of teaching Irish, (iv) Reaction to child's progress in school and (v) 'Other' comments.

Table 5.20
Parents' Questionnaire - **Volunteered general comments***

Code General Comments	Percentage of parents** (n = 89)
Irish in competition with other subjects	
1. More time should be given to other subjects (e.g. Modern Continental Languages, computers or English), and/or less time spent on Irish.	19%
2. Children should not be put under pressure (compelled) to learn Irish at primary school - Irish should be voluntary/optional.	10%
Support/lack of support for the teaching of Irish	
3. Parent is in favour of Irish and the teaching of Irish.	12%
4. Parent wants more time spent on Irish, or some subjects taught through Irish.	2%
5. Parent believes Irish is not useful or important for the child's future (whether parent actually approves of Irish or not).	11%
Concern about methods of teaching Irish	
6. Parent wants more emphasis on oral/conversational Irish in class and at playtime/lunchtime, and/or less emphasis on grammar.	13%
7. Irish class, Irish text-books should be more interesting, more fun, more attractive; more relevant to the pupil's life.	8%
8. Irish should be taught like Modern Continental Languages (using more modern methods).	7%
Reaction to child's progress in school	
9. Parent is satisfied with the progress of the child, or of children generally.	10%
10. Parent is dissatisfied with the progress of the child, or of children generally; or child is finding Irish difficult.	8%
Other comments	
11. Parent finds that the Irish taught at school now is different to his/her own, or finds Irish difficult.	3%
12. Miscellaneous	15%

* Based on Q29 of the *Parents' Questionnaire* - see Appendix 5.4.
** The percentages in this column total to more than 100% because some of the parents' comments were coded under more than one heading.

The first set of comments relate to how Irish is seen as competing with other subjects (Codes 1 & 2). The most frequent comment (19% of those who responded to this item) either suggested that more time should be given to other subjects or that less time should be given to Irish. In addition, 10% of respondents thought that children should not be put under pressure to study Irish at school or that Irish should be voluntary/optional.

The second group of response elements (Codes 3-5) indicates varying levels of support for Irish. Generally positive comments in favour of Irish and the teaching of Irish were made by 12% of parents. Two per cent of parents would like to see even more emphasis on Irish (more time teaching Irish or more time teaching other subjects through Irish). This general support for Irish is counterbalanced to a substantial degree, however, by comments from a further 11% of parents saying that Irish is not important or useful for their child's future.

Comments expressing concern about methods of teaching Irish (codes 6/7/8 - counting each multiply-coded comment just once) were made by 24% of all parents. Specifically, 13% of parents want 'more emphasis on oral/conversational Irish in class and at playtime/lunchtime, and/or less emphasis on grammar'; 8% think the 'Irish class and Irish textbooks should be more interesting, more fun, more attractive and more relevant to pupil's life', and 7% urge that 'Irish be taught like Modern Continental Languages (using more modern methods)'.

The next main theme concerns parental reactions to their children's progress in school. Comments indicating satisfaction slightly outnumber those indicating dissatisfaction: 10% of parents are 'satisfied with the progress of the child, or of children generally' while 8% are 'dissatisfied with the progress of their child/children generally, or say that their child is finding Irish difficult'

Among the 'other' comments the most frequent response (3%) is that the parent 'finds that the Irish taught at school now is different to his/her own or finds Irish difficult'. Implied in the latter, presumably, is some feeling of inadequacy in relation to helping the child with Irish homework. Finally, a further 15% of diverse response elements were coded under a 'miscellaneous' heading (see Appendix 5.4).

5.3.8 *Predicting Irish attitude/motivation and achievement from parental data*

In this concluding section, we use a regression analysis to assess the extent to which selected pupil and parent variables predict variance in (a) *Pupil achievement in Irish* and (b) *Pupil Irish attitude/motivation*. We will refer to (a) and (b) as the criterion measures, and to the various measures of parental attitude, social class and so on as the predictors. Each of the regression analyses involve the same nine predictor variables. The predictors are a subset of the measures used in the correlation matrix in Table 5.5. Generally, the predictors are selected on the basis of the strength of their correlations with *Pupil achievement in Irish* and/or with *Pupil Irish attitude/motivation*.

Pearson correlations in Table 5.5 suggest that the predictor variables themselves are inter-related in complex ways. For example, when interpreting the significant correlation between *Parent's ability in Irish* and *Pupil achievement in Irish* (r=.36) we must also take into account the fact that *Parent's ability in Irish* is significantly associated with *Social class* (r=-.35). *Social class* itself has a significant correlation with *Pupil achievement in Irish* (r=-.26). Multiple regression techniques, by controlling for these complex inter-relationships between predictor variables, allow us assess the unique contribution of each predictor to the explanation of criterion variance. Squaring the relevant Pearson 'r's' in Table 5.5, of course, gives the proportion of all criterion variance for which each predictor, considered independently, accounts. As in Chapter 3 a hierarchical regression model was used.

In the present case, perhaps due to the reduced numbers in the 'Parent Sample', *Gender of pupil* did not turn out to be significantly correlated with either *Pupil achievement in Irish* or with *Pupil Irish attitude/motivation*. Despite this, we have included it as a predictor in the two regression analyses (Tables 5.21 & 5.22) for the sake of completeness and comparability with the analyses in Chapter 3. We do not include *Location* as a predictor because all classes are in the Dublin/East Leinster area.

The nine variables were entered in the order in which they are listed below:

(1) Gender of pupil
(2) Social class
(3) Pupil general academic ability (DVRT)
(4) Parent's ability in Irish
(5) Use of Irish at home (parent's report)
(6) Attitude to learning Irish which parent encourages in the child
(7) Parent's knowledge of how Irish is taught in school
(8) Parent's own attitude to Irish
(9) Parent praises any aspect of the child's Irish achievements

Variance explained by predictor variables
It will be useful to examine these two regression analyses together in order to point out similarities and differences in the amount of criterion variance explained by the predictors in each case. It can be seen that the nine predictors explain a greater proportion of variance in *Pupil achievement in Irish* (Table 5.21) than in *Pupil Irish attitude/motivation* (Table 5.22). The proportion of total variance explained (R^2) is 32.2% in the case of achievement in Irish, while for attitude/motivation it is only 24.3%, a difference of 7.9%.

In the case of the *Pupil achievement in Irish* criterion (Table 5.21), the first four variables entered - *Gender of pupil, Social class, Pupil general academic ability* and *Parent's ability in Irish* - account for the bulk of the variance explained: 27.6% out of the total of 32.2% explained. In the case of *Pupil Irish attitude/motivation*, these same four predictors account for somewhat less of the variance explained: 14.7% of the total of 24.3%. It should be noted that almost all of this variance is attributable to one predictor - *Pupil general academic ability (DVRT)*.

Table 5.21

Multiple regression of a measure of *Pupil achievement in Irish* (listening) on pupil and parent predictor variables *(n = 150)*

Predictor variables	Multiple R	R^2	Adjusted R^2	R^2 change	F change	df	Sig F
1 Gender of pupil	.002	.000	-.006	.000	0.001	1,157	NS
2 Social class	.275	.076	.064	.076	12.77	1,156	.001
3 Pupil general academic ability (DVRT)	.488	.238	.223	.162	32.94	1,155	.001
4 Parent's ability in Irish	.526	.276	.258	.039	8.22	1,154	.01
5 Use of Irish at home (parent's report)	.553	.306	.283	.030	6.55	1,153	.01
6 Attitude to learning Irish which parent encourages in the child	.556	.309	.282	.003	0.73	1,152	NS
7 Parent's knowledge of how Irish is taught in school	.563	.316	.285	.007	1.57	1,151	NS
8 Parent's own attitude to Irish	.563	.317	.280	.000	0.06	1,150	NS
9 Parent praises any aspect of child's Irish achievements	.567	.322	.281	.005	1.12	1,149	NS

Table 5.22

Multiple regression of a measure of *Pupil Irish attitude/motivation* on pupil and parent predictor variables (*n = 150*)

Predictor variables	*Multiple R*	*R²*	*Adjusted R²*	*R² change*	*F change*	*df*	*Sig F*
1 Gender of pupil	.047	.002	-.005	.002	0.32	1,148	NS
2 Social class	.055	.003	-.011	.001	0.13	1,147	NS
3 Pupil general academic ability (DVRT)	.380	.145	.127	.142	24.16	1,146	.001
4 Parent's ability in Irish	.384	.147	.124	.003	0.43	1,145	NS
5 Use of Irish at home (parent's report)	.412	.170	.141	.023	3.97	1,144	.05
6 Attitude to learning Irish which parent encourages in the child	.423	.179	.145	.009	1.56	1,143	NS
7 Parent's knowledge of how Irish is taught in school	.434	.188	.148	.009	1.56	1,142	NS
8 Parent's own attitude to Irish	.450	.203	.157	.015	2.57	1,141	NS
9 Parent praises any aspect of child's Irish achievements	.493	.243	.194	.040	7.49	1,140	.01

The main difference between the results of the two analyses is that both *Social class* . and *Parent's ability in Irish* explain significant proportions of the variance in *Pupil achievement in Irish* but not in *Pupil Irish attitude/motivation*. *Social class* adds 7.6% to the variance explained in *Pupil achievement in Irish* while *Parent's ability in Irish*, entered later, explains another 3.9% - despite the fact that *Social class* and *Parent's ability in Irish* are themselves substantially correlated with each other (Table 5.5). *Pupil general academic ability* also adds marginally more to the variance explained in the case of achievement in Irish (16.2%) than it does in the case of Irish attitude/motivation (14.2%). It may be recalled from Chapter 3, that a similar pattern occurred in the case of our total sample of twenty classes, where both *Social class* and *Pupil general academic ability* accounted for higher proportions of variance in *Pupil achievement in Irish* (6.9% and 14.9% respectively), than in *Pupil Irish attitude/motivation* (0% and 5% respectively).

The other difference of note between the results of the two analyses is that the remainder of the predictors explain somewhat more variance in *Pupil Irish attitude/motivation* (Table 5.22) than they do in *Pupil achievement in Irish* (Table 5.21). Thus, the five predictors - *Use of Irish at home (parent's report), Attitude to learning Irish which parent encourages in the child, Parent's knowledge of how Irish is taught in school, Parent's own attitude to Irish* and *Parent praises any aspect of child's Irish achievements* - add 9.6% to the variance explained in the case of *Pupil Irish attitude/motivation* but only 4.6% in the case of *Pupil achievement in Irish*. The difference in result here is mainly due to the last of these predictors, *Parent praises any aspect of the child's Irish achievements*, which adds significantly (4%) to the variance explained in the case of *Pupil Irish attitude/motivation* but not in the case of *Pupil achievement in Irish* (less that 1% added).

The other predictor of importance in this group is *Use of Irish at home (parent's report)* which adds significantly to the proportion of variance explained in the case of both criterion measures - 3% for achievement in Irish and 2.3% for Irish attitude/motivation. Note that *Use of Irish at home (parent's report)* is not significantly correlated with two of the three previously entered predictors: *Social class* and *Parent's ability in Irish* (Table 5.5).

The failure of the remaining three predictors in this second group (predictors 6, 7 & 8) to contribute significantly to the variance explained in either analysis is presumably also due to the fact that they are all significantly correlated with one or more previously entered predictors (Table 5.5). For example, the sixth and seventh predictors *Attitude to learning Irish which parent encourages in the child* and *Parent's knowledge of how Irish is taught in school* are not only significantly correlated with each other but also with the previously entered *Parent's ability in Irish* and *Use of Irish at home (parent's report)*. The eighth variable entered, *Parent's own attitude to Irish,* is in turn, significantly correlated with the two immediately preceding variables.

In brief, then, the regression analyses show that the group of nine predictors explain somewhat more variance in *Pupil achievement in Irish* than in *Pupil Irish attitude/motivation*. The dominant predictor in both cases is the third one entered - *Pupil general academic ability*. *Social class* and *Parent's ability in Irish* are important contributors to variance explained in the case of *Pupil achievement in Irish*, but not at all in the case of *Pupil Irish attitude/motivation*. In contrast, the predictor *Parent praises any aspect of the child's achievement in Irish* makes a substantial contribution to Irish attitude/motivation, but almost none at all to achievement in Irish. *Use of Irish at home (parent's report)* makes a significant addition to the variance explained in the case of both Irish achievement and attitude/motivation.

5.4 Discussion

One strength of the present small-scale study of parents compared to previous more comprehensive sociolinguistic surveys of the general population (CLAR, 1975; Ó Riagáin and Ó Gliasáin, 1984, 1994), is that it places the parents' own children at the centre of the investigation of adult attitudes and practices in relation to Irish in primary school. Not only does this provide a very real reference point for the parents in replying to our questions, but it allows us to establish in the most direct manner possible whether there are any connections between parental attitudes and practices, on the one hand, and children's attitudes to and proficiency in Irish on the other.

Before proceeding to a discussion of these issues, we will refer to some data which allow us to extend to a number of important new variables the kind of comparison between the 'Parent Sample' and the national population which we reported on in Chapter 2. It will be recalled that in Chapter 2 we compared *Social class, Pupil general academic ability* and *Pupil achievement in Irish* in the 'Parent Sample' and in the national population. We can now broaden the basis of that comparison to include *Parent's ability in Irish* and *Use of Irish at home*, variables which have been central to a number of national sociolinguistic surveys (CLAR, 1975; Ó Riagáin and Ó Gliasáin, 1984, 1994; Ó Riagáin, 1997). Once again, it must be emphasised that the purpose of this comparison is simply to locate the group more accurately in a national context. Quite apart from this, of course, variables such as *Parent's ability in Irish* and *Use of Irish at home* are of interest in any case because they are likely on the basis of previous research to be central to parents' views and practices in relation to their children learning Irish.

5.4.1 Parental characteristics compared to the national profile

While most of our discussion here will be concerned with parental views and practices, we will begin with the key background variables of *Social class, Parent's ability in Irish* and *Use of Irish at home*. Data presented in Chapter 2 show that *Social class* in the Parent Sample does not differ significantly from the general population. In fact, the mean *Social class* rating (3.8) is virtually the same as in the general population based on census returns (3.9). On this basis at least, then, we might also have expected *Parent's ability in Irish* and *Use of Irish at home (parents' report)* to be roughly the same as in the general population. In fact, however, at some levels of ability and use, the parents in our study were superior to the general population. Similar proportions of the parents in our study (30%) and of the general public (33%) report their ability in Irish as 'parts of conversation' or better. But a greater proportion of parents in our study (41.4%) than in the general population (17-19%) report at least a minimal level of ability in Irish ('a few simple sentences'). Turning to *Use of Irish at home*, the results show that over a half of the parents in our study (56.5%) use Irish at home to some limited extent at least ('seldom' or more often), while in the general population less than one-third do so. Parents' reports concerning *Use of Irish at home* in the present study are broadly consistent with their children's own reports (see Chapter 3: section 3.4.2).

While the most obvious reason for the higher levels of parental ability and home use of Irish in the present study compared to the general population is that our sample (approximate age range 30-60) was not representative nationally, there are in fact quite plausible reasons why the parents of primary-school children might in any case differ from the general population in just the manner we have described. Parents by virtue of having children who learn Irish in school have more opportunities than the general public for contact with Irish (e.g. through supervising homework or enquiring about progress in Irish). This increased contact with the language would in itself probably justify parents in reporting slightly greater use of Irish at home and perhaps even slightly higher levels of ability in Irish. Backwash effects of this kind on use of Irish at home deriving from educational sources have already been reported in the case of all-Irish schools and the pre-school *Naíonraí* (Ó Riagáin and Ó Gliasáin, 1979; Hickey, 1997). There is no reason why similar effects might not operate, though at a generally lower level, in the case of ordinary schools. In any event, the fact that *Parent's ability in Irish* and *Use of Irish at home* are, if anything, higher than in the general population would seem to dispose of any notion that some of the more negative aspects of parental views and practices discussed below could be attributed to the selection of groups of classes which had a poor standing in relation to these important sociolinguistic variables.

It is also possible to compare the strength of association between the three background variables in the present study with their strength of association in the general population. Broadly speaking, the direction of association between the three variables in our study is the same as in various national surveys, though the strength of that association and its statistical significance is sometimes different. Taking *Social class* first, our results show a significant tendency for parents from higher *Social class* backgrounds to have higher levels of ability in Irish (r= -.35) although there is not a tendency to use Irish more often at home. Interestingly, however, when we were able to base the correlations on the responses of pupils in all 20 classes (see Chapter 3), the tendency for higher social class to be associated with greater use of Irish at home (as reported by pupils) was found to be significant (r=-.20). Nationally, *Social class* is linked, though not strongly, with both respondents' *ability in Irish* and *use of Irish*. In the CLAR (1975) national survey, for example, the socio-economic status of the respondent's father is significantly though not highly correlated (r=-.15) with the respondent's own ability in Irish. More recently, Ó Riagáin (1997) notes that 'although the social base of competent bilinguals appears to have widened, it remains firmly located within the social groups dependent on white collar occupations'. CLAR (1975) reports a positive correlation (r=.26) between *Socio-economic status* and *general adult use of Irish* (use since leaving school + current home use + work use). Ó Riagáin (1997) reports no *Social class* effect on *Use of Irish at home* among respondents reporting 'frequent' or 'occasional use of Irish', but does report some tendency for higher *Social class* to be associated with 'infrequent' use. Finally, the present study shows that while there is a weak tendency for higher *Parent's ability in Irish* to be associated with greater *Use of Irish at home*, the correlation is not statistically significant. Nationally, however, these two variables are significantly related. CLAR (1975) indicates that respondent's *ability in Irish* and *use of Irish at home* are positively correlated (r=.38). More recently, O Riagáin (1997) notes 'a close relationship between a respondent's use of Irish and his or her ability to speak Irish'. Again, it is probably because our study is confined to parents rather than adults generally - with the attendant possibility of 'school' effects on their perception of their own Irish ability and use - that the relationship between ability and use reported here does not match that in the general population.

5.4.2 *Parental characteristics and children's Irish*

All three background variables are significantly correlated with *Pupil achievement in Irish.* In other words, parents of higher social class (r=-.26), or with higher ability in Irish (r=.36) or using Irish more often at home (r=.19) tend to have children with significantly higher achievement in Irish at school. The association between the same three background variables and *Pupil Irish attitude/motivation,* however, is weaker - only greater parental *Use of Irish at home* is significantly linked with a better *Pupil Irish attitude/motivation* (r=.15).

The regression analyses confirm the robustness of these effects. Each of the three background variables, entered successively into the regression equation, makes significant additional contributions to the variance explained in *Pupil achievement in Irish.* But again, of these three background variables, only *Use of Irish at home* makes a significant contribution in the case of *Pupil Irish attitude/motivation.* Thus, any initiatives which encourage parents to use some Irish at home, even occasionally, are likely to benefit children both in terms of their attitude to Irish and their success in learning it at school. Likewise, initiatives which provide parents with an opportunity to improve their own command of Irish are likely to improve children's Irish proficiency.

How exactly does a greater use of Irish at home, or a higher level of parental ability in Irish, lead to improvements in pupil attitude or achievement? Obviously, the simple fact of parents providing a greater degree of exposure to Irish and demonstrating directly that Irish is a valid and effective means of communication is important. But other conditions conducive to improved pupil attitudes and achievement are also likely to be associated with higher levels of parental ability or more frequent use of Irish at home. For example, correlation data discussed below show that parents who use some Irish at home (a) have more positive attitudes to Irish themselves and to the notion of their child learning it at school (b) are more likely to know more about how Irish is taught (c) tend to promote a more positive attitude to learning Irish in their child and (d) are more likely to praise the child's school achievements in Irish. Each of these latter attitudes/practices is, in turn, itself linked to better pupil attitudes and achievement. We will now examine some of them in a little more detail.

5.4.3 Parents' support for the child learning Irish

We noted in the introduction to this chapter that parents' attitudes to, interest and involvement in their children's education can influence academic attitudes and achievements. Parental involvement can take a number of forms. One distinction which seems to be particularly relevant to our own results is the 'proactive' versus 'reactive' role of parents as outlined by Atkin and Bastiani (1986). These roles are seen as reflecting basic ideological beliefs about what is useful in educational terms. Reactive parents, in Atkin and Bastiani's terms, are supportive, 'showing an interest' in their child's learning, 'being a pair of ears' or 'being available'. 'Proactive' parents, on the other hand are more likely to become actively or directly involved, coaching their children and teaching them specific academic skills.

Our results suggest that while many parents are supportive of their children's learning in a reactive sense, only a minority are supportive in a proactive sense. Indeed, even some forms of 'reactive' support, for example, having favourable personal attitudes or favourable attitudes to the child learning Irish, are often missing. As in the national sociolinguistic surveys (CLAR, 1975; Ó Riagáin and Ó Gliasáin, 1984, 1994; INTO, 1985b), the majority of parents in the present study are favourable in terms both of their own attitude to Irish (64.2%) and the general approval they extend to the notion of their children being taught Irish in school (75.3%). This nevertheless leaves substantial minorities of parents who are either neutral or negative. As might be expected, parents who are personally favourable towards Irish in the present study are much more likely to be positive about their children learning Irish also (r=.75).

More favourable parental attitudes to Irish itself, and to their children learning it, are both significantly though not strongly linked to *Pupil Irish attitude/motivation* (r=.25 and r=.27). The association with *Pupil achievement in Irish* is weaker - only *Parent's own attitude to Irish* (r=.14) is significantly correlated with *Pupil achievement in Irish*. *Parent's own attitude to Irish* does not emerge as a significant predictor of either *Pupil achievement in Irish* or *Pupil Irish attitude/motivation* in the regression analyses, due mainly to the prior inclusion in the model of the background variables *Use of Irish at home* and *Parent's ability in Irish* (*Parent's own attitude to Irish* is significantly correlated with both of the latter variables: r=.30; r=.20).

More direct though still fundamentally 'reactive' support - promoting positive attitudes to learning in the child and praising the child - is often wanting. A majority of parents (69.2%) do not directly promote positive attitudes to learning Irish but 'leave it up to the child to develop his/her own attitude'. Only 29.3% 'let the child know Irish is very important'. Nevertheless, hardly any parents (1%) actually 'discourage the child from taking Irish seriously'. In this context it is worth noting that in an ITÉ national survey of sixth-grade teachers in 1985, 58% reported that 'most' parents were 'neutral' about Irish (Harris and Murtagh, 1988b). Presumably, the teachers in this case were making their judgements on the basis of whether parents *actively* supported the child's learning or not.

Praise for the child's school achievements is less common in the case of Irish than in other school subject areas (English/Mathematics/Project work): between 20-30% of parents 'hardly ever' praise Irish reading, oral Irish or Irish writing - compared to only between 2.5%-5% who 'hardly ever' praise Mathematics and English. The fact that failure to praise school achievements is very largely confined to Irish is particularly telling because it means that it is not typical of parental attitudes to school work generally. There may be a variety of reasons for this result, but at least one of them is suggested by the finding that 65.7% of parents think that Irish is of 'little' or 'no importance' as far as their child's future job is concerned. Whatever the reason, a disparity of this order in the amount of parental praise for progress in the three main primary school subjects, and the adoption by most parents of a 'neutral' attitude to the learning of one of them, is clearly a matter of concern from an educational point of view quite apart from any linguistic issues. It is also surely a factor in the substantial proportions of pupils who, on their parents' own report, either have 'no particular feelings' about learning Irish in school' (32.3%) or 'dislike learning' it (21.7%). It will be recalled that significant minorities of pupils themselves (Chapter 3, Table 3.8) do not believe they have the active support and encouragement of their parents in the task of learning Irish (e.g. 35.3% 'disagree' and 15.3% are 'neutral' in relation to the statement 'My parents are usually very interested in anything to do with my Irish schoolwork').

The correlation and regression data leave little doubt about the importance of parental praise and encouragement. *Attitude to learning Irish which parent encourages in the child* and *Parent praises any aspect of child's Irish achievements* are both linked to higher *Pupil achievement in Irish* and to more positive *Pupil Irish attitude/motivation* - correlations range from .16 to .29. Of particular significance is the fact that in the regression analysis, *Parent praises any aspect of child's Irish achievements* continues to make a significant contribution to *Pupil Irish attitude/motivation* (R^2=4%) even after *Parent's ability in Irish* and *Use of Irish at home* have been taken into account. This confirms the crucial contribution of parental praise to pupil attitude/motivation and achievement in Irish.

While the other factor just mentioned, *Attitude to learning Irish which parent encourages in child,* does not make a significant contribution to the explained variance in the regression analysis, this does not mean that it is not important. The fact that, like parental praise, it is significantly and positively correlated with both *Parent's ability in Irish* and *Use of Irish at home* suggests that praise and encouragement are two of the mechanisms by which positive background factors ultimately come to exert an influence on pupil attitude and achievement.

5.4.4 *Parents and Irish homework*

Three quarters of the parents in the present study report that their child spends more than 40 minutes per night on homework generally. This broadly corresponds to the NPC (1991) recommendation that for fifth- and sixth-grade pupils between 40 and 60 minutes is an appropriate amount of time to be allotted to homework. It is consistent also with the evidence of the second International Assessment of Educational Progress (Martin *et al.*, 1992) which we mentioned earlier in the chapter. That study found that 9 year olds spend less than one hour on homework each evening.

Proactive parental involvement in homework might take a variety of forms, such as signing or supervising homework or directly helping the child with their homework assignments. The majority of parents in the present study either supervise or sign their children's homework: 71.3% sign homework 'always/often', while only a slightly smaller proportion (66.6%) say they 'always'/'often' supervise or help with their child's homework. Findings in relation to parents' involvement in specifically Irish homework are less encouraging. More parents 'usually help' their child with Mathematics (70.2%) or English (47.5%) than with Irish generally (34.8%). Responses to a separate question show that those who help with Irish do so usually in the areas of Irish spelling (37.4%) and Irish reading (27.8%). The small discrepancy between the proportions of parents who report helping with 'Irish generally' (34.8%) and helping with Irish spelling (37.4%) may be explained by the slightly different wording of the two questions.

In this context also, parents' perceptions that their child has difficulty with a school subject may be compared with their willingness to help with that subject. Similar proportions of parents report that their child has difficulty with Mathematics and spoken Irish (27.8% and 26.8% respectively). Yet 70.2% of parents report helping with Mathematics, while only 9.1% help with oral/spoken Irish. A similar divergence arises in the case of reading. While more parents report difficulty with Irish reading (15.7%) than with English reading (6.1%), more parents help with English generally (47.5%) than help with either Irish generally (34.8%) or Irish reading specifically (27.8%). It is worth recalling also that parents are more likely to praise their child's achievements in English reading and Mathematics than in Irish reading.

In considering the implications of these findings, it must be acknowledged that the role of parents in relation to homework is extremely complex and that our information is incomplete in many respects. The points which follow, then, probably have more merit as observations on the direction of future research rather than as a definitive interpretation of the findings. One obvious problem is that our questions to parents here do not allow us to say to what extent reports of help with homework reflect (a) parents' willingness to help with different aspects of Irish or (b) how often teachers assign homework in each of these aspects. Nor can we discount the possibility that there may be some implicit accommodation between teachers, parents and pupils regarding homework. For example, it seems reasonable to suppose that, over time, teachers will tend to assign homework in those aspects of a subject which parents and pupils find acceptable and manageable and which, from the teacher's point of view, produce a successful outcome.

The low percentage of parents who report any involvement with homework in 'spoken Irish' is, nevertheless, a matter of concern. It suggests that even though the main emphasis in teaching Irish is on the spoken language, there is little or no point of contact between the vast majority of parents and children involving this aspect of school work. If, as we pointed out earlier, three quarters of the parents seldom or never speak Irish at home, and if fewer than one in ten help with 'spoken Irish' aspects of homework, there can be little opportunity for many parents to observe or praise the achievements of their children as they learn to speak the language. Both the work and achievements of pupils in this area are effectively sealed off in the school.

This is not to ignore how difficult it must be, within the present audiovisual/structural approach to teaching Irish, to identify viable homework assignments which involve speaking. The existing teaching approach does not have a strong communicative emphasis (See Chapter 7-9), and it is communicative type games and tasks which provide the most promising focus for home-based assignments involving parents and children in spoken interaction. Of course, the substantial proportions of parents who cite low levels of competence in Irish as an obstacle to helping with Irish homework (43.9%) is also a central issue here. In fact, the inclination of parents to help with Irish spelling and, to a lesser extent, Irish reading - activities which demand little more than a passive competence in the language - suggests that parental ability in Irish may often determine not only the choice about the aspect of Irish with which they should help, but perhaps even which aspects of Irish are assigned as homework. The problem is that while parent-child activity of any kind which involves Irish is likely to have a positive influence on the child's attitudes and proficiency, examining Irish spellings can easily amount to a mechanical and decontextualised linguistic exercise, providing relatively little stimulus for real interaction in Irish. Spelling exercises are also unlikely to give parents any idea of the way the child learns Irish in school or the child's speaking proficiency in the language. As we mentioned in the introduction, both parents and teachers believe (NPC, 1991; INTO, 1997) that an important function of homework is to provide parents with the opportunity to see the work the child is doing in school and to form their own judgements on how the child is progressing. We will return to some of these issues in the concluding section.

The common sense expectation that parents who help with Irish homework should have children with higher levels of pupil achievement in Irish and, perhaps, better attitudes is confounded by the correlation data. At first sight, it is curious that *Parent usually helps with Irish* is not associated with either higher *Pupil achievement in Irish* or better *Pupil Irish attitude/motivation*. The unexpectedness of this result is increased by the fact that other data show that helping with Irish is associated with many of the other parental factors which are linked with better pupil achievement and attitude - higher social class, higher parental ability in Irish, a tendency to encourage more positive attitudes to learning Irish in children, and a greater knowledge about how Irish is taught.

In fact, however, when we examine a number of other correlations, it becomes clear that the absence of an overall relationship between parental help and pupil attitude and achievement actually masks a more complicated reality. The correlation data in question leave little doubt that the kind of help which is offered by parents varies with the pupil's proficiency level. Those pupils whose parents help them with Irish reading actually tend to have significantly *lower* achievement in Irish (r=-.17) and *lower* general academic ability (r=-.18). Pupils whose parents help them with Irish grammar, in contrast, have marginally higher achievement in Irish and significantly better general academic ability and attitudes to Irish. Our interpretation of this is *not* that parental help has negative effects, but that it is pupils with lower general academic ability and lower levels of proficiency in Irish who receive help with Irish reading.

It may also be noted that children with lower levels of general academic ability in this study are more likely than other children to receive parental help with homework involving *English*, the pupils' native language (r=-.15). It is not surprising, of course, that pupils in sixth-grade who still need parental help with English - perhaps with English reading - would be of lower general academic ability. All this illustrates the complexity of the relationships between parental help with homework and pupil achievement. It is also consistent, of course, with the Martin *et al.* (1992) study mentioned earlier which showed that students who received help with homework did not achieve at higher levels in Mathematics than students who received no help.

5.4.5 *Parents' contact with school and knowledge about Irish teaching.*

The vast majority of parents have at least occasional contact with the school but not much more than a quarter (27.3%) have 'a lot' of contact. Most parents (85.4%) are 'happy' with the existing level of contact. Having more contact with the school is significantly though not strongly associated with a greater knowledge of how Irish is taught. Parents generally do not rate their knowledge of how Irish is taught very highly. A quarter of parents 'know nothing' about how Irish is taught while more than a half (56.6%) 'know only a little'. Only 17.7% 'know a lot'.

While amount of contact does not in itself appear to be critical as far as pupil performance and attitudes are concerned, knowledge of how Irish is taught does. Thus, *Parent's contact with the school* is not significantly correlated with either *Pupil achievement in Irish* or *Pupil Irish attitude/motivation*. The greater the parent's knowledge of how Irish is taught, however, the higher pupil achievement in Irish (r=.22) and the more positive pupil attitude to Irish is (r=.17). The class-level analysis also showed that parents who 'know nothing' about how Irish is taught are more commonly associated with children in low-Irish-achievement classes: in three of the four low-Irish-achievement classes for which we have parental data, the proportion who 'know nothing' ranges from 36% to 46%, while in the middle-Irish-achievement classes the percentages are all under 20. *Parent's knowledge of how Irish is taught in school*, however, did not emerge as a significant predictor in the regression analyses due to the earlier entry of *Parent's ability in Irish* and *Use of Irish at home* into the equation. Both of the latter are significantly correlated with *Parent's knowledge of how Irish is taught* (r=.37; r=.16).

Knowing more about how Irish is taught is at the nexus of a set of parental attributes which are all associated with better achievement and attitudes. Correlation data show that a greater knowledge of how Irish is taught is significantly associated with higher parental ability in Irish, better personal attitudes to Irish, more frequent use of Irish at home, the encouragement of more positive attitudes to learning Irish in children, praise for the child's achievements in Irish and a greater likelihood of helping with Irish homework generally. Thus, being well informed about the teaching of Irish appears to be one of the important ways in which more involved parents influence their children's learning of Irish. Given that at present only a minority of parents feel well informed, initiatives which would improve their knowledge might be expected to bear dividends in terms of pupil achievement and attitude.

One other specific aspect of parents' knowledge about school learning and teaching is their perception of their children's difficulties with the language. In general, parents in this study are much less likely than teachers to perceive their children as having difficulty with school subjects. Over six subjects, the median percentage (Table 5.13) of pupils whose *parents* perceive them as having difficulty (16.2%) is less than half the proportion of pupils whose *teachers* perceive them as having difficulty (40.2%). The two subject areas most frequently cited by parents as causing difficulty are Mathematics (27.8%) and spoken Irish (26.8%). Teachers agree about the relative difficulty posed by these two areas (39.9% and 47.5%) but in addition frequently mention the difficulty posed by Irish writing (48%).

The vast majority of parents think that not only is the school their child is attending 'doing everything possible' to improve their child's progress in Irish generally (83.3%) but also that they personally could not give 'any practical support as far as the teaching of Irish is concerned' apart from what they are already doing (93.4%). On the face of it, these figures might seem to leave relatively little scope for change. In relation to the former, however, it may be noted that some of the comments volunteered by parents, which we discuss in more detail below, seem to suggest that while there are concerns about materials and methods, the remedy is seen as being beyond the local school itself. Regarding the widespread belief of parents that they could not offer the school 'any practical support' in relation to Irish, it has to be presumed that the importance of praise, encouragement and help with homework - whatever about more demanding contributions such as using Irish at home - are not sufficiently well understood by parents at present. Clearly, there is considerable scope for positive intervention here.

5.4.6 *Comments volunteered by parents*

Given that comments were volunteered by only 45% of parents, it would be unwise to attach great importance to the precise percentages associated with particular categories of comment. The comments are of interest, however, in so far as they highlight the main issues about which parents feel strongly, and because these opinions are expressed in the parents' own words (Appendix 5.4).

The negative category containing the most comments (19%) focuses on the desire for more time to be spent on other subjects and less time on Irish (e.g. 'I think in this age of computerised systems etc. it would be better to allocate the time given to Irish to subjects more related to computers'). Other broadly unfavourable categories of comment express disagreement with Irish being compulsory at primary level (10%) or indicate that Irish is not useful or important for the child's future (11%). Examples of the latter categories are 'Irish should not be compulsory: students should choose to learn Irish and be encouraged to learn about their heritage.' and 'I do not see Irish as being of any practical value in today's modern commercial world'.

Nevertheless, a substantial proportion of comments are also broadly favourable or supportive: 12% express support for Irish or the teaching of Irish (e.g. 'I love the Irish language and I will encourage my child to learn it through his school years') while 2% actually want more time devoted to Irish generally. It is notable also that elsewhere in the *Parents' Questionnaire*, responding to a multiple-choice item, almost a quarter of parents (24.2%) say they would support the idea of the school their own child attended teaching 'a subject' through Irish. This figure is generally consistent with national surveys (Ó Riagáin and Ó Gliasáin, 1984, 1994), where 25% and 22% respectively of the *general public* would 'consider some form of Irish medium-education (some subjects/all-Irish) as being suitable for *most* primary school children'. Ó Riagáin (1986: 7) also reports that 24% of the public 'said they would send (or would have sent) their children to an all-Irish primary school if it was locally available'. What is interesting about the proportion responding favourably in the present study is that the question was posed specifically in terms of the school their own child was presently attending.

Assessing children's progress in Irish, 10% of comments express satisfaction while 8% express dissatisfaction. Examples of these contrasting views (see Appendix 5.4) are 'I am happy with the teaching of Irish and the results achieved at the school' versus 'Though my child has an excellent teacher and plenty of help at home, he is coming out of National School without being able to put an original sentence in Irish together. There must be something wrong somewhere'.

Comments in a number of other categories suggest that a substantial proportion of parents lay the blame for what they see as unsatisfactory progress in Irish on methods of teaching and the materials used - in this respect they largely echo the views of the pupils themselves (Chapter 4). The 'methods/materials' theme is represented by three comment categories: a desire for more emphasis on oral or conversational Irish and less on grammar (13%), that the Irish lesson and textbooks should be more interesting, more fun, more attractive and more relevant to the pupil's life (8%), and that Irish would be taught like a modern continental language, using more modern methods (7%). Examples of comments in each of these three categories are:

'More emphasis on oral work and less on grammar especially for primary school children.'
'I would like to see Irish taught as a spoken language like French or German, rather than learning poetry, stories etc. which is really of little importance when school is finished'; and
'...I would question the relevance of certain textbooks which would tend to be middle class and rural in emphasis. The methodology is unnatural, not enough emphasis on conversation'.

If we count each multiply-coded comment just once, these three categories together account for 24% of all parents. Clearly, then, the theme of unsuitable methods and materials is a dominant one. Yet, if we compare these results with replies to a number of multiple-choice questions, some contradictions emerge. For example, only 8.1% of parents overall feel that methods and materials are 'unsuitable' (Appendix 5.3, item 18) and only 14.1% of parents generally feel their child's school 'could do more' to improve their child's Irish . Perhaps it is simply that many parents are concerned about materials and methods but that they feel that fundamental choices about these matters are outside the control of individual teachers and the local school. This issue is also complicated by the low percentages of parents who feel well informed about how Irish is taught.

5.4.7 Implications and recommendations

The present situation as documented in this study is that while parents generally have positive attitudes to Irish and to the notion of their children learning it, actual commitment to and involvement in the process of children learning Irish is much less common. It also compares poorly to parental involvement in the case of other school subjects. Where active participation is present - in the form of encouragement, praise or use of Irish at home - it is associated with more positive pupil attitudes and higher pupil achievement in Irish. Even parental investment which takes the form of being well-informed about how Irish is taught - again something that is often lacking - is linked with positive outcomes for pupils.

Not surprisingly, those parents with higher levels of ability, or who use Irish at home more often, tend to be more supportive and to have children with higher levels of achievement in Irish and better attitudes to the language. Many of the forms of parental support which are lacking, however, do not depend in any direct way on the parents' ability in Irish, as such, and other factors, some of them identified here, must be responsible - doubts about the utility and importance of Irish, lack of awareness of the effect of not supporting the educational enterprise of learning Irish, or lack of knowledge of how best to help their children with Irish. Ideally, to remedy the situation, we need to respond to all these different components of the situation.

Before we outline some suggestions for change, it may be useful to reflect briefly on a number of features of the broad socio-educational context which has helped to create and maintain the relative lack of parental engagement with Irish in primary school. At the beginning of the chapter, we traced the growth of parental involvement in recent years, noting in particular the contribution of the Department of Education and Science, the INTO and the NPC to the debate. While the general difficulties and obstacles which inhibit parental involvement have been identified, involvement in the case of Irish raises personal, social and national issues which appear to be unique to this school subject. It is difficult, for example, to imagine that the attitudes of most parents to the teaching and learning of Mathematics or English would be governed by the kinds of factors which determine their attitudes to the teaching and learning of Irish - indeed our own results here provide evidence of that.

Looking back over parent-school relations at primary level as they concern Irish, and at the specific evidence produced here, it could be argued that the implicit contract in the past was that the development of proficiency in Irish in children was the work of the school. This arrangement was no doubt agreeable to parents who were either neutral or negative about Irish. Separating the two spheres also had the advantage for schools of sealing-off a potentially negative affective factor which might otherwise have undermined pupil motivation and made the teacher's task more difficult in certain cases. The increasing involvement of parents in education, however, may be expected to destabilise some of these traditional accommodations. Parents whose personal attitudes to Irish are negative, but who nevertheless want to be more involved in the education of their children, gradually will be drawn more directly into the learning process in the case of Irish. While the final outcome from the point of view of the child's education can only be positive, the degree of success in the case of Irish may well depend on how the process of change to greater parental involvement in this subject is managed and researched.

Information, expectations, praise and parent's Irish
Given the results of the present study, a number of different levels at which parents might be expected to be involved in Irish in future can be identified. At the most basic level, parents need to be informed about the benefits of more direct involvement. As Macbeth (1989: 103) points out, parents are more likely to give support and encouragement to the school's curriculum if they understand its aims and objectives. He suggests that class or group meetings between the teacher and parents 'are an appropriate mechanism for explanation and encouragement'. The NPC-Primary (1991) advocates class meetings as 'a forum for the teacher to discuss with parents the curriculum objectives, methods used for assessment of children's progress, guidelines for homework, discipline and other relevant matters'. Parents need specific information on how Irish is taught, the precise goals of

teaching it and indeed the nature of first and second-language learning in children of primary-school age. The introduction of the new curriculum in Irish will provide a useful opportunity to present this information in a fresh way. An information booklet could be prepared for parents and, indeed, certain in-class materials could be designed in such a way as to facilitate later parental involvement at home.

Particular attention should also be paid to fostering realistic expectations about what can be achieved in a primary-school programme in which the language is taught as just one subject. Evidence from Ireland and many other countries suggests that performance expectations for second- and foreign-language programmes at primary level tend to be unrealistic (Swain, 1981; Stern, 1982; Harris, 1984, 1991). Parents seem to underestimate just how hard it is for children to learn a second language in a school context. In so far as they do not use a realistic yardstick in assessing the progress of their own children in learning to speak Irish, for example, they may inadvertently belittle what has been achieved by the children. The problem may even have an intergenerational element to the extent that parents themselves may have acquired the same low self-esteem about their own language-learning performance - also based on unrealistic expectations.

Some of the misunderstanding probably arises from the common belief that children learn languages more quickly than adults. The fact is that while children often acquire languages more quickly in a *naturalistic* setting, where they are entirely surrounded by the language, this does not happen in a classroom setting. What must be borne in mind is that the motivational and other factors which can affect learning are very different in naturalistic settings compared to classrooms. For example, in a second-language classroom, unlike in a naturalistic foreign-language situation, children share a mother tongue with their peers. Thus a major motivation to learn the language - to communicate with their friends - is missing. In any event, the available research provides no clear evidence that younger children are better learners in a classroom context (though pronunciation may be an exception) (Stern, 1981: Singleton, 1995). This does not mean, however, that an early start in second and foreign-language learning is not desirable - it is indeed desirable for a variety of other important reasons (see Harris, 1991).

Parents also need to be alerted to the specific educational consequences for their own child of providing only lukewarm support, or actually withholding approval altogether, for the process of learning Irish. Having in principle committed themselves to the notion of their children learning Irish, to then remain neutral about the value and success of the enterprise, and to communicate this stance to children, is to greatly increase its chance of failure. From the point of view of building for the future, it must be counted a positive result that only 9% of parents are against the child being taught Irish (including 2% who are strongly against it), and that only 1% of parents actually discourage pupils from taking it seriously. It suggests that a call for parents to recognise and praise more explicitly their children's progress in learning to speak Irish, just as they mark progress in other subject areas, would be generally well received. It scarcely needs to be said that any specific initiative to persuade parents in this area must be conducted in a way which both respects the parents' own views regarding Irish, where these are negative, and which ultimately fully acknowledges parents' rights to promote their children's welfare in whatever way they see fit.

The quality of parental involvement in Irish is also likely to be enhanced by providing opportunities for parents to develop their own competence in Irish. On the evidence of the present study, a large proportion of parents (44%) believe their lack of ability in Irish presents a problem. This is consistent with the view of the NPC-Primary (1991) that lack of parental competence and confidence in relation to Irish and Mathematics is a source of difficulty and tension for parents who want to help. It is significant also that of those classes organized for parents in the 'Home-School-Community Liaison Scheme' (Ryan, 1995), the most popular were those which directly related to *what* the children were learning, i.e. academic skills in Irish, English, Mathematics etc. As the results here strongly suggest, improving parental ability in Irish may be an important first step in improving a range of parental attitudes and practices which are positively linked to pupil attitude and achievement in Irish.

Research on home-based activities
Setting up parent-teacher structures and providing information or language classes, even where all this is done on the basis of collaboration and choice, may not be enough to effect real change in the traditional pattern of parental involvement. We believe that it is essential to initiate a series of research and development projects which, working jointly with parents and teachers, would explore ways of bringing parents closer to what happens in the Irish class. Involvement in the learning of *spoken* Irish, the core of the Irish lesson, is particularly important and presents special difficulties for a number of reasons: the present structural-linguistic approach to teaching Irish; the difficulty for pupils of 'bringing home' or illustrating their proficiency in spoken Irish for parents; and the generally low levels of home use of Irish. Central to the solution of these problems, we believe, is the development and redefinition of the traditional notion of homework. What is needed in the case of spoken Irish are home-based activities which serve one or more of the following functions: informing parents about how Irish is taught and how much the child has learned; giving the child a chance to shine in front of the parents, to demonstrate his or her competence in speaking Irish; providing occasions for parents to recognise and praise achievements; and encouraging parents to become more directly involved in the child's learning of Irish.

The proposed new communicative approach to teaching Irish could facilitate these initiatives because communicative tasks, originally introduced in a classroom context, can often provide a natural focus for home-based interaction involving parents and children. Examples of tasks which could provide such a focus are:

1. Pupils are asked to repeat at home a simple 'survey' in Irish which had already been carried out in school. The survey might involve the pupils finding out which county/townland parents were born in; which of two television programmes the

parents preferred; which foods the parents disliked. The task of pupils might be to fill in a simple check list in Irish to record the information.

2. Activities which involved the pupil teaching his or her parents a simple game in Irish.
3. Tasks which depend for completion on parents and pupils jointly listening to Irish material on an audio tape.

Care must be taken that unrealistic demands are not made on parents' knowledge of Irish. The provision of pictorial assistance on any written Irish material would help to simplify such tasks. Even in cases where the exchanges at home take place in English, however, they are valuable in that they establish a parental link with communicative activities conducted in the Irish lesson. More generally, it might be argued that one of the criteria which should be applied to communicative speaking/listening materials which are developed for the new Irish curriculum is that a proportion of them would be adaptable for use in joint parent-child activities at home. Those activities which focus on the pupil's own life, as the best communicative materials usually do, clearly have an advantage over structural linguistic or language practice tasks.

Home-based activities which yield some 'product' or provide feedback to the teacher/class are probably preferable to those which do not. Certain kinds of home-based spoken-Irish activities which are primarily designed to inform parents about how Irish is taught and how their child is progressing, however, need *not* involve feedback to the school. For example, one teacher in the *Communicative Materials Project*, with the help of the children in his class, made a video recording of various activities in the Irish lesson, including examples of each individual child speaking Irish. Each child in turn was then allowed to take the video home. Because the video, in Irish, featured both the parents' own child and each of his/her classmates, it was viewed with great interest. There is every reason to think that this kind of approach to keeping parents informed would be successful irrespective of the approach to teaching - audio-visual, communicative or otherwise - which was adopted in the school. In the context of a communicative approach to teaching Irish, for example, pupils might make audio or video recordings in class of simple role-plays or dramas which could be brought home to parents later. The knowledge that the material would be seen at home later has the potential to heighten interest in the classroom as long as care is taken to ensure that each child has an opportunity to perform successfully.

In mentioning these examples, we are not arguing for their particular merits or practicality, but simply illustrating how the notion of homework in the case of spoken Irish might be developed in future. In fact, it is precisely because this area is so unexplored at present that a series of research and development projects is needed. Needless to say, parents and teachers would have to be involved in the development of any such initiatives. Kellaghan, Sloane, Alvarez, and Bloom (1993) point out that small discussion groups of parents, or groups of parents and teachers, can be very useful in adapting general initiatives to local conditions. Provision for choice and different levels of involvement would have to be made from the beginning. It would be critical, in particular, to be realistic about the amount of time parents could be expected to devote to home-based tasks and materials. Our proposals essentially amount to a change of emphasis in the kinds of home-based activities employed rather than an increase in the total amount of time devoted to them. The ultimate goal should be to identify the kinds of home-based tasks and materials that are congenial to the greatest range of parents and teachers and that are most helpful to children.

The home-school link in the Communicative Materials Project
The importance of collaboration and choice in developing home-based activities related to Irish is well illustrated by our experience of trying to promote some contact between the Irish class and what parents do in the home in the context of the *Communicative Materials Project* (Harris *et al.*, 1996a,b). Because of the constraints of time and personnel, an initiative on only the most modest scale could be contemplated and it was not possible to solicit the views of parents in advance. The initiative consisted of the inclusion, from time to time, in the teacher's communicative materials of information sheets for parents. It was intended that these sheets would be photocopied by the teacher and given to pupils to take home to their parents. The sheets contained phrases in Irish which the child had learnt and used at school and which could be easily adapted for use in routine interaction at home. A statement of the purpose of the information sheet was also included. It was explained that the child's progress in Irish would benefit if parents could use some of the listed phrases at home from time to time.

Only teachers could be consulted about the impact of this initiative - no assessment of parents' or pupils' reaction was possible within the scope of the project. Teachers had mixed feelings. While most believed that the basic idea was good, they felt that since only one teacher in each school was participating in the project, the conditions for involving parents were not right. They felt that a school-wide initiative that had been fully explained to all parents would have had a better chance of success. There were also suggestions about the content of the sheets - the desirability of the message to parents coming from the teacher in his or her own words (rather than in the form of a prepared note), and the possibility of providing English translations or pictorial representations of the phrases which parents were expected to use with the child. Others felt that the possibility should be explored of including in the pupil textbooks, or on prepared audio or video tapes, spoken-Irish games or tasks which would involve parents and children in interaction. In any event, our experience with this simple initiative illustrates the critical importance of careful planning and piloting, and of including parents and teachers at the design stage.

Apart from this general initiative, activities which implicitly or explicitly involved some connection with parents or home were occasionally included in lessons developed in the course of the *Communicative Materials Project*. These were usually listed as optional activities under the *Dúshláin Bhreise* heading. While we have no basis on which to evaluate the specific merits or otherwise of these suggestions, a few examples will indicate the kind of activities involved: (i) pupils are asked to invent, in consultation with their parents, a name in Irish for their own home; alternatively, they are asked to collect information from parents or grandparents about placenames associated with the latters' upbringing (ii) pupils are taught the Irish necessary to submit a request to a radio programme for a relative who is in hospital and (iii) pupils are asked to bring in a photograph of themselves when they were younger - pupils in the class must guess which pupil is represented in each photograph.

The future

Last September, ITÉ began work on a new project which will investigate more systematically how parents might support their children's efforts to acquire speaking proficiency in Irish (Harris and Ó Cathalláin, 1999, in progress). The project's long-term aim is to develop, in partnership with teachers, parents and pupils, a programme which is reasonably explicit but is also flexible enough to be applied in a range of settings. Initially, the emphasis will be on producing a booklet for parents and on developing communicative lesson units which anticipate and attempt to facilitate the involvement of parents at home. Nine schools in the east and southwest of the country, representing a range of social and educational circumstances, are involved. This number may be increased next year if results are positive. While the project is still at a very early stage, it appears so far to support the general validity of the analysis of parental involvement which we have outlined here.

Up to this point, we have been talking about parental involvement in Irish at primary level largely in educational terms. But any improvement in parental support and involvement which enhances pupil proficiency is ultimately a contribution to the larger language-promotion effort. Arguably, any such intervention also has an immediate language-revival potential in terms of the parents themselves. This is simply because, as our results here show, different aspects of parents' views and practices are all intimately connected. If in response to the kind of educational initiatives we have just been discussing, conventional parental involvement in Irish - in terms of variables such as praise, encouragement and help with homework - were to improve to the levels associated with Mathematics or English, is it not likely that the conditions for parental ability in Irish and attitude to Irish to improve would also have been created?

From a broader sociolinguistic perspective, there is a need to investigate the kinds of policy initiatives in the educational domain which will maximise backwash effects on parental ability and use of Irish at home and in the community. The Irish ability and use profile of the present sample of parents compared to the national population, already suggests the existence of such backwash effects at a low level in the case of even ordinary schools. While the effects may be small, the fact that they apply to large numbers of children makes them an important component of the language promotion effort.

6 Development of the Irish Lesson Analysis System (ILAS)

6.1 Introduction

Existing research on Irish in the primary school has tended to focus either on standards of attainment nationally or on the extent to which curriculum objectives are mastered. Apart from questionnaire-based data on teacher perceptions and practices (Harris, 1984; INTO, 1985a; Harris and Murtagh, 1988b), relatively little process-type information on the teaching and learning of Irish is available. In particular, no studies involving direct classroom observation of the Irish lesson have been carried out. In an effort to fill this gap in research, we set out in the present study to develop classroom observation instruments which would describe and analyse Irish language lessons and classroom interaction in primary school.

We have a number of aims. One of these is to establish the viability of two different types of classroom observation instruments. The first of these (*The Irish Lesson Analysis System*) describes the structure and composition of the lesson in terms of dimensions such as topics, language activities, materials and classroom organisation. The second (*The Pupil Communicative Behaviour Record*) describes pupil participation and language use based on observation of individual pupils.

Our second aim is to use the data derived from these instruments to describe the teaching of Irish generally in terms of characteristics and practices which, either currently or traditionally, are considered important in developing proficiency in the language. For example, we would like to be able to assess the relative emphasis on various types of language activities. How popular are drills? How much real or simulated communication in Irish is to be found in the typical Irish lesson? How much 'whole class' teaching occurs? How much reading aloud is employed? What materials are used? To what extent do pupils participate in the lesson and what form does this participation take?

A third aim is to establish how much variation there is, from class to class, in the composition of the Irish lesson and in pupil participation and language use. Do classes with a higher level of achievement in spoken Irish spend more time on particular kinds of activities or topics compared to classes with lower levels of achievement? How do teaching practices in sixth-grade Irish classes compare to those in first-year French foreign-language classes? How does class attention and interest vary with different kinds of activities or with different forms of classroom organisation? Do pupils of different levels of ability in Irish participate equally in class?

Chapters 6 to 9 describe the investigation of these and other issues. Three of the chapters are devoted to the *Irish Lesson Analysis System* (*ILAS*) in order to do justice to the variety of different perspectives on the Irish lesson which this instrument provides. One chapter is given over to the description of the *Pupil Communicative Behaviour Record* (*PCBR*) and the data it generates.

Chapter 6, the present chapter, gives an account of the development and use of *ILAS*, the instrument which focuses on the structure and composition of the Irish lesson.

Chapter 7 uses the direct classroom observation data derived from the *ILAS* to describe the Irish lesson in terms of *Topic, Language activity* and *Materials*.

Chapter 8 uses data from three other dimensions of *ILAS* to describe the Irish lesson in terms of *Pupil behaviour, Teacher mode of involvement* and *Classroom organisation*.

Chapter 9 describes and analyses individual pupil participation and language use during the Irish lesson using data derived from the *PCBR*.

We begin with a review of current research on the classroom processes which are presumed to be responsible for successful second-language learning. This serves to introduce the main issues which arise not only in choosing and adapting classroom observation instruments but also in interpreting the results presented in Chapters 7 and 8. We then outline the development and application of the *ILAS* and summarise the main dimensions and categories of the system. The chapter concludes with an assessment of teachers' reactions to the observation work itself and a brief discussion and commentary on selected transcripts of the observed lessons.

6.2 Classroom processes related to successful language learning

This review is not intended to be comprehensive but is limited to research which is most relevant to the present study and to the teaching of Irish. A number of issues are covered: the evolution of communicative language teaching, the experiential-analytic continuum, and the reinstatement and reconceptualisation of the analytic focus in teaching. In large part, what we will be discussing is the gradual switch which has been taking place over the last 25 years from structurally based syllabuses and teaching methods to a communicative approach. The issues to be examined are particularly relevant to the teaching of Irish at primary level at present because of the imminent switch from the audio-visual approach, which directly or indirectly has dominated Irish language teaching for the last twenty five years, to a communicative approach. As we enter this period of change, decisions will have to be made about what aspects of the existing approach must change and what aspects are worth retaining. Research on classroom-based second-language learning is likely to have a significant contribution to make to these decisions.

6.2.1 The evolution of communicative language teaching

Over the last three decades, the focus of research on second-language teaching has shifted from a concern with methods and outcomes to an attempt to understand how particular classroom processes are linked to second-language acquisition. This new research focus developed in parallel with changes in second-language pedagogy. As Mitchell (1994) points out these changes in teaching practices were prompted to a large extent by the demands of a post-war population who had a particular interest in foreign-language instruction. During the 1970's, however, existing methods, the most common being the traditional grammar-translation method and the audiolingual method, were beginning to be seen as inadequate for a number of reasons: a) lack of precise definitions of objectives, b) their narrow 'structural' approach to teaching the target language and c) their apparent lack of success in promoting worthwhile levels of fluency or communicative ability in the target language. In the grammar-translation method, the emphasis is on promoting explicit knowledge of rules, and practice in the four main skills of listening, speaking, reading and writing. The audiolingual method, on the other hand, which became popular in the 1960's is based on a behaviouristic view of language learning, in which it is proposed that language will be acquired inductively through listening, imitation and practice.

A crucial early impetus for the changes which have now taken place in second-language and foreign-language teaching was provided by the success of immersion programmes. The evidence from these programmes suggested that languages are best learned when the main focus of instruction is on 'meaning' or 'message' rather than on language practice alone. It was found that children in these programmes were achieving high levels of second-language proficiency, with no adverse effects on their native language development or overall academic achievement (Lambert and Tucker, 1972; Swain and Lapkin, 1982; Genesee, 1983). Krashen (1981, 1982, 1985) believed that the critical ingredient necessary for effective language teaching in regular 'subject-only' programmes was the provision of 'comprehensible' or meaningful input, just as happens in subject-matter teaching in immersion programmes. Learners will begin to produce language when they are ready as in first-language acquisition. Grammar should 'take care of itself,' obviating any need for an explicit focus on rules.

In line with the new emphasis on communication, more experiential modes of learning were introduced into ordinary, non-immersion classrooms. A study by Savignon (1972) indicated that introducing a 'communicative' component into an audiolingual method resulted in additional advantages for learners in terms of their ability to communicate fluently in the target language. Group work which was a feature of the new approach was thought to provide the learner with more opportunities for using the target language. Long, Adams, Mclean, and Castanos (1976) reported that the quality and quantity of learners' speech was greater in group work than in teacher-centred ('lockstep') activities. Learners were more likely to take the initiative and to negotiate meaning using a variety of language functions (requesting, clarifying , hypothesizing etc.) in the context of group work.

These ideas and results eventually culminated in the formulation of a new goal for language teaching: developing 'communicative competence'. To be competent in the language, it was argued, a learner must not only have an in-depth knowledge of its grammar and vocabulary but must also be able to use this knowledge appropriately in a range of social situations (Hymes, 1972). Canale (1983) defined 'communicative competence' as comprising four different components: grammatical, discourse, sociolinguistic and strategic competence. In the last two decades, the adoption of this new definition of language proficiency has given rise to substantial changes seen in syllabus design, teaching methodologies and materials. Much of the early development work on this new approach in second-language teaching involved groups of language teachers who cooperated in defining new 'functional based' syllabuses and attainable objectives in teaching modern languages. Many of these new syllabuses defined their objectives in terms of various language 'notions' or 'functions' (Wilkins, 1976). For example, the Threshold Level syllabuses (Van Ek, 1975) specify language-learning objectives in terms of units such as 'situations', 'activities', 'language functions', general 'notions' and 'language forms'.

Some of the more narrowly-defined 'notional-functional' syllabuses have been criticised for their lack of concern with the psychological reality of the notions and functions cited (Paulston, 1981; Long and Crookes, 1993). The recent move towards using task-based syllabuses is motivated by such concerns. Proponents of task-based language teaching (TBLT) believe that 'notional-functional' syllabuses, in common with 'structural' syllabuses, are more concerned with the units of language to be taught than with the actual learner and the learning process itself (Breen, 1987; Long and Crookes, 1992, 1993). Instead, it is argued, that the focus should be on forms which are highly motivating for the learner, and which focus on something to be 'done' rather than to be 'said' and which are derived from a 'needs analysis' of the learner group. Task-based language teaching, however, has not been adopted or evaluated to any significant extent. Some of the criticisms of TBLT are directed at the difficulty of differentiating between tasks and sub-tasks within them and of grading tasks for difficulty. The value of TBLT may be best seen in courses designed for adult learners who are learning the language for a specific purpose e.g. the BBC programme 'Get by in Italian' (BBC, 1981).

Functional approaches to language learning collectively known as Communicative Language Teaching (CLT) have had a significant impact on practice in the language classroom itself in terms of lesson content, methodology and materials. Learners are now encouraged to adopt different roles, and to engage in meaningful and socially appropriate discourse. By broadening the range of topics, activities and materials available in the classroom CLT tries to approximate as far as possible the language experiences found in natural language-learning situations. The use of the target language in the classroom is encouraged, especially for routine classroom procedures. Learners are encouraged to acquire language through using it rather than analysing it, to exploit their existing linguistic systems to the full and to learn coping strategies useful in real life situations. Error correction is generally not encouraged and in many instances is even ignored.

Other features of CLT, which are associated more with general learning theory than with the theory of 'communicative competence' focus on the role of the learner and the teacher in negotiating classroom activities and content (Mitchell, 1996). The role of the teacher is seen as that of facilitator, building up pupils' self-confidence with the aim of getting them to take charge of their own learning i.e. become 'autonomous' learners. Thus, activities which lead the pupil to reflect upon and evaluate their learning strategies are encouraged, as well as more challenging activities such as extensive reading practice and activities using authentic materials.

It will be clear from all this that CLT is not a unitary theory or method but rather a 'fluid and changing body of ideas' (Mitchell, 1994: 41), which exists in 'weak' and 'strong' versions' (Mitchell, 1988). In practice, teachers vary in the extent to which they adopt some of these communicative activities in the language. In the Bangalore Communicative Teaching Project (Prabhu, 1987; Beretta, 1992), for example, the performance of pupils involved in the experimental teaching group who were taught using a communicative task-based syllabus was compared with that of pupils who were instructed using the regular structure-based approach. Beretta (1992) reported that although pupils in the CLT programme did better, the fact that some teachers in the 'experimental' group appeared to have reverted to 'form focused' teaching made it difficult to interpret the results in any meaningful way.

6.2.2 *The experiential-analytic continuum in language teaching*

It is often difficult to find classrooms which can be called 'communicative' in every sense of the word. This and the frequent blurring of distinctions between traditional and communicative methodologies has posed problems for those concerned with straight method comparisons. A distinction which has proved useful, however, in comparing classrooms is the 'experiential' and 'analytic' continuum outlined by Stern (1990, 1992).

In the case of an 'experiential' strategy, the learner is encouraged to use the language for a purpose - to focus on the message rather than the code. The assumption is that errors will disappear gradually with exposure to rich and varied language input. The language is taught in context and approximates, as far as possible, characteristics of real language use. While this strategy is an essential feature of a communicative syllabus, Stern (1992) points out that it is not limited to this syllabus alone.

In contrast, in the 'analytic' strategy the focus is on analysing the code or the language system. The learner stands back as it were from the language, becoming familiar with specific features of it, trying them out 'safely outside the pressure of a real communicative situation'. By necessity an 'analytic' strategy decontextualizes specific linguistic features.

This analytic-experiential distinction has been used by Allen, Carroll, Burtis and Gaudino (1987) in examining communicative practices in core French-language classrooms. Observing eight classes over four different lessons they tried to establish if there were certain analytic and experiential features which were more important than others in the development of second-language proficiency. The features used were taken from the *COLT* (*Communicative Orientation to Language Teaching*), an observation scheme which had been derived from the communicative competence framework and from current theories and research in second-language teaching (Allen, Fröhlich and Spada, 1984).

The *COLT* is divided into two parts. Part I describes classroom events according to five parameters: the *activity* engaged in (e.g. drill/discussion etc.), *participant organisation* (whole class, group work etc.), *content* (topics such as management issues, form/function of language, etc.), *student modality* (listening, speaking, reading, writing) and *materials* (type, length of text). Part II describes the communicative features of both students' and teachers' verbal exchanges during the class. The seven features include *use of target language, information gap* (extent to which information is not known in advance), *sustained speech* (extent to which speakers engage in extended speech), *reaction to code or message* (drawing attention to incorrectness of form or message), *incorporation of preceding utterances* (comment, paraphrase, repetition etc.), *discourse initiation* (frequency of student initiated turns), and *relative restriction of linguistic form* (degree of restriction placed on student talk).

Allen, Carroll, Burtis and Gaudino (1987) distinguished between classes which scored high on communicative features (the 'experiential' group) and the rest (the 'analytic' group). Two classes fell into the former and six into the latter group. Allen, Swain, Harley, and Cummins (1990: 61) noted that none of these 8 classes were 'prototypically experiential or analytic' but rather 'all were intermediate along the bipolar scale'. In relation to pupils' performance on a number of grammatical, discourse and sociolinguistic features in the target language, no significant differences were found in favour of one type of classroom over another: of the two 'experiential' classes, one made the greatest gain of all eight classes in overall proficiency over the year, while the other 'experiential class' made the least gain overall.

A correlation analysis, however, revealed both positive and negative associations between achievement, on the one hand, and some 'experiential' and 'analytic' features, on the other. Gains in class achievement (on some proficiency measures) from pre-test to post-test measures were associated with relatively more time devoted to the 'experiential' features *information gap, reaction to message, topic incorporation* and *sustained speech* by the teacher. Gains were also associated with more emphasis on two 'analytic' features - activities which were *teacher directed* (teacher addressed the whole class while students worked individually) and activities in which the focus was on *form*.

Other analytic and experiential features were associated with a falling-off in class achievement. Specifically, lower class achievement was associated with more emphasis on analytic features such as *choral work, predictable information* and *display requests* in teachers speech. Somewhat surprisingly, negative associations were related to more time spent on *student speech*, even student speech which was *sustained*. Taken together, the results led Allen *et al.* (1990: 62) to conclude that 'the analytic focus and the experiential focus may be complementary, and that they may provide essential support for one another in the classroom'.

6.2.3 *Reinstating and reconceptualising the analytic focus*

The argument for and against an 'analytic' focus in CLT is ongoing. While some teachers may have abandoned explicit grammar teaching, others choose to retain some traditional grammar teaching alongside the new communicative practices. Studies in communicative ESL classrooms reveal that even though learners develop high levels of fluency and communicative ability in English they still have problems with linguistic accuracy and complexity (Spada and Lightbown, 1989; Lightbown and Spada, 1990, 1993). Two descriptive studies (Spada, 1987; Spada and Lightbown, 1993) have indicated that learners who engaged in activities which focused on form within communicative ESL classrooms had an advantage in terms of oral proficiency in the target language.

The need for an analytic focus to complement the experiential (communicative) focus is also suggested by data from immersion programmes. Despite these pupils' ability to comprehend effectively, their productive language skills and knowledge of certain grammatical rules have been found to be less well developed than that of native speakers (Harley and Swain, 1977; Genesee, 1983; Harley, 1984; Swain, 1985; Allen *et al.*, 1990). In particular, the verb system of immersion pupils seems to be simplified compared to native speakers. Swain (1985) claims that what is missing in immersion programmes is 'comprehensible output'. According to this view learners in immersion classes are not given enough opportunities to produce the target language or to negotiate meaning in the classroom context. This is supported by the finding that only about 14% of immersion student talk in teacher fronted activities were 'sustained' or more than one clause in length (Swain, 1996). More specifically, what the 'comprehensible output' hypothesis suggests is that immersion pupils are not being 'pushed' to understand the grammar of the target language. Swain believes that by getting learners themselves to focus on their output, or on the quality of their productions, they can be pushed to move from a purely semantic analysis of the language to a syntactic analysis. For example, when learners experience communicative failure they can be pushed into making their output more precise, coherent and appropriate. This 'pushed output' helps learners to reconstruct their interlanguages and thus move the acquisition process forward.

Within the last decade a number of intervention studies have investigated the effect of introducing a 'form-focused' dimension into communicative language teaching. Such programmes make an important contribution to second-language research in that they indicate new possibilities for improving the quality of learners' productions (in particular their grammatical competence) within 'communicative' programmes.

An experimental study by White (1991) investigated the effect of explicitly focusing on the correct use of adverbs within an intensive ESL programme. The results indicated greater gains (on a written task) for the instructed group compared to a control or uninstructed group. VanPatten and Cadierno (1993) compared two types of form-focused instruction in a communicative second-language programme for university students. One group of students received 'traditional' form-focused instruction (provision of rule and practice in producing sample sentences) while the other group received 'processing' instruction where the emphasis was on getting students to interpret target sentences correctly (i.e. establishing 'form-meaning' relationships). Advantages in comprehension and production were reported for subjects who received 'processing' instruction.

Three other studies have examined the effect of 'form-focused' instruction in content-based teaching in immersion programs (Harley, 1989; Day and Shapson, 1991; Lyster, 1994). Both Harley (1989) and Day and Shapson (1991) set about determining the effect of developing curriculum materials for the teaching of, or increasing awareness of, some of the more complex 'analytic features' in French immersion classes. In both studies the strategy consisted of drawing children's attention to these grammatical features and using them in communicative activities e.g. games etc. No explicit grammatical rules were provided. In Harley's experiment children's attention was drawn to the functional distinctions between the *imparfait* and the *passé composé*. Day and Shapson focused on the use of the conditional mood in hypothetical situations such as an imaginary space colony. In the latter study, students worked in pairs and participated in self-evaluation designed to raise awareness of their own language use. Both the Harley (1989) and the Day and Shapson (1991) study showed gains for the experimental classes.

More recently Lyster (1994) investigated the possibility of improving immersion pupils' sociolinguistic competence by using materials and teaching strategies which highlighted distinctions in socio-stylistic variations (in the use of formal/informal registers). Lyster believes that by focusing on form-meaning relationships, 'ostensibly fossilized forms in the immersion interlanguage may develop into more appropriate forms through a restructuring of internal representations of knowledge'. His results showed that over a period of about two months, experimental classes performed better than comparison classes on sociolinguistic measures of written and oral production.

The combined wisdom of researchers and practitioners points to the benefits of *explicitly* linking form and meaning in communicative teaching. To this end new ways of teaching grammar within a communicative programme are being explored. These include strategies such as 'consciousness raising' techniques, 'interpretation tasks' and the use of 'advance organisers'. In 'consciousness-raising' techniques (Rutherford, 1987; Sharwood Smith, 1993) the learner's attention is drawn to target structures in the input. Terrell (1991), one of the main proponents of a natural approach in L2 acquisition (see also Krashen and Terrell, 1983), acknowledges the benefits of an explicit focus on grammar within a communicative framework. She advocates the use of 'advance organisers' to draw learners' attention to a particular structure. A series of communicative activities are then engaged in which provide instances of the same structure. Finally, Ellis (1995) proposes the use of 'interpretation tasks' where learners attend to specific grammatical input and are encouraged to notice the gap between how a particular form works and how they are using it in their productions. A common feature of all these comprehension-based approaches is that they focus on the development of 'implicit' knowledge rather than 'explicit' knowledge of target language structures - there is no expectation that learners produce these target structures individually.

Despite the renewed interest in 'form-focused' instruction it would be untrue to say that the wheel has turned full circle. Rather the evidence reviewed here suggests that both 'analytic' and 'experiential' features play a significant part in second-language instruction. The challenge which faces second-language teaching lies in getting the 'form-meaning' balance right (Brumfit, 1985). This involves identifying suitable classroom activities and discourse which not only maximise the opportunities for communication but also opportunities for establishing 'form-meaning' relationships. The limited research results comparing 'analytic'/'experiential' strategies led Stern (1992: 326) to suggest that 'it is best for teachers to be open to the specific merits and drawbacks of the two strategies, and to mix them in accordance with their personal judgement on the benefits to be derived'.

The issues and research examined in this review prompt many questions about the teaching of Irish in primary school at present and about the direction which it might take in the future. At the moment the Irish programme does not appear to fit tidily into either an extreme 'experiential' or an extreme 'analytic' model. While the analytic focus is strongly represented because of the structural syllabus and audio-visual method in which present teaching has its origins, aspects of the 'second-language' (Harris, 1991) character of the programme give it an experiential focus as well. The experiential focus is manifested in a number of ways. Irish is reported to be widely used for routine classroom communication (Harris, 1983; INTO, 1985a) and to a more limited extent in about one-fifth of schools as a medium of instruction (Harris, 1983; INTO, 1985a; Harris and Murtagh, 1988a).

There are many questions about the teaching of Irish in primary school, therefore, which the direct classroom observation studies described in subsequent chapters should help to answer. How communicative is the Irish lesson at present? What should be the proper balance between 'experiential' and 'analytic' activities in any new programme? How can pupil interest and motivation and participation in learning Irish be enhanced? The studies which we are about to describe attempt at least a preliminary answer to some of these questions. As we analyse and discuss our findings in subsequent chapters we also hope to be able to make some suggestions for the future.

6.3 The ITÉ classroom observation study

6.3.1 *Adapting language classroom observation instruments*

In developing the instruments to be used in observing the Irish lesson in the *Twenty-Classes Study* we had two main aims. First, that in terms of their structure and focus the instruments would reflect both practical and theoretical aspects of Irish language teaching: (a) the kind of conceptualisation of lessons as sequences of activities organised by the teacher which teachers themselves would find natural and appropriate and (b) the aspects of classroom discourse and pupil-teacher interaction which recent work on systematic observation and second-language acquisition have identified as making important contributions to the development of second-language proficiency.

Our second aim was to use existing classroom observation systems, or an adaptation of them, if possible, since our resources would not allow us to begin the task of constructing instruments from scratch.

As it happens, there are only a handful of existing instruments which, even with substantial adaptation, would meet the requirements mentioned above. The most important of these are the Stirling System developed by Mitchell, Parkinson and Johnstone (1981) at the University of Stirling and the *COLT* system, described earlier, which originated at the Ontario Institute for Studies in Education (Allen *et al.*, 1984). Unlike earlier schemes (e.g. Wragg, 1970) which were conceptualised in terms of the kind of pupil-teacher interaction which is characteristic of teaching in the content areas (e.g.

Mathematics, History), the newer schemes which we have just mentioned acknowledge some of the unique features of the second-language classroom - e.g. the preoccupation with the medium itself, the second language, as well as with the content and function of the discourse in that medium. These two existing instruments share many features, reflecting a certain amount of agreement about the aspects of classroom practice that are important. For example, both instruments provide for the recording of information on the broad structure and composition of the lesson e.g. the main language teaching activities engaged in by the teacher as the lesson proceeds - 'drills', 'translation', 'free' or 'real' communication etc. Likewise, each provides for the systematic recording of the teaching materials used - blackboard, jotter, textbook, film strips, etc.

But there are also substantial differences between the systems which bear on the suitability to the case of the Irish lesson. Unlike the Stirling System, the *COLT* also provides for the coding of various *communicative* features of student and teacher interaction, such as length of utterance, whether the preceding utterance of the teacher or student is incorporated, the extent to which there is a real information gap between the participants and whether the student initiates conversational turns. As the research discussed earlier suggests these and other aspects of communicative interaction in the classroom may be associated with a more rapid development of proficiency in a second language (Krashen, 1982; Swain, 1985; Prabhu, 1987). Thus, the *COLT* Part II provided a better model for the *PCBR* which permitted the analysis of pupil behaviour and language use (see Chapter 9).

To describe the Irish lesson at the level of pedagogic dimensions such as language activity, topic etc. we used the Stirling System rather than the *COLT* Part 1 because the published description of some *COLT* Part I categories is quite brief. In fact, the latter system only provides for the observer *describing* the crucial dimension of a language activity (e.g. drills etc.) in his or her own words. The Stirling System, in contrast, sets out detailed guidance for *classifying* the language activities observed into twelve different types. These and other factors discussed later persuaded us that the Stirling System rather than *COLT* Part I provided a better model for a system which would describe the structure and composition of the Irish lesson.

6.4 The *ILAS*

The *ILAS* is an adaptation of the Stirling System developed by Mitchell *et al.* (1981). Central to the Stirling System, and to the *ILAS* adaptation of it, is the notion of a lesson segment. Most teachers conceptualise the language class as being composed of distinctive teaching units or events (such as 'drilling', 'repetition' etc.). The segment is designed to correspond to these 'naturalistic' teaching units. In formal terms, it is defined as a stretch of lesson discourse, having a particular topic, and involving the participants (teacher and pupils) in a distinctive configuration of roles, linguistic and organisational (Mitchell *et al.*, 1981; Mitchell, 1988). Each segment lasts for a minimum of 30 seconds and typically for between 1 and 10 minutes. Segment boundaries will often be indicated by 'framing' moves (teacher uses markers such as "Right", "*Anois*", "*Ciúnas*" etc.) and 'focusing' moves (e.g. "Put away your books, please", "*Tá go maith*", etc.) (Sinclair and Coulthard, 1975)

In practice, segments are defined in terms of five main dimensions of analysis: *Topic, Language activity, Pupil behaviour, Teacher mode of involvement* and *Classroom organisation*. For each of these five dimensions, the Stirling System defines a set of descriptive categories. In the case of *Language activity*, for example, there are categories such as 'Translation', 'Imitation', and 'Drills'. Each segment identified in the lesson discourse is allocated to one category (e.g. on each of the five dimensions). Whenever a change of categorisation occurs on any dimension, a new segment is considered to have begun. In the *ILAS* adaptation of the Stirling System, each segment is coded in relation to three other dimensions - *Materials, Class attention* and *Class interest*. Changes in categorisation on these additional dimensions, however, do not have any implications for the definition of a segment. It may be noted in passing that while in the Stirling Study, the *Materials* used in each lesson were in fact recorded, the information collected was not segment-related as it is in the *ILAS*. *Class attention* and *Class interest* were not recorded at all in the case of the Stirling System.

The Stirling System appears to have a number of advantages. First, the fact that the basic unit, the segment, coincides with the kind of unit which teachers themselves seem to use in conceptualising language lessons is, of course, an advantage in a study which is primarily descriptive and is intended to be useful to practitioners in the field. Another advantage of the Stirling System is that it was originally developed in the context of a study of an audio-visual foreign-language course. It is reasonable to expect then that its descriptive categories will be well adapted to the processes and events which are likely to be common in the teaching of Irish at primary school level because of the pre-eminence until recent times of the audio-visual *Nuachúrsaí*. Finally, at a practical level, the Mitchell *et al.* (1981) report gives an account of the Stirling System which, compared to descriptions of many other language-lesson observation systems, is unusually detailed. This both facilitated the adaptation of the instrument for our present purposes and increased the likelihood that we would be able to make useful comparisons between our results and those of previous studies which have made use of the Stirling System.

Before, turning to a more detailed description of our observation instruments it must be emphasized that both the Stirling System and *COLT* Part II were substantially revised and adapted in the course of developing the *ILAS* and the *PCBR*. This was necessary not only in order to make them suitable to the context in which Irish is taught but also for other theoretical and practical reasons. For example, we felt that the Stirling System, despite its merits, did not adequately capture the 'experiential'- 'analytic' distinction which has been developed in recent research. Consequently, we developed a new language activity category of 'Simulated communication in Irish' in the *ILAS* in addition to the 'Real communication' category in the original Stirling System in order to provide a more comprehensive description of 'experiential' activities.

6.4.1 *Short form of ILAS used by observers*

Two Irish lessons were observed in each school. The work was carried out by primary school inspectors of the Department of Education. Written instructions given to the inspectors/observers concerning the general procedure to be followed in each classroom are set out in Appendix 6.1. Two observers worked side by side, but independently, in each classroom. Observer 1 was concerned with the *ILAS* instrument. Observer 2 used the *PCBR* (see Chapter 9) to classify the general behaviour, participation and language use of three pre-selected pupils. The same inspector served as Observer 1 for both lessons within a particular class. The two inspectors switched roles as Observer 1 and 2 when they proceeded to the next school.

Observer 1 identified the main segments of classroom activity as the lesson progressed and recorded the real starting time of each segment on an A3 coding sheet (see Appendix 6.2). The observer then coded each segment on the eight dimensions according to instructions set out in a short form of *ILAS*. This Short Form of *ILAS* (Appendix 6.2) incorporates in summary form all the essential elements of the original Stirling System (definition and identification of segments, dimensions to be coded and so on) while making some changes to the number and definition of categories in each dimension. It also includes, again in summary form, a description of the three new segment-related dimensions - *Materials, Class attention* and *Class interest* - which we are adding in the case of *ILAS*. The Short Form of *ILAS* was explained to the Observers at a half-day meeting where there was ample opportunity to ask questions. It had earlier been piloted in a school which was not among those selected for the study proper. Observers were urged to conduct a 'dummy-run' in a classroom which was not involved in the project before doing the observation proper.

Each Observer made a separate audio-tape recording of each of the two lessons and was asked to recheck these recordings later if necessary in order to amplify or clarify the notes made on the prepared schedule during the class. It was explained that the present authors intended to re-examine these recordings later in order to obtain additional information and, if necessary, to correct some of the codings. In doing this later work, we would be dependent on the contextual/visually-based information supplied by the Observer who was actually present in the classroom. The Observers were asked to note down with particular care any additional in-class information which could not be inferred by us from the recordings.

The observation covered all aspects of the Irish lesson - oral/conversational Irish, Irish reading and Irish writing. If any of these three aspects were normally taught during separate periods, then the latter periods were also observed (or the reading and writing periods were added onto the oral/conversational period). The class to be observed was to include all pupils who were regularly taught Irish together, although the main focus of the study in the case of multigrade classes would be the sixth-grade pupils. The teacher was told at the very beginning that our objective was to study the typical teaching of a new lesson - not something that had been rehearsed by the class before. The observation was to continue until the class ended naturally, and was not to be terminated after some fixed period of time. The lesson was to include ordinary discipline, assignment of homework and other typical activities and was to run for an average length of time. Pupils were told by the teacher (and again by the Observer) that we were interested in finding out how children learn Irish at school and that was why the observers were present. The Observer had no part of any kind in what the teacher decided to teach or the methods used.

6.4.2 *Developing the Long Form of ILAS (used in authors' recoding)*

The present authors subsequently used the tapes to recode the lessons based on a more detailed version of *ILAS* (see Appendix 6.3). Initially, we considered this recoding as simply a reliability check. But in the event our work in recoding went far beyond this. As we proceeded, it became clear that the original short manual was not sufficiently detailed, and that even if it had been, some of the dimensions were simply too difficult to be coded fully on line by observers in the classroom. For example, initial on-line coding decisions frequently have to be revised in the light of subsequent developments in the lesson - e.g. a teacher leaves some activity but then changes his/her mind and almost immediately goes back to it again. This is the kind of situation that can only be handled satisfactorily in retrospective coding. Dimensions such as *Topic* and *Language activity*, in particular, proved to be too complex to be coded accurately on-line. We also discovered that a considerable amount of practical experience in actually applying the system was necessary in order to familiarize oneself in-depth with the various categories. Finally, we found very early on that it was necessary to become thoroughly familiar with the structure of each lesson by listening to it on tape a number of times, before we could determine segments with confidence and apply the coding system.

These and other difficulties represent shortcomings in the Short Form of the *ILAS* system itself, of course, and are not due to any shortcomings of the Observers operation of it. We are confident that the revisions which we have made to the Long Form of *ILAS* will allow it to be reliably used by Observers in future. Even if it is the Observers themselves who do the final coding in future uses of the system it is now clear from our experience that such coding should be based on tape recordings of the lesson rather than being conducted on-line as the class is in progress.

The Long Form of *ILAS* which we used in the final recoding of the lessons was developed gradually as we proceeded through the taped lessons the first few times. The process consisted of elaborating the category definitions in the Observer's Short Form of *ILAS*, reinforcing and clarifying these definitions with lists of specific marginal examples from the taped lessons, and making relatively minor adjustments to the definition of certain categories of the *Topic, Language activity* and *Pupil behaviour* dimensions (see Appendix 6.3). It also involved reinstating many portions of the text of the original Stirling System which we had deleted from the Short Form of *ILAS*.

By the end of this first examination of the tapes, the Long Form of *ILAS* was complete and a full set of data on segments and categorisation was available. The authors then independently recoded all tapes from the beginning, including rechecking segmentation and recalculating segment durations. On completion of this process, the relatively small number of disagreements revealed by comparisons between the codings of the two authors (or between codings associated with the first and second examination of the tapes) were investigated by jointly studying the relevant portions of the lessons. Minor adjustments to the definition of a small number of categories in *ILAS* were made on the basis of this. The Long Form of *ILAS* is the result. As a final check, each author took half the taped lessons and rechecked the coding of segments in the light of the final revised form of *ILAS*. The data which are presented in this chapter are all based on our recoding of 39 of the 40 lessons - the recording failed in the case of one lesson.

Our recoding of the taped lessons relied in important ways on the in-class work done by the Observers. Real starting times of each segment had been recorded by Observers in the left hand column of the original coding sheets using the Short Form of *ILAS*. Because of this we were able to relate the Observers' segmentation notes, ratings of *Class attentiveness* and *Class interest* etc. to the tapes. Specific details of how *Class attentiveness* and *Class interest* ratings were reapplied to the authors' recodings may be found in the description of the Long Form of *ILAS* in Appendix 6.3.

Final segment durations were estimated by stopwatch to the nearest second. Initial estimates of duration based on counters incorporated in Tandberg tape recorders were found to be inaccurate and had to be discarded. Unlike the Stirling Study, data on the *duration* of those segments assigned to particular categories, as well as the number of segments, are a major focus of our statistical analysis.

In the case of the Long Form of *ILAS* which we used for recoding we had to decide how detailed a description was appropriate for the purpose of the present report. The original Stirling System is presented in an appendix to Mitchell *et al.*'s (1981) own report, though a considerable amount of additional information provided elsewhere in that report is either necessary or useful in applying the system. The description of the Long Form of *ILAS* in Appendix 6.3 contains the essential elements of the original Stirling System which we are retaining, as well as an account of the key modifications to categories and dimensions which we have made. The description in Appendix 6.3, however, does not contain our operational coding specifications (which include many references to specific examples) in anything like full detail. We do provide greater detail, including specific illustrations from the classes observed, in the case of those categories which differ significantly from the Stirling System. It should be noted that the Short and Long forms of *ILAS* in Appendices 6.2 and 6.3 remain faithful wherever possible to the form of words used in the original Mitchell *et al.* (1981) description in order to facilitate comparisons between the results of the two studies. Nevertheless, given the significant modifications which we have made, no assessment of the original Stirling System should be made on the basis of the description of *ILAS* here - the original Mitchell *et al.* report should be consulted.

The eight dimensions of the Long Form of *ILAS* used in recoding the tapes - the form which is the main focus of interest here - are now summarised below. Dimensions and categories which depart from the original Stirling System are marked with an asterisk (*).

6.5 Dimensions and categories of *ILAS*

6.5.1 *Topic*

The *Topic* categories of *ILAS* describe 'what is being talked about' in the lesson segment and range over situations deriving from different course books as well as aspects of lesson content which research on classroom language learning suggests are important (e.g. topics related to pupil/teacher real life, Irish life, culture and music, the linguistics/structure of Irish itself, and routine class management).

The *Topic* dimension in *ILAS* was divided into eight categories, compared to twelve in the Stirling System. Thus, the single category 'Linguistic notions/grammar of Irish' in *ILAS* spans three corresponding narrower categories in the Stirling System: 'General linguistic notions', 'Language points (course)' and 'Language points (other)'. Mitchell *et al.*'s (1981) report sometimes uses the term 'Metalinguistic' to refer to the latter three topic categories combined. In addition, the *ILAS* category 'Fragmented/non-contextualised' is a combination of two corresponding smaller categories 'Fragmented' and 'Non contextualised' topics in the Stirling System. There is no category on the *ILAS* system directly corresponding to the 'Other' topic category in the Stirling System. Finally, the *ILAS* category 'Irish life/culture/music' corresponds to the Stirling System's category '*Civilisation Francaise*'.

- *'Linguistic notions/grammar of Irish': The discourse concerns the nature of language in general, possible ways of analysing it, or explicit analytical discussion of particular grammatical structures or semantic notions.
- *'Situation: *Nuachúrsaí'*: The discourse directly concerns a situation narrated or presented in Step A (*'Bunchomhrá'*) of the audio-visual *Nuachúrsaí* handbooks.
- *'Irish life, culture and music': The discourse concerns aspects of Irish life, culture (e.g. folklore, legend, *'piseoga'*) and music. Discussion of Irish poetry or song which extends beyond the literal meaning of the work is included here.
- 'Situation: Pupil/teacher real life': The discourse concerns aspects of the pupils' and teacher's life and interests, including home and school life, and including narrative material which directly relates to the personal experiences of the participants in the discourse.
- *'Situation: Other than *Nuachúrsaí'*: The discourse concerns specific third party situations and stories from sources other than that defined in Step A (*'Bunchomhrá'*) of the *Nuachúrsaí* handbooks.- e.g. from course books other than the *Nuachúrsaí* handbooks, or from the teacher herself/himself.
- *'Fragmented/non-contextualised': The discourse is incoherent, consisting of a series of propositions with no obvious situational relationship between them. The unity and coherence of the discourse does not rest in the content but in formal aspects of the language being practised.
- 'Routine management/organisation': The discourse concerns classroom management and organisation (e.g. discipline; setting homework).

- 'Feedback/discussing pupils' performance': The discourse concerns the transmission of information about, and/or commentary on, pupils' previous performance.

6.5.2 Language activity

The *Language activity* dimension describes the range of language activities planned and directed by the teacher (including pupil demonstrations where control temporarily passes to a pupil or group of pupils). The categories were designed to capture some of the different kinds of linguistic and communicative experiences which, on the basis of current theoretical understanding, appear to be particularly important for learning Irish or any second language in a classroom context.

A major distinction within the categories of *Language activity* relates to language practice versus communication. Language-practice categories involve the use of Irish primarily to give learners training in the manipulation of the language - the transmission of messages is incidental. In the case of 'Real communication', in contrast, the focus of attention is on meaning and on the message being transmitted. 'Simulated communication' might be thought of as intermediate between language practice and real communication.

There are 13 *Language activity* categories in *ILAS* compared to eight in the final version of the Stirling System. Notice that there is no direct equivalent of 'Simulated communication in Irish', 'Irish song/poem', 'Bilingual simulated communication' or 'Bilingual real communication' in the Stirling System. 'Drills' and 'Contextualisation exercises' were not treated as separate categories in the Stirling system.

- *'Comprehension': This category includes all Irish language practice discourse realised in a single code, which originates from a non-pupil speaker, and to which either no pupil contribution is expected, or the pupil response is secondary and occurs only in the context of comprehension checks by the teacher.
- 'Imitation': Irish practice discourse where pupils' utterances imitative of previously-provided Irish models are expected. The focus of attention is on Irish phonological or orthographic form.
- 'Transposition': Irish practice discourse where utterances are simultaneously realised in both written and spoken codes, and where the focus of attention is on the relationship between them (includes reading aloud and dictation).
- *'Contextualisation exercise': Irish practice discourse with an expected component of pupil utterances, where the focus is on the appropriacy of utterances to their discourse context. The information being transmitted is typically known, and there may therefore be non-structural constraints on pupil utterances (e.g. getting the story line right). Discourse in this category will not exhibit the systematic structural regularities which are typical of drills.
- *'Drills: Structural/vocabulary/pronunciation/spelling': Irish practice discourse in one code which has an expected component of pupil utterances, and which is structurally constrained beyond the rules of normal discourse. The focus of attention is primarily on syntactic form, although non-imitative vocabulary, pronunciation and spelling tasks are also included.

- 'Translation': This category includes discourse in which lexical meanings of Irish are made explicit through the provision of English correspondences, or through the provision of definitions in English.
- *'Simulated communication in Irish' (No direct equivalent in the Stirling System): Irish discourse (at least 80% is in Irish) which has the outer form of real communication but where there is some underlying concern with contextualised, realistic language practice as well as with the message itself. 'Simulated communication' superficially adheres to the rules of normal discourse (oral or written) but may not be truly open ended, and the pupil may not speak from a really 'personal' self. Unlike 'Real communication', where the emphasis is on pupils conveying a message as clearly and accurately as possible within the limits of their linguistic ability, pupils engaged in 'Simulated communication' may alter the 'story line' or the intended content of their utterances in order to accommodate the strengths and weaknesses in their own knowledge of the language. At the same time, 'Simulated communication' does imply that the pupil makes some creative contribution and that some element of meaning negotiation is involved.
- *'Bilingual simulated communication': Same as above but discourse is bilingual (20%-80% of talk is in English)
- *'Real communication in Irish' (more than 80% of discourse is in Irish): Irish discourse in which messages are being transmitted and in which the focus of attention is on the meaning of what is being said.
- *'Bilingual real communication': Same as for 'Real Communication in Irish' but between 20% and 80% of discourse is in English.
- *'Real communication in English': Same as for 'Real Communication in Irish' but more than 80% of discourse is in English.
- *'Irish song/poem': This category includes all Irish discourse where pupils are *reciting* a poem/prayer/song lyric or singing in Irish. This is really a topic-defined subcategory of the language activity 'Imitation' - we have categorised it as a separate language activity here because it seemed to be a quite distinct type of extended imitation.
- 'Compound': This category covers all discourse in which distinct exchanges relating to more than one of the previously defined language activity categories, but each shorter than 30 seconds, occur in complex sequences.

6.5.3 Pupil behaviour

The ways in which teachers require pupils to involve themselves in successive teaching segments is conceptualized in terms of a set of overt behavioural indicators. *Pupil behaviour* is coded in terms of seven categories of pupil involvement including the receptive modes of 'listening', 'looking' and 'reading silently', and the productive modes of 'speaking', 'reading aloud', 'doing' and 'writing'.

Each segment receives a code for the presence of each of these *seven* behaviours on the basis of teachers' intentions regarding pupil involvement. Behaviours may occur singly or in a range of combinations. Thus, a pupil might be simply 'listening', or 'listening and speaking', or 'listening, speaking and reading silently', etc. Only pupil behaviours which are integral to the dominant language activity for that segment are included. The single category of 'reading' in the Stirling System was replaced by two categories 'silent reading' and 'reading aloud' in the present *ILAS* adaptation.

- 'Listening': Pupils are considered to be in a listening mode of involvement if required to attend to any auditory language source e.g. the teacher, other pupil(s), or a tape recording.
- 'Speaking': Pupils are in the speaking mode of involvement if at that moment producing, or actively preparing to produce, spoken language (e.g. thinking of a question to ask of another pupil).
- 'Doing': Doing involves the carrying out of some non-linguistic overt physical activity in accordance with academic plans determined by the teacher (or by pupil(s) if it is a pupil-directed activity)
- *'Reading silently': Silent reading involves attending to any written text or any other graphic code (from book, blackboard etc.).
- *'Reading aloud': The pupil attends to any written text and reads it aloud or is actively preparing to read it aloud (e.g. 'round robin' reading activity or group reading aloud).
- 'Writing': Pupils are in the 'writing' mode of involvement if producing any kind of graphic text or coding, or actively preparing to do so.
- 'Looking': Looking involves attending to any non-linguistic visual stimulus. This includes visual aids such as film strips, cut outs, and also the blackboard. The pupil could also be looking at another pupil or at the teacher miming.

6.5.4 Teacher mode of involvement

This dimension was designed to capture the relationship of the teacher to the pupils, and his/her role in the discourse. Four categories were used, compared to seven in the Stirling System. The 'Monitoring' category below combines a number of categories in the Stirling System - 'Watching and helping', 'Participating', 'Working with group' and 'Working with individual'. For each segment, only one of the categories applies.

- 'Instructing': The teacher is communicating with the whole class, typically by speech, but possibly also by public writing, mime etc. and there is no expected component of public pupil response.
- 'Interacting': The teacher engages in interactive public discourse with the whole class. The typical pattern is one of question/response/reaction. While interaction is likely to be with successive pupils singly, 'readiness to speak' is required of all pupils.
- *'Monitoring' (watching/helping): The teacher is overseeing the carrying out by pupils of a pre-set task. This may involve observing a whole class oral activity (e.g. a situation drama or a pupil demonstration), or it may involve circulating among pupils who are working on individual seatwork tasks, (e.g. written exercises), and commenting privately.

- 'Not involved': The teacher is not communicating with pupils, nor in general attending to pupil activities. He/she may have given earlier instructions for a pupil activity, but is not currently monitoring it.

6.5.5 *Classroom Organisation*

This dimension is intended to collect data on the patterns of class organisation planned and implemented by the teacher. Where the class has been divided by the teacher into two or more sections, with only one section receiving the teacher's active attention for the duration of a segment (in the guise of instructing or interacting with this section of pupils) then, in the absence of any firm information on numbers, this 'active' section is considered to be the class for purposes of all coding. Where two or more classes (grade levels) are taught Irish together, only sixth-grade pupils will be considered the target class in those cases where different activities are assigned to different classes.

Only one category of *Classroom organisation* applies to each segment.

- 'Whole class': There is one central activity going on, dependent on the teacher or another source of stimulus (typically tape or film), but not on a 'pupil demonstration'.
- 'Pupil/Group Demonstration': There is one central activity going on, focused on a *pupil* or *group* demonstration. For example, one pupil may take the role of the teacher, or a group of pupils may act out a scene with the rest of the class forming an audience.
- 'Cooperative - same task': Pupils are assigned to work cooperatively in more than one group, but groups are assigned *identical* tasks.
- 'Cooperative - different task': Pupils are assigned to work cooperatively in more than one group, and groups are assigned *different* tasks (differentiated by language activity and/or pupil behaviour).
- 'Individual - same task': Pupils are set to work alone, without cooperation, but the task set is *identical* for all pupils. The pace of each pupil's activities is not dependent on other pupils or on the ongoing activity of the teacher (though there may be an eventual deadline).
- 'Individual, different task': Pupils are set to work alone, without cooperation, and at least some individuals are set tasks different from those set for others.
- 'Cooperative and individual': Some pupils are working cooperatively in one or more groups and the rest are working as individuals. Tasks may be the same or different between groups and for individuals.

6.5.6 *Materials

This dimension includes *all* materials used at any time during the lesson segment by either the pupils or the teacher. The code-number of each material used should be written in the appropriate column on the observation sheet.

It will be recalled that the introduction of new materials does not necessitate a change in segment. Only a change in one of the first five dimensions above is critical in this regard. All materials used are coded even if used for only part of the segment (e.g. 'Blackboard' is coded even if the teacher writes on the blackboard only briefly). However, materials being prepared for use in subsequent segments and which do not relate to the current segment, should *not* be coded.

While the *Materials* categories are largely the same in the *ILAS* and the Stirling System the method of collecting information on the use of these materials was different in both studies. In *ILAS*, the materials used are recorded on a segment by segment basis. In contrast, the Stirling Study used different methods of collecting information on each of two visits. On the first visit, the observers merely completed a materials checklist at the end of the lesson whereas on the second visit the observer completed a minute-by-minute coding schedule as the lesson progressed. The *Materials* categories used in ILAS are:

- '*Nuachúrsaí* handbooks': The name of the handbook e.g. '*Sean-Neidí'/'Lá Faoin Tuath*'.
- 'Other course-book/workbook': The name of the commercially produced course-book or workbook. Note that materials are coded under this heading even if only the teacher is using them.
- 'Reader'
- 'Jotter/copy'
- 'Blackboard'
- 'Wallchart'.
- 'Worksheet'.
- 'Flashcards'.
- 'Library Books'.
- 'Film strip/slide'.
- 'Cut outs'
- 'Tape'
- 'Video/film'.
- 'Overhead Projector'
- 'Photographs'
- 'Authentic materials' (specify): These include items such as posters, newspaper articles, advertisements, TV license, tax form in Irish etc.
- 'Objects'.
- 'Person' (other than pupil or teacher): For example, an outsider is brought in to the classroom and talks to the pupil about himself/herself and the pupils can ask him/her questions.
- 'Other' (any other materials not covered in the previous categories).

6.5.7 *Class attention*

The extent to which the *majority of pupils* are paying attention to the current language activity. Measured on a five point scale ranging from '1' ('Very low' attention) to '5' ('Very high' attention). This coding can only be done on line i.e. by observers in the classroom.

6.5.8 *Class interest*

The extent to which the majority of pupils are interested in the current language activity - rated on a similar five point scale to *Class attention* above.

6.6 Teachers' reactions to the observation work

One of the obvious difficulties associated with classroom observation research is the probability that it influences the very events being studied i.e. that teachers and pupils may conduct themselves differently than they would normally (Labov,1970). Certainly, the audiotaped lesson gave no strong indication of unease and self consciousness among either teachers or pupils. Whatever suggestion there may have been in pupils' or teachers' behaviour early on in the first lesson that this was a special occasion, the effect had dissipated within minutes.

Following the observation work, therefore, we asked the teachers via the *Teacher Questionnaire* (i) how typical the two observed lessons were in terms of approach/method, materials used, style of interaction with the children and, (ii) what effect, if any, the observers' presence had on their teaching (see Appendix 2.4).

Table 6.1
How typical were the two observed lessons that you taught
(in terms of methodology, materials, interaction with the pupils etc.)?

Observed lessons were	*Percentage of teachers* *N = 20*
(i) ...generally very typical	95%
(ii) ...not at all typical *	5%
	100%

* See list of comments in Appendix 2.5

All but one teacher reported that the lessons they taught were generally very typical of the usual Irish lesson (Table 6.1). Eleven of the 20 teachers gave more details. These written comments, some in Irish, others in English, are presented in Appendix 2.5. It is clear from these remarks that, even though teachers reported that the observed lessons were typical in terms of teaching approach, many felt that the presence of observers in the classroom, and the fact that the lessons were being audio taped, may have influenced both their own conduct and that of their pupils. Five of the teachers thought that they themselves and/or their pupils were more inhibited than usual. Other comments indicated that pupils showed more interest or were more cooperative than usual. One teacher from a multi-grade classroom reported spending more time with sixth-grade than usual while another teacher said he/she tried to cover more aspects of Irish than he/she would normally do within a single lesson.

When asked specifically how the teachers themselves reacted to the presence of the observers, 80% (see Table 6.2) reported that the observers had 'little' affect on their teaching while a further 20% reported that they were 'somewhat' affected. Taken together these data indicate that even though some teachers considered they themselves may have been slightly more self conscious than usual, or that their pupils behaviour may have been somewhat atypical, the overall impression was that the observation process did not change the normal Irish lesson dynamics to any significant extent.

Table 6.2
How much of an effect did you feel the observers had on you yourself and your usual teaching approach?

Observers bothered me...	*Percentage of teachers* *N = 20*
(i) ... a lot	-
(ii) ... somewhat	20%
(iii) ... very little	80%
	100%

6.7 The transcripts

In the course of developing *ILAS*, it was decided to transcribe a proportion of the Irish lessons. This transcription process played an important role in the execution of the research and particularly in the development of *ILAS*. The inclusion of a sample of these transcripts in the present report is intended to serve a number of other purposes - enriching the quantitative evidence, illustrating in a more immediate way the category definitions and providing material which may be helpful in training observers in future uses of the system. In this section we explain the function of the transcripts, describe how the extracts were selected and offer some preliminary observations on their content.

Some of the reasons for transcribing lessons as part of the research process are set out by Van Lier (1988: 238):

1. The observer needs an *estrangement device* which allows stepping out of the interaction and looking at it afresh from a detached viewpoint.

2. Analysis of interaction requires intensive immersion in the data; transcription, accompanied by multiple replays, provides such immersion.
3. Interesting phenomena often only come to light after detailed inspection of the data. That which appears at first sight incomprehensible or perfectly trivial can turn out to provide important clues to regular patterns.
4. Through recording and transcription the data become available to other researchers, who can therefore examine and criticize the analyst's interpretation.
5. Recorded and transcribed data allow for a comparison with other such data and can thus lead to cumulative research.
6. We observe selectively, and real-time coding merely enforces systematic preselection. Recorded and transcribed data, though also to some extent inevitably selective, allow for an investigation of the entire interaction in its context.

The transcription process in the present study contributed significantly to the task of modifying the Stirling System and creating *ILAS*. The transcribed lessons were useful in classifying definitions and in refining coding categories. It was sometimes difficult, for example, to decide whether particular segments should be coded in the language activity dimensions of 'Contextualisation exercise' or 'Simulated communication'. Repeated examination of segment transcripts were invaluable in helping us to identify some of the subtle differences between categories such as these.

The transcripts are intended to serve a number of purposes in the present report. First, they help to show how the category definitions of various dimensions of *ILAS* are realised in practice in Irish classrooms. Second, they illustrate some of the patterns of pupil interaction which are coded on the *PCBR* described in Chapter 9 . These include aspects such as the frequency of individual spoken contributions, the length of pupil utterances, the balance of languages used in interactions (English/Irish), whether the discourse is initiated by the teacher or pupils, whether it is a question or answer and whether it is an individual or a choral contribution.

Another advantage of transcribing data such as this is that aspects of class discourse which may be overlooked by simply listening to the tapes may be more easily identifiable in transcripts. These include features such as code switching, intonation and emphasis, repetition, hesitations and correction. Although, it was never our intention to analyse the discourse at this level of detail the transcripts help to illustrate the range of teaching contexts in which these phenomena may be observed and thus give a more complete picture of the Irish lesson.

6.7.1 Selecting lessons and extracts for transcription

In selecting lessons for transcription we had to take two main issues into consideration. To start with, our selection was constrained by the quality of the audio recordings. It would not have been practical to choose a lesson in which a lot of individual words/phrases were unclear. Another practical consideration, this time limiting the number of lessons which could be transcribed was simply the amount of time involved. Our experience in transcribing the lessons coincides with that of Van Lier (1988: 241) who considers 20 hours as a reasonable estimate of how long it takes to produce even a 'rough working transcription' of a lesson. Furthermore, he claims that 'segments to be used for close analysis and presentation will still need polishing' and that in effect 'a transcription is never finished'.

Within these general limits we tried to select as good a cross section as possible of classes in terms of socio/demographic, educational and administrative variables. In all seven of the 39 lessons were transcribed. This amounted to 152 lesson segments or just over eight and a half hours of Irish teaching time.

In Appendix 6.4 we present a sample of these 152 segments to represent the most common *ILAS Topic/Language activity* category combinations. The selection of 24 segment transcripts contains over an hour and a quarter of Irish lesson discourse. The number of pages allocated to the five largest *Topic/Language activity* combinations roughly corresponds to the proportions of *Topic/Language activity* combinations found in Table 7.13 (see Chapter 7). No more than two pages are allocated to the remaining 19 topic/activity combinations. It will be noted that in the case of three segments which were particularly long, the extract contains only the first two to three minutes of the segment. In order to give a balanced picture of different Irish language classrooms a special effort was made to ensure that selected segments were, as far as possible, evenly distributed over the seven classes from which they were selected.

Each segment transcript is identified by the class achievement rank of the class to which it relates, whether it is the first or second lesson and the duration of the entire segment (not necessarily the duration of the accompanying transcript extract). In addition each segment is introduced by a description of that segment in terms of how it was coded by the authors on each of the *ILAS* (long form) dimensions.

Full details on the transcription process, how we selected extracts, how we dealt with speech inaccuracies, and the various conventions used in the transcripts can be found in Appendix 6.4.

Given the goals and procedures above, it is clear that the transcripts cannot be taken as representative of any particular teaching style, approach or method, or of the range of teaching styles and methods generally. No generalisations about either teachers' or pupils' Irish should be based on the transcripts (see further discussion in Appendix 6.4).

While it is not intended to discuss particular transcribed lesson segments a few general points may be confirmed by a quick perusal of the material in Appendix 6.4. This examination serves to alert us to a number of issues which arise later (Chapters 7-9) in discussing the quantitative data derived from *ILAS* and *PCBR*.

6.7.2 *Preliminary observations on the transcripts*

First, note the almost exclusive use of the target language, Irish. English appears infrequently - usually single words, often simply markers used by the teachers in the context of framing or focusing moves e.g. "Right", "Look" etc. English is rarely used by the teacher to explain or translate words or phrases.

Second, except in the case of segments coded as 'Pupil demonstration' in the *Class organisation* dimension (see Appendix 6.4, Extract 8), it is almost always the teacher who initiates a change from one lesson segment to another and who directs the course of the dialogue - giving directions, allocating turns and asking questions. In the majority of segments, exchanges tend to follow the sequence 'teacher-pupil-teacher'. It will also be noted that, in general, teachers' contributions are longer than those of the pupils. This asymmetry reflects the unequal roles which are typically associated with classroom interaction (Van Lier, 1994).

The language activities *Real communication* and *Simulated communication* break this pattern by approximating naturalistic dialogue. Looking at extract 18 in Appendix 6.4 (a discussion of fires), for example, it can be seen that pupils' contributions are more spontaneous and more sustained than they are in the case of language practice segments.

Despite the fact that the teacher usually leads and dominates the discourse, the transcripts still reveal a very high level of pupil involvement in the lesson. The dialogue is brisk - there are few lengthy pauses or silent periods - and it is obvious that teachers both encourage and expect that pupils will participate even if their contributions are rather short.

7 The Irish lesson: Topic, language activity and materials

7.1 Introduction

Over the last thirty years, the focus of research on second-language teaching has shifted from a concern with methods/teaching-plans and with outcomes/results to an attempt to understand how programmes are actually implemented. The aim of this reorientation is to try to identify links between successful second-language acquisition and specific classroom processes and types of discourse. Researchers now see classroom discourse and processes, and ultimately successful learning, as a joint creation of the teacher and pupils and not simply the product of the initial teaching plan (Slimani, 1992). Thus, the earlier landmark studies of Scherer and Wertheimer (1964) and Smith (1970), which focused entirely on terminal achievement rather that on the details of method implementation by teachers, would now be seen as contributing relatively little to our understanding of classroom second-language acquisition.

The new research focus is well represented in the *Twenty-Classes Study*. The direct classroom observation data presented in this chapter and in the two succeeding ones describe, in essence, the implementation of the teacher's Irish-lesson plan. The various dimensions of *ILAS* provide a description of the same classroom events from a number of different perspectives, such as the language activities being engaged in and the forms of classroom organisation being employed. This means that the same set of lesson segments is being analysed anew in the case of each *ILAS* dimension, although the categories of each dimension sort these segments in different ways. The product of all this is a large body of individual findings which relate to each other in complex ways. In order to simplify the task of presentation, we have decided to confine the present chapter to just three *ILAS* dimensions, *Topic*, *Language activity* and *Materials*. The remaining *ILAS* dimensions will be dealt with in the next chapter. *Topic*, *Language activity* and *Materials* are considered together because they give rise to very similar general issues and because our own study shows that they are intimately linked with each other.

The complexity of the results has both positive and negative aspects. On the one hand, it means that we are provided with a very rich picture of the teaching and learning of Irish. On the other, such data provide us with the challenge of identifying a small number of reference points or themes which will bring order to our account of the results. Two such reference points are used here. The first consists of research reviewed in the last chapter which tries to identify classroom conditions which are conducive to successful second-language learning. A crucial distinction in this research is between 'experiential' activities and 'analytic' activities in the classroom (Allen *et al.*, 1987; Stern, 1990, 1992). Roughly parallel ways of stating the same distinction are (a) 'communicative' versus 'language-practice' activities or (b) 'message-focused' versus 'form-focused' activities. Virtually all the significant effects in relation to topic, language activities and materials can be understood in terms of these distinctions. While the experiential-analytic distinction is most clearly relevant in the case of *Language activity*, results relating to the two other dimensions can be seen as representing either the ramifications of that same distinction or the fine-tuning of its operation.

The second reference point is provided by comparing the present description of Irish lessons with the description of the teaching of French at first year post-primary in the Stirling Study (Mitchell *et al.*, 1981). The main focus of interest in this comparison is the difference between a second- and a foreign-language programme where both kinds of programmes have origins in the audio-visual method. Not only does the Stirling Study provide data derived from a fairly closely corresponding observation system, but the pupils involved are reasonably similar in terms of stage of schooling (sixth-grade primary in the Irish Study versus first-year post-primary in the Stirling Study). In addition, there are some significant differences between the language programmes followed which promise to make the comparison interesting.

7.1.1 *Comparisons between the Stirling and Irish studies.*

Before proceeding to the results proper - where we will frequently refer to the Stirling Study - it will be useful to give a sketch of the Irish and Stirling language programmes. Excluding 'all-Irish' (immersion) and Gaeltacht (Irish-speaking area) schools, all other children study Irish (in the vast majority of cases their second language) as a subject from the beginning of primary school. Thus, by sixth grade they have had eight years of exposure to Irish as a school subject. As we mentioned in Chapter 2, the mainly audio-visual '*Nuachúrsaí*' or 'New Courses' (Ireland: Department of Education, 1978), provided the basis for the teaching of spoken Irish in the vast majority of these 'ordinary' primary schools for many years, although courses developed by commercial publishers and others have now become much more common. Most estimates suggest that about an hour a day is spent teaching Irish - including speaking, reading and writing (Harris and Murtagh, 1988a). Questionnaire data indicate that Irish is widely used as a means of routine classroom communication, and in addition that about one-fifth of classes in ordinary schools are taught some other aspect of the curriculum, such as music or physical education, through Irish (Harris and Murtagh, 1988a).

In contrast to this language-learning situation, the Stirling Study involved post-primary students who presumably had only recently begun to study French as a foreign language. In addition, all students in the Stirling Study had followed a particular audio-visual course, while the children in the various Irish classes in the present study were sometimes taught by the teachers' own methods (see Chapter 2). Although fewer schools (n=6) and classes/teachers (n=17) were involved in the Stirling Study than in the present Irish one, more lessons were observed. And while the French lessons were much shorter than the average Irish lesson, the total observed time in the Stirling study was more than twice that of the Irish study.

7.2 Results

We begin with a presentation of background data on the lessons and on class characteristics, such as level of achievement in Irish, attitude to Irish and levels of attention and interest during the lesson. We proceed then, to the three *ILAS* dimensions *Topic, Language activity* and *Materials*. The presentation and analysis of results for each dimension has the same three part structure:

1. A description of the 39 lessons as a group (the pooled-segment analysis) in terms of the proportion of teaching time, the proportion of lesson segments and the mean segment duration associated with each category of the relevant dimension (e.g. *Topic* categories such as 'Pupil/teacher real-life situations', 'Linguistics/grammar of Irish' etc.). Except for comparative purposes with the Stirling Study, the main focus of our analysis is the proportion of teaching time rather than the number of segments. Ultimately, the proportion of all teaching time devoted to a particular *Language activity, Topic* etc. should be more important than the proportion of lesson segments devoted to it.

2. Data which indicate the extent to which *Class attention* and *Class interest* wax and wane as different *Topics, Language activities* and *Materials* are introduced. Where we report statistically significant differences between the categories of a dimension as far as mean *attention/interest* ratings are concerned, we are referring to the results of Scheffe tests conducted after a significant 'F' in an ANOVA.

3. Data and statistical tests which indicate if there is any tendency for the content and structure of the Irish lesson which is actually implemented in different classes to be related to certain academic and attitudinal characteristics of pupils or their responses to the lesson. We are interested in two issues here: (a) the extent of the between-class variation in the proportion of teaching time spent on different categories of dimensions (e.g. variations from class to class in the amount of time spent on the *Topic* category 'Pupil/teacher real life situations' or on the *Materials* category 'Other course book/workbook') (b) how these variations in lessons are related to or 'explain' pupil proficiency in Irish, attitude to Irish and the level of attention and interest they display.

4. In order to make any association between the lesson variables, on the one hand, and class characteristic variables, on the other, as salient as possible, we list the 20 classes in rank order of their achievement in spoken Irish (as in previous chapters). This list of classes is further divided into a 'high', a 'middle' and a 'low' Irish-achievement group. For the sake of simplicity we include in these tables only those categories of dimensions which were significantly correlated with at least one of the five main class measures listed above. Pearson correlations are used to test for the

significance of the association between lesson composition (as defined by the various teaching time proportions) and class achievement, and attitudinal measures.

5. Finally, in order to throw additional light on the way in which various categories of dimensions are linked, we occasionally refer to crosstabulations. For example, we might crosstabulate data on *Materials* and *Language activity* categories in order to show that certain teaching 'materials' or 'aids are more often used in the course of one *Language activity* rather than another. Results of these crosstabulations are reported as the need arises and are not presented in tabular form.

7.2.1 Background data on the lessons

Number and duration of segments

Table 7.1 shows that the 39 Irish lessons analysed consist, in all, of 828 segments. These thirty nine lessons amount to over 42 hours of teaching time, excluding breaks etc. (Table 7.2). The mean duration of segments is 3 minutes and 3 seconds, a little shorter than that reported by Mitchell *et al.* (1981) in their study of French foreign-language lessons (3 minutes, 12 seconds). Table 7.3 shows that segment durations range from 30 seconds up to 4 minutes for about three quarters of the segments in the Irish lessons. Of the remainder, only 3.6% of segments have durations greater than 10 minutes (Table 7.3).

Table 7.1
Irish Lesson Analysis System (*ILAS*) Study: Number of classes, lessons and lesson segments.

Number of classrooms observed	20
Number of sixth grade pupils in the 20 classes	533
Number of lessons analysed*	39
Number of lesson segments analysed	828

* Although 40 lessons were observed it was only possible to analyse 39 of these due to a recording failure in the case of one lesson.

Table 7.2
Duration of lessons and lesson-segments.

	Hours	*Minutes*	*Seconds*
Total duration of classes observed*	42	03	40
Average lesson duration	1	04	43
Mean segment duration		3	03
Standard Deviation (segment duration)		3	01

* Based on authors' coding of audio-tape recordings of 39 lessons.

Table 7.3
Percentage distribution of lesson segments by duration

Duration of segment (minutes)	Percentage of segments (n = 828)	Cumulative percentage
0.5-1.0	20.5	20.5
1.0 - 1.5	17.0	37.6
1.5 - 2.0	12.7	50.2
2.0 - 2.5	8.7	58.9
2.5 - 3.0	6.9	65.8
3.0 - 3.5	6.6	72.5
3.5 - 4.0	5.0	77.4
4.0 - 4.5	2.5	80.0
4.5 - 5.0	2.8	82.7
5.0 - 10.0	13.7	96.4
10.0 - 15.0	2.5	98.9
> 15.0	1.1	100.0

We now look at information on the total teaching time observed over two lessons for each of the twenty classes (Table 7.4). The results indicate substantial variation in the length of the typical Irish lesson from one classroom to the next. The average observed time over two lessons is about 2 hours 6 minutes 11 seconds (SD=34:37) with a range of 2 hours 20 minutes 23 seconds between the shortest and the longest total observation time for each class. It will be recalled (section 6.4.2), of course, that, owing to a recording failure, only one Irish lesson was included in the analysis for the class ranked 16 in terms of achievement in spoken Irish (note the low number of segments (n=20) in the case of this class). In real terms the shortest Irish lessons were observed in the case of class rank 15 with a total teaching time for the two lessons of just under one hour and twenty three minutes.

Looking now at the three achievement groups of classes it can be seen that while all classes in the high-Irish-achievement classes (ranks 1-6) spend more than two hours learning Irish during the two observed lessons, only two of the eight low-Irish-achievement classes spend this much time. In terms of segment duration, there is a range of 3 minutes 5 seconds between the shortest and the longest mean segment duration per class (last row, Table 7.4). There is no strong pattern indicating any relationship between class achievement and segment duration.

Table 7.4
Total observed teaching time, number of lesson segments and mean segment duration for each of 20 classes (listed in order of achievement in spoken Irish)

Class achievement in spoken Irish Rank* (1= highest)	Total observed teaching time (hrs: mins: secs)	Number of segments (n)	Mean segment duration (mins: secs)
1	2: 35: 31	41	3: 48
2	2: 35: 29	58	2: 41
3	3: 30: 54	62	3: 24
4	2: 20: 38	63	2: 14
5	2: 04: 41	48	2: 36
6	2: 32: 16	38	4: 00
7	1: 48: 53	29	3: 45
8	2: 36: 57	51	3: 05
9	1: 30: 24	22	4: 07
10	1: 54: 55	33	3: 29
11	2: 05: 10	39	3: 13
12	2: 20: 40	50	2: 49
13	1: 35: 18	30	3: 11
14	2: 03: 44	72	1: 43
15	1: 22: 52	28	2: 58
16	1: 10: 31	20	3: 32
17	1: 35: 31	42	2: 16
18	1: 39: 14	31	3: 12
19	2: 52: 44	36	4: 48
20	1: 47: 18	35	3: 04
Total	*42: 03: 40*	*828*	-
Class mean	*2: 06: 11*	*41.4*	*3: 12** *
Standard Deviation (SD)	*34: 37*	*14.3*	*0: 43*
Class range (max-min)	*2: 20: 23*	*52*	*3: 05*

* Based on the mean percentage of pupils in each class attaining mastery of each of 16 objectives on the ITÉ sixth-grade test of spoken Irish.
** This is the mean of the mean segment durations shown here and differs slightly from the grand mean of the original 828 segment durations (see Table 7.2)

Attention/interest, attitude and proficiency variables

As we mentioned above, we are interested in establishing if there are any connections between the structure and content of the Irish lesson implemented in different classes (as defined in terms of *ILAS*) and characteristics of these same classes such as levels of *Class achievement in spoken Irish, Class attitude to Irish* and *Class attention/interest* in Irish. The present section presents some background data on these 'class characteristics' variables and on the relationship between them. All the class characteristics variables except *Class attention* and *Class interest* have been introduced in previous chapters and so do not need any additional comment here. *Class attention* and *Class interest* do require some mention, however, because in addition to being themselves dimensions of *ILAS*, we use data from these two dimensions to evaluate class reaction to other aspects of the lesson defined by *ILAS* - e.g. we examine how *Class attention* varies as different topics or language activities are introduced in the lesson.

It will be recalled that for each segment, the observers rated the whole class on the extent to which the majority of pupils were paying attention to, and were interested in, the current activity. The class was rated on a five point scale, with '1' representing 'very low' attention (or interest) and '5' 'very high' attention (or interest). Looking at the individual mean *attention* and *interest* ratings for each of the twenty classes in Table 7.5, and the overall (grand) means of 4.3 (class attention) and 4.1 (class interest) it can be seen that (a) there is a very high level of attention and interest among pupils overall and (b) there are small but patterned variations between classes in mean *attention* and *interest* ratings. More specifically, note that the low-Irish-achievement classes have lower ratings than the high-Irish-achievement classes. The average of the *Class attention* mean ratings for the low-Irish-achievement group is 4.01 while the corresponding averages for the middle- and high-Irish-achievement classes are 4.36 and 4.7 respectively. Similarly, in the case of *Class interest* ratings, the average ratings in the low- middle- and high-Irish-achievement groups are respectively 3.71, 4.05 and 4.63.

The Pearson correlations between the five class characteristic variables are given in Table 7.6 and the means and standard deviations are given in Table 7.7. Note that the standard deviation of both *attention* and *interest* ratings (Table 7.7) is only 0.5, reflecting the generally small variations from class to class in levels of *attention* and *interest* which we saw in Table 7.5.

The general trend for higher *Class attention* and *Class interest* to be associated with classes which have higher levels of achievement in Irish (Table 7.5) is shown to be statistically significant by the Pearson correlation data in Table 7.6. Not surprisingly, perhaps, the highest correlation in Table 7.6 is between *Class attention* and *Class interest* (r = .87). Looking at rows three and four of this table, it can be seen that higher *Class attention* and *Class interest* ratings are associated with higher *Class achievement in spoken Irish* (r=.65 and r=.79 respectively). Higher *attention* and *interest* ratings also tend to be found in classes which have a more positive *Class attitude to Irish* (column two) - the correlation being somewhat stronger in the case of *Class interest* (.60) than in the case of *Class attention* (.48). A significant negative correlation (r=-.49) is found between mean *Class interest* ratings and *Class Irish-lesson anxiety* reflecting the fact that higher levels of class interest are associated with lower levels of pupil anxiety in relation to the Irish class.

Table 7.5
Mean *Class attention* and *Class interest* ratings for each of 20 classes

Class achievement in spoken Irish Rank (1=highest)	n (segments)	Class attention (mean rating) (1-5)	Class interest (mean rating) (1-5)
1	(41)	4.8	4.7
2	(58)	4.6	4.5
3	(62)	4.7	4.6
4	(63)	4.9	5.0
5	(48)	4.6	4.6
6	(38)	4.6	4.4
High-Irish-achievement classes		*4.7*	*4.63*
7	(29)	4.8	4.4
8	(51)	4.5	4.0
9	(22)	4.8	4.1
10	(33)	4.6	4.6
11	(39)	4.3	4.3
12	(50)	3.2	2.9
Middle-Irish-achievement classes		*4.36*	*4.05*
13	(30)	3.6	3.5
14	(72)	3.8	3.6
15	(28)	4.0	3.6
16	(20)	4.0	3.8
17	(42)	4.4	3.7
18	(31)	4.1	4.0
19	(36)	4.4	3.7
20	(35)	3.8	3.8
Low-Irish-achievement classes		*4.01*	*3.71*
Class mean	*41.4*	*4.3*	*4.1*
Standard Deviation (SD)	*14.3*	*.46*	*.52*
Class range (max-min)	*52*	*1.7*	*2.1*

Table 7.6
Pearson correlations between five class measures: *Class achievement in spoken Irish, Class attitude to Irish, Class Irish-lesson anxiety, Class attention and Class interest.*

Class measures	n (classes) = 20	Class achievement in Irish	Class attitude to Irish	Class Irish-lesson anxiety	Class attention
Class attitude to Irish ◊		.74**			
Class Irish-lesson anxiety ◊		-.64**	-.39		
Class attention (mean rating)		.65**	.48*	-.38	
Class interest (mean rating)		.79**	.60**	-.49*	.87**

* p <.05. ** p < .01. ◊ See Chapter 3: section 3.3.2.

Table 7.7
Means and standard deviations* of five class-level measures: *Class achievement in spoken Irish, Class attitude to Irish, Class Irish-lesson anxiety, Class attention and Class interest.*

Class measures	n (classes) = 20	Mean	Standard Deviation
Class achievement in spoken Irish		37.9	25.4
Class attitude to Irish		166.3	17.9
Class Irish-lesson anxiety		14.1	1.3
Class attention		4.3	0.5
Class interest		4.1	0.5

*In the *Twenty-Classes* sample

Other significant correlations in Table 7.6 include the positive association between *Class attitude to Irish* and *Class achievement in spoken Irish* (r = .74), and the negative association (r=-.64) between *Class Irish-lesson anxiety* and *Class achievement in spoken Irish*. It will be recalled that similar significant associations between the corresponding pupil level variables were reported in Chapter 3 (see section 3.3.3). In the case of the latter correlations, where the number of cases involved were much larger, the Pearson r's recorded were smaller, though still significant.

7.2.2 *Topic*

Table 7.8 shows the percentage of teaching time, and the percentage of segments, associated with each category of the *Topic* dimension over all lessons. Looking at the first column it can be seen that over a half of all observed segments (51.1%) are associated with the *Topic* category 'Situation: *Other than Nuachúrsaí*'. This is more than six times the proportion of segments in the nearest corresponding category ('Situation: Other course') in the Stirling Study (7.7% of all segments). The assignment of segments assigned to this *Topic* category usually means that the topics are derived from course-books (e.g. *Buail Liom*) other than the *Nuachúrsaí* handbooks. The situations may also be derived from readers or other sources, including the teacher. A specific example of the latter from the present study involved the teacher, over a number of lesson segments, discussing the repair of a puncture on a bicycle tyre.

Table 7.8
Topic: **Percentage distribution of teaching time and lesson segments, and average segment duration by *Topic*.**

Topic		*Percentage of segments*	*Proportion of teaching time* (hrs mins secs)	*Mean segment duration* (mins secs)
	Total:	(n = 828)	(42 : 3 : 40)	(3: 03)
Situation: *Other than Nuachúrsaí*		51.1	52.4	3 :08
Fragmented/non contextualised		19.8	19.6	3 :01
Situation: *Nuachúrsaí*		10.9	14.5	4 :04
Pupil/teacher real life situations		8.7	9.3	3 :15
Routine management/organisation		6.2	2.2	1 :04
Linguistics/grammar of Irish		2.2	1.3	1 :48
Irish life/culture/music		0.6	0.3	1 :33
Feedback/discussing pupil performance		0.6	0.5	2 :28
Total		100%	100%	-

The fact that 'Situation: *Other than Nuachúrsaí*' should account for so many segments in the Irish study, however, indicates the need for more differentiated *Topic* categories e.g. at the very least, topics from 'other' course-books/workbooks and readers should be in a separate category from topics related to situations set up by teachers themselves. It is possible that some of the difference in topic emphasis between the two studies can be accounted for in terms of the fact that classes in the Stirling Study followed a specific audio-visual course whereas the Irish classes used a wider variety of courses. Only one-tenth of all lesson segments in the Irish study (see Table 7.8 again) have topics associated with the *Nuachúrsaí* audio-visual course ('Situation: *Nuachúrsaí* ': 10.9%). Mitchell *et al.* (1981) reports, in contrast, that the proportion of lesson segments which had topics deriving from the recommended audio-visual French course approached one-third (31.9%).

More importantly, the data relating to these two categories in Table 7.8 indicate that while primarily course-related topics ('Situation: *Other than Nuachúrsaí* ' or 'Situation: *Nuachúrsaí* ') account for almost two-thirds (62%) of all segments in the Irish lessons, equivalent topic categories account for only two-fifths of all segments in the French lessons. The difference is made up in the Stirling Study by higher proportions of segments being devoted to three topic areas: 'Routine procedures', 'Metalinguistic' and 'Civilisation'. While these three topic categories account for 26.5% of French lesson segments, data in Table 7.8 show that in all only 9% of Irish lesson segments are assigned to equivalent topic categories ('Routine management/organisation' - 6.2%; 'Linguistics/ grammar of Irish' - 2.2%; and 'Irish life/culture/music' - 0.6%). It will be noted how rarely 'Irish life/culture/music' constitutes the segment topic. It must be borne in mind, however, that such topics are occasionally treated in terms of third party 'situations' in Irish course-books, readers etc. and so it is possible that their role is somewhat underestimated here.

An additional point here is that in the Stirling Study, the greater majority of French lesson segments associated with the three topic categories just mentioned - 'Routine procedures', 'Metalinguistic' and 'Civilisation' - involved the use of the student's native language, English. While lower proportions of segments are associated with the equivalent *Topic* categories in the Irish Study ('Routine management/organisation', 'Linguistics/grammar of Irish' and 'Irish life culture and music'), crosstabulations with language activity data presented later (see Table 7.10 below), reveal that the discourse involved in these topics is in Irish rather than in the children's native language, English. Of the three *Topic* categories just mentioned, the greatest difference between the two studies relates to 'Linguistics/grammar of Irish' (2.2%) in our study (Table 7.8, column 1) and the corresponding 'Metalinguistic' topic category (12.3%) in the Stirling Study.

There is a closer degree of correspondence between the present Irish Study and the Stirling Study in the proportion of segments allocated to the three remaining topic categories: 'Fragmented/non contextualised', 'Pupil/teacher real life' and 'Feedback/ discussing pupil performance'. A fifth of all Irish lesson discourse has no coherent topic ('Fragmented/non-contextualised': 19.8%), slightly lower than the proportion in the Stirling Study (22.5%). Many lesson segments involving the language activity 'Drills', in particular, consist of a specific syntactic structure being practised by using semantically unrelated, isolated sentences. In the case of these 'Drills', the *Topic* is categorised as 'Fragmented'. Topics relating to 'Pupil/teacher real life' situations account for 8.7% of segments in the case of the Irish lessons compared to 9.4% in the Stirling Study.

'Feedback/ Discussing pupil performance' accounts for less than 2% of segments in both the Irish and Stirling studies.

We turn now to the remaining data in the other columns of Table 7.8. In general, the percentage of all segments (column 1) which is associated with a particular *Topic* category is fairly similar to the percentage of all teaching time (column 2) associated with the same *Topic* category. Note that in the case of 'Routine management/organisation', however, the proportion of segments (6.2%), though small, does exceed the proportion of teaching time (2.2%). This simply reflects the fact that segments concerned with matters of 'Routine management/ organisation' tend to have the shortest durations (column 3). In contrast, in the case of 'Situation: *Nuachúrsaí*', the opposite is true - the proportion of teaching time (14.5%) exceeds the proportion of segments (10.9%). In other words, when lesson segments originate in the *Nuachúrsaí* they tend to last longer (an average of 4 minutes 4 seconds) than segments whose topics originate elsewhere.

An analysis of variance (ANOVA) followed by individual comparisons of means (Scheffe test), was used to test the significance of the difference between overall segment duration for the *Topic* categories. Similar tests were conducted on mean segment durations associated with the categories of the other dimensions discussed below. In the present case of the *Topic* categories, the results indicate that each of the first four more common categories in Table 7.8 ('Situation: *Other than Nuachúrsaí*', 'Fragmented/non contextualised', 'Situation: *Nuachúrsaí*', and 'Pupil/teacher real life situations') had significantly longer segment durations ($p<.05$) than the less common topic of 'Routine management/organisation'. As we hope to show below, an analysis of the kinds of *Language activities* involved in each of the *Topic* categories throws further light on the relationship between *Topic* category and segment duration.

Looking at column one of Table 7.9 it will be noted that despite some variation in *Class attention* ratings according to *Topic* category, individual comparisons (using Scheffe tests) were not statistically significant. In the case of *Class interest*, however, the mean rating for 'Pupil/teacher real life' topics (4.4) was significantly higher than for 'Fragmented/non contextualised' topics (3.9) (Scheffe test: $p<.05$).

We now look at the amount of lesson time spent on various categories of *Topic* and how this relates, if at all, to the five class measures listed earlier. Table 7.10 shows that only one category of *Topic* ('Fragmented'/'non-contextualised') is significantly correlated with *Class achievement in spoken Irish* and the direction is negative ($r=-.45$), indicating that more time spent on this topic is associated with classes having lower levels of achievement in Irish. Time spent on 'Situation: *Other than Nuachúrsaí*' topics is not significantly related to achievement in spoken Irish ($r=.41$) although the correlation approaches significance. More time on 'Situation: *Other than Nuachúrsaí*' topics is significantly associated with higher *Class interest* ratings ($r=.48$).

Table 7.9
Mean class attention and class interest ratings for the most frequent
(at least 5% of segments) *Topic* categories

Topic	n (segments)	Class attention Mean ratings (1-5) (828)	Class interest Mean ratings (1 - 5) (828)
Situation: *Other than Nuachúrsaí*	(423)	4.3	4.2
Fragmented	(164)	4.3	3.9
Situation: *Nuachúrsaí*	(90)	4.3	4.0
Pupil/teacher real life situations	(72)	4.5	4.4
Routine management/organisation	(51)	4.5	4.3
Mean rating overall	(828)	4.3	4.1

ANOVA F value = 2.26, p < .05 (*attention* ratings); ANOVA F value = 3.87, p < .01; (*interest* ratings).
See text for details of Scheffe Multiple Comparisons Test.

Table 7.11 illustrates in more detail the relationship between the amount of lesson time devoted to various topics and *Class achievement in Irish*. The tendency for 'Fragmented/non-contextualised' topics to be negatively associated with *Class achievement in spoken Irish* is indicated by the pattern of 'teaching times' in column 3. For example, in the top six (high-Irish-achievement) classes, only one has more than 20% of time devoted to 'Fragmented' topics while seven of the eight low-Irish-achievement classes have this proportion or greater. The data in column 2 show that topic situations other than those in the recommended *Nuachúrsaí* are more commonly found in high-Irish-achievement classes (13%) than in middle- (9%) or low-Irish-achievement classes (7%) though as our correlation data show the overall relationship between achievement in Irish and time spent on these topics is not significant. We also include in Table 7.11 (column 3) information on 'Pupil/Teacher real life' situations because we have already noted that *Class interest* ratings of segments associated with this topic category were significantly higher than those of 'Fragmented/non-contextualised' topics. Comparing the overall proportions of time for the three groups of classes we see that high-Irish-achievement classes are associated with more time being spent on 'Pupil/Teacher real life' situations (an average of 13% of teaching time) than either middle-Irish-achievement (9% of teaching time) or low-Irish-achievement classes (7% of teaching time). However, as we have already seen the Pearson correlation analysis showed that the pattern was not statistically significant. It is also worth noting the exceptions to overall patterns - for example, one class in the higher level group spent hardly any time at all (1% of teaching time) on 'Pupil/teacher real life' topics.

Table 7.10

Pearson correlations between proportion of Irish class time spent on categories of the *ILAS* dimensions *Topic*, *Language activity* and *Materials*, and five class measures of proficiency in Irish, attitude/motivation and pupil engagement.

ILAS dimensions: n (classes) =20 *Proportion of time spent on .*	Class achievement in spoken Irish	Class attitude to Irish	Class Irish-lesson anxiety	Class attention	Class interest
			---CLASS MEASURES---		
Topic					
Fragmented	-.45*	-.37	.17	-.13	-.30
Situation: Other than *Nuachúrsaí*	.41	.27	-.33	.21	.48*
Language activity					
Drills	-.23	-.32	.12	.04	-.13
Contextualisation exercises	-.50*	-.26	.58**	-.40	-.52*
Transposition	-.56**	-.46*	.32	-.44**	-.42
Real communication in Irish	.71**	.44*	-.61**	.41	.54**
Simulated communication in Irish	.65**	.60**	-.50*	.52*	.68**
Materials					
'No materials'	.71**	.50*	-.36	.43	.60**
Other course-book/workbook	-.51*	-.29	.28	-.19	-.49*

Only those categories of dimensions significantly correlated with at least one of the five class measures in columns 2-6 are included in this table.
* p < .05; ** p < .01.

Table 7.11

Percentage of teaching time spent on three categories of *Topic* ('Situation: other than *Nuachúrsaí*', 'Fragmented', and 'Pupil/Teacher real life situations') in each of 20 classes (listed in order of achievement in spoken Irish).

Class achievement in spoken Irish Rank (1=highest)	----------------------- *Topic* -----------------------		
	Situation: *Other than Nuachúrsaí*	Fragmented/ non-contextualised	Pupil/Teacher real life situations*
1	57	17	15
2	75	15	5
3	72	21	1
4	63	19	7
5	67	7	24
6	36	13	28
High-Irish-achievement classes	*62*	*15*	*13*
7	37	20	6
8	70	7	0
9	20	16	23
10	59	12	10
11	63	0	8
12	35	12	8
Middle-Irish-achievement classes	*47*	*11*	*9*
13	44	29	8
14	46	22	5
15	51	2	6
16	29	35	10
17	52	44	2
18	66	24	8
19	20	51	8
20	57	29	8
Low-Irish-achievement classes	*46*	*26*	*7*
Proportion of all teaching time	*52*	*20*	*9*
Class range (max-min)	*(55)*	*(51)*	*(28)*

* Pupil/Teacher real life topic was not significantly related to any class measures. However, our segment-based analysis showed that *Class interest* ratings in this category were higher than corresponding ratings in the 'Fragmented/non-contextualised' category (see Table 7.9).

The Stirling Study examined the relationship between the proportion of *segments* associated with the various categories of dimensions in each of seventeen classes and class achievement in French (Mitchell *et al.*, 1981). In the case of topic, there were two category groupings in the Scottish study which were significantly correlated with class attainment in French (i) the combined category of 'Metalinguistic' topics and (ii) the combined category of 'Routine procedures' and 'Pupil performance'. In the case of the former, more time spent discussing the structure of language was associated with higher pupil performance. In contrast, more time spent on 'Routine procedures' and 'Pupil performance' was associated with lower pupil scores in French. None of the corresponding categories in the Irish study (i) 'Linguistics/grammar of Irish', (ii) 'Routine management/organisation' and 'Feedback/discussing pupils' performance' are significantly related to achievement (data not shown in table).

7.2.3 Language activity

Table 7.12 (column 1) shows the proportion of Irish lesson segments associated with each of the *Language activity* categories of *ILAS* (see also figure 7.1). Before discussing these data in detail it may be useful to note that the Irish lessons had higher proportions of segments associated with each of the first five *Language activity* categories shown in Table 7.12 than had the Stirling Study (i.e. 'Contextualisation exercises' through 'Simulated communication in Irish'). Compensating for this, higher proportions of segments in the Stirling Study compared to the Irish study are associated with each of the remaining *Language activity* categories ('Imitation' through 'Translation'). We leave aside for purposes of this initial broad based comparison, the three small categories at the bottom of Table 7.12 which have no direct equivalent in the Stirling Study.

The first five *Language activity* categories listed in Table 7.12 account for 81.9% of all the Irish lesson segments, while equivalent categories account for not much more than half that proportion of segments in the French lessons (43.8% of all segments in the Stirling Study). Looking at the first two rows in Table 7.12, it may be seen that 32.7% of the Irish lesson segments involve 'Contextualisation exercises' and 15.2% involve 'Drills' - making 47.9% in all. In the Stirling Study only 34% of segments were assigned to the corresponding *Language activity* category 'Drill/exercise' (a broader category which approximates our 'Drills' and 'Contextualisation exercises' combined).

'Simulated Communication in Irish' accounts for 9.3% of segments in the present study. It will be recalled that there was no category directly corresponding to this one in the Stirling System. In the Stirling System, discourse of this type might have been included in the 'exercise' component of the 'Drill/exercise' category, or perhaps even in the 'Real FL' category, though this is really no more than supposition.

Figure 7.1 Percentage of all teaching time spent on various language activities.

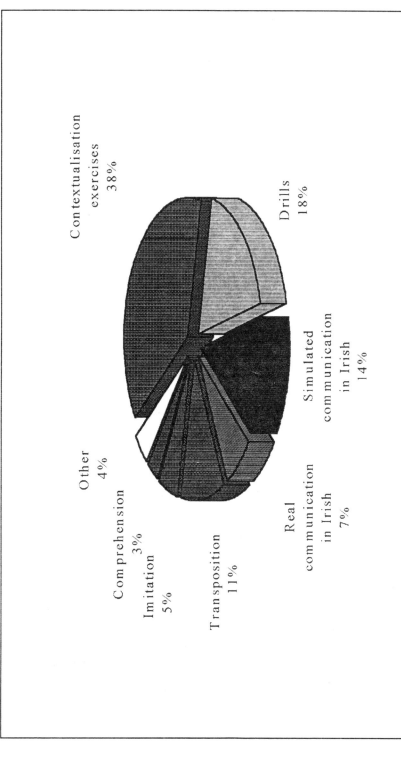

Contextualisation
exercises
38%

Drills
18%

Simulated
communication
in Irish
14%

Real
communication
in Irish
7%

Transposition
11%

Imitation
5%

Comprehension
3%

Other
4%

Table 7.12
Language activity: **Percentage distribution of teaching time and lesson segments, and average segment duration by *Language activity***

Language activity		Percentage of segments	Proportion of teaching time (hrs mins secs)	Mean segment duration (mins secs)
	Total:	(n = 828)	(42 : 3 : 40)	(3:03)
Contextualisation exercises		32.7	37.7	3:31
Drills		15.2	18.3	3:39
Real communication in Irish		12.6	6.9	1:40
Transposition (read aloud /dictation)		12.1	10.6	2:41
Simulated communication in Irish		9.3	14.3	4:40
Imitation (repeat/copy write)		5.8	4.8	2:33
Comprehension		4.7	3.0	1:55
Compound (regular cycles of activities)		1.9	1.7	2:41
Real communication in English		1.6	0.8	1:35
Translation		0.8	0.4	1:27
Irish song / poem		1.9	0.7	1:07
Bilingual real communication		1.2	0.6	1:23
Bilingual simulated communication		0.1	0.3	8:10
Total		100%	100%	---

The data for 'Real communication in Irish' (12.6%) indicate a much greater emphasis in the Irish Study than in the Stirling Study (only 1.8% of segments) on using the target language for communicating messages. In fact, if we add the proportion of segments devoted to 'Simulated communication in Irish' and 'Real communication in Irish' we can estimate that about one-fifth of all Irish lesson segments involve some kind of communication broadly defined.

Data on mean segment duration in the third column of Table 7.12 show, in addition, that 'Real communication in Irish' segments are shorter than segments associated with the other *Language activity* categories - in particular such segments are significantly shorter (Scheffe tests: $p < .01$) than those associated with 'Contextualisation exercises, 'Drills' or 'Simulated communication in Irish'.

Looking back to Table 7.8 for a moment it can be seen, in addition, that of all the topic categories, 'Routine management/organisation' is the one associated with the shortest segments (1 minute 4 seconds on average). Crosstabulations presented in more detail later (Table 7.13) reveal that 'Real communication in Irish' is the dominant language activity in this relatively small *Topic* category. While 2.2% of all teaching time is spent on 'Routine management/organisation' topics, 1.8% of this involves 'Real communication in Irish'. 'Real communication in Irish' in this context usually means the teacher giving brief instructions in Irish in the course of organising the class for the next activity - e.g. instructing pupils to take out a specific book and to open it at a specific page. Table 7.13 (fourth row) also indicates that a substantial proportion of the overall teaching time spent on 'Pupil/teacher real life' topics also involves 'Real communication in Irish' (2.3% of 9.3%). Mitchell *et al.* (1981) likewise report a tendency for 'Real FL' segments in their study to be associated with these same two topic categories and, again, to be relatively short in duration - though as we noted above the proportion of such 'Real FL' segments is quite low (1.8%) in the Stirling Study.

Returning to Table 7.12 it will be noted that in contrast to 'Real communication in Irish' segments, those segments involving 'Simulated communication in Irish' tend to be rather long in duration, running to well over four minutes on average. The proportion of all teaching time (14.3%) devoted to 'Simulated communication in Irish', therefore, exceeds the proportion of segments (9.3%).

'Transposition' activities accounted for 12.1% of all segments in the Irish Study compared to 7.4% in the Stirling Study. Crosstabulation data on *Language activity* and *Pupil behaviour* (not shown in tabular form) indicate that over 90% of the time spent on 'Transposition' activities in the Irish lessons involves 'Reading aloud' pupil behaviours.

The five remaining *Language activity* categories which have direct equivalents in the Irish and Stirling Studies are 'Imitation', 'Comprehension', 'Compound', 'Real communication in English' and 'Translation'. These categories account for only 14.8% of segments altogether in the Irish Study, compared to more than half of all the French lesson segments (56.2%) in the Stirling Study.

'Real communication in English' is involved in only 1.6% of segments in the Irish Study, in marked contrast to the Stirling Study where over one-fifth (21.3%) of all segments involve English. 'Translation' features hardly at all in the Irish lessons (less than 1% of segments) whereas it occurs in 10.6 % of the French lesson segments. And 'Imitation', an important component of audio-visual lessons, only accounts for 5.8% of segments in Irish, just under half the proportion for the same category in the Stirling Study (12.3%). This latter difference reflects presumably the greater emphasis on the audio-visual approach in the French lessons. The other two *Language activity* categories 'Comprehension' (4.7%) and 'Compound' (1.9%) are each a few percentage points lower in the Irish Study than in the Stirling Study.

Finally, the three categories 'Irish song/poem', 'Bilingual real communication', 'Bilingual simulated communication' account for a little more than three per cent of segments in the Irish lessons.

Topic and language activity

Table 7.13 further analyses the information in Tables 7.8 and 7.12 by showing how the total *teaching time* is broken down according to various combinations of *Topic* and *Language activity*. For simplicity, we have combined some of the less common language activities into broader categories. By far the largest proportion of teaching time (21.8%) is spent on 'Contextualisation exercises' based on topics in the very large 'Situation: *Other than Nuachúrsaí*' category (column one, row one). A further 10% is attributed to 'Contextualisation exercises' based on 'Situation: *Nuachúrsaí*' topics (column one, row three). The second largest proportion of teaching time is associated with the *Language activity* 'Drills' based on 'Fragmented' topics (column two, row two) - 14.4% of all teaching time.

The next most common combinations (accounting for approximately 9% of all teaching time) are 'Simulated communication in Irish' and 'Transposition' language activities, each substantially based on 'Situation: *Other than Nuachúrsaí*' topics. Finally, 'Simulated communication in Irish' and 'Real communication in Irish' language activities which use 'Pupil/teacher real life situations' as topics account for 3.9% and 2.3% respectively of teaching time. Given that this topic category accounts for only 9.3% of teaching time overall, this means that communicative language activities generally (real or simulated) are strongly associated with the 'Pupil/teacher real life' topics. We have already noted the predominance of 'Real communication in Irish' in the relatively small 'Routine management/organisation' topic category (see column 5; row 5).

Language activity: attention and interest

Attention and interest ratings corresponding to the various language activities are set out in Table 7.14. Only the first five, more common language activities listed in the table ('Contextualised exercises', 'Drills', 'Real communication in Irish', 'Transposition' and 'Simulated communication in Irish') feature in any significant differences in *mean attention* and *interest* ratings. Even within this group of frequently used language activities, differences between categories in *Class attention* ratings are never significant, though mean ratings for 'Simulated communication in Irish' (4.5) and 'Real communication in Irish' (4.6) are the highest of all. These same two language activity categories are, however, associated with significantly higher *Class interest* ratings than some of the remaining three language activity categories in this group. Specifically Scheffe Multiple Comparisons Tests showed that the mean *Class interest* rating for 'Simulated communication in Irish' (4.5) is significantly higher than for 'Transposition' (3.9), 'Drills' (4.0) (Scheffe tests: $p < .01$) and Contextualisation exercises' (4.1) (Scheffe test: $p < .05$). Meanwhile the mean *Class interest* rating for 'Real communication in Irish' (4.4) is significantly higher (Scheffe test: $p < .05$) than for both 'Tranposition' and 'Contextualisation exercises'.

Table 7.13

Topic/Language activity: Percentage distribution of teaching time by Topic/Language activity combinations

Proportion of teaching time

—————— *Language activity* ——————

Topic n (classes) = 20	Context-ualisation exercises	Drills	Simulated communication in Irish	Transposition	Real communication in Irish	Imitation	Comprehension	Combined remaining language activities*	(Total) (n =828)
Situation: *Other than Nuachúrsaí*	21.8	3.2	9.1	9.0	1.5	1.7	2.8	3.5	(52.4)
Fragmented	2.4	14.4	0.6	1.6	0.1	0.3	0.1	0.4	(19.6)
Situation: *Nuachúrsaí*	10.3	0.3	0.7	0.1	-	2.9	0.2	0.1	(14.5)
Pupil/teacher real life situations	2.5	0.4	3.9	-	2.3	-	-	0.2	(9.3)
Routine management/organisation	-	-	-	-	1.8	-	-	0.3	(2.2)
Linguistics/grammar of Irish	0.6	-	-	-	0.6	-	-	-	(1.3)
Irish life/culture/music	0.1	-	0.1	-	0.2	-	-	-	(0.3)
Feedback/discussing pupil performance	0.1	-	-	-	0.4	-	-	-	(0.5)
Total	37.7	18.3	14.3	10.6	6.9	4.8	3.0	4.5	100%

*Combined remaining language activities include 'Compound activities', 'Irish song/poem', 'Real communication in English', 'Bilingual real communication', 'Translation' and 'Bilingual simulated communication'. Each of these categories accounts for less than 2% of all teaching time.

Table 7.14
Mean *Class attention* and *Class interest* ratings for most frequent
(at least 5% of segments) *Language activity* categories

Language activity	n (segments)	Class attention Mean rating (1 - 5) (828)	Class interest Mean rating (1 - 5) (828)
Contextualisation exercises	(271)	4.3	4.1
Drills	(126)	4.3	4.0
Real communication in Irish	(104)	4.6	4.4
Transposition (read aloud/dictation)	(100)	4.2	3.9
Simulated communication in Irish	(77)	4.5	4.5
Imitation (repeat/copy write)	(48)	4.5	4.1
Comprehension	(39)	4.2	4.0
Mean rating overall	(828)	4.3	4.1

* ANOVA F value = 3.32, p < .01 (attention ratings); F = 6.33, p < .01 (interest ratings).
See text for details of Scheffe Multiple Comparisons Tests.

Language activities and class characteristics

Returning to Table 7.10 it may be seen that in relation to teaching time spent on various categories of *Language activity* and *Class achievement in spoken Irish*, the strongest association is found in the case of two communicative categories 'Simulated communication in Irish' (r=.65) and 'Real communication in Irish' (r=.71). Looking at the other columns, it can be seen that the same language activities ('Real communication in Irish' and 'Simulated communication in Irish') are significantly associated with a positive *Class attitude to Irish* (r=.44; r=.60), higher *Class interest* (r=.54; r=.68) and lower *Class Irish-lesson anxiety* (r=-.61; r=-.50). *Class attention* figures less often in these relationships, but note that it is significantly and positively associated with the proportion of time spent on 'Simulated communication in Irish' (r=.52). The pattern of relationships between some other class measures not shown in Table 7.10 are also of considerable interest. For example, a relative emphasis on 'Real' or 'Simulated communication in Irish' was found not to be related to the classes' overall general academic ability as reflected in English verbal reasoning.

In contrast to these findings, the data in column one of Table 7.10 also indicated that more time spent on 'Contextualisation exercises' and 'Transposition' type activities are associated with classes having lower levels of *Class achievement in spoken Irish* (r=-.50 and r=-.56 respectively) and these correlations were significant. Note, incidentally, that a relative emphasis on the language activity 'Contextualisation exercises' is also associated with higher *Class Irish lesson-anxiety* (r=.58) and lower levels of *Class interest* during the Irish lesson (r=-.52).

More time spent on 'Transposition' language activities is also associated with lower *Class achievement in spoken Irish* (r=-.56), with less positive *Class attitude to Irish* (r=-.46), and with lower *Class attention* mean ratings (r=-.44). It may be noted in passing that none of the language activities in the Stirling Study were significantly correlated with class attainment in French.

We now turn to the class-by-class data showing how the proportion of Irish lesson time spent on the five commonly used language activities varies according to class achievement in Irish (Table 7.15). Consistent with our correlation findings, it can be seen that 'Contextualisation exercises' and 'Transposition' are the language activities which are more characteristic of the low-Irish-achievement classes. Only 25% of all class time, on average, is spent on 'Contextualisation exercises' in high-Irish-achievement classes compared to 50% and 42% in middle- and low-Irish-achievement classes respectively. In the six high-Irish-achievement classes, only one has more than 10% of class time spent on 'Transposition', whereas 6 out of the 8 low-Irish-achievement classes have more than that proportion. We include 'Drills' in our class by class data in Table 7.15 because, as we recall from Table 7.14, segments in this category were more likely to be associated with lower levels of *Class attention* and *Class interest*. We see, however, that there is no steady pattern in the extent to which 'Drills' are used between the different Irish-achievement groups of classes.

'Simulated communication in Irish' and 'Real communication in Irish' clearly account for more teaching time in high-Irish-achievement classes. In these top six classes an average of 26% of teaching time is spent on 'Simulated communication in Irish' and 11% of teaching time on 'Real communication in Irish'. In middle-Irish-achievement classes the corresponding percentages are 10% and 8% respectively and in low-achievement classes even lower still, at 8% and 2% respectively. Note that one of the low-Irish-achievement classes has zero teaching time devoted to either 'Simulated' or 'Real communication in Irish', while the adjacent rank classes have only 1% of teaching time devoted to 'Real communication in Irish'. As our correlation analysis already indicated, the variations in *Class achievement in spoken Irish* associated with these two communicative categories are statistically significant.

Taken together these results present a positive picture of classes which place relatively more emphasis on 'Real' and 'Simulated communication in Irish' rather than on more language-practice type activities such as 'Transposition' and 'Contextualisation exercises'.

Table 7.15
Percentage of teaching time spent on five categories of *Language activity* in each of 20 classes (listed in order of achievement in spoken Irish.

Class achievement in spoken Irish Rank (1=highest)	*Language activity*				
	Contextual-isation exercises	Drills*	Simulated communic-ation in Irish	Transposition (read aloud/dictation)	Real communic-ation in Irish
1	18	17	37	3	8
2	43	13	9	15	9
3	23	32	13	5	8
4	12	14	34	6	15
5	27	18	31	6	17
6	27	13	29	5	8
High-Irish-achievement classes	*25*	*18*	*26*	*7*	*11*
7	45	20	11	3	4
8	33	18	0	18	13
9	60	10	19	6	4
10	45	5	11	20	9
11	65	0	18	5	11
12	54	9	0	12	9
Middle-Irish-achievement classes	*50*	*10*	*10*	*11*	*8*
13	42	13	16	17	2
14	48	19	8	8	1
15	40	12	15	8	8
16	54	28	0	15	0
17	40	29	0	17	1
18	44	17	8	17	0
19	39	38	6	13	1
20	31	29	8	23	0
Low-Irish achievement classes	*42*	*23*	*8*	*15*	*2*
Proportion of teaching time	*38*	*18*	*14*	*11*	*7*
Class range	*(53)*	*(38)*	*(37)*	*(20)*	*(17)*

* The category 'Drills' was not significantly related to any class measures. However, our segment-based analysis showed that *Class interest* ratings in this category were lower than corresponding ratings in the 'Simulated communication in Irish' category (Table 7.14)

7.2.4 *Materials in use*

In the Stirling Study as we mentioned in Chapter 6 (section 6.5.6), two different methods of recording usage of materials was employed. Only one of these methods, however, provides data which is amenable to comparison with the Irish Study. The Stirling method in question involved the observer recording, on a minute by minute basis, which materials were in use. In the present study, however, we recorded materials used on a segment by segment basis - and we also have available the segment duration. Teaching time associated with different materials, therefore, is the only viable basis for comparison between the Stirling Study and the Irish Study. It must be borne in mind, however, that a particular material may only be used for a fraction of the time associated with a segment. This means that the Irish Study may tend to overestimate the proportion of teaching time associated with materials compared to the Stirling Study.

Table 7.16 provides information on the extent to which various materials were used, either by pupil or teacher, in the observed Irish lessons. Looking at column 1, it can be seen that in more than a quarter of segments (26.4%) no materials at all are used. In the remaining segments, at least one material is being used. The blackboard is the most widely used of all, employed in 18.4% of segments. 'Readers' and 'Other course-books /workbooks' (such as *Buail Liom, Bog Liom* and *Anseo is Ansiúd*) are *each* used in just over 17% of segments. It should be noted that some segments may involve the use of more than one book.

The *Nuachúrsaí* handbook appears in only 10% of all lesson segments. 'Film strips', which are invariably linked to the use of the *Nuachúrsaí* by the teachers, feature in 9.1% of segments. 'Cut-outs'/'Figurines' are used in only 1.2% of lesson segments. Three other materials each account for 3% or more of segments in the Irish study - 'Worksheets' (3.4% of segments), 'Objects' (3.4% of segments) and 'Wallcharts' (3% of segments). 'Authentic materials', an important element in communicative language teaching, only account for 0.4% of segments here.

The Stirling Study, just like the Irish one, found that the blackboard and textbooks were among the most frequently used materials in the French lesson. Textbooks of any kind, however, were used for a considerably greater proportion of teaching time in the Stirling Study (37%) than in the Irish study (29.1% of teaching time represented by those segments during which 'Other course-books/workbooks' or the '*Nuachúrsaí*' handbook were used). The 'Blackboard' was used for 29% of teaching time in the Stirling Study compared to 25.4% in the Irish one. 'Readers' were in use for 10% of French lesson time compared to 14.4% of Irish lesson time.

More frequent use was made of a jotter in the Stirling Study than in the present Irish Study. Twenty eight per cent of all French lesson teaching time involved use of the 'Jotter' compared to 17.8% of teaching time in the Irish lesson. In this context it is useful to mention that results relating to *Pupil behaviour*, to be presented in Chapter 8 (see section 8.2.1), indicate that 'Writing' pupil behaviours occurred more frequently in the Stirling Study than in the Irish Study.

The Stirling Study, like the Irish one, reports relatively low use of visual aids, such as 'Slides', 'Film strips' and 'Video', even though the French course was described as an audio-visual one. 'Filmstrips' were used for only 7% of French lesson teaching time and 'Film/Video' for 1% of the time. This compares in the Irish Study to 12.1% of teaching time corresponding to segments in which 'Film strips' were in use. 'Film/Video' was not used at all in any of the Irish lessons observed.

Table 7.16
Materials: **Percentage distribution of teaching time, lesson segments, and average segment duration by *Materials***

Materials◆	Total:	Percentage of segments* (n = 828)	Proportion of teaching time * (hrs mins secs) (42: 3: 40)	Mean segment duration* (mins secs) (3:03)
'No materials' used		26.4	20.5	2:21
Blackboard		18.4	25.4	4:13
'Other' course-book/workbook		17.5	17.1	2:58
Reader		17.1	14.4	2:34
Jotter/copy		13.2	17.8	4:07
Nuachúrsaí handbook		10.0	12.0	3:39
Film strips		9.1	12.1	4:05
Objects		3.4	5.6	5:01
Worksheets		3.4	3.7	3:21
Wallcharts		3.0	3.2	3:13
Cutouts		1.2	1.5	3:52
Overhead projector		0.5	1.0	6:25
Photographs		0.4	0.8	6:36
Person (appearance)		0.4	0.7	6:16
'Authentic' materials		0.4	0.7	6:16
Tape		0.1	0.02	0:39
Other		0.5	0.3	1:59

* These columns do not add up to 100% and 828(n) because more than one type of material may be used in any one segment.
◆ Three other categories of materials - Video/Film, Library Books, Flash cards were never used.

It will be noted from the mean segment durations listed in column three of Table 7.16 that the three commonly used materials, 'Blackboard', 'Jotter/copy' and 'Film strips' are associated with longer segment durations than average: mean segment durations over four minutes long. Because the use of materials in the Stirling Study was not recorded on a segment by segment basis, comparable information is not available on the amount of time during which no materials at all were in use in that study.

Table 7.17 shows the *Class attention* and *Class interest* mean ratings for segments in which the more frequently used (in > 3% of segments) materials were present. The first row gives ratings for those segments in which no materials at all were in use. Mean *Class attention* (4.5) and *Class interest* (4.4) ratings for segments associated with this 'No materials' category are significantly higher (F =16.6 & 31.6 respectively ; p<.01) than the corresponding ratings for segments in which at least one material was in use. Examining specific materials in use, the results show that segments associated with the infrequently used materials category 'Wallcharts' (not shown in this table) have higher mean *Class attention* and *Class interest* ratings (mean ratings of 4.6 in both cases) than segments (associated with other materials). On the other hand, significantly lower mean *Class attention* and *Class interest* ratings are associated with the three materials categories 'Other course-book/workbook', 'Film strips/slides' and 'Worksheets'.

Table 7.17
Mean *Class attention* and *Class interest* ratings according to the most frequent (at least 5% of segments) *Materials* categories

Materials	n (segments)	Class attention Mean rating (1 - 5) (828)	Class interest Mean rating (1 - 5) (828)
'No materials' used	(219)	4.5**	4.4**
Blackboard	(152)	4.3	4.1
Course-book/workbook	(145)	4.2*	3.8**
Reader	(142)	4.3	4.1
Jotter/copy	(109)	4.3	4.2
Nuachúrsaí handbook	(83)	4.2	4.0
Film strips/slides	(75)	4.2*	3.9*
Overall mean	(828)	4.3	4.1

* ANOVA p < .05; ** ANOVA p < .01. In each *Materials* category, the mean ratings for segments associated with that category are compared to the mean ratings for all other segments.

Table 7.18
Percentage of lesson segments* in each of the 20 classes (listed by achievement in spoken Irish) according to three *Materials* categories

Class achievement in spoken Irish Rank (1 = highest)	--------------------- *Materials* -----------------		
	No materials used	Other course-book/ workbook**	Film strip
1	42	-	20
2	53	-	-
3	39	2	-
4	25	-	6
5	67	-	-
6	37	-	-
High-Irish-achievement classes	*44*		*4*
7	17	21	21
8	2	55	-
9	18	50	9
10	18	9	3
11	26	-	18
12	12	36	20
Middle-Irish-achievement classes	*16*	*29*	*12*
13	13	27	13
14	24	-	31
15	14	46	36
16	10	-	5
17	21	55	-
18	19	68	-
19	17	25	-
20	14	11	-
Low-Irish-achievement classes	*17*	*29*	*11*
Proportion of all lesson segments	*26*	*18*	*9*
Class range (max-min)	*(65)*	*(68)*	*(36)*

* Note teaching time is not used here. ** Other than *Nuachúrsaí* handbook

Looking back at Table 7.10 we see the extent to which teaching time spent using either 'No materials' or 'Other course-book/workbook' relates to each of the five class measures. Both categories above have significant correlations (one positive and one negative) with *Class achievement in spoken Irish*. Classes in which a greater proportion of lesson time involves 'No materials' tend to have higher levels of achievement in Irish (r = .71) while more time spent on 'Other course-book/workbook' is associated with classes having lower levels of achievement in Irish (r=-.51). Furthermore the data in column two of Table 7.10 indicate that classes in which a greater proportion of lesson time involves 'No materials' of any kind have significantly more positive *Class attitude to Irish* (r =.50) and show higher rates of *Class interest* (r=.60). Greater use of 'Other course-book/workbook', on the other hand, is associated with significantly lower levels of *Class interest* (r = -.49). Correlations between frequency of use of different teaching materials and class attainment French were not reported in the Mitchell *et al.* (1981) Stirling Study.

Finally, Table 7.18 illustrates the relationship between *Class achievement in spoken Irish* and the extent to which either of two types of materials ('Other course-book/workbook' and 'Film strips') or 'No materials' are used in each of the twenty classes. Note that the index of *Materials* used here is based on proportion of segments rather than proportion of teaching time.

The ranges listed in the last row of Table 7.18 show the overall variation across classes in the percentage of lesson segments in which the various materials are used. Two strong patterns may be observed. Consistent with earlier correlation data (Table 7.10) there is considerably less use of materials of any kind in high-Irish-achievement classes (no materials in 44% of segments on average) than in the middle-Irish-achievement classes (average of 16%) or low-Irish-achievement classes (average of 17%). The second trend relates to the use of 'Other course-book/workbook'. Five of the six high-Irish-achievement classes do not make any use at all of books in this category and in the remaining class only 2% of lesson segments involve their use. In contrast, 29% of lesson segments on average in middle- and low-Irish-achievement classes involve 'Other course-book/workbook' (and over 50% in some cases). Four of the six high-Irish-achievement classes did not use 'Filmstrips' either. Class rank 1 was an exception, however, with 'Filmstrips' being used in 20% of all lesson segments. There is no clear general relationship to be observed, however, between frequency of use of filmstrips and class achievement in Irish.

7.3 Discussion

7.3.1 Overview

It will be useful to begin with an overview of the main issues and results on which the discussion will focus. We will take the *Language activity* results first since the issues raised here will provide a context within which the data relating to *Topic* and *Materials* can be more easily understood. The discussion of *Language activity* centres around four main points.

1. English-based or partly English-based activities form a substantial component of the Stirling French foreign-language programme but are virtually unknown in the Irish programme. We attribute this to the different traditions in second-language and foreign-language teaching.

2. The overall balance between communicative activities and language practice in the Irish programme is indicated by the fact that about one-fifth of lesson segments involve communicative activities - although there are very substantial class-to-class variations.

3. A focus on language-practice type language activities tend to be associated with generally negative outcomes while communicative activities tend to be associated with generally positive outcomes. For example, those Irish classes which devote relatively more time to 'Real' or 'Simulated' communication in Irish tend, among other things, to have higher achievement in Irish and higher class interest compared to classes which devote relatively more time to language-practice activities such as 'Contextualisation exercises' or 'Transposition'.

4. Despite these findings, it is argued that aiming for a better balance than exists at present between experiential and analytic activities in the Irish lesson represents a better strategy than unqualified adherence to the dictum 'the more communicative the better'.

The experiential/analytic theme continues in the discussion of the findings relating to *Topic* and *Materials*. The main additional points made here are:

5. Communicative *Topic* categories (e.g. 'Pupil/teacher real life') tend to be associated with positive outcomes (e.g. higher class interest), while language-practice *Topic* categories (e.g. 'Fragmented') tend to be associated with negative outcomes (e.g. lower class achievement in spoken Irish, lower class interest).

6. Traditional materials, such as the blackboard, jotters and readers, are relatively frequently used in the Irish lesson, while materials (or texts) associated with recent forms of communicative language teaching, such as 'authentic' materials, are almost non-existent. Generally speaking, when Irish teachers engage in 'Real' or 'Simulated' communicative activities, these activities do not originate in course-books - either they make no use at all of materials in the course of such activities or the materials used are traditional ones such as the blackboard and the jotter. Consistent with this, use of 'No materials' tends to be associated with positive outcomes - higher class achievement in spoken Irish, better class attitude to Irish and so on. Use of course-books which are seen as alternatives to the *Nuachúrsaí* (i.e. 'Other' course-book/workbook) is associated with negative outcomes (lower class achievement in spoken Irish, lower class interest).

A concluding section of the chapter deals with some general issues which arise from the findings just reported. First we examine a paradox presented by the correlation data reported here: the fact that the communicative elements of the basically audio-visual Irish programme are associated with more 'positive' results than are the communicative elements of explicitly communicative programmes as reported in the research literature. Second, we try to identify some of the factors which in the past may have prevented teachers of weaker classes from including more communicative activities in the Irish lesson, and we consider whether the introduction of new teaching materials will help them to circumvent these difficulties. Lastly, we consider whether the introduction of communicative materials may pose certain kinds of problems for the 'all-Irish' character of language teaching at primary level, since the widespread use of Irish at present may be dependent on the routinised, predictable nature of the existing Irish lesson.

7.3.2 Language activity

The discussion of the *Language activity* results centres on the five main categories which account for most of the lesson segments and for most of the significant findings. These five categories consist of three types of *language-practice* ('Contextualisation exercise', 'Drills' and 'Transposition') and two types of *communicative* activity ('Real communication in Irish' and 'Simulated communication in Irish'). Together, these account for 81.9% of all segments in the Irish lesson but their equivalents in the Stirling Study only account for 43.8% of the French segments. For example, if we combine the proportion of segments for 'Real communication in Irish' (12.6%) and 'Simulated communication in Irish' (9.3%), we estimate that a little over one-fifth of the Irish lesson involves some communicative use of the language. By comparison, 'Real communication in French' accounts for only 1.8% of segments - and there is no language activity equivalent to 'Simulated communication' in the Stirling study.

Irish versus English
The considerably smaller proportion of segments in the Stirling study which are associated with the five main language activities is mainly compensated for by a greater emphasis on two English-language activities. Thus, 'Real communication in English' (21.3%) and 'Translation' (10.6%) - which is partly English - together account for 31.9% of segments in the Stirling Study. By comparison, these same two activities only account for 2.4% of segments in the Irish study.

In order to see how Irish lessons manage to avoid the kind of use of the pupils' native language which the French lessons engage in, we must compare the kind of topics which are associated with 'Real communication in English' in the Stirling Study and 'Real communication in Irish' in the Irish study. The Stirling study reports that 26.5% of French lesson segments are associated with three *Topic* categories - 'Routine procedures', 'Metalinguistic' and 'Civilisation' - and that these segments overwhelmingly involve the use of the student's native language, English. By comparison, only 9% of lesson segments in all are associated with the equivalent *Topic* categories in the Irish Study and crosstabulations with *Language activity* data reveal that the discourse involved is in Irish rather than in English. Thus, not only do Irish classes devote a smaller proportion of segments to these three *Topic* categories, but when they do deal with these topics, they do so in Irish.

Of the three *Topic* categories just mentioned, the one manifesting the greatest difference between the Stirling and Irish studies is 'Linguistics/grammar of Irish' (2.2% of segments in the Irish study) and the corresponding 'Metalinguistic' topic category (12.3% of segments in the Stirling Study). There are a number of factors which could account for this difference. One possibility is that because pupils in the Irish study begin instruction in Irish at a young age and continue the learning/acquisition process over a relatively long period, metalinguistic concepts and distinctions are transmitted in a more gradual and indirect way - by illustration perhaps or by informally drawing attention to significant linguistic patterns in the context of drills etc. If this assumption is correct, a consequence would be that direct discussion and explanation of metalinguistic issues, either in Irish or English, would be rarely necessary. In contrast, because the pupils in the Stirling Study presumably began French instruction only on entry to post-primary school, direct explanation and discussion of certain metalinguistic issues, through the pupils' mother tongue, may have been judged to be a faster and more efficient route to competence in the language for students of this age than a more distributed process of illustration and attention-focussing. Needless to say at this early stage in the pupils' acquisition of French, such topics would be difficult to talk about in French in any case. Our results here do not allow us, however, either to assess the merits of the two strategies, or to say whether these hypothesised strategies have any basis in fact.

It is notable also that even in those individual Irish classes where communicative activities in Irish, either 'Real' or 'Simulated', form little or no part of the lesson, the use of English is still almost never favoured. In classes where *communicative* activities in Irish are rare, the difference is made up by a greater proportion of the lesson being devoted to various kinds of Irish *language practice,* particularly 'Contextualisation exercises' and 'Transposition'. Consistent with this, there is very little evidence of code switching to be found on the audiotapes of the lessons. Where English is used, it typically consists of just a single word - either by the teacher or pupils (See sample transcripts in Appendix 6.4). Neither is there any indication from teachers' assessments of their own reactions to the observation work (Chapter 6: section 6.6) that the extensive use of Irish rather than English throughout, both for classroom communication and language practice, represents a departure from the teachers' usual approach. In any case, if teachers were in fact departing from their usual approach, we would expect pupils to exhibit extreme difficulty in understanding what was happening - and there was no evidence at all of that.

Communication versus language practice - Differences between classes
We turn now to the question of how the different kinds of language activity relate to the various class measures of Irish proficiency and attitude. The first thing to be noted is that the distinction between *communicative activities* and *language practice* is powerfully

evident in the pattern of results. Generally, *language practice* tends to be associated with negative outcomes and *communicative* activities with positive ones.

For example, when we pool the lesson segments for all 20 classes (39 lessons), we find that class interest is significantly higher for both 'Simulated communication in Irish' and 'Real communication in Irish' than it is for both 'Contextualisation exercises' and 'Transposition'. In addition, class interest is significantly higher for 'Simulated communication in Irish' segments than it is for 'Drills' segments.

When we turn to variation across classes in the proportion of lesson time devoted to each language activity, we find similar trends. With the exception of 'Drills', which do not manifest a consistent enough pattern across classes to be statistically significant, the other four main language activities once again divide, in terms of patterns of association, into the *communicative* ones ('Real communication in Irish' and 'Simulated communication in Irish') and the *language practice* ones ('Contextualisation exercises' and 'Transposition'). Specifically, both 'Contextualisation exercises' and 'Transposition' are devoted significantly more lesson time in classes which have low levels of achievement in Irish than in those which have higher levels of achievement. Correspondingly, 'Real communication in Irish' and 'Simulated communication in Irish' are devoted significantly less time in classes which are weaker in Irish.

The differences are substantial. In the top six classes in terms of achievement in Irish, for example, an average of 25% of class time is spent on 'Contextualisation exercises' compared to an average of 42% of class time in the eight weakest classes. Again, an average of 26% of time is spent on 'Simulated communication in Irish' and 11% on 'Real communication in Irish' in the top six classes, compared to averages of 8% and 2% of time respectively spent on these activities in the eight weakest classes. Combining the two communicative activities ('Real' plus 'Simulated' communication in Irish), we can say that 37% of lesson time on average is spent on communicative activities in high-Irish-achievement classes while only 10% of time is spent on them on average in the low-Irish-achievement classes. We can also examine this contrast at the level of individual classes. For example, one of the high-Irish-achievement classes (ranked 4 in terms of achievement in Irish) devotes almost 50% of teaching time to communicative activities, while one of the low-Irish-achievement classes (ranked 16 in terms of achievement in Irish) devotes zero teaching time to them.

The contrast between an emphasis on communicative activities as opposed to language practice applies not just to the association with *Class achievement in spoken Irish*, but extends also to the other four class measures such as *Class attitude to Irish, Class Irish-lesson anxiety, Class attention* and *Class interest*. Generally positive outcomes are associated with an emphasis on each of the two *communicative* language activities, while generally negative outcomes are associated with an emphasis on *language practice* activities ('Contextualisation exercises' and 'Transposition').

Of the 16 Pearson 'r' coefficients associated with the four *Language activity* categories and the four class measures just mentioned, 11 are statistically significant, 3 are marginally significant ($p < .08$) and the remaining two are in the expected direction though not significantly so. Thus, for example, classes which spend a greater proportion of lesson time on 'Contextualisation exercises' exhibit significantly higher levels of anxiety in relation to speaking in Irish during the Irish lesson, and are judged to have significantly lower levels of interest in the lesson, than other classes which spend less time on this language activity. Likewise, classes which spend more time on 'Transposition' activities have significantly less positive attitudes to Irish, and are significantly less attentive to the lesson, than classes which spend less time on this activity. In contrast, classes which spend a greater proportion of time on either of the two communicative language activities - 'Real' or 'Simulated' communication in Irish - tend to have significantly better attitudes to Irish, lower levels of anxiety in relation to the Irish lesson, higher levels of attention and/or higher levels of interest in the lesson.

More communicative equals better?
Superficially, this pattern of results may seem to suggest that we can unreservedly recommend that 'the more communicative the lesson the better' - that increasing the proportion of *communicative* activities and decreasing the proportion of *language practice* activities will improve the standing of classes on a whole range of indicators such as achievement in Irish, attitude to Irish and interest in the Irish lesson. In fact, we will have to content ourselves with a rather more modest and circumscribed conclusion than this. The kind of correlational evidence provided by this study and indeed by most studies in second-language acquisition is not strong enough to support cause-and-effect conclusions. Correlation data is fundamentally ambiguous about the 'direction-of-effect'. In addition, because a number of different variables are intercorrelated, it is extremely difficult to separate the contribution of each variable to the result of interest. This is a problem that is common in the social sciences but is particularly acute in the case of research on classroom based second-language acquisition because of the fragmented state of research and theorising, and the failure to replicate findings across different settings, cultures, ages and sociolinguistic contexts (Ellis, 1994). It will be useful to explore these issues in a little more detail at this point since basically the same ones arise later in this chapter and the next in interpreting corresponding data relating to other dimensions of *ILAS*.

Consider, for example, the significant positive correlations between *Class achievement in spoken Irish* and the proportion of class time spent on communicative language activities. It might be argued that this indicates, not as the communicative dictum suggests that a greater emphasis on communicative activities cause higher achievement in Irish, but instead that having higher *Class achievement in spoken Irish* (for whatever reason) leads to a greater emphasis on communicative activities. The underlying argument here might be that teachers of weaker classes choose not to introduce communicative activities because they believe that their pupils' level of proficiency in Irish would not allow them to benefit from such activities. Correspondingly, more able classes may be judged to have good enough Irish to profit from more communicative activities.

On purely commonsense grounds, the correlations involving *Class attention* and *Class interest* might seem more amenable to explanation in terms of the dictum 'the more communicative the better'. Here we have the evidence of the inspectors watching the reactions of pupils as the different language teaching activities unfold and their conclusion that class attention and interest are higher during *communicative* activities and lower during *language practice*. But here again, we cannot entirely discount an alternative possibility - that the critical underlying causative factor in all these cases is, at least in part, *Class achievement in spoken Irish* - that higher levels of achievement in Irish in certain classes lead to *both* the greater emphasis on communicative activities *and* the higher levels of attention and interest in these classes.

Despite these cautions about the formal evidence, notions of plausibility and commonsense have to be brought into the equation as well. Results of second-language acquisition studies such as this, in common with most other research in the social sciences, must make the best sense possible out of the evidence collected, taking due account of the characteristics of the broader language teaching context. At the very least, our data would seem to make a *prima facie* case for including a strong communicative component in all lessons if the goal is to maximise achievement in Irish and the other positive outcomes documented above. In claiming this, we are not proposing that the whole lesson should consist of communicative (or experiential) activities but merely that a balance should be struck between such activities and language practice (i.e. analytic or form-focussed activities). We concur, therefore, with the conclusion of Allen *et al.* (1990) and Allen (1992) on the basis of their classroom observation research on core French and immersion that 'the analytic and the experiential focus may be complementary, in that they provide essential support for one another in the classroom'.

7.3.3 *Topic*

Three *Topic* categories in the present study were found to be significantly related to *Class achievement in spoken Irish* and/or *Class interest*. The three categories are 'Pupil/teacher real life' (8.7% of segments), 'Situation: *Other than Nuachúrsaí*' (51.1% of segments) and 'Fragmented/non-contextualised' (19.8% of segments). The first two of these are associated with positive outcomes: either higher *Class interest* in a pooled-segment comparison between *Topic* categories, or a significant class-based correlation involving the percentage of class time spent on the *Topic* category of interest. The third *Topic* category, 'Fragmented/non-contextualised', is associated with negative outcomes: lower *Class interest* in pooled-segment comparisons, and lower *Class achievement in spoken Irish* in a class-based correlation. Not surprisingly, perhaps, the same first two *Topic* categories, i.e. those associated with positive outcomes, are common in the case of *communicative* activities while the third, associated with negative outcomes, is common in the case of one particular type of *language practice* - 'Drills'. Thus, the contrast between *language practice* and *communicative* activities continues to have significance in the case of *Topic*. Nevertheless, as we explain below, the information on *Topic* does modify and clarify aspects of the *language-practice/communicative* distinction already identified in the *Language activity* data. To illustrate this, it will be necessary to trace some of the connections between *Language activity* and *Topic* in a little more detail.

The results show that *Language activity* categories 'Simulated communication in Irish' and 'Real communication in Irish' are strongly associated - in the sense of sharing segments - with the *Topic* categories 'Pupil /teacher real life' and 'Situation: *Other than Nuachúrsaí*'. Another *Topic* category, 'Routine management/organisation', is even more strongly related to 'Real communication in Irish' but is not related at all to 'Simulated communication in Irish'. What is interesting about the 'Routine management /organisation' *Topic* category is that it is not associated with the positive outcomes, in terms of *Class interest* or *Class achievement in spoken Irish*, which are otherwise characteristic of communicative *Topics* and *Language activities* in this study. In this sense, perhaps the 'Routine management/organisation' *Topic* category can be seen as fine-tuning the *communicative/language practice* distinction as originally reflected in the *Language activity* results.

When we look more closely at 'Routine management/organisation' segments we can perhaps see more clearly what is different about the segments associated with this communicative *Topic* category. Segments in the 'Routine management/organisation' category are particularly short (1.04 minutes on average), the communication is generally quite circumscribed and tends to involve little or no spoken response from pupils e.g. the teacher gives brief instructions in Irish relating to Irish homework: (i) opening books and making a note of verbs to be studied for the next day's lesson (Appendix 6.4, extract 19) (ii) underlining spellings on various pages to be learned at home (Appendix 6.4, extract 20).

Returning now to the *Topic* categories which were associated with significant outcomes, it may be noted that 'Pupil/teacher real life' and 'Fragmented/non-contextualised' categories represent most clearly the contrasting approaches to language teaching we have been talking about - 'Pupil/teacher real life' being representative of the experiential or communicative approach and 'Fragmented/non-contextualised' being representative of a language practice or form-focused approach. Significantly, these *Topic* categories represent similar proportions of lesson segments in the Stirling and Irish studies, reflecting no doubt the audio-visual, basically form-focussed, orientation of the courses involved in both cases. A considerably greater proportion of 'Pupil/teacher real life' segments than is reported in the present Irish study would be expected in a communicatively oriented course, where the pupil's own life and communicative needs and interests would be emphasised. In contrast, an emphasis on 'Fragmented/non-contextualised' topics, that is where there is no unifying theme underlying the language activity in question (usually 'Drills'), would be at variance with a communicative approach.

It is worthwhile noting also that these class interest data relating to *Topic*, which are based on direct observations of the general behaviour of pupils during the lesson, are broadly consistent with the individual pupils' own expressed preference for materials and topics which we reported in Chapter 4. It will be recalled that pupils sought lessons which, among other things, would be 'more modern, fun, realistic, non-sexist', and they criticised the existing course materials for being 'boring, old-fashioned and repetitious'.

The remaining *Topic* category which is strongly associated both with communicative *Language activities* and with a positive outcome (higher *Class interest*), is 'Situation: *Other than Nuachúrsaí*'. Over 60% of both the segments and the lesson time devoted to 'Simulated communication in Irish' involve this *Topic* category. 'Situation: *Other than Nuachúrsaí*', however, represents an extremely large topic category, accounting for over 50% of *all* segments and lesson time, and it covers a range of language practice, particularly 'Contextualisation exercises' as well as communicative language activities. In all probability, it is the involvement of 'Simulated communication in Irish' in 'Situation: *Other than Nuachúrsaí*' which is responsible for the positive results relating to the latter topic category.

On first sight, it may appear curious that communicative activities would be associated at all with the 'Situation: *Other than Nuachúrsaí*' topic category, since the 'Other' (i.e. non-*Nuachúrsaí*) course-books in use in the classrooms in this study are not explicitly communicative in the sense that the term is now used. It must be borne in mind, however, that this *Topic* category is very broad and includes not only situations deriving from 'alternative' textbooks or readers, but also those generated by the teacher himself/herself. As we will demonstrate in the next section, it is the latter teacher-nominated topics within the 'Situation: *Other than Nuachúrsaí*' category which are associated with 'Simulated communication in Irish'.

Finally, it is interesting to note that segments involving *Nuachúrsaí* topics are not associated with either positive or negative results in terms of attention, interest, attitude to Irish or achievement in Irish.

7.3.4 *Materials*
Many of the commonly used materials in the present study are the traditional ones - 'Blackboard' (18.4% of segments and the second most common category), 'Reader' (17.1%), and 'Jotter/copy' (13.2%). None of these relatively common materials categories is significantly related to class measures of Irish proficiency and attitude. Results relating to two other common materials categories, however, are worthy of note: (a) segments in which 'No materials' are employed tend to be associated with positive outcomes (higher *Class achievement in spoken Irish*, higher *Class interest* etc.), and (b) segments in which 'Other course-book/workbooks' (i.e. alternatives to the *Nuachúrsaí*) are employed tend to be associated with negative outcomes. Once again, the *communicative* versus *language-practice* distinction helps to explain these findings and in addition the distinction itself is clarified and elaborated by them.

'No materials', the most common category of all in the *Materials* dimension, is associated with a little over a quarter of all segments. 'No materials' segments have significantly higher *Class attention* and *Class interest* ratings than other segments. The proportion of 'No materials' segments varies greatly from class to class - from a high of 67% to a low of 2%. Classes with a greater proportion of 'No materials' segments have significantly higher levels of achievement in spoken Irish, higher class interest and more positive attitudes to Irish. The strength of the connection with achievement in Irish is indicated by the fact that in classes with high levels of achievement in Irish, the mean proportion of 'No materials' segments (44%) is over two and a half times the mean proportion of 'No materials' segments in classes with middle or low levels of achievement in Irish (16% and 17%).

The use of different kinds of materials generally, of course, cannot be divorced from other aspects of the lesson and indeed it is revealing to examine the pattern of connections between 'No materials', *Topic* and *Language activity*. In brief, what such an examination reveals is that 'No materials' segments are strongly associated with communicative type *Language activity* and *Topic* categories. Crosstabulations show that 'No materials' is the *Materials* category most strongly associated with 'Simulated communication in Irish' (60% of the segments in that *Language activity* category) and to a lesser extent with 'Real communication in Irish' (34% of segments). Likewise, there is a substantial overlap between 'No materials' segments and the two *Topic* categories which are most strongly associated with 'Simulated communication in Irish'- 'Pupil teacher real life' (78% of segments in that *Topic* category involve no materials) and 'Situation: *Other than Nuachúrsaí*' (23% of segments). Given these connections - and the fact that communicative type *Language activity* and *Topic* categories tend to be associated with positive results - it is not surprising that 'No materials' segments would also be associated with positive results.

In the case of those segments which involve both 'No materials' and the *Topic* category 'Situation: *Other than Nuachúrsaí*', the implication is that the 'situation' is nominated by the teacher rather than being derived from textbooks or readers. In other words, in implementing oral/aural communicative activities in the classroom - particularly 'Simulated communication in Irish' - very often the teacher's starting point is not textbooks or other materials. Instead, communicative activities will tend to centre around topics, ideas and characters which are connected with the pupils' or the teacher's own life, or the teacher himself/herself will introduce stories, descriptions, situations and games. Whether the teacher's reason for making no use of existing materials on such occasions is that they are not considered suitable - i.e. that they are not communicative - is something that cannot be determined from our results. Neither do we know if the fact of making no use of materials in the case of communicative activities involves any difficulty or strain for teachers or if, instead, it is by preference that they dispense with materials in such circumstances. Indeed, we cannot discount the possibility that it may be precisely because such 'No materials' communicative activities involve the teacher in direct, unencumbered interaction with the class that they are associated with high levels of class attention and interest.

It might appear to follow from all this that the enterprise of making Irish teaching more communicative need not concern itself at all with the provision of specifically communicative materials. It must be borne in mind, however, that the classes which are most communicative at present, and which most often make no use of materials in the course of such communicative teaching, are also those with the highest levels of achievement in Irish. The point here is that teachers in higher ability classes may have more latitude in initiating communicative activities without the help of specifically crafted materials because high-ability pupils are able to tolerate a greater range of linguistic demands in relatively unstructured situations. Will it be as easy for teachers of low-Irish-ability classes, however, to switch to a more communicative approach? Is it not likely that in weaker classes, the teacher may be able to adopt an experiential/communicative approach only if the linguistic/communicative demands of particular tasks have been carefully tailored to the pupils' proficiency in the language? Arguably, this is a critical issue in the case of a *second-language* programme such as the Irish one. Unlike the situation in a *foreign-language* programme, the observational and transcript data would suggest that teachers of Irish at primary level do not consider it appropriate to use the pupils' home language, English, to lead-in to, or set up, a situation, game or task - something that would be considered quite acceptable in most foreign-language programmes. Thus, the provision of finely-tuned communicative materials in Irish may be an essential requirement if teachers of weaker classes are to switch to a more communicative approach and at the same time maintain the tradition of teaching Irish largely through Irish.

We turn now to 'Other course-book/workbook' (17.5% of segments). The results relating to this category are in every respect opposite to those for the 'No materials' category. Segments in which 'Other course-books/workbooks' are used have significantly lower class attention and interest ratings than other segments. Use of 'Other course-books/workbooks' is virtually non-existent in classes with high levels of achievement in Irish but is relatively common in middle- and low-Irish-achievement classes: 29% of segments on average in these latter classes and over 50% in a number of cases. Correlation data confirm that classes in which a greater proportion of segments involve the use of 'Other course-books/workbooks' have significantly lower levels of achievement in Irish and lower levels of interest than other classes.

In terms of *Language activity* connections, 'Other course-book/workbook' is associated with a range of categories but hardly at all with 'Simulated communication in Irish' (only 1.3% of segments in that *Language activity* category). While 'Other course-books/workbooks' are associated with some 'Real communication in Irish' segments, the communication in such cases does not centre on, or originate in, any material in the books themselves. Rather, the communication concerns 'Routine management/organisation' topics in which these books happen to figure in quite an incidental way e.g. the teacher may engage in real communication with the class concerning the homework to be assigned from a particular book.

Apart from the materials categories already discussed, only one other material is associated with any significant outcomes - 'Filmstrips'. Filmstrips, which provide a visual representation of the basic narrative (*bunchomhrá*) for each audiovisual *Nuachúrsaí* lesson, are used in 9.1% of lesson segments. Consistent with this, 10% of segments involve the teacher using the corresponding *Nuachúrsaí* Teacher's Handbook. Overall

'Film strips' segments receive significantly lower *Class attention* and *Class interest* ratings than other segments - something which will not come as much of a surprise given the negative comments of many pupils themselves, as reported in Chapter 4 (see section 4.4.2), in relation to the *Nuachúrsaí* generally or the use of filmstrips/projector. The proportion of segments devoted to the use of filmstrips in different classes, however, is not reliably related to any of the class measures of achievement in Irish, class attention or class interest.

It is interesting to note that, for some teachers, the use of audiovisual materials and an emphasis on communication coexist happily in the same lesson - and with impressive results. In the class ranked highest in terms of achievement in Irish, for example, 20% of the lesson segments involve the use of filmstrips, while over 40% involve 'No materials' and communicative activities: (42% of segments use 'No materials' and 45% of segments are devoted to 'Real' or 'Simulated' communication in Irish). In this regard, it may be recalled (Chapter 4) that neither dislike of the *Nuachúrsaí* nor dislike of existing lessons/materials on the basis of being boring, old-fashioned or repetitive were common themes in the spontaneous comments of pupils in high Irish-achievement classes.

Finally, authentic materials, which are normally associated with a communicative approach to language teaching, make almost no appearance in the Irish lesson at present. In the *Communicative Materials Project*, however, lesson units which made use of authentic materials (or modified 'authentic' materials) were very well received by both teachers and pupils. Among the materials of this kind that we used with good results in the *Communicative Materials Project* were ones involving Irish placenames, Irish summer colleges in Gaeltacht areas, television programme schedules and county names in Irish on vehicle registration plates. The need to modify authentic materials arises primarily from the fact that Irish is not widely enough used in the life of pupils outside Gaeltacht areas to generate a significant large range of authentic materials suited to their age and interests.

7.3.5 *Implications*

This concluding section of the chapter deals with three general issues which arise from the findings. First, why does the present study of a basically audio-visual course produce more positive findings regarding 'communication' than studies of explicitly communicative programmes often do? Second, will the provision of new communicative teaching materials be a particular help to teachers of weaker classes who wish to teach Irish more communicatively? And third, is it possible that the introduction of communicative materials will pose problems for the 'all-Irish' character of language teaching at primary level? We will now deal with each of these issues in turn.

A paradox: 'More communicative is better' in an audio-visual course.
The results of this study present us with an apparent paradox when viewed in the light of the results of a number of other studies of communicative language teaching. This consists of the fact that while the Irish second-language programme, which has its origins in the audio-visual structural tradition, would *not* be seen generally as 'communicative' in the

conventional sense (in terms of conceptualisation of the teaching process, materials etc.), our results are actually extremely favourable concerning the communicative elements in the present programme. The data show that the stronger the communicative component in Irish classes at present, the more favourable the 'outcome' is in terms of *Class achievement in spoken Irish, Class attitude to Irish, Class attention* to the lesson and so on. In contrast, in studies of language programmes where a communicative approach has *already* been installed, the performance of the more experiential or more communicative classes appear to be mixed, equivocal or actually negative (Spada and Lightbown, 1989; Allen *et al.*, 1990; Lightbown and Spada, 1990; Ullmann, 1990; Beretta, 1992).

The fact of the matter, of course, is that if the critical issue in successful learning really is the *balance* between communicative activities, as Allen *et al.* (1990) have suggested, then such apparently contradictory results are to be expected. As we pointed out earlier, our correlation findings only hold for those teaching situations in which the amount of emphasis on communication is similar to the Irish one. Thus, while we know that devoting a greater proportion of class time to communicative language activities is strongly associated with a range of positive outcomes, this result only holds with certainty in the present Irish situation where as little as 21% of lesson time (22% of lesson segments), on average, is spent on communicative activities. If this proportion were to increase twofold or more - as it might in a communicative programme - there is no certainty that the most communicative of these classes would continue to have the highest level of proficiency in Irish, the most attentive and interested pupils or the best attitude to Irish. Thus, the general Allen *et al.* 'balance' hypothesis is not undermined by the findings of the present study.

This constitutes an important reminder also that our results cannot be interpreted as evidence that language practice such as 'Contextualisation exercises', 'Transposition' and 'Drills' are either ineffective or unnecessary in the long term in developing communicative proficiency in Irish. Our results show only that classes which spend *more* time (in one interpretation *too* much time) on these language-practice activities at present, tend to have lower levels of Irish achievement, lower levels of attention and interest, poor attitudes to Irish and higher *Irish-lesson anxiety* than others. Language-practice activities have been retained by teachers over the years presumably because they have been found to be effective and we should be slow to discount their role (Van Lier, 1988).

A final question in this context is whether there is an optimum balance between *communicative/experiential* and *language-practice/analytic* activities which should be aimed for in the Irish lesson in the future. At present, the proportion of communicative activities in the Irish lesson is lower than that found in communicatively-orientated second-language classrooms. Two studies mention 40% or more as the proportion of communicative activities. Mitchell and Johnstone (1986: 126), for example, in a case study of a language classroom implementing the communicative approach reported that over the course of thirty lessons almost 40% of all activities 'were judged to have some substantive purpose for participants, real or simulated, other than the rehearsal of formal aspects of French'. A more recent study by Low, Duffield, Brown and Johnstone (1993:

69) on the teaching of foreign languages in primary school also report that '68% of teachers used 'real foreign language' more than 40% of the time during the observed lessons'. Given these data relating to *foreign*-language programmes, and the evidence from the present study on the proportion of time spent on communicative activities in the existing Irish *second*-language programme, perhaps a reasonable goal for the Irish lesson in future might be about 50% of time devoted to communicative activities.

Importance of communicative materials for weaker classes:
Why do not Irish teachers, particularly those with classes which are weaker at Irish, spend a greater proportion of lesson time on communicative activities - given the favourable outcomes as we have documented here? Although we have no direct information in this study about the teachers' views on the advantages or disadvantages of different language activities, there are one or two indications from teachers involved in the *Communicative Materials Project* which may be relevant. When teachers of weaker classes expressed reservations about emphasising communication and communicative activities, two sorts of reasons were cited: (a) that because the standard of their pupils' Irish was already unsatisfactory, they felt uneasy about taking time away from what might be considered more serious language-learning activities in order to spend it on communicative games and tasks and (b) that their weaker pupils would not, in any case, be capable of communicating in Irish even if the teacher were to attempt this approach.

The teachers' actual experience with the prepared materials supplied in the course of the project, however, did modify their initial assessments. A number of them later said that they felt that all of their pupils, even those normally fairly indifferent about Irish, were successfully learning with the new approach. In addition, they felt that the new communicative materials and activities very much represented the kind of approach that they had often privately wanted to implement, were it not for their feeling that it might appear a distraction from the 'true' task of learning and teaching Irish. In that sense the project, and particularly the provision of materials, served to legitimise a general approach that the teachers themselves already wished to implement.

The other aspect to the issue, the perception that initiating communication in Irish was forbidding and too ambitious for pupils, seems to arise in part from an interpretation of 'communication' as an open-ended, relatively unstructured discussion or debate. This interpretation of communication is not surprising, perhaps, in a situation where the lesson materials currently in use in classrooms are, by and large, not communicative in the sense that that term is now understood. Clearly, such unstructured debate or discussion might indeed have the effect of discouraging and excluding weaker children. The teachers felt that the materials supplied in the *Communicative Materials Project* managed to redefine the idea of communication or communicative activities for them in ways that were manageable and practical. The communicative games and tasks gave pupils with lower levels of ability in Irish a rare chance to publicly demonstrate their competence in the language.

An important advantage in moving to a more communicative course must be the likelihood, demonstrated in the current study, of improving class attention and interest. The experience of teachers in the *Communicative Materials Project* appeared to be that the communicative activities had the effect of storing up a certain credit with pupils, credit which could be called on later when the less congenial but necessary language practice was being conducted. Pupils seemed to be more willing to undertake the labour of learning new words and phrases prior to a communicative game or task, when they knew from previous lessons that this work was a prelude to a game or task which they were likely to find more interesting. More generally, the whole atmosphere in the Irish class seemed to improve.

This latter point is supported by our own subjective impressions as we listened again and again to the audiotapes of the lessons in the *Twenty Classes Study*. It seemed to us that in those classes which are weaker at Irish both teacher and pupil have to work very hard at the Irish lesson. The considerably greater emphasis on language practice in such classes seems to have resulted in the lesson as a whole being less relaxed, more predictable and requiring more effort than it did in other classes. In classes with higher levels of achievement in Irish, both teachers and pupils seemed to enjoy the activities more and pupils showed more initiative. This admittedly subjective impression does nevertheless fit the *Class Irish-lesson anxiety* and *Class interest* data collected by the observers in the classrooms, and is also consistent with the pupils' spontaneous comments reported in Chapter 4. It is impossible to say, of course, how much of this difference in class atmosphere can be attributed to the greater feeling of mastery and success which pupils with higher levels of achievement experience anyway, and how much is due to the greater proportion of communicative activities which are undertaken in more able classes. Our strong impression, however, was that it was the presence of communicative activities which constituted the critical element which enlivened the lessons.

Communicative materials: Benefit or threat?

As we have pointed out elsewhere (Harris, 1991), second-language programmes such as the Irish one often have a number of desirable characteristics which are not shared by foreign-language programmes generally. For example, in long-established second-language programmes, a large majority of parents tend to have at least a minimal level of competence in the language, sufficient to be helpful, for example, in supervising homework in the target language. Another characteristic of second-language programmes, and the one of most interest in the present context, is the high proportion of the target language which tends to be used in the classroom - something which is confirmed in the case of Irish by the *Language activity* data reported in the present chapter and the pupil language-use data presented in Chapter 9. An important question to be considered, then, is whether a change to a more communicative approach to teaching Irish, and particularly the provision of new communicative materials containing a diversity of tasks, games and other activities, is likely to pose any threat to the more or less 'all-Irish' character of the Irish lesson.

In weighing this possibility, it has to be acknowledged first of all that the high level of use of Irish at present may be quite dependent on the lesson being relatively predictable and routinised. This predictability both facilitates and circumscribes the kind of real communication in Irish which occurs. The predictability can be considered a positive feature of the lesson in that it reduces any pressure there might be on teachers to revert to the pupils' home language in the context of explaining new tasks or activities. Evidence that it limits communication is provided, for example, by the finding from the present study that there is little real meaning negotiation of an interactive kind in handling 'Routine management organisation' topics.

Two factors contribute to a relatively high level of routinisation and predictability in the sixth-grade Irish lesson. First, the present general approach to teaching Irish has evolved slowly over quite a long period starting from an initial orthodox and highly specified audio-visual approach. Second, pupils by the time they enter sixth grade will have been learning Irish for seven years in primary school and will be quite familiar with the range and likely sequence of language activities within the Irish class. Contrast this situation with, for example, the situation of pupils in the Stirling study who would in most cases only be starting to learn French - and indeed any language other than their native language - for the first time in First Year of post-primary school.

By definition, introducing an explicitly communicative approach to teaching Irish at primary level, with all the accompanying new tasks and different lesson structure that it will entail, will undoubtedly destabilise this existing routine in the Irish lesson. While this will obviously open up the possibility of more realistic communication, potentially it could also create more pressure to revert to English for certain kinds of explanation which were not previously necessary and thus threaten the 'all-Irish' character of the Irish lesson. A study of a communicative approach to language teaching in Scotland (Mitchell, 1988: 164) confirmed that use of the target language for all aspects of classroom management was 'the preserve of the most committed teachers only'. The teachers generally felt that while French was appropriate for simple organisational instructions (to do with seating, giving out materials etc.), it was less suitable for instructions specifically related to an activity or for explaining grammar.

It is important, therefore, that course developers would produce communicative materials which will help teachers to maintain the present 'all-Irish' character of the Irish lesson. In particular, it will require the investment of great care and creative effort to develop activities/games and tasks that will not require linguistically demanding explanations or introductions in English. The goal should be to produce materials which promote meaning negotiation, which are challenging and engaging for pupils, but which at the same time involve manageable linguistic demands. In doing this it may not always be possible to use the same range of communicative games and tasks as have been used in the early stages of post-primary modern-language courses, where the use of English to introduce certain tasks or to provide background information may be more acceptable.

8 Pupil and teacher roles and classroom organisation

8.1 Introduction

In this chapter we describe the Irish lesson in terms of the three remaining *ILAS* dimensions - *Pupil behaviour, Teacher mode of involvement* and *Classroom organisation*. As well as reporting the frequency with which the most common categories of each dimension occur (e.g. how many *Pupil behaviours* involve the pupil 'speaking', 'reading aloud' etc.) we will also investigate the categories of dimensions that are significantly linked to class attention and interest, achievement in Irish, and attitude to Irish.

As in the previous chapter, the two main reference points in discussing the results are (i) the 'communicative' versus 'language practice' orientation in language teaching and (ii) the Stirling Study of the audio-visual teaching of French at first year post-primary which uses the same set of dimensions as *ILAS* (Mitchell *et al.*, 1981). We will also consider the implications of the findings for the teaching and learning of Irish generally.

Finally, we explore two more general issues. First, we consider the nature of *Class attention* and *Class interest* and the possible reasons for the overall high levels of attention and interest which we found, and the qualitative difference between interest and attention which is indicated by the results. Second, we assess how well the *ILAS*, with its various innovations, has worked as an instrument for recording and analysing the teaching and learning of Irish. The importance of a collaborative approach to observing the Irish lesson involving researchers and teachers, and sometimes learners, is also discussed.

8.2 Results

The analysis of the data relating to *Pupil behaviour, Teacher mode of involvement* and *Classroom organisation* has the same three-part structure as the analysis of the other three dimensions described in Chapter 7.

(i) A description of the 39 lessons in terms of the proportion of teaching time, the proportion of lesson segments and the mean segment duration associated with each category of the relevant dimension. Except for comparative purposes with the Stirling study, the main focus of our analysis is the proportion of teaching time rather than the number of segments.

(ii) Data which indicate the extent to which *Class attention* and *Class interest* wax and wane as *Pupil behaviours, Teacher modes of involvement* and *Classroom organisation* change during the course of the lesson.

(iii) Data and statistical tests which indicate if there is any tendency for the proportion of teaching time spent on different categories of *Pupil behaviours, Teacher modes of involvement* and *Classroom organisation* to vary across classes and the relationship, if any, between these variations and achievement in Irish, attitude to Irish and level of class attention/interest.

A more detailed description of these three forms of analysis may be found in section 7.2 of Chapter 7.

8.2.1 Pupil behaviour

Before looking at the data on *Pupil behaviour*, it should be recalled that in the *ILAS* a given behaviour was coded as having occurred as long as it was central to the language activity in a particular lesson segment. This does not mean either that this was the only pupil behaviour which took place, or that the behaviour was sustained for the entire duration of the segment. For example, a teacher may ask pupils, in a repeating sequence, to silently read a question and then to answer that question aloud. In this case, it is clear that neither speaking nor silent reading continue for the duration of the segment. The teaching time data which we present refers, therefore, to the duration of the segments in which the behaviours occurred, not the duration of particular behaviours themselves.

Table 8.1 provides data on the extent to which various pupil behaviours were exhibited. Looking at the percentages of segments in column 1, it can be seen that pupils are listening (or were expected to be listening) as part of the activity in the case of 94.4% of all segments, and that they are speaking (or ready to speak) in the case of over two thirds of segments (67.4%). These proportions match closely those of the Stirling Study where pupils were reported as being in a 'listening' mode of involvement in 89.2% of segments and 'speaking' in 68.4% of segments. It should be pointed out here that since a substantial proportion of segments in the Stirling Study involved the use of the mother tongue, it follows that a corresponding proportion of the 'speaking' behaviours involved English rather than the target language (French).

Reading occupies a lesser but still central role in the Irish class with 'Reading silently' being involved in more segments (27.7%) than 'Reading aloud' (18.2%). If we combine both these reading categories, the overall proportion of 'reading' behaviours in the Irish study (45.9%) matches closely that reported in the Stirling Study where 47.5% of segments involved the single category 'reading'. While *Pupil Behaviour* categories in the Irish study are not mutually exclusive, these two types of reading behaviour rarely occur together in the same segment (only 1.4% of segments). Thus, adding the proportions associated with each of the two categories for the purposes of comparison with the Stirling results is not problematical.

Crosstabulations, not shown here, indicate that just under 60% of all 'Reading aloud' segments involve 'Transposition' type language activities- either individual pupils, or the whole class, read aloud extracts from their Irish reader(s) (see also Chapter 7, section 7.2.3). The remaining 'Reading aloud' segments are most commonly associated with 'Contextualisation exercises' (16%), 'Drills' (9.3%) and 'Imitation' (7.9%).

Table 8.1
Pupil behaviour: **Percentage distribution of teaching time and lesson segments and average segment duration, by *Pupil behaviour****

Pupil behaviour		Percentage of segments*	Proportion of teaching time (hrs mins secs)	Mean segment duration (mins secs)
	Total:	(n = 828)	(42 : 3 : 40)	(3:03)
Listening		94.4	88.5	2:51
Speaking		67.4	70.5	3:11
Reading silently		27.7	34.5	3:48
Looking		19.0	25.9	4:09
Reading aloud		18.2	18.4	3:04
Writing		6.8	13.2	5:57
Doing		5.1	2.3	1:24

* More than one type of behaviour can occur in any segment

'Writing', a productive pupil behaviour, occurs in only 6.8% of segments, a figure which is considerably lower than that reported in the Stirling Study (20.8%). 'Writing' segments in the Irish Study, however, are significantly longer (5 minutes 57 seconds) than segments associated with any of the other six behaviours (column 3). Comparing teaching time data with the number of segments in row 7 of Table 8.1, also it can be seen that the proportion of all *teaching time* for those segments in which 'Writing' behaviour occurs (13.2%) is almost double the proportion of all *segments* involving writing (6.8%).

Pupil behaviour which involves 'Looking' features to a smaller but still significant extent in both studies (19% of segments in the Irish Study and 28.8% in the Stirling French Study). In this context it is worth recalling the results from the previous chapter (Table 7.16) which show that purely visual stimuli (film strips/cutouts) are used in about one-tenth of all segments while objects are used to a lesser extent (3.4% of segments). Segment durations associated with 'Looking' behaviours (4 minutes 9 seconds) are longer than those associated with all other behaviours except for 'Writing'. Finally, segments in which pupils are 'Doing' something (performing a physical action other then speaking) account for the least proportion of segments (5.1% of all segments) and have the shortest durations of all (1 minute 24 seconds).

Class attention and *Class interest* ratings for segments in which each of seven pupil behaviours occur are set out in Tables 8.2. Only in the case of two pupil behaviours 'Reading silently' and 'Reading aloud' are there significant differences. In conducting these significance tests, we were obliged to compare mean ratings for each specific behaviour versus all other behaviours. We could not compare means for any two specific pupil behaviours directly because more than one behaviour could occur in any given segment. In those segments where pupils were 'Reading silently', the mean *Class attention* rating (4.2) and the mean *Class interest* rating (4.0) are significantly lower than the remaining segments in each case (ANOVA: F value = 5.32, $p < .05$ - *attention*; F value = 7.38, $p < .01$ - *interest*). Similarly, in those segments where 'Reading aloud' occurred, overall *Class attention* ratings (4.1) and *Class interest* ratings (3.8) are also significantly lower than the corresponding mean ratings for the remainder of segments (ANOVA: F value = 17.3, $p < .01$ - *attention*; F value = 29.0 $p < .01$ - *interest*).

Table 8.2
Mean *Class attention* and *Class interest* ratings for *Pupil behaviour* categories

*Pupil behaviour**	*n (segments)*	*Class attention* Mean ratings (1 - 5) (828)	*Class interest* Mean ratings (1 - 5) (828)
Listening	(782)	4.3	4.1
Speaking	(558)	4.3	4.1
Reading silently **	(229)	4.2	4.0
Looking	(157)	4.4	4.1
Reading aloud **	(151)	4.1	3.8
Writing	(56)	4.4	4.1
Doing	(42)	4.4	4.2

*Segments in which a particular behaviour occurs are compared with all remaining segments.
** Significantly different from other segments in terms of attention/interest - see text for details.

We also analysed the data in terms of the more frequent behavioural combinations (i.e. those accounting for more than 3% of all segments). This shows once again (data not in tabular form) the heavy emphasis on oral production. Of the nine main behavioural combinations identified, only three of the smaller categories, 'Listening alone' (5% of segments), 'Reading silently and Writing' and 'Listening and Doing' (3% of segments respectively) do *not* involve an oral element. The evidence of the class transcripts (Appendix 6.4), as well as the study of individual pupil communicative behaviour described in the next chapter, confirms this.

Consistent with data above relating to 'Reading aloud', the behavioural combination 'Listening and Reading aloud' is most commonly associated with 'Transposition' language activities.   Another behavioural combination - 'Listening, Speaking and Looking' - is commonly associated with segments featuring *Nuachùrsai* topics. It should also be noted that segments involving only 'Listening and Reading aloud' behaviours have significantly lower *Class interest* mean ratings (3.8) than segments involving only 'Listening and Speaking' (4.3) or 'Listening' alone (4.8).

Table 8.3
Pearson correlations between proportion of Irish class time spent on categories of the *ILAS* dimensions *Pupil behaviour* and *Classroom organisation* and five class measures of proficiency in Irish, attitude/motivation, and pupil engagement.

	---------------------- CLASS MEASURES --------------------				
ILAS dimensions: *Proportion of time spent on:*	*Class achievement in spoken Irish*	*Class attitude to Irish*	*Class Irish-lesson anxiety*	*Class attention (mean rating)*	*Class interest (mean rating)*
Pupil behaviour					
'Reading aloud'	-.68**	-.68**	.48*	-.58**	-.61**
Classroom organisation					
'Whole class'	-.16	-.05	.53*	-.29	-.37
'Pupil/group demonstration'	.28	.01	-.70**	.23	.34

Only those categories of dimensions which are significantly correlated with at least one of the five class measures in columns 2 to 6 are included in this table.
* p < .05. ** p < .01.

Turning now to the variations from class to class in the emphasis on pupil behaviour, we found that only one behaviour, 'Reading aloud', was significantly related to *Class achievement in spoken Irish* or, indeed, to any of the other four class measures. The data in the first row of Table 8.3 indicate that classes which spend more time on lesson segments involving pupils 'Reading aloud' tend to have lower achievement in spoken Irish (r=-.68), more negative attitudes to Irish and to learning Irish (r=-.68), more anxiety in relation to the Irish lesson (r=.48), and to show lower overall levels of attention (r=-.58) and interest (r=-.61) during the Irish lesson. Data not presented here in tabular form and statistical tests also indicate that devoting more time to reading aloud is not related to *Pupil general academic ability* as measured by English verbal reasoning *(DVRT)* scores.

Table 8.4

Percentage of teaching time spent on two categories of *Pupil behaviour* ('Reading aloud' and 'Reading silently') in each of 20 classes (listed in order of achievement in spoken Irish)

Class achievement in spoken Irish Rank (1=highest)	-------------- *Pupil behaviour* ----------	
	'Reading aloud'	'Reading silently'*
1	3	31
2	24	20
3	6	55
4	7	39
5	12	23
6	16	19
High-Irish-achievement classes	*11*	*31*
7	11	42
8	22	64
9	9	19
10	12	31
11	12	37
12	28	32
Middle-Irish-achievement classes	*16*	*38*
13	23	35
14	8	23
15	29	1
16	32	24
17	24	30
18	40	44
19	28	56
20	43	20
Low-Irish-achievement classes	*28*	*29*
Proportion of all teaching time	*18*	*34*
Class range (max-min)	*(40)*	*(63)*

* Although 'Reading silently' was not significantly related to any class measures, the pooled-segment analysis indicated significantly lower levels of *Class attention* and *interest* associated with 'Reading silently'.

Exactly how much time, in each class, is spent on segments during which pupils read aloud in Irish can be seen in Table 8.4. We also include 'Reading silently' in this table as it was found to be related to *Class attention* and *Class interest* at the level of individual segments (Table 8.2). The pattern of 'Reading aloud' behaviours follow the expected trend with high-Irish-achievement classes spending less time on 'Reading aloud' (11%) than either the middle- (16%) or low-Irish-achievement classes (28%). Note that in Class Rank 20, the very lowest achieving class, as much as 43% of teaching time is devoted to 'Reading aloud' behaviours. Data in column 2 of Table 8.4 show no such Irish-achievement related pattern for 'Reading silently' behaviours. Note the considerable variation across classes in the proportion of teaching time associated with those segments where 'Reading silently' occurs: a range of 63 over the 20 classes.

8.2.2 *Teacher mode of involvement*

Table 8.5 summarises data on the types of *Teacher mode of involvement* in the Irish lesson. No detailed data on teacher involvement were reported in the Stirling Study, though it is stated that teachers in the French lessons in question were 'in contact, actual or potential, with the class as a whole' in 96% of the lesson segments (Mitchell *et al.*, 1981: 31). Our own data in column 1 of Table 8.5 show that during the Irish lesson teachers are actively involved with the class - 'Interacting', 'Monitoring' or 'Instructing' - in almost 98.8% of the segments. 'Interacting', which implies that an overt pupil spoken response is involved, is the dominant mode of teacher involvement accounting for over 62.4% of all segments. This is consistent with the high proportion of 'Speaking' behaviours noted earlier (see additional evidence in the next chapter). Over a quarter (26.3%) of all segments involve the teacher 'Monitoring'. 'Instructing' (no overt pupil response expected) is less common, occurring in only 10% of segments.

Comparing columns 1 and 2, it will be noted that the proportion of segments closely matches the proportion of teaching time in the case of the two dominant modes of teacher involvement, 'Interacting' and 'Monitoring'. In the case of 'Instructing', however, the proportion of teaching time (4.8%) is less than half the proportion of segments (10%). Consistent with this, the mean duration of 'Instructing' segments (1minute 27seconds) is significantly shorter than the mean of the remaining segments (Scheffe test: $p < .01$). The relatively small proportion of 'Instructing' segments (by definition meaning that there is no overt pupil response) which we observed, and their brevity, is consistent with *Pupil behaviour* data above showing that an overt spoken response is the norm in the Irish lesson.

Mean attention and interest ratings associated with different teacher modes of involvement indicate that segments where the teacher is 'Not involved' in the current language activity have marginally lower mean *Class attention* and *Class interest* ratings than all other categories of teacher involvement - though the difference is not significant. None of the *Teacher mode of involvement* categories are significantly correlated with the five class measures in Table 8.3 and thus the relevant correlations are not included. For this reason also we do not present a table showing time spent on various *Teacher modes of involvement* in each of the twenty classes.

Table 8.5
Teacher mode of involvement: **Percentage distribution of teaching time and lesson segments and average segment duration by** *Teacher mode of involvement.*

Teacher mode of involvement		Percentage of segments	Proportion of teaching time (hrs mins secs)	Mean segment duration (mins secs)
	Total:	(n = 828)	(42:3:40)	(3:03)
Interacting		62.4	66.6	3:15
Monitoring		26.3	26.4	3:03
Instructing		10.0	4.8	1:27
Not involved		1.2	2.3	5:50
Total		100%	100%	-

It may be worth noting that a greater emphasis on 'Interacting', is a feature of classes with higher levels of *Pupil general academic ability* (r=.47), while 'Monitoring' is associated with classes with lower levels of *Pupil general academic ability* (r= -.54).

8.2.3 Classroom organisation

Table 8.6 provides data relating to the proportion of lesson segments and the proportion of teaching time associated with five different types of *Classroom organisation*. Only three forms of organisation - 'Whole class', 'Individual: same task', and 'Pupil/group demonstration' - involve a substantial proportion of either lesson segments or of teaching time. Most segments (column one) involve whole-class teaching (85.6%). Pupils working independently, but on identical tasks (e.g. a writing task based on the same exercise in a course-book), accounts for 6.2% of segments.

The Stirling results relating to French foreign-language teaching correspond fairly closely to these findings - 88.7% of segments were coded as 'Whole class' and 8.4% as 'Individual: same task'. However, there was a slightly greater emphasis on 'Pupil/group demonstration' in the present Irish Study (7.5%) than in the Stirling Study (2%). Pupils working in pairs or in small groups on the same task - 'Co-operation: same task' - a form of classroom organisation which is associated with communicative language teaching - was a very rare occurrence in the Irish lesson (0.5% of all segments) as were instances of pupils working alone on different tasks (0.2% of segments). No instances at all of groups of pupils working together, each group on a different task, were recorded.

Table 8.6
Classroom organisation*: Percentage distribution of teaching time and lesson segments, and average segment duration by *Classroom organisation

Classroom organisation	Total:	*Percentage of segments* (n = 828)	*Proportion of teaching time (hrs mins secs)* (42 : 3 : 40)	*Mean segment duration (mins secs)* (3:03)
Whole class		85.6	80.9	2:53
Pupil/group demonstration		7.5	6.3	2:34
Individual: same task		6.2	11.7	5:46
Co-operation: same task		0.5	0.8	5:10
Individual: different task		0.2	0.3	4:03
Total		100%	100%	-

Looking now at teaching time, a notable point is that in the case of 'Individual: same task', the proportion of teaching time (11.7%) exceeds the proportion of segments (6.2%), reflecting the fact (column 3) that segments associated with this type of classroom organisation tend to be rather long (mean segment duration of 5 minutes 46 seconds). Individual comparisons show that the mean segment duration for 'Individual: same task' is significantly longer than for 'Pupil/group demonstration' and ' Whole class' (Scheffe test: $p < .01$). Crosstabulations (not shown here in tabular form) reveal that segments classified as 'Individual: same task' in the Irish study typically involve written tasks. More generally, regarding mean segment duration and *Classroom organisation*, note that since 'Pupil/group demonstration' involves the whole class (mostly as an audience for the demonstration perhaps) mean durations for the first two 'whole class' type segments listed in Table 8.6 are shorter than for the remaining 'group' and 'individual' task segments.

In Table 8.7 we look at the variation in *Class attention* and *Class interest* ratings across *Classroom organisation* categories. The only significant differences are found between 'Pupil/group demonstration' and the two other major classroom-organisation categories of 'Whole class' and 'Individual: same task'. Individual comparisons show that the *Class attention* mean ratings for segments associated with the two latter categories (4.3 in each case) are significantly lower than the *Class attention* mean rating for the 'Pupil/group demonstration' category (4.7) (Scheffe test: $p < .01$ and $p < .05$ respectively). Similarly, the *Class interest* mean ratings for 'Whole class' and

'Individual: same task' (4.1 in each case) are also significantly lower than for corresponding ratings in 'Pupil/group demonstration' segments (4.7) (Scheffe test: p < .01).

Table 8.7
Mean *Class attention* and *Class interest* ratings in the most frequent
(at least 5% of segments) *Classroom organisation* categories

Classroom organisation	*n (segments)*	*Class attention* Mean rating *(1 - 5)* (828)	*Class interest* Mean rating *(1 - 5)* (828)
Whole class	(709)	4.3	4.1
Pupil/group demonstration	(62)	4.7	4.7
Individual : same task	(51)	4.3	4.1
Overall mean	(828)	4.3	4.1

* ANOVA F = 6.46, p < .01 (*Class attention*); F = 11.18, p < .01 (*Class interest*). (See text for details of Scheffe tests).

Looking back now at Table 8.3 it can be seen that none of the *Classroom organisation* categories are significantly correlated with *Class achievement in spoken Irish*. The absence of any consistent pattern of association between the most common forms of classroom organisations and achievement in Irish can also be seen in the class by class data presented in Table 8.8. Table 8.8 does show, however, the consistently strong emphasis on whole class teaching. Only in the case of one class (class rank 4) was a minority of class time (34%) devoted to 'Whole class' teaching (44% is spent on 'Pupil/group demonstration' in that class).

Two categories of *Classroom organisation*, however, have significant correlations (one negative and one positive) with *Class Irish-lesson anxiety*. Classes in which more time was spent on 'Pupil/group demonstration' have overall significantly lower levels of anxiety in relation to the Irish lesson than other classes (r=-.70) while more time spent on 'Whole class' forms of organisation was associated with significantly higher levels of *Irish-lesson anxiety* (r=.53) (see Table 8.3).   Finally, an emphasis on 'Pupil/group demonstration' is associated with a slight but not significant tendency for *Class achievement in spoken Irish* to be higher (r = .28), and with a significantly lower level of *Pupil general academic ability* (r =-.46) (data not shown in tabular form).

Table 8.8.
Percentage of teaching time spent on three categories of *Classroom organisation*
('Whole class', 'Individual: same task' and 'Pupil/group demonstration')
in each of 20 classes (listed in order of achievement in spoken Irish)

Class achievement in spoken Irish Rank (1 = highest)	---------------- *Classroom organisation* ------------		
	Whole class	*Individual: same task*	*Pupil demonstration*
1	97	3	0
2	82	14	4
3	71	11	18
4	34	17	44
5	91	9	0
6	99	0	1
High-Irish-achievement classes	*79*	*9*	*11*
7	80	20	0
8	93	7	0
9	81	19	0
10	66	21	4
11	56	26	9
12	85	8	7
Middle-Irish-achievement classes	*77*	*17*	*3*
13	82	18	0
14	91	6	3
15	86	0	14
16	89	11	0
17	75	22	3
18	91	9	0
19	84	12	4
20	90	9	0
Low-Irish-achievement classes	*86*	*11*	*3*
Proportion of all teaching time	*81*	*12*	*6*
Range (max-min)	*(65)*	*(26)*	*(44)*

8.3 Discussion

In the first part of the discussion we focus on results relating to each of three dimensions of *ILAS - Pupil behaviour, Teacher mode of involvement* and *Classroom organisation,* and we consider the implications for the teaching and learning of Irish. We then turn to two more general points. One of these concerns the attention and interest ratings: why are attention and interest rates so high generally, and why are interest ratings consistently lower than attention ratings and more sensitive to measures of pupil reaction to the lesson? The second general point concerns the success of the *ILAS* as an instrument for describing and analysing the teaching and learning of Irish. A collaborative approach to classroom observation by researchers, teachers and, in some contexts involving pupils, is recommended.

8.3.1 Pupil behaviour

Only two pupil behaviours - 'Reading aloud' and, to a considerably lesser extent, 'Reading silently' - are associated with significant effects in the present study. Consequently, we will begin with these two kinds of reading and proceed then to the other behaviours.

Reading is involved in 46% of the segments overall, roughly equivalent to the proportion found in the Stirling study. The Stirling study, however, did not distinguish between 'Reading aloud' (18.2% of segments in the present study) and 'Reading silently' (27.7% in the present study). As the results show, the distinction is important. 'Reading aloud' is associated with a number of significant effects. In the pooled-segment analysis, for example, 'Reading aloud' segments are associated with significantly lower mean *Class interest* and mean *Class attention* ratings than other segments. In the class-level analyses, classes which devote more time to 'Reading aloud' are significantly more likely to have lower achievement in spoken Irish, less positive class attitude to Irish, higher levels of anxiety in relation to the Irish lesson and reduced levels of attention to and interest in the Irish lesson.

Segments in which 'Reading silently' were involved were associated with just two significant outcomes: in the pooled-segment analysis, those segments in which pupils were 'Reading silently' have significantly lower mean *Class interest* and mean *Class attention* ratings than all other segments. It is interesting to note that in the Stirling Study, which combined these two kinds of reading, no significant connections were found between reading and achievement in French.

'Reading aloud' segments were found almost invariably to involve language practice and to be particularly strongly associated with 'Transposition' - language practice in which utterances are translated from one code to another. The 'Reading aloud' data contributes important information to our interpretation of 'Transposition', however, since it establishes that reading-to-speaking (i.e. reading aloud) rather than listening-to-writing (dictation) activities were involved in all but a minority (1 out of 10) of 'Transposition' segments (see Chapter 7: section 7.2.3). 'Reading aloud' is also involved in forms of language practice other than 'Transposition': over one-third of 'Reading aloud' segments involve 'Contextualisation exercises', Drills' or 'Imitation'. The connection between 'Reading aloud' and 'Transposition' is unique because in the case of 'Transposition' segments, reading aloud (combined with listening) is not just one component of a complex activity but constitutes the whole activity and lasts for the duration of the entire segment. Behaviours occurring in the context of other language activities may last for only portions of a segment.

It is no surprise, therefore, that the pattern of association between variables such as class achievement, class interest etc. and 'Reading aloud', should be virtually identical to the pattern of association between these same variables and 'Transposition' and, indeed, other types of language practice such as 'Contextualisation exercises'. 'Reading aloud', of course, need not necessarily involve 'Transposition' or indeed any other type of language practice, and thus the pattern of association between 'Reading aloud' and variables such as *Class achievement in spoken Irish* and *Class interest* need not always follow the 'negative' direction found here. 'Reading aloud' in a different language learning context might well be associated with *communicative* language activities, and indeed even in the present study a small proportion of the instances of 'Reading aloud' were communicative. An example of a communicative type 'Reading aloud' activity would be where a pupil reads to the class the results of a survey of preferences regarding television programmes which had been conducted within the class. In such cases, the relationship of 'Reading aloud' to variables such as *Class achievement in spoken Irish* and *Class interest* might well be different to here.

Teachers of low-Irish-achievement classes seem to particularly favour 'Reading aloud' language practice: 43% of all teaching time in the class with the very lowest achievement in Irish of all, and 28% of teaching time on average in low-Irish-achievement classes generally, are devoted to 'Reading aloud'. If 'Reading aloud' is associated with the negative outcomes documented here, does this mean it has no merit as an activity? In that case, why do teachers continue to make use of it? We have suggested previously that teachers may feel that the kind of routine 'Reading aloud' activities that we have been describing, though relatively mechanical, are rewarding for those pupils who have few other opportunities to display their competence in Irish. Such an assumption on the part of teachers would certainly be consistent with the data in Chapter 4 showing that pupils prefer reading in Irish to other activities involving Irish. But if this is the case, why do the ratings of the observers show a fall in *Class interest* during lesson segments where reading aloud is involved?

We would like to argue here that there may be no real conflict between the pupil stated preferences for reading and the perception of the observers regarding *Class interest*. Quite often in this study, 'Transposition' consisted of a series of individual pupils reading aloud one at a time while the rest of the pupils listened. It is quite reasonable that pupils, thinking of *themselves* reading aloud in such circumstances, would say they 'like reading' - since the activity would tend to provide them with the feeling of being competent in this aspect of Irish. In contrast, inspectors observing the same class as a whole during the very same activities - where only one pupil is reading aloud, perhaps haltingly, and the rest of the pupils are simply following the text silently - might observe a fall off in class interest generally. The probable success of reading aloud activities in motivating individual pupils, therefore, must be weighed against the evidence that there is a price to be paid in terms of class interest more generally.

But quite apart from the effect on individual pupil motivation and general class interest, there must also be doubt about the real contribution of mechanical reading aloud activities either to literacy or general proficiency in Irish in the case of pupils as old as those in sixth grade.

The weight of research evidence points to the need for reading to be contextualised, personalised and meaningful if it is to be of long term value in promoting literacy in second-language learners (Murtagh, 1989; Krashen, 1993). Among the conclusions of an international study of reading (Neville Postlethwaite and Ross, 1992) 'the more effective school is one where the teachers emphasize, above all, the understanding of what is read'. Significantly in terms of our results, Southgate, Arnold and Johnson (1981) found a negative correlation between progress in first language reading achievement of seven to nine year olds and the amount of time that teachers spent listening to them read aloud.

Second-language reading also, must in general, serve some communicative purpose beyond practice as such. A purely skill-building approach to reading, with little or no emphasis on the message, runs the risk that the activity will turn into a mere test and that it will generate little personal interest on the part of the pupil. This is not to say that the development of lower-order skills is not important, but that this should be seen in the context of the ultimate goal of reading - communicating messages.

At the very least, therefore, our results suggest that a law of diminishing returns may apply to the assignment of large proportions of time in low-Irish-achievement classes to language-practice type reading-aloud activities such as 'Transposition' and 'Contextualisation exercises'.

The results just outlined had a considerable influence on the approach to Irish reading adopted in the *Communicative Materials Project*. They showed the importance of providing reading tasks which engage the interest of the whole class by permitting pupils with relatively basic reading skills in Irish to engage in communicative, contextualised reading in Irish. In the report on the *Communicative Materials Project* (Harris *et al.*, 1996a,b) we emphasised the importance of providing a range of authentic reading texts, equivalent as far as practicable to the range which are available in English to pupils in the ordinary course of their lives. The report also emphasised the importance of integrating reading activities with other listening, speaking and writing activities in the same communicative tasks. We felt that in order to emphasise the communicative nature of Irish reading, the present practice of having a separate reader composed mainly of narratives should be abandoned in the new Irish programme and, instead, that the reading component of each teaching unit would be physically integrated with other communicative material relating to the listening, speaking and writing components in pupil's text book. In proposing this, we were at pains to point out that we were not underestimating the importance of stories in Irish for pupils, and indeed we recommended that a special series of non-course books in Irish, geared to the real interests of primary school pupils, should be developed. The aim of this latter series, we suggested, would be to allow pupils to read independently in Irish for pleasure and interest, both inside and outside school, rather than simply for language practice.

We turn now to results relating to the remaining categories of *Pupil behaviour*. The results show that pupils were considered to be 'Speaking' for about two thirds of the segments and 'Listening' for nearly 95% of the segments in the Irish lesson. Neither speaking nor listening behaviours in the Irish study are related to any of the other variables we studied such as *Class interest* or *Class achievement in spoken Irish*. While the proportions of 'Listening' and 'Speaking' behaviours in the present study are roughly equivalent to the Stirling study, the significance of the occurrence of speaking and listening behaviours is different in the case of the Irish study in that the pupils' native language, English, was rarely involved. In the Stirling study, also, it was found that more time spent on segments in which pupils were required to speak was associated with higher performance on the French test.

To understand the likely reason for this lack of association between the amount of emphasis on speaking/listening and the class variables, and indeed to appreciate the significance of the 'Speaking' and 'Listening' data generally, three points must be taken into account: (1) *Pupil behaviour* categories are so basic and general (e.g. 'Speaking') that data relating to them are difficult to interpret in isolation from data relating to other dimensions, particularly *Language activity*; (2) Instances of a particular behaviour, as defined here, can represent either the occurrence of that behaviour, or simply the readiness of pupils to exhibit the behaviour; and (3) a particular behaviour is coded as occurring as long as it is central to the activity involved - thus, it is not necessarily the only behaviour involved, nor is it necessarily sustained for the whole segment.

Regarding the first point, note that 'Speaking' could consist of a large variety of spoken utterances and contexts of use, including both communication and language practice. In view of these diverse origins, it is not surprising that the proportion of class time spent on segments involving 'Speaking' is not significantly related to variables such as *Class achievement in spoken Irish, Class attitude to Irish* and *Class interest*. This is particularly so given the other evidence here that an emphasis on language-practice has entirely contrasting patterns of association with class achievement in Irish, class interest etc. compared to an emphasis on communicative type activities. Thus, while on the face of it, the high proportion of 'Speaking' behaviours occurring may represent the Irish lesson in a positive light, the reality is that the true significance of this finding is difficult to assess. Fortunately, we were able to resolve some of these issues, and to demonstrate the importance of 'speaking', in a more focussed study of individual pupil behaviour reported in the next chapter.

None of the remaining *Pupil behaviours*, 'Writing', 'Looking' or 'Doing', show any significant association with variables such as *Class achievement in spoken Irish* or *Class interest*. Only 6.8% of segments involved writing compared to 20.8% of segments in the

Stirling Study. 'Writing' segments were almost twice as long as other segments. Typically, written assignments were given towards the end of the lesson, or before a break, and pupils were required to work individually with the support of the teacher. Writing assignments begun towards the end of the Irish lesson were often finished at home. Although one of our transcript extracts (Appendix 6.4: extract 11) shows how 'Simulated communication' was realised through the written mode, most segments involving writing were not communicative in character. Frequently, pupils were simply required to produce in written form essentially the same content which had been covered in earlier lesson segments (e.g. rehearsed answers to comprehension type questions) and thus the material was highly predictable.

8.3.2 *Classroom organisation and teacher mode of involvement*

Data from the *Classroom organisation* and *Teacher mode of involvement* dimensions illustrate the active, central role of the teacher in the Irish lesson, either 'Interacting' with pupils (62.4% of segments) or 'Instructing' (10% of segments), all of this within a predominantly 'Whole-class' context (85.6% of segments and 80.9% of teaching time). The 'Whole class' focus in the teaching of Irish is very similar to the situation in the teaching of French in the Stirling study. Small-group work (a form of classroom organisation often associated with communicative language teaching) is extremely rare in the Irish lesson (less than 1% of segments).

A questionnaire based survey of Irish sixth-grade teachers, covering all school subjects, also suggests that the 'whole-class' emphasis is common, though not as strong as in Irish (Burke and Fontes, 1986). In the Burke and Fontes study also, teachers reported that in a typical school day the amount of whole-class teaching time is just over 60% on average. The remainder of the time is spent on pupils working together in groups (18%) or individually (18%). It must be borne in mind, however, that subject by subject information was not requested in the Burke and Fontes (1986) study. The possibility must be considered, therefore, that some subjects (such as 'Arts and Crafts') may involve more group work than others (such as Irish).

One category of *Classroom organisation* 'Pupil/group demonstration' while not very common, occurs a little more frequently in the present Irish study (7.5% of segments) than in the Stirling Study (2% of segments). In this form of classroom organisation, which may be seen perhaps as intermediate between small-group and whole-class forms of organisation, a pupil or group of pupils leads or directs the lesson activity while the rest of the class functions as an 'audience' - perhaps answering or otherwise interacting with the demonstrating pupils. The teacher usually retains a monitoring role. It may appear that 'Pupil/group demonstration' should be categorised as a form of small-group activity. The fact that there is one central activity going on, albeit with 'demonstrating' and 'audience' groups having different roles, means that there is also a whole-class dimension to 'Pupil/group demonstration'.

Only just over half the classes devote any time, and usually very little time, to this form of organisation. One high-achievement class spends 44% of lesson time on it, however, and another spends 18%. Segments in which a 'Pupil/group demonstration' occurs have higher *Class attention* and *Class interest* mean ratings than either 'Whole class' or 'Individual: same task' forms of classroom organisation. There is also a significant tendency for classes which devote a greater proportion of teaching time to 'Pupil/group demonstration' forms of organisation to have lower levels of *Irish-lesson anxiety* and for classes which devote a greater proportion of time to 'Whole class' forms of organisation to have higher levels of *Irish-lesson anxiety*. This result is of interest because the measure of *Irish-lesson anxiety* used is based on the individual pupil's own report. Thus, we have evidence both from the pupils themselves and from the classroom observers, indicating a positive response to the 'Pupil/group demonstration' form of classroom organisation.

'Pupil/group demonstration' segments are associated with both communicative and language practice type activities e.g. 'Simulated communication in Irish', 'Drills' and 'Contextualisation exercises'. This seems to increase the possibility that it really is the form of classroom organisation involved, rather than *Language activity*, which is responsible for the favourable results relating to *Irish-lesson anxiety, Class attention* and *Class interest*. This also suggests that where language practice is necessary, 'Pupil/group demonstrations' may have a better chance of securing a positive response from pupils than more traditional 'Whole class' approaches. There are indications in the literature on second-language classroom research that situations in which pupils have more control of talk engender higher rates of interest and are associated with a wider variety of communicative acts and syntactic structures than situations which are predominantly teacher controlled (Cathcart, 1986; Dickinson, 1987; Holec, 1987). Listening to the tapes of the lessons, it seemed to us that the whole class, and not just the demonstrating group, acquire a sense of ownership/autonomy in relation to the lesson, a feeling of being in charge which appears to be highly motivating.

It is interesting to note that communicative activities in the Irish lesson are not associated with forms of classroom organisation typically considered characteristic of such an approach to language teaching. Despite the fact that 21.9% of segments involve communicative language activities, small-group forms of organisation are virtually non-existent. In fact, nearly all 'Real communication in Irish' segments, and two thirds of 'Simulated communication in Irish' segments, involve the whole class - a form of classroom organisation normally associated with language practice. Most of the remaining 'Simulated Communication in Irish' segments are associated with the 'Pupil/group demonstration' form of organisation.

The present study, therefore, provides little information about the potential of small-group based, interactive type communicative activities in any new approach to teaching Irish. On the face of it, 'Simulated communication in Irish' activities using a 'Pupil/group demonstration' form of classroom organisation would seem to be the most attractive to pupils. It is interesting in this context to note that teachers in the *Communicative Materials Project*, particularly those with weaker classes, did not generally find communicative activities with a small-group form of classroom organisation viable. Pair-work was considered viable, however, for some kinds of materials and tasks. Among the objections mentioned were the limited linguistic ability of pupils, the amount of preparation and disorder involved and the difficulty of getting the class settled down again. But as we point out in Chapter 9 problems such as these are not 'insurmountable' and 'can be averted by careful planning' (Sheils, 1988). It is also likely that difficulties which arise when group work is first undertaken diminish the more pupils become used to working together.

As a result of the teachers' response, as well as the results of the present study, most of the communicative games and tasks which we proposed in the *Communicative Materials Project* report (Harris *et al.*, 1996a,b), though primarily whole-class based, often had a pupil/group demonstration element. Many of the activities were of the type that could also be implemented in small-group form (in which case they would normally make somewhat greater demands on the linguistic abilities of the pupils). Task/games involving competing teams/groups of children, but with a whole class dimension, were very successful. In any event, the available evidence would suggest that in developing communicative materials for Irish in primary school, tasks should be selected which do not constrain the teacher too much as regards classroom organisation. Given the general agreement about the value of small-group work in a communicative context (Long, Adams, McLean and Castanos, 1976; Long and Porter, 1985; Pica and Doughty, 1985; Ellis, 1994; see also Chapter 9: section 9.4.3), the long term goal should be to evolve towards at least an increase in the proportion of small-group tasks and activities in the Irish lesson.

8.3.3 Attention and interest

We turn now to some more general issues to which the observation study gives rise. While we have already discussed what the attention and interest data reveal about pupils' immediate reaction to a variety of aspects of the Irish lesson, a few questions about attention and interest still remain. For example, why are attention and interest ratings so high generally? The overall mean rating of 4.3 for attention and 4.1 for interest (out of a maximum of 5) represents a very high level of engagement with the lesson. As we shall see in the next chapter, ratings of the attentiveness of individual pupils are broadly consistent with these *ILAS* ratings of *Class attention*, although significant variations between different types of pupils within classes are also uncovered. While teachers can take justifiable pride in these results, it is important to reflect on the means by which they are achieved. This is especially so in the light of the frequently negative comments about the Irish lesson by pupils reported in Chapter 4 which might have led us to expect attention and interest to be lower.

One partial explanation for the good ratings may be that the observation process itself produced exceptional pupil behaviour. Taking into account the comments of some of the teachers on the observation work (see Chapter 6, section 6.6), it is possible that pupils, for entirely laudable reasons, may have been eager to exhibit a high level of involvement in the lesson, to put on their best performance, as it were, in the presence of visitors. Arguably, however, it would have been difficult for pupils to maintain, over the period of two full lessons, behaviour which departed in a significant way from their normal behaviour.

Certainly, listening to the audiotapes of the lessons, it is difficult to find any great evidence of self-consciousness among the pupils after the first few minutes.

Perhaps a more likely explanation is that the whole-class, teacher-centred focus of interaction, and the frequency of short-answer questions (see Chapter 9), discourages disengagement from the lesson by pupils. If this is so, a further question emerges: what kind of engagement with the lesson is maintained in this way? Since many of the teachers' questions are of a routine, predictable nature (see also Chapter 9), it is possible that many pupils are able to answer correctly while listening and attending with a rather narrow and shallow focus on the lesson. Pupils' level of real spontaneous interest in the lesson material - more accurately reflecting some of this negative reaction to the Irish lesson recorded in Chapter 4 - may be masked by the requirement to attend well enough to be able to answer the teacher's questions.

This brings us to a second issue: why is it that attention is consistently rated more highly than interest by the observers and that the statistical analyses show that interest ratings are a more subtle measure than attention ratings of pupils' reactions to the different dimensions of the lesson? The differential sensitivity of attention and interest ratings is shown in a number of ways. For example, while both *Class attention* and *interest* are strongly and positively related to measures of achievement in Irish and attitude to Irish, *Class interest* is more highly correlated in both cases. In addition, while *Class attention* and *interest* are negatively related to *Class Irish-lesson anxiety*, the association is significant only in the case of *Class interest*. More generally, *Class interest* is significantly related to a number of *ILAS* categories/dimensions to which *Class attention* is not: the *Topic* 'Situation: Other than *Nuachúrsaí*', the *Language activities* 'Real communication in Irish' and 'Contextualisation exercises', and the use of 'No Materials'.

Clearly, then, the observers made a real distinction between the two variables. Implicitly, they recognise that the notion of 'interest' refers to a more spontaneous or voluntary component of the pupil's reaction to the lesson than 'attention' does - there is a sense in which attention, but not interest, can be commanded or insisted upon. In other words, 'interest' is a little less amenable to being managed by the teacher's questioning and interaction strategies than 'attention' is.

Notwithstanding these points, it has to be acknowledged that pupil enjoyment and interest cannot be the sole criterion of worth in evaluating language learning materials and activities. Activities or topics which do not attract high levels of interest may nevertheless be essential to effective learning. For example, we noted in Chapter 4 that while pupils in high-Irish-achievement classes dislike grammar-related activities, this would not be sufficient reason for abandoning such activities - indeed they may be crucial to success. But in the long-term, the inherent attractiveness of lesson content for pupils, its capacity to stimulate their interest, cannot be disregarded. In the *Communicative Materials Project*, we tried to achieve some balance between what appeared to be more interesting activities and less interesting, but necessary, activities. In each lesson, any necessary formal linguistic work was quickly followed by communicative games and tasks which had more direct appeal for pupils. Over time, pupils learned that whatever language practice was done initially always had an immediate purpose, in the sense that this new linguistic knowledge was put to use to 'do' something later in the unit. Such productive engagement helps to foster 'intrinsic motivation' among pupils (Crookes and Schmidt, 1991).

8.3.4 The ILAS: Modifications and potential

We turn now to an assessment of how well the ILAS has worked as an instrument for recording and analysing the teaching and learning of Irish at primary level. We feel that all the main innovations which we introduced - mentioned briefly below - should be retained in any future use of the instrument. In addition, we hope that the inclusion in the present report of the long form of *ILAS* (Appendix 6.3), together with transcripts of segments from the Irish lessons (Appendix 6.4), will be useful in the future training of observers.

The addition of the two 'high-inference' dimensions of *Class attention* and *Class interest*, which we have just been discussing, is a useful advance on the Stirling System. The fact that these 'on-line' ratings of pupil reactions were conducted on a segment by segment basis allowed us to link them to changes in other lesson dimensions such as *Topic, Language activity, Pupil behaviour, Teacher mode of involvement, Classroom organisation* and *Materials*. The addition of the 'Simulated communication in Irish' category to the *Language activity* dimension was also an improvement compared to the original Stirling System, with strong associations being revealed between the new category and a variety of positive learning outcomes. The 'Simulated communication in Irish' category will be particularly valuable in analysing Irish lessons when a more communicative approach to teaching is introduced in schools.

The large proportion of lesson segments in which 'Reading aloud' occurred, and the evidence of its association with significant learning outcomes, justified our decision to make this a separate category of *Pupil behaviour* (rather than have one broad 'reading' category as in the Stirling System). The decision to incorporate the recording of *Materials* into a segmental analysis of the lesson was also successful. While the method of recording materials in the present study was not as detailed as that used in the Stirling System (where it was done on a minute-by-minute basis), the fact that it was linked to segments helped to reveal the association between, on the one hand, the 'No materials' category and, on the other, communicative language activities and topics, as well as changes in attention and interest. It is difficult to see how these relationships would have emerged in a non-segment-based analysis and recording.

All this confirms the usefulness of segment-based observation instruments, though the need remains for ongoing revision of the various descriptive categories and dimensions in order to keep them in line with changing theoretical understandings. While there has been a move away from segment-based observation systems (Mitchell, 1989), in favour of discourse and interaction-based systems (Allen, Fröhlich and Spada, 1984; Ullmann and Geva, 1984), we believe that because teachers apparently conceptualise lessons in terms of segments (Mitchell *et al.*, 1981) they will continue to interpret innovations, and incorporate them into their teaching repertoire, in a fundamentally segmental-type way. In other words, we can expect a segmental analysis of lessons to continue to represent at least one level of psychological reality as far as teachers are concerned, irrespective of what new perspectives on language teaching emerge.

8.3.5 *Observing the Irish lesson in future: functions and participants*

In the present study we have used two direct observation instruments, the *ILAS* and the *PCBR* (described in Chapter 9), to explore the implementation of the Irish curriculum and to identify those activities and conditions which are associated with better learning outcomes. Our approach involved 'outside' observers using instruments based on the current best understanding of which classroom processes contribute to successful learning. While this has apparently been successful, and perhaps was a necessary first step, classroom observation with different goals from ours, and using very different approaches, can also contribute to the improvement of pupil proficiency. In particular, classroom observation in which the role of the teacher as observer and interpreter is central, can add a different and important perspective to our understanding of the learning process (Nunan, 1996; Bell, 1997).

Classroom observation conducted by teachers in their own classroom, or in the classrooms of other teachers, can bring different issues in language teaching into focus, enhance programme implementation, facilitate understanding of new approaches, promote the diffusion of innovation, improve teachers' insight into their own performance and more generally contribute to professional development. Ullmann (1991) argues that teachers benefit by becoming aware of the complex dynamics which influence their own teaching strategies. She also believes that teachers should be taught to use instruments and procedures which help them focus their observation in a systematic way. Gebhard, Gaitan and Oprandy (1987), for example, found that although trainee teachers benefitted from the process of observing, the experience was enhanced when they were given guidance in how to observe systematically.

Burns (1990) points out that if second-language teaching is to become more communicative, teachers need opportunities to gain greater understanding of the interactional processes in their own classrooms. Ford (1991) describes the development of an observation scheme to help teachers who were learning to implement cooperative learning situations in Core French classrooms. The scheme comprised two parts (a) a checklist designed to remind teachers to incorporate all the important facets of group-work activities and (b) an observation instrument (such as the *COLT*) which helped determine if students in cooperative activities displayed those discourse features believed to be important for promoting second-language learning. Thornbury (1996) reports how trainee teachers were taught to analyze class discourse, looking out for communicative features such as the use of 'referential questions', 'feedback on content', 'wait time' and 'student initiated turn' (see Chapter 9). Trainees reported a heightened awareness of those instances where their teaching strategies were less communicative, an awareness which in some cases resulted in improved classroom practice. Finally, Mitchell (1989: 205) describes how teachers who became involved in action research on communicative methodology reported that the participation 'provided them with a valuable opportunity for self-appraisal and (in some cases) methodological reorientation'.

This expanded conception of the role of observation in investigating classroom processes must not omit the view of the learner. Galton and Simon (1980: 186) argue that 'teaching tactics both mediate and are themselves mediated by the pupil's behaviour'. We have already seen in Chapter 4 that pupils can provide unique information on second-language learning. Peacock (1997) reinforces this point when he illustrates the mismatch which can exist between teachers' and pupils' views on the appropriateness and enjoyableness of materials in use in second-language classrooms. One way in which learners could become involved in the observation process is by analysing, along with their teacher, selected activities from previous lessons, such as errors and their resolution, communication breakdown and cultural issues (Van Lier, 1988).

There are more general advantages for second-language learning research in widening the observation process. Classroom observation provides teachers, supervisors and researchers with a common language for describing language teaching (Fanselow, 1988). This is turn stimulates analytic inquiry into the language teaching process itself and helps teachers discover their underlying beliefs, goals, practices etc. In this way, the gap between theory and practice may be reduced and a richer data base becomes available for theory building. As Allwright (1992) points out, this should gradually lead to the development of a common agenda both in terms of the issues to be investigated and the procedures to be used.

9 Pupil participation and language use in the Irish lesson

9.1 Introduction

Teachers have always been concerned with the extent to which pupils involve themselves in the lesson in progress: how frequently different individuals volunteer answers or comments, how closely they attend to ongoing activities, and the quality and accuracy of their contributions. In second and foreign-language classes, the contributions of pupils have had an even more important role, in so far as pupil speech is seen as providing both the evidence of, and the mechanism for, language learning. More recently, as we outlined in Chapter 6, teacher and pupil language-use has caught the attention of researchers in a new way as the emphasis in classroom second-language learning research shifted from the study of teaching methods to a concern with the relationship between different kinds of classroom discourse and successful language learning (Chaudron, 1988; Allen and Carroll, 1988; Allen, Swain and Harley, 1988; Ellis, 1994).

Despite the perceived importance of pupil talk in the second-language classroom, research indicates that, as in the case of *first* language classrooms, it is teachers who tend to do most of the talking. About two-thirds of classroom speech can be attributed to the teacher, mostly as soliciting and reacting moves, with students uttering most of the responding moves (Bialystok, Frohlich and Howard, 1978; Ramirez, Yuen, Ramey and Merino, 1986). Furthermore, pedagogic discourse appears to be more restricted than naturalistic discourse (Kasper, 1986; Pica and Long, 1986; Ellis, 1994). In particular, the proportion of unpredictable and sustained speech in the second-language classroom seems to be very small (Allen and Carroll, 1988). The nature and length of pupil discourse, of course, will be determined in many instances by the kinds of questions asked. Studies have found that 'display' questions are more common than 'referential' questions in second-language classrooms, in comparison with out-of-class interactions between native and non-native speakers (Long and Sato, 1983; White and Lightbown, 1984; Early, 1985; Ramirez *et al.*, 1986; Johnston, 1990). Display questions are those to which the answer is already known by the teacher. They are characteristic of language practice or form-focused activities and typically elicit short predictable answers from pupils. Referential questions, in contrast, are associated with real communication and with tasks involving meaning negotiation and they tend to elicit more complex output from pupils (Ellis, 1994).

Other communicative features of classroom interaction which are considered important to the development of second-language proficiency were discussed more fully in Chapter 6. Allen and Carroll (1988) and Allen *et al.* (1988), for example, argue for the importance of (a) whether reactions to an utterance in the target language focus on the language itself (e.g. correcting a mistake in grammar) or on the message (e.g. correcting an error of fact in the message), (b) the extent to which speakers engage in extended discourse as opposed to restricting their utterances to a minimum (a word or phrase) and (c) whether or not preceding utterances are incorporated in the listener's reaction, by way of comment, clarification of content, or elaboration.

One of the traditional concerns of language teachers which has attracted the attention of researchers in recent years is the nature and extent of pupil participation in classroom discourse and the relationship of this participation to eventual achievement in the target language. The evidence in the international literature, however, is conflicting. Studies by Seliger (1977), Naiman, Fröhlich, Stern and Todesco (1978) and Strong (1983, 1984) report positive correlations between various measures of learner participation/output (e.g. actual speech, amount of verbal interaction, hand-raising) and second-language proficiency. Other researchers (Day, 1984; Ely, 1986) have found no such relationship. Even where positive correlations have been established, the question of whether increased second-language proficiency results from more production, or vice versa, remains unanswered.

Another aspect to the relationship between pupil ability in the target language and pupil participation in class relates to the frequency with which teachers use questions to elicit responses from different pupils. Mizon (1981) and Early (1985), for example, found that teachers used more questions when addressing second-language learners than when conversing with native speaking students in mother-tongue classrooms. One possible explanation for this is that questions may facilitate interactions involving less proficient students by clearly establishing both the topic and who is expected to speak next (Chaudron, 1988).

The extent to which the learner is exposed to *comprehensible input* is yet another aspect of classroom discourse which has attracted attention in recent years (Krashen, 1985). According to Krashen's model, humans acquire language by understanding messages rather than by consciously focusing on form. The model also posits a mental screen between the learner and the environment, a screen which is activated by affective factors (e.g. anxiety, self confidence) and which controls the amount of input a pupil converts into intake. In order for comprehensible input to result in successful language acquisition, therefore, the learner must be 'open' to the input or have a 'low affective filter'. To be maximally effective, the input must also contain a new aspect of the language which the learner has not yet acquired but is ready to acquire (Krashen, 1991). Thus, the quality of pupil attention and interest, as well as appropriateness of language content and context, may be important predictors of success in second-language acquisition.

The present chapter examines some of these issues of classroom language use and pupil participation in the context of the teaching and learning of Irish at sixth grade in primary school. The instrument we use is the newly constructed *Pupil Communicative Behaviour Record (PCBR)* already referred to briefly in Chapter 6. The main issues we concentrate on are (a) the frequency of individual pupil speech in Irish and silence during the Irish lesson (b) the communicative features of pupil utterances (c) variations in language use and attentiveness in pupils who have different levels of ability in Irish (d) the frequency of 'other' kinds of pupil 'behaviour' during the Irish lesson, such as reading, writing and choral speech and (e) whether factors such as the size of the class and the kinds of teaching activities which are emphasised are linked to the frequency of individual pupil speech, silence and other behaviours.

9.2 Method

9.2.1 Sample

Within each of the twenty sixth-grade classes in the study, one pupil of high ability in Irish, one of middle ability in Irish and one of low ability in Irish was randomly selected. In this way, pupils of different ability levels in Irish and from different types of classes contributed to the picture of pupil language use which finally emerged. The initial categorisation of pupils as high, middle and low ability in Irish was done by the class teacher. An observer then randomly selected one pupil from each of the three ability groups to be the focus of study. Due to replacements (see section 9.2.3.1 below) a total of 66 pupils rather than the initially selected 60 pupils was observed. This group comprised 34 girls and 32 boys. The teacher did not know which pupils were the target of the observation. In each class, two observers worked side by side, one using the *PCBR*, which is the subject of the present chapter, and the other using the *ILAS* which was described in Chapter 6.

9.2.2 Instrument

The development of the Pupil Communicative Behaviour Record (PCBR)
While the *ILAS*, based on the Stirling system, provides us with a general description of the classroom practice of Irish teachers, it is limited by the fact that it is structured around fairly large planning or lesson-activity 'segments'. Thus, it fails to register in detail the characteristics of communicative interaction in the classroom or indeed the more transient events and experiences which may have a bearing on how successfully pupils learn a second language. For example, teachers and pupils sometimes digress briefly from the formal lesson plan to make some personal or individual contribution in the target language. 'Real communication' exchanges of this kind, concerned with classroom management, discipline, or with life outside the school may command relatively high interest and attention among pupils (See Appendix 6.4, extracts 18-20*)*. While such events may be very relevant to the development of second-language proficiency, their brevity precludes them from being recorded in a lesson-segment type observation instrument. Existing lesson-segment type observation systems also fail to describe the extent to which different types of pupils are engaged with the activity in progress, or

indeed whether they are participating in the lesson in a manner which is at all consistent with the pedagogic goals of the activity. The *ILAS* is a considerable improvement on previous segment-based systems in at least providing an on-line measure of how pupils in *general* in the class were engaging with the lesson.

The observation system described below, the *PCBR*, tries to overcome these limitations by focusing on individual pupil participation and language use. In developing the instrument, account was taken of research which tries to identify those features of pupil interaction with the teacher and with other pupils which are important for second-language learning. In particular, we relied on the *COLT* (Part II) observation scheme which was discussed in Chapter 6 (Allen, *et al.*, 1984; Allen, *et al.*, 1987; Allen, *et al.*, 1990). *COLT* was developed in the context of a five year Development of Bilingual Proficiency (DBP) project in Toronto. The system allows for the recording of such communicative features of classroom interaction as target language use, information gap, length of utterance, reaction to code or message, incorporation of preceding utterances, discourse initiation by teacher or student, and relative restriction of linguistic form.

While we adapted major features of *COLT* Part II in describing certain pupil behaviours (e.g. see 'Pupil speaks individually' category below), we did not attempt any detailed communicative categorisation in relation to other pupil behaviours (e.g. where the pupil is engaged in 'other' behaviours such as choral speech, reading or writing). This is not to suggest that reading and writing activities do not vary widely in the kind of communicative interaction they involve. It is simply that it would have been beyond our resources to collect this information in the time available. In addition, since it would have required access to, and evaluation of, pupils' written products it would have raised entirely new issues in the research. Another difference is that the *PCBR* examines only *pupil* language and communication, and does not specifically examine teacher discourse. Finally, unlike *COLT* Part II, *PCBR* records the pupil's ability in Irish, as rated by the teacher, an item of information that proved very interesting in interpreting the other data generated by the system.

Categories of the Pupil Communicative Behaviour Record
The *PCBR* defined behaviour under three main headings: *(1) Pupil speaks individually, (2) Pupil is silent* and *(3) Other pupil behaviour* (see Appendix 9). Behaviours under each main heading could be coded in relation to a range of language use or other descriptive categories:

(1) Pupil speaks individually
'Language used': 'Irish' was ticked if the utterance was in Irish or mostly in Irish, and 'English' if the utterance was in English or mostly in English.
'Asks a question': This category was relevant if the pupil asked a question. There were two options - 'pseudo' and 'genuine'. 'Pseudo' would be the appropriate option where the question was only posed as part of a drill or some other practice (and the answer to it was, therefore, highly constrained and predictable). The 'genuine' question option might be

ticked when the pupil, for example, having been reading, decides on his/her own initiative to ask the teacher for an explanation of some word he/she did not understand.

'Answers': This category was ticked if the pupil answered a question, and was coded as 'predictable' or 'unpredictable'.

'Length of utterance': The sub-categories here were 'one word', 'clause', 'sentence', and 'sustained' and were intended to measure the extent to which the pupils engaged in extended or restricted discourse.

'Takes turn': This category was intended to capture the situation where the pupil took the initiative in some fundamental way, departing from the formal agenda of the lesson to some extent (asking questions or making comments unprompted by the teacher). These could consist either of (a) question-forms or phrases which might be used routinely in class communication but which in the specific instance observed were not related to the ongoing lesson ('routine') or (b) 'new' or original contributions.

'Interaction type': Each pupil's spoken contribution was coded in relation to one of two sub-categories, 'pupil-pupil' or 'pupil-teacher'.

(2) Pupil is silent (or engaged in non-task related pupil-pupil exchange)

This main heading was relevant if the pupil was silent during a particular activity e.g. listening more or less attentively. Being silent does not include engagement in any *Other* behaviour such as silent reading or writing (see below). This heading was also relevant if the pupil was not actually engaged in any formal language activity or task but was chatting to neighbouring pupil(s) (i.e. non-task-related exchanges). There were two categories to be ticked in the case of *Silent* behaviours: 'Attending' ('high'/ 'moderate'/ 'low') and 'Disruptive' ('high' / 'moderate' / 'low'). In the case, for example, where a pupil was not engaged at all in the task, but was chatting loudly to his/her neighbours, the rating might consist of ticking 'low' for 'Attending' and 'moderate' or 'high' for 'Disruptive'.

(3) Other pupil behaviour

There were four categories under this heading: 'Choral speech', 'reading silently', 'reading aloud', and 'Writing'. Only one of these four would be ticked for a particular pupil behaviour. We also asked the observers to place a tick in the adjacent categories of 'Attending' and 'Disruptive', to indicate the manner in which the task was performed (even if the pupil is *not* silent e.g. choral reading aloud or choral speech).

9.2.3 *Procedure*

The inspector observed the selected pupils, one at a time in succession, and recorded various aspects of their behaviour. This record was made by placing ticks in the appropriate columns of an A3 size coding sheet (see Appendix 9) which listed the behavioural categories and sub-categories of the *PCBR*. A full description of the categories of the *PCBR*, as well as directions for carrying out the observation work, were given in a manual which had been previously studied by the observers and which could also be referred to during the observation work itself (Appendix 9). The observers had earlier been involved in a training session during which the coding schedules and method of categorising and recording behaviours were explained in detail.

The observation work proceeded in five-minute sequences, with the first three minutes being given over to observing the target pupil, and the last two minutes being used to record more fully his/her behaviour on the coding sheet. Two full lessons were observed in each class. The same three pupils were observed in Lesson 1 and Lesson 2 except in the few instances where substitutions had to be made due to pupils being absent etc. (see below).

Within any one three-minute observation period, it was possible that more than one type of pupil behaviour would occur. For example, a pupil might be engaged in a question-and-answer type spoken interaction with the teacher in the first minute of the observation period, after which there might be a whole-class choral response, followed by yet another exchange between the same pupil and his/her teacher in the last minute of the observation period. In such a case, three different pupil behaviours would be coded for that observation period. The observer would code each new behaviour by drawing a line within the row for that unit on the *PCBR* coding sheet and placing ticks in the relevant categories for each new behaviour. Thus, the number of pupil behaviours recorded for each lesson is substantially greater than the number of observation units.

In general the *PCBR* might be described as a low-inference instrument, that is to say that the categorisation required by the observer is so straightforward and unambiguous that there seems to be little subjective element involved. There are two aspects of the *PCBR*, however, where that is not the case. The first arises under the 'Asks a question' and 'Answers' headings discussed earlier where the observer must categorise features such as, 'pseudo'/ 'genuine' question, 'predictable'/'unpredictable' answer. These would seem to involve high inference ratings. This may be contrasted with low inference judgements, such as whether a pupil speaks or remains silent, which leave little room for ambiguity. The other aspect of the *PCBR* which involves high inference judgements is the rating of the pupils' level of attentiveness or disruptiveness during silent periods.

Additional coding guidelines

In general, we tried to analyse the observers' *PCBR*-based record of pupil behaviour as it was presented to us, intervening only where the operation of the coding system seemed to be inconsistent or ambiguous. The kinds of problems encountered, and the manner in which we resolved them are set out briefly below and are discussed in more detail in Appendix 9 (see section - Additional Coding Guidelines).

(1) Complex behaviours: Observers opted to represent some *Complex* pupil behaviours by placing ticks under more than one of the main headings. For example, where a pupil was contributing to a group discussion and was also taking notes, the behaviour might be coded as *Complex,* consisting of *Pupil speaks individually* and *Other pupil behaviour* (i.e. 'Writing'.)

(2) Mutually exclusive categories/subcategories ticked: The solution here depended on the particular categories/subcategories ticked. In those instances where ticks were made in more than one of the categories under the *Other pupil behaviour* heading, the observer's accompanying notes, or coterminous data from the *ILAS* schedule for that lesson (completed by the second observer) usually provided sufficient information to resolve the conflict. In the case of the 'Language' category, however, ticks under both 'Irish' and 'English' subcategories was interpreted as 'half Irish/half English', while in those instances where no language was recorded (no ticks made) 'Irish' was assumed to be the language used as long as the 'Interaction type' was 'pupil-teacher' (see Appendix 9).

Where other mutually exclusive categories/subcategories were ticked, both were disregarded except in the case of the graded subheadings in the 'Length of utterance' category. Here, superior categories (longer utterances) were accepted in favour of inferior ones (shorter utterances). The 'Takes turn' category seems to have been misunderstood by at least some observers. Many placed ticks in the 'Takes turn' category as well as in the adjacent 'Asks a question' or 'Answers' categories. Only those behaviours which were coded under the 'Takes turn' category *alone* were included as instances of the kind of genuine pupil initiative which this category was intended to capture.

(3) Unequal numbers of pupils/Pupil replacements: At the beginning of an observation period, the preselected pupil with high ability in Irish was always observed first, thus producing more behaviours for higher ability pupils. This was taken into account in all analyses since we used proportions rather than actual numbers of behaviours. Four target pupils who were absent for the second lesson were replaced by pupils of corresponding ability in Irish. Two pupils were replaced for other reasons (see Appendix 9) for the second observation period - making a total of six substitutions in all.

(4) Incomplete codings: In instances where behaviours were only partially coded we simply accepted the incomplete data presented .

9.2.4 Analysis

Most of the data we present here consists of the relative frequency of occurrence of different categories of pupil behaviour (aggregated over classes and pupils). We use *chi square* (Ferguson, 1976) to test for differences in the distribution of these frequencies. Frequency of behaviours rather than of observation units is used as the dependent variable, because using units involves some loss of information in cases where more than one behaviour occurs during the observation period. Chi-square statistics are quoted here primarily as a means of distinguishing between more important and less important trends in the data for these particular pupils and classes. Reporting these statistics should not be seen as implying any claims about the population of schools and classes generally.

The actual pupil behaviour observed may be determined by, or linked to, a wide variety of factors, including characteristics of the pupils themselves (e.g. ability in Irish, gender) or of the class or teaching (e.g. the size of the class or the nature of the teaching process). Our main focus in the analysis is on pupil characteristics though we also examine class/teaching characteristics. In the case of pupil characteristics, for example, we examine how frequently pupils of different levels of ability in Irish (e.g. 'high' ability-in-Irish', 'low' ability-in-Irish') speak individually in Irish or remain silent. Another concern is the extent to which pupils are generally 'Attending' or being 'Disruptive' during *Silent* behaviours.

In the case of class/teaching characteristics, our investigation is exploratory and is confined to a correlation analysis of the relationship between behavioural propensities (e.g. the propensity for pupils in the class to remain silent) and class/teaching characteristics (e.g. class size; the amount of teaching time devoted to communicative activities). Class-/teaching-group size would seem likely, on commonsense grounds alone, to be important to pupil participation: pupils should have a proportionately better chance of 'getting their turn', as it were, in a small class. Ideally we would like to establish if there are any connections between pupil behaviour and the particular language activities which are implemented by the teacher.

9.3 Results

The results are divided into five sections. The first section reports the relative frequency of occurrence of the main behaviours - individual speech, silence and 'other' pupil behaviour. The following three sections analyse each of the main behaviours in more detail. For example, in the case of individual pupil speech we investigate whether its frequency varies according to ability in Irish and gender. We also describe linguistic/communicative features of pupil speech, including whether it is in Irish or English, the length of the pupil's utterance, whom the interaction involves and whether the utterance consists of a question, an answer or some other type of contribution. In the last section, we examine class variations in pupil behavioural propensities.

Before turning to the results proper some background data on the observation work will be useful. Table 9.1 distinguishes between the number of observation units (i.e. the three minute periods during which the pupil was monitored) and the number of behaviours coded in each of these observation units. Data in the first two rows provide information on the distribution of units. Two-thirds (67.4%) of the observation units contain just one behaviour. A little less than a quarter (23.8%) of units have two behaviours recorded, while the remaining 8.8% of units have three or more behaviours recorded. Overall, then, the number of behaviours (778) exceeds the number of observation units (534).

A different perspective on the units/behaviour distribution is provided by the data in the last two rows of Table 9.1. It can be seen that less than half of all behaviours (46.3%) occur in units containing only that behaviour - even though such one-behaviour units, as we have just pointed out, account for two thirds of all units. At the other extreme, just over a fifth of all behaviours (21.1%) are seen in multiple-behaviours units. Close to a third of all behaviours (32.6 %) are observed in two-behaviour units.

Table 9.1
Number of behaviours and observation units in the *PCBR* study* .

PCBR* study n = 66 pupils	----------- *Composition of unit* ---------			
	Units with one behaviour	*Units with two behaviours*	*Units with three or more behaviours*	*Total units/ behaviours*
Number of observation units	360	127	47	534
Percentage of observation units	*67.4*	*23.8*	*8.8*	*100%*
Number of behaviours	360	254	164	778
Percentage of behaviours	*46.3*	*32.6*	*21.1*	*100%*

*Pupil Communicative Behaviour Record

9.3.1 *Frequency of the main behaviours*

Table 9.2 shows the distribution of pupil behaviours according to the main language/communication headings of the *PCBR*. About one fifth of the behaviours (20.2%) consist of the pupil being *Silent*, presumably listening/looking. About half the behaviours involve the pupil speaking individually (i.e. composed of 41.6% of cases where the pupil simply speaks individually (*Individual only*) and another 8.2% of *Complex* behaviours where the pupil speaks while also being involved in other activities such as 'Writing'. A little less than a third of behaviours (29.9%) are classified as *Other only* (i.e. choral speech, reading or writing apart from *Complex* behaviours).

A pie chart of these distributions is shown in Figure 9.1. Bear in mind that the *Complex* component may be joined with either of the adjacent components since it includes both *Pupil speaks individually* and *Other* behaviours.

Another perspective on the different linguistic/communicative activities is provided by the number and percentage of *units* in which particular categories of behaviour occur. We can ask, for example, in how many units is there at least one instance of the pupil speaking individually. Clearly, since more than one category of behaviour may occur in any unit, we must decide in advance what priority should be assigned to different categories of behaviours if we are to divide the 534 units into mutually exclusive sets. For the purposes of the present analysis we decided to give priority to units in which one of two mutually exclusive behaviours occurred: (a) units in which the pupil was observed to speak individually at least once (though other behaviours, either simultaneous or successive could also occur) and (b) units in which the pupil remained silent for the whole observation period.

Table 9.2
Distribution of pupil behaviours according to language/communication category.

Behavioural Category	Number of behaviours	Percentage of behaviours
1. *Individual only* (Pupil speaks individually)	324	41.6
2. *Complex* (Pupil speaks individually and also reads or writes i.e. elements of (1) above & (3) below	64	8.2
3. *Other only* (Pupil is engaged in choral speech, reading or writing but excluding (1) & (2) above).	233	29.9
4. *Silent* (Pupil is silent)	157	20.2
Total	*778*	*100%*

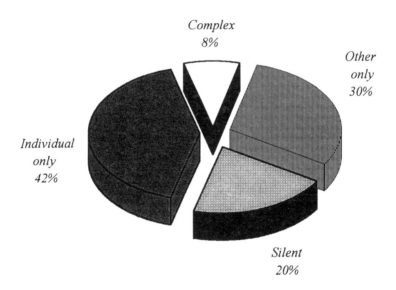

Figure 9.1 Distribution of pupil behaviours according to language/communication category.
(see Table 9.2 for an explanation of the titles)

We set out the data in Table 9.3 in such a way that units of these two kinds are clearly distinguished. Note that the observed pupil speaks at least once in nearly half (48.4%) of all the units. This 48.4% is made up of the 38.9% of all units in which the pupil speaks individually and the 9.5% of all units which involve *Complex* behaviours (*Pupil speaks individually* plus *Other*). Similarly, by combining the percentages in rows two and three it can be seen that in almost 40% of units the pupil is engaged in some form of *Other* behaviour i.e. 'Choral speech', 'Reading' or Writing'. Finally, in just over a fifth of all observation units (21.9%) the pupil remains *Silent* throughout.

Looking back to Table 9.2 for a moment and comparing the data there with the data in Table 9.3 it can be seen that the proportions associated with the four main categories of pupil behaviour remain more or less the same whether we are counting behaviours (Table 9.2) or the observation units containing these behaviours (Table 9.3).

Figure 9.2 provides in graphic form a more detailed breakdown of behavioural categories by unit composition. This breakdown is presented as background information only and we are not using it to support any new conclusions. It shows the distribution of the main behavioural headings (*Pupil speaks individually*, *Silent* etc.) in relation to the number of behaviours which a unit contains. It can be seen (column 4) that *Silent* behaviours are most likely (74%) to occur in observation units where *Silent* is the only behaviour occurring. Instances of the pupil speaking individually, on the other hand (column 1), are more likely to occur in units containing more than one behaviour. Over a third (35%) of the instances of the pupil speaking occur in conjunction with one other behaviour (i.e. in two-behaviour units). A further 39% of individual speaking behaviours occur in units with three or more behaviours. Thus, only about a quarter (26%) of all instances of the pupil speaking individually occur in units where that behaviour is the only one recorded.

Table 9.4 shows the number of pupil behaviours in *Other* categories i.e. not *Silent* and not *Pupil-speaks-individually*. We include here the *'Other'* behaviour component of *Complex* behaviours i.e. cases where the pupil spoke individually but was also engaged in some other behaviour such as reading or writing. The frequency of each subcategory of behaviour (e.g. 'Choral speech') is expressed as a percentage of *Other* pupil behaviours (n = 297) and also as a percentage of all pupil behaviours (n = 778). It can be seen that 38.1% of all pupil behaviours are classified as *Other* i.e. 'Choral speech', 'Reading' or 'Writing'. The combined reading behaviours ('reading aloud'/'silent reading') make up 14.1% of all behaviours, while 'Writing' and 'Choral speech' closely follow with 12.3% and 11.7% respectively. It is worthy of note, perhaps, that even in Irish classes at sixth-grade, 'Choral speech' makes up a small but not negligible proportion of pupil behaviours.

These results indicate a high level of overt definite pupil participation in class. While pupils remain silent without being involved in any other behaviour for one fifth of the units, data presented below indicate that they are most often listening with a moderate or high level of attention during these periods. For the rest of the time, they are switching in and out of different forms of participation in class - speaking individually or chorally, reading, or writing. In particular, there is a high level of individual spoken contributions by pupils.

Table 9.3
Distribution of observation units by the four main categories of pupil behaviour.

Behavioural Category	Observation units	
	n	*Percentage of units*
1. *Individual only* (Pupil speaks individually)	208	38.9
2. *Complex* (Pupil speaks individually *and also* reads or writes). Excludes small number of units counted under 1 above.	51	9.5
3. *Other only* (Pupil is engaged in choral speech, reading or writing). Excludes units counted under 1 & 2 above.	158	29.6
4. *Silent* (Pupil is silent for the whole unit)	117	21.9
Total	534	100%

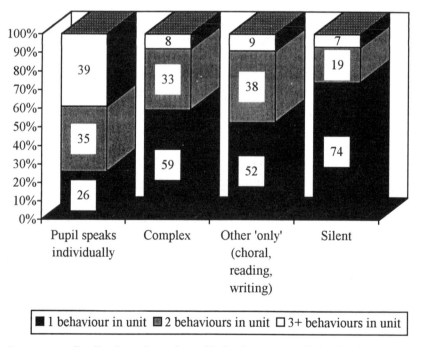

Figure 9.2 Percentage distribution of number of behaviours per unit by the four main categories of behaviour.

Table 9.4
Distribution of *Other** pupil behaviours according to sub-category of behaviour involved.

'Other' behaviour	n (behaviours)	Percentage of *Other* category behaviours (n = 297)	all behaviours (n = 778)
Choral speech	91	30.6	11.7
Silent reading	64	21.5	8.2
Reading aloud	46	15.5	5.9
Writing	96	32.3	12.3
Total *Other*	297	100%	38.1

* Including *Complex* behaviours (n = 64)

This pattern of participation by targeted pupils as revealed by data from the *PCBR* is confirmed by a similar perceived high level of participation by pupils as reported by inspectors in the *Global Rating of Lesson* instrument (Appendix 2.3, Q23). Inspectors reported that in over 90% of the classes, less than 20% of the pupils could be classified as adopting a passive role (or resisting involvement) in the Irish class.

9.3.2 Individual pupil speech

Tables 9.5-9.8 provide a more detailed analysis of various characteristics of pupils' individual spoken contributions - the general communicative function of their utterances and to whom they speak (to other pupils or to the teacher). We also examine the manner in which these utterance characteristics vary with ability in Irish and gender.

Pupil ability in Irish
Table 9.5 shows the distribution of instances of the pupil speaking individually according to his or her ability in Irish. It can be seen that while 61.6% of all behaviours recorded for 'higher ability-in-Irish' pupils involve the pupil speaking individually, only 36.3% of the behaviours of pupils with a 'lower' level of ability in Irish involve individual speech. A chi-square analysis confirms that the frequency of the pupil speaking individually is distributed significantly differently over the three ability levels in Irish (chi square = 34.4; df=2; p <.001). A similar significant result is obtained if the ability grouping is based on the sixth-grade ITÉ test of spoken Irish (listening test only) rather than on teachers' ratings (chi square = 54.4; df =2; p < .001).

Table 9.5 also shows that more behaviours of all kinds are recorded for 'higher ability-in-Irish' (40.9%) compared to 'middle' (31.9%) and 'lower ability-in-Irish' (27.2%) pupils. As we pointed out earlier (also see Appendix 9) this unequal distribution of behaviours is due to the fact that in each lesson the 'higher ability-in-Irish' pupil was always observed first. Thus, 197 three-minute observation units were completed for pupils of higher ability-in-Irish, 180 units for pupils of middle ability-in-Irish and 157 units for pupils of lower ability-in-Irish. These correspond roughly to proportions of .37, .34 and .29. of all units respectively. Units which relate to pupils of the 'middle' level of ability-in-Irish are represented in the proportion expected (one-third). Units related to 'higher' ability-in-Irish pupils are slightly overrepresented and units related to 'lower' ability-in-Irish' pupils are slightly underrepresented.

Table 9.5
Percentage distribution of instances of *Pupil speaks individually * according to pupil's ability in Irish (n = 66 pupils)

| | *Percentage of behaviours* | | |
| | *Pupil speaks individually* | *Pupil does not speak individually* | *Total* |
Pupil ability in Irish (as rated by teacher)	n=388	n=390	(n = 778)
Higher	61.6	38.4	40.9
Middle	46.4	53.6	31.9
Lower	36.3	63.7	27.2
Total	49.9	50.1	100%

* Almost always in Irish. Includes *Complex* behaviours.

Since more observations were made of pupils with 'higher' ability-in-Irish than of those with lower ability-in-Irish, and since the former tend to speak more often as we established earlier, the overall frequency with which pupils generally tend to speak individually may be somewhat overestimated. Nevertheless, note that even in the case of 'lower' ability-in - Irish pupils, 36.3% of all their behaviours involve individual speech (Table 9.5). The unequal distribution does not affect the validity of our conclusions, however, since it is taken into account in comparing the proportion of behaviours in different categories associated with pupils of different ability levels in Irish.

It may be mentioned in passing, that the proportion of units associated with the three levels of ability in Irish translates into the following total observation times: nine hours 51 minutes observation time for 'higher' ability-in-Irish pupils; nine hours exactly for 'middle' ability-in-Irish pupils; and seven hours and 51 minutes for 'lower' ability-in-Irish pupils - a total of 26 hours 42 minutes observation time altogether. Note that this is less than the forty-plus hours of teaching observed in the case of *ILAS*. The difference is primarily due to the fact that only 3 out of every 5 minutes were observed in the case of *PCBR*, the other two minutes being devoted to recording what had been observed.

Length of utterance
Table 9.6 shows the distribution of instances of the pupil speaking individually according to (a) 'Length of utterance' ('word', 'clause', 'sentence', 'sustained') and (b) *Pupil ability in Irish*. It can be seen (last row, Table 9.6) that only 13.4% of all spoken utterances are longer than a single sentence (i.e. 'sustained'). Most utterances (52.9%) are one sentence long, while just under one fifth (18.7%) consist of no more than one word. Regarding *Pupil ability in Irish*, a chi-square analysis confirms what is already clear from an inspection of Table 9.6 - that there is no significant relationship between the pupil's proficiency in Irish and the length of his/her spoken contributions (chi square=5.03; df=6; NS). In other words, while pupils with higher ability in Irish are more likely to speak individually in class, as we have just shown, they are no more likely than less able pupils to speak at greater length on each occasion. One possible interpretation of this is that the kind of exchanges which are possible or expected are so constrained by the lesson format itself - by the form of the teacher's language or by precedent within the class - that being of higher ability in Irish, being capable, for example, of more sustained contributions, is irrelevant. We return to this issue in the context of an analysis of the role of class and teaching characteristics in the next section.

Table 9.6
Percentage distribution of instances of *Pupil speaks individually* according to length of utterance and pupil ability in Irish.

Percentage of behaviours

Pupil ability in Irish	'one word' n=70	'clause' n=56	'sentence' n=198	'sustained' n=50	Total* (n=374)
Higher	20.3	15.1	48.4	16.1	51.3
Middle	16.7	16.7	56.5	10.2	28.9
Lower	17.6	12.2	59.5	10.8	19.8
Total	18.7	15.0	52.9	13.4	100%

* 'Length of utterance' was not recorded for a further 14 instances of *Pupil speaks individually*

Gender
Virtually equal proportions of behaviours in the case of boys (50.9%) and of girls (49.6%) involve speaking individually and the difference between them, therefore, is not significant

(chi square= .07; df=1; NS). In terms of 'Length of utterance', there was some tendency, though not a statistically significant one, for boys to make proportionally more single-word and clause-level contributions than girls, while girls had proportionately more sentence-level and sustained utterances than boys (chi square 6.5; df=3; NS). Neither was any significant relationship found between gender and ability-in-Irish as rated by the teacher (Pearson's r = .04; NS).

Language used and Interaction type

Table 9.7 presents further data on individual spoken contributions, this time focused on the participants and on the language chosen. The table consists of a crosstabulation of 'Interaction type' ('pupil-pupil' or 'pupil-teacher') and the amount of Irish used ('Irish', 'English, or 'half-Irish and half-English'). The first thing to be noted is that Irish (or mostly Irish) is the predominant language choice in interactions (91% of interactions are entirely in Irish). While 18% of 'pupil-pupil' lesson-related interactions are in English (or 'half-and-half'), however, only 6% of 'pupil-teacher' interactions are in English. We exclude from the analysis of 'Language used' informal non-task-related chatting/gossiping among pupils - coded as *Silent* behaviour in the present study - which is almost certainly conducted in English. In the case of a further 12% of 'pupil-pupil' interactions, the language used was not recorded - presumably because the observer could not hear the dialogue in question.

Table 9.7
Language used in pupil-pupil and pupil-teacher interactions.

	Percentage of behaviours			
	'Interaction type'			
Language	'pupil-pupil' (n=50)	'pupil-teacher' (n=316)	'Interaction type' not recorded (n=22)	Total* (n=388)
Irish	70.0	94.0	95.5	91.0
English	12.0	5.7	4.5	6.4
Half & half	6.0	0.3	-	1.0
Language not recorded	12.0	-	-	1.5
Total	12.9	81.4	5.7	100%

*Includes *Complex* behaviours.

The chi-square analysis carried out involves combining the 'English' and 'half and half' language categories in order to obtain satisfactory cell frequencies. Thus, two categories of 'Interaction type' and only two categories of 'Language' are represented in the analysis. Cases where data on either language or interaction type were missing are disregarded. The result confirms that the language used is distributed differently in 'pupil-pupil' and 'pupil-teacher' interactions (chi square=9.31; df=1; p<.01). Pupils more often use some English when talking to each other in a *lesson* context than when they are talking to the teacher - although as we have just pointed out, use of Irish is quite high overall (over 90%) in lesson-related interaction.

The small number of 'pupil-pupil' interactions which occur militate against any clear pattern emerging in relation to pupil ability. A chi-square analysis, not shown here, showed no evidence that the likelihood of 'pupil-pupil' interactions as opposed to 'pupil-teacher' interactions occurring was affected by the pupils' ability in Irish (chi square = .02; df = 2; NS).

Type of utterance
Table 9.8 shows the distribution of instances of the pupil speaking individually according to the kind of utterance involved - (a) Questions ('Asks a question') (b) Answers or (c) as instances of the pupil taking the initiative in a more fundamental way (i.e. 'Takes turn').

The most frequent type of pupil utterances were 'Answers'. It may be seen that roughly two thirds (65.2%) of utterances involve the pupil making a 'predictable' answer (mostly, presumably, to teacher questions). A further 17.5% of utterances were rated as 'unpredictable' answers. Thus, 82.7% of all exchanges consisted of the pupil answering, with the ratio of 'predictable' to 'unpredictable' answers being 65/17 approximately. Incidentally, if we look at 'sustained' utterances only, we find a much better balance between 'predictable' and 'unpredictable' answers. Of the 50 individual utterances which were coded as 'sustained' (See Table 9.6), only 42% were coded as 'predictable' answers while 36% were 'unpredictable' answers. The proportion of 'predictable' to 'unpredictable' answers is much lower for longer utterances (42/36), therefore, than it is for utterances generally in these classes (65/17).

Returning now to Table 9.8, it can be seen that less than 4% of pupil utterances were coded as 'Questions', a little less than half of these (1.8%) being considered 'genuine' (as opposed to 'pseudo' questions which are posed as part of language practice or formal exercises of some kind).

It will be recalled from our description of problems in coding the *PCBR* that observers sometimes placed ticks in mutually exclusive categories. One such example are those instances where observers ticked the 'Takes turn' category as well as one or other of the adjacent 'Asks a question' and 'Answers' category (see Appendix 9 - Additional Coding Guidelines). Filtering out those behaviours which were included in more than one category, we found that only 3.1% of utterances could be unambiguously interpreted as evidence of the pupil taking the conversational initiative (i.e. 'Takes turn'). Because of this ambiguity, we will not be basing any of our conclusions on the 'Takes turn' data.

Table 9.8
Distribution of instances of *Pupil speaks individually* according to the type of pupil contribution.

	Pupil speaks individually		
Type of utterance	*n*	*Percentage of behaviours*	*Total %*
Pupil 'Answer'			
'predictable'	*253*	65.2	
'unpredictable'	*68*	17.5	82.7
Pupil 'Question'			
'pseudo'	*8*	2.1	
'genuine'	*7*	1.8	3.9
Both 'Answer' & 'Question'	*3*	0.8	0.8
Pupil 'Takes turn'*			
'routine'	*5*	1.3	
'new'	*7*	1.8	3.1
None of the above	*37*	9.5	9.5
Total	*(388)*	100%	100%

* Other than those behaviours coded under 'Answer' and 'Question' above.

Due to the small number of pupil behaviours in the 'Asks a question' category, it was not feasible to examine differences in the distribution of pupil behaviours in the 'Answers' and 'Asks a question' categories according to pupil ability.

Finally in this respect, looking at the last row of Table 9.8 it can be seen that just under a tenth (9.5%) of all individual pupil utterances were not assigned to any of the three main sub-categories - 'Asks a question', 'Answers' or 'Takes turn'.

9.3.3 Silence

Tables 9.9 - 9.11 analyse cases where the pupil is silent. Being silent, in the special sense defined in the *PCBR* Coding Guidelines (Appendix 9), may involve the pupil listening more or less attentively or it may involve the pupil chatting to other pupils about non-task related issues, being entirely inattentive to the formal lesson, or even being disruptive. For this reason, we examine data on different aspects of silence - how often pupils were silent, how the frequency of this behaviour related to *Gender* and *Pupil ability in Irish*, and how attentive or disruptive the pupil was during the observation period. Recall that being 'silent' in the sense it has been defined here does not include *Other* activities such as silent reading or writing.

Ability in Irish and 'Silent' behaviours
Table 9.9 shows that pupils who are of 'lower' ability-in-Irish are more than twice as likely (31.6%) to be silent as pupils who are of 'higher' ability-in-Irish (12.6%). A chi-square analysis confirms that the tendency to remain silent is distributed significantly differently across ability levels in Irish (chi square = 28.58; df = 2; p<.01). Using achievement on the ITÉ sixth grade test of spoken Irish instead of teachers' ratings as the measure of ability in Irish yields a similar pattern of results (chi square = 29.13; df = 2; p < .01).

Table 9.9
Percentage distribution of instances of *Pupil is silent* according to *Pupil ability in Irish*.

Pupil ability in Irish	Percentage of pupil behaviours		
	Pupil is 'Silent' (n=157)	'Rest' of pupil behaviours (n=621)	Total (n=778)
Higher	12.6	87.4	40.9
Middle	20.2	79.8	31.9
Lower	31.6	68.4	27.2
Total	20.2	79.8	100%

In cases where pupils remained silent for the whole observation unit (not shown here in tabular form) we again found that the tendency to remain silent varied significantly with ability in Irish - pupils who were of 'lower' ability-in-Irish stayed silent for the whole unit in 23.6% of cases whereas pupils who were of 'higher' ability-in-Irish stayed silent for the whole unit in only 8.2% of cases (chi square = 24.2, df=2, p < .01).

Ability in Irish and 'Attentiveness'
Table 9.10 shows that low levels of 'Attentiveness' to the lesson are relatively uncommon, occurring in just 15.4% of all behaviours where pupils are silent. It also shows the distribution of different levels of 'Attentiveness' during silent periods according to *Pupil ability in Irish*. It can be seen that in more than three-fifths of those cases (62.5%) where 'high' ability-in-Irish' pupils are silent, a high level of attentiveness to the Irish lesson is exhibited. During similar silent periods involving 'low' ability-in-Irish' pupils, however, a high level of attentiveness is exhibited in only a quarter of the cases (25.8%). A chi-

square analysis based on all silent behaviours confirms that there is a significant difference in the distribution of attention levels across levels of ability in Irish (chi square=14.8; df=4; p<.01).

When we limit our analysis to instances where pupils were silent for the whole observation unit the same pattern emerges i.e. higher levels of attentiveness among the 'higher' ability-in-Irish pupils (chi square = 6.75; df=2; p <.05). In other words, whether we look at all silent behaviours, or just those silent behaviours which last for the whole 3 minute observation unit, higher levels of attentiveness to the lesson are characteristic of pupils with higher levels of ability in Irish.

Table 9.10
Levels of attentiveness associated with *Silent* behaviour as a function of *Pupil ability in Irish*.

Pupil ability in Irish	*Percentage of behaviours*			
	High attentiveness (n=62)	*Moderate attentiveness (n=70)*	*Low attentiveness (n=24)*	*Total (n=156)*
Higher	62.5	27.5	10.0	25.6
Middle	40.0	48.0	12.0	32.1
Lower	25.8	53.0	21.2	42.3
Total	39.7	44.9	15.4	100%

Ability in Irish and 'Disruptiveness'
We also examined data on levels of 'Disruptiveness' ('high', 'moderate', 'low') during silent periods among pupils with different abilities in Irish (data not shown here). Overall, a 'low' level of disruptiveness is the norm - 89.1% of all silent behaviours are associated with a low level of disruptiveness. However, among the relatively small group (10.9%) who are disruptive to some degree ('high'/'moderate'), there is a significant variation in frequency of disruptiveness between pupils of different levels of ability in Irish. In order to carry out a chi-square analysis on this data, levels of disruptiveness had to be combined because of the low observed frequencies in 'high' and 'moderate' disruptiveness cells. When this was done, expected frequencies in all but one of the six cells (3 x 2) were greater than 5 (chi square=6.94; df = 2; p < .03). The test confirms that pupils with lower levels of ability in Irish are disproportionately represented at the 'high'/'moderate' disruptiveness categories.

Gender, 'Attentiveness' and 'Disruptiveness'

The proportion of silent versus 'non-silent' behaviours did not differ significantly (chi square = 1.64; df=1; NS) for boys and girls (data not presented in tabular form). We also examined levels of attentiveness during silent periods in relation to *Gender* and this time we did find a difference. Data in Table 9.11 show a tendency for a 'high' level of attentiveness during silent periods to be associated with girls rather than with boys. Of those cases where girls remained silent, 43.9% were assigned 'high' attentiveness ratings by observers, compared to only 17% for boys. Similarly, only 8.8% of girls' silent behaviours were given 'low' attentiveness ratings as opposed to 32.1% for boys (chi square=13.95; df=2; p<.01). The possibility that the gender-related difference in attentiveness ratings might be explained in terms of differences in ability in Irish can probably be discounted since, as we reported earlier, no significant relationship between *Gender* and *Pupil ability in Irish* was found in the present study.

The significant gender-related differences, however, are confined to attentiveness ratings: no significant variation in the levels of disruptiveness were recorded for boys and girls.

Table 9.11
Levels of attentiveness during *Silent* behaviour as a function of pupil *Gender*.

Gender		*High attentiveness* n=34	*Moderate attentiveness* n=54	*Low attentiveness* n=22	*Total* n=110
		Percentage of behaviours			
Boys	(n=53)	17.0	50.9	32.1	48.2
Girls	(n=57)	43.9	47.4	8.8	51.8
Total		30.9	49.1	20.0	100%

9.3.4 'Other' pupil behaviours

We also examined the distribution of various categories of *Other pupil behaviour* - 'Choral speech', 'reading aloud' 'silent reading' and 'Writing' - according to *Pupil ability in Irish* (data not show in tabular form). In each case we carried out a chi-square analysis to establish whether the particular behaviours were distributed differently across ability levels in Irish. None of the chi-square tests produced a significant result.

This is not really surprising in the case of at least some of these behaviours since they do not allow the same scope for individual pupil variation that behaviours classified as

Silent or *Pupil speaks individually* do. For example, 'Choral speech' being a class level activity tends to include all pupils - unless individuals are prepared to resist involvement rather obviously. Similarly, since 'Writing' normally involves pupils working individually on equivalent tasks, non-engagement would soon become apparent to the teacher and would presumably provoke some sanction. In both these cases, it is difficult to see how *Pupil ability in Irish* could be related to the frequency of occurrence of the behaviour in question.

Variation in the frequency with which pupils read aloud might seem to be a more likely possibility in relation to ability in Irish. The fact that no such relationship was detected here, however, may suggest that all pupils are considered capable of this activity and so, in general, are often nominated to perform in some arbitrary fashion (e.g. simply next-in-line etc.). Incidentally, it may appear inconsistent initially that only 5.9% of all pupil behaviours consist of 'reading aloud' (Table 9.4), given that *ILAS* data presented in Chapter 8 (Table 8.1) showed that 'reading aloud' occurred in 18.2% of segments. The difference is due in part to the fact that in the case of *ILAS* 'reading aloud' was counted as a behaviour as long as pupils were in a state of readiness to read aloud - though at any one time only one pupil might be reading aloud. In contrast, in the case of the *PCBR* data currently under discussion, 'reading aloud' would count as a behaviour only if the target pupil was actually the one reading at the time the observation was made.

9.3.5 Class/teaching characteristics and pupil behaviour

Up to this point, we have concentrated on the relationship between pupil language/ communication behaviours (such as *Pupil speaks individually* or *Silence*) and individual pupil characteristics (such as *Pupil ability in Irish* and *Gender*). In this section, we explore the possibility of a relationship between these same pupil behaviours and certain characteristics of either the classes in which the pupils are taught or the teaching approaches used. For example, are pupils in large classes more likely to remain silent than those in small classes? Are pupils in those classes which spend a greater proportion of the Irish lesson on 'Real communication in Irish' more likely to speak individually than those in other classes? To answer these and similar questions, we first need to develop class-level measures of the various behavioural propensities e.g. 'Propensity to speak individually', 'Propensity to remain silent' and so on. We can then establish the strength of any statistical association between class behavioural propensities and characteristics of classes or teaching.

Pupil behavioural propensities
In order to reflect the extent to which pupils generally in each class have a relatively greater or lesser propensity to manifest each behaviour, we aggregate individual behavioural data to the class level. It must be appreciated that since we have observations for only three pupils per class, our behavioural propensity measures have a very narrow base in each class. The first step in the process is to obtain a single score in each of the behavioural categories we intend to examine (e.g. *Pupil speaks individually*) for each of

the three pupils observed in each class. This is done by totalling for each pupil all recorded instances of a particular behaviour during *both* observed lessons, and then expressing this number as a percentage of the total number of behaviours recorded for that pupil. The mean of the resulting three pupil-scores is taken as the class score for that particular behavioural propensity. The latter averaging process is necessary in order to balance the contribution of pupils of high-, middle- and low-ability in Irish within each class to each behavioural propensity score.

Four class behavioural propensity measures were developed:

1. *Propensity to speak individually* in the Irish class (including *Complex*).
2. *Propensity to make a 'sustained' spoken contribution* in the Irish class. (While we had found that the frequency of 'sustained' utterances was not related to *Pupil ability in Irish*, it is plausible to expect that in highly structured classes such a propensity may be related to class level factors such as teaching method and language activity).
3. *Propensity to be engaged in 'Other' behaviours* (such as 'Choral speech', 'Reading' or 'Writing'). This refers to *Other only*, excluding *Complex*.
4. *Propensity to remain silent* in the Irish class.

Class characteristics

Because of the exploratory nature of this part of the analysis, only a small number of variables from the full range for which we have measures, will be considered. Eight class measures ('characteristics') in all are used:

1. *Class achievement in spoken Irish* (Mean percentage of pupils in each class attaining mastery of each of 16 objectives on the ITÉ test - see Chapter 2).
2. *Size of sixth-grade group in the class.*
3. *Total class size* (Total number of pupils in teaching group).
4. *Proportion of class time spent on 'Drills'* (*Language activity* category in *ILAS*).
5. *Proportion of class time spent on 'Contextualisation exercises'* (*ILAS*).
6. *Proportion of class time spent on 'Transposition'* (*ILAS*).
7. *Proportion of class time spent on 'Simulated communication in Irish'* (*ILAS*).
8. *Proportion of class time spent on 'Real communication in Irish'* (*ILAS*).

The first 'class characteristic' variable *Class achievement in spoken Irish* is the same as that used to rank each of the twenty classes in terms of achievement in Irish in previous chapters. The next two variables, *Size of sixth grade in class* and *Total class size*, are included because a national survey (Harris, 1983) indicated that the number of pupils in sixth grade within a particular class was a significant predictor of achievement in spoken Irish: small teaching groups tend to have significantly higher achievement in Irish.

The remaining five 'class characteristic' variables (no.'s 4-8) relate to the teaching of Irish. They consist of the proportion of class time spent on the five most common *ILAS* language activities (see Chapter 7: section 7.2.3). Many other dimensions of *ILAS*, such as *Topic, Materials* or *Classroom organisation* could also have been studied.

Between-class variations in behavioural propensities

Table 9.12 shows the Pearson correlation coefficients between the eight class-characteristics variables and the four behavioural propensity measures. The correlation coefficient in each cell is based on 20 pairs of data points corresponding to the 20 classes in the study. We will begin with the first three class-characteristic variables listed above.

Table 9.12
Pearson correlations between four class behavioural propensities and eight class characteristics

	-------------- *Pupil propensity to $^{\phi}$... --------*			
		make a	*be*	
	speak	*'sustained'*	*engaged in*	*remain*
	individually	*spoken*	*'Other'*	*silent*
Class characteristics n (classes)=20		*contribution*	*behaviours*	
Class achievement in spoken Irish	.53**	.53**	-.42*	-.33
Size of sixth grade group in class	-.64**	-.27	.51**	.39*
Total class size	-.55**	-.23	.28	.53**
ILAS measures				
Proportion of class time spent on:				
'Contextualisation exercises'	-.55**	-.41*	.57**	.20
'Drills'	-.06	-.27	-.10	.20
'Transposition'	-.46*	-.24	.32	.34
'Real communication in Irish'	.25	.34	-.16	-.20
'Simulated communication in Irish'	.63**	.51**	-.60**	-.28

$^{\phi}$ See text for explanation. * p < .05. ** p < .01.

Class achievement in spoken Irish is significantly correlated with three behavioural propensities: (i) 'Pupil propensity to speak individually', (ii) 'Pupil propensity to make a sustained contribution', and (iii) 'Pupil propensity to be engaged in 'other' behaviours'. Classes with higher levels of achievement in spoken Irish tend to have pupils who speak individually in the Irish class more often (r=.53), and produce 'sustained' utterances more often (r =.53), than classes with lower levels of achievement in spoken Irish. These same classes with higher levels of achievement in spoken Irish are significantly less likely (r=-.42) to be engaged in *Other* behaviours (such as 'Choral speech', 'Reading' and 'Writing') compared to classes with lower levels of achievement.

We turn next to the relationship between the two class size variables - *Size of sixth-grade group in class* and *Total class size* - and the various behavioural propensities. Correlations in Table 9.12 (rows 1 and 2) show that as classes (or sixth-grade groups within multigrade classes) become larger, there is a significant tendency for pupils to make fewer individual spoken contributions (r =-.64 and -.55) and to more often remain silent (r=.39 and .53). Larger sixth-grade groups within classes are also associated with a greater propensity for pupils to be engaged in 'Other' behaviours ('Choral speech', 'Reading' or 'Writing') (r=.51).

We now look at the relationship between the various behavioural propensities and the class characteristic measures consisting of the proportion of class time spent on the five most common *ILAS Language activity* categories. First, it may be noted that *Propensity to remain silent* is not significantly correlated with any of the five teaching variables. For the sake of clarity, it will be useful to first state the results regarding the remaining three behavioural propensities in very general terms. It should be emphasised in advance that only some of these results on which the generalisation is based are statistically significant. The correlations indicate that the three forms of language practice ('Contextualisation exercises', 'Drill' and 'Transposition') tend to be associated with a reduced propensity to speak individually, a reduced propensity to make a sustained spoken contribution and an increased propensity to engage in 'Other' behaviours. The two forms of communicative *Language activity* ('Simulated communication in Irish' and 'Real communication in Irish'), in contrast, tend to be associated with an increased propensity to speak individually, an increased propensity to make sustained spoken contributions and a decreased propensity to be engaged in 'Other' behaviours.

All seven statistically significant correlations in this group are consistent with the general statement above which indicates contrasting behavioural propensities for language-practice type activities and communicative activities. In the case of 'Real communication in Irish' and 'Drills', however, none of the correlations with the behavioural propensity measures are significant. The language-practice/communicative contrast is most clearly illustrated by 'Simulated communication in Irish' and 'Contextualisation exercises'. The correlations show that as classes spend more time on 'Simulated communication in Irish', there is a significant tendency for pupils to speak individually more often (r =.63) and to make sustained contributions more often (r =.51), but to engage in 'Other' behaviours ('Choral speech', 'Reading' and 'Writing') less often (r = -.60). In contrast, as classes spend more time on 'Contextualisation exercises', pupils are significantly less likely to speak individually (r =-.55) or to make sustained contributions (r =-.41) and significantly more likely to engage in 'Other' pupil behaviours (r =.57). More time spent on 'Transposition' - a form of language practice - is also associated with classes in which pupils are significantly less likely to speak individually (r = -.46).

In passing, it should be noted that even though 'Contextualisation exercises' (a form of language-practice) correlates positively with *Other* behaviours in the present study, this does not necessarily mean that *Other* behaviours always involve language practice. Writing, for example, may be communicative and may involve meaning negotiation. But we cannot say anything directly about the communicative character of the various components of *Other* behaviour here because we did not analyse written/reading material from a 'meaning negotiation' point of view. More importantly, we cannot say how important a role such activities may play in determining the standard of Irish which is currently achieved.

We also looked at the relationship between, on the one hand, *Class attitude to Irish* and *Class Irish-lesson anxiety* and, on the other, the behavioural propensities (data not in tabular form). Significant correlations were found only in the case of *Class Irish-lesson anxiety*: the higher the levels of anxiety during the Irish lesson, the less likely pupils were either to speak individually (r=-.54) or to produce sustained utterances (r=-.53) and the more likely they were to remain silent (r=.44).

9.4 Discussion

The *PCBR* has proved to be an effective instrument for revealing the pattern of pupils' involvement in the Irish lesson and the manner in which different kinds of behaviour are related to factors such as gender and ability in Irish. We have also succeeded in documenting some of the interactive characteristics of pupils' spoken contributions and in estimating the level of attentiveness and disruptiveness which different kinds of pupils exhibit during periods when they are silent. And finally we have been able to identify a number of connections between certain class characteristics (e.g. class size, language-teaching activities) and various aspects of pupil behaviour in the Irish class (the tendency for pupils to make sustained spoken contributions, to remain silent and so on.)

Before considering some of the broader implications of our findings it is important to recall two limitations of our approach. First, as in other studies of this kind, we have no way of quantifying how representative of conditions in Irish classrooms generally are the events (e.g. pupil behaviours or language teaching activities) which we observed in these particular classrooms on these particular days. The fact that we set out to demonstrate relationships between such transient events and more enduring characteristics of pupils and classes (such as gender or class size) implies a claim, of course, that the events in question are reasonably typical and that the relationships revealed are stable.

Second, the tests of statistical significance which we report have sometimes been applied to sets of data which are not always independent, specifically in those cases where we study different aspects of fundamentally the same set of behaviours. Thus, for example, we examine how frequently pupils of different ability levels remain silent in class and in a different context we compare the level of attentiveness of these same groups of pupils during the same periods of silence. In arriving at conclusions, we try to minimise these shortcomings by looking for converging evidence and consistency in the pattern of results over different kinds of data. The fact that we have such a wide range of data available to us in the present study provides considerable protection against biased interpretations.

9.4.1 Main findings

One of the more important findings of the study is that about half of all behaviours recorded during the three minute observation period consisted of the pupil speaking individually - and in Irish in 91% of the cases. This finding is of interest in the light both of the focus in the primary school curriculum on developing competence in speaking the language, and the fact that the Irish class in ordinary schools is the main, and sometimes the only situation where we can be absolutely sure that the majority of pupils actually use the language. This is not to disregard the fact either that Irish is often used to a limited extent for routine communication in ordinary schools (Harris, 1984; INTO, 1985a) or that a small minority of parents use Irish at home. The finding is also important to the extent that many teachers and parents would probably consider a high rate of individual spoken contributions by pupils as evidence of the general vitality and success of the Irish lesson.

Any satisfaction we might feel at the fact that pupils speak individually so frequently during the Irish lesson must be tempered, however, by three other findings of the study (1) that pupil speech is not produced very often in the context of real communication or of meaning negotiation (2) that the frequency of individual speech is not at all evenly distributed over different kinds of pupils in the classroom and (3) that those with lower levels of ability in Irish who remain silent are less attentive to the lesson than those with higher levels of ability in Irish who remain silent. We will now look at each of these issues in more detail.

Regarding the first point, it may be noted that individual pupil speech most frequently took the form of answers (82.7% of all utterances) and these were in general short, predictable responses to 'display' questions from the teacher, something which is characteristic of language practice rather than real communication or meaning negotiation. This figure is not very different to that reported by Politzer, Ramirez and Lewis (1981) where 90 % of all student moves were found to be responses. Indeed, if we were to add in those instances of 'Choral speech' which were answers in the present study, the results might well be closer still.

A substantial proportion of the utterances of our pupils were very short, something which must raise doubts about the effectiveness, as language practice, of this kind of language use. Only 13.4% of pupil utterances were sustained beyond the single-sentence level and 18.7% consisted of just single words. While the remaining 67.9% of utterances consisted of clauses or whole sentences, even this may give a somewhat misleading impression of the linguistic sophistication of pupils' responses. This is because of the pedagogic practice in Irish-language classrooms, as in classrooms generally, of requiring pupils to incorporate part of the teacher's question or prompt into their answers in order to make a complete sentence. On the positive side, it must be acknowledged that the number of sustained utterances which were recorded in this study probably does not represent a particularly low proportion for a non-immersion classroom - it certainly compares very favourably with a study of French *immersion* classrooms where less than 15% of student turns were coded as sustained (Allen, *et al.*, 1988). Answers consisting of sustained pupil utterances in the present study, incidentally, were much more likely to be coded as 'unpredictable' (i.e. occurring in the context of meaning-negotiation) than were shorter answers consisting of a single word, a clause or a sentence. In other words, longer utterances in Irish are more likely than shorter ones to be communicative in character.

The second aspect of the high frequency of individual pupil speech in Irish which is undesirable is that its occurrence varies substantially, and to a statistically significant degree, according to the ability of the individual pupil in Irish. For example, only 36.3% of the behaviours of pupils who have lower levels of ability in Irish involve individual speech, compared to 61.6% of the behaviours of pupils with higher ability in Irish. If frequent individual speech really is conducive to an improvement in the pupil's command of Irish, then it seems as if those most in need, pupils with lower levels of ability in the language, are the ones least likely to be engaged in it.

What are pupils with lower ability in Irish doing while those with a better command of the language are engaging in individual speech interactions? There are two indications, one indirect, the other direct, that they are listening/looking rather than engaging in some other language-learning task more in tune with their particular level of ability in Irish. First, we know from observation data derived from *ILAS* that the most common form of classroom organisation during the Irish lesson is 'whole class' and that the most common teacher mode of involvement with pupils is 'interacting' (see Chapter 8). Thus, on the basis of this information alone, it is unlikely that pupils with lower levels of ability in Irish will be engaged in different individual tasks (e.g. involving silent reading or writing) or working in pairs or groups on language or communication tasks. In fact, regarding this last point, it may be noted that only 12.9% of individual speech behaviours (and only 6.4% of all behaviours) involve pupil-pupil exchanges. The second kind of evidence that those with lower levels of ability are listening/looking while the more able pupils make individual spoken contributions is the finding that those who have lower ability in Irish are more than twice as likely to be silent as pupils who have higher ability in Irish, and this difference is statistically significant.

This brings us to the third issue - that the silence of 'lower-ability-in-Irish' pupils is not the same as the silence of 'higher-ability-in-Irish' pupils. Pupils with higher levels of ability in Irish are much more likely than pupils with lower levels of ability in Irish to be rated as 'highly attentive' during these periods of silence. Likewise, low levels of attention are more common in pupils with lower levels of ability in Irish. While boys and girls are equally likely to be silent, girls are significantly more attentive during these silent periods. It may be recalled from Chapter 3 (section 3.3.3) that girls also had significantly more positive *Irish attitude/motivation* than boys.

Notwithstanding all this, it must be noted that low levels of attentiveness (15.4%) and high/moderate levels of disruptiveness (10.9%) during silent periods are relatively uncommon. This is broadly consistent with the 'whole-class' attention data derived from the *ILAS* (see Chapter 8). Finally, it is clear from the data here that pupils are not indifferent about issues of speech and silence in the Irish class. We found, for example, that classes in which pupils are less likely to speak also have significantly higher levels of *Irish-lesson anxiety*. Higher anxiety is also associated with a significantly lower propensity to make sustained contributions in class and a significantly greater propensity to remain silent.

9.4.2 *Explaining differential pupil participation in the Irish class*

Before outlining possible ways to change this situation, assuming that change is feasible, it will be useful to consider briefly some of the factors which may lie behind the emphasis on individual speech in the Irish lesson and the uneven participation by pupils.   This exploration is necessarily speculative since we have no information from teachers about the strategies they may have been pursuing, or even whether they were aware of the variation in participation which we discovered.   Nevertheless, we hope that our observations may at least serve as working hypotheses which might be tested in future studies.

Listening to the tape recordings of the lessons made by the observers and examining the transcripts of these (see Appendix 6.4), the impression is compelling that an important secondary goal of teachers in so frequently soliciting individual spoken contributions from pupils may simply be to maintain attention to the lesson more generally. In other words, the actual language practice provided by these exchanges is only part of the desired result - equally important is generating a high level of expectation among pupils that they will be nominated to speak.   The brevity of the exchanges which are typical of the Irish lesson means that individual pupils can be required to speak at just about any time.   In this situation, it may not matter too much that the content of display questions do not always engender a high level of interest *per se* among pupils, since their attention is guaranteed by the high likelihood of having to 'perform'.

The problem for pupils who are weaker at Irish is that, for whatever reason, they seem to have a much lower probability of either being asked to perform or of volunteering to perform. Without the same motivation of imminent public performance which more able pupils have, lower ability pupils are probably more dependent on the intrinsic interest of the lesson material to keep them engaged - an interest which may not be high when 'display' type questions predominate. Admittedly, there is a possibility that some instances of 'silence' on the pupil's part may consist of an inability to respond (orally) to a question or prompt from the teacher, rather than from non-involvement, disinterest or actual resistance. Since we only observed and recorded the pupil's behaviour and speech, and not the teacher's, we have no way of identifying which instances of silence represent an inability to respond. The evidence we have presented that lower-ability-in-Irish pupils are not as attentive as higher-ability pupils during periods of silence, however, seems to undermine the notion that inability alone could be sufficient general explanation for the observed differences in speech and silence.

Another perplexing issue is whether it is teachers or pupils who ultimately determine how often pupils speak. Are teachers the more important in this respect in that it is they who nominate the pupils to speak?   Or is it the pupils who play the larger part by volunteering to answer? As mentioned earlier, the evidence in the international literature concerning the relationship between pupil participation and second-language development is conflicting (Seliger 1977; Naiman *et al.*, 1978; Strong, 1983, 1984; Day, 1984; Ely,

1986). Ellis (1994), reviewing these studies alongside others relating to the effect of quantity of practice on specific grammatical structures believes that, on balance, the interpretation that 'proficiency causes participation' is more plausible.

Even if Ellis is correct - and the correlational evidence is ambiguous - this does not mean either that teachers of Irish routinely leave it up to weaker pupils to decide on their own level of participation in class, or that lower levels of participation by weaker pupils are due to any lack of effort on the teacher's part. It is plausible to think that in making decisions about which pupil to nominate to speak, teachers are trying to achieve an optimum balance between a range of concerns - e.g. not slowing the class down too much; ensuring that there is a high proportion of successful (correct) public exchanges in Irish in order to provide a good language model for pupils in general, and so on. Teachers may also be trying to take account, for example, of the discomfort for weaker pupils of being nominated to speak in situations where there is a high probability that their answer, or failure to answer, will expose them to embarrassment. Teachers may feel that certain weaker pupils will do better at Irish in such circumstances by listening to the (linguistically correct) public exchanges involving the more able pupils. Again, it must be borne in mind that these are only speculations and that much more wide-ranging research would be needed to establish the connections between pupil behaviour and teachers' strategies.

Issues of pupil participation are not unique either to the Irish class or to schools in Ireland and indeed such issues have always concerned educationalists. Good (1981), for example, claimed that low-achievers develop a strategy of remaining passive in class over time - not responding when called, not volunteering, asking fewer questions and approaching the teacher less often. Subsequent research by Good, Slavings, Hobson Harel and Emerson (1987) appears to support the 'passivity model'. In the study, the questioning behaviour of pupils from kindergarten, Grades 1, 3, 6, 7, 9 and 12, during mathematics and language arts classes was observed. While the mean number of questions per observation period was fairly constant across grade levels, low-achievers in upper grades asked fewer questions than low-achievers in lower grades. In fact, low-achievers in kindergarten tend to ask more questions than their peers. While low-achieving pupils continued to be active participants up to third grade, they had become relatively passive by sixth grade. Good *et al.* (1987: 94) suggest that 'the ways in which low-achieving students present themselves - by asking frequent questions - may inadvertently lead to teacher and peer feedback that, in subtle ways, undermines the initiative of these students over time'. Gipps (1994: 31) also illustrates how low-achieving pupils, feeling threatened or anxious to please the teacher, may 'attempt to avoid being picked on to answer questions, or to get the teacher to give as many clues as possible until the 'correct' answer is framed for them'. It scarcely needs to be said that we have no way of knowing whether these specific phenomena observed in British and American schools are also characteristic of Irish schools or of the teaching of Irish. At the very least, however, these studies suggest that the issues of pupil participation and language use which we have identified in the case of Irish may also occur, to a greater or lesser extent, in the case of other subjects in Irish schools.

9.4.3 *Control, turn-taking and wait time.*

Are there changes which could be made to the existing teacher-focused, whole-class approach which might improve pupil participation and communicative language use? The research literature has identified two promising factors (a) ceding more control to pupils, particularly in relation to turn-taking and (b) increasing wait-time for responses. In relation to the first of these, McHoul (1978) points out that in order to cope with potential transition and distribution problems, most classroom discourse tends to be organised so that there is a strict allocation of turns, with tight control being exercised over who speaks to whom. As a result, there is relatively little turn-by-turn negotiation, and competition and individual student initiatives are discouraged. In this kind of situation, as Van Lier (1988) points out, learners have no need to attend carefully to classroom talk (as they would in ordinary conversations in order to identify those potential transition points when they might take their turn). In other words, a significant source of intrinsic motivation is lost.

In classrooms where this kind of control is relaxed, the consequence can be seen in the content of interactions, the frequency of pupil initiatives and the general levels of engagement. Cathcart (1986) studied the different kinds of communicative acts performed by Spanish speaking children in a variety of school settings (recess, seatwork, free play, ESL instruction, playhouse, interview and story telling) and found that situations where the learner had control of the talk were characterized by a wide variety of communicative acts and syntactic structures. Where the teacher had control, pupils were more likely to produce single-word utterances, short phrases and formulaic chunks. Consistent with this, studies by Midorikawa (1990) and Robson (1992) indicate that when learners are given the opportunity to ask questions, they automatically elect to use open referential-type questions. Allen, *et al.* (1988) show that in immersion classrooms also, extended talk is more likely to occur when students initiate an interaction and have to 'find their own words'. They suggest that teachers provide more opportunities for student-initiated talk and for asking more open-ended questions. Other positive effects of allowing more control to pass to pupils are documented in the present study (Chapter 8: section 8.3.2) where we found that *Class attention* and *Class interest* was higher, and *Irish-lesson anxiety* was lower, during lesson segments in which a 'Pupil/group demonstration' form of classroom organisation was used.

Such changes are likely to benefit all pupils, not just those who have difficulty with Irish. Traditional classroom learning conditions also have limitations for pupils with higher levels of ability in Irish. Results of the present study, for example, suggest that pupils' contributions in class can often be so strongly governed by the form of the teacher's questions or prompts, that the higher level of ability in Irish which many of them possess is not reflected in the content of their utterances. For example, despite the strong association between ability in Irish and frequency of individual pupil speech found here, no association was detected between ability and length of utterance. While acknowledging that it is always problematical to try to assign a 'positive' interpretation to the acceptance of the null hypothesis, a strong expectation of a difference does seem reasonable in this case i.e. other things being equal, more able pupils should be expected to produce more sustained utterances than less able ones. If what we are suggesting is actually true, then existing lesson structures not only produce a certain kind of frustration in more able pupils, but the more extended and enriched linguistic input which such pupils might be expected to produce is denied to all pupils.

Another significant factor determining participation is 'wait time'. In a study of ESL secondary-school classrooms, White and Lightbown (1984) found that teachers rarely gave enough time for students to formulate answers before repeating, rephrasing or redirecting the question to another student. The shorter the wait time, the fewer and the shorter the student responses. They found some teachers asking up to four questions per minute, with overall about 40% of the questions receiving no response and up to 64% being repetitions of previous questions (as many as nine repetitions of the same question). They claim that the success rate of students responding to subsequent repetitions of questions was quite low, lower often than the rate of response to questions asked only once. Of course, this may simply mean that easy questions are answered quickly, without being redirected, while the redirected difficult questions continue to pose problems for students.

We already noted in Chapter 3 (section 3.4.2) the possibility that a longer wait-time might reduce pupils' anxiety and increase their self-confidence by giving them time to think about the question and formulate their response (Tsui 1996; Long, Brock, Crookes, Deicke, Potter and Zhang, 1984). A greater wait-time can also result in longer pupil utterances, and an increase in the participation of less able pupils (Holley and King, 1971; Long *et al.*, 1984; White and Lightbown, 1984). Holley and King (1971) propose at least a five-second wait time and report that teachers in third-level German classes who waited that long obtained an increase in responses following initial hesitations. Gipps (1994: 30) urges teachers to use strategies which 'allow *maximum levels of sustained interaction* (author's emphasis) with all pupils' giving them more time, but also 'offering speculations, hypotheses and conjectures' which 'stimulates more talk, questions and ideas from the pupils and generates discussion between them'.

While acknowledging the good sense of all this, it must be admitted that there are probably limits to the extent to which participation can be improved within existing classroom structures. Increasing wait time may help less able pupils but it may also pose new problems of lesson dynamics in a situation where the engagement of pupils is still fundamentally maintained by the pace of the ('display') question-and-answer exchanges, rather than by the inherent challenge or interest offered by the lesson material itself. Thus more basic changes may be needed.

9.4.4 A greater emphasis on communication

We have described in previous chapters some of the circumstances which are linked to low levels of achievement in Irish and poor attitudes to Irish: a feeling among many pupils that they do not have the active support of their parents in the task of learning the language, a poor self-image regarding their own ability to learn Irish, difficulties in understanding the lesson or the teacher, and feelings of apathy, discouragement and even anxiety about learning the language in school. Clearly, any initiatives which ameliorate these difficulties also have the potential to improve pupil participation in class. In this concluding section, however, we consider specifically how a communicative emphasis in language teaching could enhance pupil participation and language use. First, we discuss the *PCBR* data which show that pupil participation and language use are better in those classes which have certain characteristics such as smaller numbers of pupils and, more importantly in the present context, a greater emphasis on communicative activities. Second, based in part on the *Communicative Materials Project*, we examine the benefits of adopting a more developed communicative approach to teaching Irish, one which would take greater account of research on the link between certain types of classroom interaction and successful learning.

Class size, communicative teaching and pupil participation: PCBR data
The *PCBR* data present a coherent picture of the relationship between class characteristics (such as class size and teaching activities) and various pupil behavioural propensities. For example, we found that as sixth-grade classes (or sixth-grade groups within multi-grade classes) become smaller, pupils are significantly more likely to engage in individual speech and less likely to remain silent. This result is consistent with the commonsense notion that any one pupil in a small class group is more likely to have an opportunity to speak than in a large class, assuming that teachers have a roughly constant rate at which they nominate pupils to speak. It has to be acknowledged, nevertheless, that the whole issue of class size is extremely complex and remains fundamentally unresolved in the research literature. One thing on which there is agreement, however, is that the nature of pupil-teacher interaction may be as important as group size as such (Galton, Simon and Croll, 1980; Kumar, 1992). Galton *et al.* (1980), for example, found that while each individual pupil received less attention in larger classes, the effect was not strong. This was because teachers tended to compensate for large class sizes by spending a greater proportion of time interacting with pupils as individuals or in small groups. We return to this general issue of the size of the teaching group in the context of the discussion of small-group work below.

PCBR data also show that the kind of teaching activity engaged in affects pupil participation. As classes spend more time on 'Simulated communication in Irish', for example, there is a significant tendency for pupils to speak individually more frequently and to make sustained contributions more often (correspondingly, they engage less often in 'other' behaviours such as choral speech, reading and writing). In contrast, as classes spend more time on 'Contextualisation exercises', a form of language practice, pupils are significantly less likely either to speak individually or to make sustained contributions (and significantly more likely to engage in 'other' behaviours).

While the picture is coherent, it is not unambiguous in every respect. One of the difficulties, as with virtually all correlational studies, is partial correlation. The problem applies particularly here in the case of those correlations involving *Class achievement in spoken Irish*. For example, we know from previous studies (Harris, 1983) that higher levels of *Class achievement in spoken Irish* are significantly more likely in smaller sixth-grade classes or teaching groups than they are in larger classes and groups. We also know from Chapter 7 that this same variable, *Class achievement in spoken Irish*, is positively correlated with the proportion of class time spent on 'Simulated communication in Irish'. The critical complication is that higher *Class achievement in spoken Irish* is also significantly associated with higher *Propensity to speak individually* (a class-level effect which mirrors the relationship between *Pupil ability in Irish* and *Pupil speaks individually* at the pupil level). Thus, it may be the higher achievement in Irish, rather than the small numbers in class or the emphasis on 'Simulated communication in Irish', which produces the better individual pupil-participation results. In other words, it is not possible to conclusively link particular pupil behavioural propensities either to class size or to language teaching activities - *Class achievement in spoken Irish* is always a potential alternative explanation for the differences observed.

There are two aspects to the *PCBR* results, however, which are not undermined by problems of partial correlation and which do suggest a real link between language teaching activities and particular kinds of pupil participation and language use. First, there is the difference between 'Real' and 'Simulated' communication in Irish as far as connections with behavioural propensities are concerned. The results show that an emphasis on 'Simulated communication in Irish', but not an emphasis on 'Real communication in Irish', is associated with more individual pupil speech, more sustained utterances and fewer 'Other' pupil behaviours. Since both 'Real' and 'Simulated' activities are communicative, and since both are positively correlated with *Class achievement in spoken Irish*, their different relationships with the various pupil behavioural propensities cannot be explained on the basis of the kind of partial correlation problem mentioned above.

We can explain these divergences, however, by looking more closely at the differences between 'Real' and 'Simulated' communication activities. It may be recalled from the *ILAS* data presented in Chapter 7 that a substantial proportion of 'Real communication in Irish' activities concern classroom management topics and involve short one-sided directions from the teacher - little or no individual pupil response is required. Such classroom management topics never involve 'Simulated communication in Irish'. Thus, the differential connections between 'Real' and 'Simulated' communication and the various behavioural propensities identified here are consistent with specific characteristics of each type of language activity as identified in Chapter 7.

Second, it will be recalled that the analyses of individual pupil behaviour described in the earlier part of the Results section showed that the production of sustained utterances is *not* related to pupil ability in Irish. In the latter analyses, 'class' factors were effectively eliminated because we aggregated differences between 'high', 'middle' and 'low' ability-in-Irish pupils over all classes. When we allow 'class' factors to enter, as we do when we correlate *Class achievement in spoken Irish* and *Propensity to make a sustained spoken contribution*, we do find a significant association. Note also that *Propensity to make a sustained spoken contribution* is significantly and positively correlated with the proportion of class time spent on 'Simulated communication in Irish' but negatively correlated with the proportion of time spent on 'Contextualisation exercises'. Taken together, these findings suggest that the frequency of sustained utterances is more sensitive to the language activity involved (and perhaps to other class-level factors) than it is to individual factors such as pupil ability in Irish. These results also suggest, of course, that it would be worthwhile at some future date to examine the contribution of the other *ILAS* dimensions of language teaching studied here - such as topic, learning materials and classroom organisation to pupil participation and language use.

A more developed communicative approach to teaching Irish
The link which we have established in the *PCBR* data between communicative teaching activities and improvements in pupil participation and language use applies, of course, to the kind of primary-school Irish programme which we examined in the *Twenty-Classes Study*. That is a programme in which an explicitly communicative approach - in the sense that that term is now understood - has yet to be implemented. If the beneficial effects of communicative teaching activities on participation and language use are to be fully realised, therefore, the new curriculum will have to promote a more developed version of communicative teaching than exists at present. This version should incorporate a greater number of those features which research and practice have now identified as conducive to successful learning: use of authentic materials, tasks involving meaning negotiation, small-group work, communication repair and learner feedback. To illustrate how some of these factors might affect pupil participation and communicative language use, we will examine two of them in more detail: small-group work and tasks involving meaning negotiation.

Long and Porter (1985) summarize the main pedagogic arguments in favour of group work - it increases language-practice opportunities, it improves the quality of student talk, it helps to individualise instruction, it promotes a positive affective climate and it motivates learners to learn. In particular, this more private and negotiable context of language use should reduce some of the social risk for less able pupils who wish to make use of whatever Irish they have. There is evidence too that small-group work provides more opportunities for meaning negotiation if the tasks are of the required 'information-exchange' type (Pica and Doughty, 1985; Ellis, 1994). Long, Adams, McLean and Castanos (1976) found that small groups provide more opportunities for language production and a greater variety of language use in initiating discussion, asking for clarification, interrupting, competing for the floor and joking. The quality of interaction appears to be enhanced if the learners comprising the pair/group are heterogeneous with regard to sex and proficiency level. It is also interesting to note Porter's (1986) conclusion that there is very little evidence that learners pick up each others linguistic errors. The need for some caution in relation to group work in some instances, however, is suggested by the work of Wong-Fillmore (1982, 1985).

One of the problems, as we found out both in the *Twenty Classes Study* and in the *Communicative Materials Project*, is that most teachers do not appear to be enthusiastic about group work in teaching Irish. It is possible that many of the perceived organisational and learner problems associated with group work, however, can be overcome by good design and implementation. Lyle (1996) recommends (i) that all children should work on the same task at the same time (ii) that the teacher should have a clear view of the type of learning he/she wants to take place (iii) that the task should be well structured and attention be given to the composition of the group and the groups' previous experiences of each other.   Similarly, Shaw (1996) points out the need for instructions and tasks to be clear and focused, and for learners to be trained in how to behave in group situations e.g. taking responsibility.   Davis (1997) suggests that teachers use a checklist of task components to ensure that the task is being carried out as planned.   Davis also believes that tasks should be given an appropriate time allotment to allow students at different levels to complete their work.   Finally, Sheils (1988) gives some practical advice in relation to seating arrangements, formation of groups and preparation of activities.

Davis (1997) points out that group work is often used as an 'endpoint' in a traditional language practice sequence, serving only as a check to see if learners can display their knowledge of whatever language forms were being studied.   Such display activities are not truly communicative or learner centred.   He argues that in a communicative classroom whose syllabus is organised by tasks, group work is a natural form of organisation and can come at any point in the instructional sequence.

We turn now to the issue of task characteristics and meaning negotiation.   There is evidence that specific characteristics of communicative tasks determine the kind of language use and interaction which occur.   The existence of an information gap between participants is often considered to be critical because it leads to the exchange of information and meaning negotiation.   A number of studies (Long, 1980; Doughty and Pica, 1986; Newton, 1991) show that 'two-way' tasks result in more negotiation than 'one-way' tasks.   An example of a two-way task would be one where each of the participants hold part of the information needed to complete it.   A one-way task might involve giving instructions or telling a personal story.   A second important feature is that the task should involve the learner planning his or her output.   Planned tasks 'stretch' interlanguages further, and promote 'destabilization' more, than unplanned tasks (Long, 1989).   Studies reviewed in Ellis (1994) also suggest that learners produce more complex and more target-like language when they have time to plan their output.   A third significant point is whether the task is 'closed' or 'open'.   A closed task involves participants reaching a single correct or small finite set of solutions - detecting the differences between two pictures or identifying the perpetrator of a crime.   An open task is one where there is no predetermined solution - as in free conversation, debate, ranking activities and suggesting preferred solutions to problems.   Long (1989) concludes that closed tasks produce more negotiation work, and more useful negotiation, than open tasks.   He also argues that closed tasks result in more topic- and language-recycling, more feedback, more feedback-incorporation, more rephrasing and more precision.   But open-ended tasks also have their merits.   Jones (1991) points out that open-ended tasks afford learners greater interactive freedom to practise conversational skills, such as topic selection and change.

In arguing for a greater emphasis on communication in teaching Irish, and one which is better attuned with the findings of classroom research, we are not discounting the importance of an analytic focus or, indeed, of language practice.   As we pointed out in Chapter 6 and in Chapter 7, there is evidence that form-focused and communicative activities are complementary. Van Lier (1988) argues that certain ritualistic language-practice elements of the second-language classroom such as choral work, display questions and repetitions help to provide a secure and supportive environment for children as they gradually develop their second-language skills. This 'scaffolding' process is similar to the way in which young children are supported by caretakers in the development of their first language, through games, rituals etc. Disposing of such routines on the basis that they are not authentic enough would, according to Van Lier (1988: 227), amount to 'premature surgery'. He suggests that language activities can be structured in such a way that a 'scaffold' is first provided for the learners' participation and then is systematically and gradually disassembled. Prabhu (1990: 173) also argues that because teaching is a form of recurrent social encounter between teachers and learners - 'with self-images to protect' and 'personalities to cope with' - it needs 'a certain degree of routinisation to make it sustainable or even endurable'.

What we are proposing here, then, is not a revolution, not the wholesale replacement of existing practices, but simply the beginning of a change in direction. It would be foolish, in particular, to undervalue what has been achieved and is being achieved with existing approaches. We have already documented some of the positive outcomes of Irish language teaching in primary schools, particularly the fact that most pupils have an opportunity to speak Irish of some kind quite often. And anyone who is familiar with Irish language classrooms will have been impressed by the energy, fluency and pace of the typical Irish lesson at present. Thus, the advantages and disadvantages of change will have to be carefully weighed. Ultimately, it is teachers themselves who will decide how far it is desirable to go in this new direction, and indeed there is no reason why there should not be some variation from teacher to teacher in the extent to which the communicative emphasis is incorporated into a new approach.

10   Summary and conclusions

10.1 Introduction

The research and development work on Irish in primary schools reviewed here goes beyond the relatively simple parameters of earlier national surveys conducted by ITÉ in the late 1970's and 1980's. The *Twenty-Classes Study* provides a close-up picture of the process of teaching and learning Irish based on direct observation of 40 Irish lessons. It also presents an account of the views of both pupils and parents - two participants in the educational process whose perspectives on Irish in primary school have not previously been investigated. In addition, it describes the development of a range of new classroom-observation and questionnaire-type instruments which were necessary to gather these new data. These instruments will allow much more comprehensive investigations of Irish in primary school in the future than has been possible up to now.   Finally, the *Communicative Materials Project* allows us to test out practical solutions to many of the problems identified in the research study.

The chapter is in three sections. First, we give a very brief overview of a few of the main themes and findings (section 10.2 below). A detailed summary of each chapter follows in section 10.3. Descriptions of the new instruments, as well as a discussion of implications and recommendations arising from the findings of each part of the study, are nested within the chapter summaries. Finally, in section 10.4 we consider the kinds of structures which are needed to implement our recommendations and to support the teaching of Irish in a more proactive and comprehensive way in the context of national language policy.

10.2 Main themes and findings

In order to provide a general framework within which the summaries in the next section can be integrated, we begin with one or two points from each chapter.

- Although the *Twenty-Classes Study* involved a relatively small number of classes/ schools, these were carefully selected to give the research a national dimension as far as possible. We were concerned with the geographical distribution as well as with levels of *Pupil achievement in Irish, Pupil general academic ability* and *Social class.* The data presented in Chapter 2 show that the crucial characteristics of the sample accord quite well with the national picture, bearing in mind the relatively small number of classes and pupils involved.
- The investigation of Irish attitude/motivation indicates that pupils are reasonably well disposed towards the Irish language itself and towards the idea of integrating with the

Irish-language-speaking 'group'. But motivation, or actual commitment to learning Irish, is less positive. In addition, it is motivation, rather than 'integrative' attitudes which is most strongly related to success in learning Irish. A substantial minority of pupils also do not believe that they have the support and encouragement of their parents in the task of learning Irish. Where parental encouragement is present, it has a positive effect on pupil achievement in Irish and an even stronger effect on attitude/motivation. Pupils tend to have a poor estimation of their ability in Irish compared to other subjects and a substantial minority are anxious about speaking Irish in class.

- Pupils' reactions to the Irish lesson, expressed in their own words, indicate that they often experience the materials and lesson content as boring, old-fashioned and repetitious. They would like a course which is more modern, more fun and more realistic, with a greater emphasis on conversations and games. General apathy /discouragement, and unhappiness at not being able to understand the lesson or the teacher, are themes which feature frequently in classes with low levels of achievement in Irish.

- When parents themselves were surveyed they were generally positive about Irish and supportive of the notion of their children being taught Irish in school. In practice, however, many have a lukewarm, hands-off attitude to the enterprise of their children actually learning Irish: a majority of parents do not directly promote positive attitudes to learning Irish; they are much less likely to praise their child's achievements in Irish than in other subjects; and they are less likely to help with homework in Irish than other subjects.

- The direct observation of the Irish lessons revealed that an emphasis on communication is associated with generally positive outcomes: higher achievement in Irish, higher levels of class attention and class interest during the observed lessons and lower levels of *Irish-lesson anxiety*. Generally negative outcomes are associated with traditional language-practice activities. Classes in which teachers spend a greater proportion of time without using any materials at all tend to have higher levels of achievement in Irish.

    Compared to foreign-language classrooms at first-year post-primary, sixth-grade primary Irish classes make greater use of the target language and are more communicative (a greater proportion of time is spent on 'Simulated' and 'Real communication' in the target language).

- Only two pupil behaviours - 'Reading aloud' and, to a considerably lesser extent, 'Reading silently' - are associated with significant outcomes. Classes which devote more time to activities involving the pupil 'Reading aloud' are significantly more likely to have lower achievement in spoken Irish, less positive class attitude to Irish, higher levels of anxiety in relation to the Irish lesson and reduced levels of attention to and interest in the Irish lesson. 'Reading silently' segments have significantly lower mean *Class interest* and *Class attention* ratings than all other segments.

    Data from the *Classroom organisation* and *Teacher mode of involvement* dimensions illustrate the active, central role of the teacher in the Irish lesson, either

'Interacting' with pupils or 'Instructing' (72% of segments), all of this within a predominantly 'Whole-class' context (85.6% of segments). Pupils working together in small groups, a form of classroom organisation very much associated with communicative language teaching, accounts for less than 1% of segments. 'Pupil/group demonstration' segments, while not very common (7.5% of all segments) are associated with higher *Class attention* and *Class interest* than other segments. Classes which devote more time to 'Pupil/group demonstration' forms of organisation also have lower levels of *Irish-lesson anxiety*.

- Other observation work which focused on *individual* pupils showed that about half of all pupil behaviours in class consisted of the pupil speaking individually - and in Irish in 91% of cases. The results also showed that (i) pupil speech is not produced very often in the context of real communication or of meaning negotiation, (ii) pupils with lower levels of ability in Irish speak less often than other pupils, (iii) when those with lower levels of ability in Irish are silent they are less attentive to the lesson than those with higher levels of ability who remain silent, and (iv) classes which emphasise communicative activities are associated with higher levels of individual pupil speech and have pupils who are more likely to make sustained contributions.

The classroom observation work can be seen as a way of examining the likely effects of introducing the communicative approach prior to its actual introduction. In so far as the classes currently emphasising communication can be taken to represent the effect of introducing a communicative approach more generally, it can be said that the results of this study make a *prima facie* case for a communicative approach to teaching Irish at primary level.

10.3 Summaries of individual chapters.

10.3.1 Chapter 1 - Introduction

Chapter 1 presents the background to the report and briefly describes the main projects on which it is based: the *Twenty-Classes Study*, the *Communicative Materials Project* and the *Teaching through Irish Project*. It also outlines the structure of the report itself.

10.3.2 Chapter 2 - The Twenty-Classes Study in a national context

Chapter 2 describes the methodology of the study and presents a range of background information which is necessary to determine how much weight can be attached to our findings in a national context. It begins with a review of research on achievement in Irish at primary level. This is followed by a description of the ten instruments used to collect data from parents, pupils and teachers, including the four new instruments which are the main focus of the study. The remainder of the chapter presents and discusses data relating to the 20 classes and compares these to data at a national level.

Achievement in Irish, general academic ability and social class

Because the selection of classes was fundamentally informal, it is important to establish that they are at least broadly representative. We want to establish two kinds of representativeness: (a) that average *Pupil achievement in Irish, Pupil general academic ability* and *Social class* in the selected sixth-grade classes do not differ substantially from the national population and (b) that the selected classes as a group represent the full range of achievement in Irish nationally, while maintaining an overall balance between weak and strong classes.

The results indicate that we have been reasonably successful. First, in terms of achievement in Irish, the mean percentage of pupils in the sample attaining mastery of sixth-grade objectives in Irish is not statistically different from the mean percentage nationally. In addition, both in terms of the range of achievement in Irish across classes, and the balance between classes with high, middle and low levels of achievement in Irish, the sample mirrors the national picture quite well. Second, while *Pupil general academic ability* (measured by a test of verbal reasoning in English, the *DVRT*) in the sample is significantly lower than nationally, the difference in practical terms is fairly small - mean *DVRT* standard scores only differ by 1.5. Third, while pupils in the sample come from significantly lower *Social class* backgrounds than the general population, this effect is largely an artifact of the poor quality of information about *Social class* which happened to be available to us in the case of certain pupils whose parents were long-term unemployed. We argue that the real *Social class* standing of pupils in the sample is not very different from those nationally.

The results also show clearly that lower *Pupil general academic ability* and lower *Social class* predominate among pupils and classes with low levels of achievement in Irish. Mastery of sixth-grade objectives in Irish shows a steady and substantial increase according to increasing levels of *Pupil general academic ability*. In addition, more than twice the proportion of pupils in the highest *Social-class* group than in the lowest *Social-class* group attain mastery of objectives. Correlation and regression analyses of these relationships are reported in Chapter 3 and in Chapter 5.

Some ordinary schools produce very high levels of achievement in spoken Irish. For example, the mean percentage of pupils attaining mastery of each objective in spoken Irish in the highest-achieving class is 81.3% - a level of achievement which may not be too far off that attained in many all-Irish schools. It is argued that even if the proportion of such schools nationally is small, their absolute number ensures that they make a considerable contribution to the general language-promotion effort.

The Parent Sample

Chapter 2 also had a number of secondary aims. One of these is to establish the extent to which the smaller sub-group of classes involved in the Parents' Survey *(the Parent Sample)* differs from the larger group of twenty classes (what we call the *Total Sample*) as well as from classes nationally. While *Pupil achievement in Irish* in the *Parent Sample* was found to be substantially lower than it is nationally, this outcome was expected since all the Parent-Survey schools were either in Dublin or in the surrounding counties in East Leinster. Earlier research (Harris, 1983) had shown that Dublin classes have lower levels of achievement in spoken Irish than classes from other regions. This did not undermine the representativeness of the *Parent Sample* in other respects, however, as shown by the fact that *Pupil general academic ability* and *Social class* in this group of classes does not differ significantly from the situation nationally.

Socio-demographic and educational variables
Another goal of Chapter 2 was to provide a more complete picture of the 20 selected classes by presenting data on a number of socio-demographic and educational variables. These variables had been linked in previous research to achievement in Irish e.g. class size, gender composition of classes, urban-rural and regional location, Irish-medium instruction and course-method (Harris, 1983). While we do not claim to have achieved the kind of balance and representativeness in relation to these socio-demographic and educational variables which would be produced by random sampling, the results show that the classes selected for the study reflect the whole range of values and categories of these variables.

Pupil interest in and difficulty with Irish
Finally, we present data on teachers' perceptions of pupils' ability in Irish, their interest in Irish and their experience of difficulty with various school subjects. The teachers' ratings allow us to place performance in Irish in the present study in the context of performance in other subjects, such as Mathematics or English reading, without conducting a large amount of direct testing. The results show that teachers tend to judge large proportions of pupils as having difficulty with Irish. This is particularly so in the case of spoken Irish. Even in the high-Irish-achievement group of classes, which are considerably better than the national average, substantial proportions of pupils are often perceived as having difficulty with this subject. One way of construing data on perceived pupil difficulty with school subjects is that they indicate the extent to which there is a gap between the level of performance expected by the teacher and the actual performance of pupils. We argue that if the high expectations which appear to be characteristic of Irish are to have a positive influence on outcome, they must be accompanied by frequent opportunities for pupils to experience success in learning, and to receive feedback on their progress which is both affirmative and of a high quality. Otherwise, pupil esteem in relation to their ability to develop speaking proficiency in Irish may suffer. This issue is taken up again in Chapter 4.

10.3.3 Chapter 3 - Pupils' attitude and motivation in relation to Irish

The study of Irish attitude/motivation described in Chapter 3 provides the first account of primary-school pupils' affective response to Irish and to the learning of Irish. The chapter has two main objectives: (i) to establish how positive or negative are the different components of pupils' *Irish attitude/motivation* and (ii) how strongly are each of these affective components related to achievement in Irish. The instrument used to measure attitude/motivation also included a scale to measure the pupil's self-concept in relation to his/her Irish ability and a scale to measure the extent to which Irish is used at home.

Main characteristics of pupils' Irish attitude/motivation
The results show that of the two main affective clusters studied, *Integrativeness* and *Motivation*, pupils' integrative attitudes are the more positive. That is to say, they are generally well-disposed towards the Irish language itself and towards the idea of integrating with the Irish-language 'community' or 'group' - they tend to be favourable towards Irish speakers, they wish to be more closely associated with the Irish language and, in a broader context, they are open to other languages and language groups. In contrast, the components of *Motivation*, what might be paraphrased as commitment to actually learning Irish, are less positive. *Motivation* items and scales, focused on such things as the strength of pupils' desire to learn Irish, on the intensity of the effort which they are prepared to commit to learning Irish and on the amount of satisfaction which they experience in learning it, all tend to elicit less positive responses.

One specific contrast between *Integrativeness* and *Motivation* consists of the affective reaction of pupils to second/foreign languages generally versus Irish. The results show that pupils' disposition to the general idea of learning a second/foreign language is more positive than their attitude to learning Irish. At the level of classes, over 60% of pupils in 19 out of the 20 classes agree that they 'would like to learn a foreign language in school' even if they 'didn't *have* to do it'. By contrast, only 6 out of 20 classes have that many pupils agreeing that they 'really enjoy learning Irish'. The preference gap between Irish and foreign languages is particularly clear among pupils in low-Irish-achievement classes: while all the low-Irish-achievement classes have a majority of pupils who 'would like to learn a foreign language', only one of these low-achievement classes has a majority who 'really enjoy learning Irish'. In half of the high-Irish-achievement classes, however, the proportion who are positive about learning Irish slightly exceeds the proportion who are interested in learning a foreign language. The results relating to the Irish/foreign-language comparison must be interpreted with caution, however, since for most pupils the 'second/foreign language' item concerns their affective reaction to a hypothetical situation, while the 'learning Irish' item refers to their actual experience.

Perception of parental encouragement, self-concept and anxiety
Data from the *Parental encouragement* scale shows that a substantial minority of pupils do not believe that they have the support and encouragement of their parents in the task of learning Irish. On the positive side, however, in response to an item from the *Use of Irish at home* scale, about half the pupils report at least some use of Irish at home. This is consistent with the reports of home use from parents themselves (Chapter 5).

Data from the *Irish-ability self-concept* scale, and responses to other individual items, indicate that pupils tend to have a poor estimation of their ability to speak Irish compared to their ability in other school subjects. The proportion of pupils agreeing that they are 'better' than 'most pupils' in the class, is smallest in the case of Speaking Irish (30.7%), a little larger for Mathematics (36.7%) and is greatest for English Reading (57.5%).

Results relating to *Irish-lesson anxiety* items show that somewhere between a quarter and a half of pupils, depending on the question, admit to anxiety, lack of confidence or embarrassment about speaking Irish in class.

Relationship between attitude/motivation and achievement in Irish

The correlation and regression analyses attempt to assess the importance of overall *Irish attitude/motivation* (and its individual components) in relation to achievement in Irish, using other important variables which affect achievement in Irish (*Pupil general academic ability, Social class, Parental encouragement*) as a standard of comparison. The correlation and regression analyses also give an indication of which kinds of initiatives designed to improve pupils' Irish achievement and attitudes might succeed.

Overall *Irish attitude/motivation* is strongly and positively related to achievement in Irish ($r=.40$) - pupils with more positive attitude/motivation do better at Irish. The only variable which is more strongly related to achievement in Irish than this is *Pupil general academic ability* as measured by the DVRT ($r=.47$). At the level of classes also, *Irish attitude motivation* is strongly and positively related to achievement in Irish ($r=.74$). Responses to one item give an indication of the range of attitude/motivation over the 20 classes: in the class with the highest achievement in Irish, 100% of pupils agree (slightly or strongly) that they 'really enjoy learning Irish'; in two of the low-Irish-achievement classes less than 20% of pupils agree.

While all six main components of *Irish attitude/motivation* are significantly correlated with achievement in Irish, the three components of the *Motivation* cluster are somewhat more strongly related ($r = .34$ to $.35$) to achievement than are the three components of *Integrativeness* ($r = .22$ to $.29$). *Attitude to learning Irish* (a *Motivational* scale indicating the amount of satisfaction which pupils experience in learning Irish) is the component most closely related to achievement in Irish, while *Interest in second/foreign languages* (an *Integrativeness* scale) is the least strongly correlated.

Higher *Irish-lesson anxiety* in pupils is associated with significantly lower levels of *Pupil achievement in Irish.* The fact that this scale measures anxiety about *speaking* Irish is interesting in the light of classroom observation data to be presented later (Chapters 8 and 9) which shows that pupils with lower levels of ability in Irish speak individually in the Irish class less often.

The regression analyses show that when four individual and socio-demographic factors (mainly *Pupil general academic ability, Location* and *Social class*) are entered first into the equation, they account for most of the variance (33.4%) in *Pupil achievement in Irish.* Two home factors (*Parental encouragement* and *Use of Irish at home*) entered later only contribute an additional 3% to the explained variance. The *Irish attitude/motivation index*, entered last, adds a further 4.1%. When the various components of Irish attitude/motivation were entered individually as predictors of achievement, only three emerged as significant - the two motivation scales, *Attitude to learning Irish* and *Motivational intensity to learn Irish,* and *Irish-lesson anxiety.*

When we consider the factors which are related to, or determine, attitude/motivation (as opposed to Irish achievement) the picture is much different: this time it is the two home variables (*Parental encouragement* and *Use of Irish at home*) which are most important. Together, these two variables explain the bulk of the variance in *Irish attitude/motivation* (27.8%). The four individual and socio-demographic factors are less important, explaining only 14.3% of the variance in attitude/motivation.

Promoting positive attitudes to learning Irish in primary school
Tackling the problems of motivation and anxiety in learning Irish which are revealed by our results is important not only on educational grounds, but also in the context of the societal effort to promote the wider use of Irish. Poor pupil/attitude motivation also represents a great problem for teachers day to day. Thus, a high priority must be accorded to the development of a positive attitude to Irish as a curricular objective in its own right, and to identifying ways of improving attitudes.

Attitude to learning Irish (a measure of pupil satisfaction with the learning experience) is important for two reasons: (i) because so many pupils in low-Irish-achievement classes have poor attitudes and (ii) because this is the factor which is most strongly related to achievement in Irish.

Clearly initiatives which influence home factors - *Parental encouragement* and *Use of Irish at home* - are also critical. Ways of improving parental and home support for Irish are taken up in some detail in Chapter 5. But correlation data presented in other chapters also indicate the central role of in-class factors in determining attitude to learning Irish. For example, in Chapter 7 we show that classes which spend more time on communicative activities have significantly better overall Irish attitude/motivation and lower *Irish-lesson anxiety* (i.e. less anxiety about speaking in Irish in class). The difficulty which pupils in low-Irish-achievement classes have in understanding the lesson/teacher, and the more widespread dislike of 'boring, old-fashioned and repetitive' lessons and materials (Chapter 4), are very likely part of the problem also.

The correlation data indicate, predictably enough, that *Irish-lesson anxiety* is governed by in-class factors, but that *Irish-ability self concept* is related to both home and in-school factors. We argue that the maintenance of pupil self-esteem in relation to learning Irish requires realistic expectations and achievable goals, opportunities to experience success in learning Irish, and adult recognition and praise for achievements (both at home and at school).

One reassuring finding is that for the great majority of pupils in sixth class, integrative attitudes are relatively positive. These attitudes are important because they help to maintain motivation during the long task of acquiring Irish. In the *Communicative Materials Project* (see Chapter 1), we investigated various approaches to the development of positive integrative attitudes, placing considerable emphasis on Irish culture and authentic materials in a way that was intended to be enjoyable for pupils and relevant to their own lives. Among the activities included were learning Irish dancing, exploring the Irish-language origins of local Irish place names, role-plays/drama related to trips to the Gaeltacht or Irish Summer College, and so on. Arguably, such activities have a particularly important role in developing positive attitudes in a case such as Irish where most pupils have little or no contact with the language outside school. We also suggest that questions such as why children learn Irish, what use they might expect to make of it and why it is of value should be raised and answered in the classroom.

10.3.4 Chapter 4 - Pupils' views on the Irish lesson in their own words

In this chapter, we analyse pupils' views, expressed in their own words, on their experience of learning Irish. Pupils wrote responses to three prompts (at the end of the *Pupil Questionnaire*):

1. 'What I don't like about the Irish lesson'
2. 'What I do like about the Irish lesson'
3. 'How I would like to change the Irish lesson.'

We transcribed pupils' responses, assigned them to different thematic categories, and selected a sample of responses for illustrative purposes (see Appendix 4). In many instances the same basic theme takes different forms, and is reinforced, in responses to each of the three questions. We also investigated the connections between the level of success which is achieved by pupils in learning to speak Irish and the kinds of themes and issues which emerge in their evaluation of the Irish lesson.

Main themes and their relationship to achievement in Irish
The three main themes evident in pupils' responses are (i) the suitability of existing lesson content and materials, (ii) comprehension difficulties and apathy in low-Irish-achievement classes, and (iii) the popularity of Irish reading.

With regard to the first of these themes, pupils identify particular sources of dissatisfaction and propose definite remedies in relation to lesson content and materials. They dislike both *Nuachúrsaí-related activities and materials* (at 30% the most common theme of all) and the fact that the existing courses/lessons are *boring old fashioned and repetitious* (15%). The objection to the *Nuachúrsaí* reoccurs in responses to the question about desired 'change', with 6.1% wanting to *dispense with film strips/projector* and 4.9% wanting *less or no use of the Nuachúrsaí*.

In contrast, what they like in the way of lesson content and materials are *conversations, games, drama, songs and poems* (25.7%). This same theme emerges in response to the desired 'changes' question, with *more conversations, games, drama, songs and poems* being mentioned by 13.6% of pupils, and a desire to make the lesson *more modern, more fun, more realistic, and non-sexist* by 16.1% of pupils. More generally, they simply want *new materials* (8%).

Use of the *Nuachúrsaí*, however, is not always associated with negative pupil reaction - 8.4% of pupils actually like them. Nor are the objections equally strong in all classes.

Dislike of *Nuachúrsaí-related activities and materials*, or dislike of existing materials on the basis that they are *boring* etc., are not common themes in any of the high-Irish-achievement classes.

What distinguishes objections to the *Nuachúrsaí* and the desire for new materials is the pervasiveness of the themes - their re-occurrence in different forms in response to all three questions. This, together with the strength of feeling evident in many of the pupils' comments (Appendix 4), leaves little doubt that what a substantial proportion of them really want is the replacement of the *Nuachúrsaí*. Evidence that dislike of the *Nuachúrsaí* is concentrated in the middle-Irish-achievement group of classes increases the importance of the issue because this group represents the largest proportion of classes nationally in terms of Irish achievement.

The second broad theme relates to two concerns frequently expressed by pupils in low-Irish-achievement classes: (a) apathy, discouragement and a general desire to disengage from the learning of Irish and (b) an inability to understand the lesson or teacher. These concerns emerge in response to all three write-in questions, but particularly in the form of expressed 'dislikes' and a desire for change. These issues do also appear occasionally in middle- and high-Irish-achievement classes, but to a considerably lesser extent.

Direct observation data presented in Chapter 7 provide some confirmation of the apathy and disengagement evident in the pupils' comments - ratings made by the inspectors show that pupils in low-Irish-achievement classes show much less interest in the lesson than those in high-Irish-achievement classes. These results are also consistent with the evidence of higher *Irish-lesson anxiety* and less positive attitudes to Irish in low-Irish-achievement classes (Chapter 3). The direct comments of pupils, however, are more revealing and more convincing than other kinds of evidence. In addition, the pupils' own remarks succeed in highlighting 'difficulty in understanding' as at least one significant source of the apathy and negativity.

It is important not to either understate or overstate the scale of the problems revealed by these results. The main group of low-Irish-achievement classes, where apathy/negativity and difficulty in following the lesson were common, fall just within the lowest 10% of classes nationally in terms of achievement in Irish. Nevertheless, the results identify a significant educational problem in terms of the absolute numbers of pupils affected.

The third theme in pupils' comments is the popularity of Irish reading: *Reading or specific readers* constitutes the most commonly expressed 'like' comment overall (28% of pupils). Despite this, a substantial proportion (14.5%) dislike reading and only 4.5% actually want more of it. There is no clear evidence of variation between high-, middle- and low-Irish achievement classes in relation to this theme. No particularly strong reasons for either disliking or liking Irish reading emerge in the pupils' comments.

It is not surprising that pupils should like Irish reading, assuming that the material was at an appropriate level of difficulty and was geared to their interests. The popularity of this activity may simply reflect the fact that the reading material available is generally better geared to pupils' interests than the material used in the oral portion of the lesson (such as the *Nuachúrsaí* or 'alternative' courses). But another likely factor is that it is easier for pupils to perceive their progress in the case of reading than it is in the case of spoken Irish. Pupils can see that they are proceeding steadily through their reader as the year unfolds. There may be a more general message here for the design of the new Irish courses following the launch of the new curriculum: pupils need to be regularly told what they are going to learn, what skills they are going to acquire and, having completed a particular section of the course itself, what they then know or can do.

Some of the lesser themes in pupils' comments relate to 'grammar/spelling' and 'written' exercises. A measure of disagreement emerges in relation to these. Just over 16% of pupils dislike grammar-related activities while 6.3% like them, and 13.9% of pupils dislike written exercises while 16.7% like them. It is worth noting that though the most common 'dislike' in high-Irish-achievement classes is either grammar or spelling, these same aspects do not feature as a common 'dislike' in any of the low-Irish-achievement classes. This shows that we must be careful in making claims about the relationships between pupils' likes/dislikes and successful learning. For example, we could hardly claim that because grammar or spelling are disliked in high-Irish-achievement classes, we should dispense with them altogether. Indeed the pupils' success may in part be determined by just these activities. To put it another way, if Irish lessons or courses of a completely different kind to the present ones were introduced, some other elements of these new courses might well become the focus of pupils' complaints.

Implications for the future

The development of new courses for Irish following the introduction of the new curriculum will provide an opportunity to respond to some of the problems identified by the pupils themselves here. Certainly, the communicative orientation in itself should help, if we take the positive responses of pupils to communicative lesson segments in the present study as an indication (See Chapter 7). But the success of new courses will depend to a considerable extent on other factors. Accommodating the needs of pupils who have lower levels of achievement in Irish, for example, or making lesson material 'more modern, more fun, more realistic' depends on the excellence of research-and-development work, and on the success of creative enterprises, which have yet to begin in earnest. A communicative orientation in itself will not solve these problems.

Improvements may also depend on factors other than materials or lesson content - on changes in teaching practices and classroom atmosphere, for example, which improve the self-esteem and participation rates of pupils in low-Irish achievement classes (See Chapter 9). The reaction to the guidelines in the *Communicative Materials Project*, which represented a preliminary attempt to find ways of responding to some of the concerns of pupils, showed the value of ascertaining and taking account of their views. As we argue in the concluding section of the present report, however, additional resources need to be provided so that the kind of research-and-development work carried out in the *Communicative Materials Project* can be continued and, indeed, accelerated.

10.3.5 *Chapter 5 - Parents' views and practices in relation to Irish*

In this chapter we (a) describe the collection of information on parental attitudes and practices in relation to Irish by means of a questionnaire sent to parents via the individual child and (b) establish the usefulness of such information in explaining pupil achievement in spoken Irish and attitude to Irish.

While we have a considerable amount of information on public attitudes to Irish, we do not have detailed information specifically on the attitudes and practices of parents who have children in primary school. Because the present small-scale study of parents places the parents' own children at the centre of the investigation of adult attitudes and practices in relation to Irish it provides them with a very real reference point in replying to our questions.

The questionnaire was distributed to seven of the original classes in the *Twenty-Classes Study*. All these 'parent' classes were in Dublin and surrounding areas, either in the 'middle-Irish-achievement' or 'low-Irish-achievement' groups. Before describing our findings in detail, we first of all want to consider the comparability of these classes with the population of classes nationally.

Parental ability in Irish and use of Irish at home
We already know from statistical tests reported in Chapter 2 that *Pupil general academic ability* and *Social class* in the *Parent Sample* do not differ significantly from the situation nationally. In Chapter 5 we extended the comparison with the national situation to include two other key home-background factors (*Parents' ability in Irish* and *Use of Irish at home*), using information derived from the Parents' Questionnaire. These variables are of particular interest because of their potential to influence children's attitude to Irish and achievement in Irish.

On the basis of *Pupil general academic ability* and *Social class* data alone we might have expected *Parent's ability in Irish* and *Use of Irish at home* (parents' report) to be roughly the same as in the general population. In fact, at some levels of ability and use, however, the parents in our study were superior to the population nationally. We argue that the fact of having children learning Irish at primary school affords parents more opportunities than the general public for contact with Irish. This may be at least partly responsible for the differences in adult ability and use between parents in the present study and in the national population.

The correlation analyses show that *Social class*, *Parent's ability in Irish* and *Use of Irish at home* are all significantly and positively correlated with *Pupil achievement in Irish*. Of these, however, only greater parental *Use of Irish at home* is significantly linked with better *Pupil Irish attitude/motivation*. The regression analyses confirm the robustness of these effects. This suggests that any initiatives which would encourage parents to use some Irish at home, even occasionally, are likely to benefit children both in terms of their attitude to Irish and their success in learning it at school. Likewise, initiatives which provide parents with an opportunity to improve their own command of Irish should also lead to improvements in children's proficiency. At present, a large proportion of parents (44%) believe that their lack of ability in Irish is an obstacle to helping their child with Irish. In fact, the inclination of parents to help with Irish spelling and, to a lesser extent, Irish reading - activities which demand little more than a passive competence in the language from parents - suggests that ability in Irish may often determine not only the aspect of Irish with which parents help, but perhaps even which aspects of Irish the teacher chooses to assign as homework.

Praise, support and involvement

Another issue of interest relates to parental support for children learning Irish. The results show that while parents generally have positive attitudes to Irish and to the notion of their children learning it, actual commitment to and involvement in the process of children learning Irish is much less common. There are a number of indications of this in the data.

First, a majority of parents (69.2%) do not directly promote positive attitudes to learning Irish but 'leave it up to the child to develop his/her own attitude'. Only 29.3% 'let the child know Irish is very important'. Nevertheless, hardly any parents (1%) actually 'discourage the child from taking Irish seriously'.

Second, praise for the child's school achievements is less common in the case of Irish than in other school subject areas (English/Mathematics/Project work): between 20-30% of parents 'hardly ever' praise Irish reading, oral Irish or Irish writing - compared to only between 2.5%-5% who 'hardly ever' praise Mathematics and English. The fact that failure to praise school achievements is very largely confined to Irish is particularly telling because it means that it is not typical of parental attitudes to school work generally. There may be a variety of reasons for this result, but at least one of them is suggested by the finding that 65.7% of parents think that Irish is of 'little' or 'no importance' as far as their child's future job is concerned.

Third, in relation to homework, more parents 'usually help' their child with Mathematics (70.2%) or English (47.5%) than with Irish generally (34.8%). Oral/Spoken Irish is the aspect of Irish with which parents are least likely to help (9.1%). The low levels of praise and help in the case of oral Irish seems surprising given that (along with Mathematics) Spoken Irish is the subject most frequently cited by parents as causing difficulty for the child.

What is of particular significance in the results of the correlation analyses is that where active participation on the part of parents is present - in the form of encouragement, praise or help with homework - it is associated with more positive pupil attitudes and higher pupil achievement in Irish. The regression analysis confirms the influence of one variable in particular, *Parent praises any aspect of child's Irish achievements*, in terms of its contribution to overall *Pupil Irish attitude/motivation*. These results match those in Chapter 3 where we based our analyses on *pupils'* perceptions of parental encouragement - there, too, there were strong effects of parental support on the child's attitude/motivation in relation to Irish.

The vast majority of parents have at least occasional contact with the school, but not much more than a quarter (27.3%) have 'a lot' of contact. Having more contact with the school is significantly associated with a greater knowledge of how Irish is taught. Parents generally, however, do not rate their knowledge of how Irish is taught very highly. A quarter of parents 'know nothing' about how Irish is taught, while another half (56.6%) 'know only a little'. What is important, once again, is that even parental investment which takes the form of being well-informed about how Irish is taught is linked with positive outcomes for pupils. Knowing more about how Irish is taught is at the nexus of a set of parental attributes - higher parental ability in Irish, better personal attitudes to Irish, more frequent use of Irish at home, the encouragement of more positive attitudes to learning Irish in children, praise for the child's achievements in Irish and a greater likelihood of helping with Irish homework generally - all of which are associated with better pupil achievement and attitudes. Thus, being well informed about the teaching of Irish appears to be one of the important ways in which more involved parents influence their children's learning of Irish.

Parents' comments
General comments were volunteered by 45% of parents. The negative category containing the most comments (19%) focuses on the desire for more time to be spent on other subjects and less time on Irish. Other broadly unfavourable categories of comment express disagreement with Irish being compulsory at primary level (10%) or indicate that Irish is not useful or important for the child's future (11%). Nevertheless, a substantial proportion of comments are also broadly favourable or supportive. Twelve per cent of parents express support for Irish or the teaching of Irish (e.g. "I love the Irish language and I will encourage my child to learn it through his school years") while 2% actually want more time devoted to Irish generally. In assessing children's progress in Irish, 10% of parents express satisfaction (8% express dissatisfaction). Comments in a number of other categories suggest that a substantial proportion of parents lay the blame for what they see as unsatisfactory progress in Irish on methods of teaching and the materials used - in this respect they largely echo the views of the pupils themselves (Chapter 4).

Responses to another multiple-choice item, however, show that most parents (83.3%) believe that the school 'is doing everything possible' to improve their child's progress in Irish generally - only 14.1% feel it 'could do more'. This may suggest that while parents are concerned, they feel that fundamental choices about methods and materials are outside the control of individual teachers and the local school.

Implications and recommendations
It is argued that, in the past, there was an implicit understanding that the development of proficiency in Irish in children was the work of the school. This was presumably agreeable to those parents who were either neutral or negative about Irish. It also had the advantage for schools of sealing-off a potentially negative affective factor which might otherwise have undermined pupil motivation. The increasing involvement of parents in education, however, may be expected to destabilise some of these traditional accommodations. Parents whose personal attitudes to Irish are negative, as well as those who are positive,

will gradually be drawn more directly into the learning process in the case of Irish. While the final outcome from the point of view of the child's education can only be positive, the degree of success in the case of Irish may well depend on how the process of change is managed and researched.

Parents could become more involved in Irish at different levels and in different ways. The NPC-Primary (1991) advocate class meetings as 'a forum for the teacher to discuss with parents the curriculum objectives, methods used for assessment of children's progress, guidelines for homework, discipline and other relevant matters'. Another possibility is that an information booklet for parents could be prepared. The introduction of the new curriculum in Irish will provide a useful opportunity to investigate these possibilities in a new context.

At the most basic level, parents need to be informed about the benefits of more direct involvement in the case of Irish. In addition, they should be alerted to the specific educational consequences for their own child of providing only lukewarm support, or actually withholding approval altogether, for the process of learning Irish. Information on how Irish is taught, the precise goals of teaching it and the nature of first and second-language learning in children of primary school age is also required. Finally, attention should be paid to fostering realistic expectations about what can be achieved in a primary-school programme in which the language is taught as just one subject.

Setting up parent-teacher structures and providing information or even language classes, however, may not be enough to effect real change in the traditional pattern of parental involvement. An argument is made for a series of research-and-development projects which would explore ways of bringing parents closer to what happens in the Irish class. Involvement in the learning of spoken Irish, the core of the Irish lesson, is particularly important. New home-based activities which go beyond the traditional definition of homework could be used to inform parents about what the child has learned and provide an opportunity for the child to demonstrate his or her competence in speaking Irish and for parents to recognise and praise the progress being made. Communicative tasks, originally introduced in a classroom context, can often provide a natural focus for home-based interaction involving parents and children. Home-based activities which yield some 'product' or provide feedback to the teacher/class are particularly useful.

Even those activities which do not involve feedback to the school can be useful. Pupils from one class involved in the *Communicative Materials Project*, for example, took home a video recording of various activities in the Irish lesson, including examples of each of the children speaking Irish. We also describe our experience in that project of using simple information sheets in Irish for parents. More recently, ITÉ has begun work on a new project which investigates more systematically ways in which parents could support their children's efforts to acquire speaking proficiency in Irish (Harris and Ó Cathalláin, 1999, in progress).

Specific initiatives designed to inform or persuade parents in this area must be conducted in a way which both respects the parents' own views regarding Irish, where these are negative, and which ultimately fully acknowledges parents' rights to promote their children's welfare in whatever way they see fit. It is essential that parents and teachers would be involved at the planning stage and that there would be provision for choice and different levels of involvement from the beginning.

We must also be realistic about the amount of time available to parents. The focus should be on redistributing the time which parents already spend with their children on Irish homework to new, more useful activities rather than increasing the overall amount of time.

10.3.6 Chapter 6 - The development of the Irish Lesson Analysis System

A major aim of the *Twenty-Classes Study* was to use direct classroom observation to describe the process of teaching and learning Irish in primary school. In order to this we developed two instruments, the *Irish Lesson Analysis System (ILAS)* and the *Pupil Communicative Behaviour Record (PCBR)*. In developing these instruments we had two concerns. First, that in terms of their structure and focus, the instruments would reflect both practical and theoretical aspects of Irish language teaching: (a) the kind of conceptualisation of lessons as sequences of activities organised by the teacher which teachers themselves would find natural and appropriate and (b) the aspects of classroom discourse and pupil-teacher interaction which recent research on second-language acquisition have identified as making important contributions to the development of second-language proficiency. Our second goal was to use an adaptation of existing classroom observation systems, if possible, since our resources would not allow us to begin the task of constructing entirely new instruments.

Chapters 6 to 9 describe the observation work. The first three of these chapters are devoted to the *ILAS*, in order to do justice to the variety of different perspectives on the Irish lesson which this instrument provides. Chapter 6, summarised here, describes the development and application of the *ILAS*, an observation instrument which focuses on the structure and composition of the Irish lesson. The second observation instrument, *PCBR*, is dealt with in Chapter 9 and analyses pupil participation and language use during the Irish lesson.

Research on classroom language learning

Chapter 6 begins with a review of current research on the classroom processes presumed to be responsible for successful second-language learning. This serves to introduce the main issues which arise not only in choosing and adapting classroom observations instruments but also in interpreting the data they generate. The review covers the evolution of communicative language teaching, the experiential-analytic continuum in second-language teaching and more recent efforts to reconceptualise and reinstate the analytic focus in teaching. In large part, what we discuss is the gradual switch which has been taking place over the last 25 years from structurally-based syllabuses and teaching methods to a communicative approach. The issues examined are particularly relevant to the Irish situation, where we are about to change from an audio-visual/structural-linguistic approach to a communicative approach in the new curriculum (MacSuibhne, 1996). As we enter this period of change, decisions will have to be made about what aspects of the existing approach must change and what aspects are worth retaining. Research on classroom based second-language learning is likely to have a significant contribution to make to these decisions.

The development of the Irish Lesson Analysis System
We then proceed to describe the development and use of the *Irish Lesson Analysis System* in the present study. The *ILAS* is an adaptation of the Stirling System developed by Mitchell *et al.* (1981). The unit of analysis is the 'lesson segment'. This is designed to correspond to 'naturalistic' teaching units (events such as 'drilling', 'repetition' etc.). A segment lasts typically for between 1 and 10 minutes. Segments are defined in terms of six main dimensions of analysis - *Topic, Language activity, Pupil behaviour, Teacher mode of involvement, Classroom organisation* and *Materials* - and their associated categories. In the case of *Language activity*, for example, there are categories such as 'Translation', 'Imitation', 'Contextualisation exercises' and 'Simulated communication in Irish'. Each segment was also coded in relation to two other pupil related dimensions *Class attention* and *Class interest* i.e. the extent to which pupils in general were paying attention to or were interested in the current activity.

Two Irish lessons were observed in each school. The work was carried out by primary-school inspectors of the Department of Education. Two observers worked side by side, but independently, in each classroom. Observer 1 was concerned with the *ILAS* instrument. Observer 2 used the *PCBR* (see Chapter 9) to classify the general behaviour, participation and language use of three pre-selected pupils.

Observer 1 identified the main segments of classroom activity as the lesson progressed and coded each segment on the eight dimensions according to instructions set out in a short form of *ILAS* (Appendix 6.2). The observation covered all aspects of the Irish lesson - oral/conversational Irish, Irish reading and Irish writing. The teacher was told at the very beginning that our objective was to study the typical teaching of a new lesson - not something that had been rehearsed by the class before. Each observer made a separate audio-tape recording of each of the two lessons. The present authors subsequently used these tapes to recode some dimensions of the lessons based on a more detailed version of *ILAS*. The data analysed here are based on these recodings.

Following the observation work, we asked the teachers (i) how typical the two observed lessons were in terms of approach/method, materials used, style of interaction with the children and, (ii) what effect, if any, the observers' presence had on their teaching. The results of the teachers' assessments are reviewed in Chapter 6 and their comments are presented in Appendix 2.5. All but one teacher reported that the lessons they taught were generally very typical of the usual Irish lesson. A majority (80%) also reported that the observers had 'little' effect on their teaching.

A proportion of the Irish lessons were transcribed and a sample of them is included in the present report (Appendix 6.4). The transcripts are intended to serve a number of purposes - to enrich the quantitative evidence, to illustrate in a more immediate way the category definitions of *ILAS* and to provide material which may be helpful in training observers in future. The final section of Chapter 6 describes how the extracts were selected and offers some preliminary observations on their content.

10.3.7 Chapter 7 - The Irish lesson: Topic, language activity and materials

The various dimensions of the *Irish Lesson Analysis System (ILAS)* provide a description of the same classroom events from a number of different perspectives, such as the language activities being engaged in and the forms of classroom organisation being employed. In order to simplify the task of presenting the results, Chapter 7 is confined to a description of the Irish lesson in terms of just three *ILAS* dimensions: *Topic, Language activity* and *Materials*. The remaining dimensions are dealt with in Chapter 8.

Two main reference points are used in analysing and interpreting the results. The first consists of research reviewed in Chapter 6 which tries to identify classroom conditions which are conducive to successful second-language learning. A crucial distinction is made in this research between 'experiential' activities and 'analytic' activities (Allen *et al.*, 1987; Stern, 1990, 1992) or 'communicative' versus 'language-practice' activities. Virtually all the significant effects reported in Chapter 7 can be understood in relation to this distinction. The second reference point is provided by comparing the present description of Irish lessons at sixth-grade with the description of the teaching of French at first year post-primary in the Stirling Study (Mitchell *et al.*, 1981). The main focus of interest in this comparison is the difference between a second- and a foreign-language programme, where both programmes have origins in the audio-visual method.

Language activity
The five main categories of *Language activity* consist of three types of *language-practice* ('Contextualisation exercises', 'Drills' and 'Transposition') and two types of *communicative* activity ('Real communication in Irish' and 'Simulated communication in Irish'). Together, these account for 81.9% of all segments in the Irish lesson but their equivalents only account for 43.8% of the French segments in the Stirling Study. About one-fifth of the Irish lesson segments involve communicative activities - although there are very substantial class-to-class variations. By comparison, only 1.8% of segments in the Stirling Study could be classified as communicative.

Another important difference between the two studies was that English-based or partly English-based language activities formed a substantial component of the Stirling programme but are virtually unknown in the Irish programme. We attribute this to the different traditions in second- and foreign-language teaching. It is suggested that because pupils in the Irish study begin instruction in Irish at a young age, and continue the learning/acquisition process over a relatively long period, metalinguistic concepts and distinctions are transmitted in a more gradual and indirect way through the target language. In contrast, because pupils in the Stirling Study presumably began French instruction only on entry to post-primary school, direct explanation and discussion of certain metalinguistic issues through the pupils' mother tongue may have been judged to be a faster and more efficient route to competence in the language.

Both class-level analyses and the pooled-segment analyses indicate that generally positive outcomes are associated with an emphasis on *communicative* language categories while generally negative outcomes are associated with an emphasis on *language-practice* categories.

When we pool segments for all observed lessons, we find that *Class interest* is significantly higher for segments involving both 'Simulated communication in Irish' and 'Real communication in Irish' than it is for those involving both 'Contextualisation exercises' and 'Transposition'. In addition, *Class interest* is significantly higher for 'Simulated communication in Irish' segments than it is for the language-practice 'Drills' segments.

When we turn to variation across classes in the proportion of lesson time devoted to each activity, we find similar results. The two language-practice activities 'Contextualisation exercises' and 'Transposition' are devoted significantly more lesson time in low-Irish-achievement classes than in high-Irish-achievement classes. Correspondingly, the two communicative activities 'Real communication in Irish' and 'Simulated communication in Irish' are devoted significantly less time in classes which are weaker in Irish. Combining the two communicative activities ('Real' plus 'Simulated' communication in Irish), we can say that 37% of lesson time on average is spent on communicative activities in high-Irish-achievement classes while only 10% of time is spent on them on average in low-Irish-achievement classes. We can also examine this contrast at the level of individual classes. For example, one of the high-Irish-achievement classes (ranked 4 in terms of achievement in Irish) devotes almost 50% of teaching time to communicative activities, while one of the low achievement in Irish classes (ranked 16 in terms of achievement in Irish) devotes zero teaching time to them.

A correlation analysis indicates that the significant positive association with an emphasis on communicative activities, and the significant negative association with language practice, does not just apply to *Class achievement in spoken Irish*. It also extends to the other four class measures. *Class attitude to Irish*, *Class attention* and *Class interest* are significantly better in classes which emphasise communication while *Class Irish-lesson anxiety* is significantly lower.

Superficially, this pattern of results may seem to suggest that 'more communicative' is always better: that increasing the proportion of *communicative* activities, and decreasing the proportion of *language-practice* activities, will improve achievement in Irish and attitude to Irish, raise levels of attention and interest, and lower anxiety about speaking in class. It is argued, however, that aiming for a *balance* between experiential and analytic activities represents a better strategy. Such a strategy is also consistent with the conclusion (Allen *et al.*, 1990: 62) that 'the analytic and the experiential focus may be complementary, in that they provide essential support for one another in the classroom'. Nevertheless, our results make a *prima facie* case for including a strong communicative component in all Irish lessons at primary level.

Topic

Three *Topic* categories in the present study were found to be significantly related to *Class achievement in spoken Irish* and/or *Class interest*. These categories are 'Pupil/teacher real life' (8.7% of segments), 'Situation: *Other than Nuachúrsaí*' (51.1% of segments) and 'Fragmented/non-contextualised' (19.8% of segments). The first two of these are associated with positive outcomes: either higher *Class interest* in a pooled-segment comparison between *Topic* categories, or a significant correlation between the percentage of class time spent on the relevant *Topic* category and *Class interest*. The third *Topic* category, 'Fragmented/non-contextualised', is associated with negative outcomes: lower *Class interest* in pooled-segment comparisons, and lower *Class achievement in spoken Irish* in a class-based correlation.

Not surprisingly, perhaps, the same first two *Topic* categories, i.e. those associated with positive outcomes, are common in the case of *communicative* activities while the third, associated with negative outcomes, is common in the case of one particular type of *language practice* - 'Drills'. Note incidentally that 'Situation: *Other than Nuachúrsaí* includes not only situations derived from 'alternative' textbooks or readers, but also situations generated by the teacher himself/herself - and it is the latter which are associated with communicative activities.

Thus, the contrast between *language practice* and *communicative activities* continues to have significance in the case of *Topic*. Nevertheless, the information on *Topic* does modify and clarify aspects of the *language-practice/communicative* distinction already identified in the *Language activity* data. For example, we show how the 'Routine management/organisation' *Topic* category, which is often associated with one-sided *Real communication in Irish*, is not linked to the positive outcomes that other communicative *Topic* categories are.

The two topic categories 'Pupil/teacher real life' and 'Fragmented/non-contextualised' reflect most clearly the contrasting approaches to language teaching we have been talking about - 'Pupil/teacher real life' being associated with an experiential or communicative approach and 'Fragmented/non-contextualised' with a language practice or form-focused approach. It is worth noting that these *Topic* categories represent similar proportions of lesson segments in the Stirling and Irish studies, reflecting no doubt the audio-visual, basically form-focused, orientation of the courses involved in both cases. A considerably greater proportion of 'Pupil/teacher real life' segments than is reported here would be expected in a communicatively oriented course. An emphasis on 'Fragmented/non-contextualised' topics, that is where there is no unifying theme underlying the language activity in question (usually 'Drills'), would be at variance with a communicative approach.

Materials in use

Many of the commonly used materials are the traditional ones - 'Blackboard' (18.4% of segments and the second most common category), 'Reader' (17.1%), and 'Jotter/copy' (13.2%). None of these categories are significantly related to class measures of Irish proficiency and attitude. 'No materials', the most common category of all, is associated with a little over a quarter of all segments. The proportion of 'No materials' segments varies greatly from class to class - from a high of 67% to a low of 2%. Classes with a greater proportion of 'No materials' segments have significantly higher levels of achievement in Irish, higher class interest and more positive attitudes to Irish. Pooled-segment comparisons also show that 'No materials' segments receive significantly higher class attention and class interest ratings than other segments. Crosstabulations show that 'No materials' segments are strongly associated with communicative-type *Language activity* and *Topic* categories. It appears that in implementing oral/aural communicative activities in the classroom - particularly 'Simulated communication in Irish' - the teacher's starting point very often is not textbooks or other materials, but topics/ideas/characters connected with either the pupils' or teacher's own life, or stories, descriptions, situations and games introduced by the teacher himself/herself.

It must be borne in mind, however, that the classes which are most communicative at present, and which most often use no materials in the course of such communicative teaching, are also those with the highest levels of achievement in Irish. The situation may not be as easy for teachers of low-Irish-achievement classes. Thus, the provision of communicative materials which are finely tuned to the pupils' proficiency in the language may be an essential requirement in enabling teachers of the latter classes to teach communicatively.

We turn now to the use of course-books which are seen as alternatives to the *Nuachúrsaí* - 'Other course-books/workbooks'. The results relating to this category are exactly opposite to those for the 'No materials' category. Use of 'Other course-books/workbooks' is virtually non-existent in classes with high levels of achievement in Irish but is relatively common in middle- and low-Irish-achievement classes. Segments in which 'Other course-books/workbooks' are used (17.5% of segments) receive significantly lower class attention and interest ratings from observers than other segments. Correlation data confirm that classes which emphasise the use of 'Other course-books/workbooks' have significantly lower levels of achievement in Irish and lower levels of interest than other classes.

Conclusion and implications
In the concluding section of Chapter 7 we consider three general issues which arise from the findings (i) why does the present study of a basically audio-visual course produce more positive findings regarding 'communication' than studies of explicitly communicative programmes often do? (ii) will the provision of new communicative teaching materials be a particular help to teachers of weaker classes? (iii) will the introduction of communicative materials pose problems for the 'all-Irish' character of language teaching at primary level?

The first point concerns the apparent paradox that the communicative elements of the present Irish programme are associated with more clearly 'positive' results than are the communicative elements of explicitly communicative programmes (Spada and Lightbown, 1989; Allen *et al.*, 1990; Lightbown and Spada, 1990; Beretta, 1992). In the latter studies, the performance of more communicative classes appears to be mixed, equivocal or actually negative. It is argued, however, that if the critical issue in successful learning is getting the balance between communicative and analytic activities right (Allen *et al.*, 1990), then such apparently contradictory results are to be expected. If the proportion of communicative segments in the present programme (22%) were to double, for example, there is no guarantee that the most communicative classes would continue to have (as at present) the highest levels of proficiency in Irish, the most attentive and interested pupils and the most positive attitudes to Irish. The issue is that the *balance* between experiential and analytic activities would have changed. This constitutes an important reminder also that our results cannot be interpreted as evidence that language practice activities are either ineffective or unnecessary in developing communicative proficiency in Irish (Van Lier, 1988). Looking at evidence elsewhere, we suggest that a reasonable goal for the Irish lesson in future might be devote about 50% of the time to communicative activities.

Regarding the second issue above, we ask why do not teachers (particularly in low-Irish achievement classes) already elect to spend more lesson time on communicative activities, given that such activities are associated with the positive outcomes documented here. Two sorts of reasons emerged in the *Communicative Materials Project*: (a) where teachers felt that the standard of their pupils' Irish was already unsatisfactory, they were often uneasy about taking time away from what might be considered more serious language-learning activities in order to spend it on communicative games and tasks; and (b) some teachers felt that their weaker pupils would not, in any case, be capable of communicating in Irish even if the teacher were to attempt this approach. Their actual experience with the prepared communicative materials supplied in the course of the project, however, did modify these initial assessments. Later on the teachers felt that the materials managed to redefine the idea of 'communication' or 'communicative activities' in ways that were manageable and practical and which would be accessible to all children. They felt that weaker children, in particular, were benefiting. Thus, the provision of the right kinds of communicative materials may be a critical factor in allowing teachers to switch to a communicative approach.

Finally, we consider whether the introduction of communicative materials may pose certain kinds of problems for the more or less 'all-Irish' character of Irish-language teaching at primary level. It is noted first that the relatively high level of use of Irish at present may be quite dependent on the lesson being predictable and routinised. While this predictability makes communication in Irish possible, it also limits its scope. Introducing an explicitly communicative approach to teaching Irish, with all the accompanying new tasks and different lesson structure that that will entail, will undoubtedly destabilise existing routines. Although this will obviously open up the possibility of more realistic communication, it could also create more pressure to revert to English for certain kinds of explanation which were not previously necessary. A study of a communicative language teaching in Scotland (Mitchell and Johnstone, 1986; Mitchell, 1988, 1989) reports that while teachers felt that French was appropriate for simple organisational instructions in the classroom, they believed that it was less suitable for instructions specifically related to an activity or for explaining grammar. It is important, therefore, that course developers would produce communicative materials and tasks which will allow teachers to maintain the present 'all-Irish' character of the Irish lesson.

10.3.8 *Chapter 8 - Pupil and teacher roles and classsroom organisation*

Chapter 8 analyses classroom observation data relating to three *ILAS* dimensions: *Pupil behaviour, Teacher mode of involvement* and *Classroom organisation*. Our main objectives are: (a) to describe pupil and teacher roles and forms of classroom organisation and (b) to determine the relationship of these to achievement in Irish, class attention, class interest, attitude to Irish and *Irish-lesson anxiety*. As in the previous chapter, the two main reference points in discussing the results are (i) the 'communicative' versus 'language practice' orientation in language teaching and (ii) the Stirling Study of the audio-visual teaching of French at first year post-primary. In the concluding section of the chapter we explore a few more issues relating to attention and interest and the future of *ILAS*.

Pupil behaviour

The results show that pupils were considered to be 'Speaking' for about two thirds of the lesson segments and 'Listening' for nearly 95% of the segments. These proportions match closely those of the Stirling Study. Reading is involved in 46% of the segments overall, roughly equivalent again to the proportion found in the Stirling study. The Stirling study, however, did not distinguish between 'Reading aloud' (18.2% of segments in the present study) and 'Reading silently' (27.7% in the present study). *Pupil behaviour* which involves 'Looking' features in 19% of segments - less than in the Stirling Study (28.8%). 'Writing' behaviours are significantly longer than segments associated with any of the other six behaviours but occur in only 6.8% of segments (considerably lower than the 20.8% reported in the Stirling Study). Finally, segments in which pupils are 'Doing' something (performing a physical action other then speaking) account for the least proportion of segments (5.1%).

Only two pupil behaviours - 'Reading aloud' and, to a considerably lesser extent, 'Reading silently' - are associated with significant effects. In the pooled-segment analysis, for example, 'Reading aloud' segments are associated with significantly lower mean *Class interest* and mean *Class attention* ratings than other segments. In addition, classes which devote more time to 'Reading aloud' are significantly more likely to have lower achievement in spoken Irish, less positive class attitude to Irish, higher levels of anxiety in relation to speaking in Irish and reduced levels of attention and interest in class. Segments in which 'Reading silently' was involved were associated with just two significant outcomes: in the pooled-segment analysis, they have significantly lower *Class interest* and *Class attention* ratings than all other segments. In the Stirling Study, which combined these two kinds of reading, no significant connections were found between reading and achievement in French.

'Reading aloud' segments in the Irish study were found to almost invariably involve language practice and to be particularly strongly associated with 'Transposition'- a language activity in which utterances are translated from one code (e.g. listening or reading) to another (e.g. writing or speaking).

Teachers in classes which have low levels of achievement in Irish seem to particularly favour reading-aloud of the language practice kind. It is argued that teachers may feel that despite the fact that 'Reading aloud' activities of this kind are relatively mechanical, they are rewarding for those pupils who have few other opportunities to display their competence in Irish. Such an assumption on the part of teachers would be consistent with pupils' own reports (see Chapter 4) that they prefer reading in Irish to other activities involving Irish. The probable success of reading-aloud activities in motivating individual pupils, however, must be weighed against the evidence that there is a price to be paid in terms of class attention and interest more generally.

It is important to point out also that the pattern of association between 'Reading aloud' and variables such as *Class achievement in spoken Irish* and *Class interest* need not always follow the 'negative' direction found here. 'Reading aloud' in another teaching context might equally well have been associated with *communicative* language activities and with positive outcomes such as a higher interest and lower anxiety.

The insights provided by these results had a strong influence on the approach to Irish reading adopted in *Communicative Materials Project*. This involved an emphasis on the kind of communicative reading activities which would capture the interest of all pupils, even those with very low levels of academic achievement. In the report on the *Communicative Materials Project* (Harris *et al.*, 1996a,b) the value of integrating reading with listening, speaking and writing in the same communicative tasks was stressed. It was also argued that the practice of having a separate, mainly narrative-based 'reader' should be discontinued and instead that the reading component of each unit would be physically integrated with other communicative material relating to listening, speaking and writing in the pupil's textbook. This is not to underestimate the importance of stories and of children's literature in the classroom. Indeed, we suggest that a new series of non-course books in Irish tailored to the more general or leisure reading interests of Irish children should be developed.

It might appear surprising that the frequency of 'speaking' behaviours is not significantly related to variables such as *Class achievement in spoken Irish, Class attitude to Irish* and *Class interest*. The explanation lies mainly in the fact that the definition of speaking adopted in *ILAS* was relatively loose: 'speaking' referred to both readiness to speak as well as to actual speech and did not distinguish between speech which was sustained for the whole segment from shorter contributions within segments. In addition, the high frequency of speaking behaviours means that 'speaking' occurred in a wide range of contexts, including both language practice and communication. Chapter 9 reports on a more focused study of individual speech in which we demonstrate its importance more clearly.

Classroom organisation and teacher mode of involvement
Data from the *Classroom organisation* and *Teacher mode of involvement* dimensions illustrate the active, central role of the teacher in the Irish lesson, either 'Interacting' with pupils (62.4% of segments) or 'Instructing' (10% of segments), all of this within a predominantly 'Whole-class' context (85.6% of segments). This is typical of the emphasis on 'whole class' teaching in Irish primary schools (see Burke and Fontes, 1986) and is very similar to the situation regarding the teaching of French in the Stirling study. Another form of classroom organisation, 'Individual: same task', is associated with 6.2% of segments.

The organisational category, 'Pupil/group demonstration', while not very common, occurs more frequently in the Irish study (7.5% of segments) than in the Stirling Study (2% of segments). In this category, a pupil or group of pupils leads or directs the lesson activity while the rest of the class functions as an 'audience' - perhaps answering or otherwise interacting with the demonstrating pupils. The teacher usually retains a monitoring role.

Segments in which 'Pupil/group demonstrations' occur have higher *Class attention* and *Class interest* mean ratings than either 'Whole class' or 'Individual: same task' forms of classroom organisation. There is a significant tendency for classes which devote a greater proportion of time to 'Pupil/group demonstration' forms of organisation to have lower levels of *Irish-lesson anxiety* and for classes which devote a greater proportion of time to 'Whole class' forms of organisation to have higher levels of *Irish-lesson anxiety*. 'Pupil/group demonstration' segments are associated with both communicative and language-practice type activities. This would suggest that it really is the form of classroom organisation involved, rather than language activity as such, which is responsible for the favourable results in relation to attention, interest and anxiety. This also suggests that where language practice is necessary, 'Pupil/group demonstrations' may have a better chance of securing a positive response from pupils than more traditional 'Whole class' approaches.

Pupils working together in small groups, a form of classroom organisation very much associated with communicative language teaching, accounts for less than 1% of segments. Teachers in the *Communicative Materials Project*, particularly those with weaker classes, often felt that communicative activities with a small-group form of classroom organisation were not viable due to the limited linguistic ability of pupils, the amount of preparation and disorder involved, and the difficulty of getting the class settled down again. As a result most of the communicative games and tasks which we proposed in the report on the *Communicative Materials Project* (Harris *et al.*, 1996a,b) had a whole-class dimension and, where possible, a pupil/group demonstration or 'competing-team' element. In the longer term, however, we suggest (see Chapter 9) that the teaching of Irish should include a greater proportion of small-group activities.

ILAS: General observations and future use

Finally, a number of more general questions about the *ILAS* data and about the future use of the instrument are discussed. One issue is why ratings of attention and interest are so high generally (especially in the light of the frequently negative pupil comments about the Irish lesson reported in Chapter 4). It is suggested that present forms of classroom organisation (whole-class, teacher-centred) and interaction patterns (e.g. very frequent display questions requiring short answers from pupils) actually discourage disengagement from the lesson by pupils. It is possible, however, that many pupils are able to answer correctly while listening and attending with a rather narrow and shallow focus on the lesson. Another issue is why interest ratings are generally lower than attention ratings and more sensitive to features of the lesson such as language activity and topic. It is argued that the notion of 'interest' refers to a more spontaneous component of the pupil's reaction to the lesson than 'attention' does and that this aspect of pupil engagement is less amenable to being managed by the teacher's questioning and interaction strategies.

All the main innovations introduced into *ILAS* were successful and should be retained in future uses of the instrument. The addition of the two 'high-inference' dimensions of *Class attention* and *Class interest* is a useful advance on the original Stirling System. The fact that these 'on-line' ratings of pupil reactions were conducted on a segment by segment basis allowed us to link them to changes in *Topic, Language activity, Pupil behaviour,* and *Classroom organisation.* The addition of the 'Simulated communication in Irish' category to the *Language activity* dimension was also an improvement on the original system, with strong associations being revealed between the new category and a variety of positive learning outcomes. The large proportion of lesson segments in which 'Reading aloud' occurred, and the evidence of its association with significant learning outcomes, justified our decision to make this a separate category of *Pupil behaviour* (rather than have one broad 'reading' category as in the Stirling System). The decision to incorporate the recording of *Materials* into a segmental analysis of the lesson was also successful. All this confirms the usefulness of segment-based observation instruments, though the need remains for ongoing revision of the various descriptive categories and dimensions in order to keep them in line with changing theoretical understandings.

While the present study using 'outside' observers was successful and, perhaps, a necessary first step in studying the Irish lesson, it is important to point out that classroom observation with different goals, and using very different approaches, can contribute to the improvement of pupil proficiency. In particular, classroom observation in which the role of the teacher as observer and interpreter is more central can provide a different and important perspective to our understanding of the learning process (Nunan, 1996; Bell, 1997). Action research conducted by teachers themselves in which they observe their own or other teachers' classrooms can help them to understand and evaluate their own instructional practices. It is important, therefore, that teachers are given the training necessary for using observation procedures. Pupils can also contribute to action research in the classroom. One example of this is where pupils, in association with their teacher, analyse and evaluate selected activities from previous lessons, such as errors and their resolution (Van Lier, 1988). We have already shown in Chapter 4 how pupils' views can contribute significantly to our understanding of the teaching and learning process.

Finally, it is argued that classroom observation provides teachers, inspectors and researchers with a common language for describing teaching, which in turn stimulates analytic inquiry into the process itself and helps teachers discover their underlying beliefs, goals, practices etc. In this way, the gap between theory and practice may be reduced, and a richer data base will become available for theory building.

10.3.9 Chapter 9 - Pupil participation and language use in the Irish lesson

While the *ILAS* provides us with a broad-based description of the classroom practice of Irish teachers, it fails to register in detail the characteristics of communicative interaction in the classroom. It also fails to describe the extent to which different types of pupils are engaged with the lesson activity in progress, or indeed whether they are participating in the lesson in a manner which is at all consistent with the pedagogic goals of the activity. The *Pupil Communicative Behaviour Record (PCBR)*, overcomes these limitations by describing individual pupil participation and language use. In developing the instrument account was taken of research which tries to identify those features of the classroom which are important for second-language learning. In particular, we took account of the *COLT* observation system (Allen, *et al.*, 1984; Allen, *et al.*, 1990) which allows for the recording of communicative features of classroom interaction.

Sample and instrument

Individual pupils of high, middle and low levels of ability in Irish were observed in each class and over two lessons. The inspector observed the selected pupils, one at a time, and recorded various aspects of their behaviour. The observation work proceeded in five minute sequences, with the first three minutes being given over to observing the target pupil, and the last two minutes being used to record more fully his/her behaviour on the coding sheet.

The *PCBR* defined behaviour under three main headings: *(1) Pupil speaks individually, (2) Pupil is silent* and *(3) Other pupil behaviour*. Behaviours under each main heading could be coded in relation to a range of language use or other descriptive categories. *Individual pupil speech* was categorised in terms of the 'Language used' (Irish/English/half-and-half), the 'Length of utterance' and whether the utterance was a 'Question' or an 'Answer' etc. Other descriptive categories related to individual pupil's speech were also used. In cases where the pupil was silent, two categories 'Attending' and 'Disruptive' were rated as being high/moderate/low. *Other* behaviours consisted of four categories: 'Choral speech', 'Reading silently', 'Reading aloud', and 'Writing'.

Speech and silence

About one-fifth of the behaviours consist of the pupil being *Silent*, presumably listening/looking. Levels of attention were generally high, and levels of disruptiveness were low, during these 'silent' behaviours. For example, just 15.4% of all silent behaviours were associated with low levels of attentiveness, while high/moderate levels of disruptiveness occurred in only 10.9% of all silent behaviours. *Other* behaviours (38.1%) consist of choral speech, reading or writing. The combined reading behaviours ('reading aloud'/'silent reading') make up 14.1% of all behaviours, while 'Writing' and 'Choral speech' follow closely with 12.3% and 11.7% respectively.

One of the more important findings of the study, however, is that about half of all behaviours recorded during the three minute observation period consisted of the pupil speaking individually - and in Irish in nine out of ten cases.

These results indicate a high level of overt definite pupil participation in class. This is of interest in the light of the fact that the Irish class in ordinary schools is the main, and sometimes the only situation where we can be absolutely sure that the majority of pupils actually use the language. The findings are also important to the extent that many teachers and parents would probably consider a high rate of individual spoken contributions by pupils as evidence of the general vitality and success of the Irish lesson.

These positive results must be viewed in the light of three less positive findings. First, individual pupil speech most frequently took the form of answers (82.7% of all individual utterances) and these were in general short, predictable responses to 'display' questions from the teacher, something which is characteristic of language practice rather than real communication or meaning negotiation. Only 13.4% of all pupil utterances were longer than a single sentence (i.e. 'sustained'). Answers which were sustained were much more likely to be coded as 'unpredictable' (i.e. occurring in the context of meaning-negotiation) than were shorter answers consisting of a single word, a clause or a sentence. No significant gender differences were found in the main behaviours of interest here.

The second characteristic of individual pupil speech in Irish which is undesirable is that its occurrence actually varies substantially according to the pupil's ability in Irish. It seems as if the pupils most in need of opportunities to speak in Irish, those with lower levels of ability in the language, are the ones least likely to be engaged in it.

The third issue is that pupils with higher levels of ability in Irish are much more likely than pupils with lower levels of ability in Irish to be rated as 'highly attentive' during these periods of silence. Likewise, low levels of attention during periods of silent listening are more common in pupils with lower levels of ability in Irish. While boys and girls are equally likely to be silent, girls are significantly more attentive than boys during silent periods.

Finally, we found that classes in which pupils speak individually less often have significantly higher levels of *Irish-lesson anxiety*.

Explaining pupil participation
We argue that an important secondary goal of teachers in so frequently soliciting individual spoken contributions from pupils may simply be to maintain attention to the lesson more generally. It is suggested that the problem for pupils who are weaker at Irish is that, for whatever reason, they have a much lower probability of either being asked to perform or of volunteering to perform. Without the motivation provided by imminent public

performance, lower ability pupils are more dependent on the intrinsic interest of the lesson material to keep them engaged - and we know from Chapter 4 that pupils generally are often very critical of Irish lesson materials.

Another issue to which the results give rise is whether teachers or pupils ultimately determine how often pupils speak. Teachers are most likely trying to achieve an optimum balance between a range of concerns - e.g. not slowing the class down too much, ensuring that there is a high proportion of successful (correct) public exchanges in Irish in order to provide a good language model for pupils in general, and so on. Teachers may also be trying to take account of the discomfort for weaker pupils of being nominated to speak in situations where their answer, or failure to answer, is likely to expose them to embarrassment. Another possibility is that low-achievers themselves develop a strategy of remaining passive in class over time - not responding when called, not volunteering, asking fewer questions and approaching the teacher less often (Good *et al.*, 1987).

The research literature has identified a number of changes which could be made to the existing teacher-focused, whole-class approach which might improve pupil participation and communicative language use: ceding more control to pupils, particularly in relation to turn-taking and increasing wait-time for responses. Most classroom discourse tends to be organised so that there is a strict allocation of turns, with tight control being exercised over who speaks to whom. As a result, there is relatively little turn-by-turn negotiation, and competition and individual student initiatives are discouraged (McHoul, 1978; Van Lier, 1988). In classrooms where this kind of control is relaxed, the benefits can be seen in the content of interactions, the frequency of pupil initiatives and the general levels of engagement (Cathcart, 1986; Allen, *et al.*, 1988; Midorikawa, 1990; Robson, 1992). Other positive effects of allowing more control to pass to pupils were documented in Chapter 8. Research also indicates that greater 'wait-time' results in longer pupil utterances as well as an increase in the participation of less able pupils (Holley and King, 1971; Long *et al.*, 1984; White and Lightbown, 1984). Even if increasing wait time does help less able pupils, however, the strategy may ultimately pose other problems of lesson dynamics in a situation where the engagement of pupils is primarily maintained by the fast pace of the ('display') question-and-answer exchanges, rather than by the inherent challenge or interest offered by the lesson material itself. Thus, more basic changes may be needed.

A greater emphasis on communication

In the final section, we discuss the contribution which a communicative approach to teaching Irish could make to improving pupil participation and language use. Two broad areas are examined. First, we consider the finding from the *PCBR* data that pupil participation and language use are better in those classes which have certain characteristics such as smaller numbers of pupils and a greater emphasis on communicative activities. Second, we examine the likely benefits of adopting a more developed communicative approach to teaching Irish.

Taking the first of these issues, we found that as sixth-grade classes (or sixth-grade groups within multi-grade classes) get smaller, pupils are significantly more likely to speak individually and less likely to remain silent. The *PCBR* data also show that as classes spend more time on 'Simulated communication in Irish' there is a significant tendency for pupils to speak individually more often and to make sustained contributions more often. In contrast, as classes spend more time on 'Contextualisation exercises', a form of language practice, pupils are significantly less likely either to speak individually or to make sustained contributions. While the results produce a coherent picture, it is not an entirely unambiguous one. The fact that *Class achievement in Irish* is significantly correlated with *Class size* and *Proportion of time spent on 'Simulated communication'* means that we cannot conclusively link pupil behavioural propensities to either of the latter. Notwithstanding these problems of partial correlation, additional exploratory analyses add weight to the indications that pupil participation and language use are sensitive to particular characteristics of the kind of communicative language teaching activity which are involved.

The second point is that Irish-language teaching at primary level should gradually assimilate the full range of strategies, ideas, teaching materials and tasks which research and practice relating to the communicative approach have linked to successful learning. Among the features which appear to be important are meaning negotiation, learner feedback, communication repair, use of authentic materials and small-group work. We focus on two of these in particular: small-group work and tasks involving meaning negotiation.

It has been shown that a greater emphasis on group work increases the opportunity for pupils to speak, improves the quality of pupil talk, helps to individualise instruction, promotes a positive affective climate for learning and provides more opportunities for meaning negotiation (Long and Porter, 1985; Pica and Doughty, 1985; Ellis, 1994). Increasing the amount of individual pupil speech occurring in more one-to-one communicative activities in the Irish lesson would reduce the need for such a high rate of individual pupil speech in a whole-class context. This more private and negotiable context of language use should also reduce some of the social risk for less able pupils who wish to make use of whatever Irish they have. One of the problems, as we found out in the *Twenty-Classes Study* and in the *Communicative Materials Project*, is that most teachers do not appear to be enthusiastic about group work in teaching Irish. In the longer term, however, many of the perceived organisational and learner problems associated with it may be surmountable through good design and implementation (Lyle, 1996; Shaw, 1996; Davies, 1997).

A number of studies have also demonstrated, that the kind of language use and interaction which is promoted by a task may be related to specific characteristics of that task. Long (1980), Doughty and Pica (1986) and Newton (1991) show that 'two-way' tasks result in more negotiation of meaning than one-way tasks. Another critical feature is whether or not the task involves the learner planning his or her output. Planned tasks 'stretch' interlanguages further, and promote 'destabilization' more, than unplanned tasks

(Long, 1989; Ellis, 1994). A third important feature is whether the task is 'closed' (has a single correct or small finite set of solutions) or 'open' (no predetermined solution). Closed tasks tend to produce more negotiation work, more topic and language recycling, more feedback and more feedback-incorporation than open tasks Long (1989). On the other hand, open-ended tasks may afford learners great interactive freedom to practise conversational skills such as topic selection and change (Jones, 1991).

While arguing for a communicative approach to teaching Irish which would incorporate current best practice, it is emphasised that our results cannot be used to dismiss the contribution of an analytic focus or indeed the value of a certain amount of language practice. Van Lier (1988) points out, for example, that language practice can provide a secure scaffold for second-language learners, just as various kinds of games and rituals are employed by caretakers to support young children's first-language acquisition. Prabhu (1990: 173) makes the further point that language practice helps to render the kind of 'recurrent social encounter' involved in teaching and learning endurable by bringing a certain amount of routinisation to it. The optimum balance between experiential /communicative and analytic/language-practice activities in teaching Irish at primary level is something that will only emerge over time and it may well vary from teacher to teacher.

10.4 Implications

In the course of this report we have presented a wide range of new research findings and practical information concerning the teaching and learning of Irish in ordinary primary schools. Arising directly from these, we have proposed various initiatives which we believe would improve pupil achievement and attitude/motivation. The initiatives relate to matters such as the involvement of parents, changes in teaching methods and practices, and the development of teaching materials. To implement even these recommendations, however, would require a research-and-development effort considerably greater than that which is presently in place. But the real scale and importance of the task of supporting Irish in primary school can only be determined by enlarging our frame of reference. Two issues in particular are important: (a) the crucial role of ordinary primary schools within the larger national effort to promote bilingualism and the wider use of Irish and (b) the implications for the teaching of Irish of the fact that, outside Gaeltacht areas, Irish is a minority second language. In this concluding section, we argue that when account is taken of these issues, as well as the findings and recommendations of the present report, it is clear that a new body is needed to provide a comprehensive support system for Irish in ordinary primary schools.

Taking the language revival issue first, the point here is that ordinary primary schools have a central role in reproducing speaking proficiency in Irish in each new generation. There are a number of reasons for this. First, there is the fact that the overwhelming majority of children learn Irish in ordinary schools (rather than in the considerably smaller number of Gaeltacht or all-Irish schools). Thus, any initiative which enhances the success of such schools has the potential to affect large numbers of pupils and, thereby, make a substantial contribution to the language-revival effort. It must be borne in mind too - as we showed in Chapter 2 - that a small but significant minority of ordinary schools produce levels of achievement in Irish which approach or equal the average level obtaining in all-Irish schools. Second, exposure to Irish at primary level is probably both more intense, and more focused on speech and conversation, than it is at post-primary level. The informal use of Irish for school and class communication, and the teaching of parts of other subjects partly or wholly through Irish, are more common at primary than at post-primary. At post-primary, the language tends to be restricted to the Irish lesson, in part because teachers at this level are subject specialists. At primary, every teacher is an Irish teacher. Thus, for the majority of pupils, primary school provides the most sustained exposure to the spoken language that they will ever have. These schools have a special importance for the language in other ways too: they lay the groundwork for further language learning at post-primary and third level and, to the extent that they provide the first introduction to Irish, they can have a considerable influence on long-term attitudes towards Irish.

The minority second-language status of Irish is another factor to be taken into account. The key sociolinguistic consequence for the teaching of Irish is that pupils have little or no interactive contact with the spoken language outside school. The resulting paradox is that while pupils learn to speak Irish in school in order to use it in their own lives, they know that there are very few occasions outside (particularly involving their peers) in which there might be either a real need, or even an opportunity, to speak it. The problems which this presents for teachers and schools are set out in some detail in Harris *et al.* (1996a,b). For present purposes, we can enumerate just a few of them. First, it is more difficult for both teachers and pupils to identify a proximal goal or motivation outside school for learning to speak the language in the classroom. In addition, in teaching the language, and in developing tasks and materials for use within the classroom, it is more difficult to identify situations, contexts and even language registers which make the prospect of using Irish credible or plausible. Another result is that the range of authentic Irish-language materials and the volume of commercially-produced resources available for teaching and learning Irish at this level bears no comparison with that available in the case of the major European languages.

These all represent challenges rather than insurmountable difficulties. We mention them here merely to make the case that structures and resources equal to the task must be provided. The response required has both creative and research-and-development dimensions. The creative challenge is, in some respects, analogous to that confronted by Irish-programme makers in TnaG and RTÉ - and indeed by Irish dramatists and writers - who wish to use Irish to reflect and incorporate life outside Gaeltacht areas. But the creative work in the case of primary schools needs to be backed up by, and located within, a sustained research-and-development enterprise - to identify educational problems and possibilities, to set up pilot programmes, and to ensure that adequate provision is made for in-service training.

We believe, therefore, that a representative body should be established under the auspices of the Department of Education and Science to provide a support system for the teaching and learning of Irish in ordinary primary schools, and to elaborate and particularise the implications of government policy in this area. Essentially, what is required is a long-term exercise in educational and language planning focused on the complex interaction between the school on the one hand and the home/community on the other. Included on the proposed body would be representatives of all those involved in the teaching and promotion of Irish, as well as those whose active cooperation has the potential to enhance the efforts of schools e.g. teachers, teachers' unions or representative bodies, Colleges of Education, the NPC, the NCCA, ITÉ, Bord na Gaeilge, TnaG, RnaG, RTÉ, An Gúm, the commercial educational publishers, business and commerce and Irish-language, social and sporting organisations. A body of this kind is needed because the pace of existing work needs to be accelerated; because the division of responsibilities between existing agencies does not facilitate decisive, sustained action; and because the quality and efficiency of the work itself would be enhanced if there was a greater element of partnership and inter-agency co-operation and sharing of ideas.

While we focus only on the needs of ordinary primary schools in the present discussion, some of our arguments also apply to all-Irish and Gaeltacht schools. Indeed, all-Irish and Gaeltacht schools have additional needs which are analysed in some detail in the report on the *Communicative Materials Project* (Harris *et al.*, 1996a,b). The needs of Irish-medium schools are also acknowledged in the Education Act (1998) (Section 31). It must be noted also that we do not consider here the extent to which the functions of the proposed body might be similar to those envisaged in the Education Act or indeed to the 'Institute of Teaching Resources' suggested recently by the INTO (INTO, 1998a,b). Our concern on this occasion is simply to try to define the scope and importance of the work which would be carried out by a body with a representative and inter-agency character to support the teaching of Irish in ordinary schools.

Among the functions of the proposed body would be:

1. To provide a support system for the teaching and learning of Irish, taking account both of the educational aspects of the issue and the national aim of promoting bilingualism and the wider use of Irish.

2. To adopt a proactive approach towards this task - finding out what teachers, parents and pupils require in the way of materials etc.; identifying the problems and possibilities which exist in relation to teaching and learning Irish; and establishing pilot schemes and commissioning research to investigate new ways of responding to these.

3. To coordinate the production of textbooks and audio, video and IT-based teaching and learning materials.

4. To identify in-service needs generally, and to ensure, in particular, that adequate training and support is provided for teachers who are involved in new initiatives relating to Irish.

5. To establish what various agencies and institutions could contribute to developing a more supportive out-of-school environment for primary school pupils learning Irish; to coordinate the work of these various bodies; and to function as a forum for ideas and debate in this area.

Until relatively recently, the Department of Education and Science was directly responsible for nearly all aspects of Irish at primary level - for the Irish curriculum itself, for the development of the teaching materials for oral Irish (implicitly recognising the special needs of this subject) and more generally for the teaching of Irish in the context of state policy on Irish. Because the curricular and materials-development responsibilities of the Department of Education and Science are now partialled out between the NCCA and the commercial publishers, there is no longer a single agency which has active day-to-day responsibility for supporting the teaching and learning of Irish in the context of language promotion and revival. These arrangements represent a change of status which is probably more significant for Irish than it is for other school subjects. This is not the only reason, however, why a new body is needed. Even if the Department were to retain control of materials development in the case of oral Irish, for example, it still could be argued that, in practice, its role in supporting Irish is not defined broadly enough. To say this is not in any way to criticise the present work either of the Department of Education and Science or other agencies such as the NCCA, Bord na Gaeilge or ITÉ. We can readily point out, for example, the role of the Department's Inspectorate in the present study, and the work of the representative NCCA Irish Curriculum Committee which completed its work last year. The point rather is that an inter-agency, coordinating body, with a focused, proactive approach to supporting the teaching and learning of Irish, is a better way to proceed.

Just one of the reasons why such a body is required is that many aspects of materials production in the case of Irish are fundamentally non-profitable. Commercial publishers are constrained by the entirely reasonable requirement to make a profit. But this can sometimes have undesirable consequences for the kind of teaching materials which are produced - it normally means that the emphasis has to be on producing a book to be sold to each pupil. It can be argued, for example, that in the vacuum left in recent years as the *Nuachúrsaí* gradually fell out of favour, the economics of educational publishing have had a greater impact on how oral Irish was taught. Irrespective of the merits of these commercially-produced materials in themselves, the fact of the matter is that the teaching of the oral aspect of the language is more dominated by pupil texts now than it was heretofore. If a more active monitoring agency had been in place during this period, developments such as these would have been anticipated, identified and responded to much earlier. None of this is to deny the important role that educational publishers have played in the case of Irish in the past and indeed collaborative ventures between publishers and the proposed new body would be very desirable in the future.

What we are proposing in any case is considerably more than a centre which would assign authors to produce textbooks or other teaching materials in the conventional way. There are advantages, as the *Communicative Materials Project* showed, in having applied linguists working side by side with a consultative group of teachers, who try out new materials and approaches in their own classrooms and report back their experiences and the reaction of pupils. But this kind of once-off approach to development work is not sufficient given the challenges which the sociolinguistic position of Irish presents - and particularly in a period of great change in second-language teaching generally.

The issues which Irish-language materials development and teaching at primary level must constantly confront are discussed in some detail in Harris *et al.* (1996a,b). We can take just one of these issues, language registers, for illustrative purposes here. Because the day-to-day experiences of most children of primary-school age outside the Gaeltacht has not yet found expression in Irish, Irish-language registers appropriate to many situations of interest to them have yet to evolve. Consequently, pupils often feel ill at ease using forms of language that they associate with the formality of school rather than with 'real' life outside. It will require an ongoing effort to find innovative solutions to problems such as these. As we pointed out in the report on the *Communicative Materials Project*, a number of strategies may be needed - e.g. involving creative writers in Irish as well as those with educational expertise directly in materials development, and soliciting the opinions of pupils themselves about ways of using Irish in their own lives.

Creating opportunities for young people to influence the evolution of the language is an important enterprise in its own right, of course, since it is young people who bring vitality and change to any language. Experimentation and failure are an inevitable part of this process of innovation. The alternative is the provision of learning materials which can all too quickly acquire the dated characteristics of which pupils complained so often in the *Twenty-Classes Study*. It scarcely needs to be said that the introduction of a communicative approach to teaching Irish will not, in itself, solve the problems we have been talking about here - although their existence, and the need to respond to them, is brought more clearly into focus with a communicative approach. In structural-linguistic or language-practice based approaches, or where the emphasis is on narrative texts, the realities of using the language for real communication may never be confronted and so sociolinguistic issues can be more easily obscured or ignored.

The *Teaching through Irish Project* carried out by ITÉ illustrates another way in which the proposed body could take more decisive steps in support of Irish at primary level. The project (see Chapter 1) involved the development of materials for teaching Science and Art through Irish at third and fourth grade in ordinary primary schools (Harris and Mac Giollabhuí, 1998a,b,c). The project is instructive in a number of ways. First, it raises the question of why such materials were not developed earlier, and why the content-based teaching option has not been more vigorously promoted before now - given that a substantial minority of teachers already conduct a small amount of Irish-medium instruction, mainly in music and physical education (Harris 1983, 1993; Harris and Murtagh, 1988a; INTO, 1985a). Second, because the project was a limited one, designed simply to explore possibilities in the area, Irish-medium materials suitable for other grades and subjects have not yet been developed. Third, the project illustrates how in-service workshops can be used to develop innovative approaches to the teaching of Irish. It also serves as a model for how a limited programme of instruction through Irish in ordinary schools could be promoted more widely on an entirely voluntary basis. Workshops allow teachers an opportunity to share experiences and to provide mutual support as they respond to the new professional challenges presented by teaching through Irish.

One of the functions of the body now proposed would be to identify and exploit precisely these kinds of possibilities at the earliest possible moment. While the ITÉ project makes an initial contribution, the further initiatives now needed - materials-development for other grades and subjects, and the establishment of pilot schemes and in-service - can only be undertaken by a body with a different, more extensive brief. Without the support and validation provided by a comprehensive scheme, it will continue to be difficult for individual teachers, acting alone, to choose this teaching option. In that case, the potential for Irish-medium teaching in ordinary schools which was uncovered by this ITÉ project will almost certainly remain dormant.

The critical feature of the proposed body, however, is the organic link which it would provide between the different activities needed to support Irish, and the direct contact which would be established between people and agencies capable of contributing solutions. Very few of the issues we have been discussing can be tackled in isolation - materials development, in-service training for teachers, or pilot schemes to involve parents. The strategies which we have discussed for involving parents in their children's efforts to learn to speak Irish, for example, would be greatly strengthened if new classroom learning materials were to incorporate tasks which anticipated the involvement of parents, or if there could be joint planning and coordination of supportive television programmes and the development of in-class materials.

The various partners in this enterprise do not need to have a consensus on matters relating to Irish in order to be effective. The experience of partnership in economic and social matters at a national level shows that all that is needed is attitudes and values that are good enough to sustain public cooperation - the partners do not have to agree on their ultimate social vision (National Economic and Social Forum, 1997). Deliberation which is 'problem-solving and practical' in character will tend to produce consensus in the long-term, but this is an outcome rather than a precondition of partnership. Finally, there is another side to all this - the possibility that solving problems of relevance to primary schools may provide guidance and direction for the language-promotion and revival effort nationally. Some of the enduring problems in the two domains are the same: how to energise people to actually begin using the language for real communication and how to identify and cultivate registers and contexts of use which facilitate the switch to Irish. If we can find practical solutions to some of these problems in a school context, there is every reason to expect that we will be able to apply them in the larger language-promotion domain.

Bibliography

Allen, J.P.B. (1992) Instructional processes and the development of communicative competence. *IRAL,* 30 (1), 1-20.

Allen, J.P.B. and Carroll, S. (1988) Analytic and experiential dimensions in Core French classrooms. *Canadian Modern Language Review,* 45, 43-64.

Allen, J.P.B., Carroll, S., Burtis, J. and Gaudino, V. (1987) The Core French Observation Study. In B. Harley, P. Allen, J. Cummins and M. Swain (eds) *The development of bilingual proficiency: Final report. Vol. II: Classroom treatment.* Toronto: Modern Language Centre, Ontario Institute for Studies in Education.

Allen, J.P.B., Fröhlich, M. and Spada, N. (1984) The Communicative Orientation of Language Teaching: An observation scheme. In J. Handscombe, R.A. Orem and B.P. Taylor (eds) *On TESOL '83.* Washington, D.C.: TESOL.

Allen, J.P.B., Swain, M. and Harley, B. (1988) Analytic and experiential aspects of core French and immersion classrooms. *Bulletin of the CAAL,* 10 (2) , 59-68.

Allen, J.P.B., Swain, M., Harley, B. and Cummins, J. (1990) Aspects of classroom treatment: Toward a more comprehensive view of second language education. In B. Harley, P. Allen, J. Cummins and M. Swain (eds) *The development of second language proficiency.* New York: Cambridge University Press.

Allwright, D. (1992) Exploratory teaching: Bringing research and pedagogy together in the language classroom. *Revue de Phonétique Applique,* 103-104, 101-18.

Angoff, W.H. (1971) Scales, norms, and equivalent scores. In R.L. Thorndike (ed), *Educational measurement* (2nd ed.). Washington, D.C.: American Council on Education.

Applebee, A. N., Langer, J.A. and Mullis, I.V.S. (1989) *Crossroads in American education: The nation's report card. A summary of findings.* Princeton, N.J.: Educational Testing Service.

Atkin, J. and Bastiani, J. (1986) 'Are they teaching?': an alternative perspective on parents as educators. *Education,* 3-13, 18-22.

Bartley, D.E. (1970) The importance of the attitude factor in language dropout: A preliminary investigation of group and sex differences. *Foreign Language Annals,* 3, 383-93.

Bell, J.S. (1997) Introduction: Teacher research in second and foreign language education. *Canadian Modern Language Review,* 54 (1), 3-10.

Bennett, J. (1997) Values and primary education: The Irish language textbooks, 1988-96. *Oideas,* 45, 23-31.

Beretta, A. (1992) What can be learned from the Bangalore Evaluation. In J.C. Alderson and A, Beretta (eds) *Evaluating second language education.* Cambridge: Cambridge University Press.

Bialystok, E., Frohlich, M. and Howard, J. (1978) Variables of classroom achievement in second language learning. *Modern Language Journal,* 62, 327-335.

Bord na Gaeilge/Irish Marketing Surveys (1982) Youth Market Survey - Attitudes to the Irish language. Unpublished Report. Dublin: Author.

Bord na Gaeilge: An Coiste Comhairleach Pleanála (1986) *Irish and the education system: An analysis of examination results.* Dublin: Author.

Bourdieu, P. (1974) The school as a conservative force: Scholastic and cultural inequalities. In J. Eggleston (ed) *Contemporary research in the sociology of education.* London: Methuen.

Bourdieu, P. (1977) *Outline of a theory of practice.* Cambridge: Cambridge University Press.

Boyle, J.P. (1987) Intelligence, reasoning and language proficiency. *Modern Language Journal,* 71 (3), 277-88.

Breathnach, L. (1983) *Tar Liom: Gramadach, Cleachtaí agus Aistí.* Dublin: Gill and Macmillan.

Breathnach, L. (1984) *Bog Liom: Foclóir, Gramadach agus Cleachtaí.* Dublin: Gill and Macmillan.

Breathnach, L. (1988) *Buail Liom: Comhrá, Aistí, Gramadach agus Cleachtaí.* Dublin: Gill and Macmillan.

Breen, M.P. (1987) Learner contributions to task design. In C.N. Candlin and D. Murphy (eds) *Language learning tasks.* (Lancaster Practical Papers in English Language Education, Vol 7, 23-46). Englewood Cliffs, JJ: Prentice-Hall.

British Broadcasting Corporation (1981) *Get by in Italian.* London: British Broadcasting Corporation.

Brown, S. and McIntyre, D.I. (n.d) Segments-unit for analysis of recorded lessons, Unpublished paper, Department of Education, University of Stirling.

Brumfit, C.J. (1985) *Literature and literature teaching: From practice to principle.* Oxford: Pergamon.

Bullock, A. (1975) *A language for life.* Report of the Bullock Committee. London: HMSO.

Burke, A. and Fontes, P.J. (1986) Educational beliefs and practices of sixth-class teachers in Irish primary schools. *Irish Journal of Education,* 20, 51-77.

Burstall, C. (1975) Factors affecting foreign-language learning: A consideration of some relevant research findings. *Language Teaching and Linguistics Abstracts,* 8, 105-25.

Burstall, C. (1979) Primary French in the balance. In J. Pride (ed) *Sociolinguistic aspects of language learning and teaching.* Oxford: Oxford University Press.

Burstall, C., Jamieson, M., Cohen, S. and Hargreaves, M. (1974) *Primary French in the balance.* Windsor, Berks.: NFER.

Canale, M. (1983) From communicative competence to communicative language pedagogy. In J. Richards and R. Schmidt (eds) *Language and communication.* Harlow: Longman.

Carmines, E.G. and Zeller, R.A. (1979) *Reliability and validity assessment.* London: Sage.

Carroll, J.B. (1979) Twenty-five years of research on foreign language aptitude. In K.C. Diller (ed) *Individual differences and universals in language learning aptitude.* Rowley, Mass.: Newbury House.

Cathcart, R. (1986) Situational differences and the sampling of young children's school language. In R. Day (ed) *Talking to learn: Conversation in second language acquisition.* Rowley, Mass.: Newbury House.

Chaudron, C. (1988) *Second language classrooms: Research on teaching and learning.* Cambridge: Cambridge University Press.

Chen, C. and Stevenson, H.W. (1989) Homework: A cross-cultural examination. *Child Development,* 60, 551-561.

Clément, R., Gardner, R.C. and Smythe, P.C. (1977) Motivational variables in second language acquisition. A study of Francophones learning English. *Canadian Journal of Behavioural Science,* 9, 123-33.

Clément, R., Gardner, R.C. and Smythe, P.C. (1980) Social and individual factors in second language acquisition. *Canadian Journal of Behavioural Science,* 12, 293-302.

Clément, R., Smythe, P.C. and Gardner, R.C. (1978) Persistence in second language study: Motivational considerations. *Canadian Modern Language Review,* 34, 688-94.

Cockcroft, W.H. (1982) *Mathematics counts.* Report of the Enquiry into the Teaching of Mathematics. London: HMSO.

Cohen, J. and Cohen, P. (1975) *Applied multiple regression/Correlation analysis for the behavioural sciences.* London: John Wiley & Sons.

Committee On Irish Language Attitudes Research (CLAR) (1975) *Report.* Dublin: Stationery Office.

Cooper, H. (1989) Synthesis of research on homework. *Educational Leadership,* 47, 85-91.

Cronbach, L.J. (1951) Coefficient alpha and the internal structure of tests. *Psychometrika,* 16, 297-334.

Crookes, G. and Schmidt, R.W. (1991) Motivation: Reopening the research agenda. *Language Learning,* 41 (4), 469-512.

Cummins, J. (1984) *Bilingualism and special education: Issues in assessment and pedagogy.* Clevedon: Multilingual Matters.

Davis, R.L. (1997) Group work is not busy work: Maximising success of group work in the L2 classroom. *Foreign Language Annals,* 30 (2), 265-79.

Day, R. (1984) Student participation in the ESL classroom or some imperfections of practice. *Language Learning ,* 34, 69-102.

Day, E.M. and Shapson, S.M. (1991) Integrating formal and functional approaches to language teaching in French immersion: An experimental study. *Language Learning,* 41(1), 25-58.

Dickinson, L. (1987) *Self-instruction in language learning.* Cambridge: Cambridge University Press.

Dörnyei, Z. (1990) Conceptualising motivation in foreign language learning. *Language Learning,* 40, 45-78.

Dörnyei, Z. (1994) Understanding L2 motivation: On with the challenge. *Modern Language Journal,* 78 (4), 515-23.

Doughty, C. and Pica, T. (1986) Information gap tasks: Do they facilitate second language acquisition? *TESOL Quarterly,* 20 (2), 305-26.

Dye, J. S. (1989) Parental involvement in curriculum matters: Parents, teachers and children working together. *Educational Research,* 31 (1), 20-35.

Early, M. (1985) Input and interaction in content classrooms: Foreigner talk and teacher talk in classroom discourse. Unpublished Ph.D. dissertation, University of California at Los Angeles.

Egan, O. and Archer, P. (1985) The accuracy of teachers' ratings of ability: A regression model. *American Educational Research Journal,* 22 (1), 25-34.

Ellis, R. (1994) *The study of second language acquisition.* Oxford: Oxford University Press.

Ellis, R. (1995) Interpretation tasks for grammar teaching. *TESOL Quarterly,* 29 (1), 87-105.

Ely, C. (1986) An analysis of discomfort, risktaking, sociability, and motivation in the L2 classroom. *Language Learning,* 36, 1-25.

Epstein, J.L. (1983) *Homework practices, achievements, and behaviours of elementary school children.* Baltimore: JohnsHopkins University Press.

Fanselow, J.F. (1988) 'Let's see': Contrasting conversations about teaching. *TESOL Quarterly,* 22 (1), 113-30.

Ferguson, G.A. (1976) *Statistical analysis in psychology and education.* London: McGraw-Hill.

Feyten, C.M. (1991) The power of listening ability: An overlooked dimension in language acquisition. *Modern Language Journal,* 75 (2), 173-80.

Fontes, P. and Kellaghan, T. (1977) *The new primary school curriculum: Its implementation and effects.* Dublin: Educational Research Centre.

Fontes, P., Kellaghan, T. and O'Brien, M. (1981) Relationships between time spent teaching, classroom organization, and reading achievement. *Irish Journal of Education,* 15 (2), 79-91.

Ford, E. (1991) Criteria for developing an observation scheme in cooperative language learning. *Canadian Modern Language Review,* 48 (1), 45-63.

Galton, M. and Simon, B. (eds) (1980) *Progress and performance in the primary classroom.* London: Routledge & Kegan Paul.

Galton, M., Simon, B. and Croll, P. (1980) *Inside the primary classroom.* London: Routledge & Kegan Paul.

Gardner, H. (1993) *Frames of mind: The theory of multiple intelligences.* London: Fontana Press.

Gardner, R.C. (1979) Social psychological aspects of second language acquisition. In H. Giles. and R. St. Clair (eds) *Language and social psychology.* Oxford: Basil Blackwell.

Gardner, R.C. (1985a) *The Attitude/Motivation Test Battery: Technical report.* Department of Psychology, University of Western Ontario.

Gardner, R.C. (1985b) *Social psychology and second language learning: The role of attitudes and motivation.* London: Edward Arnold.

Gardner, R.C. and Lambert, W.E. (1959) Motivational variables in second language acquisition. *Canadian Journal of Psychology,* 13, 266-72.

Gardner, R.C. and Lambert, W.E. (1972) *Attitudes and motivation in second language learning.* Rowley, Mass.: Newbury House.

Gardner, R.C. and MacIntyre, P.D. (1991) An instrumental motivation in language study: who says it isn't effective? *Studies in Second Language Acquisition,* 13, 57-72.

Gardner, R.C. and MacIntyre, P.D. (1993) A student's contributions to second-language learning. Part II: Affective variables. *Language Teaching,* 26, 1-11.

Gardner, R.C. and Smythe, P.C. (1981) On the development of the Attitude/Motivation Test Battery. *Canadian Modern Language Review,* 37, 510-25.

Gardner, R.C., Clément, R., Smythe, P.C. and Smythe, C.L. (1979) *The Attitude/Motivation Test Battery - revised manual.* Research Bulletin No.15. London, Canada: Language Research Group, University of Western Ontario.

Gardner, R.C., Lalonde, R.N. and Pierson, R. (1983) The socio-educational model of second language acquisition: An investigation using LISREL causal modeling. *Journal of Language and Social Psychology,* 2 (1), 1-15.

Gardner, R.C., Smythe, P.C., Clément, R. and Gliksman, L. (1976) Second-language acquisition: A social psychological perspective. *Canadian Modern Language Review,* 32, 198-213.

Gebhard, J.G., Gaitan, S. and Oprandy, R. (1987) Beyond prescription: The student teacher as investigator. *Foreign Language Annals,* 20 (3), 227-32.

Genesee, F. (1976) The role of intelligence in second-language learning. *Language Learning,* 26, 267-80.

Genesee, F. (1983) An invited article. Bilingual education of majority-language children: The immersion experiments in review. *Applied Psycholinguistics,* 4, 1-46.

Genesee, F. (1987) *Learning through two languages: Studies of immersion and bilingual education.* Cambridge, Mass.: Newbury House.

Gipps, C. (1994) What we know about effective primary teaching. In J. Bourne (ed) *Thinking through primary practice.* London: Routledge/Open University.

Gliksman, L., Gardner, R.C. and Smythe, P.C. (1982) The role of the integrative motive on students' participation in the French classroom. *Canadian Modern Language Review,* 38, 625-47.

Good, T. (1981) Teacher expectations and student perceptions: A decade of research. *Educational Leadership, 38,* 415-23.

Good, T.L., Slavings, R.L., Hobson Harel, K. and Emerson, H. (1987) Student passivity: A study of question asking in K-12 classrooms. *Sociology of Education, 60,* 181-99.

Gordon, M.E. (1980) Attitudes and motivation in second language achievement: A study of primary school students learning English in Belize, Central America. Unpublished doctoral dissertation, University of Toronto.

Gorman, W.G. (1968) The construction and standardization of a verbal reasoning test for age range 10 years, 0 months, to 12 years, 11 months, in an Irish population. Unpublished doctoral dissertation. University College Dublin, Ireland.

Greaney, V. (1978) Trends in attainment in Irish from 1973 to 1977. *Irish Journal of Education, 12,* 22-35.

Greaney, V. and Kellaghan, T. (1984) *Equality of opportunity in Irish schools: A longitudinal study of 500 students.* Dublin: Educational Company of Ireland.

Hallan, S. and Cowan, R. (1998) Is homework important for increasing educational attainment. Paper presented at the British Psychological Society Annual Conference, Exeter.

Hannan, D.F. and Shortall, S. (1991) *The quality of their education.* Dublin: Economic and Social Research Institute (ESRI).

Hannan, D., Breen, R., Murray, B., Watson, D., Hardiman, N. and O' Higgins, K. (1983) *Schooling and sex roles: Sex differences in subject provision and subject choice in Irish post-primary schools.* Dublin:, ESRI General Research Series, Paper No 113.

Hannon, P. and Jackson, A. (1987) *The Banfield Reading Project. Final report.* National Children's Bureau.

Harley, B. (1984) How good is their French? In H. Stern (ed) *The immersion phenomenon. Language and Society, 12,* 55-60

Harley, B. (1989) Functional grammar in French immersion: A classroom experiment. *Applied Linguistics, 10* (3), 331-59.

Harley, B. and Swain, M. (1977) An analysis of verb-form and function in the speech of French immersion pupils. *Working Papers on Bilingualism, 14,* 31-40.

Harris, J. (1982) Achievement in spoken Irish at the end of primary school. *Irish Journal of Education, 16* (2), 85-116.

Harris, J. (1983) Relationships between achievement in spoken Irish and demographic, administrative and teaching factors. *Irish Journal of Education, 17* (1), 5-34.

Harris, J. (1984) *Spoken Irish in primary schools.* Dublin: Institiúid Teangeolaíochta Éireann.

Harris, J. (1988) Spoken Irish in the primary school system. *International Journal of the Sociology of Language, 70,* 69-87.

Harris, J. (1991) *Foreign language teaching in primary schools: Issues and research. Part 1.* In Irish National Teachers' Organisation (ed) *Foreign language teaching in primary schools: Issues and research.* Dublin: Irish National Teachers' Organisation.

Harris, J. (1993) An Ghaeilge labhartha sa gnáthscoil: Fadhbanna is féidearthachtaí sa ré nua. *Teangeolas, 32,* 50-8.

Harris, J. and Mac Giollabhuí, S. (1998a) *Lean den ealaín! Ealaín trí Ghaeilge do na gnáthscoileanna. Lámhleabhar an mhúinteora.* Dublin: Institiúid Teangeolaíochta Éireann.

Harris, J. and Mac Giollabhuí, S. (1998b) *Bain triail as! Eolaíocht trí Ghaeilge do na gnáthscoileanna. Lámhleabhar an mhúinteora.* Dublin: Institiúid Teangeolaíochta Éireann.

Harris, J. and Mac Giollabhuí, S. (1998c) *Bain triail as! Eolaíocht trí Ghaeilge do na gnáthscoileanna. Leabhar an dalta.* Dublin: Institiúid Teangeolaíochta Éireann.

Harris, J. and Murtagh, L. (1987) Irish and English in Gaeltacht primary schools. In G. Mac Eoin, A. Ahlqvist, D. Ó hAodha (eds) *Third International Conference on Minority Languages: Celtic Papers. Multilingual Matters 32.* Clevedon: Multilingual Matters.

Harris, J. and Murtagh, L. (1988a) National assessment of Irish-language speaking and listening skills in primary-school children: Research issues in the evaluation of school-based heritage-language programmes. *Language, Culture and Curriculum,* 1(2), 85-130.

Harris, J. and Murtagh, L. (1988b) Ability and communication in learning Irish. Unpublished.

Harris, J. and Murtagh, L. (1991) Scéim Phíolótach i dteagasc na Gaeilge sa Bhunscoil. Report: Part 1. The contribution of pupils and parents to achievement in spoken Irish. Unpublished report submitted to the Department of Education.

Harris, J. and Murtagh, L. (1992) Scéim Phíolótach i dteagasc na Gaeilge sa Bhunscoil. Report: Part II. A direct observation study of 40 Irish lessons. Unpublished report submitted to the Department of Education.

Harris, J. and Murtagh, L. (1996) Topic and language activity in teaching Irish at sixth grade in primary school: A classroom observation study. In T. Hickey and J. Williams (eds.) *Language, education and society in a changing world.* Dublin: IRAAL (Clevedon: Multilingual Matters).

Harris, J. and Murtagh, L. (1997) Speech and silence in the Irish language class. In A. Ahlqvist and V. Capkova (eds.) *Dán do oide.* Dublin: Institiúid Teangeolaíochta Éireann.

Harris, J. and Ó Cathalláin, S. (1999) A partnership approach to developing parental support for Irish in primary school. Dublin: Institiúid Teangeolaíochta Éireann. In progress.

Harris, J., Hickey, M., Ní Chonaill, M. and Murtagh, L. (1982) *Béaltriail Ghaeilge Institiúid Teangeolaíochta Éireann. II.* (Lámhleabhar an Scrúdaitheora, Freagarleabhar, agus 6 théip) (*The Institiúid Teangeolaíochta Éireann Oral Irish Test. II.* Examiner's handbook, Answer book, and 6 tapes). Dublin: Institiúid Teangeolaíochta Éireann.

Harris, J., Murtagh, L., Hickey, M., De Nais, D. and Ó Domhnalláin, T. (1978/1985) *Béaltriail Ghaeilge Institiúid Teangeolaíochta Éireann. VI.* (Lámhleabhar an Scrúdaitheora, Freagarleabhar, agus 2 théip) (*The Institiúid Teangeolaíochta Éireann Oral Irish Test. VI.* Examiner's handbook, Answer book, and 2 tapes). Dublin: Institiúid Teangeolaíochta Éireann.

Harris, J., Ó Néill, P., Uí Dhufaigh, M. and Ó Súilleabháin, E. (1996a) *Cúrsaí nua Gaeilge na bunscoile: Moltaí agus ábhar samplach. Imleabhar I: Naíonáin Shóisearacha - Rang 2.* Dublin: Institiúid Teangeolaíochta Éireann.

Harris, J., Uí Dhufaigh, M., Ó Néill, P. and Ó Súilleabháin, E. (1996b) *Cúrsaí nua Gaeilge na bunscoile: Moltaí agus ábhar samplach. Imleabhar II: Rang 3-6.* Dublin: Institiúid Teangeolaíochta Éireann.

Hickey, T. (1997) *Early immersion education in Ireland: Na naíonraí./An luath-thumadh in Éirinn: Na naíonraí.* Dublin: Institiúid Teangeolaíochta Éireann.

Holec, H. (1987) The learner as manager: managing learning or managing to learn? In A. Wenden and J. Rubin (eds) *Learner strategies in language learning.* Englewood Cliffs, N.J.:Prentice Hall.

Holley, F.M. and King, J.K. (1971) Imitation and correction in foreign language learning. *Modern Language Journal,* 55, 494-98.

Holt, J. (1994) How children learn ... and fail. In A. Pollard and J. Bourne (eds) *Teaching and learning in the primary school.* London: Routledge/Open University.

Horwitz, E.K., Horwitz, M.B. and Cope, J. (1986) Foreign language classroom anxiety. *Modern Language Journal,* 70 (2), 125-32.

Hymes, D. (1972) On communicative competence. In J. Pride and J. Holmes (eds) *Sociolinguistics.* Harmondsworth: Penguin.

Institiúid Teangeolaíochta Éireann (1980) *Modern Languages Syllabus Project for Post-Primary Schools: Skeleton syllabus.* Dublin: Author.

Ireland (1998) Education Act.

Ireland: Central Statistics Office (1986) *Classification of occupations.* Dublin: Central Statistics Office.

Ireland: Central Statistics Office (1993) *Census 86. Vol 7: Occupations.* Dublin: Central Statistics Office.

Ireland: Department of Education (1978) *Lá Faoin Tuath/Sean Neidí: Cúrsa Comhrá Gaeilge le haghaidh ranganna sinsearacha.* Dublin: Stationery Office.

Ireland: Department of Education (1990a) *Report of the Review Body on the Primary Curriculum.* (Quinlan Report). Dublin: Stationery Office.

Ireland: Department of Education (1990b) *Report of the Primary Education Review Body.* Dublin: Stationery Office.

Ireland: Department of Education (1990c) *Pilot project on Home/School/Community Liaison. Draft job description.* Dublin: Author.

Ireland: Department of Education (1993) Tuarascáil Staitistiúil (Statistical Report) 1992/93. Dublin: Stationery Office.

Ireland: Department of Education (1994a) *Gender equity. Action Research Report. Exploring the gender gap in primary schools.* Dublin: Department of Education.

Ireland: Department of Education (1994b) Tuarascáil Staitistiúil (Statistical Report) 1993/94. Dublin: Stationery Office.

Ireland: Department of Education (1995a) Tuarascáil Staitistiúil (Statistical Report) 1994/95. Dublin: Stationery Office.

Ireland: Department of Education (1995b) *White Paper on Education: Charting our Education Future.* Dublin: Stationery Office.

Ireland: Department of Education and Science (1997) Pilot project on modern languages in national schools. Circular 45/97.

Irish National Teachers' Organisation (INTO): Education Committee. 1976. *Primary school curriculum: Curriculum questionnaire analysis.* Dublin: Author.

Irish National Teachers' Organisation (1985a) *The Irish language in primary education: Summary of INTO survey of teachers' attitudes to the position of Irish in primary education.* Dublin: Author.

Irish National Teachers' Organisation (1985b) *The Irish language in primary schools: Summary of the main findings of a survey of public attitudes by the Market Research Bureau of Ireland.* Dublin: Author.

Irish National Teachers' Organisation (1996a) *Primary school curriculum: An evolutionary process.* Dublin: Author

Irish National Teachers' Organisation (1996b) *Effective school organisation.* Dublin: Author.

Irish National Teachers' Organisation (1997) *Parental involvement: Possibilities for partnership.* Dublin: Author.

Irish National Teachers' Organisation (1998a) The curriculum for primary schools. Background paper. INTO Consultative Conference on Education, Limerick. Dublin: INTO.

Irish National Teachers' Organisation (1998b) Irish in the primary school: A discussion document. INTO Consultative Conference on Education, Limerick. Dublin: Author.

Johnston, M. (1990) Teacher questions in the academic language-content classroom. Unpublished paper, Tokyo: Temple University Japan.

Jones, F. (1991) Classroom riot: Design features, language output and topic in simulations and other communicative free-stage activities. *System, 19,* 151-69.

Kasper, G. (ed) (1986) *Learning, teaching and communication in the foreign language classroom.* Aarhus: Aarhus University Press.

Keith, T., Reimers, T., Fehrman, P., Potterbaum, S. and Aubey, L. (1986) Parental involvement, homework and TV time: direct and indirect effects on high school achievement. *Journal of Educational Psychology,* 78 (5), 373-80.

Kellaghan, T. and Fontes, P.J. (1988) Gender differences in self-concept. *Irish Journal of Education,* 22, 42-52.

Kellaghan, T. and Macnamara, J. (1972) Family correlates of verbal reasoning ability. *Development Psychology,* 7, 49-53.

Kellaghan, T., Macnamara, J. and Neuman, E. (1969) Teachers' assessments of the scholastic progress of pupils. *Irish Journal of Education,* 2, 95-104.

Kellaghan, T., Madaus, G.F. and Airasian, P.W. (1982) *The effects of standardized testing.* London: Kluwer-Nijhoff Publishing.

Kellaghan, T., Sloane, K., Alvarez, B. and Bloom, B.S. (1993) *The home environment and school learning: Promoting parental involvement in the education of children.* San Francisco: Jossey-Bass.

Kraemer, R. (1990) *Social psychological factors related to the study of Arabic among Israeli Jewish high school students.* Unpublished doctoral dissertation, Tel-Aviv University.

Krashen, S. D. (1981) *Second-language acquisition and second-language learning.* Oxford: Pergamon.

Krashen, S. D. (1982) *Principles and practice in second-language acquisition.* Oxford: Pergamon.

Krashen, S. D. (1985) *The input hypothesis: Issues and implications.* London: Longman.

Krashen, S. D. (1991) The input hypothesis: An update. In James E. Alatis (ed) *Georgetown University Round Table on Languages and Linguistics. 1991.* Washington, D.C.: Georgetown University Press.

Krashen, S. D. (1993) *The power of reading: Insights from the research.* Colorado: Libraries Unlimited, Inc.

Krashen, S. and Terrell, T. (1983) *The natural approach: Language acquisition in the classroom.* Oxford: Pergamon.

Kumar, K. (1992) Does class size really make a difference? - Exploring classroom interaction in large and small classes. *RELC Journal,* 23 (1), 29-47.

Labov, W. (1970) The study of language in its social context. *Studium Generale, 23,* 30-87.

Labov, W. and Fanshel, D. (1977) *Therapeutic discourse: Psychotherapy as conversation.* New York: Academic Press.

Lalonde, R.N. and Gardner, R.C. (1985) On the predictive validity of the attitude/motivation test battery. *Journal of Multilingual and Multicultural Development,* 6 (5), 403-12.

Lambert, W.E. and Tucker, G.R. (1972) *The bilingual education of children: The St. Lambert experiment.* Rowley, Mass.: Newbury House.

Levin, I., Levy-Schiff, R., Appelbaum-Peled, T., Katz, I., Komar, M. and Meiran, N. (1997) Antecedents and consequences of maternal involvement in children's homework: A longitudinal analysis. *Journal of Applied Developmental Psychology,* 18, 207-27.

Lightbown, P. and Spada, N. (1990) Focus on form and corrective feedback in communicative language teaching: Effects on second language learning. *Studies in Second Language Acquisition,* 12, 429-48.

Lightbown, P. and Spada, N. (1993) *How languages are learned.* Oxford: Oxford University Press.

Likert, R. (1932) A technique for the measurement of attitudes. *Archives of Psychology.* No. 140.

Liu, X. (1989) A survey and analysis of English language learning anxiety in secondary school students in the People's Republic of China. MA dissertation, East China Normal University, People's Republic of China.

Livingston, S.A. and Zieky, M.J. (1982) *Passing scores: A manual for setting standards of performance on educational and occupational tests.* Princeton, N.J.: Educational Testing Service.

Long, M.H. (1980) Inside the 'black box': Methodological issues in classroom research on language learning. *Language Learning,* 30 (1), 1-42.

Long, M.H. (1989) Task, group, and task-group interactions. University of Hawaii *Working Papers in ESL,* 8, 1-26.

Long, M.H. and Crookes, G. (1992) Three approaches to task-based syllabus design. *TESOL Quarterly,* 26 (1), 27-56.

Long, M.H. and Crookes, G. (1993) Units of analysis in syllabus design: The case for task. In G. Crookes and S.M. Gass (eds) *Tasks in a pedagogical context: Integrating theory and practice.* Clevedon: Multilingual Matters.

Long, M. and Porter, P. (1985) Group work, interlanguage talk, and second language acquisition. *TESOL Quarterly,* 19, 207-28.

Long, M.H. and Sato, C.J. (1983) Classroom foreigner talk discourse: forms and functions of teachers' questions. In H.W. Seliger and M.H. Long (eds) *Classroom-oriented research in second language acquisition.* Rowley, Mass.: Newbury House.

Long, M., Adams, L., Mclean, M. and Castanos, F. (1976) Doing things with words: verbal interaction in lockstep and small group classroom situations. In John Fanselow and Ruth Crymes (eds) *On TESOL '76.* Washington D.C.: TESOL.

Long, M.H., Brock, C.A., Crookes, G., Deicke, C., Potter, L. and Zhang, S. (1984) *The effect of teachers' questioning patterns and wait time on pupil participation in public high school classes in Hawaii for students of limited English proficiency.* Technical Report No. 1. Honolulu: Centre for Second Language Classroom Research, Social Science Research Institute, University of Hawaii at Manoa.

Low, L., Duffield, J., Brown, S. and Johnstone, R. (1993) *Evaluating foreign languages in primary schools.* Stirling: Scottish CILT.

Lukmani, Y.M. (1972) Motivation to learn and learning proficiency. *Language Learning,* 22, 261-73.

Lyle, S. (1996) An analysis of collaborative group work in the primary school and the factors relevant to its success. *Language and Education,* 10 (1), 13-31.

Lynch, K. (1985) An analysis of some presuppositions underlying the concepts of meritocracy and ability as presented in Greaney and Kellaghan's study. *Economic and Social Review,* 16 (2), 83-102.

Lyster, R. (1994) The effect of functional-analytic teaching on aspects of French immersion students' sociolinguistic competence. *Applied Linguistics,* 15 (3), 263-87.

Macbeath, J. and Turner, M. (1990) *Learning out of school: Homework, policy and practice.* A research study commissioned by the Scottish Education Department. Glasgow: Jordanhill College.

Macbeth, A. (1989) *Involving parents: Effective parent-teacher relations.* Oxford: Heinemann Educational.

Maccoby, E.E. and Jacklin, C.N. (1974) *The psychology of sex differences.* Stanford, Ca.: Stanford University Press.

MacIntyre, P.D. and Gardner, R.C. (1989) Anxiety and second-language learning: Toward a theoretical clarification. *Language Learning,* 39 (2), 251-75.

MacIntyre, P.D. and Gardner, R.C. (1991) Language anxiety: Its relation to other anxieties and to processing in native and second languages. *Language Learning,* 41, 513-34.

MacIntyre, P.D., Noels, K.A. and Clément, R. (1997) Biases in self-ratings of second-language proficiency: The role of language anxiety. *Language Learning,* 47 (2), 265-87.

Mac Mathúna, L. (1985) The potential for Irish-English dual-medium instruction in the primary school. *Teanga, 5,* 57-71

MacSuibhne, A. (1996) Gaeilge na Bunscoile: Taitneamh, éagsúlacht agus cumarsáid. *Comhairle: Information Bulletin.* Dublin: National Council for Curriculum and Assessment.

Maertens, N.W. and Johnson, J. (1972) Effects of arithmetic homework upon the attitudes and achievements of fourth, fifth, and sixth grade pupils. *School Science and Mathematics,* 72, 117-26.

Marjoribanks, K. (1979) *Families and their learning environments. An empirical analysis.* London: Routledge and Kegan Paul.

Martin, M. and Kellaghan, T. (1977) Factors affecting reading attainment in Irish primary schools. In V. Greaney (ed) *Studies in reading.* Dublin: Educational Company of Ireland.

Martin, M.O., Hickey, B.L. and Murchan, D.P. (1992) The Second International Assessment of Educational Progress: Mathematics and Science findings in Ireland. *Irish Journal of Education,* 26. Special Edition.

McHoul, A. (1978) The organization of turns at formal talk in the classroom. *Language and Society,* 7, 183-213.

Merttens, R. and Vass, J. (1987) Parents in schools: Raising money or raising standards? *Education 3-13,* 15 (2), 23-7.

Midorikawa, H. (1990) An exploratory study of the relationship of teacher questions to learner output. Unpublished paper. Tokyo: Temple University Japan.

Miller, G.W. (1971) *Educational opportunity and the home.* London: Longman.

Mitchell, R. (1988) *Communicative language teaching in practice.* London: Centre for Information on Language Teaching and Research.

Mitchell, R. (1989) Second language learning: Investigating the classroom context. *System,* 17 (2), 195-210.

Mitchell, R. (1990) Evaluation of second language teaching projects and programmes. *Language, Culture and Curriculum,* 3 (1), 3-17.

Mitchell, R. (1994) The communicative approach to language teaching: An introduction. In A. Swarbrick (ed) *Teaching modern languages.* London: Routledge/The Open University.

Mitchell, R. (1996) Language, education and applied linguistics in a changing world. In T. Hickey and J. Williams (eds) *Language, education and society in a changing world.* Clevedon/Dublin: Multingual Matters/IRAAL.

Mitchell, R. and Johnstone, R. (1986) The routinization of communicative methodology. In C. J. Brumfit (ed) *The practice of communicative teaching. (ELT Documents 124).* Oxford: Pergammon Press.

Mitchell, R., Parkinson, B. and Johnstone, R. (1981) *The foreign language classroom: An observational study.* Stirling Educational Monographs No. 9. Department of Education, University of Stirling.

Mizon, S. (1981) Teacher talk: A case study from the Bangalore/Madras cummunicational ELT project. M.A. Thesis, University of Lancaster, England.

Mortimore, P., Sammons, P., Stoll, L., Lewis, D. and Ecob, R. (1988) *School matters: The junior years.* London: Open Books.

Muchnick, A.G. and Wolfe, D.E. (1982) Attitudes and motivations of American students of Spanish. *Canadian Modern Language Review,* 38, 262-81.

Murtagh, L. (1989) Reading in a second or foreign language: Models, processes, and pedagogy. *Language, Culture and Curriculum,* 2 (2), 91-105.

Naiman, N., Fröhlich, M., Stern, H. and Todesco, A. (1978) *The good language learner. Research in Education Series,* No 7. Toronto: The Ontario Institute for Studies in Education.

National Economic and Social Forum. (1997) *A framework for partnership - Enriching strategic consensus through participation. Forum Report No 16.* Dublin: Author.

National Parents Council - Primary (1991). Issues in Education (1): Homework. Dublin: Author.

National Parents Council - Primary (1998) *The Parents Programme 1995-1997: Achievements, evaluation and learning.* Dublin: Author.

Neville Postlethwaite, T. and Ross, K.N. (1992) *Effective schools in reading: Implications for educational planners.* The Hague: The International Association for the Evaluation of Educational Progress.

Newton, J. (1991) Negotiation: Negotiating what? Paper presented at SEAMEO Conference on Language Acquisition and the Second/Foreign Language Classroom, RELC, Singapore.

Norton, J.E. (1984a) Towards the design of a communicative syllabus for Irish in the primary school. *Studies in Education,* 2 (1), 22-38.

Norton, S. (1984b) Bridging the formal and informal fields of Irish language learning at primary level. In D.M. Singleton and D.G. Little (eds) *Language learning in formal and informal contexts.* Dublin: Irish Association of Applied Linguistics.

Nunan, D. (1996) Hidden voices: insiders' perspectives on classroom instruction. In K.M. Bailey and D. Nunan (eds) *Voices from the language classroom.* Cambridge: Cambridge University Press.

Ó Conchúir, D. agus Ó Súilleabháin, E. (1991) *Modh an Aoibhnis.* Indreabhán, Conamara: Cló Iar-Chonnachta Teo.

Ó Domhnalláin, T. and Ó Gliasáin, M. (1976) *Audio-visual methods v. A.B.C. methods in the teaching of Irish.* Dublin: Institiúid Teangeolaíochta Éireann.

Ó Dubhghaill, A. (1983) *Anseo is Ansiúd.* Dublin: C.S. Ó Fallúin.

Ó Fathaigh, M. (1991) *Learning Irish in second-level schools: Attitudes, motivation and achievement.* Dublin: Comhar na Múinteoirí Gaeilge.

Ó Riagáin, P. (1982) The influence of social factors on the teaching and learning of Irish. In W.F. Mackey *et al.* (eds) *Contemporary perspectives on the teaching of Irish.* Dublin: Bord na Gaeilge.

Ó Riagáin, P. (1986) *Public and teacher attitudes towards Irish in the Schools. A review of recent studies.* Occasional Paper 6. Dublin: Institiúid Teangeolaíochta Éireann.

Ó Riagáin, P. (1997) *Language policy and social reproduction: Ireland 1893-1993.* Oxford: Clarendon Press.

Ó Riagáin, P. and Ó Gliasáin, M. (1979) *All-Irish primary schools in the Dublin area.* Dublin: Institiúid Teangeolaíochta Éireann.

Ó Riagáin, P. and Ó Gliasáin, M. (1984) *The Irish language in the Republic of Ireland 1983: Preliminary report of a national survey.* Dublin: Institiúid Teangeolaíochta Éireann.

Ó Riagáin, P. and Ó Gliasáin, M. (1994) *National survey on languages 1993: Preliminary report.* Dublin: Institiúid Teangeolaíochta Éireann.

Osborne, A.F. and Milbank, J.E. (1987) *The effects of early education: A report from the Child Health and Education Study.* Oxford: Clarendon Press.

Paschal, R.A., Weinstein, T. and Walberg, H.J. (1984) The effects of homework on learning: A quantitative synthesis. *Journal of Educational Research,* 78 (2), 97-104.

Pattison, P. (1989) Pupil motivation and oral communication skills. In G.M. Willems and P. Riley (eds) *Foreign language learning and teaching in Europe.* Amsterdam: Bureau Lerarenopleiding & Free University Press.

Paulston, C. B. (1981) Notional syllabuses revisited: Some comments. *Applied Linguistics,* 2 (1), 93-5.

Peacock, M. (1997) Comparing learner and teacher views on the usefulness and enjoyableness of materials. *International Journal of Applied Linguistics,* 7 (2), 183-200.

Pica, T. and Doughty, C. (1985) The role of group work in classroom second language acquisition . *Studies in Second Language Acquisition Research,* 7, 233-48.

Pica, T. and Long, M. (1986) *The linguistic and conversational performance of experienced and inexperienced teachers.* In R. Day (ed) *Talking to learn: Conversation in second language acquisition.* Rowley, Mass.: Newbury House.

Plowden, Lady B. (1967) *Children and their primary schools. Volumes 1 & 2.* A report of the Central Advisory Council for Education in England. London: HMSO.

Politzer, R., Ramirez, A. and Lewis, S. (1981) Teaching standard English in the third grade: classroom functions of language. *Language Learning,* 31, 171-93.

Porter, P. (1986) How learners talk to each other: input and interaction in task-centred discussion . In R. Day (ed) *Talking to learn: Conversation in second language acquisition.* Rowley, Mass.: Newbury House.

Prabhu, N.S. (1987) *Second language pedagogy.* Oxford: Oxford University Press.

Prabhu, N.S. (1990) There is no best method - why? *TESOL Quarterly,* 24 (2), 161-76.

Pritchard, R. (1987) Boys' and girls' attitudes towards French and German. *Educational Research,* 29 (1), 65-72.

Ramage, K. (1990) Motivational factors and persistence in foreign language study. *Language Learning,* 40, 189-219.

Ramirez, J.D., Yuen, S.D., Ramey, D.R. and Merino, B. (1986) *First year report: Longitudinal study of immersion programs for language minority children.* Arlington, V.A.: SRA Technologies.

Robson, G. (1992) Individual learner differences and classroom participation: A pilot study. Unpublished paper. Tokyo: Temple University Japan.

Rutherford, W.E. (1987) *Second-language grammar: Learning and teaching.* London: Longman.

Ryan, S. (1995) *The Home-School-Community Liaison Scheme: Summary evaluation report.* Dublin: Educational Research Centre.

Sasaki, M. (1993) Relationships among second-language proficiency, foreign language aptitude, and intelligence: A structural equation modeling approach. *Language learning,* 43 (3), 313-44.

Savignon, S. (1972) *Communicative competence: An experiment in foreign language teaching.* Philadelphia: Center for Curriculum Development.

Scherer, A. and Wertheimer, M. (1964) *A psycholinguistic experiment in foreign language teaching.* New York: McGraw-Hill.

Seliger, H. (1977) Does practice make perfect? A study of the interaction patterns and L2 competence. *Language Learning,* 27, 263-78.

Sharwood Smith, M. (1993) Input enhancement in instructed SLA: Theoretical bases. *Studies in Second Language Acquisition,* 15 (2), 165-79.

Shaw, P.A. (1996) Voices for improved learning: The ethnographer as co-agent of pedagogic change. In K.M. Bailey and D. Nunan (eds) *Voices from the language classroom.* Cambridge: Cambridge University Press.

Sheils, J. (1988) *Communication in the modern languages classroom*. Strasbourg: Council of Europe.

Sinclair, J.McH. and Coulthard, R.M. (1975) *Towards an analysis of discourse*. London: Oxford University Press.

Singleton, D. (1995) Introduction: A critical look at the critical period hypothesis in second language acquisition research. In D. Singleton and Z. Lengyel (eds) *The age factor in second language acquisition*. Clevedon: Multilingual Matters.

Skehan, P. (1982) Memory and motivation in language aptitude testing. Unpublished Ph.D. thesis, University of London.

Skehan, P. (1990). The relationship between native and foreign language learning ability: Educational and linguistic factors. In H. Dechert (ed) *Current trends in European second language acquisition research*. Clevedon: Multilingual Matters.

Skehan, P. (1998) *A cognitive approach to language learning*. Oxford: Oxford University Press.

Slimani, A. (1992) Evaluation of classroom interaction. In J.C. Alderson and A. Beretta (eds) *Evaluating second language education*. Cambridge: Cambridge University Press.

Smith, P.D. (1970) *A comparison of the cognitive and audiolingual approaches to foreign language instruction: The Pennsylvania Foreign Language Project*. Philadelphia: Center for Curriculum Development.

Southgate, V., Arnold, H. and Johnson, S. (1981) *Extending beginning reading*. London: Heinemann Educational Books.

Spada, N.M. (1987) Relationships between instructional differences and learning outcomes: A process-product study of communicative language teaching. *Applied Linguistics, 8,* 137-61.

Spada, N. and Lightbown. P.M. (1989) Intensive ESL programs in Quebec primary schools. *TESL Canada Journal, 7,* 11-32.

Spada, N. and Lightbown P.M. (1993) Instruction and the development of questions in L2 classrooms. *Studies in second language acquisition, 15* (2), 205-24.

Stern, H.H. (1982) *Issues in early core French: A selective and preliminary review of the literature 1975-1981*. Toronto: City of Toronto Board of Education.

Stern, H.H. (1990) Analysis and experience as variables in second language pedagogy. In B. Harley, P. Allen, J. Cummins and M. Swain (eds) *The development of second language proficiency*. Cambridge: Cambridge University Press.

Stern, H.H. (1992) *Issues and options in language teaching*. Oxford: Oxford University Press.

Stevenson, H.W., Chen, C. and Uttal, D.H. (1990) Beliefs and achievements: A study of black, white and Hispanic children. *Child Development, 61,* 508-23.

Strong, M. (1983) Social styles and second language acquisition of Spanish-speaking kindergarteners. *TESOL Quarterly, 17,* 241-58.

Strong, M. (1984) Integrative motivation: Cause or result of successful second language acquisition? *Language Learning, 34,* 1-14.

Swain, M. (1981) Linguistic expectations: Core, extended and immersion programs. *Canadian Modern Language Review, 37,* 486-97.

Swain, M. (1985) Communicative Competence: Some roles of comprehensible input and comprehensible output in its development. In S. Gass and C. Madden (eds) *Input in second language acquisition*. Rowley, Mass.: Newbury House.

Swain, M. (1996) Integrating language and content in immersion classrooms: Research perspectives. *Canadian Modern Language Review, 52* (4), 529-48.

Swain, M. and Lapkin, S. (1982) *Evaluating bilingual education: A Canadian case study*. Clevedon: Multilingual Matters.

Terrell, T.D. (1991) The role of grammar instruction in a communicative approach. *Modern Language Journal*, 75, 52-63.

Thornbury, S. (1996) Teachers research teacher talk. *ELT Journal*, 50 (4), 279-88.

Tizard, B. and Hughes, M. (1984) *Young children learning, talking and thinking at home and at school*. London: Fontana.

Tizard, B., Mortimore, J., and Burchell, B. (1988) Involving parents from minority groups. In Bastiani, J. (ed) *Parents and teachers 2: From policy to practice*. Windsor: N.F.E.R. Nelson.

Tizard, J., Schofield, W. and Hewison, J. (1982) Collaboration between teachers and parents in assisting children's reading. *British Journal of Educational Psychology*, 52, 1-15.

Toomey, D. (1993) Parents hearing their children read: a review. Rethinking the lessons of the Haringey Project. *Educational Research*, 35 (3), 223-36.

Tremblay, P.F. and Gardner, R.C. (1995) Expanding the motivation construct in language learning. *Modern Language Journal*, 79 (4), 505-18.

Trylong, V.L. (1987) Aptitude, attitudes, and anxiety: A study of their relationships to achievement in the foreign language classroom. Unpublished doctoral dissertation, Purdue University..

Tsui, A.M.B. (1996) Reticence and anxiety in second language learning. In K.M. Bailey and D. Nunan (eds) *Voices from the language classroom*. Cambridge: Cambridge University Press.

Ullmann, R. (1990) Using complementary approaches to evaluate second-language programmes. *Language, Culture and Curriculum*, 3 (1), 19-38.

Ullmann, R. (1991) Teachers, administrators, and researchers work together in classroom observation research: A professional development opportunity. *Canadian Modern Language Review*, 48 (1), 77-89.

Ullmann, R. and Geva, E. (1984) Approaches to observation in second language classes. In C. J. Brumfit (ed) *Language issues and educational policies* (ELT Documents 119). Oxford: Pergamon Press.

Van Ek, J. (1975) *The Threshold Level*. Strasbourg: Council of Europe.

Van Lier, L. (1988) *The classroom and the language learner*. London: Longman.

Van Lier, L. (1994) Language awareness, contingency and interaction. *AILA Review*, 11, 69-82.

VanPatten, B. and Cadierno, T. (1993) Explicit instruction and input processing. *Second Language Acquisition*, 15, 225-43.

Walberg, H. (1979) *Educational environments and effects*. Berkeley: McCutchan.

Wells, G. (1985) *Language development in the pre-school years*. Cambridge: Cambridge University Press.

Wesche, M., Edwards, H. and Wells, W. (1982) Foreign language aptitude and intelligence. *Applied Psycholinguistics*, 3, 127-40.

White, L. (1991) Adverb placement in second language acquisition: Some effects of positive and negative evidence in the classroom. *Second Language Research*, 7, 133-61.

White, L. and Lightbown, P. (1984) Asking and answering in ESL classes. *Canadian Modern Language Review*, 40, 288-344.

Wilkins, D.A. (1976) *Notional syllabuses*. Oxford: Oxford University Press.

Wong-Fillmore, L. (1982) Instructional language as linguistic input: Second language learning in classrooms. In L. Wilkinson (ed) *Communicating in the classroom*. New York: Academic Press.

Wong-Fillmore, L. (1985) When does teacher talk work as input. In S. Gass and C. Madden (eds) *Input in second language acquisition*. Rowley, Mass.: Newbury House.

Wragg, E.C. (1970) Interaction analysis in the foreign language classroom. *Modern Language Journal*, 54 (2), 116-20.

Appendix 1.1

Sample lesson from the *Communicative Materials Project*[1]

Easaontú faoin Teilifís

Cuspóirí: Go mbeadh an páiste in ann iarraidh ar dhaoine eile rudaí a dhéanamh.
Áiseanna: Bileog do gach páiste. Téip.

Cur Chuige:

○ Abair, "Tá Seán, Áine agus Mamaí sa bhaile. Tá Seán ag imirt cluiche ríomhaire ar an teilifíseán. Éistigí leis an téip anois".

Téip

Áine: *Gabh mo leithscéal, a Sheáin. Tá an clár is fearr liomsa ag tosú anois.*

Seán: *ÁÁÁ - tá mé ag baint úsáide as an teilifíseáin chun cluiche ríomhaire a imirt - tá mé ag imirt Fifa Sacar.*

Áine: *Is féidir leat an cluiche ríomhaire a imirt nuair a bheidh mo chlársa thart. Brostaigh.....*

Seán: *Ná bí ag cur isteach orm, a Áine. Tá ag éirí go geal liom - sin cúl eile.*

Mamaí: *A Sheáin - bíonn tú ag imirt cluichí ríomhaire ar an teilifís gach lá! Déan do chuid obair bhaile anois.*

○ Stop an téip anseo. Pléigh na féidearthachtaí don chuid eile den sceitse leis an rang. Seinn an chuid eile den téip agus pléigh na difríochtaí.

Seán: *ÁÁÁ, a Mhamaí - tabhair cúig nóiméad eile dom, más é do thoil é.....Áine, más é do thoil é! Déanfaidh mé do chuid jabanna sa teach anocht duit.*

Áine: *Maith go leor - ach ná déan dearmad. Is féidir liomsa dul trasna an bhóthair go teach Nóra. Beidh sise ag féachaint ar an gclár céanna.*

○ Pléigh leis na páistí na difríochtaí idir an méid a tharla ar an téip agus na tuairimí a bhí ag an rang roimh ré.

○ Roinn an rang ina ghrúpaí, triúr i ngach grúpa. Iarr orthu an sceitse a chleachtadh le cabhair na bileoige. Roghnaigh roinnt grúpaí chun an dráma a léiriú.

---

[1] Gníomh 17, Aonad 1, Rang 4 from *Cúrsaí Nua Gaeilge na Bunscoile: Moltaí agus Ábhar Samplach* (Harris *et al.*, 1996b). Print size and other material reduced from original A4 format. Pupils would have encountered some of the vocabulary required here in previous lessons. Note that the Pupil's Material (the 'bileog') is not distributed until after pupils have listened to the sketch in its entirety.

Teacher's Material (continued)

Dúshlán Breise:

1. Múin téarmaí a bhaineann leis an teilifíseán -
    scáileán   'cnapaire'
    sruthanna   cnaipe
    aeróg   teilifíseán inaistrithe
    sruthanna eachtrannacha   sos na bhfógraí

2. Pléigh na nósanna a bhíonn ag na páistí sa bhaile maidir leis an teilifís.
    An bhféachann an chlann go léir le chéile ar an teilifís riamh? - Cén clár?
    An mbíonn easaontú faoi chláir éagsúla ar chainéil éagsúla?
    Conas a réitítear na haighnis sin?

3. Pléigh fógraí ar an teilifís, mar shampla:
    Na cinn is mó a thaitníonn le páistí.
    Na cinn is measa.
    An gcreideann na páistí na rudaí a deirtear sna fógraí?

    Iarr ar na páistí a bheith ag faire amach don fhógra is fearr a fheiceann siad ag an
    deireadh seachtaine. Iarr orthu nóta a dhéanamh d'aon Ghaeilge a chloiseann siad nó a
    fheiceann siad ar fhógraí. Pléigh na torthaí Dé Luain.

4. Déan suirbhé ar an méid ama in aghaidh na seachtaine a mbíonn na páistí ag féachaint ar
    an teilifís.

5. Pléigh na buanna atá ag an Raidió i gcomórtas leis an teilifís:
    - An mbíonn daoine fásta agus daoine óga ar aon intinn faoi chláir?
    - Cá bhfuil teacht ar *Raidió na Gaeltachta* agus *Raidió na Life* ar an raidió féin?

6. Iarr ar na páistí pictiúir a bhaineann leis na cláir is mó a thaitníonn leo a ghearradh
    amach (as an *RTE Guide* agus araile). I gcomhpháirt leis na páistí, cum teidil Ghaeilge do
    na cláir sin - ní gá aistriúchán díreach i gcónaí. Déan 'Colláis' de na pictiúir agus na
    teidil Ghaeilge agus croch suas é.

7. Iarr ar na páistí a gcuid fógraí féin a scríobh agus iad a chur os comhair an ranga i
    bhfoirm drámaí.

Pupil's Material

Áine: *Gabh mo leithscéal, a Sheáin. Tá an clár is fearr liomsa ag tosú anois.*

Seán: *ÁÁÁ - tá mé ag baint úsáide as an teilifíseáin chun cluiche ríomhaire a imirt - tá mé ag imirt Fifa Sacar.*

Áine: *Is féidir leat an cluiche ríomhaire a imirt nuair a bheidh mo chlár críochnaithe. Brostaigh.....*

Seán: *Ná bí ag cur isteach orm, a Áine. Tá ag éirí go geal liom - sin cúl eile.*

Mamaí: *A Sheáin - bíonn tú ag imirt cluichí ríomhaire ar an teilifís gach lá! Déan do chuid obair bhaile anois.*

Seán: *ÁÁÁ, a Mhamaí - tabhair cúig nóiméad eile dom, más é do thoil é.....Áine, más é do thoil é! Déanfaidh mé do chuid jabanna sa teach anocht duit.*

Áine: *Maith go leor - ach ná déan dearmad. Is féidir liom dul trasna an bhóthair go teach Nóra. Beidh sise ag féachaint ar an gclár céanna.*

Appendix 1.2

Sample lessons from the *Teaching through Irish Project*

Sample lessons in Science and Art for third and fourth grades are presented on the following pages. The material is reduced from the original A4, two-colour format.

Science
Pages 360 to 364 below contain a lesson on static electricity. Material from the teacher's handbook (three pages) is followed by material from the pupil's textbook (two pages). The *Obair Bhreise* section of the original lesson is omitted here. The extracts are from Lesson 18 of *Bain Trial As: Eolaíocht trí Ghaeilge do na Gnáthscoileanna* (Harris and Mac Giollabhuí, 1998b,c).

Art
Pages 365 to 368 contain a lesson on 'Marbling'. This appears as Lesson 4 in *Lean den Ealaín: Ealaín trí Ghaeilge do na Gnáthscoileanna* (Harris and Mac Giollabhuí, 1998a).

Leictreachas Statach

EOLAÍOCHT *18* **BUNCHEACHT**

Réamhábhar

Cuspóir
A léiriú gur féidir leictreachas statach a chruthú trí rudaí a chuimilt dá chéile.
[Tá dhá shaghas leictreachais ann; leictreachas statach agus sruthleictreachas].

Áiseanna
*   Píosaí beaga páipéir, balún, cíor, *biro* plaisteach, geansaí, mála, scian, banda leaisteach, rialóir adhmaid, rialóir plaisteach, peann luaidhe, scriosán, 20p, bosca lóin agus leabhair.
*   Leabhar an Dalta, Leathanaigh 48 agus 49.

Foclóir

banda leaisteach (*elastic band*)	leictreachas statach (*static electricity*)
bolgán (*light bulb*)	ómra (*amber*)
cíor (*comb*)	téipthaifeadán (*tape recorder*)
cuimil (*rub*)	scriosán (*eraser*)
geansaí olna (*woollen jumber*)	sruthleictreachas (*current electricity*)
greamaigh (*stick*)	stróic mé (*I tore*)
in aghaidh	

Imchaint an Cheachta

An bhfuil peann plaisteach ag aon duine?
An bhfuil an peann sin déanta as plaisteach?
Cad as a bhfuil an rialóir déanta?
Cad a cheapann tusa, a ....?
B'fhéidir go bhfuil an ceart agat.

Bain triail as arís.
Cuimil é de do gheansaí arís.
Ar thóg sé suas an píosa páipéir?
An bhfuil tú ag féachaint ar Chuid B?
Ar chuir tú tic sa bhosca?
An bhfuil pinn luaidhe daite agat?

Cur Chuige

Nóta

Déantar leictreachas statach nuair a chuimlítear nithe áirithe dá cheile, go speisialta aon rud atá déanta as plaisteach. Nuair a chuimlítear peann plaisteach de gheansaí olna, nó de ghruaig, tógann sé an leictreachas ón ngruaig nó ón ngeansaí. Ní féidir le peann luaidhe é sin a dhéanamh mar go bhfuil sé déanta as adhmad.

Timpeall na bliana 600 R. Ch. fuair na Gréagaigh amach go bpiocfadh ómra suas píosaí páipéir tar éis é a chuimilt d'éadach. Sa séú haois déag rinne William Gilbert trialacha le hómra agus thug sé an rud céanna faoi deara. B'eisean an chéad duine a d'úsáid an focal 'leictreachas' mar go bhfuil sé bunaithe ar 'lektron', an focal Gréigise ar ómra.

Réamhrá

■ Pléigh leis na daltaí na háiteanna go léir sa seomra ranga ina bhfuil leictreachas. Abair, mar shampla:

> Tá leictreachas ag dul go dtí an bolgán, tá leictreachas ag dul isteach sa téipthaifeadán agus tá leictreachas sa soicéad. An bhfuil leictreachas in aon áit eile? Cad a cheapann sibh? An bhfuil leictreachas sa pheann seo? agus araile.

■ Cuir aer isteach i mbalún (ná bíodh an balún rómhór) agus taispeáin do na daltaí é. Níl aon leictreachas statach ar an mbalún faoi láthair, ach cuimil an balún de ghruaig nó de gheansaí olna agus triail arís é. Abair:

> Tá balún agam. Tá aer istigh sa bhalún. An bhfuil leictreachas ar an mbalún seo?

Pléigh é seo leis an rang. Tabhair an balún do dhalta éigin agus abair leis/léi:

> Cuir an balún in aghaidh an bhalla .... Cad a tharla? Sea .... thit an balún. Níor ghreamaigh sé den bhalla.

1

An Léiriú

■ Tabhair an balún do dhalta eile. Abair:

> Cumil an balún de do chuid gruaige. [Is leor é a chuimilt timpeall 10-20 uair. Féach Léaráid 1]. Anois cuir an balún in aghaidh an bhalla. Cad a tharla? ....
> Sea, ghreamaigh an balún den bhalla. Cén fáth ar ghreamaigh sé? [Féach Léaráid 2]

Pléigh é seo leis an rang. Mura bhfuil an freagra acu abair:

> Tá leictreachas ar an mbalún. Tháinig an leictreachas ón ghruaig. Is leictreachas statach é seo.

[Scríobh na focail 'Leictreachas Statach' ar an gclár dubh]

2

■ Nuair atá an triail sin pléite agat leis na daltaí faigh peann plaisteach (*biro*) agus cuir píosaí beaga páipéir ar an mbord. Iarr ar dhalta éigin an peann a chuimilt dá chuid/cuid gruaige idir 10-20 uair. Ansin tógfaidh an peann suas na píosaí beaga páipéir. Cinntigh go bhfuil na píosaí páipéir chomh beag agus is féidir. Abair:

> A ...., seo duit peann plaisteach. Cuimil an peann de do chuid gruaige. Anois cuir an peann in aice leis na píosaí páipéir. Cad a tharla? .... Sea, thóg an peann suas na píosaí páipéir. Cén fáth ar tharla sé sin?

Mura bhfuil an freagra acu abair:

> Thóg an peann an leictreachas ón ghruaig. Tá leictreachas sa pheann anois. Is leictreachas statach é sin.

Obair na nDaltaí

> Anois, féach ormsa arís. Tá rialóir adhmaid agam. Anois, a ...., cuimil an rialóir de do gheansaí/do chuid gruaige fiche uair. .... An dtógfaidh an rialóir suas an píosa páipéir? Cad a cheapann tú? Lámha suas na páistí a deir, 'Tógfaidh'. Sibhse osclaígí na Leabhair ar Leathanach 48 agus cuirigí tic sa bhosca in aice le 'Tógfaidh' ar an Leathanach i do Leabhar. Anois lámha suas na páistí a deir 'Ní thógfaidh'. Sibhse, cuirigí tic sa bhosca in aice le 'Ní thógfaidh'. Anois cuir an rialóir in aice leis an bpíosa páipéir. Ar thóg sé suas an píosa páipéir? .... Níor thóg sé. Cén fáth?

Mura bhfuil an freagra acu abair:

> Níor thóg an rialóir leictreachas statach as an ngruaig/ngeansaí. Níl aon leictreachas sa rialóir. Cuirigí tic sa bhosca in aice le 'Níor thóg sé' ar do leathanach.

■ Déan amhlaidh leis na nithe eile ar an liosta. Is féidir iad a chuimilt de ghruaig nó de gheansaí olna. Bí cúramach leis an gcíor – ná lig do dhaltaí ach a gcíor féin a úsáid. Ansin abair leo tic a chur sa bhosca ceart.

■ Nuair atá siad críochnaithe le Cuid A, abair:

> Anois féach ar Chuid B, Leathanach 49. Féach ar Uimhir 1. Scríobh síos na rudaí a thóg suas na píosaí páipéir. .... Anois féach ar Uimhir 2. Scríobh síos na rudaí <u>nár</u> thóg suas na píosaí páipéir.

■ Nuair atá siad críochnaithe le Cuid B léigh an scéal leo atá i gCuid C. Abair:

> Anois féachaigí ar Chuid C. Tá scéal beag le léamh. An féidir leatsa an scéal sin a léamh, a ....?

Léigh, pléigh agus mínigh an scéal do na daltaí. Ansin abair leo pictiúr den scéal a tharraingt sa bhosca folamh. Abair:

> Féach ar an mbosca folamh. Tarraing pictiúr den scéal sa bhosca sin le do pheann luaidhe. Nuair atá an pictiúr críochnaithe agat, dathaigh é le do chriáin/do phinn luaidhe daite/do mharcóirí.

Mar Chríoch

■ Pléigh leictreachas statach ar bhonn níos leithne leis na daltaí, mar shampla, sa charr, ag siúl ar bhrat urláir agus an tintreach.

Leictreachas Statach

EOLAÍOCHT *18* **BUNCHEACHT**

Focail le foghlaim

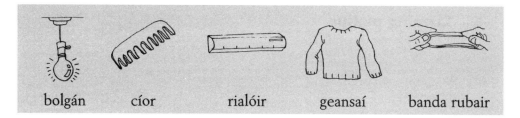

| bolgán | cíor | rialóir | geansaí | banda rubair |

A   Cuir ✔ sa bhosca ceart.

	Ainm an Ruda	Cad a cheapann tú?		Ar thóg sé suas na píosaí páipéir?	
1	Rialóir adhmaid	Tógfaidh	☐	Thóg sé	☐
		Ní thógfaidh	☐	Níor thóg sé	☐
2	Bosca lóin	Tógfaidh	☐	Thóg sé	☐
		Ní thógfaidh	☐	Níor thóg sé	☐
3	20p	Tógfaidh	☐	Thóg sé	☐
		Ní thógfaidh	☐	Níor thóg sé	☐
4	Scriosán	Tógfaidh	☐	Thóg sé	☐
		Ní thógfaidh	☐	Níor thóg sé	☐
5	Mála	Tógfaidh	☐	Thóg sé	☐
		Ní thógfaidh	☐	Níor thóg sé	☐
6	Scian	Tógfaidh	☐	Thóg sé	☐
		Ní thógfaidh	☐	Níor thóg sé	☐
7	Banda rubair	Tógfaidh	☐	Thóg sé	☐
		Ní thógfaidh	☐	Níor thóg sé	☐
8	Cíor	Tógfaidh	☐	Thóg sé	☐
		Ní thógfaidh	☐	Níor thóg sé	☐

B Déan liosta.

1 Ainmnigh na rudaí a thóg suas na píosaí páipéir: ....

....

2 Cad iad na rudaí <u>nár</u> thóg suas na píosaí páipéir? ....

....

C Tarraing pictiúr.

Stróic mé píosaí beaga páipéir agus chuir mé ar an mbord
iad. Ansin chuimil mé an rialóir plaisteach fiche uair de mo chuid
gruaige. Chuir mé an rialóir in aice leis na píosaí páipéir agus
thóg sé suas iad.

Marmarú

$\mathcal{4}$

Réamhábhar

Cuspóir
A chur ar chumas na ndaltaí an próiseas marmaraithe a fhiosrú agus úsáid a bhaint as an bpáipéar marmaraithe ina gcuid ealaíne féin.

Áiseanna
•péint ola (ceithre dhath nó mar sin), •biotáille bhán, •pailéid (leis an phéint agus an bhiotáille bhán a mheascadh), •dhá bháisín, •páipéar láidir, •scuabanna, •sean-nuachtáin

[**Nóta:** Is féidir péint mharmaraithe a fháil i gcuid de na siopaí. Tá sí réidh le húsáid díreach ón bhfeadán].

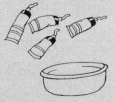 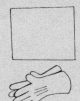 

Foclóir

anonn agus anall *(to and fro)*	nuachtáin
báisín	patrún *(pattern)*
biotáille bhán *(white spirit)*	péint mharmaraithe *(marbling paint)*
bolgán aeir *(air bubble)*	plaisteach *(plastic)*
faoin uisce	próiseas *(process)*
feadán *(tube)*	róthiubh *(too thick)*
in imeartas *(contrasting)*	scuab
leath bealaigh *(halfway)*	spréigh *(spread)*
measc	tanaithe *(thinned)*

Imchaint an Cheachta

Tabhair dom an scuab sin, le do thoil, a ....

Cheannaigh mé an bhiotáille bhán sa siopa.

Caithfidh tú bheith cúramach.

Féach, tá an phéint ag snámh ar bharr an uisce.

Ná lig don phéint dul ar do chuid éadaí.

An bhfuil páipéar ag gach duine?

Tóg amach go cúramach é.

Cuir síos ar an nuachtán é.

Tá sé fliuch go fóill.

Ná doirt an t-uisce.

Nach bhfuil an patrún sin go hálainn!

Cur Chuige
Réamhrá

■ Taispeáin agus pléigh samplaí de mharmarú leis na daltaí roimh ré, más féidir. Bíonn
samplaí de le fáil go minic taobh istigh de chlúdaigh seanleabhar.
Murar féidir leat samplaí de mharmarú a fháil, d'fhéadfá sampla de do chuid féin a
dhéanamh roimh ré, é a úsáid mar chlúdach leabhair agus é a phlé leis na daltaí.
Abair:

Féach ar an leabhar/gcóipleabhar seo. Féach ar an gclúdach. Tá an clúdach go deas.
An bhfuil clúdach mar sin ar do leabharsa? Cad iad na dathanna atá ann? Sea, tá
dearg agus gorm ann. Aon dath eile? Tugtar marmarú air sin. Ar mhaith libh marmarú
a dhéanamh? Ceart go leor.

■ Roghnaigh na dathanna a ba mhaith leat a úsáid. Bain úsáid as dathanna atá in imeartas lena
chéile agus a dhéanfaidh patrúin dheasa ag an deireadh, mar shampla, na dathanna dearg
agus gorm.

Obair na nDaltaí

■ Abair:

Clúdóidh mé an bord le sean-nuachtáin chun é a choinneáil glan. Tá dhá bháisín
agam anseo. Cuirfidh mé uisce sa bháisín seo. Anois cuirfidh mé uisce sa bháisín eile.
Líon na báisíní leath bealaigh suas le huisce. [Féach Léaráid 1]

1    **2**

Nóta

*Má bhíonn an phéint róthiubh, titfidh sí go bun an bháisín. Sin an chúis go
gcaithfidh tú í a mheascadh le beagán den bhiotáille bhán ar dtús ionas go
snámhfaidh sí ar bharr an uisce. Déan an meascadh tú féin seachas ligean do
dhaltaí é a dhéanamh, mar ní mór duit bheith an-chúramach leis an bhiotáille
bhán agus leis an phéint ola ar eagla go ndoirtfeadh siad ar éadaí na ndaltaí,
nó go ndoirtfeadh an báisín sa seomra ranga. Is leor trí nó ceithre bhraon de
gach péint ag an tús agus de réir mar atá sí á húsáid is féidir cúpla braon eile a
chur san uisce ó am go chéile.*

*Bí cinnte go bhfuil spás ullmhaithe agat sa seomra leis na pictiúir a fhágáil ina
luí ann fad atá an phéint ag triomú. Is féidir iad a chrochadh an lá dár gcionn.*

Roinn an rang ina dhá ghrúpa agus tabhair báisín do gach grúpa. Abair:
  Seasaigí in aice leis an mbáisín. Bígí cúramach agus ná doirtigí an t-uisce.
  Tá péint agam. Tá ceithre dhath agam – dath gorm, dath dearg, dath buí agus dath glas. Tá biotáille bhán agam sa bhuidéal seo.
[Féach Léaráid 2]

Measc beagán den phéint ghorm agus den bhiotáille bhán go dtí go mbíonn an meascán in ann rith cosúil le dúch. Abair:
  Tógfaidh mé an phéint ghorm agus meascfaidh mé í leis an bhiotáille bhán.

3

Anois tógfaidh mé an phéint dhearg agus cuirfidh mé beagán den bhiotáille bhán tríd sin freisin. Anois tá an dath dearg measctha.
Déan amhlaidh leis na dathanna go léir – gach dath ar phailéad leis féin – go dtí go mbíonn siad tanaíthe agus leachtach agus gur féidir leis an phéint rith isteach san uisce ina bhraonta.
[Féach Léaráid 3]

4

5

Nuair atá na péinteanna measctha ar na pailéid, cuir isteach sa bháisín iad agus spréigh timpeall ar bharr an uisce iad le peann luaidhe nó le cos scuab phéinteála.
[Féach Léaráidí 4 agus 5]. Abair:
  Anois cuirfidh mé na péinteanna isteach san uisce agus spréifidh mé timpeall ar bharr an uisce iad le mo pheann luaidhe.

6

7

■ Tabhair páipéar do gach dalta. Roghnaigh dalta as grúpa amháin. Abair leis/léi:
Cuir do pháipéar anuas go cúramach ar an uisce. Fág ar snámh ar bharr an uisce é ar feadh nóiméid.
Léirigh é seo más gá. Bí cinnte nach bhfuil aon bholgáin aeir faoin bpáipéar.
Le do scuab cuir do pháipéar anonn agus anall ar bharr an uisce. Ná cuir faoin uisce é. Anois tóg amach an páipéar go cúramach as an mbáisín. Tá beagán uisce ar an bpáipéar. Scaoil an t-uisce atá ar an bpaipéar isteach sa bháisín. Cuir do pháipéar anuas go cúramach ar an nuachtán. Tá patrún deas ar bharr do pháipéir anois.
[Féach Léaráidí 6 agus 7]

■ Abair leis na daltaí eile:
Anois déanaigí go léir an rud céanna. Fágaigí na pictiúir ar na nuachtáin go dtí amárach mar tá an phéint fliuch. Beidh siad tirim amárach.

■ Lig do na pictiúir triomú sula gcuirtear ar taispeáint iad.

Mar Chríoch

■ An lá dar gcionn ba chóir duit na pictiúir a chur ar taispeáint ar na ballaí sa seomra ranga agus na torthaí a phlé leis na daltaí. Cuir ceisteanna, mar shampla:
Cá bhfuil do phictiúrsa, a .... Ó, feicim anois é. Tá an patrún sin go hálainn. Cad iad na dathanna atá ann? Cé leis an pictiúr seo? Tá sé sin go han-deas freisin.

■ Is féidir leis na daltaí an páipéar marmaraithe a úsáid le téacsleabhair nó cóipleabhair a chlúdach. Caithfidh siad clúdach plaisteach a chur orthu ina dhiaidh sin ar eagla go rachadh an phéint ar na lámha.

■ D'fhéadfadh na daltaí boscaí pinn luaidhe a chlúdach leis an bpáipéar marmaraithe chomh maith, faoi mar atá léirithe sa léaráid atá in aice le teideal an cheachta seo ar Leathanach 11.

■ D'fhéadfadh na daltaí na samplaí den mharmarú a rinne siad a ghearradh suas ina bpíosaí beaga agus pictiúir eile a chruthú astu.

Appendix 2.1

Twenty-Classes Study: **Instructions for the examiner**

Nóta don Scrúdaitheoir

Ord riartha
Táthar ag súil go ndéanfar an obair idir 22 Bealtaine agus 2 Meitheamh. Ach is féidir tús a chur leis an tástáil ar 18 Bealtaine, más gá, agus leanúint léi chomh fada leis an 9 Meitheamh.

Éilíonn dírbhreathnú beirt chigirí agus iad ag obair taobh le chéile. Ní mór, mar sin, machnamh a dhéanamh ar an gcaoi ina rachfaí i mbun oibre i scoileanna cúpláilte. Déanfar roinnt moltaí faoi seo ag an gcruinniú a thionólfar ar 17 Bealtaine do na cigirí a bheidh páirteach sa tionscadal.

Seo a leanas an t-ord inar ceart na ceistiúcháin agus na trialacha a riaradh. Ní mór a mheabhrú go riarfar *Ceistiúchán don Dalta* ar dtús, agus nach gcuirfear aon cheann de na trialacha teanga go dtí go mbeidh deireadh leis an dírbhreathnú.
- *(1)* *Ceistiúchán don Dalta*
- *(2)* *Áireamh an Mhúinteora ar na daltaí de réir cumais*
- *(3)* *Dírbhreathnú dhá cheacht ag beirt chigirí*
  - *(i) Córas Dírbhreathnaithe ITÉ - I (Breathnóir 1)*
  - *(ii) Coras Dírbhreathnaithe ITÉ - II (Breathnóir 2)*
  - *(iii) Observers' Global Rating of Lesson*
- *(4)* *Ceistiúchán don Oide*
- *(5)* *Béaltriail Ghaeilge ITÉ-VI*
- *(6)* *Drumcondra Verbal Reasoning Test*

1. Ceistiúchán don dalta
Ní mór don chigire treoracha don dalta agus na míreanna féin a léamh amach os ard. Gheofar gach eolas faoi riaradh na trialach sa treoirleabhar *Ceistiúchán don Dalta - Treoracha*. Riarfar *Ceistiúchán don Dalta* ar dtús i gcaoi nach mbeidh aon róthionchar ag an aird a thabharfar ar an nGaeilge le linn dírbhreathnaithe agus tástála ar dhearcadh nó ar bharúlacha na ndaltaí. D'fhéadfaí é a riaradh le linn don chigire a chéad chuairt a thabhairt ar an scoil chun socruithe na trialach a dhéanamh agus an seomra ranga a fheiceáil - i gcás nach mbeifear ag tosú ar an obair féin an lá céanna. Níl fáth ar bith nach mbeadh achar áirithe idir riaradh *Ceistiúcháin don Dalta* agus cur i gcrích na coda eile den obair. Is fiú iarraidh ar an oide treise a chur le ráiteas an chigire i dtaobh an ghá atá le freagraí fírinneacha a thabhairt ar na ceisteanna uile - freagraí a bheidh ar fáil do lucht taighde amháin.

2. Áireamh an Mhúinteora ar na Daltaí de réir Cumais
Fad is a bheidh *Ceistiúchán don Dalta* á riaradh ag an gCigire, iarrtar ar an oide eolas a thaifead i dtaobh daltaí ghrád 6 (cumas agus spéis sa Ghaeilge, deacrachtaí le hábhair scoile éagsúla agus

slí bheatha na dtuismitheoirí). Ar an lámh eile, d'fhéadfadh an cigire *Áireamh an Mhúinteora ar na Daltaí de Réir Cumais* a thabhairt don oide le comhlánú ar a chaoithiúlacht nuair a théitear chun cainte leis an scoil ar dtús.

Ní mór chuige seo leathanach cuí de *Áireamh an Mhúinteora ar na Daltaí de Réir Cumais* a thabhairt don oide nuair a bheidh *Ceistiúchán don Dalta* réidh le riaradh. Féadfaidh an cigire a mhíniú don oide cén t-eolas atá le soláthar aige. Coinneoidh an cigire na leathanaigh chomhlánaithe in áit shábháilte mar gheall ar an gcineál eolais atá iontu.

3. *Dírbhreathnú*

Beidh beirt bhreathnóirí i mbun dírbhreathnaithe ag obair taobh le taobh ach iad neamhspleách ar a chéile. Ina theannta sin:

(a) Aimseoidh *Breathnóir 1* na príomhchodanna gníomhaíochta sa seomra ranga. Aicmeoidh sé agus breacfaidh sé síos iad de réir sceidil réamhullmhaithe *Córas Dírbhreathnaithe ITÉ - I*.

(b) Aimseoidh *Breathnóir 2* iompar agus úsáid teanga na ndaltaí a roghnaíodh roimh ré de réir sceidil réamhullmhaithe *Córas Dírbhreathnaithe ITÉ - II*.

(c) Déanfaidh gach breathnóir taifead fuaime den dá cheacht.

(d) A luaithe is a bheidh deireadh leis an rang, comhlánfaidh an bheirt bhreathnóirí an seicliosta *Observers' Global Rating of Lesson* i gcomhar le chéile. (Lorgaíonn sé seo eolas níos iomláine ar ghníomhaíocht sa rang agus ar iompar daltaí agus an oide le linn ceacht áirithe). Beidh seicliosta comhlánaithe ar fáil *do gach ceacht.*

Tig leis na breathnóirí éisteacht leis an téip athuair más gá d'fhonn na nótaí a bhreacadh ar an sceideal le linn an cheachta a sheiceáil nó cur leo. Tá dréacht threoirleabhar don bhreathnóir ar fáil ina bhfuil -

    (i)   eolas faoin dóigh le tasc an bhreathnóra a mhíniú don oide

    (ii) eolas faoin dóigh le taifead fuaime a dhéanamh sa seomra ranga

    (iii) cúntas ar *Córas Dírbhreathraithe ITÉ -I* and *II*

    (iv) treoir i dtaobh chomhlánú an Obervers' Global Rating of Lesson.

4. *Ceistiúchán don Oide*

Ní mór don chigire cóip den cheistiúcháin agus clúdach ar a bhfuil seoladh ITÉ a chur isteach i gclúdach eile agus é a thabhairt don oide nuair a bheidh an obair dhírbhreathnaithe thart. Tig leis an oide an ceistiúchán a chomhlánú fad is a bheidh *Triail Éisteachta an BG-VI* nó an *DVRT* ar siúl.

Ní ceart go bhfaigheadh an t-oide ranga cóip den *Ceistiúcháin don Oide* go dtí go mbíonn an obair dírbhreathnaithe thart. Fáth amháin atá leis seo ná go mbaineann cuid de na ceisteanna le frithghníomhú an oide i gcás an bhreathnaithe féin. Caithfidh an Cigire 'Uimhir an Ionaid' a scríobh isteach sna spásanna cuí ar chlúdach an cheistiúcháin sula scaoileann sé leis. Tá sé seo fíor-thábhachtach mar ní bheidh aon bhealach eile ag ITÉ leis na ceistiúchain éagsúla a aithint ona chéile níos déanaí - ní scríobhfaidh an t-oide a ainm ar an gceistiúchán agus cuirfidh sé an chóip chómhlánaithe isteach i gclúdach le seoladh ITÉ air, gan aon rud seachas 'uimhir an ionaid' ar an gceistiúchán féin. Tabharfaidh an toide an clúdach dúnta seo ar ais *don chigire le cur ar aghaidh chuig ITÉ.*

Seo an rud atá le déanamh ag an gCigire, mar sin. Gheobhaidh sé clúdach dúnta le haghaidh gach oide agus istigh ann beidh

    (a) cóip bhán de Ceistiúchán don Oide

    (b) litir ó ITÉ faoin gceistiúchán

(c) clúdach le seoladh ITÉ air a bheidh le húsáid ag an oide féin.

Ba cheart an clúdach sin a thabhairt don oide díreach taréis an obair dhírbhreathnaithe a bheith críochnaithe.

5. Béaltriail Ghaeilge ITÉ - VI (BG-VI)
Le riaradh ar dhaltaí rang VI amháin.

Seo leanas na hábhair do BG-VI
(a) Freagarleabhar do gach dalta.
(b) *Lámhleabhar an Scrúdaitheora* (Léibhéal Rang 6) (dath dearg).
(c) Téip (cáiséad) don *Triail Éisteachta* (dath dearg).
(d) *Leathanach Tuairisce don Triail.*

Tá gach eolas faoin modh riaracháin agus faoin gcóras marcála i Lámhleabhar an Scrúdaitheora. B'fhiú dhá phointe a lua anseo, áfach:

(1) Cuirtear an Triail Éisteachta ar na daltaí ar dtús

(2) Ní chuirtear ach leath na gceisteanna sa Triail Chainte ar gach dalta toisc í a bheith fada. Tá cur síos i Lámhleabhar an Scrúdaitheora ar conas a dhéantar amach *cé acu leath* den Triail Chainte a ba cheart a chur ar gach dalta.

6. DVRT (Drumcondra Verbal Reasoning Test)
Seo leanas na hábhair don DVRT:
(a) 'Practice Test' do gach dalta.
(b) 'Drumcondra Verbal Reasoning Test 1' do gach dalta.
(c) DVRT 'Instructions for administration'.
Beidh staduaireadóir, nó uaireadóir ar a bhfuil lamh soicind ag teastáil chomh maith.

Sé an DVRT an triail dheireannach a chuirtear ar na daltaí, taréis BG-VI a bheith críochnaithe ar fad. Ní miste maidin nó iarnóin a bheith saor don DVRT. B'fhearr nach mbeadh aon dalta á thástáil ar BG-VI an leathlá sin. Is leor uair a chloigh nó mar sin, áfach, don DVRT féin. Cuirfear an DVRT ar dhaltaí uile ghrád 6 atá sa rang.

- Nuair a bhíonn an DVRT thart, scríobh isteach 'uimhir an dalta' agus 'uimhir an ionaid', san ord sin sa chúinne clé ar bharr'chlúdach gach DVRT.
- Má tharlaíonn sé go mbíonn dalta áirithe rang 6 i láthair don DVRT, nach raibh i láthair don Triail Éisteachta in hiomláine, ní bheidh aon 'uimhir an dalta' ar fáil don dalta sin. Sa chás sin scríobh isteach "as láthair don Bhéaltriail" agus 'uimhir an ionaid' ina dhiaidh sin ar chlúdach an DVRT.
- Má tharlaíonn sé go mbíonn dalta áirithe a bhí i láthair do chuid éigin den Bhéaltriail Ghaeilge as láthair don DVRT, scríobh nóta faoin dalta ar an *Leathanach Tuairisce*.
- Tá 'dáta breithe' tábhachtach i gcás an DVRT. Mar sin, bí cinnte go bhfuil an spás cuí líonta ar chlúdach an DVRT.
- Ní gá don scrúdaitheoir an DVRT a scóráil - déanfaidh ITÉ an obair sin.
- Tá gach eolas faoin DVRT sa Leabhrán *'Instructions for Administration'*.

Uimhir an Ionaid
Tabharfar 'uimhir an ionaid' do gach uile scoil agus bainfear úsáid as an uimhir sin amach anseo chun cóipeanna de na trialacha a aithint óna chéile. Ba cheart 'uimhir an ionaid' a bheith ar gach doiciméad (freagarleabhar, Leathanach Tuairisce, 7rl.) a chuirfear ar ais chuig ITÉ.

Nóta

Má aimsíonn tú easnamh nó dearmad tábhachtach san ábhar seo, nó in ábhar ar bith eile, iarrtar ort glaoch a chur ar John Harris le do thoil. Cuirfear na scrúdaitheoirí ar an eolas faoin easnamh sin láithreach.

Appendix 2.2

Teacher's rankings of pupils

Teacher's Rankings of Pupils

Instructions

Please fill in the information at the top of the large sheet first.
Use additional sheets if necessary

Column A
Pupil Name: Full name of each sixth-grade pupil in your class (as he/she will write it on the cover of the tests). Write the names in the order under which they appear in the roll book - including absent pupils.

Column B
Pupil Ability In Irish: Part of the class observation will involve one of the inspectors monitoring three individual pupils in the class. Because this is such a small number, it is important to get as good a cross-section of ability levels in Irish as possible. Therefore, within each class the inspector will randomly select one pupil from the top, middle and bottom ability levels in Irish. Only that inspector will know which pupils are being monitored.

We will depend on your knowledge of the pupils' abilities in Irish to divide them into three groups of approximately equal size -
1. a "higher ability in Irish" group,
2. a "middle ability in Irish" group and
3. a "lower ability in Irish" group.

In the ability column, therefore, please write a '1' (one) beside the name of each pupil who you consider to be in the highest ability group in Irish, '2' opposite each pupil you consider to be in the middle ability in Irish group and '3' beside the name of each pupil in the lower ability Irish group. Once you have rated each pupil as belonging to the top, middle or bottom category as regards ability in Irish, the inpector will then be able to randomly select one pupil from each ability level. (*Pupil Ability In Irish* is the *only* item of information from the TEACHER'S RANKING which the inspector will use in selecting pupils)

Column C
Pupil Interest In Irish: The pupil's interest in Irish is to be rated on a 5 point scale: 1 = very high; 2 = high; 3 = fair; 4 = low; 5 = very low.

| Column D | **Pupil Difficulty With Various Subjects:** Your assessment of whether the pupil experiences difficulty in school with a number of aspects of Irish, English and Maths. The information sought is :
d = *difficulty* experienced with this subject;
nd = *no difficulty* experienced with this subject.
Either 'd' or 'nd' should be written under *each of the seven* subject headings for *each* pupil. |

| Column E | **Occupation Of Pupil's Parents/Guardians:**
This information is needed in order to be able determine the pupils socio-economic background. Socioeconomic status is a very important variable in this kind of educational linguistic research. Needless to say, the information on socioeconomic background will be treated as strictly confidential and this document will be destroyed as soon as it is coded in numerical terms. Two items of information are sought on the *main earner* only, whether it is the father or mother, or the male or female guardian. |

(i) **Full Title** of the parent or guardian's occupation (or former occupation if retired, redundant or unemployed), whichever parent is the main earner. For example, if the father is unemployed but the mother is employed, then she is the main earner.

If the parent who was the main earner is now unemployed (i.e. receiving financial assistance from the state), please indicate whether it is long term (more than 2 years) or short term (less than 2 years). If you are in doubt about how to classify a particular occupation, simply give as much information as possible. Write any explanatory notes you wish in the margin.

(ii) **Type of Work Done**: Although the title itself will often be self-explanatory (e.g. bus conductor), more detail will sometimes be needed on the type of work done. For example, if you list the job title as "Civil Servant", the type of work done might be that of a clerical assistant, tax inspector or staff officer etc.

Here are some examples of the kind of information required:

Full Title: Civil Servant (Retired)

Type of Work Done: Administrative Officer, Department of Finance

Full Title: Small farmer/part time barman

Type of Work Done: 40 acres mixed farming/works in hotel at night

Full Title: Factory worker (longterm unemployed)

Type of Work Done: Machinist in clothing factory

Full Title: Farmer

Type of Work:120/150 acres mixed farming

Full Title: Nurse

Type of Work Done: Private Nursing Home for the elderly

Áireamh an Mhúinteora ar na Daltaí de Réir Cumais

Treoracha

Líon isteach an t-eolas, le do thoil, ag barr an leathanaigh mhóir i dtús báire.
Bain úsáid as leathanaigh breise más gá.

Colún A **Ainm An Dalta:** Ainm iomlán gach dalta séú grád i do rangsa (faoi mar a scríobhfaidh sé/sí é ar chlúdach na dtrialacha). Scríobh síos na hainmneacha san ord ina bhfuil siad ar an rolla - ag cur san áireamh daltaí atá as láthair.

Colún B **Cumas An Dalta Ar An nGaeilge:** Mar chuid den bhreathnú ranga a dhéanfar, beidh ar dhuine de na cigirí measúnú a dhéanamh ar *thrí* dhalta ar leith sa rang. Toisc gur líon an-bheag é seo, tá sé an-tábhachtach go dtiocfaí ar thrasghearradh, chomh cruinn agus is féidir, de na leibhéil chumais Ghaeilge sa rang. Dá bhrí sin is é a dhéanfaidh an cigire dalta amháin a roghnú 'gan aird' as gach leibhéal cumais Ghaeilge sa rang: barrleibhéal, meánleibhéal agus bunleibhéal. Ní bheidh a fhios ag aon duine ach amháin ag an gcigire áirithe sin féin cé hiad na daltaí a bhfuil measúnú á dhéanamh orthu.

Beimid ag brath ar an eolas atá agatsa, mar mhúinteoir, ar chumas na ndaltaí ar an nGaeilge, chun iad a roinnt i dtrí ghrúpa a bheidh mórán ar chomh-mhéid lena chéile:-
1. grúpa 'ardchumas Gaeilge'
2. grúpa 'meánchumas Gaeilge'
3. grúpa 'lagchumas Gaeilge'

Mar sin beidh ortsa, le do thoil, an figiúr '1' a scríobh sa cholún cumais i ndiaidh gach dalta atá sa ghrúpa is airde cumas Gaeilge, dar leat; beidh ort an figiúr '2' a scríobh i ndiaidh ainm gach dalta atá sa ghrúpa meánchumas Gaeilge, agus '3' i ndiaidh ainm gach dalta sa ghrúpa lagchumas Gaeilge'.

Nuair a bheidh gach dalta áirithe mar sin agatsa in ord de réir cumais Ghaeilge, beidh an cigire in ann dalta amháin a roghnú 'gan aird' as gach leibhéal cumais sa rang. (Is é *CUMAS AN DALTA AR AN nGAEILGE* an t-aon mhír amháin eolais ar an *LIOSTA DALTAÍ* a mbainfidh an cigire feidhm as agus daltaí á roghnú aige).

Colún C **SPÉIS AN DALTA SA GHAEILGE:** Ní mór spéis gach dalta sa Ghaeilge a mheas ar scála 5 phointe :- 1 = an-ard; 2 = ard; 3 = cuibheasach; 4 = íseal; 5 = an-íseal.

Colún D **DEACRACHT AN DALTA LE hÁBHAIR ÉAGSÚLA:** Is é atá i gceist anseo do thuairim féin faoi cé acu an mbíonn nó nach mbíonn deacrachtaí ar scoil ag an dalta áirithe le gnéithe éagsúla den Ghaeilge nó den Bhéarla, nó le Matamaitic i gcoitinne. An tuairim nó an t-eolas atá á lorg againn anseo
    d = *bíonn* deacracht aige/aici leis an ngné seo;
    gd = *ní bhíonn* deacracht aige/aici leis an ngné seo;

Ba cheart 'd' nó 'gd' a scríobh faoi *gach teideal de na seacht ngnétheideal* i gcás gach dalta ar leith.

Colún **SLÍ BHEATHA THUISMITHEOIR/CHAOMHNÓIR AN DALTA**: Is gá an
E t-eolas seo chun cúlra socheacnamaíochta an dalta a chinntiú.

 Ní gá a rá go gcoimeádfar an t-eolas seo go h-iomlán faoi rún agus scriosfar an doiciméad seo chomh luath is a bheidh sé códaithe in uimhreacha againn.

Iarrtar an chéad dá mhír eile eolais i leith *an phríomhshaothraí amháin*, is cuma cé acu an t-athair/mháthair, caomhnóir fireann/baineann é/í.

(i) *Teideal iomlán na slí beatha* (nó hath-shlí beatha má tá sé/sí ar pinsean, iomarcach nó gan obair), i gcás cibé duine atá mar phríomhshaothraí. Mar shampla, má tá an t-athair dífhostaithe agus an mháthair fostaithe, is í an mháthair an príomhshaothraí sa chás sin.

An tuismitheoir a bhí tráth ina p(h)ríomhshaothraí, má tá sé/sí as obair anois (i.e. ag fáil cúnamh airgid ón stát), abair cé acu díomhainteas fadtéarmach (níos mó ná dhá bhliain) nó gearrthéarmach (níos lú ná dhá bhliain) é. Má tá amhras ort faoin gcaoi inar cheart slite beatha áirithe a aicmiú, tabhair oiread eolais agus is féidir leat.

(ii) *SAGHAS OIBRE A DHÉAN(ANN/ADH)) SÉ/SÍ*: Cé go míneoidh an teideal é féin go minic (e.g. fear ticéad bus), beidh eolas breise ag teastáil i gcásanna áirithe ar an saghas oibre a dhéantar, mar shampla, más é 'Státseirbhíseach' an teideal b'fhéidir gurb é an saghas oibre a bheadh i gceist ná obair oifigigh chléireachais, nó chigire chánach, nó oifigigh foirne etc.

 Seo roinnt samplaí den saghas eolais atá ag teastáil:

Teideal iomlán: Státseirbhíseach (Ar pinsean).

Saghas oibre a dhéan(ann/adh) sé/sí: Oifigeach Riaracháin, An Roinn Airgeadais.

Teideal iomlán: Feirmeoir beag/fear tábhairne páirtaimsireach.

Saghas oibre a dhéan(ann/adh) sé/sí: 40 acra feirmeoireacht mheasctha/ag obair i dteach ósta istoíche.

Teideal iomlán: Oibrí monarchan (gan obair fhadtéarmach).

Saghas oibre a dhéan(ann/adh) sé/sí: Ag obair ar inneall i monarcha éadaí.

Teideal iomlán: Feirmeoir.

Saghas oibre a dhéan(ann/adh) sé/sí: 120/150 acra feirmeoireacht mheasctha.

Teideal iomlán: Banaltra.

Saghas oibre a dhéan(ann/adh) sé/sí: Ag obair i dTeach Príobháideach Banaltrais.

Ainm an Mhúinteora _____

Áireamh an Mhúinteora ar na Daltaí de réir Cumais*
(Daltaí rang a sé amháin)

Ainm na Scoile: _____
Seoladh: _____

A	B	C	D							E
AINM AN DALTA (Rang a sé amháin)	**CUMAS AN DALTA AR AN nGAEILGE**	**SPÉIS AN DALTA SA GHAEILGE**	**DEACRACHT AN DALTA LE hÁBHAIR ÉAGSÚLA** (d=deacracht, gd=gan deacracht)							**SLÍ BHEATHA AN TUISMITHEORA/CHAOMHNÓRA** (an tuismitheoir is mó a thuilleann airgead/pá)
	1='grúpa 'ard - chumas Gaeilge' 2='grúpa 'meán-chumas Gaeilge' 3=grúpa 'lag - chumas Gaeilge'	1=an-ard 2=ard 3=cuibheasach 4=íseal 5=an-íseal	*Gaeilge*			*Béarla*			*Mata-maitic*	(i) Teideal iomlán na slí bheatha/na hath-shlíbeatha (ii) An saghas oibre a dhéan(ann) sé/sí
			G ó bhéal	*G* léamh	*G* scríobh	*B* ó bhéal	*B* léamh	*B* scríobh		
										Teideal Iomlán: Saghas oibre a dhéan(ann) sé/sí:
										Teideal Iomlán: Saghas oibre a dhéan(ann) sé/sí:
										Teideal Iomlán: Saghas oibre a dhéan(ann) sé/sí:
										Teideal Iomlán: Saghas oibre a dhéan(ann) sé/sí:
										Teideal Iomlán: Saghas oibre a dhéan(ann) sé/sí:

*Form reduced from original A3 size.

Appendix 2.3

Observers' Global Rating of Lesson: Item used in Chapter 9

Completed jointly by Observer 1 and Observer 2 for <u>each lesson.</u>

23. **What percentage of the pupils appeared to adopt an entirely passive role or to actually resist involvement, in the lesson?**

☐ % of passive or resisting pupils.
Can you add any comments?
....
....

Results:

		Percentage of classes	
Percentage of pupils adopting passive role	*n =*	*Lesson 1 (20)*	*Lesson 2 (20)*
0 - 10%		70.0	85.0
11 - 20%		20.0	10.0
21% - 30%		5.0	0.0
31% or more		5.0	5.0
		100%	100%

Appendix 2.4

Teacher Questionnaire: **Selected items**

Q17. **Cén modh teagaisc a úsáideann tú agus tú ag múineadh Gaeilge ó <u>bhéal/comhrá</u> <u>Gaeilge</u> ag léibhéal Rang VI? (Cuir tic i mbosca amháin).**

    a)   Modh Closamhairc amháin ('Lá Faoin Tuath'/'Sean Neidí').   ☐

    b)   Modh ABC.   ☐

    c)   Meascán: Modh Closamhairc agus Modh ABC   ☐

    d)   Do mhodh féin.   ☐

         Más é do mhodh féin atá i gceist tabhair breis eolais anseo
         le do thoil:

         _____

         _____

         _____

Q. 32. **Ag cur san áireamh a bhfuil d'eolas tugtha agat thuas, léirigh anseo an méid iomlán ama *in aghaidh na seachtaine* a thugtar do mhúineadh *ábhar* eile (seachas an Ghaeilge) trí Ghaeilge i do rangsa? (Cuir tic i mbosca amháin).**

    (i)   Ní thugtar aon am   ☐

    (ii)   Tugtar níos lú ná uair a chloig   ☐

    (iii)   Tugtar idir uair agus 2 uair a chloig.   ☐

    (iv)   Tugtar idir 2 agus 3 huaire a chloig   ☐

    (v)   Tugtar idir 3 agus 4 huaire a chloig.   ☐

    (vi)   Tugtar idir 4 agus 5 huaire a chloig.   ☐

    (vii) Tugtar níos mó ná 5 huaire a chloig.   ☐

AN tSLÍ INA nDEACHAIGH AN BREATHNÚ RANGA LE DÉANAÍ I gCION ORT

Q69. Cé chomh tipiciúil is a bhí an dá cheacht a mhúin tú i an dá bhreathnadóir sheachtracha (i.e. maidir le do chur chun teagaisc, leis na hábhair a úsáideach, le stíl na hidirghníomhaíochta leis na daltaí etc.)? **Cuir tic i mbosca amháin.**

    (i) An dá cheacht a breathnaíodh bhí siad tipiciúil ar fad   ☐ 1

    (ii) An dá cheacht a breathnaíodh ní raibh siad tipiciúil ar chor ar bith   ☐ 2

Cuir síos aon léiriú nó aon mhíniú is mian leat:

_____

_____

_____

_____

Q70. Cé chomh fada is a mhothaigh tú gur chuir na breathnadóirí as duit féin agus do do ghnáth-theagaisc? **(Cuir tic i mbosca amháin).**

    (i) Chuir na breathnadóirí as go mór dom   ☐ 1

    (ii) Chuir na breathnadóirí as dom cuid mhaith   ☐ 2

    (iii) Is beag má bhí aon tionchar ag na breathnadóirí   ☐ 3
          ar mo chuid teagaisc ar chor ar bith.

Appendix 2.5

Teachers' reactions to the observation work

Written responses to part 2 of Q69. on the Teacher Questionnaire

School Class. No*	Comment
1	Bhí níos mó suim ag na daltaí sa rang Ghaeilge nuair a bhí na cigírí istigh, go háirithe ar an chéad lá. Bhí siad ag déanamh iarracht ag an Ghaeilge ar an lá sin - ní raibh siad ina gcodladh! Bhí mise "an deas" freisin - níl sé sin tipiciúil! Ach rinne mé ceacht tipiciúil.
2	Ní dóigh liom go raibh na páistí chomh réidh chun cainte is a bhíonn siad de ghnáth - eagla orthu faoi na téipthaifeadáin i mo thuairim.
4	It wasn't typical from the point of view that the children paid more attention than normal. The first day they were very tired as we had a concert the previous night. Some of the kids who usually act up paid more attention than they've ever shown. In other ways they were inhibited by the presence of others and were very quiet during the first class but more co-operative during the second.
8	Bhí an dá cheacht bunaithe ar thimpeallacht na ndaltaí. Thaispeáin mé mo mhodhanna múinte sa Ghaeilge agus bhí suim an-mhór ag na daltaí sa scéim. Bhí mé cúthail i dtosach ach i gceann tamaill níor thug mé aon aird ar na breathnadóirí. Thug na breathnadóirí an mhisneach dom agus bhí mé an uaibhreach as na daltaí.
9	Chuaigh mo thréimhse sa Fhrainc agus an cúrsa Ardteastas san Oideachais go mór i gcion orm. Táim an-tugtha leis an modh chumarsáideach le cluichí cainte le hobair i ngrúpaí anois. Bainim úsáid as Gaeilge don chuid is mó sa Rang. Tá fonn orm deis a thabhairt do na páistí comhrá a dhéanamh. Foghlaimíonn duine teanga chun cumarsáid a dhéanamh.

School Class No.	Comment
10	Chuir na breathnadóirí agus na téipthaifeadáin as do na daltaí.
12	Bhí an dá cheacht tipiciúil go leor ach amháin nach ndearna mé an phíosa scéalaíochta a cumadh do na daltaí. Rinne me dearmad glan orthu (na breathnadóirí) tar éis cúpla nóiméad ach déarfainn gur ullmhaigh mé an dá cheacht beagáinín níos fearr ná mar is gnáth.
13	Tá rang IV go rang VI agamsa agus de gnáth ní chaithim an méid ama sin le Rang VI. Bheadh níos mó le déanamh ag na ranganna eile de ghnáth.
14	Normally I would have spent an awful lot more time at each individual area - say Grammar. I tried to squeeze everything in the 1½ hrs. approx to give a general impression of what I do or attempt to do.
15	Leanas leis na ceachtanna díreach mar a dheinim gach lá. An dán a mhúineas bhí sé déanta cheana ag Rang a VI nuair a bhíodar i Rang V ach nua do Rang a V.
20	Bhí na ceachtanna tipiciúil go leor maidir le mo chur chun teagaisc agus leis na hábhair a úsáideadh ach bhíos an-neirbhíseach toisc easpa taithí agam ar bheith ag múineadh ós comhair cuairteoirí. Déarfainn go raibh na taifeadáin ag cur isteach ar na páistí an chéad lá agus ní raibh siad ró-bhríomhar ach oiread tar éis deireadh seachtaine fada.

* These ranks are the same ones used throughout the report to represent the *Twenty Classes* (see Chapter 2).

Appendix 3.1

Pupil Questionnaire: Instructions for administration

The Pupil Questionnaire is largely based on an adaptation of the widely used *Attitude /Motivation Test Battery* which was originally validated and standardised on samples of anglophone Canadian students in grades 7 to 11. The one-third or so of the questionnaire items at the end, however, are new.

No time limit is set for administration of the Pupil Questionnaire. Unlike the original form of the test, the items here are read aloud by the examiner. Consequently, pupils are answering each item more or less simultaneously, so that the overall pace will be decided by the slowest pupils.

The activities of the examiner should be as unobtrusive as possible. Moving from one pupil to another or looking at a pupil's answers should be kept to a minimum - except to ensure that the correct question is being answered. Disruptive behaviour on the part of pupils, such as talking or making unnecessary noise, should be discouraged. Any extraneous noise or disruption could influence pupils' answers.

Should questions be asked about the meaning of a particular item, it is important that the exmainer's answers remain within the meaning and, as far as possible, within the vocabulary of the printed item. If it is necesary to explain a particular item, it is best to stay as close to the original item as possible. Of course, care should be taken not to influence the student to respond in any particular way.

When reading the items aloud to the pupils, the examiner should use a normal speaking rate and tone. Proceed to the next item briskly once the last pupil has marked his or her answer. In the case of the first one or two practice items, the examiner should say both the item statement and the answer options aloud. For the remainder of the items, however, only the statement is said aloud. The assumption is that even very poor readers will know the left to right order of the answer options by then.

TO BE READ ALOUD BY THE EXAMINER TO THE PUPILS
(Words to be spoken by the examiner are emphasised.)

"You are being asked to answer this questionnaire so that we can find out more about how children learn Irish and what they think and feel about it. Your answers will only be seen by the people who are doing the research. No one in the school or anywhere else is allowed to see your answers. Although we ask for your name on the cover of the Questionnaire, this is only because we must be able to keep your questionnaire together with other questionnaires which you will be asked to answer in a few days.

We want to find out what you really think and feel, so we are depending on you. If you really do not want to answer any particular question on this questionnaire, however, you do not have to

384 Teaching and learning Irish in primary school

- but we <u>hope</u> you will not leave any questions out. Please raise your hand if you are not sure what to do.
First, please write your name, class and school on the cover.
Now open your booklet and look at the three practice questions."
[Hold up a copy of the pupil's booklet to show practice items]

"Now, I am going to read each question out loud while you read it in your questionnaire. Some people will agree and others will disagree with the statements. There are no right and wrong answers since many people have different opinions.
Look at the first one."

The examiner should now write out the first practice sentence and the five answer options on the blackboard, setting them out as they are in the pupil's booklet.

Cork footballers are better than Dublin footballers.

1	2	3	4	5
Strongly Disagree	Slightly Disagree	Neutral	Slightly Agree	Strongly Agree

Say the item statement once you have written it down. Then say each of the options aloud once or twice, proceeding each time from left to right and pointing to each option as you say it. This is to ensure, as far as possible, that poor readers will be able to identify the answer options simply from the left to right order, since the options will not be spoken aloud by the examiner on the test items proper.

Explain the word 'neutral' by saying that it means *"when you are in between when you don't agree or disagree"* (or some broadly similar form of words).

Then, when you have the attention of the class, repeat the statement for the first practice item:
"Cork footballers are better than Dublin footballers". Now, what do you think about that? Do you agree or disagree? If you feel certain that Cork footballers really <u>are</u> better than Dublin footballers, then draw a circle around "strongly agree", just below the sentence.

[Demonstrate drawing a circle around the relevant words on the blackboard, then erase the circle again]

Strongly Disagree	Slightly Disagree	Neutral	Slightly Agree	Strongly Agree

"If you agree, but only just a little bit, then draw a circle around 'slightly agree'. If you <u>don't</u> think that Cork footballers are better than Dublin footballers, then draw a circle around either 'strongly disagree' or 'slightly disagree', whichever best describes how you feel. If you have no opinion or are not sure whether you agree or disagree, draw a circle around 'neutral'. Remember we want you to give <u>your</u> opinion."
[Pause]
"You must only draw a circle around <u>one</u> of the choices. Some people would circle 'strongly disagree, others would circle 'strongly agree', and still others would circle 'slightly agree' or 'slightly disagree'. If you are not really sure whether you agree or disagree draw a circle around

'neutral'. There is no right or wrong answer on this questionnaire. All that is important is say what your feeling is."

[Check that each pupil has given only one answer. If the class gives a choral response, explain that for the other items they must work quietly on their own. Leave the five options written on the blackboard during the test. Please make sure that circles drawn around individual options have been erased.]

"Now look at the next statement. I will read it out loud. Then draw a circle around which words say how you feel - Do you 'strongly disagree' or do you 'slightly disagree'? Are you 'neutral'? Do you 'slightly agree' or do you 'strongly agree'?

'Summer holidays from school are too long'.

Do you agree or disagree?

Now draw a circle around which words say how you feel about the statement - "Summer holidays from school are too long".

[Don't say the specific answer options aloud again - unless you feel it is necessary. You could perhaps point towards the answer options on the blackboard.]

"Don't waste too much time thinking about it. Draw a circle around your answer as soon as you can. On the other hand, please do not be careless as it is important that we find out your true feelings.

Now, the next statment:

'Glenroe is a good programme'.

Mark your answer by drawing a circle around the words which say how you feel.

[Pause]

Now, before we begin I want to see if you know what a foreign language is."

[Ask a few questions to establish that pupils understand what a foreign language is.]

"Right, turn to page 2 and I will read out the statements. Each time, circle the answer which tells how you feel about the statement. Don't wait for me to tell you to mark your answer. Just do it yourself when I read the statement out loud. Are you ready?"

First read the item identification number on the left of each statement. Then read the statement after a moment's pause. In general, do not repeat the statement aloud. If an interruption (or a general lapse of attention) occurs while you are speaking, or while the pupils are recording their responses, the item number and statment should be repeated in full. Emphasise the number of the item being repeated and check that pupils who have already marked down an answer do not record the same answer again to the next item by mistake.

Item options, as mentioned above, are not spoken aloud. The last three items (78, 79 and 80) are "write in" questions. Give as much time as necessary for pupils to write in any comments they have. Encourage pupils, if necessary, to respond to these items, explaining that we want their opinions and suggestions.

Since the items on the test were originally intended to be read silently by the pupil, some of them may be rather difficult to read aloud fluently. It would be desirable, therefore, to read quickly through the booklet yourself beforehand to become familiar with the phrasing of the items.

If possible, go right through all the items without a break. If you feel that pupils are becoming restless, however, it may be desirable to give a short break while pupils remain in their seats. Care should be taken that pupils begin with the correct item after the break.

When booklets are being collected, check that each has a name, age and class written on the front cover.

(Note: If you have any observations to make on individual items or on pupils' reactions to them, we would be very interested to hear them.)

Ceistiúchán don Dalta

Pupil Questionnaire

Ainm _____

Rang _____

Scoil _____

Institiúid Teangeolaíochta Éireann

PRACTICE QUESTIONS

Cork footballers are better than Dublin footballers.

1	2	3	4	5
Strongly Disagree	Slightly Disagree	Neutral	Slightly Agree	Strongly Agree

Summer holidays from school are too long.

1	2	3	4	5
Strongly Disagree	Slightly Disagree	Neutral	Slightly Agree	Strongly Agree

"Glenroe" is a good programme.

1	2	3	4	5
Strongly Disagree	Slightly Disagree	Neutral	Slightly Agree	Strongly Agree

Appendix 3.2

Pupil Questionnaire: Item-response data[*]

Item No.	Percentage of pupils choosing response options on each item.....				
	Strongly Disagree	Slightly Disagree	Neutral	Slightly Agree	Strongly Agree

Irish Attitude/Motivation Scales

Integrativeness scales

(1) Attitude to Irish speakers (10 items)

2. Most people who speak Irish are friendly and easy to get along with.

5.9	15.5	35.1	28.4	14.7

6. The more I get to know people who speak Irish, the more I want to learn it.

11.6	18.0	18.0	32.0	20.0

12. The Irish language is an important part of Ireland and the Irish people.

2.4	3.3	6.1	24.7	63.1

17. Some of the best people in Ireland are Irish speakers.

14.9	16.5	23.5	26.7	18.0

23. If Ireland lost the Irish language and the Irish way of life, it would really be a great loss.

2.4	4.7	4.3	17.1	71.0

40. People in our country who only speak English should try harder to learn the Irish language.

8.6	12.0	11.8	29.2	38.2

42. People who speak Irish help to make the Irish way of life special and different from other countries.

3.9	8.6	13.3	32.9	41.0

---

[*] (N pupils = 490). Items here are grouped according to the relevant scales. Item numbers indicate the order in which the items appeared on the *Pupil Questionnaire*.

Item No.	Percentage of pupils choosing response options on each item.....				
	Strongly Disagree	**Slightly Disagree**	**Neutral**	**Slightly Agree**	**Strongly Agree**

47. People who speak Irish help to keep alive an old and beautiful part of the Irish way of life.

	1.8	5.3	7.1	26.1	59.0

49. I would like to know more people who speak Irish.

	12.0	22.2	23.3	23.1	19.0

52. People who speak Irish are friendly, nice and interesting.

	6.3	15.1	35.1	27.6	15.3

(2) Integrative orientation to Irish (4 items)

15. Learning Irish is important for me because it will allow me to meet and talk to different kinds of people.

	8.8	15.7	13.7	36.3	25.1

27. It is important for me to learn Irish because it will make it easier for me to take part in things like Slógadh, feiseanna and Irish music.

	12.9	14.5	17.8	32.4	22.0

36. Learning Irish is important because it will make me feel more at home with people who speak Irish.

	7.8	12.7	12.9	35.9	30.4

37. It is important to learn Irish because it will help me to read Irish books and to understand Irish songs, stories and television programmes.

	5.1	9.0	9.2	34.9	41.2

(3) Interest in second/foreign languages (10 items)

3. If I were visiting a foreign country I would like to be able to speak the language of that country.

	1.8	1.0	3.3	15.7	77.8

5. Even though countries which speak other languages are not right beside Ireland, it is still important to learn foreign languages.

	2.4	4.3	4.7	27.3	60.8

11. I wish I could speak another language, besides English, really well.

	1.6	1.0	2.2	12.4	82.2

Item No.	Percentage of pupils choosing response options on each item.....				
	Strongly Disagree	**Slightly Disagree**	**Neutral**	**Slightly Agree**	**Strongly Agree**

14. I would like to be able to read books written in another language, besides English.
3.9   3.9   5.3   28.2   58.4

18. I often wish I could read newspapers and magazines in another language besides English.
4.9   7.3   9.0   30.4   48.0

21. Learning another language, besides English, can be very enjoyable.
2.9   8.0   14.7   32.9   41.2

31. I would really like to learn a lot of foreign languages.
1.4   10.0   6.7   28.0   53.5

43. If I went to another country for a while I would try hard to learn the language of that country - even if I could get by using English.
3.7   6.3   11.0   35.3   43.1

50. I would like to learn a foreign language in school even if I didn't <u>have</u> to do it .
4.7   6.3   8.8   31.4   48.4

53. I like meeting and listening to people who speak other languages besides English.
3.5   9.0   12.9   32.2   42.0

Motivation scales

(4) Desire to learn Irish (7 items)

54. If there were Irish-speaking families living near me, I would like to speak Irish to them.
7.3   12.4   12.9   38.6   28.4

60. Compared to subjects like Maths and English reading, I don't like Irish very much.
15.7   22.7   9.8   26.7   24.9

61. During the Irish lesson, I wish that only Irish was spoken.
32.2   28.6   11.2   16.3   11.0

62. If there was a chance to speak Irish outside school, I would like to try speaking it.
24.7   21.6   12.0   26.7   14.7

70. I would like to visit the Gaeltacht.
19.0   12.7   13.1   23.9   31.2

Item No.	Percentage of pupils choosing response options on each item.....				
	Strongly Disagree	Slightly Disagree	Neutral	Slightly Agree	Strongly Agree

71.   I would not like to go to a Summer course in Irish.

| | 23.3 | 24.7 | 8.0 | 15.7 | 28.0 |

72.   I would like to spend less time learning Irish at school.

| | 19.8 | 27.6 | 14.3 | 19.6 | 18.2 |

(5) Motivational intensity to learn Irish (5 items)

56.   To be honest, I don't really try very hard to learn Irish at school.

| | 25.9 | 30.4 | 8.4 | 22.2 | 12.4 |

58.   During the Irish lesson I put up my hand to answer very often.

| | 8.0 | 27.6 | 11.4 | 31.8 | 20.8 |

59.   I often think about what I have learned in my Irish lesson when the day is over.

| | 22.4 | 23.7 | 11.4 | 31.0 | 11.2 |

63.   I don't go to too much trouble with my Irish homework.

| | 21.8 | 30.8 | 12.0 | 25.7 | 8.8 |

68.   I try to understand Irish programmes on television.

| | 23.1 | 16.9 | 12.4 | 33.3 | 14.1 |

(6) Attitude to learning Irish (10 items)

7.   Learning Irish is a waste of time.

| | 47.6 | 23.7 | 9.8 | 11.6 | 6.9 |

13.   When I leave school, I will give up learning Irish completely because I am not interested in it.

| | 28.0 | 25.5 | 21.2 | 12.4 | 12.2 |

20.   I really enjoy learning Irish.

| | 19.2 | 21.8 | 11.0 | 28.2 | 19.4 |

25.   I love learning Irish.

| | 22.4 | 23.5 | 11.6 | 24.9 | 17.1 |

30.   Irish is an important school subject.

| | 6.3 | 11.8 | 9.8 | 29.4 | 42.2 |

Item No.	Strongly Disagree	Slightly Disagree	Neutral	Slightly Agree	Strongly Agree
	Percentage of pupils choosing response options on each item.....				

35. Learning Irish is really great.

21.4	25.1	11.0	27.6	14.5

39. I hate Irish.

34.1	23.5	7.8	17.3	16.9

44. The time I spend learning Irish, I would rather spend on other subjects.

14.9	26.3	13.1	23.3	21.8

46. I think that learning Irish is boring.

23.9	24.9	10.2	23.3	17.3

51. I want to learn as much Irish as possible.

14.7	23.1	12.4	26.9	22.7

Other scales

(7) Instrumental orientation to Irish (4 items)

4. Learning Irish is important for me only because I'll need it for my job or career when I am older.

24.1	23.5	9.2	21.0	21.8

10. Learning Irish in school is important for me because people will have more respect for me if I speak Irish.

24.9	24.7	18.0	23.5	8.6

24. I think it is important for me to learn Irish because it may be useful to me someday in getting a good job.

6.7	7.1	10.0	33.3	42.4

34. Learning Irish is important because it will make me a more knowledgeable person.

12.9	17.8	18.6	32.2	18.2

(8) Irish-lesson anxiety (5 items)

9. It embarrasses me to put up my hand and say something aloud during the Irish lesson.

43.3	20.2	10.0	16.1	10.0

22. I don't feel sure of myself when I am speaking out loud in Irish during the Irish lesson.

14.3	22.2	11.8	33.5	17.6

Item No.	Percentage of pupils choosing response options on each item.....				
	Strongly Disagree	**Slightly Disagree**	**Neutral**	**Slightly Agree**	**Strongly Agree**

28. I get nervous and mixed up when I am speaking in my Irish class.

| | 18.2 | 19.0 | 7.8 | 34.3 | 20.0 |

32. I always feel that the rest of the pupils in my class are better at speaking Irish than I am.

| | 12.2 | 21.4 | 11.4 | 31.2 | 23.1 |

45. I am afraid that the other pupils in the class will laugh at me when I speak Irish.

| | 36.9 | 21.4 | 8.8 | 19.4 | 12.9 |

(9) Parental encouragement (10 items)

1. My parents try to help me with my Irish.

| | 11.6 | 11.0 | 14.7 | 34.5 | 27.6 |

8. My parents feel that because we live in Ireland, I should learn Irish.

| | 11.4 | 15.7 | 23.1 | 24.3 | 24.9 |

16. My parents feel that it is important that I work hard at my Irish until I finish school.

| | 3.9 | 7.1 | 12.9 | 26.9 | 48.6 |

19. My parents encourage me to ask my teacher for help if I am having problems with my Irish.

| | 5.5 | 4.3 | 11.0 | 22.4 | 56.3 |

26. My parents often tell me how important Irish will be for me when I leave school.

| | 11.6 | 18.8 | 13.7 | 30.4 | 25.1 |

29. My parents think I should spend more of my time on my Irish lessons.

| | 13.1 | 20.4 | 25.9 | 26.9 | 13.1 |

33. My parents really encourage me to work hard at my Irish.

| | 9.4 | 16.9 | 16.1 | 32.9 | 24.1 |

38. My parents are usually very interested in anything to do with my Irish schoolwork.

| | 12.9 | 22.4 | 15.3 | 31.2 | 17.3 |

41. My parents encourage me to practice my Irish as much as possible.

| | 12.2 | 22.2 | 17.6 | 29.2 | 18.2 |

48. My parents feel that I should really try to learn Irish.

| | 8.6 | 12.0 | 20.0 | 30.6 | 28.4 |

Item No.	Strongly Disagree	Slightly Disagree	Neutral	Slightly Agree	Strongly Agree

Percentage of pupils choosing response options on each item.....

Non-AMTB based scales

(10) Irish-ability self-concept (6 items)

66. I am better than most pupils in my class at speaking Irish.

| 22.0 | 25.5 | 21.6 | 22.7 | 8.0 |

67. By the time I finish school, I will be able to speak Irish quite well.

| 7.3 | 11.6 | 15.9 | 35.7 | 29.2 |

73. I understand most of what the teacher says in Irish at school.

| 9.0 | 12.0 | 7.6 | 40.4 | 30.6 |

75. I am better than most pupils in my class at Irish writing.

| 13.5 | 18.2 | 30.0 | 28.2 | 9.8 |

76. I am better than most pupils in my class at Irish reading.

| 10.8 | 21.8 | 23.5 | 32.0 | 11.4 |

77. I am better at speaking Irish than I am at doing Maths.

| 38.6 | 22.0 | 11.2 | 12.7 | 15.1 |

(11) Use of Irish at home (3 items)

55. My mother sometimes speaks Irish at home.

| 58.8 | 11.2 | 7.1 | 15.9 | 6.3 |

64. My father sometimes speaks Irish at home.

| 50.2 | 14.3 | 9.2 | 15.3 | 9.0 |

74. No one at home ever speaks Irish.

| 21.4 | 29.4 | 6.1 | 12.4 | 30.0 |

Miscellaneous items (3 items)

57. I am better than most pupils in my class at Maths.

| 22.7 | 20.4 | 19.6 | 22.2 | 14.5 |

Item No.	Percentage of pupils choosing response options on each item.....				
	Strongly Disagree	Slightly Disagree	Neutral	Slightly Agree	Strongly Agree
69.	I am better than most pupils in my class at English reading.				
	5.9	13.9	22.4	37.3	20.2
65.	My parents are proud of how much Irish I have learned at school.				
	8.6	8.0	25.5	32.7	24.9

Appendix 4

Pupils' comments

Sample responses to write-in items at the end of the *Pupil Questionnaire*

Conventions used in transcription.

- Punctuation and spelling errors corrected.
- Irish words/phrases are printed in italics.
- Direct translations of words/phrases are enclosed in round brackets ( ) and included immediately after the word/phrase to which they apply.
- Additional background information is enclosed in square brackets [ ].
- Teachers' names (when used by pupil) have been deleted and replaced with <teacher's name>.

Item 78   "What I don't like in the Irish lesson."

- *A   Nuachúrsaí-related activities/materials (n=14)*
1. I don't really like the *Comhrá* [in this context 'Comhrá' = Nuachúrsaí] .
2. I don't like the projector because I see no point in rattling off sentences.
3. I don't like the *Comhrá* and changing the sentences into the *aimsirí* (tenses).
4. The *Comhrá* can be very boring and old fashioned. The books seem to tell us about boys and never really girls and some stories are not very interesting.
5. I do not like the *Teilgeoir* (Projector) that much and it is too long sometimes.
6. I don't like the *Teilgeoir* because the pictures are no good, and the storyline is always the same old "Mammy! I'm off *faoin tuath* because *tá an ghrian ag taitneamh"* (Mammy! I'm off 'to the country' because 'the sun is shining').
7. I don't like the *Comhrá* which we have to repeat from the teacher.
8. I do not like the Film strip [Projector].
9. I do not like *Buntús* [another name for the *Nuachúrsaí*] or standing up.
10. Doing Irish on the screen and doing the tenses.
11. I don't like going to the *Comhrá*. And I don't like spending that much time doing Irish in the morning. And most people shout so you can't concentrate.
12. *Comhrá* is not a nice lesson.
13. Is when the teacher is asking lots of questions and doing the Projector.
14. I don't like doing the questions and answers and Projector.

- **B Difficulty in understanding generally (n=8)**
1. Teacher goes too fast. And asks the better people and doesn't give the weaker ones a chance. And he lets off all the good people who speak Irish and get it wrong.
2. What I don't like in the Irish lesson is when the teacher is speaking Irish and I can't understand what he is saying.
3. Not being told what basic words mean and just being made to repeat them.
4. I don't like when the teacher asks something and I don't understand it.
5. I don't like when I don't understand what people are saying. Or when I get a question I don't understand.
6. Is when the teacher says something in Irish and she does not tell you what it is in English.
7. I don't like Irish at all because I don't understand it - even the teacher gets mad with me sometime because I do not know it and we do it every day.
8. What I don't like about the Irish lesson is if you get homework and you don't understand and no-one in your house has a clue about Irish - you're stuck.

- **C Grammar-related activities (n=8)**
1. I don't like learning *briathra* (verbs) - it is boring and there are a lot of more interesting things in Irish than running down *Dhún mé, Dhún tú,* ('I closed', 'You closed') etc.
2. I don't like the Irish verbs and the *briathra* and the *Chéad, Dara, Triú, Ceathrú agus Cúigiú Díochlaonadh* (first, second, third, fourth and fifth declensions).
3. In the Irish lesson I don't like learning the nouns, pronouns, picking out what is masculine or feminine. The *briathra* (verbs), *briathra neamhrialta* (irregular verbs).
4. VERBS [pupil's emphasis] because I knew the English language before I learned my English verbs so I don't think you should learn as much verbs as we do.
5. I don't like *Comhrá* or *inné, gach lá* (yesterday, everyday) and *amárach* (tomorrow) words which you have to change to past and future.
6. I don't like the Irish - Today, Tomorrow, Yesterday because I get confused in them.
7. In Irish I don't like e.g. *aige, leis, mé, tú* [pronouns]. I don't like the way people always ask the teacher the English word for the Irish word.
8. I don't like Irish Grammar.

- **D Boring, old fashioned, repetitious course & materials (n=7)**
1. In the Irish lesson I don't like when the reading is said over and over again.
2. It's a bit boring because sometimes it's just basic.
3. I don't like the way the books and the *Comhrá* are old fashioned and mostly about boys. They are also very boring.
4. I don't like the way boys are always the popular people. I would like fashionable things and real life - the brothers and sisters are friendly - as at home we fight we are not always very friendly.
5. It is not very interesting. Nobody takes an interest in the lesson. We keep going over the same thing.
6. I don't like it when we have to say the sentence over and over again - and I dislike translation! And also it's quite boring.
7. I find them boring unuseful crap and it is no good to me because I have no intention of staying here or learning the Irish so I'm not going to learn it.

- *E Reading activities and specific readers (n=7)*
1. I don't really like the reading because it takes too long to read one story.
2. I don't like the stories in the *Fás* [name of Irish reader] book.
3. I don't like *Seal ag Léamh* [name of Irish reader].
4. I don't like having to read words off the blackboard after the Irish reading.
5. I don't like reading because I am no good at it.
6. I don't like the reading because most of the story I don't understand and most meanings.
7. I don't like reading in the Irish lesson.

- *F Written exercises including essays, answers etc. (n=7)*
1. I don't like writing questions and answers. And when my teacher has explained something what's the point of writing it down?
2. Writing stories and writing Irish questions out of the Irish workbook *Lean Den Obair* [name of workbook], spelling.
3. I don't like writing essays in Irish. I also don't like learning all the different rules.
4. I don't like writing compositions. I don't like *Comhrá*. I don't like explaining poems in Irish. I don't like spelling tests.
5. Writing Irish and the teacher does not make it easier for me to understand.
6. I don't like writing in the Irish lesson.
7. I don't like doing Irish questions and writing out stories.

- *G Spelling exercises (n=5)*
1. I don't like Irish spellings. Projector. Verbs.
2. I don't like Irish spelling but I am good at them.
3. What I don't like about the Irish lesson is getting Irish spellings.
4. I don't like Irish spellings or Irish essays.
5. Learning Irish spellings especially the ones with *fada*'s (long vowel accent) on them.

- *H Irish-lesson anxiety, low self-esteem etc. (n=4)*
1. In the reading I get mixed up and get given out to. I'm not so good at Irish.
2. Because I am no good at it and most other people that are good at it laugh at me and the Irish spellings are too hard and essays are too hard.
3. I don't like when the teacher asks me questions because if I get it wrong I get embarrassed.
4. I don't like talking in Irish because I get all mixed up. I also don't know which word to put in if I am stuck.

- *I Generally negative about Irish lesson (n=4)*
1. That there is too much time spent at it. Any other language would be much more enjoyable.
2. I don't like anything in Irish.
3. Why should you learn Irish? I will never need it. It is stupid. The way you spell 'A' is 'é'. It is the worst subject ever made for school.
4. I think it is a waste of time and we should be learning other languages. The chances of us speaking all Irish again are 100-1.

- *J Generally positive about Irish lesson (n=2)*
1. I like everything about the Irish Lesson. There is nothing that I do not like about it.
2. What I don't like in the Irish lesson is it is too short.

- *K Drama, poems, songs (n=2)*
1. I don't like learning Irish poetry during the Irish lesson.
2. I do not like the songs in the Irish lesson.

- *'Other' comments (n=3) and minor categories (n=2)* - *Dislike teaching through Irish, Dislike stories*
1. When the teacher gets cross; when I get too much homework.
2. I don't like long words.
3. People who try to destroy the Irish lesson on purpose.
4. I don't like Geography in Irish.
5. I don't like Irish questions or some Irish stories.

End of sample comments for Q 78.

Item 79 - "What I do like in the Irish Lesson."

- *A Reading activities and specific readers (n=14)*
1. What I do like is the Irish reading.
2. I like reading simple stories and learning Irish spellings. I like learning Irish poems when I understand them.
3. Reading a story and answering the questions.
4. I like Irish reading because you get a chance to read on your own and everything is explained.
5. Reading the *Seal ag Léamh* [name of reader].
6. I like reading my Irish book and I like answering questions in the book.
7. I like reading even though some of the time I don't understand it in English.
8. I like the reading because our teacher explains it all in English so that we understand it.
9. I like reading.
10. I like when we are doing our Irish reading and when I never make a mistake.
11. I like reading out loud in class.
12. Reading the stories because they are quite interesting.
13. I like the Irish Reading.
14. I like Irish reading competitions.

- *B Conversation, drama, games, songs, poems (n=13)*
1. I like the plays in Irish - it gives me a chance to speak oral Irish. It is interesting and is good for helping to improve your Irish.
2. I like speaking our news in Irish.
3. Doing plays, poems and Geography in Irish.
4. Playing games in Irish.
5. I like drama the way can you act out stories because it is fun and we learn while doing it.

6. I like acting out Irish poems and learning them.
7. Irish reading. Having conversations, talking about the News.
8. I like Irish songs and I like our game. The teacher picks an Irish thing and we have to ask her questions about it in Irish.
9. I like playing Bingo and having reading competitions.
10. Sometimes <teacher's name> asks people to tell him what they done over the weekend in Irish.
11. I really like when teacher lets us talk about things in Irish like dogs, school, holidays etc.
12. I like normal everyday conversations in Irish and talking about the pictures.
13. I like reading in the lesson. Or having a conversation in Irish with the teacher.

- **C Written exercises including essays, answers etc. (n=8)**
1. Irish writing.
2. I love doing Irish writing and doing essays because I like doing research and Irish writing is brilliant.
3. I like writing essays in Irish and learning new words and phrases.
4. Writing and doing the questions in our books.
5. I like the Irish writing and the book called *Tar Liom* [name of course-book].
6. I like writing essays sometimes in Irish.
7. I like writing Irish stories or discussing pictures. I also like playing games that help you with Irish.
8. I love writing stories because I can put it my own way; not following rules. I like talking (in Irish) about what we see in the *Comhrá*.

- **D Stories generally, picture stories, creative writing (n=7)**
1. General Irish: stories.
2. I like making up Irish stories and answering questions about a picture.
3. I like to write short stories or short poems about things. I think the picture story in our work book is a good idea. I like them best.
4. I like the good stories in the book.
5. I love writing stories.
6. I like reading and making up stories and things like that because it is exciting to read them.
7. I like drawing pictures and making up my own stories.

- **E Oral Irish practice, answering questions (n=5)**
1. I like answering Irish questions out of the stories.
2. I like answering the questions. But I would like if we could speak to an Irish person. We have never done this and it would be a change.
3. I like most of the oral Irish.
4. I like oral Irish because you don't have to do any writing when you are talking Irish.
5. I like answering questions. I like spellings and I like changing Irish into past tense.

- **F Nuachúrsaí-related activities/materials (n=4)**
1. I like doing the Irish *Comhrá* and Irish story.
2. The *Buntús* is very enjoyable and the pictures explain it clearly. I like it.

3. I like in the mornings when we do the projector and the pictures come on and we say a sentence and answer a question on the picture.
4. I like it when we are doing the Irish filmstrip.

- **G Pupil likes nothing about Irish (n=4)**
1. I like nothing in the Irish lesson because I think it's boring.
2. I don't like anything about Irish.
3. I like not a thing in Irish because it is hard.
4. There is nothing I really like about the Irish lesson.

- **H Being able to understand, explanations, translations etc. (n=4)**
1. I like it because the teacher tells us what the question and answers means.
2. I like it sometimes when I can understand what people are saying to me.
3. When the teacher explains the Irish stories into English and explain words to us.
4. I like Irish when you know what you're talking about. And you don't get embarrassed in front of your friends. It's great fun when you know it.

- **I Spelling exercises (n=4)**
1. I like doing the spelling of the Irish lesson.
2. I like Irish spellings because it is really nice to do Irish spellings.
3. I like the way the teacher asks us questions or asks us spellings in Irish.
4. Spelling tests and Irish reading.

- **J Grammar-related activities (n=3)**
1. I like the *Díochlaonadh*'s (declensions) and the verbs and the Irish reading.
2. I like translating the Irish stories into English and changing the verbs into different tenses.
3. I like the dramas and song in the Irish lesson and learning the nouns and verbs because they are interesting.

- **K Learning about our own language, culture, identity etc. (n=3)**
1. It helps to keep alive the customs and makes it easier to learn Irish history.
2. I like the feeling that I am keeping up Irish heritage. I like knowing that I know a little about our very own language.
3. I do like the thought of keeping our Irish culture and language especially with the abolition of all borders in European countries in 1997.

- **'Other' categories (n=5) and minor categories (n=3)** - *Using a particular course-book, Humour/funny stories, Pupil likes everything about Irish.*
1. I like everything in the Irish lesson especially the irregular verbs. I usually prefer grammar to essays but essays are also interesting.
2. Doing other subjects through Irish.
3. Learning the names of fish, animals, birds.
4. Is the *Lean den Obair* [name of work-book] because the questions are not too hard and the *Líonta* [name of reader] because it has good stories.
5. When the teacher says it is all right to take out the *Nua Litriú 2* [vocabulary book].

6.	When we learn new things about Irish and the *Buail Liom* [name of course-book] questions and stories.
7.	The bits of funny things that would happen in the stories.
8.	I like everything in the Irish lesson.

End of sample comments for Q 79.

Item 80 - "How I would like to change the Irish lesson."

- 	*A Make it more modern, fun, realistic, non-sexist (n=8)*
1.	Make it more enjoyable - maybe by going on small tours in Irish and making the lesson shorter.
2.	The *Comhrá* is very old fashioned. They should bring it up to date and everything is about boys, he done this, and he done that, and the women are always seen in the kitchen washing the dishes or cooking.
3.	If we did more fun work, like plays, chatting, and games, we would be more eager to work. Make the *Comhrá* more exciting, more exciting stories. Not *An Dochtúir* (The Doctor) but *Timpiste sa charr* (A car accident).
4.	I would like real life - sisters fighting and so on. When children look at happy sisters and brothers getting along they think something is wrong with their family.
5.	Make every story into a play. Go on Irish nature walks. The whole class go on an Irish weekend.
6.	More enjoyable film strips and more enjoyable text books and more enjoyable lessons.
7.	Make it more interesting with some funny stories and help people enjoy themselves.
8.	Make it more exciting by talking about everyday things like divorce or separation, death, drugs and alcohol.

- 	*B Make it easier to understand - more explanations/translations (n=7)*
1.	I would like to have English with Irish, like when you read in Irish then explain what you read in English.
2.	To understand the words.
3.	That the teacher can spend more time at Irish and spend more time helping people who don't understand things.
4.	I would like to make it easier for the people that think it is too hard and lose interest in it.
5.	By putting English beside it.
6.	I would change it by explaining Irish a bit more and not doing essays.
7.	I would make the Irish books a bit easier to understand.

- 	*C More conversation, drama, games, poems, songs (n=7)*
1.	More drama and less verbs, *briathra*'s (verbs) etc.
2.	I think we should do more games through Irish and less projector and Irish reading.
3.	More poems but a bit better.
4.	I would like to have a lot more oral Irish. And some plays.

5. I wouldn't change much about the Irish lesson - the way it is - but I'd add more conversation about up to date Irish stories.
6. I would like to cut out the *Buntús* (*Nuachúrsaí*) and have more games and riddles.
7. I would like to change it by having to speak Irish right through the Irish lesson so that I can understand more of the Irish words.

- **D *Would not like any change (n=6)***
1. Well I don't really want to change the Irish lesson because sometime it could be fun doing it.
2. I wouldn't like to change anything.
3. I don't want anything to change.
4. I think that the Irish lesson is just right and I wouldn't change it in any way.
5. I would not like to change anything in Irish for I love it.
6. I wouldn't like to change the Irish lesson because I enjoy learning Irish and I think it would be a shame to stop the teaching of it.

- **E *Less emphasis on Irish, including Irish homework (n=5)***
1. Irish should be only half an hour or 40 minutes long - not an hour.
2. I would not spend that much time at Irish.
3. I would like to get rid of Irish Homework.
4. I would like to do less Irish.
5. Give a little less Irish homework.

- **F *New Materials (n=4)***
1. Having a video to show the Irish.
2. I would like to change it by having more interesting books and do things that help you with Irish, that are more enjoyable rather than hating Irish with boring things.
3. I would like to change the film strip and make it more up to date and put better stories in the *Líonta* [name of reader].
4. I would like to change it with a new *Comhrá* and new interesting stories and fashion. The girls in some stories are real frightened of everything and that the boys come to save the day. [sic]

- **G *Dispense with Nuachúrsaí filmstrips/projector (n=3)***
1. I would like to change the Irish lesson by not using the projector.
2. By not using the projector.
3. I would like to get rid of the projector.

- **H *Less/no use at all of the Nuachúrsaí (n=2)***
1. I wouldn't have *Comhrá* and I'd make everything more interesting.
2. Not so much *Comhrá* and more talking to each other.

- **I *More time devoted to Irish and more teaching through Irish (n=2)***
1. I would like to change the Irish lesson by spending more time at the lesson and only speaking Irish and getting homework based on Irish only.

2.   I would like to have Irish spoken during *Sos* (short break) and lunch breaks as I believe that you would be a more fluent Irish speaker.

- *J Stop teaching Irish altogether (n=2)*
1.   I would like to stop it altogether.
2.   I wouldn't like to change it at all. I wish we never did it at all.

- *K More Irish reading (n=2)*
1.   Longer at reading, less speaking, a little less writing.
2.   I would like more reading.

- *'Other' comments (n=6) and minor categories (n=6)* - *Less grammar, Fewer/easier spellings, Less/no reading, More grammar, Less/no writing, More writing.*
1.   I would like if there was more History in the Irish stories and less long words.
2.   To learn more about the Irish language. To learn more about Ireland.
3.   I would like to change the Irish lesson by doing more oral work - to get better at it and stories too, and up date the *Comhrá* - make it more interesting.
4.   I wouldn't mind what way we learned it.
5.   I would like to get a good Irish teacher to do the Irish lesson who knows a good bit of it.
6.   The teacher should put people into groups and ask each other questions.
7.   I would like to change the Irish lesson by doing less grammar and more reading.
8.   I would like more Irish reading and less spelling.
9.   To have no reading.
10.   To have more verbs in the Irish lesson.
11.   I would like to change it by having no writing just reading and playing '20 Questions'.
12.   I'd change it by doing more writing and less learning.

End of sample comments for Q 80

Appendix 5.1

Parents' Questionnaire: Note to inspector

1. Each pupil will be given a sealed envelope with an ID number in the top right hand corner to be brought home to his/her parents. Each envelope contains:
   (a) A copy of the Parents' Questionnaire which has the same ID on the cover as on the above mentioned envelope.
   (b) An explanatory letter for parents.
   (c) A pre-addressed envelope for returning the completed questionnaire.

2. Since each returned Parents' Questionnaire will have only an ID number on the cover, we need to know which ID number goes with which pupil for purposes of analysis. On the 'List of ID's'[1], therefore, please write in beside each ID number the name of the pupil who is to receive the envelope with that ID. It is important that this 'List of ID's be returned to ITÉ when compiled by the inspector, since this will allow us to link each Parents' Questionnaire with a particular pupil.

   Probably the most simple way to compile the list is to copy the relevant names from the roll book onto the 'List of ID's' and then distribute the envelopes so that each pupil receives the envelope with the correct ID.

   The inspector, if possible, should be the one to distribute the envelope to the pupil. It might also be a good idea to write either the child's first name or the parents' name on the envelope you hand to each child (in case any of the children themselves inadvertently mix up their envelopes later on). It should be emphasised to the children that they must give the actual envelope they receive to their parents.

   Finally, as an extra precaution, the teacher might be asked to write the pupil's initials (only) on each envelope as it returns.

3. Although each envelope contains an English version of the Parents' Questionnaire at present, copies of the Irish version are also being made available. If parents require the Irish version they will note this on the returning envelope. In such cases, the relevant pupils ID from the list should be copied onto an Irish version of the Questionnaire and, along with a pre-addressed envelope, returned to the parents.

4. Each teacher and principal should first be given a copy of the Parents' Questionnaire and covering letter and given time to examine them (perhaps while the inspector is filling in the list of names). If possible, these blank copies should be collected later. Needless to say the work should proceed only if the teacher and principal have no objection.

John Harris

---

[1] The list of ID's, with lines alongside for writing in each pupil's name, followed on two additional separate pages. These pages are not reproduced here.

Appendix 5.2

Parents' Questionnaire: **Letter to parents**

Leagan Gaeilge ar chúl
**SCÉIM PHÍOLÓTACH I dTEAGASC NA GAEILGE
PILOT SCHEME ON TEACHING OF IRISH**

Dear Parent/Guardian,

      Over the last few weeks your child's class (6th class) has been involved in a study of the teaching and learning of Irish. This study is being carried out in a number of schools by the Department of Education in association with Institiúid Teangeolaíochta Éireann (The Linguistics Institute of Ireland). An important part of this work is to determine parents' views on the teaching and learning of Irish. We would be grateful, therefore, if you would answer the questions on the enclosed questionnaire. The completed questionnaire should be placed in the enclosed envelope, and given to your child to return to the school by Friday, 23rd June.

     *   YOUR OPINIONS ARE REQUIRED FOR GENERAL RESEARCH PURPOSES ONLY AND WILL HAVE NO EFFECT, ONE WAY OR ANOTHER, ON YOUR CHILD OR ON THE SCHOOL.
     *   ONLY OUR RESEARCHERS WILL SEE YOUR REPLIES.
     *   NO INDIVIDUAL PUPIL OR PARENT WILL BE IDENTIFIED IN REPORTING THE RESULTS.
     *   YOUR CHILD'S TEACHER KNOWS THAT YOUR OPINIONS ARE BEING SOUGHT.

WE EARNESTLY ASK FOR YOUR COOPERATION SINCE THE SUCCESS OF THE STUDY DEPENDS ON A HIGH RESPONSE RATE

IF YOU <u>DO NOT WISH TO RESPOND</u> TO THIS QUESTIONNAIRE JUST PLACE A TICK (✓) IN THE BOX AND RETURN THIS SHEET <u>AND</u> THE BLANK QUESTIONNAIRE IN THE ENCLOSED ENVELOPE.

IF YOU WOULD PREFER AN IRISH FORM OF THIS QUESTIONNAIRE PLEASE RETURN THE MATERIALS AND WRITE 'LEAGAN GAEILGE AG TEASTÁIL' ON THE ENVELOPE. WE WILL SEND YOU AN IRISH VERSION PROMPTLY.

WE ARE INTERESTED ONLY IN YOUR <u>OWN</u> PERSONAL OPINIONS - THERE ARE NO RIGHT OR WRONG ANSWERS.
THANK YOU   GO RAIBH MÍLE MAITH AGAT.

English on reverse side
SCÉIM PHÍOLÓTACH I dTEAGASC NA GAEILGE

A Thuismitheoir/Chaomhnóir, a Chara,

Bhí staidéar ar siúl le roinnt seachtainí anuas sa rang a bhfuil do pháiste ann (Rang VI) maidir le teagasc agus le foghlaim na Gaeilge. Tá an staidéar seo ar siúl i roinnt scoileanna ag an Roinn Oideachais i gcomhar le hInstitiúid Teangeolaíochta Éireann. Is cuid thábhachtach den staidéar seo é dearcadh na dtuismitheoirí ar theagasc agus ar fhoghlaim na Gaeilge a fháil amach. Bheimis buíoch díot, mar sin, ach na ceisteanna as an gceistiúcháin atá leis seo a fhreagairt, le do thoil. Ba cheart an ceistiúchán comhlánaithe a chur sa chlúdach iniata, é a dhúnadh agus a thabhairt do do pháiste lena thabhairt ar ais ar scoil faoin Aoine, 23ú Meitheamh.

* IS LE hAGHAIDH TAIGHDE GHINEARÁLTA AMHÁIN ATÁ DO THUAIRIMÍ AG TEASTÁIL AGUS NÍ BHEIDH TIONCHAR ACU, BEALACH AMHÁIN NÓ BEALACH EILE, AR DO PHÁISTE NÁ AR AN SCOIL.
* NÍ FHEICFIDH AON DUINE ACH AN LUCHT TAIGHDE DO CHUID FREAGRAÍ.
* NÍ LUAFAR AINM DHALTA AR BITH NÁ AINM THUISMITHEORA AR BITH IN AON TUAIRISC AR THORTHAÍ AN TAIGHDE SEO.
* TÁ FHIOS AG AN MÚINTEOIR ATÁ AG DO PHÁISTE GO BHFUIL DO THUAIRIMÍ Á LORG AGAINN.

IARRAIMID FAOI DHÍOGRAIS ORT CABHRÚ LINN MAR NÍ ÉIREOIDH LEIS AN STAIDÉAR SEO MURA dTIOCFAIDH FREAGRAÍ Ó LÍON ARD TUISMITHEOIRÍ/CAOMHNÓIRÍ.

MURAR MIAN LEAT AN CEISTIÚCHÁN SEO A LÍONADH, ÁFACH, CUIR TIC(✓) SA BHOSCA ANSEO AGUS CUIR AN CEISTIÚCHÁN AGUS AN LEATHANACH SEO ISTEACH SA CHLÚDACH ATÁ LEIS AGUS CUIR AN tIOMLÁN AR AIS CHUIG AN SCOIL ARÍS LE DO THOIL.

MÁS MAITH LEAT LEAGAN GAEILGE DEN CHEISTIÚCHÁN SEO A FHÁIL, NÍ GÁ ACH AN tÁBHAR GO LÉIR A CHUR AR AIS GO DTÍ AN SCOIL AGUS 'LEAGAN GAEILGE AG TEASTÁIL' A SCRÍOBH AR AN gCLÚDACH. CUIRFIMID LEAGAN GAEILGE DEN CHEISTIÚCHÁIN CHUGAT LÁITHREACH.

**NÍL SPÉIS AGAINN ACH I DO THUAIRIMÍ PEARSANTA FÉIN - NÍL FREAGRAÍ CEARTA NÁ MÍCHEARTA AR NA CEISTEANNA.
GO RAIBH MÍLE MAITH AGAT**

Appendix 5.3

Parents' Questionnaire[*] : Item-response data

The following note to parents appeared on the inside of the front cover of the *Parents' Questionnaire* (English version):

The Questionnaire should be completed by the parent (or guardian) who has the greater involvement in the child's school work i.e. the parent who usually buys school books, supervises homework, attends meetings in the school and so on. In the case where both parents are equally involved in the child's school work, either parent may fill in the Questionnaire. Most questions can be answered by placing a tick (✓) in a box. In those cases where a reply is to be written in, you may answer in either English or Irish. Where there is a reference below to 'the school', this means the school your child is attending at present.

Please complete this questionnaire yourself, without consulting your child.

Percentages of parents choosing various response options (N = 198)

BACKGROUND

1. **What is your relationship to the child who brought home this questionnaire (e.g. father, mother, guardian (aunt), etc.)?**
(i)	Mother	67.7%
(ii)	Father	27.8%
(iii)	Guardian	0.5%
(iv)	No information	4.0%

2. **What is the occupation of the main earner in the house? (If the main earner is now unemployed, please give the last full-time job, followed by the word 'unemployed' in brackets.)**

    see Chapter 2, Tables 2.7 and 2.11 for details on social class and unemployment.

---

[*] Most questions in the *Parents' Questionnaire* booklet were answered by ticking one of the boxes beside the various answer options or, less commonly, by ticking 'as many boxes as necessary'. In the listing below we have omitted both the answer boxes and the 'tick one box' instructions in order to make room for the item data. Where relevant we have noted in italics instances in which the respondent could 'tick as many boxes as necessary'.

3.   When were you born?

(i)	Between 1920-1929	1.0%
(ii)	Between 1930-1939	10.6%
(iii)	Between 1940-1949	43.4%
(iv)	Between 1950-1959	44.9%
(v)	Since 1960	--

4.   When you were growing up, what language(s) were spoken in your home?

(i)	English only	90.4%
(ii)	English and Irish, but mostly English	9.1%
(iii)	English and Irish, half and half	--
(iv)	English and Irish, but mostly Irish	--
(v)	Irish only	--
	No response	0.5%

5.   What is your general attitude to Irish now?

(i)	Strongly in favour	16.7%
(ii)	Somewhat in favour	47.5%
(iii)	No particular feelings	22.7%
(iv)	Somewhat against it	9.1%
(v)	Strongly against it	2.5%
	No response	1.5%

6.   How would you describe your ability to speak Irish?

(i)	No Irish	9.1%
(ii)	Only the odd word	20.7%
(iii)	A few simple sentences	41.4%
(iv)	Parts of conversations	22.2%
(v)	Most conversations	4.0%
(vi)	Native speaker ability	1.0%
	No response	1.5%

7.   How often, if ever, is Irish spoken by anyone in your home at present?

(i)	Very often	0.5%
(ii)	Often	2.5%
(iii)	Occasionally	19.2%
(iv)	Seldom	34.3%
(v)	Never	41.9%
	No response	1.5%

YOUR CHILD AND IRISH

8. **How do you feel about your child being taught Irish in primary school?**
    (i)   Strongly in favour   29.3%
    (ii) Somewhat in favour   46.0%
    (iii) No particular feelings   13.6%
    (iv) Somewhat against it   7.1%
    (v)   Strongly against it   2.0%
          No response   2.0%

9. **How important do you think Irish is as far as your child's future job is concerned?**
    (i)   Very important   11.6%
    (ii) Important   22.2%
    (iii) Of little importance   50.0%
    (iv) Not important at all   15.7%
          No response   0.5%

10. **How does your child generally feel about learning Irish in school?**
    (i)   My child likes learning Irish   42.9%
    (ii) My child has no particular feelings about learning Irish   32.3%
    (iii) My child dislikes learning Irish   21.7%
          No response   3.0%

    If your child dislikes learning Irish, can you give any additional information?

    Summary of main volunteered reasons
    - *Finds Irish difficult to learn*   6.0%
    - *Thinks it is unnecessary/irrelevant*   5.5%
    - *Child finds it boring*   2.5%

11. **How often would you praise your child's school achievements in the following subjects?**
    (Tick one box in each row)

	I praise my child's ...	Often	Occasion-ally	Hardly ever	No response
(a)	English reading	64.6%	29.3%	5.1%	1.0%
(b)	Mathematics	68.7%	26.8%	3.0%	1.5%
(c)	English writing	61.1%	32.8%	2.5%	3.5%
(d)	Project work	59.1%	28.8%	6.6%	5.6%
(e)	Irish reading	41.4%	32.8%	20.2%	5.6%
(f)	Oral/spoken Irish	33.8%	28.8%	30.3%	7.1%
(g)	Irish writing	41.9%	31.8%	20.2%	6.1%

12. **What general attitude towards learning Irish in school do you try to encourage in your child?**

(i)	I let my child know that Irish is very important	29.3%
(ii)	I leave it up to my child to develop his/her own attitude to Irish	69.2%
(iii)	I discourage my child from taking Irish seriously	1.0%
	No response	0.5%

THE SCHOOL AND IRISH

13. **How much contact do you have with the school your child is attending?**

(i)	No contact at all	--
(ii)	Practically no contact	5.1%
(iii)	Occasional contact	67.7%
(iv)	A lot of contact	27.3%

14. **Are you satisfied with the amount of contact you have with the school?**

(i)	I'm happy with the level of contact I have with the school.	85.4%
(ii)	I would like more contact with the school.	14.6%
(iii)	I would like less contact with the school.	--

15. **How much time do you think your child spends learning Irish in school each day? (Please write in the number of minutes.)**

____ minutes each day approximately

Summary of responses

(i)	*1-40 minutes each day, approximately*	24.7%
(ii)	*40-60 " " "*	56.1%
(iii)	*60-100 " " "*	10.1%
(iv)	*100+ " " "*	2.0%
	No response	7.1%

16. **Are you satisfied with the amount of time spent on Irish in your child's school?**

(i)	The amount of time spent on Irish is just right	73.7%
(ii)	Less time should be spent on Irish	15.2%
(iii)	More time should be spent on Irish	8.6%
	No response	2.5%

17. **How much do you know about the way your child is taught Irish in school (e.g. what workbooks, readers etc. are used, how much emphasis is placed on speaking, reading and writing etc.?)**

(i)	I know nothing about how Irish is taught	25.3%
(ii)	I know a little about how Irish is taught	56.6%
(iii)	I know quite a lot about how Irish is taught	17.7%
	No response	0.5%

18. **What is your opinion of the methods and materials (workbooks, readers, etc.) which are used to teach your child Irish?**

(i)	Very suitable	16.2%
(ii)	Suitable	54.5%
(iii)	Unsuitable	8.1%
(iv)	Very unsuitable	1.0%
(v)	No opinion	19.7%
	No response	0.5%

19. **Does the school your child attends teach any subjects, apart from Irish, through Irish?**

(a)	(i)	Yes	7.6%
	(ii)	No	74.2%
	(iii)	I don't know	16.7%
		No response	1.5%

(b)	If **NO**, would you <u>support</u> the idea of the school teaching a subject through Irish?		
	(i)	Yes	24.2%
	(ii)	No	51.5%
		No response	24.2%

20. **Does your child have difficulty in school with any of the following subjects? Place a tick in the box beside any subject your child has difficulty with. If your child does not have difficulty with a subject, just leave that box empty.** *(Tick as many boxes as necessary)*

    My child <u>has difficulty</u> with

(a)	English reading	6.1%
(b)	Mathematics	27.8%
(c)	Irish reading	15.7%
(d)	Spoken/oral Irish	26.8%
(e)	English writing	6.6%
(f)	Irish writing	16.7%

21. **Is there anything you feel the <u>school</u> could do to improve your child's progress in Irish generally?**

    (i)   No, the school is doing everything possible   83.3%

    (ii)   Yes, the school could do more   14.1%

If **YES**, please give more information, if possible.

    Summary of main volunteered reasons

- *More emphasis on oral Irish*   6.1%
- *More individual attention*   2.0%
- *Irish should be more fun/more interesting*   1.5%
- *More emphasis on Irish culture*   1.5%
- *Use more audio/visual equipment/language labs*   1.0%

22. **Do you think <u>you</u> could give the school any practical support as far as the teaching of Irish is concerned (apart from what you are already doing)?**

    (i)   Yes   5.6%

    (ii)   No   93.4%

    No response   1.0%

If **YES**, please give details of what form this support might take.

    (Summary of main volunteered suggestions)

- *Speak more Irish at home*   3%
- *By attending Irish classes for parents*   1%

HOMEWORK

23. **How much time, on average, does your child spend on <u>all</u> his/her homework each night?**

    _____ minutes each night, on average

    Summary of responses

    (i)   *Between 1-40 minutes each night*   20.7%

    (ii)   "   *41-60* "   "   40.4%

    (iii)   "   *61-100* "   "   22.2%

    (iv)   "   *101-120* "   "   12.6%

    No response   4.0%

24. **How often, if ever, do you sign your child's homework?**
(i)	Always	46.0%
(ii)	Often	25.3%
(iii)	Occasionally	21.7%
(iv)	Seldom	2.5%
(v)	Never	4.0%
	No response	0.5%

25. **How often, if ever, do you supervise (or help with) your child's homework (e.g. examine tables, listen to the child reading aloud, check that writing is satisfactory etc.)?**
(i)	Always	23.2%
(ii)	Often	43.4%
(iii)	Occasionally	25.8%
(iv)	Seldom	5.6%
(v)	Never	2.0%

26. **If you help with your child's homework, what subjects do you <u>usually</u> help with?**
(Tick as many boxes as necessary.)

(a)	Mathematics	70.2%
(b)	English	47.5%
(c)	Irish	34.8%
(d)	History/Geography	37.9%
(e)	Environmental Studies	13.1%
(f)	Arts & Crafts	15.2%
(g)	Other (give details)	--

27. **If you help with your child's IRISH homework, what aspects of Irish do you usually help with?** *(Tick as many boxes as necessary.)*

(a)	Irish reading	27.8%
(b)	Irish writing	15.7%
(c)	Oral/spoken Irish	9.1%
(d)	Irish grammar	18.2%
(e)	Irish poetry	8.6%
(f))	Irish spelling	37.4%

28. **If you do <u>not</u> help with your child's IRISH homework, what is your main reason for not doing so?**

    (i)   I am not interested in school work generally   --
    (ii)   I don't have enough time usually   3.5%
    (iii) I don't agree with Irish being taught   1.5%
    (iv)   I am not very good at Irish myself   43.9%
    (v)   Other reason

    _____

    _____

    Summary of main volunteered reasons
    - *Parent says his/her child does not need help*   8.6%
    - *Parent says he/she was never taught Irish at school (educated abroad)*   0.5%
    - *Parent thinks "Irish is a dead language,*
      - better to teach foreign languages"   0.5%
    - *Parent asks "what good will my child get out of it?"*   0.5%
    - *No response*   41.0%

29. **Do you have any general comments?**

    _____
    _____
    _____

    See Appendix 5.4 for general comments by parents.

THANK YOU FOR COMPLETING THIS QUESTIONNAIRE

GO RAIBH MÍLE MAITH AGAT !

Appendix 5.4

Parents' comments (Item 29 *Parents' Questionnaire*)

Sample Comments[1]   *Codes*[2]

Irish in competition with other subjects

1. More time should be given to other subjects (e.g. Modern Continental Languages, computers or English), and/or less time spent on Irish

'I think in this age of computerised systems etc. it would be better to allocate the time given to Irish to subjects more related to computers.'   1

'I think more time should be spent on other languages.'   1

'I think there is two much emphasis on Irish in schools to-day. I think our children should have a choice of a foreign language which would be more useful to them when they leave school.'   1

'I don't think it is a good idea to spend too much time on Irish.'   1

'In my opinion it would be far more beneficial to have French and German taught at primary level than Irish.'   1

'I think that if a child has difficulty with subjects at school they are wasting good time learning Irish particularly in primary school.'   1

'I think that other languages should be taught besides Irish.'   1

'In my own view the fact that Irish is taught leaves less time for English which is much more important.'   1

---

[1] Minor errors and omissions in the original comments have been corrected. Names of schools have been deleted. The comments listed here represent 85% of those volunteered. Those omitted either duplicate the contents of other comments or else relate to the 'miscellaneous' category.

[2] See Table 5.20 in text for summary of these codes. Note that as each parent's reply may contain more than one response element, more than one code may be assigned to each written reply.

'I do not encourage but nor do I discourage my child learning Irish but I would prefer if they were taught a live European language instead of Irish.'   1

'I think that a continental language should be introduced into the primary curriculum along with Irish, because of our membership of the EEC.'   1

2. *Children should not be put under pressure (compelled) to learn Irish at primary school - Irish should be voluntary/optional.*

'As we are now members of the EEC I think more emphasis should be
placed on the teaching of some of the official languages of the   1
Community. While I would encourage the learning of Irish on a   2
cultural basis, I would make it a non-compulsory subject.'

'I am against Irish being compulsory at primary level. I would like to see French or   2
German being taught instead. For families wanting Irish there are all-Irish schools.'   1

'I feel too much emphasis is put on Irish - it's not needed very often after school and if   2
left to learn like other languages such as French/German etc., where there is no pressure   1
it would probably be more popular. (N.B. Failed Leaving Cert on account of Irish).'

I don't think children should be put under pressure to learn Irish .'   2

'Irish should not be compulsory: students should choose to learn
Irish and be encouraged to learn about their heritage.'   2

'I would not object to my child learning Irish providing she wishes to and it would be
of help to her future.'   2

Support/lack of support for the teaching of Irish

3. *Parent is in favour of Irish and the teaching of Irish.*

'Child has attended Irish courses each year during summer holidays and there is
attachment on the part of the family for aspects of Irish culture.'   3

'Is maith liom bheith ag labhairt Gaeilge agus Béarla.'   3

'I love the Irish language and I will encourage my child to learn it through his school
years.'   3

'Yes, I would like my child to be good at Irish.'   3

'I travel abroad and find my identity through Irish most important. Irish should be encouraged.'   3

'We are interested in keeping the Irish language alive and we try and keep our child as interested as we are.'   3

'I would like to see Irish being used more, but only if the child has a liking for the   3
language - not to be forced on those who have no interest at all in it.'   2

4. Parent wants more time spent on Irish, or some subjects taught through Irish.

'Not enough Irish taught in schools'   4

5. Parent believes Irish is not useful or important for the child's future (whether parent actually approves of Irish or not).

'What good is Irish to my child if she has to emigrate to another country for work which is happening every day in Ireland.'   5

'I agree with the teaching of Irish but I think it has no benefit jobwise.'   5

'I do not see Irish as being of any practical value in today's modern commercial world.'   5

'Most of my children, and I suspect most children, resent having to learn Irish which they feel will have little value to them in the future. It imposes an added scholastic burden on an already crowded curriculum.'   5

'Presently the educational system is so academically geared that Irish has become irrelevant to career prospects.'   5

'My own education was greatly hampered by Irish, I have never at any time benefited from my knowledge of Irish.'   5

'I think it is nice for children to learn Irish, but I don't feel they will use it in later life. I learned Irish at school, but never used it afterwards.'   5

'Irish is nice as part of one's heritage but I don't see why so much time is spent on a subject that is not used in everyday life. Most jobs cater for English speaking people. Better use of time spent would be to teach a child a trade or maybe even read or write   5
English.'   1

Concern about methods of teaching Irish.

6. *Parent wants more emphasis on oral/conversational Irish in class and at playtime/lunchtime, and/or less emphasis on grammar*

'Perhaps schools should devote one lunchtime each week to the speaking of Irish totally by both teachers and pupils.'   6

'More emphasis on oral work and less on grammar especially for primary school children.'   6

'I would like to see Speech and Drama done in primary school in Irish and English.'   6

'Perhaps if Irish was encouraged and spoken during playtime it might help.'   6

'I think too much time is involved in the teaching of grammar and not enough time spent in developing the historical and cultural aspects of Irish.'   6

'Let's speak the language. I find it sad to see pupils doing poetry and literature and regarding it as a chore. I believe they would like to speak Irish from an early age. Forget all the emphasis on grammar. I realise some grammar is necessary - one has to have the basics. My French pupils enjoy French tapes and conversations. I do grammar to make conversation possible. Why don't we look to Wales. I was very impressed on a visit last year to hear Welsh spoken in shops and on buses. Wouldn't it be wonderful if we could see that happening in Ireland.'

6
3

'I would like to see more subjects taught through Irish and less emphasis placed on Irish grammar.'

6
4

7. *Irish class, Irish text-books should be more interesting, more fun, more attractive, more relevant to the pupil's life.*

'Irish books have no interest for the pupils - too simple minded, and rural children of 10-12 are very well informed - Irish teaching should inform at their general maturity level.'   7

'I would like to see Irish made more interesting - *Comhrá* (projector) is dull, out of date. Also here on the east coast children are not in touch with spoken Irish outside school and find it is a dead language. Most parents discourage it here and let their children hear them saying they were useless at it in school themselves.'   7

'To make Irish enjoyable to learn.'   7

'I would like the pressure taken off grammar and the natural love of the language to 7
be kept on, as it was when she was in earlier classes.' 6

'As I've indicated earlier, I would question the relevance of certain textbooks which
would tend to be middle class and rural in emphasis. The methodology is unnatural, 7
not enough emphasis on conversation.' 6

'Make Irish more fun to do, such as trips to the Gaeltacht.' 7

8. Irish should be taught like Modern Continental Languages (using more modern methods).

'I would like to see Irish taught in the schools like a modern language. I think
children would enjoy it more.' 8

'As a school subject I would like to see Irish being treated like any other
continental language.' 8

'I would like to see Irish taught as a spoken language like French or German, rather
than learning poetry, stories etc. which is really of little importance when school is 6
finished.' 8

'More time should be given to the speaking of Irish, the history, beauty of the Irish 6
language. More modern methods applied to the teaching of same as in the case of the 8
teaching of French/German. The Irish language is part of our culture and 3
therefore is very important.'

'I think Irish should be taught in the same way as German, French and Spanish. I was
taught through Irish in primary school and I hated it. Today I speak more Spanish
than Irish.' 8

Reaction to child's progress in school

9. Satisfied with the progress of the child, or of children generally

'I am very pleased with the standard of Irish our young people have
received from the teachers in this school.' 9

'I am happy with the teaching of Irish and the results achieved at the school.' 9

'I feel that the school is doing a good job and we are pleased with the child's progress.' 9

'Overall I'm pleased with the way my daughter is being taught Irish and other subjects
in her school.'　9

'I am lucky that my child is of average intelligence and does not find any subject too
difficult.'　9

'I think the standard of Irish in my child's school is excellent.'　9

'We are delighted with our child's progress in school. As regards spoken Irish,
we strongly feel that our daughter would benefit more by learning to speak French　9
or German.'　1

'Happy the way things are.'　9

10.　Dissatisfied with the progress of the child/children generally or child is finding Irish difficult.

'My daughter has no problem with Irish but my son age 9, finds it hard to pick up.　10
I don't think it should be forced on children. I don't think Irish is important.'　2
　5

'Ba chóir go mbéadh líofacht cuíosach maith ag páistí tar éis 8 mbliana ar scoil - ní hé
sin an chás!'　10

'Though my child has an excellent teacher and plenty of help at home, he is coming
out of National School without being able to put an original sentence in Irish together.
There must be something wrong somewhere.'　10

'My child fell back in Irish over past few months - was average up until then. I just
don't know what happened - and it's a most important year with moving to new
school!'　10

'I have children at various stages - 2 already finished school - the standard generally
has gone down especially in Maths and Irish, allowing for difference in abilities. The
textbooks also are most uninteresting. Why not have Roald Dahl or Judy Bloom　10
'as Gaeilge'? I know more children who hate 'Peig' than like it - this is a reality.
Also I do not like the privileges given to Irish speakers and all-Irish schools. It creates
division and jealousy instead of liking for the language. We already have enough
division. The ability to use the language seems to come from, or possibly the　7
proximity to, an Irish-speaking school.'

'I feel the teaching of Irish in schools in present times is incorrect - not teacher's fault.
I don't know the answer.'　10

Other

11. Irish taught at school now is different to his/her own, or finds Irish difficult

'I found that as my child went from class to class, his teacher had a different
pronunciation of Irish words and this made it difficult for me to help him.'   11

'I am not very good at Irish myself and it seems to have changed a great deal since I
was in school, so I find it hard to help my child with it.'   11

'The little I learned about Irish in school is completely different to today's Irish.'   11

12. Miscellaneous [1]

'It should be 'all-Irish' or none!'

'If Irish was used more often in every-day life it would make it easier to learn in school.'

'I don't discourage Irish and leave it up to herself. If she showed more interest I'd probably send
her to 'An Ghaeltacht' to improve it and I'd be in favour of teaching other subjects through
Irish.'

'It might be useful to conduct a similar survey on a European language (e.g. French)
instead of Irish.'

'I would have thought one comment was obvious - Irish is not an international language.'

'Irish is important (re Q.9) but only when the job in question requires it.'

'My two younger children attend [name of an all-Irish school] and I also attend the parents' Irish
nights.'

'Adult classes for parents who are not good at Irish.'

'1. Easpa trealaimh scannallach m.s. stiallscannáin.
2. Easpa díograise is tacaíochta ó chigirí áirithe.
3. Plean scoil reasúnta ach cinnte don Ghaeilge.
4. Athoiliúnt rialta do mhúinteoirí.'

(end of comments)

---

[1] Comments without a specific code number were included in the 'miscellaneous' category of Table 5.20 in
the main text.

Appendix 6.1

Twenty-Classes Study: Observers' Manual

General procedure

During the lesson

Two observers in each classroom, working side by side, but independently, each observer making a separate audio tape-recording of each of the two lessons.

Observer 1: Identifies, classifies and notes down the main segments of classroom activity during the lesson according to the prepared schedule *Coras Dirbhreathnaithe ITÉ - I* (*Irish Lesson Analysis System*)[1]. Half-minute to ten minute segments, average three and a half minutes. Section 2, below[2], gives further information on how to code the segments of the lesson along various dimensions.

Observer 2: Classifies the general behaviour and language use of three pre-selected pupils according to the prepared schedule *Coras Dirbhreathnaithe ITÉ - II* (*Pupil Communicative Behaviour Record*). Further information in section 3 below.[3]

The 'anchor' inspector in each school serves as Observer 1, and the 'guest' inspector serves as Observer 2. The same inspector serves as Observer 1 for *both* lesson 1 and lesson 2 in a particular class.

Immediately after <u>each</u> lesson

(a) *Observers' Global Rating Of Lesson[4]*: The two observers jointly fill in a check list which refers to that lesson and seeks a more *global* description of classroom activity and pupil/teacher behaviour. Thus, there will be a completed *Observers' Global Rating of Lesson* for *each* lesson.

(b) Each observer may need to recheck the tape recording in order to amplify or check the notes made on the prepared schedule during the class.

---

[1] For the purposes of the present report in English, the original titles in Irish - *Córas Dírbhreathnaithe I* and *Córas Dírbhreathnaithe II* - are changed to the *Irish Lesson Analysis System (ILAS)* and the *Pupil Communicative Behaviour Record (PCBR)* respectively. The English translation of *Córas Dírbhreathnaithe* is 'Direct Observation System'.

[2] Section 2 of the original instructions to the Observers which contained the coding guidelines for *ILAS* is to be found in Appendix 6.2 here.

[3] Section 3 of the original instructions which contained the coding guidelines for *PCBR* now appears in Appendix 9.

[4] See Appendix 2.3 for *Observers' Global Rating of Lesson*.

General strategy

If the recordings are of reasonable quality, we in ITÉ can go back over them to obtain additional information and, if necessary, to correct some of the codings. In doing this later work on the tapes, however, we will have to depend very much on the contextual/visually-based information supplied by the Observer who was actually present in the classroom in order to make sense of the audio recordings. It is critical, therefore, that the Observers note down with particular care any additional in-class information which could not be inferred by us from the recordings. The motto might be "if in doubt, make a note of it."

Each Observer first records the word "start" at the beginning of the tape, then stops the tape right there until the lesson begins. One tape recorder should be placed reasonably near the blackboard or the teacher's desk, the other as centrally as possible in the classroom. Tape recorders fitted with a separate microphone should be used if at all possible. As soon as the teacher is ready, but before the lesson begins, the Observers should start the two tape recorders simultaneously. When the Observers are seated, and ready to begin filling in the schedules, they should signal the teacher to begin the lesson as soon as is convenient. The two tapes should be stopped simultaneously after the lesson. Observation and recording should run for as long (or as short!) as the lesson itself does.

Blank C90 tapes will be provided, and a separate tape should be used for each lesson. Each cassette should be clearly identified with the Observer's name, the name of the school and the class teacher, and an indication of whether it contains a recording of the first or second lesson. Since each side of the C90 runs for 45 minutes, some convenient way of stopping side A of the tape and turning to side B must be found - without disrupting the class any more then is necessary and without losing a significant part of the lesson. The best arrangement might be to arrange beforehand with the teacher that you will signal him or her when you wish to pause for a moment to turn over the tape (this should be at the end of a segment). Once 35 minutes have elapsed, perhaps the Observer could start to watch out for a suitable break in the lesson. The stopping and restarting of Observer 1's and Observer 2's tapes should be synchronised as carefully as possible. The time at which the last segment of the lesson on side A (before tape-turning) ended and the time at which the new segment of the lesson on side B began should be noted in the appropriate place on the Observers' Schedules.

The lesson to be recorded

The "lesson" is intended to include *oral/conversational Irish*, *Irish reading* and *Irish writing*. If any of these three are taught during separate periods, then the latter periods should also be observed. If that is not convenient for the Observer, perhaps the teacher could be asked to join the reading and writing periods onto the oral/conversational period.

The teacher should be told at the very beginning that our objective is to study typical teaching of a *new lesson* - not something that has been rehearsed by the class before. The lesson should include ordinary discipline, assignment of homework and other typical activities. Pupils should be told by the teacher (and again by the inspector) that we are interested in finding out how children learn Irish at school and that is why the observers are present.

The class is considered to include all pupils who are regularly taught Irish together, although the main focus of the study in the case of multigrade classes will be the sixth-grade pupils. Observer 2 will be directly concerned with only *three* of the *sixth-grade* pupils.

It may be helpful to the Observers if the teacher can indicate in a very general way beforehand how the lesson will unfold in terms of activities, how long the lesson will run and so on. The Observer's role here, however, is to make only a very general verbal enquiry and the teacher should not be pressed in any way for a detailed plan of any kind, nor should the teacher be expected to adhere during the lesson to what he or she may have indicated at the beginning.

The Observer must have no part of any kind in what the teacher decides to teach or the methods used. The aim is that the teacher should teach a *typical lesson for an approximately average length of time*. The observation should run until the class ends naturally, and not just terminate after some fixed period of time. If the teacher wants you to offer an opinion on whether to use this or that book, or a particular lesson, it should be explained that *the choice should be made by the teacher* and, as far as possible, should be *typical of what he or she usually does*.

It is particularly important to make this clear if the initial approach to the school suggested that the teacher had been selected because he or she used the audio-visual approach, for example. The original basis for selection should be set aside at this stage, and the teacher informed that she should proceed to teach the lesson in as nearly a typical fashion as possible.

If the teacher plans to use a coursebook or textbook during the lesson, the Observers may find it useful to consult the book beforehand (or indeed afterwards). But the book should not be consulted by the Observers during the class in case, consciously or unconsciously, this would impose any constraints on the teacher. The task of the Observer is to observe what *actually* happens and, as far as possible, not to interfere with or influence events in any way.

It is very desirable that the Observers would do a 'dummy-run' using the schedules in a classroom before doing the observations proper. If there are any questions or difficulties at that stage, please phone John Harris.

All schedules and tapes are to be returned to ITÉ.

In any event, it would be well worthwhile checking the classroom in advance to establish the location of sockets etc. and to choose a suitable vantage point for the observation.

Appendix 6.2

Irish Lesson Analysis System (ILAS): **Short form**[1]

Segment

For the purposes of this study the lesson is broken up into segments. A *segment* is defined as a *stretch of lesson discourse, having a particular topic, and involving the participants (teacher and pupils) in a distinctive configuration of roles, linguistic and organisational.* Most teachers conceptualize the language class as being composed of distinctive teaching units or events. The segment is designed to correspond to these 'natural' units.

Each segment is a stretch of the Irish lesson which lasts for a *minimum of 30 seconds*. Typically segments will last for between 1 and 10 minutes. Segment boundaries will often be indicated by 'framing' and 'focusing' moves. 'Framing' is when the teacher uses markers such as "Right", "Anois", "Ciúnas" etc. followed by a silent stress. A focusing move, on the other hand, usually sums up the activity just completed (e.g. "Put away your books", "Tá go maith", etc.) or launches a new topic or activity, helping pupils to see where they are going and describing what will occur (e.g. the teacher says "Anois, déanfaimid píosa beag filíochta/gramadaí", "Éist leis na habairtí seo agus scríobh síos i do chóipleabhar iad" etc.).

There will be occasions, however, where the teacher will move from one activity (segment) to another without giving any signals. This may happen where a particular pattern has been established in the Irish class over time where certain activities logically follow others, thus freeing the teacher from having to overtly refer to, or announce, a changeover. For example, a language activity such as 'imitation' may always be followed by another language activity such as a particular question and answer drill.

Each *segment* is defined in terms of five separate dimensions:
1. *Topic*
2. *Language Activity*
3. *Pupil Behaviour*
4. *Teacher mode of involvement*
5. *Classroom organisation*

If there is a change in categorisation or any of these dimensions, a new segment has begun. Three further dimensions are considered in relation to each segment, although these dimensions don't define a segment:
6. *Materials*
7. *Class attentiveness*

---

[1] This is the version of *ILAS* used by the observers. A sample of the *ILAS* coding sheet used by the obsrevers may be found on the last page of this Appendix. *ILAS* is adapted from the Stirling System by kind permission of the authors. No assessment of the original Stirling System should be made on the basis of the summary description of *ILAS* categories here.

8. Class interest.

These are the eight dimensions which are coded as the lessons proceed. The real starting time of each segment is first recorded in the left hand column and the segment is then coded on each of the eight dimensions. In practice, the first and second dimensions, *Topic* and *Language Activity*, are central to the identification of segments. With short segments you may have to work very fast, but you will find that the categorisations or coding of many dimensions (e.g. pupil attentiveness) do not change very often from one segment to the next.

Please draw a line right across the observation sheet after each segment.

The various dimensions which are coded are now considered in more detail:

Topic - What is being talked about.

The following categories are used in coding the 'topic' discussed:

1. *Linguistics/grammar of Irish*:   The discourse concerns the nature of language in general, possible ways of analysing it, analytical discussion of particular grammatical structures, etc.
2. *Situation: Nuachúraí*: The discourse concerns a third party situation narrated or presented in 'Lá Faoin Tuath'/'Sean Neidí'.
3. *Irish life/ culture/music*: Aspects of Irish life, culture and music.
4. *Situation: pupil/ teacher real life*: Concerns pupils'/teacher's real life.
5. *Situation: other than Nuachúraí:* Other third party situations (e.g. from other books).
6. *Fragmented/ non-contextualised*: The discourse concerns no coherent, topic (its unity and coherence rest in formal aspects of the language being practised).
7. *Routine management/organisation*: The discourse concerns classroom management and organisation, including things like the setting of homework, discipline etc.
8. *Feedback/discussing pupils previous performance*: The discourse consists of the teacher discussing/commenting on the pupil's previous performance. The topic is more concerned about how the pupil has performed rather than the linguistic content itself.

Language activity

The range of language activities planned and directed by the teacher. This dimension is concerned with aspects of the linguistic experience provided for pupils which appear to be particularly important for learning Irish or any second language. The categories of this dimension are summarised under three main headings

1. The balance of Irish and English.
2. The extent to which Irish is used for real or simulated communication.
3. The various types of 'language practice' (i.e. not communication).

Simulated communication does not have a real purpose (apart from the exercise itself). The content and form is rather predictable, there are limits on what can be said (not open ended) or no real new information is involved.

Real communication is purposeful, relatively unpredictable, open-ended and involves the transmission of new information.

The set of categories for this dimension is:

Language Practice
   1.   Comprehesion

2. Imitation
3. Transposition
4. Drill/ contextualisation excercise
5. Translation

Simulated Communication

6. Simulated communication in <u>Irish</u>
7. <u>Bilingual</u> simulated communication

Real communication

8. Real communication in <u>Irish</u>
9. <u>Bilingual</u> real communication
10. Real communication in <u>English</u>

Other

11. Irish song/poem
12. Compound (regular cycles of above)

Each segment is coded under only *one* of the above 1-2 language activities. This is the single most important dimension to code. If in doubt about coding, please write a brief description of the language activity.

Language Practice

1. *Comprehension:* Focus on global comprehension of lexical meaning (e.g. listening or reading comprehension).

2. *Imitation:* Pupils' behaviour (spoken or written) imitates a given model (e.g. spoken repetition or copy writing).

3. *Transposition:* Irish practice-discourse realised simultaneously in both written and spoken codes, where the focus of attention is on the relationship between them (e.g. reading aloud = transposition from written to spoken mode; dictation = transposition form spoken to written mode).

4. *Drill/contextualisation exercise:* Irish-practice discourse with an expected component of pupil utterances, where the focus of attention is on syntactic form and/or the appropriateness of utterances to their discourse context (e.g. structural or question-and-answer drills).

5. *Translation:* Discourse in which lexical meanings of Irish are made explicit through English, (I -> E,) or vice versa (E -> I) (e.g. translation exercises or the giving of 'vocabulary' notes).

Simulated Communication

6. *Simulated communication in Irish:* Irish practice discourse which has the outer form of real communication but in which there is *no real new information being communicated*. The focus of attention is on the excercise, per se. The discourse is relatively predictable. It is not open ended and there are limits to what can be said compared to equivalent real communication. Consists of activities such as role play, drama etc.

7. *Bilingual simulated communication:*

Same as above but discourse is *bilingual* (in Irish and English) rather than in Irish only.

Real Communication

8. *Real communication in Irish*: Irish discourse in which real new information is being transmitted, and the focus of attention is on the meaning of what is being said. The discourse is unpredictable, purposeful, open ended and unconstrained.

9. *Bilingual real communication*: Same as above but discourse is bilingual (Irish and English)

10. *Real communication in English*: Same as above but all discourse is in English.

Other

11. *Irish song/poem*: Pupils learning/saying poem or singing in Irish.

12. *Compound*: All discourse involving brief occurrences of more than one of the above categories, in regular, structured sequence.

Pupil behaviour

Six 'channels of communication' are coded here, three receptive and three productive. The categories were as follows:

1. Listening
2. Speaking
3. Doing (productive)
4. Reading
5. Writing
6. Looking (receptive).

For each segment write down the numbers (up to six) which apply to the pupils.

1. *Listening*: Pupils are considered to be in a listening mode of involvement if required to attend to any auditory language source e.g. teacher, other pupil, tape recording, etc.

2. *Speaking*: Speaking, or actively preparing to speak in Irish.

3. *Doing*: Carrying out some non-linguistic overt physical activity in accordance with teacher's plan eg. drawing a picture, taking out books, mime etc.

4. *Reading*: Reading involves attending to any written textbook, blackboard etc.

5. *Writing*: Producing any kind of graphic text or coding, or actively preparing to do so.

6. *Looking*: Looking involves attending to any non-linguistic stimulus, usually visual aids eg. film strips, cut outs, blackboard, person doing mime etc.

These six channels might be activated singly or in a range of combinations. Thus a pupil might simply be 'Listening' ('1'), or 'Listening and Speaking' (1,2), or 'Listening, Speaking, Reading (1,2,4) etc.

Teacher mode of involvement

1. *Instructing*: The teacher is leading, explaining, reading or writing. There is no component of public pupil response. Pupil may be required to respond privately - take down notes etc.

2. *Interacting*: The teacher is involved in verbal interactions with one or more pupils - typically question/response/reaction. Involves public pupil response.

3. *Monitoring*: The teacher is actively correcting or monitoring some <u>pre-set</u> task e.g. listening to and correcting a pupil who is reading out loud, or watching and correcting a pupil demonstration, circulating among pupils and marking seatwork tasks/homework individually etc.

4. *Not involved*: The teacher is doing none of the above i.e. not communicating with or monitoring pupils. For example, pupils may be involved in some activity teacher set earlier and teacher may be silently correcting homework or preparing materials for next segment/lesson etc.

For each segment write down the number (one only) of the category which applies.

Class organisation

1. *Whole class*: One central activity going on, dependent on the teacher or another source of stimulus, but not on a 'pupil demonstration'; the class functions as one group.

2. *Pupil demonstration*: One central activity going on, focuses on a pupil demonstration (e.g. one pupil taking the role of teacher, or a group of pupils acting out a scene with the rest of the class forming an audience).

3. *Cooperative, same task*: Pupils are assigned to work cooperatively in <u>more than one</u> group, but groups are assigned <u>identical</u> tasks.

4. *Cooperative, different task*: Pupils are assigned to work cooperatively in <u>more than one</u> group, and groups are assigned <u>different</u> tasks.

5. *Individual, same task*: Pupils are set to work alone, without cooperation, but the task set is <u>identical</u> for all pupils.

6. *Individual, different task*: Pupils are set to work alone, without cooperation, and at least some individuals are set tasks different from those set for others.

7. *Cooperative and individual*: Some pupils are working cooperatively and the rest are working as individuals. Tasks may be the same or different.

For each segment write down the number (one only) of the category which applies to the segment.

Materials

For each segment <u>all</u> materials used are to be specified i.e write down the code number of <u>each</u> material used. The following are the range of items that may be used and coded.

1.   *Nuachúrsaí handbook*: Specify whether "Sean-Neidí"/"Lá Faoin Tuath"
2.   *Commercially produced <u>course-book/workbook</u>*: (name) e.g. 'Bog liom'; 'Anseo is Ansiúd'; 'Slí na nÓg' (i), 'Fás' (i), "Seal ag Léamh"; "Lean den Obair" etc.
3.   *Reader* (name)
4.   *Jotter/copy*
5.   *Blackboard*
6.   *Wallchart*
7   *Worksheet*
8.   *Flashcards*
9.   *Library Books*
10. *Film strip/slide*
11. *Cut outs*
12. *Tape*
13. *Video/film*

14.   *Overhead Projector*
15.   *Photographs*
16.   *Authentic materials*: e.g. newspaper articles, advertisements, T.V. licence, tax form in Irish etc.
17.   *Objects*
18.   *Person*: e.g. an outsider is brought in to the classroom and talks to the pupil about himself/herself and the pupils can ask him/her questions.
19.   *Other*: any other materials not covered in the previous categories.

Class attentiveness

The extent to which the majority of pupils are paying attention to the current language activity. It is measured on a five point scale representing 'very low' attention to 'very high' attention on the part of pupils. Write one number under this heading for each segment.

Class interest

The extent to which the majority of pupils are interested in the current language activity. Write one number under the heading for each segment.

Patterns of expectation

An important concept to guiding you in carrying out the 'segmentation' of lesson discourse according to the system is that of the 'pattern of expectation' obtaining at any given moment during the process of instruction. Apart from the clues to segment boundaries inherent in framing and focusing moves, decisions regarding segmentation and the characterisation of successive segments on the various dimensions do not depend on the quality of any *individual* utterances produced by teacher or pupils. They depend rather on the *shared understandings between teacher and pupil regarding what sort of utterance is appropriate at particular moments in the lesson.*

This concept is particularly helpful in applying the categories of the Pupil Behaviour dimension. If one coded a new segment every time a pupil started or stopped speaking, for example, there might be hundreds of segments in a lesson, and this would vitiate the whole purpose of the system. The difficulty disappears if the concept of 'pattern of expectation' is followed through logically. A segment was taken to be 'Speaking' if a pupil speaking-readiness component was built into the pattern. The pupil speaking involved could not just be an aside, but must be an integral part of the pattern of expectation; but with this proviso it could be a very small part of the total activity of the segment.

Brief events within a segment which are *inconsistent with the way in which the segment as a whole is characterised* are to be disregarded provided the existing 'pattern of expectation' was not disrupted by the intrusive event sufficiently for the latter to succeed in establishing an alternative pattern.

IRISH LESSON ANALYSIS SYSTEM

(SHORT VERSION)

Córas Dírbhreathnaithe ITÉ - 1

Dáta: _____

Ceacht: 1 nó 2

Uimhir an Ionaid: _____

Ainm an Chigire: _____

Múinteoir: _____

Ainm na scoile: _____

Seoladh: _____

SEGMENT	TOPIC	LANGUAGE ACTIVITY	PUPIL BEHAVIOUR	TEACHER MODE OF INVOLVEMENT	CLASSROOM ORGANISATION	MATERIALS	CLASS ATTENTIVENESS	CLASS INTEREST
Began at (actual time of day)	1 = Linguistics/ grammar of Irish	LANGUAGE PRACTICE 1 = Comprehension (read/listen)	1 = Listening	1 = Instructing	1 = Whole class	1 = Nuachúrsaí handbook (name)	1 = very low	1 = very low
	2 = Situation: Nuachúrsaí	2 = Imitation (repeat/copy write)	2 = Speaking	2 = Interacting	2 = Pupil demonstration	2 = Other course book/workbook (name)	2 = low	2 = low
	3 = Irish life/ culture/ music	3 = Transposition (read aloud/dictation)	3 = Doing	3 = Monitoring	3 = Cooperation: same task	3 = Reader (name)	3 = fair	3 = fair
	4 = Situation: pupil/ teacher real life	4 = Drill/exercise [1] (structured drills/Q. & A.)	4 = Reading [2]	4 = Not involved	4 = Cooperation: different task	4 = Jotter/copy	4 = high	4 = high
	5 = Situation: other than Nuachúrsaí	5 = Translation (1 → E or E →I)	5 = Writing		5 = Individual: same task	5 = Blackboard	5 = very high	5 = very high
	6 = Fragmented/non contextualised	SIMULATED COMMUNICATION 6 = Simulated communication in Irish (role play/drama)	6 = Looking		6 = Individual: different task	6 = Wallcharts		
	7 = Routine management/ organisation	7 = Bilingual simulated communication			7 = Cooperation & individual	7 = Worksheets		
	8 = Feedback/ discussing pupil performance	REAL COMMUNICATION 8 = Real communication in Irish				8 = Flashcards		
		9 = Bilingual real communication				9 = Library books		
		10 = Real communication in English				10 = Filmstrip/slide		
		OTHER 11 = Irish song/poem				11 = Cut outs		
		12 = Compound (regular cycles of above)				12 = Tape		
						13 = Video/film		
						14 = Overhead Projector		
						15 = Photographs		
						16 = 'Authentic' materials (newspapers, etc.)		
						17 = Objects		
						18 = Person (appearance etc)		
						19 = Other (name)		

1. The *Language activity* ategory 'Drill/exercise' is this short version is represented by two separate categories Contextualisation exercises (4a) and Drills (4b) in the long version of ILAS.

2. The *Pupil behaviour* category 'Reading' is subdivided, in the long version of ILAS, into 'Reading aloud' (4a) and 'Reading silently'. (4b).

Appendix 6.3

Irish Lesson Analysis System (ILAS): **Long form**[1]

The basic unit of analysis - The segment.

The function of this unit is to distinguish the general pedagogic strategies used by the teachers: that is, to identify classroom events which appear distinctive in their intended effects on the development of pupils' competence in Irish. Brown and McIntyre (n.d.) emphasise the importance of analysing teaching behaviour using units which a) are "as easily comprehensible as possible to teachers", and b) "divide up the lesson in similar ways to those in which teachers tend to conceptualise their activities". Second and foreign language teachers describe their lessons as composed of 'presentations', 'drills', 'exercises' and so on; the segment unit being proposed here is intended to carve up classroom events so as to correspond broadly with such teachers' descriptions.

The segment unit proposed for the analysis of the Irish lessons is defined as *a stretch of lesson discourse, having a particular topic, and involving the participants (teacher and pupils) in a distinctive configuration of roles, linguistic and organisational.* In making this definition operational, five critical dimensions of analysis were established: *Topic, Language activity, Pupil behaviour, Teacher mode of involvement,* and *Classroom organisation.* For each of these five dimensions a set of categories was worked out. Each segment identified in the lesson discourse was to be allocated to one category on each dimension. Whenever a change of categorisation occurred on any dimension, a new segment was considered to have begun. The information collected for each segment, therefore, indicates (a) what is being talked about, (b) what language is being spoken, for what purpose, and (c) what the involvement of the individuals present in the lesson is.

The analysis of lessons into strings of discrete segments cannot be done mechanically through the application of a completely explicit set of low inference discourse analysis procedures. While it is necessary to be as explicit as possible about the criteria upon which decisions concerning segmentation are made, it is pointless to pretend that to some degree, the observer's intuitive sense of what goes with what will not play a role. Acceptance of this view allows us to go along with Brown and McIntyre, when they say:

---

[1] Adapted from the Stirling System with the kind permission of the authors (Mitchell, Parkinson and Johnstone, 1981). The present description of *ILAS* draws on material in an appendix to the Mitchell *et al.* (1981) report, though it also incorporates material from the main body of the report from time to time. While categories in most dimensions of the Stirling System have been modified for the present version, some of them considerably so, the original form of words is retained wherever possible. In a small number of cases portions of the original text which turned out not to be critical to our study have been omitted. This long version of *ILAS* was used by the present researchers (along with the observers original codings using the shorter version of *ILAS*) to recode the Irish lessons from the audio-tapes. This subsequent coding provides the data for the present report.

"There may... within a segment be brief events which are inconsistent with the way in which the segment as a whole is characterised, but classroom segments exist as long as their outlines, their identifying patterns persist". They go on to propose a minimum length of time, arbitrarily chosen, "for which the dominant activity, the stable pattern, must persist even if there are short lived behaviours that are inconsistent with the segment features within that time".

In the present *ILAS* adaptation of the original Stirling System, each segment is also coded in relation to three secondary dimensions - *Materials, Class attention* and *Class interest*. Changes in categorisation on these additional dimensions, however, do not have any implications for the definition of a segment. While in the Stirling Study, information on the materials used in each lesson was in fact recorded, the information was not segment-related as it is in the case of *ILAS* here. *Class attention* and *Class interest* were not recorded at all in the Stirling System. Categories of all eight dimensions will be described later. Categories/dimensions which depart from, or which have no direct equivalent in the Stirling system are marked with an *.

Guidelines for the identification and coding of segments

1. Each segment is a stretch of the Irish lesson which lasts for a minimum of 30 seconds. Typically segments will last for between 1 and 10 minutes.
2. Segments in a lesson are numbered consecutively on the leftmost column of the coding sheet.
3. The start of the first segment is indicated
    a) by the first public utterance by the teacher to the whole class, or
    b) by the start of the recording, if the teacher is already speaking to the whole class when recording gets under way.
4. For the identification of the second and subsequent segments, the observer listens for the potential segment beginnings. That is the observer listens for the teacher moves which create new expectations about the type of discourse which is to be permitted in the lessons. These will usually, though not always, be explicit framing and focusing moves.

    In framing moves the teacher may use markers such as "Right", "Anois", "Now", "Ciúnas" "OK" etc. followed by a silent stress. A focusing move, on the other hand, usually sums up the activity just completed (e.g. "Ceart go leor", "Is féidir libh é sin a chríochnú anocht", "Right, fágfaimid mar sin é", "Tá go maith", etc.) or launches a new topic or activity, helping pupils to see where they are going and describing what will occur (e.g. the teacher says "Anois, deanfaimid píosa beag filíochta/gramadaí", "Eist leis na habairtí seo agus scríobh síos i do chóipleabhar iad" etc.).

    Having identified such moves, the observer then listens to what follows, to discover whether the new set of discourse rules actually comes into force. If the ongoing discourse does appear to be constrained by the teacher's new set of discourse rules, for a period lasting at least 30 seconds, the existence of a new segment is recognised (unless the conditions outlined in 8 below apply). The segment is then categorised on the 5 dimensions listed above, in accordance with the appropriate definitions and ground rules.

As already indicated, framing or focusing moves and segment boundaries do not always coincide. These 'mismatches' may occur for the following reasons:

*   False starts: Where the teacher attempts to alter the patterns of discourse in the lesson by use of some sort of framing move, but fails to implement the new pattern (e.g. because pupils are still finishing off the previous task). Such a move is regarded as a

false start, and is not taken to be the start of a new segment. This is the case even if subsequent attempts to start the same new pattern are successful. The successful starter should be taken as the segment beginning, and the period between the first unsuccessful starter and the successful starter is dealt with as prescribed in paragraphs 7 and 15.

- Non-differences: It may also happen that framing moves may signal a 'transition' between lesson activities having identical categorisations on all dimensions of the analysis system and therefore counting as one segment in terms of the system.
- Abrupt shifts: There will be occasions, where teachers move from one activity to another without giving any overt signal in terms of framing or focusing moves. In these abrupt shifts the pupils are expected to infer from internal evidence what the character of the new activity is to be. (e.g. a teacher might move from a repetition activity to a question-and-answer session in this way).

5. Should the process of transition from one segment to another be prolonged, and if it is not possible to locate a specific successful starting move for a following segment, the time taken in ambiguous transition should be measured and divided between the earlier and later segments.

6. When teacher moves are observed which explicitly bring to an end the established discourse pattern, and/or establish a new set of interim discourse rules and expectations, the segment is considered to have ended.

7. Candidate segments which last less than 30 seconds are subsumed in neighbouring ones. If the rules applying in the preceding and following stretches of discourse are identical, the candidate segment shorter than 30 seconds is ignored and its time added to the single segment recognised in the surrounding discourse. If a candidate segment of less than 30 seconds occurs between stretches of discourse which are recognised to be different segments, it is added to that segment it most resembles (i.e. the one with the largest number of identical category entries on the 5 dimensions). If the number of identical categories is the same, the time is divided between the two neighbouring segments.

8. Some candidate segments lasting longer than 30 seconds will also not be recognised as independent segments. This will be the case where the observer/coder judges that, although the type of discourse actually recorded has changed from that prescribed by the teacher, the public expectations regarding the discourse rules currently in force have merely been suspended, rather than definitively cancelled, and where this observer/coder judgement is confirmed by the subsequent reappearance of the previously established pattern. The typical event likely to be refused segment recognition, even if lasting longer than 30 seconds, is when the teacher gets involved in disciplinary action directed at a minority of pupils, but there is an ongoing expectation that whole class activity will be resumed at any moment.

    If discourse rules have been suspended, not cancelled for an interruption, the interruption may or may not form a segment. If it a) lasts 30+ seconds and b) establishes a clear pattern of discourse rules of its own which temporarily override the pattern of the interrupted segment, and if pupils have something to do, it is coded as a segment in its own right. If both these conditions do not apply it is not a segment.

9. It can be expected that the vast majority of segments will be teacher initiated, and that the pattern and sequencing of segments will be controlled. Occasional instances of pupil-initiated segments may occur, however, where the teacher appears to alter the rules of discourse in response to a pupil utterance. Thus, for instance, a pupil question may lead to the establishment of a segment discussing some aspect of civilisation apparently not pre-planned by the teacher.

For a pupil-initiated stretch of discourse to qualify as a segment, however, it must be public discourse to which the majority of the pupils are required to attend. Because pupil-initiated segments are actualised only if the teacher accepts and builds on the initiation, these segments should be timed from the teacher's acceptance of the initiation.

10. If a change occurs in the rules governing the pattern of discourse at a particular moment, which in the observer's judgement constitutes a cancellation of the pattern previously obtaining, and if the new pattern persists for at least 30 seconds, a new segment is to be identified, as previously outlined.

11. The observer should note on the coding sheet, under the heading of *Language activity*, the initiating move taken to be the first move from each segment. The segment will be timed from the start of the relevant utterance, and its time noted on the coding sheet, to the nearest second.

12. Under conditions of group or individual work, where pupils have been allocated to different tasks (topics, activities and/or involvement), parallel segments could be claimed to exist. However, no attempt will be made to code parallel segments. Where they occur, only that segment in which the greatest number of pupils is involved will be coded. In coding from tapes, of course, it may often be impossible to estimate numbers. Where the class has been divided by the teacher into two or more sections, with only one section receiving the teachers active attention for the duration of a segment (in the guise of instructing or interacting with this section of pupils) then, in the absence of any firm information on numbers, this 'active' section is considered to be the class for purposes of all coding. Where two or more classes (grade levels) are taught Irish together, only sixth-grade pupils will be considered the target class in those cases where different activities are assigned to different classes.

13. Tape turning: In the original instructions the two observers in each class (cf. Appendix 6.1), each of whom were making a separate audio recording of the lesson, were advised that, as far as possible, they should try to stop and turn over tapes simultaneously at the end of a segment. They were to signal their intention to the teacher who in turn would pause giving the observers time to turn the tapes and to note the new starting time at the onset of the next segment. In the event, this procedure was not always implemented (e.g. the teacher did not pause for the changeover/the changeover took place in the middle of a segment/ tapes were not turned over by both observers simultaneously).

   However, such anomalies did not prove to be a major problem for the authors during recoding since there was always enough information, either on the tapes themselves or from the Observers' notes and changeover times, to resolve any such potential problems. For example, if it was clear that the class was only temporarily suspended to allow the changeover, then the time involved in the changeover was merely subtracted from the total segment length. If the changeover took place in the middle of a segment and the lesson did not stop, then the changeover time was not subtracted and the segment length calculated in the usual way.

14. External interruptions exceeding 30 seconds which halt class activity (e.g. visitors with messages for teacher, summoning of teacher outside classroom), should be left uncoded and their time deducted from the lesson total. Their presence should however, be indicated, and length noted. Events preceding and following this type of interruption are coded separately in the first instance, but if they turn out to be identical, are considered to form one segment. If, however, the class has something to do coding continues and the teacher mode of involvement is coded as 'not involved' (thus probably starting a new segment).

15. Teachers' procedural discourse outlining a specific substantive task, which is carried out immediately afterwards, does not constitute a separate segment. It is regarded as an introductory part of the segment in which the task is carried out. This is the case even if the task gets under way with a delay long enough to exceed 30 seconds. The teacher's statement outlining the task is still taken as opening the segment.

However a separate segment (topic being 'routine management/organisation') is coded a) if matters like drawing margins, giving out books, become the dominant concern in their own right, b) if the introduction appears to relate to the lesson as a whole, or some other larger unit, rather than to the immediately succeeding segment, and c) if the introduction relates to a task to be carried out later and after an interval (e.g. homework), or to a task which is not in fact carried out immediately afterwards due to a change of plan or the end of the lesson (but does not substantially discuss or rehearse the linguistic content of the task).

16. Tapes: When a tape or other non-living audio source is used to produce classroom discourse, it is considered a direct substitute for the teacher, and the discourse is coded in the usual way, except for the category of *Teacher mode of involvement*.

Segments in which the teacher is attending to a tape monologue, or attending to pupils and tape engaged in interactive discourse, are coded 'Monitoring' on the *Teacher mode of involvement* dimension. Where the teacher is not attending to the tape, his/her mode of involvement may be categorised in the usual way.

The dimensions of *ILAS*

With two exceptions the Long Form of *ILAS* has the same number of categories in each dimension as the Short Form of *ILAS*, and these categories are listed in the same order and with more or less the same titles. The categories which were changed in developing the Long Form of *ILAS* are as follows: (1) In the case of the *Topic* dimension, Category 2 of the Short Form ('Situation: Nuachúrsaí') refers to third party situations narrated in the *Nuachúrsaí* handbooks *Lá Faoin Tuath/Sean Neidí* (Ireland: Department of Education, 1978) whereas it refers only to such situations narrated in Step A (the Bunchomhrá) of the lessons in these handbooks in the Long Form of *ILAS*. (2) In the *Language activity* dimension, the 'Drill/exercise' category of the Short Form of *ILAS* becomes two separate categories - 'Drills' and 'Contextualisation exercises' in the Long Form; and (3) In the *Pupil Behaviour* dimension, the single category 'Reading' in the Short form becomes two separate categories 'Reading aloud' and 'Reading silently' in the Long Form.

Topic

The *Topic* categories of *ILAS* describe 'what is being talked about' and range over situations deriving from different course books, as well as aspects of lesson content which research suggests are important e.g. topics related to pupil/teacher real life, Irish life, culture and music, the linguistics/structure of Irish itself, and routine class management.

A feature of second language lessons, as compared with other types of classroom discourse, is that what is being talked about is frequently of only secondary importance. The primary aim is frequently to provide pupils with opportunities to practise and develop a variety of language skills (rather than the transmission to them of any substantial body of knowledge - as it would be in Mathematics, for example). Nevertheless, the development of an understanding of the culture and way of life associated with the second language (e.g. Irish) are now also regarded as important secondary objective. Furthermore, there is a growing awareness of the importance of using the second language in situations which relate to the real life needs and interests of pupils. Finally, conscious analysis and discussion of the structure and rules of the target language may have a contribution to make to the development of competence in the language. The *Topic* categories of *ILAS* were designed to reflect these concerns with lesson content. There are eight categories in *ILAS* compared to 12 in the original Stirling System. Categories which depart from the Stirling System are marked with an asterisk*.

1 *Linguistic notions/grammar of Irish
The discourse concerns the nature of language in general, possible ways of analysing it or explicit analytical discussion of particular grammatical structures or semantic notions.

Examples form only a minor part of the discourse, explanations and definitions being the dominant issue. In practical terms, therefore, this means that the language activity associated with this topic category usually involves 'Real communication in Irish'. Language practice which mainly consists of grammar drills with little analytical discussion of the grammatical structures or semantic notions, and no coherent topic, would be excluded from this category.

2 *Situation: Nuachúrsaí
The discourse directly concerns a situation narrated or presented in *Step A* (*Bunchomhrá*) of the *Nuachúrsaí* handbooks.

The essential constituents of a 'situation' are one or more characters in a specific physical location, engaged in coherent linguistic and/or non-linguistic activity plausibly related to that location. The text in question may be directly narrated, in whole or in part, or the situation may be discussed; in the latter case, participants are factually accurate concerning the situation as presented in the text (e.g. characters must be correctly identified). The use or non-use of mime or drama in the presentation of situations should not influence categorisation decisions on this dimension.

If the topic of the *Bunchomhrá* changes as the lesson progresses to other new material (e.g. in *Step D* exercises) the *Topic* category 'Situation: Other' (see below) applies rather than the present one. Discourse based on workbook (e.g. *Lean den Obair*) exercises whose lessons are *directly* linked to those in the corresponding *Nuachúrsaí* handbooks are included in this category.

3 *Irish life/culture/music
The discourse concerns aspects of Irish life, culture (e.g. folklore, legend, 'piseoga') and music. Discussion of Irish poetry or song which extends beyond the literal meaning of the work is included here. The reciting of an Irish poem or the singing of an Irish song is excluded from this category (see below 'Situation: Other').

4 Situation: pupil/teacher real life
The discourse concerns aspects of the pupils' and teacher's life and interests, including home and school life, and including narrative material which directly relates to the personal experiences of the participants in the discourse.

Participants may tell the truth about themselves or not, but any fantasy is voluntary. Discourse related to current affairs, local, national or international news are also included here. In the case of Irish, this *Topic* category will frequently be associated with 'Simulated' and 'Real communication' language activities. But it may also be associated with *Language activities* such as 'Contextualisation exercises'.

5 *Situation: Other than Nuachúrsaí
The discourse concerns specific third party situations and stories other than those presented in *Step A* (*Bunchomhrá*) of the *Nuachúrsaí* lessons.

The situations may be narrated, acted out or discussed. The category includes topics from other coursebooks, from readers or from narratives recounted by the teacher as part of the more traditional *ABC* oral/aural method of teaching Irish. *Obair na maidine* ('morning work') is included here *if* the discussion develops in a thematically coherent way *and if* the emphasis is on promoting general communication or conversational skills (rather than on merely providing a very loose topical link between the elements of a drill). Singing songs, reciting poems or discussing their literal meaning also come under this topic heading. Games such as *Fiche Cheist (Twenty Questions)* and situations related to other content teaching areas - e.g. history, geography - are normally categorised here.

6 *Fragmented/non-contextualised topics
The discourse is incoherent, consisting of a series of propositions with no obvious situational relationship between them. The unity and coherence of the discourse does not rest in the content but in formal aspects of the language being practised.

Typically, but not exclusively, drill type language activities will be 'Fragmented' in nature. Examples:

1. Structural and vocabulary drills practised in *Step C* of the *Nuachúrsaí* (*Cleachtadh múnlaí agus foclóra*) will usually be assigned to this *Topic* category since any thematic link to the basic narrative of the lesson are really incidental, tenuous, and/or are not sustained.

2. Memorized narratives used as a framework for drills (e.g. verb tense practice such as the traditional verb-tense practice sequence *D'éirigh mé ar a hocht a chlog; Chuir mé mo chuid éadaigh orm;* etc.) would be coded as 'Fragmented/non contextualised'.

7 Routine management/organisation
The discourse concerns classroom management and organisation. The category includes discipline, and also the setting of homework if the linguistic content of the homework is not substantially discussed or rehearsed.

Activities assigned to this *Topic* category will often be quite short in duration and may involve the use of relatively little Irish (because of their routine nature - getting out books, settling down etc.).

8 Feedback/discussing pupils previous performance
The discourse involves the transmission of information about, and/or commentary on, pupils' previous performance.

An instance is the collecting of marks after a test. In this category may be included also the public correction of written exercises and tests, provided that discussion of the actual mechanics of marking has greater salience than both the ostensible topic of the exercise etc. and the language points underlying possible mistakes.

Language activity

This dimension of the system was designed to investigate the range of language activities planned and directed by the teacher (including pupil demonstrations where control temporarily passes to a pupil or group of pupils). The categories were designed to capture some of the different kinds of linguistic and communicative experience which, on the basis of current theoretical understanding, appear to be particularly important for learning Irish or any second or foreign language in a classroom context. The categories are designed to provide information on matters such as:

1. The popularity of various types of language practice (i.e. not communication).
2. The extent to which Irish is used in the classroom for any substantive 'communicative' purpose i.e. for real communication.
3. The balance of Irish and English.

A major distinction within the categories of *Language activity* relates to language practice versus communication. Language-practice categories involve the use of Irish primarily to give learners training in the manipulation of the language - the transmission of messages is incidental. In the case of 'Real communication', in contrast, the focus of attention is on meaning and on the message being transmitted. 'Simulated communication' might be thought of as intermediate between language practice and real communication.

There are 13 *Language activity* categories in *ILAS* compared to eight in the final version of the Stirling System. Notice that there is no direct equivalent of 'Simulated communication in Irish', 'Irish song/poem', 'Bilingual simulated communication' or 'Bilingual real communication', in the Stirling System. 'Drills' and 'Contextualisation exercises' were not treated as separate categories in the Stirling system.

In cases where *Language activity* categories have been changed or adapted from the Stirling system, specific examples of the language activity from the present study are given.

Instructions on coding *Language activity* in the context of 'Pupil/group demonstration' are given in the *Classroom organisation* section below.

Language Practice (categories 1-5 below)
1 *Comprehension
This category includes all Irish language practice discourse realised in a single code, which originates from a non-pupil speaker, and to which either no pupil contribution is expected or the pupil response is secondary and occurs only in the context of comprehension checks by the teacher. The primary focus of attention is typically on the lexical meaning of the discourse.

The message may be new, or known. Where the message is new, the decision to allocate the discourse to this category rather than to that of 'Real communication in Irish' will depend on where the focus of attention is believed to lie i.e. on the message or the lexical items. This category includes the playing through of a prescribed narrative or dialogue, with or without accompanying pictures, and other listening comprehension activities.

2 Imitation
This category includes all Irish language practice discourse in one code, where pupils' utterances imitative of previously-provided Irish models are expected. The focus of attention is on Irish phonological or orthographic form.

The category includes both the production and reproduction of model utterances, in the course of pronunciation and or writing practice. The typical instance of 'Imitation' is the activity of repetition, where modelling and imitative moves follow each other in interactive sequence. The recitation of previously memorised material is also to be categorised here, as long at it can be related to a previously provided model. Copy writing is another realisation of imitative discourse. Recognition of imitative discourse is helped by the total predictability of pupil utterances, which must conform in phonological or orthographic detail to the model previously provided.

3 Transposition
This category includes all Irish practice discourse where utterances are simultaneously realised in both written and spoken codes, and where the focus of attention is on the relationship between them (e.g. reading aloud/dictation).

Transposition provides practice in relating the codes and in making translations from one to the other. That is, it involves input in one mode, oral or written, and output in another. There must be pupil output in some productive mode. The category includes reading aloud and dictation. It does not include comprehension activity (See category 1 above) taking place with pupils' books open. However, where the teacher positively directs pupils' attention to the written code, even if he/she also supplies an oral rendering of the text, the discourse will be categorised here (as long as an oral rendering is also required of the pupils).

4a *Contextualisation exercise

This category includes all Irish practice disourse with an expected component of pupil utterances, where the focus is on the appropriacy of utterances to their discourse context.

The information being transmitted is typically known, and there may therefore be non-structural constraints on pupil utterances (e.g. getting the story line right). Discourse in this category will not exhibit the systematic structural regularities which are typical of drills, though the substance and form of utterances will still be largely predictable.

Typical instances are question and answer sequences, oral or written. Also included are the acting out of pre-prepared dialogues but *excluding both* (a) strictly memorised dialogues (which would be coded under 'Imitation', and (b) more loosely rehearsed role-play dialogue where the learner makes a creative input or where there is some element of meaning negotiation (which would be coded under 'Simulated communication'). Other instances relate to the production of oral or written prepared compositions which do not involve any creative input from the pupil.

Examples:
1. *Nuachúrsaí Step BI exercises (Cur i bhfeidhm an bhunchomhrá):* The questions being asked are designed to elicit, clarify or elaborate on utterances already covered in the basic narrative *(Bunchomhrá).*
2. *Nuachúrsaí Step BII exercises (Cur i bhfeidhm an bhunchomhrá:* Exercises where the content is sometimes only loosely related to the topic of the *Bunchomhrá*, would come under the heading 'Contextualisation exercises' instead of 'Drill' because they involve question and answer sequences in which there is an emphasis on utterance/discourse relationships rather than on repetitive structural or new-vocabulary drills.
3. Exercises based on the story line presented in the *Nuachúrsaí* filmstrips: General questions about the narrative relating to the *Nuachúrsaí* filmstrips (not necessarily those questions in the *Nuachúrsaí* handbook).
4. Exercises in reader: Oral or written question-and-answer sequences designed to test pupils' comprehension of a story covered in an Irish language reader. In the case of written question-and-answer sequences, the material would often have been covered orally beforehand.
5. Questions on teacher-presented narrative: The teacher asks pupils questions designed to test the pupils comprehension of a story which the teacher has previously recounted to the pupils.

4b *Drills: Structural/vocabulary/pronunciation/spelling

This category includes all Irish practice discourse in one code which has an expected component of pupil utterances, and which is structurally constrained beyond the rules of normal discourse. The focus of attention is primarily on syntactic form (although non-imitative vocabulary, pronunciation and spelling tasks are also included).

Opportunities are provided for manipulating the paradigmatic and syntagmatic relationships obtaining within particular syntactic structures of Irish. The constraints are either made explicit by the teacher, or are implicit in models supplied by the teacher.

The typical instance is the pattern drill where the teacher lays down constraints relating to a particular structure, and then elicits a series of utterances (oral or written) exemplifying it from pupils. The information being carried is typically known, and there is only secondary emphasis on meaning even in the case of contextualised drills. Pupil utterances are at least partly predictable as far as structure is concerned.

Examples:

1. *Structural exercise:* (a) *Nuachúrsaí Step C* exercises: The teacher presents the children with a sentence already encountered in the basic narrative (*Bunchomhrá*) e.g. *Níorbh fhada go bhfuair Mamaí boladh glasraí dóite* and then elicits similar utterances beginning with the same structure provided in the model *Níorbh fhada go ......* followed by a different but appropriate verb/phrase ending. (b) Structural drills may also be implemented in written form e.g. pupils, as part of an exercise from the coursebook *Buail Liom*, rewrite sentences such as *B'éigean dom an (oscail:doras),* making the necessary changes in the words within brackets.

2. *Vocabulary exercise: Nuachúrsaí Step BII* exercises (*Foclóir Breise*): These exercises involves the teaching of additional vocabulary which goes beyond the meaning of the discourse (story line) in question.

3. *Pronunciation exercise:* The pupil's task is to find words in a written text which contain a particular sound e.g. 'á'.

4. *Spelling exercise:* The pupils are asked to spell aloud words from memory (which have not been previously rehearsed i.e. not 'Imitation').

5 Translation

This category includes discourse in which lexical meanings of Irish are made explicit through the provision of English correspondences, or through the provision of definitions in English. The Irish units being explained may range in length from morphemes to entire narratives.

The category includes all translation exercises, as well as the taking/giving of vocabulary notes with English equivalents. The category must include items in English and corresponding items of Irish in the subject matter being considered. The language used to organise the activity, and to comment on correspondences, could be Irish, English or non-existent.

Simulated communication (categories 6-7 below)

6 *Simulated communication in Irish (No direct equivalent in the Stirling System)

This category includes all Irish discourse (more than 80% is in Irish) which has the outer form of real communication but where there is some underlying concern with contextualised realistic language practice as well as with the message for its own sake. 'Simulated communication' superficially adheres to the rules of normal discourse (oral or written) but may not be truly open ended, and the pupil may not speak from a really 'personal' self.

Unlike real communication, where the emphasis is on pupils conveying a message as clearly and accurately as possible within the limits of their linguistic ability, pupils engaged in 'Simulated communication' may alter the story line or the intended content of their utterances in order to accommodate the strengths and weaknesses in their own knowledge of the language. At the same time, 'Simulated communication' does imply that the pupil makes some creative contribution and that some element of meaning negotiation is involved. The teacher may prompt or coax the pupil to develop his or her contribution, as long as a real element of pupil initiative remains. Excluded from this category, therefore, are dialogues which have such a formulaic (teacher-determined) structure that the pupils' task consists of no more than the reproduction of well rehearsed lines in a predetermined scenario. Activities of this latter kind should be coded as 'Contextualisation exercises'.

The distinction between 'Simulated communication' and 'Contextualisation exercise' may occasionally be difficult to draw in practice. A borderline example encountered in the present study involved a discussion about an actual event in the classroom which, because it was virtually entirely teacher led and controlled, was finally judged to fall within the category of 'Contextualisation exercise'. Another situation in which the language activity was coded as 'Contextualisation exercise' was where the teacher, in the context of a discussion of an entirely realistic and topical subject, asked questions in such a way that they either incorporated or strongly implied the expected answers. Although many teacher-pupil discussions concerning real life topics are intended as simulated communication exercises, they cannot be assigned to this category in the present system unless some significant freedom to determine the development of the discourse is clearly ceded to the pupil.

Examples:
1. Discourse involved in certain kinds of role play and drama, which mimic real life situations in a manner consistent with the above definition.
2. Pupils in a demonstrating group mime actions while the rest of the class formulate the sentences which describe the actions of the demonstrating group.
3. *Nuachúrsaí Step D* (*Saorchomhrá Cruthaitheach - free creative conversation*): Some of the language activities recommended under this heading fall within the category of 'Simulated communication', as long as pupils can influence the course of the exercise, drama, role play etc.
4. Games such as *Fiche Ceist* (*Twenty Questions*): Even though the questions tend to follow a very predictable pattern in the Irish lesson at this level (i.e. the same kinds of questions are regularly asked each time the game is played), nevertheless the game does involve an information gap which is gradually redefined as the game proceeds.
5. Pupils formulate questions: Language activities which involve pupils formulating questions to be answered by other pupils (e.g. the pupil in the role of teacher) are categorised as 'Simulated communication' even if the questions relate to a familiar story/situation. If the activity is to be assigned to this category, however, the demonstrating pupils must have freedom to choose and formulate the questions themselves (i.e. to introduce some creative element into the exercise), even though their linguistic ability may limit the kinds of questions they are capable of formulating.
6. Written simulated communication: Pupils write a letter to a friend (as an open-ended task), although in effect they largely limit themselves to structures/vocabulary already practised earlier in the lesson.

7 * Bilingual simulated communication
Same as above but discourse is bilingual (20% - 80% of talk is in English).

Real communication (categories 8-10 below)

8 *Real communication in Irish (more than 80% of discourse is in Irish)
This category covers all Irish discourse in which messages are being transmitted and the focus of attention is on the meaning of what is being said.

Messages are defined, for example, as (i) statements containing information (referential or other) which is new to the hearer, or thought by the speaker to be new to him/her (ii) requests for information the speaker does not have (iii) commands to the hearer concerning some action the speaker wants carried out. This contrasts with practice language, where language is produced primarily to give learners training in the manipulation of Irish, and any transmission of messages is incidental. There are no structural or content constraints restricting the allocation of Irish discourse to this category.

Nevertheless, in this category the teacher may modify the language used to suit the pupils' level of competence. The teacher may also take more of the initiative in order to compensate for pupils' linguistic limitations, as long as he/she responds to the pupils' contributions. The provision of occasional words or idioms by the teacher or the translation of English words in passing - occurrences which would be common in certain kinds of 'real life' communication between native and non-native speakers - is permitted under this heading as long as more than 80% of the main discourse consists of real communication in Irish.

Examples:
1. Discussion of grammatical points or imparting new information to pupils on a particular grammatical structure are included here. Real communication can also occur when the teacher gives instructions in Irish with no expected component of immediate public pupil oral response but where the pupils are expected to respond non-verbally (e.g. taking out jotters and preparing a page for an essay) or are expected to act on the instructions at a later date (e.g. homework and how it is to be done). The essential requirements, that the discourse is purposeful and the emphasis is on meaning, are still met.
2. 'Real communication' is also involved if pupils are reading/writing in order to understand/communicate messages and not just doing reading or writing for the sake of the linguistic exercise itself. For example, a pupil may have to read a set of instructions in Irish which are to be acted upon - the focus of the activity then is on the message being communicated in the text.

9 *Bilingual real communication
Same as for 'Real communication in Irish' above but the discourse is bilingual (between 20% and 80% of discourse is in English, remainder in Irish).

10 *Real communication in English
Same as for 'Real communication in Irish' but practically all discourse is in English (more than 80% of discourse in English).

Other activities (categories 11-12 below)

11 *Irish song/poem (no direct equivalent in the Stirling system)
This category includes all Irish discourse where pupils are *reciting* a poem/prayer/song lyric or singing in Irish.

This is really a topic-defined subcategory of the language activity 'Imitation' - we have categorised it as a separate language activity here because it seemed to be a quite distinct type of extended imitation. All other discourse or practice discourse, apart from recitation, relating to songs/poems (choral reading of poems, line by line imitation, discussing the words or meaning of songs etc.) should be coded according to other appropriate categories above.

12 Compound

This category covers all discourse in which distinct exchanges relating to more than one of the previously defined language activity categories, but each shorter than 30 seconds, occur in complex sequences.

Discourse allocated to this category is to be distinguished from that where stray exchanges of another character occur as intrusions into a particular language activity by the regularity of the exchange sequences, and by the fact that alternation is determined by teacher initiative (rather than pupil initiative or pupil error).

Where a body of material is covered using two or more activities in compound fashion, if a particular case of one of the activities lasts for more than 30 seconds, it is not considered to be a new segment.

If an intrusive activity occurs non-systematically within a compound segment, but lasts less than 30 seconds, it is discounted as in other kinds of segment. If it lasts longer than 30 seconds it is an interruption and is coded as an independent segment.

Where a 'Drill' or 'Contextualisation exercise' is elaborated to include systematic pupil repetition of correct responses, it will still be coded as 'Drill' or 'Contextualisation exercise', and not as 'Compound'.

Pupil behaviour

The ways in which teachers require pupils to involve themselves in successive teaching segments is described in terms of overt pupil behaviours. *Pupil behaviour* is coded in terms of seven categories of pupil involvement including the receptive modes of 'Listening', 'Looking' and 'Reading silently', and the productive modes of 'Speaking', 'Reading aloud', 'Doing' and 'Writing'. The single category of 'Reading' in the Stirling System was replaced by two categories 'Reading silently' and 'Reading aloud' in the present *ILAS* adaptation.

Each segment receives a code for the presence of each of these seven behaviours on the basis of teachers intentions regarding pupil involvement. Behaviours may occur singly or in a range of combinations.

Only pupil behaviour which is integral to the dominant language activity for that segment should be included. Behaviours do not have to be sustained over the whole segment in order to be coded as having occured. Pupil behaviours during intrusive activities should *not* be considered. So, if the teacher writes something essential on the board during a particular activity to which the pupil must attend, the pupil behaviour 'Reading silently' will be noted. In the case where there is *no* expectation that the pupils should attend to the written code (e.g. where the teacher writes something on the blackboard which relates to a another task which has not yet been introduced or discussed) no behaviour code should be noted.

1 Listening

Pupils are considered to be in a listening mode of involvement if required to attend to any auditory language source e.g. the teacher, other pupil(s), or a tape recording.

2 Speaking

Pupils are in the speaking mode of involvement if at that moment producing, or actively preparing to produce spoken language (e.g. thinking of a question to ask of another pupil).

3 Doing
Doing involves the carrying out of some non-linguistic overt physical activity in accordance with academic plans determined by the teacher (or by pupil(s), if it is a pupil-directed activity). Examples include drawing a picture, taking out books, mime etc.

4a *Reading silently
Silent reading involves attending to any written text or any other graphic code (from a book, the blackboard etc.)

4b *Reading aloud
The pupil attends to any written text and reads it aloud or is actively preparing to read it aloud.

In a *round robin* reading activity where pupils read aloud one by one, the pupil behaviour is coded 'Listening' and 'Reading aloud' because each pupil is actively preparing to read aloud. If a group are reading aloud in unison, the pupil behaviour codes should be the same (i.e. 'Listening' and 'Reading aloud'). The logic for this is that it is assumed that the pupils are listening to the other pupils in order to keep in step with the activity itself and are themselves actively reading aloud. Similarly, in choral recitation, the pupils are assumed to be listening as well as speaking .

5 Writing
Pupils are in the 'writing' mode of involvement if producing any kind of graphic text or coding (e.g. correcting homework, doing choice tests), or actively preparing to do so.

6 Looking
Looking involves attending to any non-linguistic visual stimulus. This includes visual aids such as film strips, cut outs, and also the blackboard. The pupil could also be looking at another pupil or at the teacher miming. Pupils are considered to be looking at a visual stimulus only if they have been directed to do so or the looking behaviour is an intrinsic element of the learning activity. An incidental reference to a visual item is not enough to be coded as '+ looking'. Looking behaviour does *not* involve situations where the pupil is looking at a person as a normal part of attending to what he/she is saying (e.g. pupils looking at a teacher who is instructing).

Additional coding guidelines for *Pupil behaviour*

The definitions just provided make explicit what is meant by 'Listening' etc. in the case of individual pupils. In observing the interaction of a teacher with a class of 30 or so pupils, however, it is clearly probable that at any one time, individuals or groups of individuals may be involved in different ways in the ongoing lesson. Different pupils may have been allocated a variety of tasks, on a group or individual basis, which involve the activation of different sets of communicative channels. And even within whole class activities, different pupils may be allocated different communicative roles. Thus, an individual pupil or a small group may be given some task of demonstration, and the rest of the pupils may be required to form an audience for this minority.

The following guidelines are proposed for applying the category set in terms of communicative channels to class and group involvement:

1. In whole class interactive discourse, pupil responses may be choral or individual. Where they are choral, clearly all pupils are involved in the same way. Where they are individual, that is, when the rule 'only one person speaks at a time' is in operation, the observer must decide whether the teacher has restricted in any way the obligation on all pupils to be *ready* to contribute to the discourse, at any moment, if called on. This would be the case, for instance, if the teacher had instructed most of the pupils to form an audience for some kind of oral demonstration activity being carried out by a minority of pupils or by an individual.

If this has happened the majority cannot be regarded as being in an active 'speaking' mode. But if no such restrictions have been imposed, the operation of the 'one at a time' rule cannot be regarded as cancelling out the 'Speaking' mode for all.

2. In whole class activities, the mode of involvement of the majority of the pupils will be used to categorise the discourse. Thus, in the case cited above, if most pupils are playing audience while one or two have the sole right to speak, the whole class must be coded as 'Listening' and 'Looking' only, and not 'Speaking'.

3. In group activities, the problem is more complex. Different groups and individuals may have been instructed to use a different selection of communication channels (*Pupil behaviours*), in parallel. The teacher may be interacting with any, or none, of these. The small amount of group work known to occur allows an arbitrary solution to be adopted: as with whole class activities, the mode of involvement of *the majority* only will be coded. This may sometimes necessitate guesswork.

In general, in judging involvement, the central interest is not what the children actually do, but what the teacher intends them to do or gives them a chance to do. We in any case, have a much better guide to teacher intentions than to pupils' inner mental states, in the complex of directions and hints with which the teacher tries to convey his or her intentions to the pupils. The judgements concerning which pupil channels are intended by the teacher to be active at any particular moment, and in particular concerning *changes of state* in the different channels, must therefore be made mainly on the basis of any procedural discourse, in particular on teachers' focussing moves. Additional secondary clues can be gathered from the range of materials immediately available (if a film strip is being shown it seems safe to judge that the teacher means the children to look at it, even if no explicit instruction is given).

The procedure being proposed here for the observer in relation to this dimension is a continuous monitoring of all seven categories of *Pupil behaviour*, independently recording any changes of state which may occur in any behaviour at any time. That is different from that proposed in relation to all other dimensions, where the observer must allocate events to one or other of a mutually exclusive set of complex categories.

The *general rule* to be applied, therefore, when coding *Pupil behaviour* is to include only those pupil behaviours which involve the majority of the pupils in the class and which are intended by the teacher to be integral to the current language activity.

Teacher mode of involvement

This dimension was designed to capture the relationship of the teacher to the pupils, and his/her role in the discourse. Four categories were used, compared to seven in the Stirling System. The 'Monitoring' category below combines a number of categories in the Stirling System - 'Watching and helping', 'Participating', 'Working with group' and 'Working with individual'. For each segment, only one of the categories applies.

1 Instructing

The teacher is communicating with the whole class, typically by speech, but possibly also by public writing, mime etc. and there is no expected component of public pupil response. Pupils may simply be required to attend, or they may be required to respond privately, typically in writing - taking down notes etc.

If the teacher is producing public writing for the pupils to copy or operate on, and there is no expected public pupil response component, one of the two situations may apply:

(i) The period of teacher writing is substantially coterminous with the period provided for pupil response - the pupils are apparently supposed to keep up with the teacher, and completion of their task is expected (though not necessarily achieved) within 30 seconds of the teacher ceasing to write. In this case, the teacher is 'Instructing' and the classroom organisation category (see next section) is 'Whole class'.

(ii) The teacher goes ahead of the pupils, and does not expect them to complete their task within 30 seconds after he/she finished writing. In this case there is no public communication in real time, and so the relevant category of *Classroom organisation* (See description in next section) is 'Individual' and the *Teacher mode of involvement* is *not* 'Instructing'.

Common classroom experience suggests that public teacher writing is normally accompanied by general monitoring of classroom activity and, therefore, in the absence of information to the contrary, the coder should regard the teacher as 'Monitoring' (See third category below) during this activity.

2 Interacting

The teacher engages in interactive public discourse with the whole class. The typical pattern is one of question/response/reaction. While interaction is likely to be with successive pupils singly, 'readiness to speak' is required of all pupils. Substantial patterned *public* pupil responses are required. Typically oral, these may occasionally take other forms e.g. writing on the blackboard, performing public mime.

Pupils' response may be non-verbal. However, where pupils respond *privately* (e.g. in writing) to teachers' oral cues this is *not* 'Interacting'. Pupil responses, verbal or non-verbal, must be contributions to a public discourse for 'interaction' to occur.

3 *Monitoring

The teacher is overseeing the carrying out by pupils of a pre-set task. This may involve observing a whole class oral activity (e.g. a situation drama or a pupil demonstration), or it may involve circulating among pupils who are working on individual seatwork tasks, (e.g. written exercises), and commenting privately on their work. When a tape is being played publicly in a whole class situation the teacher is considered to be 'Monitoring'.

We also include here instances where the teacher is participating in an activity along with all students. For example, the teacher may sing, or repeat taped utterances, with pupils.

4 Not involved

The teacher is not communicating with pupils, nor in general attending to pupil activities. He/she may have given earlier instructions for pupil activity, but is not currently monitoring it. For example, pupils may be involved in some activity the teacher set earlier and the teacher may be silently correcting homework or preparing materials for the next segment/lesson etc.

Classroom organisation

This dimension is concerned with the patterns of class organisation which are intended and implemented by the teacher. There are seven categories as in the original Stirling Study. Only one category applies to each segment.

1 Whole class

There is one central activity going on, dependent on the teacher or another source of stimulus (typically tape or film), but not on a 'Pupil demonstration'. The class functions as one group and the pace of each pupil's activities is determined from moment to moment by the teacher, and/or a central stimulus source and/or class activities, e.g. class discussion.

A typical example is where each pupil takes it in turn to read aloud from their reader (round robin). Another example is where each pupil is ready to ask another pupil a question based on a passage read, but is simultaneously ready to answer any other pupil's question.

2 Pupil/Group demonstration (a special case of 'whole class')
There is one central activity going on, focussed on a pupil or group demonstration. For example, one pupil may take the role of the teacher, or a group of pupils may act out a scene with the rest of the class forming an audience

This category could be considered a special case of group work (as in the examples below), but given the interdependent nature of the roles assigned to the different groups of pupils it was decided to treat it effectively as a special case of 'whole class' work. This has implications for the coding of the 'Language activity': if the larger non-demonstrating group is required to make productive responses ('Speak' and/or 'Write' and/or 'Do'), the activity of this non-demonstrating group is coded. In other cases, the activity of the demonstrating individual or group is coded. This category of *Classroom organisation* will be used even when the teacher is one of the demonstrating group, providing that he/she is not simply acting as teacher to a subset of the class.

3 Cooperative: same task
Pupils are assigned to work cooperatively in more than one group, but groups are assigned identical tasks.

4 Cooperative: different task
Pupils are assigned to work cooperatively in more than one group, and groups are assigned different tasks (differentiated by language activity and/or pupil behaviour).

5 Individual: same task
Pupils are set to work alone, without cooperation, but the task set is identical for all pupils. The pace of each pupil's activities is not dependent on other pupils or on the ongoing activity of the teacher (though there may be an eventual deadline).

6 Individual: different task
Pupils are set to work alone, without cooperation, and at least some individuals are set tasks different from those set for others.

7 Cooperative and individual
Some pupils are working cooperatively in one or more groups and the rest are working as individuals. Tasks may be the same or different between groups and for individuals.

For each segment, only one *Classroom organisation* category above is considered to apply.

Materials

This dimension includes *all* materials used at any time during the lesson segment by either the pupils or the teacher. The code-number of each material used should be written in the appropriate column on the observation sheet.

It will be recalled that the introduction of new materials does not necessitate a change in segment. Only a change in one of the first five dimensions above is critical in this regard. All materials used are coded even if used for only part of the segment (e.g. 'Blackboard' is coded even if the teacher writes on the blackboard only briefly). However, material being prepared for use in subsequent segments and which do not relate to the current segment, should *not* be coded.

Listed below is the range of items used which may be coded.

1.   **Nuachúrsaí handbooks** - Specify the name of the handbook e.g. *'Sean-Neidí'/ 'Lá Faoin Tuath'*.

2. **Other course book/workbook** - Give the name of the commercially produced course book or workbook e.g. 'Bog liom'; 'Anseo is Ansiúd'; 'Slí na nÓg; 'Lean den Obair' etc. Note that materials are coded under this heading even if only the teacher is using them.
3. **Reader.**
4. **Jotter/copy.**
5. **Blackboard.**
6. **Wallchart.**
7. **Worksheet.**
8. **Flashcards.**
9. **Library Books.**
10. **Film strip/slide.**
11. **Cut outs.**
12. **Tape.**
13. **Video/film.**
14. **Overhead Projector.**
15. **Photographs.**
16. **Authentic materials:** These include items such as posters, newspaper articles, advertisements, TV license, tax form in Irish etc.
17. **Objects.**
18. **Person** (other than pupil or teacher): For example, an outsider is brought into the classroom and talks to the pupils about himself/herself and the pupils can ask him/her questions.
19. **Other** (any other materials not covered in the previous categories).

Class attentiveness (No equivalent in the Stirling System)

This dimension is designed to capture the extent to which the majority of pupils are paying attention to the current language activity. It is measured on a five point scale representing 'very low' attention (a rating of '1') to 'very high' attention (a rating of '5') on the part of pupils. This coding can only be done online i.e. by the observers in the classroom.

Only one point on the rating scale is assigned to each segment.

Class interest (No equivalent in the Stirling System)

The extent to which the majority of pupils are interested in the current language activity is rated on a similar five point scale to that above.

Notes on authors' recoding of *Class attentiveness* and *Class interest.*

The original coding of attention and interest was carried out by the observers in the classroom as the segments of the lesson actually unfolded. In the case of the authors' recodings of the lessons based on audio recordings, however, which is the basis for the present analysis, we had to depend entirely on these original data since visual information would be critical in making judgements of this kind.

In order to handle those cases where the segment boundaries as originally determined by the observer in the classroom did not match new boundaries in the authors' recodings of segments, and where attention or interest ratings by the observers actually varied across the relevant segments, we had to develop a systematic procedure for calculating new attentiveness and interest values from the original data provided by the observer. It should be stressed that in the majority of cases the identification of segment boundaries by the observers and the authors either matched very closely, or else diverged in ways which were not problematical as far as recalculating attentiveness and interest ratings were concerned e.g. the observers' attentiveness or interest ratings often remained stable over quite a few segments.

The following examples illustrate the kinds of situations that actually arose, or that could have arisen, and the manner in which the recalculation was accomplished:

1. The starting times of the observer's first segment (segment I-1) and the authors' first segment (segment A-1) corresponded but the authors judged the segment to be longer than the observer did, so that our first segment (A-1) temporally overlapped part of the observer's second segment (I-2). In such cases the class attentiveness and interest ratings for our new segment (A-1) were taken as the same as the ratings of the original observer's segment (I-1), if the duration of the latter accounted for 50% or more of the new segment (A-1).

2. The starting times of segment A-1 and I-1 correspond, but the authors' first segment (A-1) temporally overlapped all of the observer's second segment (I-2). In this instance the attention and interest ratings for our first new segment (A-1) were calculated as the mean of the observer's ratings for his/her first two segments (I-1 and I-2). A similar procedure was applied if the authors' new segment temporally overlapped three or more of the observer's segments.

3. The authors judged that a new segment (A-2) occurred at some point during the observer's first segment (I-1) but the A-2 segment did not finish until the end of the observer's second segment (I-2). Assuming that the observer's rating actually changed from segment I-1 to segment I-2, the rating chosen for our new segment (A-2) was taken to be the observer's rating associated with the lesson segment, or the portion of the lesson-segment, which accounted for the greater proportion of the temporal overlap with A-2.

Appendix 6.4

Lesson transcripts

Transcribing the lessons

All recording study was done on audio cassettes tapes. Video recording was not used for a number of reasons: it would be more disruptive and invasive than audiotaping, and the cost and time involved in training observers would be prohibitive

Two separate audio recordings were made of each lesson as a protection against the possible malfunction of one of the machines. Each of the two observers sat at different ends of the classroom, recording the lesson on high quality C90 cassettes.

Transcription necessitates frequent replaying of small fragments of lesson discourse. It was important, therefore, to have a robust playback mechanism. We also had to estimate segment durations. Bearing these requirements in mind, we chose the Tandberg Educational recorder/player. Unfortunately, we found that the real-time counter was not completely accurate and varied from machine to machine. Consequently all segment durations had to be rechecked using stop watches.

There were a few stages to the transcription process. We began by selecting the better quality tape recording. We then listened to the tape a few times in order to become familiar with the structure and content of the lesson before beginning the transcription proper.

It has been estimated that one lesson can take about 20 hours to transcribe. But this is a conservative estimate. Van Lier (1988: 241) argues that such a product 'will be a rough working transcription' and that 'segments to be used for close analysis and presentation will still need polishing'. He cites the work of Labov and Fanshel (1977) who 'found that after years of working on one relatively short recording, they were still making non-trivial changes to the transcription'. Of course, the nature of the dialogue and the quality of the recording are significant factors in determining how much time is needed to produce an accurate transcript.

The quality of the tape recordings varied rather widely. The teacher's speech was invariably distinct and easily transcribed. In the case of pupils, however, it was often quite difficult to determine what exactly was being said. Nevertheless, pupil utterances which seemed on a first hearing to be completely unintelligible, were often decoded through repeated playbacks and the use of contextual information. Enlisting the assistance of colleagues also proved very helpful in resolving ambiguous dialogue. As Van Lier (1988: 240) points out 'a fresh ear may get it right the first time'.

Background information which would help in interpreting class discourse was assembled and consulted both before and during the transcription process. These sources included:

1. Teachers' reports via the *Teacher Questionnaire* (see Appendix 2.4)
2. Pupils names from the 'Teacher's rankings of pupils' (see Appendix 2.2)

3. Notes made by the inspectors on the *Irish Lesson Analysis System* (*ILAS*) coding sheet regarding materials etc.
4. The actual course-books/workbooks/film strips which were being used by teachers and pupils. For example, transcribing reading-aloud activities (*Transposition*) was greatly simplified by having access to the appropriate readers. Similarly, being able to refer to the *Nuachúrsaí* handbooks and film strips when transcribing *Nuachúrsaí*-related activities frequently helped to clarify uncertainties.

Selecting the sample extracts

The extracts included here are selective in two ways:

1. Seven full lessons from seven different classes were initially transcribed. These particular classes were selected so as to achieve an optimal mix of the social, demographic and educational conditions prevailing in the 20 classes.
2. From these seven transcripts, we selected 24 lesson segments. These segments were chosen so as to represent the relative frequency of, and time spent on, various combinations of the *Topic/Language activity* categories of *ILAS* (see Table 7.13). It will be noted that in the case of three segments which were particularly long, the extract contains only the first two to three minutes of the segment.

The 24 extracts altogether contain over an hour and a quarter of Irish-lesson discourse and run to 39 pages. They are listed under the 17 most frequent *ILAS* topic/language activity combinations. The number of pages allocated to the most frequent combinations roughly corresponds to the proportions for these combinations in Table 7.13. No more than two pages are allocated to the remaining combinations.

The transcript of each segment is identified by the Irish-achievement ranking of the class (1 = highest, 20 = lowest) from which the extract is taken, the lesson number (first or second lesson) and the location of the segment (segment number) within that lesson (e.g. Class 2, lesson 1, segment 5). Each extract is also preceded by a list of the characteristics of that segment in terms of each of the eight *ILAS* coding dimensions.

Given the goals and procedures just outlined, it is clear that the transcripts here cannot be taken as representative of any particular teaching style, approach or method, or of the range of teaching styles and methods generally.

Accuracy of transcripts

The transcriptions were intended to be as detailed and as accurate as possible as far as *classroom interaction* was concerned. Like Van Lier (1988: 242), we include 'all that was said and by whom it was said'. It is a well established fact that spontaneous speech, even in a first language, is replete with errors, self-corrections, false starts and disfluency of various kinds. Since it was not an objective of this study to analyse the teachers' Irish, mispronunciations and relatively minor grammatical errors at the individual-word level (e.g. word-initial changes or word-endings) in the teachers' speech are not recorded unless the teachers themselves drew attention to them by self-correction. No changes in word order or in other aspects of discourse were made.

Grammatical mistakes and more serious mispronunciations in the pupils' speech have been recorded, however, as they often give rise to interactions which, for a short period at least, become the focus of the lesson. English words and phrases in both the teachers' and pupils' speech were transcribed directly as spoken and are printed in italics. It scarcely needs to be said that no assessment of either teachers' or pupils' use of Irish should be based on the extracts here which were neither selected or transcribed with this purpose in mind.

Although our aim was to be as inclusive as possible, we did not want to produce a script that was overly complex. Thus, non-verbal contextual information is kept to a minimum and is included only when it assists the overall interpretation of an utterance.

In those cases where all efforts to decode a troublesome sequence of speech failed we simply marked the discourse as unintelligible using the conventions listed below (an asterisk * representing each unintelligible word). No attempt was made to guess either the content of unclear utterances or the identity of a speaker who was not readily recognised. In cases where there is uncertainty regarding what has been said, the utterances are enclosed in angular brackets.

Conventions for transcription[1]

- The speaker is indicated in the left-hand margin.
  The letter 'T' is used to indicate the teacher speaking.
  The letter 'P' indicates a pupil speaking where it is not possible to identify him/her by name.
  P1:   Indicates the first contribution by a particular pupil in a sequence of spoken exchanges between that pupil and another speaker (usually the teacher). P2 indicates that pupil's second contribution and so forth.
  Pupils: This refers to a situation where more than one pupil is engaged in choral speaking - (usually the whole class or a particular group of pupils e.g. a demonstrating group).
- In order to maintain the anonymity of schools and participants, pupils' names, place names and all other identifying information or references have been changed or deleted. Where place names and references to specific locations have been deleted the missing speech is indicated by curved brackets enclosing an asterisk representing each word deleted e.g. (* *)
- First names taken from the following list of common Irish girls' and boys' names are used as substitutes for actual names of those pupils whom we were able to identify from the recordings:
  Aisling, Anne, Aoife, Breda, Carol, Caroline, Catherine, Ciarán, Claire, Clíona, Conor, Colette, David, Deirdre, Eimear, Elanor, Emma, Fiona, Fionnula, Gemma, Helen, Jason, Jennifer, Joan, John, Julie, Linda, Maeve, Máire, Mairéad, Mark, Mary, Michael, Niamh, Nora, Orla, Patricia, Patrick, Paul, Paula, Pauline, Rachael, Rebecca, Rita, Róisín, Seán, Sinéad, Siobhán, Tara, Tomás, Úna, Yvonne.
- The following surnames were used as substitutes for real ones in the text:
  Garvey, Greene, Martin, Mac Aogáin, Ní Néill, Ó Briain, Ó Floinn, Ó Riain, Ó Sé,

Other conventions

' '   Text which is being read aloud is enclosed in single quotes ' '. Text which is being read aloud from Irish readers is printed exactly as it is spoken (even though the readers themselves were consulted during the transcription process).

" "   Double quotes indicate direct speech in a reading text.

A-B-C   Spellings (where the pupils or teacher spell a word aloud) are indicated by capital letters each separated by a hyphen.

---

[1]   Partly based on Wells (1985).

?	A question mark is used at the end of utterances where an interrogative meaning is considered to have been intended.
!	An exclamation mark is used at the end of an utterance considered to have exclamatory intention.
'	An apostrophe is used for normal contractions and elision of syllables.
italics	English words and phrases are printed in italics.
CAPS	Capitals are used where part of an utterance receives unusually heavy stress to convey emphasis or contrastive meaning.
*	Asterisks are used to indicate unintelligibility, for whatever reason. The number of asterisks corresponds as closely as possible to the number of words judged to have been uttered.
...	Stops are used to indicate pauses. One stop is used for a very short pause. Thereafter, the number of stops used corresponds to the estimated length of the pause in seconds.
..8..	Pauses over 5 seconds in length are indicated by the number corresponding to the length of the pause (e.g. 8 seconds).
___	Underlining: Where utterances overlap because two or more speakers speak at once, the overlapping portions are underlined. In the present context, underlining usually means that pupil(s) and teacher are speaking simultaneously.
-	A hyphen indicates a hiatus, either because the utterance is incomplete or because the speaker makes a fresh start at the word or utterance.
[ ]	Contextual information is enclosed in square brackets.
( )	Interpretations of utterances and descriptions of intonation where applicable are enclosed in round brackets and included immediately after the utterances to which they apply. Only rising intonation (in the case of statements which function as questions) is indicated in the present transcripts .
< >	Utterances, or parts of utterances, about which there is doubt are enclosed in angular brackets; where two interpretations are possible they are both given, separated by an oblique stroke (/).
(sic)	Words emanating from pupils which are transcribed without correction.

Contextualisation exercises - Situation: Other than Nuachúrsaí

Extract 1.

Rank 12, lesson 1, segment 10	Segment duration: 5 mins 24 secs
Topic:	*Situation: Other than Nuachúrsaí* *(Fiaclóir - The Dentist)*
Language activity:	*Contextualisation exercise*
Pupil behaviour:	*Listening, speaking, looking*
Teacher mode of involvement:	*Interacting*
Classroom organisation:	*Pupil demonstration*
Materials:	*Nuachúrsaí film strip, objects*
Class attentiveness:	*Fair*
Class interest:	*Fair*

T: *Right. So*, bhí scuab fiacla ag an bhfiaclóir. Ar aghaidh leat, tabhair aire anois. Bhí scuab fiacla ag an bhfiaclóir. Bhí sé ag múineadh rud éigin don bhuachaill, agus céard a rinne sé? Céard a dúirt an fiaclóir an uair sin? Seo an buachaill. Tar amach anseo. Ha! Ha! Hee! Hee! Tá mise ag breathnú anois. Suígh síos ansin. Is mise an fiaclóir. Mmm. Cad is ainm duit?

Conor: Conor Greene.

T: Conor is ainm dom. Go maith. *Now.* Oscail do bhéal anois. Mmm. Mmm. Mmm. Cad tá i mo lámh agam?

P: Pionsúr.

T: Pionsúr. Bhuel, *not yet.* Sin an pionsúr. Sin an pionsúr. *OK..* Cad tá i mo lámh agam anois?

P: Instealladh. Instealladh.

T: *No.*

P: Scáthán mór.

T: An bhfuil a bhéal mór go leor?

P: Scáthán.

T: Sin scáthán mór. Scáthán?

P: Beag.

T: Scáthán beag. Tá scáthán beag agam. Oscail do bhéal. Mmm. Cad tá á dhéanamh agam anois? ..... *Right.* Bhuel? Bhuel * (pupil name).

P: D'fhéach - D'fhéach an fiaclóir leis * * *

T: Is mise an fiaclóir. Cuir ceist ormsa. Is mise an fiaclóir. Tá mé ag - Tá tú -?

P: * * *

T: *No*, tá tú. *You are.* Bí ag caint mar gheall ormsa. Tá tú ag - ?

P: Tá tú ag ... féachaint i, i gob *.

T:	Go maith. Tá mé ag féachaint isteach anseo agus tá scáthán i mo lámh agam. *Right.* Mmm. Tá *problem* agat anseo, tá fadhb agat anseo. *Problem* mór, fadhb mhór anseo. An raibh tusa ag lí popreoite?
Conor:	Níl.
T:	An RAIBH?
Conor:	Bhí.
T:	An raibh tú ag ithe milseán?
Conor:	Bhí.
T:	Bhí. Mmm. *OK.* Caithfidh mé rud éigin a dhéanamh duit....... *Now,* Conor. Cad a dhéanfaidh mé leis sin?
Conor:	Instealladh a thabhairt dom.
T:	Cad a dhéanFAIDH mé?
P:	Thóg tú instealladh do Conor.
T:	Éinne eile? Seán.
Seán:	Tabharfaidh tú.
T:	Tabharfaidh mé. Cad a dhéanfaidh mé arís?
P:	Tabharfaidh tú.
T:	Cad a dhéanfaidh mé?
P:	Tabharfaidh tú.
T:	Tabharfaidh mé. Cad a dhéanfaidh mé, Michael?
Michael:	Tabharfaidh tú instealladh do Conor.
T:	Tabharfaidh mé instealladh dó. Heh! Heh! Heh! * thug mé an t-instealladh dó. Ar ghortaigh mé thú?
Conor:	Ní.
T:	Níor ghortaigh. Bzzzz (Drill noise). An bhfuil druil agam in áit éigin? Bzzz! *OK.* Rud éigin. Seo an - ? (rising intonation)
Tomás:	Druil.
T:	*OK.* Seo an druil. Cad a dhéanfaidh mé leis an druil? Ó, caithfidh mé pionsúr a fháil ar dtús. Ah. Mionphionsúr. *Now,* féach ar an 'Nua-Litriú' (name of book). Cad tá á dhéanamh agam anois? Ah! [teacher makes a sound imitating the extraction of a tooth] Tá mé ag - ? ...
P:	Ag tarraingt.
P:	Ag stoitheadh fiacaile.
T:	Ag stoitheadh fiacaile. Cad tá á dhéanamh agamsa, Paul?
Paul:	Ag stoitheadh fiacaile
T:	Ag? *Can you give me another word?*
Paul:	Ag .. tarraingt.
T:	Ag tarraingt. Tá mé ag tarraingt na fiacaile. Tá mé ag tarraingt na fiacaile anois. Feicim, Conor, go bhfuil píosa beag ansin, tá sé lofa. Tá sé lofa. Caithfidh mé - .. bhuel?
P:	Druil.
T:	Druileáil a dhéanamh air. ZZzzzzzzz! (drilling noise) Tá sé glan anois. Caithfidh mé rud éigin a chur isteach ann ... Tabharfaidh mé?
P:	Líonadh * *
T:	Caithfidh a fhiacla, a chuid fiacla a - a líonadh. Tá fiacail amháin ansin agus caithfidh mé an fhiacail sin a - ? (rising intonation)

Pupils:	Líonadh.
T:	Líonadh. Caithfidh mé é a - ? (rising intonation)
Pupils:	Líonadh
T:	Abair é sin, John Greene. Caithfidh tú - ?
John:	A líonadh.
T:	é - an fhiacail a líonadh. Cad a dhéanfaidh mé, Jason?
Jason:	Caithfidh tú an fiacla a líonadh.
T:	Caithfidh mé na fiacla a líonadh. *OK*. Fiacail amháin atá ann. Anseo, tá scuab agam. Scuab. Scuab. Cuirfidh mé rud éigin ar an scuab. Cad a chuirfidh mé? Cad a cuirfidh mé ar an scuab? Patrick?
Patrick:	Slaod fiacla.
T:	Slaod. Go maith. Cuirfidh mé slaod. Cén sort scuaibe é? 'Oral B' atá scríofa air. Cén sort scuaibe é?
P:	*Oral B.*
T:	*Oral B.* Cén sort scuaibe? Scuab don úrlar, an ea? Cén sort scuab?
P:	Scuab fiacla.
T:	Scuab fiacla. Tá sé ansin in áit éigin. Scuab fiacla. Tá scuab fiacla agam. Agus cuirfidh mé an - Chuir mé an slaod air. Anois, Conor, oscail do bhéal. Dún do fhiacla. Nuair a bhíonn tú ag glanadh do chuid fiacla, glan mar seo iad. Suas agus síos, suas agus síos. Agus ansin, beidh mé - *or* beidh tú ceart go leor ansin. Beidh tú ceart go leor. *Now.* An raibh tú ag ithe milseán? An bhfuil tú ag ithe mórán popreoite?
P:	Níl.
T:	Go maith. *OK.* Ith bia folláin agus beidh fiacla ceart go leor agat.

(end of segment).

Extract 2.

Rank 3, lesson 1, segment 17	**Segment duration = 2 mins 52 secs**
Topic:	*Situation: Other than Nuachúrsaí ('Timpiste rothair' - A cycling accident)*
Language activity:	*Contextualisation exercise*
Pupil behaviour:	*Listening, speaking, reading silently*
Teacher mode of involvement:	*Interacting*
Classroom organisation:	*Whole class*
Materials:	*Blackboard*
Class attentiveness:	*Very high*
Class interest:	*High*

T:	Ach féach anois ar an méid atá déanta. Focal eile ar timpiste, anois. Beagáinín dul siar. * anois go tapaidh.
P:	Tionóisc.

T:	Tionóisc. Cé hiad na buachaillí a bhí amuigh ag rothaíocht?
P:	Seán agus Ciarán.
T:	Cá bhfuair siad na rothair?
P:	Fuair siad na rothair do bhreithlá.
T:	Dá bhreithlá. Cár chuaigh siad ag rothaíocht?
P:	Chuaigh siad ag rothaíocht faoin tuath.
T:	David, cén sort lae a bhí ann?
David:	Eh Lá fuar
T:	Arís?
David:	Fuar.
T:	Ceart. Bhí sé fuar. Aon rud eile mar gheall air? Cad a bhí ar an dtalamh?
P:	Sleamhain.
T:	Bhí an talamh sleamhain. Maith an fear. Bhí - Cad a bhí ar an dtalamh, mar sin?
P:	Sioc.
T:	Sioc agus sneachta, b'fhéidir, agus leac oighir ar na locha. *Now.* Cá - Cad a dhein siad nuair a chuaigh siad suas go dtí barr an chnoic, Tomás Ó Floinn.
Tomás:	Bhí picnic againn.
T:	Bhí picnic- ? (rising intonation)
Tomás:	Acu.
T:	Maith an fear. Bhí picnic acu. *Now*, nuair a bhí ag - nuair a bhí siad ag teacht anuas, cad a dhein siad? Cad a dhein siad, Deirdre?
Deirdre:	Phreab siad ar na rothair.
T:	Ceart. Conas a bhí siad ag gluaiseacht agus iad ag teacht anuas le fána, Sinéad?
Sinéad:	Bhí siad ag rothaíocht ar nós na gaoithe.
T:	Ceart. Arís (rising intonation).
Sinéad:	Bhí siad ag rothaíocht -
T:	Ceart.
Sinéad:	ar nós na gaoithe.
T:	Ceart. *Now*, bhí sé sin maith go leor. An raibh siad ag rothaíocht go cúramach? Eh .. An raibh siad ag rothaíocht go CÚRamach * (pupil name)?
P1:	Bhí.
T:	Eh?
P2:	Bhí.
T:	Níor mhínigh mé an focal sin, is dóigh liom. 'Go cúramach' - le cúram. 'Cúramach' *means 'careful'*. An raibh siad ag rothaíocht go cúramach?
P3:	Ní raibh siad ..
T:	Ag rothaíocht.
P4:	Ag rothaíocht.
T:	Go cúramach.
P5:	Go cúramach.
T:	Ní raibh. Conas atá a fhios agaibh nach raibh siad ag rothaíocht go cúramach? Anne?
Anne:	Mar bhain siad na lámha de na cluasa.
T:	Mar bhain siad na lámha de na cluasa. Agus dúirt mé go raibh siad cosúil le rud éigin - go raibh siad cosúil le rud éigin .. - go raibh siad cosúil le rud éigin? (rising intonation)
P:	Bhí siad cosúil le dhá fhaoileán.
T:	Ceart. Conas a tharla go raibh siad cosúil le dhá fhaoileán? Mínigh é sin, a Sheáin.

Seán: Mar bhí na (sic) dá lámh amach acu agus bhí siad cosúil le dhá fhaoileán ag eitilt trasna na spéire.

T: Ceart. Agus, ansin, go tobann, chuala siad scréach na gcoscán. *Now* ..

Extract 3.

Rank 8, lesson 1, segment 3	Segment duration = 8 mins 55 secs
Topic:	*Situation: Other than Nuachúrsaí (Maidin na Bainise - The morning of the Wedding)*
Language activity:	*Contextualisation exercise*
Pupil behaviour:	*Listening, speaking, reading silently, looking*
Teacher mode of involvement:	*Interacting*
Classroom organisation:	*Whole class*
Materials:	*Blackboard, photographs*
Class attentiveness:	*High*
Class interest:	*High*

T: *Right. Now.* Píosa an-bheag eile *now* atá le déanamh, - agus caithfidh mé an *chart* seo a bhaint mar ní bheidh slí agam na rudaí go léir a scríobh ar an gclárdubh. *Now.* Maidin na bainise. Beidh an bhainis againn amárach, an dtuigeann sibh? Táimid ag ullmhú inniubh. An dtuigeann sibh?

Pupils: Tuigimid.

T: *Right. Now,* táimid ag ullmhú. *Now,* maidin na bainise atá ann. *Now.* Maidin na bainise. Cad tá le déanamh ag an bhrídeog? .. *Now,* éiríonn sí ar maidin, agus, ar dtús - ? (rising intonation)

Pupils: ..9.. * * * * * [pupils whispering/murmuring]

T: *No*, sula dtéann siad go dtí na gréithre. Ná bac leis na gréithre fós. Bíonn ort dul isteach sa - ? (rising intonation)...

P: Seomra folctha.

T: Seomra folctha. *Good.* An-mhaith. Agus cad a ghlacann tú ann? *Bath?* Ó bhí sé agaibh cheana. Glacann tú - ?

P: *Miss, Miss.* Níonn tú do aghaidh agus do lámh..

T: *No, yes...* Glacann tú folcadh nach ea? *A bath.* Nach ea? Glacann tú - ? (rising intonation)

Pupils: folcadh.

T: * * * * Glacann tú - ?

Pupils: Folcadh

T: Sa seomra folctha. Cad a dhéanann tú ansin? *Now,* an duine seo. Bhuel, a Shinéad?

Sinéad: Chuaigh sé go dtí an *hairdressers.*

T: *Now,* an aimsir láithreach atá ag teastáil, *now.*

P: Téann siad go dtí -

T: An-mhaith. Téann siad go dtí an - ? (rising intonation)

Pupils: .. gruagaire.

T:	Go maith. Ansin, tagann sí abhaile, agus cad a chuireann sí uirthi féin? *Oh, my Lord.*
P:	Cuireann sí an gúna uirthi.
T:	An gúna? (rising intonation)
Pupils:	bainise
T:	Féach ar an gceann seo [Teacher shows a wedding photograph]
Pupils:	Aaaahhh! (gasps of admiration)
T:	* * agus cuireann sí an gúna - ?
Pupils:	Bainise. <u>An gúna bainise.</u>
T:	*Now.* Cad as a ndéantar gúna bainise? Cad as a ndéantar gúna bainise?
Pupils:	*Miss, Miss, Miss.*
T:	*Now*, cad as a bhfuil an ceann seo déanta, b'fhéidir? *Look,.* An stuif sin.
P:	*Lace.*
T:	*Lace. Now*, an Ghaeilge atá ar *'lace'* ná lása. Agus cad eile?
Pupils:	*Miss, Miss, Miss.*
T:	..Tá sé déanta de lása agus *now*, féach! *Now.* Féach an stuif seo. *Look.* An stuif sin.
P:	*Satin.*
T:	*Satin.* * * * * Sról, sról. Sin an Ghaeilge atá ar *satin* An dtuigeann sibh?
Pupils:	<u>Sról.</u>
T:	Cuirfidh mé *'satin'* ansin. [writes word on blackboard]. *Right.* Sról. *So*, de gnáth, bíonn sé déanta de - ? (rising intonation)
Pupils:	Sról, lása.
T:	Lása, lása agus an ceann seo, tá sé maisithe, maisithe, *decorated with*, nach ea. Tá sé maisithe <u>le sról.</u> Tá sé - (rising intonation)?
Pupils:	Maisithe le sról.
T:	Tá sé maisithe le - ? [writing word on blackboard]
Pupils:	sról.
T:	Tá sé maisithe le sról. Agus cad a chuireann sí ar a ceann?
Pupils:	Em *veil.*
T:	*Now.* An rud seo, nach ea? *Now*, caille bhrídeoige an Ghaeilge atá ar sin.
Pupils:	<u>Caille bhrídeoige.</u>
T:	*The wedding veil.* Caille <u>bhrídeoige.</u> Caille bhrídeoige. *Now......* [Teacher writes word on blackboard] Caille <u>bhrídeoige.</u> Cad de a bhfuil sé déanta? Cad as a bhfuil sé déanta?
Pupils:	Lása.
T:	Lása. Tá sé - Tá sé déanta de - ?
Pupils:	Lása.
T:	Agus bíonn bláthanna ar barr chun í a choimeád ar do cheann. Tá ciall ann, nach ea? *Right, right,* * * * * * *Right. Now*, rachaimid siar air go han-tapaidh ar fad. *Now*, ar dtús, cad a bhí againn anseo?
Pupils:	Fáinne pósta.
T:	Cuir suas na lámha a chailíní, más é bhur dtoil é. *Right.* Máire?
Máire:	Fáinne pósta.
T:	*Right.* Úna. Cathain a fhaigheann tú fáinne pósta?
Úna:	......
Pupils:	*Miss, Miss.*

T: Faigheann tú fáinne pósta nuair a - ? .. *Come on*, déan iarracht.
Úna: Phósann tú
T: Nuair a phósann tú. Sin an méid. *Come on.* Go maith. Faigheann tú fáinne pósta nuair a - ? (rising intonation)
Pupils: Phósann tú.
T: *Right.* Cá bpósann daoine de ghnáth? ...
P1: Séipéal
T: An abairt go léir, *now*. Pósann - Póstar, nó pósann daoine de ghnáth - ?
P2: Pósann siad sa séipéal.
T: Sa séipéal. Agus - ?
Pupils: I bparóiste an chailín.
T: I bparóiste - ?
Pupils: An chailín.
T: *Now*, an lá sin.. ar an lá sin, cad tugtar ar an gcailín? Lámha in airde.
P1: Lánúin.
T: An bheirt acu le chéile. An cailín?
P2: Brídeog.
T: An bhrídeog. An - ?
Pupils: Bhrídeog
T: Agus ar an mbuachaill?
P: An fear céile.
T: An fear céile. An-mhaith. Agus an bheirt acu le chéile, Deirdre?
Deirdre: An lánúin.
T: An lánúin. An-mhaith ar fad. *Now*, cé a bhíonn ag cuidiú leo? An abairt - an abairt iomlán atá ag teastáil uaim. *Right*, Rachael? Beidh tú níos fearr an uair seo, le cúnamh Dé.
Rachael: Bíonn na cailíní coimhdeachta ag cabhrú leo.
T: Ag cabhrú leis an gcailín, nach ea? Agus cé a bhíonn ag cabhrú leis an bhfear céile?
Pupils: Na fir (tionlacáin) (mispronunciation of last syllable).
T: *No*, na fir tionlacAIN. Na fir tionlacain. Tionlacain. Agus an cailín beag?
Pupils: Cailín na bláthanna.
T: Cad a bhíonn á dhéanamh ag an gcailín sin. Bíonn sí ag tabhairt aire leis - ar an rud sin, nach ea? Bíonn sí ag tabhairt aire don chaille. Bíonn sí ag tabhairt aire don?
Pupils: Caille.
T: Bíonn sí ag tabhairt aire don chaille, nach ea?
Pupils: Sea.
T: Sin an jab atá aici, nach ea? *Right. Now.* Cad a thugtar ar an rud seo? Lámha in airde. Anois, bhuel Yvonne?
Yvonne: Fáinne gealltanais
T: Fáinne?
Pupils: Gealltanais.
T: Agus nuair a fhaigheann tú fáinne gealltanais, bíonn tú - ?
Pupils: Geallta.
T: Bíonn tú - ?
Pupils: Geallta.
T: *Right. Now.* Anois, bhí an gúna bainise aici. Cad as a dhéantar gúna bainise? Déantar - an abairt iomlán, *now. Come on.* Anne.

Áine:	<u>Déantar gúna bainise</u>
T:	As?
Anne:	Lása agus sról.
T:	An-mhaith. An-mhaith. Agus cad tugtar ar an rud seo?
Pupils:	Lása.
T:	Bhuel, tá a fhios agam go bhfuil sé déanta as lása, ach an rud féin ..
Pupils:	Caille.
T:	Caille - ? (rising intonation)
Pupils:	Caille bhrídeoige.
T:	Caille - ?
Pupils:	Bhrídeoige
T:	Caille - ?
Pupils:	Bhrídeoige.
T:	*Right. Now.* Mí na Meala. Cad tá le déanamh acu le haghaidh an rud seo? Bíonn orthu a gcuid - ? (rising intonation)
Pupils:	Airgid a mhalartú.
T:	Airgead na hÉireann a mhalartú ar airgead na - ? (rising intonation)
Pupils:	Spáinne
T:	Nó airgead na Gréige, nó pé áit a bhfuil siad ag dul ann. *Right.* Cad eile atá le déanamh acu sula bpósann siad? *Come on.* Na rudaí seo go léir atá uaim. Bhuel, Claire?
Claire:	Má bhíonn teach ceannaithe acu, téann siad go dtí an banc chun morgáiste -
T:	a - ?
Claire:	a fháil.
T:	An-mhaith. Chun morgáiste a fháil. Aon rud eile a dhéanann siad, Eva?
Eva:	Tagann an eh an grianghrafadóir agus, em..
T:	Cad a dhéanann siad leis an ngrianghrafadóir? Cuireann siad - ?
Pupils:	In áirithe -
T:	Cuireann siad in - ?
Pupils:	<u>áirithe</u>
T:	é. Cuireann siad in - ?
Pupils:	áirithe é.
T:	An dtuigeann tusa 'in áirithe'?
P:	* *
T:	*Right, right.* Cuireann siad - ?
Pupils:	in áirithe é.
T:	Cuireann siad in áirithe é. Aon rud eile? An t-óstán agus - ? (rising intonation)
Pupils:	an séipéal agus an sagart.
T:	agus rudaí mar sin. *Right. Now.* Is leor sin don lá inniu, is dócha.

(end of segment)

2. Drill - Fragmented topics

Extract 4

Rank 3, lesson 1, segment 1	Segment duration = 3 mins
Topic:	*Fragmented*
Language activity:	*Drill (verbs)*
Pupil behaviour:	*Listening, speaking*
Teacher mode of involvement:	*Interacting*
Classroom organisation:	*Whole class*
Materials:	*None*
Class attentiveness:	*Very high*
Class interest:	*Very high*

T: Anois eh ar maidin, tosnóimid arís leis na briathra. Rithfimid siar anois ar na briathra i dtosach agus beidh muid ag leanacht ar aghaidh inniu leis an Modh Coinníollach, ach tosóimid leis an Aimsir Láithreach, Chaite agus Fháistineach arís. Obair na maidine anois. Cad a dhéanann tusa gach maidin, eh Sinéad?

Sinéad: Dúisíonn mé gach maidin ar a hocht a chlog.

T: Litrigh, Ciarán.

Ciarán: D-U-I-S-E-O-I-N-N.

T: Mícheart.

P: D -U-I-S-Í-O-N-N.

T: Ceart. Cad eile a dheineann tú?

P: Preabann mé amach ar an urlár.

T: Litrigh.

P: P R E A B A N N, preabann.

T: Em .... Cad eile a dheineann tú, Ciarán Ó Sé?

Ciarán: Téann mé

T: Cén áit?

Ciarán: Téann mé síos go dtí an seomra folctha

T: Amach os ard.

Ciarán: Téann mé síos go dtí an seomra folctha

T: Litrigh 'téann'.

P: T-É-A-N-N, téann.

T: Cad eile a dheineann tú?

P: Scuabann -Scuabann mé mo fhiacla.

T: Litrigh 'scuabann', David.

David: S-C-U-A-B-A-N-N.

T: Scuabann mé m'fhiacla. Cad mar gheall ar d'ingne?

P1:   Níonn tú do ingne.

T: Cad a dhéanann TUSA?

P2:   Níonn mé mo ingne.

T:	Litrigh 'níonn'
P:	N-Í-O-N-N. Níonn.
T:	Cad mar gheall ar an tuáille? Cad a dhéanann tú leis an tuáille?
P:	Tirimíonn mé mo aghaidh agus mo lámha.
T:	Litrigh 'tirimíonn', 'tirimíonn', eh Claire?
Claire:	T-R-I-O-M-A-N-N. Tirimíonn.
T:	Ní hea. Éinne eile, anois? Tirimíonn.
P:	T-R-I-O -
T:	Ní hea.
P:	T-R-I-M -
T:	Ní hea. TIrImíonn. (emphasizes 'i' sounds) Éinne eile, anois?
P:	T-I-R-I-M-Í-O-N-N.
T:	Ceart. Maith an fear. Tirimíonn mé m'aghaidh agus mo lámha. *Now,* sin an Aimsir Láithreach. Aimsir Láithreach an rud a dhéanann muid gach lá. Críochnaíonn an Aimsir Láithreach ar Í-O-N-N, E-A-N-N. Dúisíonn mé. Preabann mé. Téann mé. Éiríonn mé. Anois, cad mar gheall ar inné? Cad a dhein mé? Dúisíonn mé gach lá. Cad a DHEIN mé maidin inné?
P:	Dhúisigh mé maidin.
T:	Cad a dhein MISE maidin inné?
P:	Dhúisigh tú.
T:	Cad a dheineamar maidin inné, eh Ciarán?
Ciarán:	Dhúisíomar.
T:	Dhúisíomar. Litrigh 'dhúisíomar', Niamh.
Niamh:	D-H-Ú-I-S-O-M-A-R
T:	Mícheart. A Sheáin?
Seán:	D-H-Ú-I-S-I-O-M-A-R, dhúisíomar.
T:	Dhúisíomar maidin inné ar a hocht a chlog. Phreabamar amach ar an urlár. Litrigh 'phreabamar', Conor Ó Briain.
Conor:	P-H-R-E-A-B-A-I-M
T:	Mícheart. PhreabAMAR. Triail arís é.
Conor:	P-H-R-E-A-B-A-M-A-R.
T:	Ceart. P-H-R-E-A-B-A-M-A-R, phreabamar. Phreabamar amach ar an urlár. Chuamar go dtí an seomra codlata. D'osclaíomar doras, doras an chófra éadaigh. D'osclaíomar. Litrigh d'osclaíomar, eh Lisa. D-, uaschama - .
Lisa:	D-, uaschama, O-S-C-L-A-I-M
T:	A-Í-O-M-A-R, d'osclaíomar doras an chófra éadaigh. *So,* Anois .....

(end of segment)

Extract 5.

Rank 4, lesson 1, segment 20	Segment duration = 3 mins 55 secs
Topic: *Language activity:* *Pupil behaviour:* *Teacher mode of involvement:* *Classroom organisation:* *Materials:* *Class attentiveness:* *Class interest:*	*Fragmented* *Drill [Céim B: Nuachúrsaí]* *Listening, looking* *Monitoring* *Pupil/Group demonstration* *Nuachúrsaí handbook & film strip:* *['Lá Faoin Tuath', Lesson 8]* *Very high* *Very high*

[This lesson was unusual in that the pupils themselves directed a substantial part of it. In the following activity a demonstrating group of pupils practise the vocabulary exercises found in Céim B of the *Nuachúrsaí* 'Lá Faoin Tuath' handbook - Lesson 8)]

Pupils: Foclóir Breise.

P: Troscán. Em Troscán. Sin bord agus cathaoireacha agus eh, rudaí mar - rudaí mar sin. T-R-O-S-C-Á-N.

P: Táilliúir. Táilliúir. Bíonn táilliúir ag ag em deisiú éadaithe em éadaí do em daoine agus em ag ag cuir '*patch*anna' (correct word is 'paistí') agus mar sin ar éadaithe. T-Á-I-L-L-I - I- -Ú-I-R.

P: Em. Leabhair eolais: Sin leabhair a usáidtear chun rudaí a fháil amach. Bíonn gach rudaí - em bíonn beagnach gach rudaí i leabhair eolais faoi daoine, agus faoi daoine a rinne rudaí speisialta agus tíortha. L-E-A-B-H-A-I-R E-O-L-A-I-S.

Conor: Saighdiúir. Saighdiúir. Bíonn saighdiúir le Gardaí de gnáth agus cúpla bhliain ó shin nuair a fuair fear amach as an priosiún bhí na saighdiúirí ag féachaint eh leis na Gardaí agus bíonn sé - bíonn gunnaí leo agus bíonn éadaí glasa orthú. Saighdiúir. S-A-I-G-H-D-I-Ú-I-R.

Pupils: Céard * * * * * * * a mháistir?

T: Tá <sé/sin> go deas.

P: Em An Céim a Ceathair.?

    [Projector is switched on and all pupils look at pictures]

P: Siúinéir is ea athair Máiréad.

P: Báicéir is ea athair Séamus.

Deirdre: Gruagaire is ea athair Tomás.

Pádraig: Siopadóir is ea athair Síle.

Conor: Tiománaí is ea athair Mícheál.

P: An chéad cheann eile.

P: Téann sí go dtí - ..

Pupils: An Briathar.

    [Here the projector is switched off. In the following exercise pupils select a verb and different pupils list/recite (rapidly) the different tense and person forms of that verb].

P: Tá an briathar 'ól' againn agus tá Deirdre ag tosnú.
Deirdre: Anois tá mé ag ól - Tá mé, Tá tú, Tá sé, Tá sí, Táimid, Tá sibh, Tá siad.   An Saorbhriathar: táthar. Níl mé ag ól. An bhfuil mé ag ól?
P: Inné - D'ól mé tae. D'ól mé, D'ól tú, D'ól sé, D'ól sí, D'ólamar, D'ól sibh, D'ól siad. An Saorbhriathar: Óladh. Níor ól sé. Ar ól sé?
P: Gach lá ólaim bainne. Ólaim, ólann tú, ólann sé, ólann sí, ólaimíd, ólann sibh, ólann siad, An Saorbhriathar, óltar. Ní ólann sé bainne. An ólann sé bainne?
P: Amárach, ólfaidh mé bainne. Ólfaidh mé, ólfaidh tú, ólfaidh sé, ólfaidh sí, ólfaimid, ólfaidh sibh, ólfaidh siad. An Saorbhriathar, ólfar. Ní ólfaidh mé bainne. An ólfaidh mé bainne?
Conor: * * * d'ólainn, d'óltá, d'óladh sé, d'óladh sí, d'ólaimis, d'óladh sibh, d'ólaidís, An Saorbhriathar. D'óltaí. Ní óladh sé liomanáid. An óladh sé tae?
[Projector switched on again and demonstrating pupils describe pictures using the correct prepositional pronouns.]
P: An chéad cheann eile, mas é do thoil é? [Céim 3]
Deirdre: D'iarr sé uirthi leabhar a fháil dó.
P: D'iarr Máire air leabhar a fháil di eh.
Deirdre: D'iarr sé uirthi an doras a dhúnadh.
P: D'iarr sí uirthi a paidreacha a rá.
Conor: D'iarr sí uirthi an carr a ghlanadh.
P: D'iarr sí uirthi instealladh a fháil.
P: D'iarr sí uirthi mála a chur suas.
Pupils: An chéad cheann eile. [Céim 4]
P: Bhí beirt nó triúr sa leabharlann roimpi.
Conor: Bhí an máistir isteach romham ar maidin.
P: Chuaigh mé - Ar chuaigh tú go dtí an leabharlann? Agus bhí beirt nó triúr isteach romhat, Deirdre.
Deirdre: Tá Séamus Mac Aogáin thíos ansin agus bhí beirt nó triúir páistí isteach romh - istigh roimhe ar maidin.
P: Em Tá Máire Ó Néill thíos ansin agus bhí an máistir istigh roimpi ar maidin.
P: Bhí - Bhí an máistir istigh - istigh romhainn ar maidin. An raibh an máistir istigh romhaibh? Agus bhí an máistreas istigh rompu sa seomra eile.
Pupils: Romham, romhat, roimhe, roimpi, romhainn, romhaibh, agus rompu sa seomra eile. An chéad cheann eile.
P: Ceard atá á léamh aige? [Céim 5]
P: Céard tá á léamh aige?
P: Tá leabhar á léamh aige - agam .
Deirdre: Céard atá á scríobh agat?
Conor: Tá litir á scríobh aige.
P: Céard atá á ghlanadh agat?
P: Tá- tá an fhuinneog á ghlanadh agam.
Conor: Céard tá á bhriseadh aige?
P: Tá an fhuinneog á bhriseadh aige.
Conor: Céard tá á cheannach aige?
P: Tá milseáin á cheannach aige.
Pupils: Sin an méid.
(end of segment)

3. Contextualisation exercises - Situation: Nuachúrsaí [1]

Extract 6.

Rank 10, lesson 1, segment 3	Segment duration = 18 mins 19 secs (first 3 minutes only)
Topic:	*Situation: Nuachúrsaí ('Dóiteáin' - A fire)*
Language activity:	*Contextualisation exercise*
Pupil behaviour:	*Listening, speaking, looking*
Teacher mode of involvement:	*Interacting*
Classroom organisation:	*Whole class*
Materials:	*Nuachúrsaí handbook & film strip ('Sean Neidí', Lesson 34 - 'Dóiteáin')*
Class attentiveness:	*Very high*
Class interest:	*Very high*

T: *All right.* Féach anois air seo..... *Right.* An féidir le héinne cur síos a dhéanamh ar an bpictiúr sin le bhur dtoil? Bhuel, Rachael?

Rachael: Bhí deatach * * * * * agus bhí daoine ag rith ar an sráid

T: Maith an cailín. Ag rith ar an tsráid. Ana-mhaith. Yvonne?

Yvonne: Em. Bhí cailín le gúna glas ar a rothar.

T: Maith an cailín. Tá cailín ag marcaíocht ar, nó ag rothaíocht ar, rothar. Ana-mhaith. Colette?

Colette: Em. Bhí na daoine ag * * * * * * *

T: Ana-mhaith ar fad. Maith an cailín. Máire?

Máire: B'fhéidir go mbeadh em na daoine sa bhaile mór agus em bhí siad ag siopadóireacht.

T: B'fhéidir go raibh siad ag siopadóireacht. Maith an cailín. Éinne eile? Catherine?

Catherine: Em. Bhí an tine mór - bhí an tine mór agus bhí na daoine eagla.

T: Bhí eagla ar na daoine. Maith an cailín. Niamh?

Niamh: Bhí dhá simléar ar an díon.

T: Ana-mhaith. Bhí dhá shimléar ar an díon. Cad tá ag teacht amach as an díon? Cad tá ag teacht amach as an díon? Bhuel, Sinéad?

Sinéad: Bhí a lán deatach ag teacht amach as.

T: Ana-mhaith. Agus cén dath atá air? Cén dath atá air, Mary?

Mary: Dubh

T: Maith an cailín. Dath dubh *Right*, aon rud eile atá le feiceáil sa phictiúr sin. Claire?

Claire: Tá a lán - tá a lán fuinneoga ar - ar an teach.

T: Ar an teach. Maith an cailín. Tá a lán fuinneog ar an teach. Em, an gceapann tú go bhfuil gach rud ciúin sa tsráid? An bhfuil gach rud ciúin sa tsráid? Bhuel ?

P1:   Níl

---

[1] Where only an extract from a segment is given, it is possible that the portion not reproduced has a bearing on the coding.

T:	Bhuel, tá - ? (rising intonation)
P2:	Tá daoine * * ag iarraidh * fios a chur ar an mbriogáid dóiteáin.
T:	Ana-mhaith. Chun fios a chur ar an mbriogáid dóiteáin. Ana-mhaith. Deirdre?
Deirdre:	Em ní - ní raibh em aon drithlí sa - ag teacht amach - teacht amach as an simléar ach em. mar dá mbeadh * * * * siad ag dul isteach sa teach beidh * * * *
T:	Ana-mhaith ar fad. An féidir leat an focal drithlí a mhíniú don rang? An bhfuil a fhios ag gach duine cad is brí le drithlí?
Deirdre:	*Sparks or* *
T:	*Sparks.* Maith an cailín. Maith an cailín. Anois, féach ar an bpictiúr seo. Cé atá le feiceáil sa phictiúr seo? Bhuel, Joan?
Joan:	Tháinig garda ar an treo agus -
T:	Os ard anois...
Jane:	Tháinig garda ar an treo agus bhí sé ag caint leis na daoine.
T:	Bhí sé ag caint leis na daoine. Agus, cad tá á rá aige, an gceapann sibh? Cad tá á rá ag an ngarda? Em, bhuel Yvonne?

(end of 3 minute extract)

Extract 7

Rank 9, lesson 2, segment 4	**Segment duration=23mins 51secs (first 3 minutes of segment only)**
Topic:	*Situation: Nuachúrsaí ('Dóiteáin' - A fire)*
Language activity:	*Contextualisation exercise*
Pupil behaviour:	*Listening, speaking, looking*
Teacher mode of involvement:	*Interacting*
Classroom organisation:	*Whole class*
Materials:	*Film strip (Sean Neidí: Lesson 34)*
Class attentiveness:	*Very high*
Class interest:	*High*

[In this segment the teacher asks pupils questions based on the pictures from the *Nuachúrsaí* film strip - Lesson 34.]

T:	Anois, Tomás, or eh - Cuir an rud ar siúl, más é do thoil é. Dún cúpla dallóg ansin dom, Deirdre .. 15 .. Léigh é sin dom anois.
Pupils:	'An Roinn Oideachais. Sean-Neidí. Cúrsa Comhrá Gaeilge le haghaidh ardranganna. Rialtas na hÉireann, naoi déag seachtó naoi. Rang a sé, ceacht a tríocha ceathair.'
T:	Tá go maith. An chéad phictiúr eile. Cad a chuala na páistí?
Pupils:	Chuala na páistí adharc á séideadh.
T:	Cén sort adhairce a chuala siad á séideadh, adharc cairr an ea?
Pupils:	Adharc an bhriogáid dóiteáin.

T:	Adharc an bhriogáid dóiteáin. Chuala siad adharc an bhriogáid dóiteáin. Cén fáth go raibh an bhriogáid dóiteáin ag teacht agus an adharc á séideadh?
Pupils:	Mar bhí tine ..
T:	Mar bhí tine trí thine, an ea?
Pupils:	Mar bhí teach, siopa -
T:	Teach a bhí trí thine, an ea?
Pupils:	Bhí siopa, siopa, siopa.
T:	Bhí siopa trí thine, nach ea?
Pupils:	Sea.
T:	Cá raibh an siopa?
Pupils:	* * * .
T:	Cá raibh an siopa?
Pupils:	Bhí an siopa .. sa chathair.
T:	Sa chathair, nó sa sráidbhaile, nach ea?
Pupils:	Sea.
T:	An raibh a lán daoine ar an tsráid?
Pupils:	Bhí a lán daoine ar an tsráid.
T:	Cad a bhí san aer?
Pupils:	Bhí deatach san aer.
T:	An chéad phictiúr eile. Cá ndeachaigh na buachaillí nuair a chuala siad an adharc á séideadh?
Pupils:	Chuala -
T:	Cá NDEACHAIGH siad?
Pupils:	Chuaigh siad timpeall an chúinne
T:	Chuaigh siad timpeall an chúinne. Ar shiúil siad nó ar rith siad, meas tú?
Pupils:	Rith siad.
T:	Cén fáth ar rith siad, meas tú?
Pupils:	Chun an * * an tine * * * [many different suggestions being given by pupils].
T:	Ach cén fáth ar rith siad? Cén fáth nár shiúil siad?
Pupils:	Mar * * * * * * (many different suggestions again)
T:	An raibh deifir orthu?
Pupils:	Bhí deifir orthu.
T:	Ar eagla go mbeadh pé rud a bhí ann imithe, nach ea?
Pupils:	Sea.
T:	*So*, rith siad. Ar stop éinne iad?
Pupils:	Stop an garda iad.
T:	Sagart paróiste a stop iad, an ea?
Pupils:	Ní hea.
T:	Máistir scoile?
Pupils:	Ní hea.
T:	Cé a stop iad?
Pupils:	Stop an garda iad.
T:	Cén fáth ar stop an garda iad?
Pupils:	Mar * * * (many different suggestions from pupils)
T:	Mar?
Pupils:	Mar * * * (pupils repeat their suggestions)
T:	B'fhéidir go mbeadh - (rising intonation)?

Pupils: * contúirt * * *.
T: Contúirt ar an tsráid, nach ea?
Pupils: Sea.
T: Áit a raibh an tine. Ar stop sé gach duine?
Pupils: Stop sé gach duine.
T: An chéad phictiúr eile.

[This general pattern of interaction continues for remainder of segment.]

(end of 3 minute extract)

4. Simulated communication in Irish - Situation: Other than Nuachúrsaí

Extract 8.

Rank 4, lesson 1, segment 22	**Segment duration = 2 mins 2 secs**
Topic:	*Situation: Other than Nuachúrsaí (Word game - Twenty Questions)*
Language activity:	*Simulated communication in Irish*
Pupil behaviour:	*Listening, speaking*
Teacher mode of involvement:	*Monitoring*
Classroom organisation:	*Pupil demonstration*
Materials:	*None*
Class attentiveness:	*Very high*
Class interest:	*Very high*

P: An Smaoineamh. (name of word game - a version of '20 Questions')
Ciarán: Tá mise ag smaoineamh ar rud éigin a bhí sa Bhuntús agus ceist, a Mháistir, an bhfuil cead agam an rud seo a dhéanamh mé féin?
T: Tá.
Ciarán: Go raibh maith agat, a mháistir, agus tosnóidh mé ansin.
P: Cé mhéad litir atá sa focail seo?
Ciarán: Cúig
P: Cá bhfaigheann tú an rud seo de ghnáth?
Ciarán: Is féidir leat é a fháil aon áit.
P: An rud teibí é?
Ciarán: Ní rud teibí é.
P: Cén dath a bhíonn ar an rud seo?
Ciarán: Ó! Bíonn an dath donn agus dubh.
P1:   An bhfuil an rud seo - An bhfuil an rud seo sa seomra seo?
Ciarán: Anois?
P2:   Sea.
Ciarán: Níl.

P:	Em. Em .
Ciarán:	Rómhall agus * * * * *.
P:	An féidir leat an rud seo a cheannach?
Ciarán:	Is féidir leat an rud seo a cheannach.
P:	An bhfuil sé mór nó beag?
Ciarán:	D'fhéadfadh é a bheith mór nó beag.
P:	An féidir leat é seo a thabhairt suas i do láimh?
Ciarán:	Is féidir.
P	An féidir an rud seo a ithe?
Ciarán:	Is féidir.... Em. Rómhall. Tá bua * * * <caite> go léir. Is casúr é.
P:	Tá mise ag smaoineamh ar rud éigin a bhí sa Bhuntús. Agus ceist agam, a Mháistir, an bhfuil cead agam an rud seo a dhéanamh mé féin?
T:	Gabh mo leithscéal.
P:	Ní féidir leat casúr a ithe
T:	Ní féidir leat casúr a ithe.
Ciarán:	Ach dúirt mé nach féidir leat.
Pupils:	Dúirt tú "is féidir leat".
Ciarán:	Déanfaidh mé ceann eile.
T:	Caithfidh mé na marcanna a thabhairt do Niamh.
Niamh:	Tá mise ag smaoineamh ar rud éigin a bhí sa Bhuntús. Agus ceist agam, a Mháistir, an bhfuil cead agam an rud seo a dhéanamh mé féin?
T:	*
Niamh:	Go raibh maith agat a mháistir, agus tosnóidh mé ansin.
P:	Cé mhéad litir atá ann?
Niamh:	Tá trí déag litir.
P:	An rud teibí é?
Niamh:	Ní rud teibí é.
P:	Cá bhfaigheann tú an rud seo de ghnáth?
Niamh:	Ar an talamh, de ghnáth.
P:	Cé mhéad fhocal atá ins an <rud seo>?
Niamh:	Fhocal, fhocal (sic) amháin.
P:	An bhfuil an rud seo trom?
Niamh:	Tá. D'fheadfadh é -
P:	Is leabharlann é.
Niamh:	Ní leabharlann é.
P:	<u>Cén dath a bhíonn ar an rud seo?</u> (Two pupils speak almost simultaneously)
Niamh:	Sin ceist amaideach, mar ní rud teibí é. * * * .
Pupils:	* * * * <b'fhéidir>
P:	Is leabharlannaí é.
Niamh:	IS leabharlannaí é.
P:	<Cé mhéad> marcanna?
T:	Cúig déag.

(end of segment).

Extract 9

Rank 3, lesson 1, segment 11	Segment duration = 4 mins 49 secs
Topic:	*Situation: Other than Nuachúrsaí*
Language activity:	*Simulated communication in Irish (role play)*
Pupil behaviour:	*Listening, speaking*
Teacher mode of involvement:	*Monitoring*
Classroom organisation:	*Pupil demonstration (2 pupils answering questions about their birthday & presents)*
Materials:	*None*
Class attentiveness:	*High*
Class interest:	*Very high*

T: *Now.* Nuair a bhíonn breithlá agat, bíonn féasta agat, agus do dheineamar é sin cheana mar gheall ar an bhféasta agus an, eh, an eh, an eh - ithe agus an scléip agus an spórt a bhí agaibh. Anois, tar amach agus déanfaimid beagáinín beag cainte anois ar an mbreithlá sin. Tar amach Seán Garvey, Máire Ní Néill - agus Máire Ní Néill (same girl).

  Now, sibhse anois a bheidh ag caint mar gheall ar an mbreithlá i dtosach, mar dul siar. Cuir tú féin in aithne, a Sheáin.

Seán: Is mise Seán Garvey agus bhí mo bhreithlá agam ar an ceathrú lá déag de Mhí na Márta.

Máire: Is mise Máire Ní Néill agus bhí mo bhreithlá ar an t-aonú lá de Mhí Aibreáin.

T: *Now,* cuirigí ceisteanna orthu. Lean ar aghaidh. Ceist uait. Gach duine anois le ceist.

P: A Sheáin, cén aois a bhí tú?

Seán: Bhí mé trí bhliain déag d'aois, an lá sin.

T: Eh.

P: A Sheáin, an raibh féasta agat?

Seán: Bhí féasta mór agam sa bhaile an tráthnóna sin agus thug mé cuireadh do mo chairde go léir.

P: Déan cur síos ar do fhéasta.

Seán: Bhí cáca mór againn agus bhí reóan agus trí choinneall déag air.

T: Ceist air anois.

P: Cé rinne - Cé a rinne do cháca milis?

Seán: Rinne mo Mhamaí an císte milis agus fuair sí a lán rudaí san siopa agus fuair sí reóan agus plúr agus bainne.

T: Tá go maith.

P: A Mháire, cad a fuair tú do do bhreithlá?

Máire: Fuair mé em rothar deas nua agus em fuair mé a lán beart ó fear an phoist.

P: A Mháire, an raibh tú sásta leis na féiríní?

Máire: Bhí mé an-sásta leis na féiríní.

P: Cén sort beart - beartanna a fuair tú?
T: Arís?
P: Cén sort beartanna a fuair tú?
Máire: Fuair mé scairf agus * agus gúnaí nua agus a lán rudaí eile.
T: Em. *
P: Cad eile a fuair tú?
Máire: Fuair mé em ..... fuair mé em airgead ó mo athair agus mo mháthair.
T: Go maith.
P: A Sheáin, ar fuair (sic) tú aon rud ó fear an phoist.
Seán: Eh Fuair mé a lán litir agus em cártaí ó fhear (sic) an phoist.
T: Ciarán?
Ciarán: A Sheáin, cé mhéad cairde a bhí agat ag do bhféasta?
Seán: Bhí timpeall deich cairde agam ag an bhféasta agus bhí an-spórt againn ag éisteacht le céirníní agus ag imirt peile.
T: Sea. Deichniúr. Duine beirt triúr, nuair a bhíonn tú ag caint ar dhaoine.
P: Cén sort bronntanas a fuair tú?
Seán: Fuair mé bríste nua agus fuair mé rothar deas nua freisin ó mó athair.
P: Déan cur síos an rothar.
T: AR an rothar
P: Ar an rothar.
Seán: Bhí fráma dearg air agus bhí slabhra - slabhra glas, agus bhí triotháin dhonna agus ..
T: Tá go maith. David, níor chuir tú aon cheist go fóill. Ceist. *Come on.*
David: Cad a, cad chuige an cloigín?
T: Arís?
David: Cad chuige an cloigín?
T: Sea. Cad chuige an cloigín?
Seán: Nuair a bhíonn mé ag druidim le cúinne, * tharraing mé an cloigín.
T: "Tharraing mé", a dúirt sé. Ní dóigh liom. Cad a dhein sé leis an gcloigín? Focal eile?
P: Bhuail.
T: Bhuail mé an cloigín. Ceart. Ceist anois. Lean ar aghaidh.
P: Cár chuaigh tú ag rothaíocht tar éis an *
Seán: Chuaigh mé ag rothaíocht suas an bóthar ard.
T: Sea. Aon cheist eile anois? David?
David: Conas a polladh ar an roth?
T: Conas?
David: Conas a polladh ar an roth?
T: Bhuel, níl a fhios agam...
P: Conas a dheisigh a - a athair an roth?
T: Ach ní raibh éinne ag caint mar gheall ar pholl sa rothar go fóill.
P: Ar polladh do roth riamh?
Seán: ..Polladh mo roth nuair a bhí mé ag dul síos an bóthar ard.

(end of segment)

5. Transposition - Situation: Other than Nuachúrsaí

Extract 10

Rank 10, lesson 1, segment 9	Segment duration = 4 mins 51 secs

Topic:	*Situation: Other than Nuachúrsaí ('Dóiteán' - A fire.)*
Language activity:	*Transposition (read aloud)*
Pupil behaviour:	*Listening, reading aloud*
Teacher mode of involvement:	*Monitoring*
Classroom organisation:	*Whole class*
Materials:	*Reader (Seal ag Léamh I, page 88)*
Class attentiveness:	*Very high*
Class interest:	*Very high*

T: *OK.* Tosóimid anois ag léamh. Dóiteán. Tosaigh ag léamh, le do thoil, Helen.
Helen: 'Bhí Aindí tuirseach tar éis an lae.'
T: Go maith. Sinéad?
Sinéad: 'Cuir sé an teilifís ar shiúl.'
T: Ar SIÚL.
Sinéad: 'Ar siúl agus shuígh sé síos dó féin.'
T: 'Dó féin'. *Right.* Máire?
Máire: ' "Beidh <tíotáin> (mispronounced) amháin." '.
T: Beidh - ? (rising intonation)
Máire: ' "Beidh <tiotáin> (sic)" '
T: ToitÍN.
Máire: 'Toitín amháin. ' "Beidh toitín amháin agam anois," ar seisean leis féin, "agus ansin rachaidh mé a codladh." '
T: A chodladh. *Right.* Aoife?
Aoife: 'Chuir sé an toitín sa chiseán nuair a bhí críochnaithe aige leis'.
T: Joan?
Joan: 'Suas an staighre leis ansin agus chuaigh sé a chodladh.'
T: *Right.* Caroline?
Caroline: 'Ní raibh an toitín múchta i gceart aige.'
T: *Right.* Eimear?
Eimear: 'Dúisigh Aindí.'
T: Go maith, DHúisigh Aindí. Rita Martin?
Rita: ' "Nach bog an aimsir í", ar seisean leis féin. "Tá sé an-te anseo istigh" '.
T: *Right.* Fionnula?
Fionnula: 'Chuir sé a shrón san aer.'
T: Maith an cailín. Mairéad?
Mairéad: Eh ' "Ce - .. Cén - .. Cén boladh é sin?" ar seisean leis féin.'

T:	Maith an cailín. Cén boladh é sin? *Right*. Úna?
Úna:	'Lig sé béic as. "Deatach! Tine! Ó go sábhálá Dia sinn. Tá an teach trí thine." '
T:	Maith an cailín. Orla?
Orla:	'Léim sé as a leaba.'
T:	*Right*. Carol?
Carol:	'D'oscail sé an doras.'
T:	*Right*, Elanor?
Elanor:	'Dhún - Dhún sé go tapaidh arís é, áfach'
T:	Go maith. Fiona?
Fiona:	'Bhí bun an tí ar fad trí thine.'
T:	Maith an cailín. Patricia?
Patricia:	'Thosaigh sé ag <casacht> (mispronunciation) mar bhí an deatach ag teacht isteach faoin doras.'
T:	Maith an cailín. Féach anois go géar - ag casacht - ? (rising intonation).
Patricia:	Casachtach.
T:	Maith an cailín. *Right*, Siobhán?
Siobhán:	' "Níl aon dul as agam," ar seisean leis féin. "Caithfidh mé triail a bhaint as an bhfuinneog." '
T:	*Right*. Tara?
Tara:	'D'oscail sé an fhuinneog.'
T:	*Right*. Em, Linda?
Linda:	'Faoin am seo, bhí cuid de na comharsana bailithe taobh amuigh.'
T:	*Right*. Clíona?
Clíona:	' "Faigh dréimire," a bhéic fear acu.'
T:	*Right*. Em Tara, ar léigh tusa? Maeve?
Maeve:	' "Cuir fhios ar an.." '
T:	Cuir - ?
Maeve:	' " Cuir fhios.." '
T:	Cuir - ? (rising intonation)
Maeve:	' "FIOS ar an mbriogáid dóiteán," arsa fear eile.'
T:	*Right*. Nora?
Nora:	' "Léim, Aindí! Léim!" arsa fear eile fós'.
T:	*Right*. Maith an cailín. Rebecca?
Rebecca:	' "Fan nóiméad, Aindí," arsa athair Phóil.'
T:	*Right*. Aisling?
Aisling:	Em, ' "Beidh blaincéad mór láidir againn i gceann nóiméid agus beidh tú em abál- .. abál- .. abál- "' (mispronouces beginning of word)
T:	Ábalta.
Aisling:	' "Ábalta léim." '
T:	Maith an cailín. *Right*. Emma?
Emma:	'D'oscail siad amach an blaincéad agus rug ceathair - ceathrar fear ar na cúinní.'
T:	*Right*. Rebecca? *You read*. Em, Jennifer?
Jennifer:	' "Léim anois, Aindí," arsa duine acu.'
T:	*Right*. Em, Róisín?
Róisín:	'Bhí Aindí díreach chun léim nuair a stop sé go tobann.'
T:	Go maith. Julie?
Julie:	' "Mo bhriste (sic) ," ar seisean.'

T:	*No, not* 'mo bhriste', 'mo - ? (rising intonation)
Julie:	bhriste.
T:	Ní hé - mo - ?
Julie:	' "Mo bhrístí (sic)," ar seisean.'
T:	"Mo bhrÍste," ar seisean. Go maith. Deirdre?
Deirdre:	' "Rinne mé dearmad glan ar mo bhríste." '
T:	*Right.* Breda?
Breda:	'Isteach leis arís.'
T:	Em, Go maith. Orla? Ar léigh tusa? Rita, ar léigh tusa?
Rita:	'Bhí an seomra lán de deatach agus bhí Aindí ag casachtach.'
T:	Go maith. Lámha suas éinne nár léigh go fóill. *Right*, Yvonne?
Yvonne:	'Tharraing sé a bhríste féin, rith sé go dtí an fhuinneog - fhuinneog agus léim sé amach.'
T:	Maith an cáilín. Pauline?
Pauline:	'Bhris an blaincéad an titim, ach mar sin féin ghortaigh Aindí a chos agus a lámh.'
T:	Maith an cailín. Mary?
Mary:	' "Conas atá tú?" arsa athair Phóil leis.'
T:	*Right.* Gemma?
Gemma:	' "Níor cheart dom gearán," arsa Aindí.'
T:	*Right.* Em, Rachael?
Rachael:	' "Féach an - ... D'fhéach.. - " '
T:	' "D'fhéadfadh an - " ' ..
Rachael:	' "D'fhéadfadh an scéal bheith i bhfad níos measa." '
T:	Maith an cailín. Em, Paula?
Paula:	' "Nach mór an -" '
T:	Bhuel, ar ais arís go dtí an tús, le do thoil.
Paula:	'Bhí Aindí tuirseach tar éis an lae.'
T:	Ana-mhaith. Ar léigh gach duine anois?
P:	'Chuir sé an teilifís ar siúl agus suigh sé síos dom féin.'
T:	'DÓ féin.' *OK.* Maith an cailín.

(end of segment)

6. *Simulated communication in Irish - Pupil/Teacher real life situations*

Extract 11

Rank 9, lesson 2, segment 6	**Segment duration=17 mins (2 minute extract)**
Topic:	*Situation: pupil/teacher real life ('Timpiste a tharla' - 'An accident')*
Language activity:	*Simulated communication in Irish*
Pupil behaviour:	*Writing*
Teacher mode of involvement:	*Interacting*
Classroom organisation:	*Individual: same task*
Materials:	*Jotter/copy, Overhead projector*
Class attentiveness:	*Very high*
Class interest:	*Very high*

[Pupils start writing an essay which had been set by the teacher in a previous segment. The title of the composition is 'Timpiste a tharla': the pupils must write about an accident which happened to them or which they witnessed. The majority of the class are concentrating on writing the essay. Although the pupils are allowed to ask questions if they need help, the main pupil behaviour involved is writing.

This is a short extract from an unusually long segment]

P: An scríobhfaimid san Aimsir Chaite?

T: Ins an Aimsir Chaite, sea. Sin a dúirt mé. Scríobh é ins an Aimsir Chaite. .. 8 ..
Agus cuirigí ceisteanna orm anois, aon fhocal nach féidir libh a litriú, aon fhocal nach féidir libh a rá i gceart i nGaeilge. Tá foclóir ar gach binse freisin, nach bhfuil?

Pupils: Sea. Tá.

T: Úsáid é sin freisin. Munar féidir libh na focail a fháil sa bhfoclóir, cuir ceisteanna ormsa. .. 15 ..

P: *Final. Final.* Conas a déarfá *'final'*?

T: Cluiche ceannais. .. 10 .. Cluiche ceannais .....

P: Conas a déarfá *'one night'*?

T: Éinne? Conas a déarfá *'one night'*

P: Oíche amháin.

T: Oíche amháin .. 20 .. Ceist anois?

P: Conas a litríonn tú 'hÉireann'?

T: Inis dom - Inis dom an abairt.

P: Cluiche ceannais na hÉireann.

[The teacher's response to this request is inaudible. It is possible that the teacher writes the word on the board or in the pupil's copybook.]

[The segment continues for another 15 minutes during which the pupils continue writing and individual pupils occasionally ask the teacher for help with spellings or in translating English words into Irish]

(end of extract)

7. Drills - Situation: Other than Nuachúrsaí

Extract 12

Rank 3, lesson 1, segment 20	Segment duration =1 min 53 secs
Topic:	*Situation: Other than Nuachúrsaí* *('Na Cuairteoirí' - 'The Visitors')*
Language activity:	*Drill*
Pupil behaviour:	*Listening, speaking, reading silently*
Teacher mode of involvement:	*Interacting*
Classroom organisation:	*Whole class*
Materials:	*Reader (Seal ag Léamh I: pages 70-71)*
Class attentiveness:	*High*
Class interest:	*High*

T: *Now.* Rang a sé. "Ní dhéanfaidh mé". Cad dúirt Uncail Pól? "Ní dhéanfaidh mé," arsa Pól. Deirdre?
Deirdre: Dúirt - Dúirt Pól nach déan - nach dhéan sé air.
T: Níl sé ceart. Ciarán
Ciarán: Dúirt Pól nach ndéanfaidh sé dearmad air.
T: Nach - ? (rising intonation)
Ciarán: Nach ndéanfaidh- ndéanfaidh. Nach ndéanfaidh -
T: Nach ndéanFADH sé dearmad air. Abair é sin, gach duine. Dúirt Uncail Pól nach ndéanFADH sé. Arís.
Pupils: Dúirt Uncail Pól nach ndéanfadh sé.
T: Arís.
Pupils: Dúirt Uncail Pól nach ndéanfadh sé.
T: Dúirt Pól nach ndéanfadh sé dearmad air. Mar, nuair a chuaigh siad isteach ins an scoil ansin, an cuimhin libh cad a tharla? Cad dúirt an máistir, a Sheáin?
Seán: Dúirt sé beidh foireann na peile ag imirt Dé - Dé Déardaoin.
T: Ceart. Now, dúirt sé go *what*? Sinéad?
Sinéad   Go mbeadh.
T: Ceart. An Modh Coinníollach. Go mbeadh foireann peile ag imirt. ' "Cén t-am a thiocfaimid le chéile," arsa an múinteoir. "Bígí ag geata na scoile ag a ceathair a chlog", arsa an múinteoir.' *Now*, a Sheáin, cuir claoninsint ar sin. "Dúirt an múinteoir leo -"
Seán: Go mbeadh.
T: *No.* Bheith.
Seán: Bheith ag geata na scoile ag a ceathair a chlog.
T: Ceart. ' "Is leor a bheith déanach uair amháin sa tseachtain," arsa Tomás.' Cad dúirt Tomás? .... Dúirt sé GUR leor a bheith déanach uair amháin sa tseachtain. *Now*, nuair a shroich sé an baile ansin, dúirt sé le Mamaí gur bhuail Uncail Seán leis *etcetera*.

(end of segment)

8. *Imitation - Situation: Nuachúrsaí*

Extract 13

Rank 4, lesson 1, segment 17	**Segment duration = 1 min 15 secs**
Topic:	*Situation: Nuachúrsaí*
	('An Leabharlann' - 'The Library')
Language activity:	*Imitation*
Pupil behaviour:	*Listening, looking*
Teacher mode of involvement:	*Monitoring*
Classroom organisation:	*Group demonstration*
Materials:	*Film strip/slide, Nuachúrsaí handbook*
	'Lá Faoin Tuath': Lesson 8
Class attentiveness:	*Very high*
Class interest:	*Very high*

Pupils: An scannán ....
[Demonstrating group (5 pupils) setting up the film strip]

P: Brostaigh Seán ...
[The demonstrating pupils then take it in turn to describe the pictures on the filmstrip by reciting phrases from the 'Bunchomhrá' (basic narrative for each lesson found in the *Nuachúrsaí* handbook)]

P: 'Ceacht a hocht. Rang a sé. Cúrsa Comhrá Gaeilge le haghaidh ardranganna. An Roinn Oideachais. Báile Átha Cliath.' (Reading from filmstrip)

P: Bhí suim ag ... Tá suim ag Máiréad sa - sa léitheoireacht. [Picture 1]
Téann sí go dtí an leabharlann gach seachtain. [Picture 2]
Siúinéir ab ea é a athair. [Picture 3]

P: Dé hAoine seo caite d'iarr - d'iarr sé - leabhar adhmadóireachta a fháil dó ón leabharlann dó. [Picture 4]
Bhí beirt nó triúir sa leabharlann roimpi. [Picture 5]
Chonaic sí scéalta staire ar an tseilf sa chúinne. [Picture 6]

P: Thóg sí an leabhar. [Picture 7]
Em. Chuaigh sí trasna chun caint leis an leabhar - leabharlannaí. [Picture 8]
"Céard atá uait an tseachtain seo, a Mháiréad?" [Picture 9]
"Tá leabhar staire uaim." [Picture 10]

P: "Ba mhaith liomsa leabhar adhmadóireacht do mo athair." [Picture 11]
"Céard atá á dhéanamh aige anois." [Picture 12]
"Cófra beag do mo sheomra codlata." [Picture 13]
"Tusa peata - peata do athar gan dabht!." [Picture 14]

(end of segment)

9. Comprehension - Situation: Other than Nuachúrsaí.

Extract 14

Rank 10, lesson 1, segment 5	Segment duration = 1 min 3 secs
Topic:	*Situation: Other than Nuachúrsaí ('Dóiteán' - Fire).*
Language activity:	*Comprehension (listen)*
Pupil behaviour:	*Listening*
Teacher mode of involvement:	*Instructing*
Classroom organisation:	*Whole class*
Materials:	*Reader (Seal ag Léamh I, page 90)*
Class attentiveness:	*High*
Class interest:	*High*

T: Anois, em féach anois. *Now.* Ná hosclaigí le bhur dtoil 'Seal ag Léamh'. Ná hosclaigí 'Seal ag Léamh'. Léifidh mise an chuid nua den scéal seo. *All right?* Agus éistigí go géar, le bhur dtoil. *So,* dúnaigí na leabhair. *OK.* ....
' "Léim anois, Aindí", arsa duine acu. Bhí Aindí díreach chun léim nuair a stop sé go tobann. "Mo bhríste!" ar seisean. "Rinne mé dearmad glan ar mo bhríste". Isteach leis arís. Bhí an seomra lán de dheatach agus bhí Aindí ag casachtach. Tharraing sé a bhríste air féin, rith sé go dtí an fhuinneog agus léim sé amach. Bhris an blaincéad an titim, ach, mar sin féin, ghortaigh Aindí a chos agus a lámh. "Conas atá tú?" arsa athair Phóil leis. "Níor cheart dom gearán," arsa Aindí. "D'fhéadfadh an scéal bheith i bhfad níos measa" '.

(end of segment)

Extract 15

Rank 8, lesson 1, segment 13	Segment duration = 1 min 51 secs
Topic:	*Situation: Other than Nuachúrsaí ('An Bhainis' - The Wedding)*
Language activity:	*Comprehension (read/listen)*
Pupil behaviour:	*Listening, reading silently*
Teacher mode of involvement:	*Instructing*
Classroom organisation:	*Whole class*
Materials:	*'Other' course-book: ('Anseo is Ansiúd 3', page 59.)*
Class attentiveness:	*Very high*
Class interest:	*High*

T: *Now*, deirfiúr - *now*. Nílim ach chun píosa an-bheag de seo a dhéanamh anocht agus cuir de glanmheabhair é mar is gnáth. An dtuigeann sibh? Cuir de glanmheabhair é mar - is - gnáth. 'Deirfiúr le Liam is ea Cáit.' An dtuigeann sibh é sin?

Pupils: Tuigimid.

T: 'Phós sí Máirtín Ó Murchú as Luimneach an samhradh seo caite. Thug sí cuireadh dá cairde go léir chun na bainise.' Cuireadh, *invitation*. Cairde, *'friends'*. 'Ní bhfuair cairde Liam aon chuireadh.' Cén fáth? Ní raibh sé chun pósadh. * * * * nach ea? 'Fuair Cáit a lán bronntanas óna cairde.' *Now*, féach ar na rudaí a fuair sí. 'Fuair sí cúpla foireann gréithre.' Gréithre - cupáin agus fochupáin agus plátaí. An dtuigeann sibh?

Pupils: Tuigimid.

T: 'Cúpla cur scian' - scian agus forcanna agus spúnóga, 'cóir throscáin' - troscán, *'furniture'* - bhí sé sin againn cheana - 'agus a lán rudaí eile. I bparóiste Cháit a bhí an pósadh.' *The wedding was in Kate's parish. Right.* 'Nuair a shroich Liam an séipéal bhí Muintir Uí Mhurchú i láthair.' *When Liam reached the church the Murphy family were present.* Bhí siad i láthair. *Present. Right.* Nuair atá an rolla á mharcáil agam, má tá tú i láthair, cuirim *correct mark* nach ea agus má tá tú as láthair cuirim *duck egg*, nach ea. *Right.* Is leor sin.

(end of segment)

10. Contextualisation exercises - Pupil/Teacher real life situations

Extract 16

Rank 16, Lesson 2, segment 1	Segment length = 6 mins 57 secs (first 2 minutes of segment)
Topic:	*Pupil/teacher real life*
Language activity:	*Contextualisation exercise*
Pupil behaviour:	*Listening, speaking*
Teacher mode of involvement:	*Interacting*
Classroom organisation:	*Whole class*
Materials:	*None*
Class attentiveness:	*High*
Class interest:	*High*

T: *Right.*
Pupils: As a phóca a thóg sé -
T: * * * * *
P: * * * * *
T: Cé mhéad duine i do chlann, Mary?
Mary: Ceathair cinn.
T: Ainmnigh iad.
Mary: Mo mhamaí, mo dhaidí, mo dhearthair agus mé
T: Agus cé hé an duine is óige i do chlann, do dhearthair nó tusa?
Mary: Mo d⟨h⟩earthair an duine is óige.
T: Agus cén aois é?
Mary: Tá sé ocht bliana d'aois.
T: An bhfuil sé ag dul ar scoil?
Mary   Tá sé ag dul ar scoil.
T: Agus cén rang ina bhfuil sé?
Mary: Tá sé i rang .. i rang a ceathair.
T: I rang a ceathair. *Right. OK..* Cén caitheamh aimsire atá agat, Tomás? ... Cén
            caitheamh aimsire atá agat? Patrick? Is maith liom -
Patrick: Is maith liom bheith ag snámh agus is maith liom bheith ag imirt peile.
T: Ag imirt peile. An féidir leat snámh?
Patrick: Is féidir liom snámh.
T: *Right.* Cé acu is fearr leat, bheith ag snámh san fharraige nó bheith ag snámh sa linn
            snámha?
Patrick: Is maith liom bheith ag snámh sa linn snámha.
T: Sa linn snámha. *Right. OK..* Ceart go leor. Cén chaitheamh aimsire atá agat,
            Anne?
Anne: Is maith liom bheith ag snámh - Is maith liom bheith ag snámh agus ag agus ag
            cispheil.

T: Ag imirt cispheile. An raibh tú ag imirt cispheile aréir?
Anne: Bhí mé ag imirt cispheile aréir.
T: Cá háit?
Anne: Ins an .. (*) (placename)
T: (*). (placename) Agus an raibh an bua ort, nó an bua agat?
Anne: Ní raibh an bua agam
T: *Right.* Agus an raibh áthas ort?
Anne: Ní raibh áthas -
T: Conas a bhí tú? Bhí - ?
Anne: Bhí mé brón -
T: Bhí mé brónACH. Bhí mé brónach nó bhí brón orm. An raibh tuirse ort?
Anne: Ní raibh tuirse *.
T: An raibh tuirse ort?
Anne: Bhí tuirse *.
T: Bhí tuirse <u>ORM</u>. *Right. OK.* Agus cén t-am a tháinig tú abhaile?
Anne: Tháinig mé abhaile em...
T: An raibh sé go luath nó an raibh sé déanach san oíche?
Anne: Déanach san oíche.

(end of extract)

11. Contextualisation exercise - Fragmented topic

Extract 17

Rank 9, lesson 2, segment 1	Segment duration = 1 min 17 secs
Topic:	*Fragmented*
Language activity:	*Contextualisation exercise*
Pupil behaviour:	*Listening, speaking*
Teacher mode of involvement:	*Interacting*
Classroom organisation:	*Whole class*
Materials:	*None*
Class attentiveness:	*Very high*
Class interest:	*Very high*

T: Anois, a bhuachaillí agus a chailíní, cén - cén lá atá ann inniu?
Pupils: Lá .
T: Cén lá atá ann inniu?
Pupils: Déardaoin Céadaoin (pupils giving different replies)
T: Dé Céadaoin. Cén lá a bhí ann inné?
Pupils: Dé Máirt.
T: Cén lá a bheidh ann amárach?

Pupils:	Beidh Déardaoin. Déardaoin .
T:	Amárach Dé - ? (rising intonation)
Pupils:	Déardaoin.
T:	Cén lá a bhí ann arú inné?
Pupils:	Arú inné bhí * * Dé <u>Luain.</u>
T:	Is arú amárach?
Pupils:	Arú amárach Dé hAoine.
T:	Agus cén mhí atá ann?
Pupils:	An * *
T:	Cén MHÍ atá ann?
Pupils:	Mí Bealtaine.
T:	Tá - ?
Pupils:	Mí Bealtaine.
T:	Cén séasúr atá ann?
Pupils:	Seo an Samhradh.
T:	An Samhradh atá ann. Cén sort aimsire atá ann inniu? .. An bhfuil an lá go breá?
Pupils:	Tá an lá go breá.
T:	An bhfuil eh scamaill sa spéir?
Pupils:	Tá scamaill sa spéir.
T:	An bhfuil báisteach ag titim?
Pupils:	Níl báisteach ag titim.
T:	An bhfuil an talamh fliuch?
Pupils:	Níl an talamh fliuch.
T:	An bhfuil an ghrian ag taitneamh?
Pupils:	Tá an ghrian ag taitneamh.
T:	An féidir an ghrian a fheiceáil inniu?
Pupils:	Ní féidir an ghrian a fheiceáil inniu.
T:	Cén fáth?
Pupils:	Mar tá scamaill sa bhealach.
T:	Mar tá na scamaill sa bhealach.

(end of segment)

12. Real communication in Irish - Pupil/Teacher real life situations

Extract 18

Rank 10, lesson 1, segment 2	Segment duration = 4 mins 19 secs

Topic:	*Situation: Pupil/teacher real life*
	(A fire that pupil witnessed/heard of)
Language activity:	*Real communication in Irish*
Pupil behaviour:	*Listening, speaking*
Teacher mode of involvement:	*Interacting*
Classroom organisation:	*Whole class*
Materials:	*None*
Class attentiveness:	*Very high*
Class interest:	*Very high*

T: An bhfaca éinne sa rang seo dóiteán riamh? An bhfaca éinne sa rang seo dóiteán? Jennifer?

Jennifer: Bhí dóiteán i (*). (placename)

T: An raibh? Agus cá bhfuil (*)? Nó cén sórt ruda é (*)? An (*) é?

Jennifer: Is (*) é.

T: Is (*) é. Go maith. Agus cathain a bhí an dóiteán ann?

Jennifer: * * * * * * * *.

T: An tseachtain seo caite an ea? Maith an cailín. *All right.* Ar chuala sibh faoi aon dóiteán a bhí in Éirinn. Ar chuala sibh faoi thine mhór a bhí in Éirinn. Bhuel, Clíona?

Clíona: Cúpla cúpla em - Chuala mé ar an raidió go raibh em - go raibh dóiteán. Níl a fhios agam cá - cá raibh sé ach em gur thit tintreach - do bhuail tintreach ar chrann agus thosaigh em an - chuaigh an - an crann go léir suas i lasracha.

T: Ana-mhaith. Maith an cailín. Ana-mhaith. Deirdre?

Deirdre: Em Cúpla bhliain ó shin em bhí dóiteán mór em i (*) (placename).

T: Ana-mhaith. I (*). Agus cad a tharla an oíche sin?

Deirdre: Em Gach - gach duine em - daoine a bhí isteach sa seomra fuair siad bás.

T: Fuair siad bás. Fuair siad bás. Maith an cailín. Agus cén sórt áite í an (*)? An pictiúrlann é?

Deirdre: Em, eh - bhí ceol pop -

T: *Yes.* Maith an cailín. Bhí popceol á sheinm ann. *All right* agus cad a bhí á dhéanamh ag na cailíní agus ag na buachaillí ann?

Deirdre: Ag damhsa.

T: Ana-mhaith ar fad. *Right.* Ar chuala sibh faoi aon dóiteán eile? Bhuel Tara?

Tara: Chonaic mé carr trí thine sa bóthar? Bhí sé - bhí sé em -

T: Tar éis timpiste a bhí ann, an ea? Sea. Maith an cailín. Agus ar gortaíodh éinne?

Tara: Ní *

T: Go maith. *Right.* Pauline?

Pauline: Chonaic mé tine em * * *.

T: Maith an cailín. Sa (*) atá in aice leatsa, nach ea ? (* * *).

Pauline: *Yeah.*

T: *Right.* Agus ar gortaíodh éinne nó ar maraíodh éinne? An raibh éinne gortaithe? An raibh?

Pauline: Ní raibh.

T: Ní raibh. Go maith.

T: Éinne eile? Bhuel Siobhán?

Siobhán: Bhí tine mór sa (* *). (placename)

T: Ó go maith agus cá bhfuil (* *)?

Siobhán: Em *.

T: Faoin tuath an ea?

Siobhán: *No.* Sa chathair.

T: Sa chathair. Maith an cailín. Agus cén sórt siopa é sin?

P: (* *).

T: (* *). An-mhaith. Agus an raibh em - An ndeachaigh an *shop* suas i lasracha, an gceapann tú? An ndeachaigh an SIOPA - gabh mo leithscéal - an SIOPA suas i lasracha?

P: Níl a fhios agam.

T: Níl a fhios agat. *All right.*

(end of segment)

13. Real communication in Irish - Routine management/organisation

Extract 19

Rank 3, lesson 1, segment 9	**Segment duration = 58 secs**
Topic:	*Routine management/organisation*
Language activity:	*Real communication in Irish*
Pupil behaviour:	*Listening, writing*
Teacher mode of involvement:	*Instructing*
Classroom organisation:	*Whole class*
Materials:	*Jotter/copy, Other course-book or workbook (Réamhobair Gramadaí)*
Class attentiveness:	*High*
Class interest:	*High*

T: Anocht, anois, is féidir libh an Modh Coinníollach a dhéanamh arís as an leabhairín beag gramadaí sin. Tabhair dom leabhar gramadaí nóiméad, duine éigin. Sea. Osclaigí suas eh leathanach a - a tríocha - leathanach a fiche hocht, is dóigh liom.

Now. An Modh Coinníollach, briathra mírialta ansin. Dhúnfainn, dhúnfá, dhúnfadh sé, dhúnfaimís, dhúnfadh sibh, dhúnfaidís agus dhúnfaí. *Now.* Bí á dhéanamh sin anocht agus amárach, leanfaimid ar aghaidh leis an mbriathar saor ansin agus leis an gclaoninsint ins an Modh Coinníolladh. *So,* féachaigí air sin - féachaigí air sin anois ins an leabhar beag gramadaí anocht.

(end of segment)

Extract 20

Rank 8, lesson 1, segment 9	**Segment duration = 2 mins 36 secs**
Topic:	*Routine management/organisation*
Language activity:	*Real communication in Irish*
Pupil behaviour:	*Listening, doing*
Teacher mode of involvement:	*Instructing*
Classroom organisation:	*Whole class*
Materials:	*Other course-book (photocopy handout)*
Class attentiveness:	*Very high*
Class interest:	*High*

T: *Now.* Cuir líne faoi na *spellings* seo don oíche anocht.
..25.. * * ** ..... [pupils getting ready]
Right. Now. Ar an gcéad leathanach 'an gúna bainise' ar an triú líne - 'an gúna bainise' - cuir líne faoi. *Now.* 'Bhí Síle ar bís' an chéad cheann i dtosach, 'Bhí Síle ar bís' .. agus ag an mbun 'Bhí Mámaí ar bior'. *Right.* An chéad leathanach eile. An chéad leathanach eile. 'Go healaíonta', ar an gceathrú líne 'go healaíonta' - '*artfully*', '*skilfully*'. Agus an líne ina dhiaidh sin, 'an fáinne gealltanais', 'an fáinne gealltanais'.
Now, faoin bpictiúir 'Mí na Meala'.... *No,* cuir an líne faoi. Agus ag an deireadh 'an taispeántas'. Cé mhéad atá ansin? A haon, dó, trí, ceathair, cúig, sé, seacht.
Now, em ar an leathanach deireanach anois - *Wait now till we see.* 'Airgead Shasana a mhalartú', 'airgead Shasana a mhalartú'. Tá ocht gcinn ansin, nach bhfuil? Aon, dó, trí, ceathair, cúig, sé, seacht, ocht. Is leor sin. *Right.*
Now, beidh an briseadh againn anois, is dócha, agus beidh an chuid eile tar eis a haon déag. *Right.*

(end of segment)

14. Imitation - Situation: Other than Nuachúrsaí

Extract 21

Rank 8, lesson 1, segment 14	Segment duration = 2 mins 15 secs

Topic:	*Situation: other than Nuachúrsaí ('An Bhainis' - The Wedding)*
Language activity:	*Imitation (repeat)*
Pupil behaviour:	*Listening, reading aloud*
Teacher mode of involvement:	*Interacting*
Classroom organisation:	*Whole class*
Materials:	*Other course-book (Anseo is Ansiúd 3 - page 59)*
Class attentiveness:	*Very high*
Class interest:	*High*

T: 'Deirfiúr le Liam is ea Cáit.' Le chéile.
Pupils: 'Deirfiúr le Liam is ea Cáit.'
T: 'Phós sí Máirtín Ó Murchú as Luimneach an samhradh seo caite.'
Pupils: 'Phós sí Máirtín Ó Mhurchú as Luimneach an samhradh seo -'
T: *No, no, no.* 'Phós sí Máirtín Ó' - ? (rising intonation)
Pupils: 'Murchú'
T: Níl aon 'h' ansin - 'as Luimneach' ...
Pupils: an samhradh seo caite.
T: 'Thug sí cuireadh dá cairde' - dá cairde, *her friends.* Níl aon 'h' ann, dá cairde, *her friends* - 'go léir chun na bainise.'
Pupils: 'Thug sí cuireadh dá cairde go léir chun na bainise.'
T: 'Ní bhfuair cairde Liam aon chuireadh.'
Pupils: 'Ní bhfuair cairde Liam aon chuireadh.'
T: 'Fuair Cáit a lán bronntanas óna cairde.'
Pupils: 'Fuair Cáit a lán bronntanas óna cairde.'
T: 'Fuair sí cúpla foireann gréithre.'
Pupils: 'Fuair sí cúpla foireann gréithre.'
T: 'Cúpla cur scian.'
Pupils: 'Cúpla cur scian.'
T: Eh em 'cur scian'.. - *cutlery sets, sets of cutlery.*
        'Cóir throscáin' - *pieces of furniture* 'agus a lán rudaí eile.'
Pupils: 'Cóir throscáin agus a lán rudaí eile.'
T: 'I bparóiste Cháit a bhí an pósadh.'
Pupils: 'I bparóiste Cháit a bhí an pósadh.'
T: 'Nuair a shroich Liam an séipéal bhí Muintir Uí Mhurchú i láthair.'
Pupils: 'Nuair a shroich Liam an séipéal bhí Muintir Uí Mhurchú i láthair.'

T: Nóiméad amháin go léifidh mé an teachtaireacht? ..25..
           [Teacher reads message delivered by pupil]

(end of segment)

15. Transposition - Fragmented topic

Extract 22

Rank 16, lesson 2, segment 10	**Segment duration = 2 mins 40 secs**
Topic:	*Fragmented*
Language activity:	*Transposition (read aloud)*
Pupil behaviour:	*Listening, reading aloud*
Teacher mode of involvement:	*Interacting*
Classroom organisation:	*Whole class*
Materials:	*Reader (Fás G - pages 58-59)*
Class attentiveness:	*High*
Class interest:	*High*

T: *Right.* Tógaigí amach 'Fás G', le bhur dtoil.   Leathanach caoga hocht agus
           leathanach caoga naoi, caoga hocht agus caoga naoi ..15 ..
           [Pupils taking out Readers - Tape turned over here - approximately 20 seconds of the
           lesson not recorded]
Pupils: *Teacher! Teacher! Teacher!*
T: * * * eh Niamh?
Niamh: Thaitin an éan -
T: Thaitin ? (rising intonation)
Niamh: Thaitin na héin agus na <u>héisc</u> ag - leis.
T: Léigh amach an abairt ina bhfuil an ceann eile freisin, Catherine.
Catherine: Thaitin siad go mór leis.
T: *Right.* Léigh amach an abairt in a bhfuil an focal 'chonaic'. -
P: *Teacher! Teacher!*
T: Chonaic. Yvonne? Chonaic - ?
Yvonne: Chonaic Fionn iasc beag ag snámh ar bharr an uisce.
T: Go maith. Léigh amach an abairt ina bhfuil an focal 'lámha'. 'Lámha'. Orla?
Orla: Ach bhí an t-iasc aige ina lámha.
T: *Right.* Léigh amach an abairt in a bhfuil an focal 'cairde'.   Cara amháin, níos mó ná
           cara amháin, cairde.
P: *Teacher, teacher*
T: Léigh amach an abairt ina bhfuil an focal 'cairde', le bhur dtoil. Anne?
Anne: Ach ní raibh cairde mar sin <u>aige</u>.
T: Léigh amach an abairt in a bhfuil an focal 'is minic'. 'Is minic'.
Pupils: *Teacher! Teacher!*

T:	Tomás?
Tomás:	Is minic a suigh sé ag féachaint orthu.
T:	*Right.* Léigh amach an abairt ina bhfuil an focal eh.. 'seanmhná'. Seanmhná, *old women*, seanmhná. Léigh amach an abairt ina bhfuil an focal 'seanmhná'. Seanmhná.
Pupils:	*Teacher! Teacher!.*
T:	Bhuel, Joan?
Joan:	Isteach sa teach leis agus thaispeáin sé do na * * * seanmhná é.
T:	*Right.* Léigh amach an abairt in a bhfuil an focal 'ar bith'. Ar bith. Níl airgead ar BITH agam. Níl aon airgead ar bith agam. Ar bith?
P:	*Teacher! Teacher!*
T:	Bhuel?
P:	Ní raibh cara ar bith aige.
T:	Go maith. Léigh amach an abairt ina bhfuil an focal eh ..'cluichí'. 'Cluichí'. 'Cluichí'.
Pupils:	*Teacher! Teacher! Teacher! Teacher!*
T:	Paul?
Paul:	...Ba mhaith...
T:	Ba mhaith leis -
Paul:	Ba mhaith leis cluichí a ...imirt le ... le buachaillí (other pupil and teacher help this pupil with words he finds difficult to pronounce) ... dá aois féin.
T:	*Right. OK.*

(end of segment)

16. Compound - Situation: Other than Nuachúrsaí

Extract 23

Rank 3, lesson 1, segment 22	**Segment duration = 4 mins 57 secs**
Topic:	*Situation: Other than Nuachúrsaí*
Language activity:	*Compound (Comprehension & Contextualisation exercise)*
Pupil behaviour:	*Listening, speaking, reading silently*
Teacher mode of involvement:	*Interacting*
Classroom organisation:	*Whole class*
Materials:	*Reader (Seal ag Léamh I - page 73) Blackboard*
Class attentiveness:	*Very high*
Class interest:	*Very high*

| T: | *Now.* Tosnóimid ar an gceacht nua léitheoireachta anois. 'Déardaoin nó Dé hAoine?' an teideal atá air. |

	Now. 'Chuaigh Pól agus Niamh abhaile go tapaidh ón scoil tráthnóna Déardaoin.'
	Focal eile, bhí sé againn ar maidin, Conas a chuaigh siad abhaile, a Chiaráin Uí Shé?
Ciarán:	Rith siad abhaile go tapaidh.
T:	Go maith. Go tapaidh. Ar shlí eile?
P:	Go tobann.
T:	Go tobann.
P:	Ar nós na gaoithe.
T:	Ar nós na gaoithe. Sea. 'Bhí Mamaí bocht an-tuirseach.' Bhí sí an-tuirseach. Cén fáth, n'fheadair?
P:	Mar bhí sí ag glanadh an teach.
T:	Ag glanadh an tí. Go maith. Agus, is dócha, ag obair ó mhaidin go hoíche. 'Bhí an teach glanta aici' - Sea, tá an ceart agat - 'ó bhun go barr do na cuairteoirí.' Do na cuairteoirí (rising intonation)?
P:	*For the visitors.*
T:	Sea. As Gaeilge - do na daoine a bhí le teacht. ' "Déanaigí deifir leis an obair - obair bhaile anois", ar sise.' Déanaigí deifir leis an obair bhaile. *Now,* abair é sin ar slí éigin eile. A Thomáis?
Tomás:	Brostaigh leis an obair bhaile anois.
T:	Ceart. Maith an fear. Nó déan an obair bhaile (rising intonation) - ?
P:	Go tapaidh.
T:	Go tapaidh. * * *. 'Bhuail an chlog a ceathair. Bíonn Aint - ' ... *Now,* * . ' "Bíonn Aintín Máire anseo timpeall a ceathair , de ghnáth," arsa Mamaí.' Anois, Déardaoin anois agus tá Mamaí ag súil le Aintín Mháire. An bhfuil sí ag teacht? Deirdre?
Deirdre:	Ní raibh sí ag teacht. Bhí sí ag teacht ar Dé hAoine.
T:	Ceart. De ghnáth. 'Bhuail an clog leathuair tar éis a ceathair.' Leathuair tar éis a ceathair. ' "Tá siad déanach inniu," arsa Mamaí.' *Now,* 'tá siad déanach' ?
P:	*She'll be late today.*
T:	As Gaeilge. A Sheáin?
Seán:	Tá siad mall.
T:	Tá siad mall. Ceart. Tosnaigh le 'níl', Ciarán Ó Riain?
Ciarán:	Níl siad in am.
T:	Ceart. ' "Níl siad in am," arsa Mamaí. Leis sin, chuala siad cnag ar an ndoras.' David. Cnag. Cad a dhein siad?
David:	Bhuail - bhuail - bhuail siad an cnag .
T:	Ceart. Maith an fear. Bhuail siad cnag ar an ndoras. Chuala siad cnag ar an ndoras. *Now,* b'fhéidir - b'fhéidir gur - An cuimhin libh an dán beag a dheineamar .. mar gheall ar an ndoras?
P:	An baschrann.
T:	An baschrann. An cuimhin libh? Subh milis ar bhaschrann an dorais. Sea. B'fhéidir gur bhuail siad baschrann an dorais. Sea. ' "Sin iad anois iad," arsa Mamaí agus rith sí amach chun fáilte a chur rompu. Baineadh geit aisti nuair a d'oscail sí an doras. An múinteoir a bhí ann. "An bhfuil Pól istigh?," ar seisean. "Tá cluiche againn tráthnóna." "Tráthnóna inniu!" arsa Mamaí agus ionadh uirthi. "Is ea," arsa an múinteoir agus ionadh airsean freisin.' Freisin?
P:	*Also*
T:	As Gaeilge? Freisin? Bhí fearg airsin freisin?

P: Em, chomh maith.

T: Chomh maith. Ceart. ' "Is ea", arsa an múinteoir agus ionadh airsin freisin anois. "Nach ndúirt Pól é sin leat?" "Tar amach anseo, a Phóil," arsa Mamaí agus fearg uirthi.' *Now.* Abair é sin ar shlí eile - bhí fearg uirthi?

P: Bhí crosta uirthi

T: Bhí sí, nó -

P: Bhí sí crosta.

T: Ceart. Nó bhí sí ar - ?

P: Buile.

T: Ar buile. 'Chonaic Pól go raibh fearg ar an múinteoir freisin. "Ó", arsa Pól. "Inniu atá an cluiche againn! Amárach atá Aintín Máire ag teacht, mar sin - is ea, sin é a dúirt Uncail Seán liom ceart go leor." "Nach deas an teachtaire é - " '
Now, teachtaire. Teachtaire? ... Teachtaire. [teacher writes word on blackboard] Duine a théann amach ar theachtaireacht, chun rud a dhéanamh. I mBéarla, *'messenger'*. Do chuaigh sé amach ar theachtaireacht. Teachtaire, duine a théann amach chun jab beag a dhéanamh. Uaireanta glaonn do Mhamaí ort agus tugann sí airgead duit agus deir sí leat "rith síos an baile agus faigh na rudaí seo dom". Ansin, téann tusa amach ar theachtaireacht.
- arsa an múinteoir . ' "Nach deas an teachtaire é", ar seisean. "Is deas, go deimhin", arsa Mamaí agus fearg uirthi. "Féach anois cad atá déanta agat", ar sise le Pól. " Tá gach rud trí chéile agat agus ní hé an chéad uair agat é" '.

(end of segment)

17. *Real communication in Irish - Situation: Other than Nuachúrsaí*

Extract 24

Rank 3, lesson 1, segment 28	**Segment duration = 1 min 55 secs**
Topic:	*Situation: Other than Nuachúrsaí*
Language activity:	*Real communication in Irish*
Pupil behaviour:	*Listening, speaking, reading silently*
Teacher mode of involvement:	*Interacting*
Classroom organisation:	*Whole class*
Materials:	*Blackboard*
Class attentiveness:	*Very high*
Class interest:	*Very high*

T: Anois, déanfaimid aiste bheag anois - aiste bheag. Anois, an cuimhin libh an comhrá a bhí ar siúl againn ar maidin? Bhíomar ag caint mar gheall ar bhreithlá agus cad iad na bronntanaisí a fuair siad don bhreithlá arís agus mar gheall ar thimpiste?

P: Fuair siad rothair.

T: Ceart. Agus chuaigh siad amach ag rothaíocht. Anois, déanfaimid beagáinín scríbhneoireachta anois - scríbhneoireachta ar, em, .. ar eh, Cad a dhéanfaimid? Déanfaimid turas, eh turas rothaíochta. Déanfaimid, mar sin, 'Turas a dhein mé'. Eh Seo teideal na haiste anois, T-U-R-A-S [Teacher writes title on blackboard].
        Turas a dhein mé. Sé sin, scríobhfaidh sibh beagáinín dom ar - bunaithe ar an rothar nua agus mar a chuaigh sibh amach ag rothaíocht. Anois. Beidh focail mar seo á n-úsáid agam. Rothar deas nua. Rothar deas nua. [Teacher writing on blackboard]
        Now, níl mé chun na habairtí a thabhairt díobh in aon chor. Déanaigí féin suas na habairtí. Rothar deas nua. Beidh sibh ag caint ar mar a fuair sibh an rothar. Conas a fuair sibh an rothar? Más maith libh, is féidir libh beagáinín cúntais a thabhairt ar an rothar, ar chodanna an rothair. Tá codanna an rothair thuas ansin, féach. An diallait, agus na cluasa, agus fráma an rothair agus an teannaire.

(end of segment)

(End of transcript extracts)

Appendix 9

Pupil Communicative Behaviour Record: Coding guidelines[*]

The observer will observe three pupils, one at a time in succession, and record various aspects of each pupil's behaviour on the *Pupil Communicative Behaviour Record (PCBR)*. The observation work will proceed in 5 minute units for each pupil, with the first three minutes of each unit being given over to actually observing the pupil, and the 4th and 5th minute being used to record events on the observation sheet. In a 30 minute class, therefore, each of the three targeted pupils would be observed twice (2 x 3 x 5).

First, the teachers' rating of pupils sheet (Áireamh an mhúinteora ar na daltaí de réir cumais - see Appendix 2.2) should be used to randomly select one pupil from each of the three ability groupings in Irish (high/medium/low ability). The pupil selected from the high ability group should be referred to as 1 in the *Pupil* column of the *Pupil Communicative Behaviour Record* sheet to indicate to us that this is the *high ability* pupil. If you wish you can add in the pupil initials beside the number, as an aid to your work. Likewise, the pupils selected from the *middle* and *lower* level ability in Irish groups are numbered 2 and 3 respectively. We have printed in these numbers (1, 2, and 3) on the observation sheet to indicate the individual high, medium and low ability pupils so as to remind you of the order in which pupils are to be observed.

This is how the work proceeds:

Pupil 1 3 minutes observation.
       2 minutes to record events on the sheet.

Pupil 2 3 minutes observation.
       2 minutes to record events on the sheet.

Pupil 3 3 minutes observation.
       2 minutes to record events on the sheet.

Then back to *Pupil 1* again and proceed as before.

Generally, recording events consists of putting one tick (✓) in each relevant cell. If there is a change in pupil behaviour during the 3 minute observation period, please draw a line across the page, within the row corresponding to that pupil, and record a new series of ticks to describe new behaviour as done in Fig 1 below.

---

[*]A copy of the *Pupil Communicative Behaviour Record* may be found on the last page of this appendix.

Fig. 1

Pupil 1,2,3	LANGUAGE		ASKS A QUESTION		ANSWERS		LENGTH OF UTTERANCE				TAKES TURN		INTERACTION TYPE	
	Irish	English	Pseudo	Genui-ne	Predic-table	Unpre-dictable	One word	Clause	Sent-ence	Sust-ained	Rout-ine	New	Pupil-pupil	Pupil-teacher
1	✓									✓			✓	
	✓				✓		✓							✓
2														

The same three pupils are to be observed in Lesson 1 and Lesson 2. The particular targeted pupils should be indicated on the sheet with the Teachers' ratings of pupils.

Write explanatory notes whenever necessary.

Categories of Pupil Behaviour

We will now consider briefly the headings under which pupil behaviour is categorised in the *Pupil Communicative Behaviour Record.*

There are three main headings

(1)   If The Pupil Speaks Individually

(2)   If The Pupil Is Silent

(3)   Other Pupil Behaviour

The latter two general headings will apply frequently and so we will begin with these. Take the second main heading, for example *(2) If The Pupil Is Silent*

Fig. 2

IF THE PUPIL IS SILENT (or non-task related e.g. chatting/whispering)					
ATTENDING			DISRUPTIVE		
H	M	L	H	M	L
	✓				✓

pupil = moderately attentive not disruptive

Suppose the pupil is silent, while the teacher is reading aloud to the class. Here you would place a tick under *one* of the letters 'H' (high), 'M' (moderate) or 'L' (low) for *each* of the subheadings ATTENDING and DISRUPTIVE to indicate how attentive or disruptive the pupil was. Thus, if the pupil happened to be *fairly* attentive and *not at all disruptive* then you might place two ticks as in Fig 2 above.

On the other hand, if the pupil was not engaged at all in the task, but was chatting rather loudly to neighbouring pupils, you might place the two ticks under 'L' for ATTENDING and 'M' for DISRUPTIVE, depending on just how inattentive or disruptive you felt he or she was, as in Fig 3 below.

Fig. 3

IF THE PUPIL IS SILENT (or non-task related e.g. chatting/whispering)					
ATTENDING			DISRUPTIVE		
H	M	L	H	M	L
		✓		✓	

pupil is not attending to the task and is moderately disruptive

Now consider the third main heading: (3) *Other Pupil Behaviour.*

If the pupil is engaged in choral speech along with other pupils, then place a tick in the appropriate cell. If he/she is reading aloud, either alone or with other pupils, then place a tick under the 'aloud' category of READING. Likewise, if the pupil is reading silently, or writing, the category in which a tick is to be placed is clear.

Only one of the four subheadings of the general heading OTHER PUPIL BEHAVIOUR, however, should be ticked for a pupil at any one time. The only exception is where the pupil's behaviour changes within an observation unit - in which case you should draw a horizontal line within the row for that pupil before placing, below the new line, another tick to reflect the change in behaviour.

Important: Even if you place a tick under one of the four subheadings of OTHER PUPIL BEHAVIOUR, you should also place ticks, as appropriate, in the adjacent categories of ATTENDING and DISRUPTIVE, to indicate the manner in which the task is being performed. For example, suppose a pupil is engaged in a writing task, but is attending poorly to it (e.g. is listening occasionally to another pupil who is chatting). The following might be a description of his or her behaviour:

Fig. 4

IF THE PUPIL IS SILENT (or non-task related e.g. chatting/whispering)						OTHER PUPIL BEHAVIOUR				
Attending			Disruptive			Choral Speech	Reading		Writing	
H	M	L	H	M	L		silent	aloud		
		✓			✓				✓	

Pupil is writing although <u>not</u> attending well to it. Pupil is <u>not</u> disruptive.

Finally, turning to the general heading (1) *If the Pupil Speaks Individually* (this excludes non-task related *chatting* etc.). This heading will apply less often than *Other Pupil Behaviour* in most classrooms. If the pupil *does* speak individually, then the following three subheadings are *always* relevant: *Language, Length Of Utterance* and *Interaction Type.*

Language requires no comment except to say that an utterance is counted as *Irish* if *most* of it is in Irish; *English* if *mostly* in English. In the case of LENGTH OF UTTERANCE the category *sustained* indicates that a stretch of discourse longer than a sentence is involved - e.g. a memorised poem being recited individually by the particular pupil being observed. However, it would also be appropriate to place a tick under *sustained* if the observed pupil was engaged with another pupil in discussing a library book in Irish which they had earlier read, or if they were engaged in some other form of simulated dialogue. In the latter kind of discussion, the individual phrases used by the pupil in his/her conversational turns may be quite short, but he/she is sustaining a longer stretch of discourse *overall*. Incidentally, you do not have to be able to hear every single word of such a discussion in order to code it. The kind of pupil-pupil discussion just described might be coded thus:

Fig. 5

IF THE PUPIL SPEAKS INDIVIDUALLY													
LANGUAGE		ASKS A QUESTION		ANSWERS		LENGTH OF UTTERANCE				TAKES TURN		INTERACTION TYPE	
Irish	English	Pseudo	Genuine	Predic-table	Unpre-dictable	One word	Clause	Sent-ence	Sust-ained	Routine	New	Pupil-pupil	Pupil-teacher
✓									✓			✓	

Note in Fig 5 above that we have not placed a tick under either of the subheadings ASKS A QUESTION or ANSWERS. This is because these subheadings do not really apply to sustained discourse - they are only relevant to more isolated question and answer exchanges. The really important thing, however, is that for each occasion when a targeted pupil speaks individually the three main subheadings have ticks: LANGUAGE, LENGTH OF UTTERANCE and INTERACTION TYPE.

Consider another LENGTH OF UTTERANCE category: *One word*. Suppose that during an observation unit the targeted pupil gave one-word answers in Irish to the teacher on two separate occasions (in response to two different drill-type questions). These two successive utterances might be coded as follows:

Fig. 6

IF THE PUPIL SPEAKS INDIVIDUALLY													
LANGUAGE		ASKS A QUESTION		ANSWERS		LENGTH OF UTTERANCE				TAKES TURN		INTERACTION TYPE	
Irish	English	Pseudo	Genuine	Predic-table	Unpre-dictable	One word	Clause	Sent-ence	Sust-ained	Routine	New	Pupil-pupil	Pupil-teacher
✓				✓		✓							✓
✓				✓		✓							✓

We have ticked the category *predictable* under ANSWERS in Fig 6 because the question being answered is not open-ended. As long as the pupil actually knows the Irish construction being drilled, then the answer he/she can give is entirely predictable. This need not always be the case, of course. For example, in the context of informal conversation *(Comhrá Neamhfhoirmiúil)*, a pupil might be asked their opinion about the puppet characters Zig and Zag ("Cad é do thuairim faoi *Zig & Zag?*") and his/her reply in Irish in *this* case would probably be coded as *unpredictable*.

ASKS A QUESTION is the relevant subheading when the *pupil* asks a question. This category can be ticked under two sub-headings: *pseudo* or *genuine* - *pseudo* being the situation where the question is only posed as part of a drill or some other practice (and the answer to it is, therefore, highly constrained and predictable). The *genuine* category of ASKS A QUESTION might be ticked, for example, when the pupil has been reading silently and then suddenly says out loud that he/she doesn't understand what they are reading ("*Ní thuigim é seo - cad is* R-Í-O-M-H-A-I-R-E ?")

In the case of ASKS A QUESTION and ANSWERS the pupil is presumed to be speaking in the context of a fairly set lesson plan. There is a special heading TAKES TURN, however, which is intended to capture the situation where the pupil takes the initiative in a more fundamental way and departs from the formal lesson structure to some extent. An example of this - which would fit in the *routine* category of TAKES TURN - might be where the pupil volunteers to clean the blackboard "*An nglanfaidh mé an clár dubh, a Mháistir?*") An example which would fit in the category *new* of TAKES TURN would be where the pupil comments that it is raining and asks if the football game will take place today (*"Tá sé ag cur báistí anois. An mbeidh aon chluiche againn inniu?"*)

Note that in each of the above cases of a pupil speaking individually, LANGUAGE, LENGTH OF UTTERANCE and INTERACTION TYPE subheadings are *always* used to describe the pupil behaviour, while ASKS A QUESTION, ANSWERS and TAKES TURN may or may not be used - depending on the type of utterance.

Finally, it should be noted that we have not ticked the adjacent sub-headings of ATTENDING and DISRUPTIVE when the behaviour of the targeted pupil fits under the general heading of IF THE PUPIL SPEAKS INDIVIDUALLY. This is because we assume that when the pupil speaks individually he or she must usually be attending to the class and can hardly be disruptive (Note again that we exclude disruptive *chatting* of a non-task related kind from the general heading IF THE PUPIL SPEAKS INDIVIDUALLY. However, if you feel that ATTENDING and DISRUPTIVE subheadings are still relevant to the behaviour you observed under the former heading, please place a tick/ticks in the relevant categories as you see fit.

Additional coding guidelines for the *PCBR*

(1) Complex behaviours

While the *PCBR* coding guidelines stated that the various categories of *Other pupil behaviour* such as writing, reading aloud etc. were to be treated as mutually exclusive, no specific guidance was given about the simultaneous use of the major headings *If the pupil speaks individually* and *Other pupil behaviour*. In the event, the observers opted to represent some *Complex* pupil behaviours by placing ticks under both these main headings. For example, in one case the target pupil was part of a group engaged in a discussion, but he had also been assigned to make written notes on what was happening. Thus, the observer recorded a series of ticks in categories under the *If the Pupil speaks individually* heading while also placing a tick in the 'writing' category under the *Other pupil behaviour* heading. Again here, the observers' notes were useful in confirming how they applied the system.

(2) Mutually exclusive categories/subcategories ticked

We list here some of the most common instances where observers ticked incompatible categories/subcategories. Many observers wrote notes on the coding sheets describing the target pupil's behaviour and these served to confirm that the scheme was being implemented in a manner consistent with the instructions. In a small number of cases, these notes were used to resolve ambiguities or inconsistencies in coding.

a) The instructions specified that only one category in the category *Other pupil behaviour* could be ticked in coding pupil behaviour at a given time (i.e. *choral speech*, or *silent reading*, or *reading aloud'* or *writing*). This was based on the assumption that only one of these behaviours could be exhibited at a time. Pupils of course might change rapidly from one behaviour to another during an observation unit, but this would be adequately handled within the system by drawing a line on the *PCBR* record sheet and inserting a new series of ticks to represent the new behaviour. In the few instances where observers placed ticks under more than one of these categories to describe an *Other pupil behaviour*, their own accompanying notes usually provided sufficient information to allow the researchers to resolve the conflict in line with the instructions. For example, on a few occasions, both *choral speech* and *reading aloud* were simultaneously ticked, but it was clear from the observers notes and the *ILAS* schedule that choral reading aloud was the observed pupil behaviour - the tick under *choral speech* was intended to distinguish individual reading from *choral reading*. Since the instructions had specified that reading aloud covered both individual and choral reading, we disregarded the unnecessary tick relating to choral speech. In one instance where more than one category of *Other pupil behaviour* was ticked without explanation, however, both ticks were disregarded.

b) Instructions for the implementation of *PCBR* stated that in the case of *Language*, 'Irish' was to be interpreted as mostly or all Irish, while 'English' meant mostly or all English. In a small number of cases where both 'Irish' and 'English' categories were ticked, we assumed that what was intended was 50% Irish, 50% English. In cases where no tick was placed under *Language* at all, we assumed that the language spoken was Irish, as long as the behaviour was coded as *Interaction type*: 'pupil-teacher'. This assumption about language can be justified on the basis that the overwhelming majority of public exchanges between pupils and teachers in all classrooms were in Irish, something which can be confirmed from the *Observer's Global Rating* results and the lesson transcripts in Appendix 6.4. We reasoned also that in the very small number of cases where the language used was English, it was implausible that the observer would overlook the coding of such a relatively rare and noticeable occurrence. In the cases where *Interaction type* was 'pupil-pupil', however, we took missing *Language* data at face value - we assumed that the observer had been unable to identify the language pupils were using (since pupil-pupil exchanges are not really public) and that the omission of a tick under the *Language* category simply reflected this.

c) In the case of double ticks under the *Length of utterance* category, where only one subheading should have been selected, we disregarded the tick associated with the subordinate linguistic category - e.g. we would disregard a tick under 'sentence' in favour of a tick under 'sustained'.

d) In the small number of instances where incompatible subheadings were ticked (e.g. *Interaction type* identified as both 'pupil-pupil' and 'pupil-teacher'), both ticks were disregarded.

e) One category of pupil behaviour requires special mention, since it seems to have been misunderstood by at least some observers: *Takes turn*. The intention was that the *Takes turn* category would be used only when the pupil took the initiative in a fundamental way in making a spoken contribution, to such an extent that he or she consciously departed from the lesson structure. In the instructions for *PCBR*, behaviour of this kind had been explicitly contrasted with the adjacent categories of *Asks a question* and *Answers*, categories which were to be used in the case of the more common and circumscribed pupil contributions which were governed by the set lesson plan.

   Observers, however, sometimes placed ticks in the *Takes turn* category as well as in either the *Asks a question* or *Answers* categories. The probability is that what the observers meant to indicate by this pattern of ticks was that the pupil had taken the initiative in making his or her contribution - e.g. by raising his/her hand. This was not the intended use of the *Takes turn* category, however, since the pupil in the example mentioned might simply be offering to answer ordinary questions addressed to the class by the teacher, and not really taking the more fundamental kind of conversational initiative which had been specified in the instructions. Because of this apparent misunderstanding on the part of some observers, it was decided to analyse data under the heading *Takes turn* in relation to whether the adjacent categories of *Asks a question* and *Answers* were also ticked (i.e. filtering out behaviours which had been coded under 'question' or 'answer'.

f) Although the instructions specified that 'sustained' utterances did not apply to isolated utterances associated with pupil 'questions' and 'answers', in the event observers chose to code the majority of 'sustained' utterances under one of the three categories 'Asks a question', 'Answers' or 'Takes turn'.

(3) Unequal numbers/Pupil replacements

a) When the *PCBR* data was examined it became apparent that, in both lessons, 'high' ability in Irish pupils were always observed first, followed by 'middle' ability in Irish pupils and, then 'lower' ability in Irish pupils. Furthermore, one observer reverted to the first (high ability pupil) after a class break in each lesson. Thus, we ended up with more pupil observation units and behaviours (and consequently more observation time) for higher ability pupils than for the rest and, likewise, more observation units for middle ability in Irish pupils than for lower ability in Irish pupils. The imbalance in numbers of pupils at the various ability-in-Irish levels was taken into account in all analyses, however, since we used proportions rather than actual numbers of pupil behaviours in conducting statistical tests.

b) In the case of two classes two target pupils were missing for the second lesson and had to be replaced. In one class the observer substituted three new randomly selected pupils in the appropriate 'Irish ability' categories as new targets of observation while in the other case the observer simply replaced the two missing pupils with pupils of corresponding ability. An unintentional replacement occured in another class where, in the first observed lesson a pupil of level 2 ability-in-Irish was mistakenly observed instead of a pupil of level 3 ability-in-Irish thereby reducing the number of observation units for the 'lower' ability pupils in that particular class. In these six cases, we accepted the substitutions, simply correcting pupil identification data so that the relevant achievement and attitudinal information was linked to the substituted target pupils. Fortunately, taken overall, replacements were equally distributed between the ability levels. These substitutions meant that only 54 pupils were observed for *both* lessons while twelve pupils were observed during one lesson only. Thus, *PCBR* data was collected for a total of 66 pupils rather than the projected 60 pupils

(4) Incomplete codings

The instructions for applying *PCBR* indicated that if there was a change in pupil behaviour during the three-minute observation period, a line should be drawn across the page within the row corresponding to that pupil and a new series of ticks recorded to describe the new behaviour. Sometimes, however, even though the actual line was omitted, the presence of aligned rows of ticks across subheadings made it quite clear that a change in pupil behaviour was being signalled. In such cases, we treated the additional rows of ticks as if lines had been drawn.

Where pupil behaviour was only partially coded according to the *PCBR* scheme, for example, ticks placed only in *Language* and *Interaction type* (pupil-pupil or pupil-teacher), we simply accepted the data available.

PUPIL COMMUNICATIVE BEHAVIOUR RECORD
(Córas Dírbhreathnaithe ITÉ - II)

Dáta: _____

Ceacht: 1 nó 2 _____

Uimhir an Ionaid: _____

Ainm an Chigire: _____

Múinteoir: _____

Ainm na scoile: _____

Seoladh: _____

OBSERV-ATION UNIT	PUPIL 1, 2, 3	IF THE PUPIL SPEAKS INDIVIDUALLY											IF THE PUPIL IS SILENT (or non-task related e.g. chatting/whispering)						OTHER PUPIL BEHAVIOUR			
		LANGUAGE		ASKS A QUESTION		ANSWERS		LENGTH OF UTTERANCE				TAKES TURN		INTERACTION TYPE		ATTENDING			DISRUPTIVE			CHORAL SPEECH	READING		WRITING
Began at		Irish	English	Pseudo	Genuine	Predic-table	Unpre-dictable	One word	Clause	Sentence	Sustained	Routine	New	Pupil-pupil	Pupil-teacher	H	M	L	H	M	L		silent	aloud	
	1																								
	2																								
	3																								
	1																								
	2																								
	3																								
	1																								
	2																								
	3																								

*Reduced from original A3 size.

Author index

Subject index